# Fodor's

# ISRAEL

6th Edition

**Where to Stay and Eat for All Budgets**

**Must-See Sights and Local Secrets**

**Ratings You Can Trust**

Fodor's Travel Publications   New York, Toronto, London, Sydney, Auckland
**www.fodors.com**

**FODOR'S ISRAEL**

**Editors:** Linda Cabasin, Ruth Craig, Caroline Trefler

**Contributors:** Judy Balint, Andrew Collins, Judy Stacey Goldman, Mike Hollander, Andrea Lehman, Rachel Klein Lisberg, Mike Rogoff, Miriam Feinberg Vamosh
**Editorial Production:** Aviva Muse-Orlinoff
**Maps:** David Lindroth, Inc., *cartographer*; Rebecca Baer and Bob Blake, *map editors*
**Design:** Fabrizio La Rocca, *creative director*; Guido Caroti, *art director*; Jolie Novak, *senior picture editor*; Melanie Marin, *photo editor*
**Cover Design:** Pentagram
**Production/Manufacturing:** Robert Shields

Sixth Edition

ISBN: 1–4000–1668–1

ISBN-13: 978–1–4000–1668–6

ISSN: 0071–6588

**SPECIAL SALES**
This book is available at special discounts for bulk purchases for sales promotions or premiums. Special editions, including personalized covers, excerpts of existing books, and corporate imprints, can be created in large quantities for special needs. For more information, write to Special Markets/Premium Sales, 1745 Broadway, MD 6-2, New York, New York 10019, or e-mail specialmarkets@randomhouse.com.

**AN IMPORTANT TIP & AN INVITATION**
Although all prices, opening times, and other details in this book are based on information supplied to us at press time, changes occur all the time in the travel world, and Fodor's cannot accept responsibility for facts that become outdated or for inadvertent errors or omissions. So **always confirm information when it matters,** especially if you're making a detour to visit a specific place. Your experiences—positive and negative—matter to us. If we have missed or misstated something, **please write to us.** We follow up on all suggestions. Contact the Israel editor at editors@fodors.com or c/o Fodor's at 1745 Broadway, New York, NY 10019.

PRINTED IN THE UNITED STATES OF AMERICA

10 9 8 7 6 5 4 3 2 1

# Be a Fodor's Correspondent

Your opinion matters. It matters to us. It matters to your fellow Fodor's travelers, too. And we'd like to hear it. In fact, we *need* to hear it.

When you share your experiences and opinions, you become an active member of the Fodor's community. That means we'll not only use your feedback to make our books better, but we'll publish your names and comments whenever possible. Throughout our guides, look for "Word of Mouth," excerpts of your unvarnished feedback.

Here's how you can help improve Fodor's for all of us.

Tell us when we're right. We rely on local writers to give you an insider's perspective. But our writers and staff editors—who are the best in the business—depend on you. Your positive feedback is a vote to renew our recommendations for the next edition.

Tell us when we're wrong. We're proud that we update most of our guides every year. But we're not perfect. Things change. Hotels cut services. Museums change hours. Charming cafés lose charm. If our writer didn't quite capture the essence of a place, tell us how you'd do it differently. If any of our descriptions are inaccurate or inadequate, we'll incorporate your changes in the next edition and will correct factual errors at fodors.com *immediately*.

Tell us what to include. You probably have had fantastic travel experiences that aren't yet in Fodor's. Why not share them with a community of like-minded travelers? Maybe you chanced upon a beach or bistro or B&B that you don't want to keep to yourself. Tell us why we should include it. And share your discoveries and experiences with everyone directly at fodors.com. Your input may lead us to add a new listing or highlight a place we cover with a "Highly Recommended" star or with our highest rating, "Fodor's Choice."

Give us your opinion instantly at our feedback center at www.fodors.com/feedback. You may also e-mail editors@fodors.com with the subject line "Israel Editor." Or send your nominations, comments, and complaints by mail to Israel Editor, Fodor's, 1745 Broadway, New York, NY 10019.

You and travelers like you are the heart of the Fodor's community. Make our community richer by sharing your experiences. Be a Fodor's correspondent.

Nesi'ah tovah! (Or simply: Happy traveling!)

Tim Jarrell, Publisher

# CONTENTS

# ABOUT THIS BOOK

### Our Ratings

Sometimes you find terrific travel experiences and sometimes they just find you. But usually the burden is on you to select the right combination of experiences. That's where our ratings come in.

As travelers we've all discovered a place so wonderful that its worthiness is obvious. And sometimes that place is so unique that superlatives don't do it justice: you just have to be there to know. These sights, properties, and experiences get our highest rating, **Fodor's Choice,** indicated by orange stars throughout this book.

Black stars highlight sights and properties we deem **Highly Recommended,** places that our writers, editors, and readers praise again and again for consistency and excellence.

By default, there's another category: any place we include in this book is by definition worth your time, unless we say otherwise. And we will.

Disagree with any of our choices? Care to nominate a place or suggest that we rate one more highly? Visit our feedback center at www.fodors.com/feedback.

### Budget Well

Hotel and restaurant price categories from ¢ to $$$$ are defined in the opening pages of each chapter. For attractions, we always give standard adult admission fees; reductions are usually available for children, students, and senior citizens. Want to pay with plastic? **AE, D, DC, MC, V** following restaurant and hotel listings indicate whether American Express, Discover, Diner's Club, MasterCard, and Visa are accepted.

### Restaurants

Unless we state otherwise, restaurants are open for lunch and dinner daily. We mention dress only when there's a specific requirement and reservations only when they're essential or not accepted—it's always best to book ahead.

### Hotels

Hotels have private bath, phone, TV, and air-conditioning and operate on the European Plan (aka EP, meaning without meals), unless we specify that they use the Continental Plan (CP, with a continental breakfast), Breakfast Plan (BP, with a full breakfast), or Modified American Plan (MAP, with breakfast and dinner) or are all-inclusive (including all meals and most activities). We always list facilities but not whether you'll be charged an extra fee to use them, so when pricing accommodations, find out what's included.

### Many Listings
- ★ Fodor's Choice
- ★ Highly recommended
- ⊠ Physical address
- ✢ Directions
- ⓓ Mailing address
- ☎ Telephone
- 🖷 Fax
- ⊕ On the Web
- ✉ E-mail
- 🎫 Admission fee
- ☉ Open/closed times
- ▶ Start of walk/itinerary
- Ⓜ Metro stations
- ▭ Credit cards

### Hotels & Restaurants
- 🏨 Hotel
- 🛏 Number of rooms
- ⚴ Facilities
- ¶◯¶ Meal plans
- ✕ Restaurant
- 🕭 Reservations
- 👗 Dress code
- ↘ Smoking
- 🍷 BYOB
- ✕🏨 Hotel with restaurant that warrants a visit

### Outdoors
- 🏌 Golf
- ⛺ Camping

### Other
- ☻ Family-friendly
- 🛈 Contact information
- ⇨ See also
- ⊠ Branch address
- ☞ Take note

# WHAT'S
# WHERE

| | |
|---|---|
| **JERUSALEM**<br> | To most visitors Jerusalem means the Old City, its ancient walls embracing sites sacred to three of the world's great religions: Judaism, Christianity, and Islam. Here you'll find the Western Wall, perhaps the holiest Jewish site; the dazzling gold-top Dome of the Rock, the Muslim sanctuary marking the site from which the prophet Muhammad is said to have ascended to heaven; as well as the Via Dolorosa, the route Jesus walked to Calvary. The Old City takes you back in time with its narrow stone alleyways and arches and the streets are crowded with travelers, pilgrims, and vendors of everything from fresh produce to Bedouin caftans and videocassettes. Your senses may be overwhelmed here by the intense colors; the aromas of turmeric, fenugreek, fresh mint, and cardamom-spiced coffee; and the blare of Arabic music and the Babel of languages. "New Jerusalem" is an intriguing contrast to the Old City: it's very much of the present, with a lively pedestrian mall on Ben Yehuda Street and Nahalat Shiva, lined with shops and sidewalk cafés. Some compare a visit to Jerusalem to eating a very rich meal: it's fabulous but sometimes a little hard to digest! Even the less tumultuous places to visit, like the serene synagogue of the Hadassah Hospital with its 12 Chagall stained-glass windows, the Israel Museum, and the sobering Yad Vashem Holocaust Memorial can take a lot out of you—but this is Jerusalem: a heady mix of profound sensations both worldly and emotional to which no one can remain indifferent. |
| **SIDE TRIPS FROM JERUSALEM**<br> | A few miles east of Jerusalem is the Judean Desert, a bleak landscape of dramatically sculpted cliffs. If you love the desert, this is the place to begin its exploration, which you can do in a variety of ways, from the comfort of your air-conditioned car while keeping to the main roads, to a jeep ride, a hike, or even a camel trek. A visit to Qumran, where the Dead Sea Scrolls were found, is the perfect complement to seeing the scrolls in the Israel Museum in Jerusalem. To experience the Dead Sea, take a float on the salty water—it's too buoyant for swimming—and slather on the famously curative black mud. Not far from here looms Masada, the mountain-top remains of King Herod's palace-fortress. Also a short trip from Jerusalem—when politics allow—is Bethlehem, Jesus's birthplace. In the town's center is the Church of the Nativity, built over what is thought to be the grotto where he was born. Just outside Jerusalem is a wine route, with many new wineries—you'll also find fresh goat cheese made by local farmers. |

# WHAT'S
# WHERE

| TEL AVIV | |
|---|---|
|  | Tel Aviv is Israel's economic and cultural center, and its beautiful beaches and seaside promenade, vibrant with cafés and good times, hug the Mediterranean. The energy of the city buzzes at the outdoor Carmel Market, where crowds jostle in search of knickknacks and fresh produce, and at the twice-weekly Nahalat Binyamin street market. Tel Aviv is also the place where you'll find Israel's cultural diversions including the Israel Philharmonic and the up-and-coming New Israeli Opera—both based at the Tel Aviv Performing Arts Center. There are a variety of performances at the Suzanne Dellal Cultural Center in the charmingly renewed Neveh Tzedek quarter, where restaurants, cafés, and designer jewelry and fashion boutiques could easily occupy half a day. The ancient port city of Jaffa, now annexed to Tel Aviv, dates from at least biblical times; among its charms is a bustling flea market. Some say that the galleries, gift shops, and cafés of restored Old Jaffa are too touristy but in summer there is an arts festival which is great for mingling with the locals. The restaurants in Tel Aviv, with cuisines from around the world, are the best in the country, and many are clustered around the city's newest hub, the old Port in North Tel Aviv. Tel Aviv is also where Israeli nightlife is found so if, like the locals, you want to party till the wee hours, take a nap in the late afternoon to prepare for the post-sundown scene in the Florentine quarter and other trendy locales. |
| **HAIFA AND THE NORTHERN COAST**<br><br> | Wending your way along the Mediterranean coast, you're never too far from a sandy beach, a comfortable hotel, or a delicious meal of fresh fish. But the coast offers more than pampering: it has layers of history to uncover, as well as rugged Mt. Carmel for hiking. In Haifa, Israel's third largest city and home of one of its two ports, the golden dome of the Baha'i Shrine and Gardens dominates the skyline. The Crusader city of Akko is a stone's throw north of Haifa, and a walk along the Old City's ramparts gives a hint of the major commercial port it was in its medieval heyday. These ramparts surround the Old City with its market, fishing port, subterranean Crusader Halls, and restored Turkish Bath, along with the magnificent 18th-century El-Jazzar Mosque. South of Haifa in Caesarea, where Herod built a major seaport, the vast remains of the Roman city include an amphitheater which, along with Byzantine and Crusader ruins, make Caesarea a magnet for history lovers. Take it all in and then enjoy a swim at the beach in view of the Roman aqueduct's arches. |

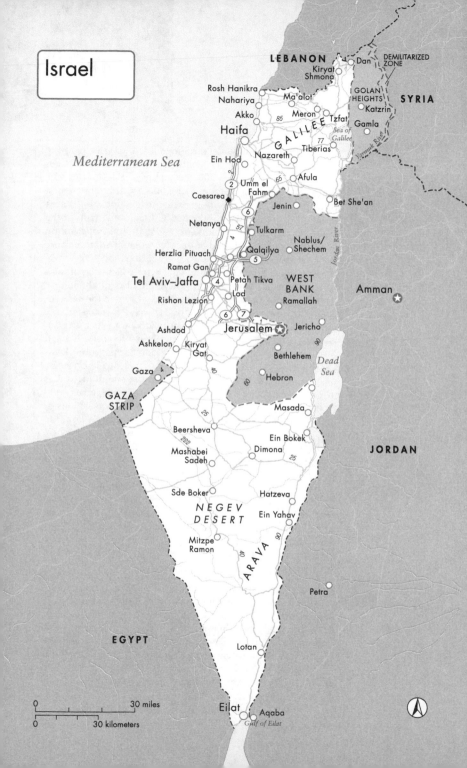

# WHAT'S WHERE

The Galilee's verdant valleys, rolling hills, and lyrically lovely Sea of Galilee are wonderful counterparts to the historical riches found here. The lake is 700 feet below sea level and surrounded by steep hills, and the area has a warm climate and subtropical greenery. In spring, nature lovers flock to the area to enjoy the wildflowers, hike Mt. Gilboa, and swim in the springs at Gan Hashelosha National Park. You can relax on the Galilee beaches—the public ones are woefully short on basic amenities, but an overnight at a beachside hotel solves the problem—and dine on freshly caught St. Peter's fish (tilapia) at a restaurant by the water's edge. There are also an abundance of significant historical and archaeological sites in the area, including the excavations at Zippori, where a Roman-era city with exquisite mosaics and a sophisticated aqueduct was uncovered, and Bet She'an, where the best-preserved Roman theater in Israel can be explored. Megiddo (Armageddon) was one of history's greatest battlegrounds thanks to its strategic location between Egypt and Mesopotamia, and modern digs have uncovered layers of civilization from as long ago as 4000 BC, including a palace from King Solomon's time, remains of 5,000-year-old temples, and a Canaanite-period gate. Nazareth, once a tiny village where Jesus is believed to have grown up, is now a jangling, busy city. Around the Sea of Galilee are the famed sites of Jesus's ministry: tradition says Jesus performed the miracle of the multiplication of the loaves and fishes at Tabgha, and in Capernaum, where Jesus called many of his disciples, are the ruins of a fifth-century AD synagogue—its gleaming white columns and steps perch on the site of an even earlier synagogue, perhaps the one where Jesus taught. Farther south, along the Jordan's eucalyptus-bordered banks, is Yardenit, where Christian pilgrims come to be baptized in emulation of Jesus's own experience in the Jordan's waters.

In this area you can satisfy an interest in active sports, charming country-style bed-and-breakfasts, and historical treasures—amid natural pools, streams, and majestic mountain peaks. In the summer, the sacred hilltop city of Tzfat (Safed)—which was a haven for Sephardic Jews fleeing the Inquisition and the center of Jewish mysticism (the Kabbalah)—comes alive with a Klezmer music festival, and the many art galleries welcome visitors, with artists often in residence. Opportunities for hiking abound: Mt. Meron, site of the tomb of the ancient sage Rabbi Shimon Bar Yochai, has hiking trails with spectacular

vistas, and to the north there are great trails amid the lush nature reserves of the Upper Hula Valley. The Gamla Nature Reserve, renowned for bird-watching, is nearby. Mt. Hermon, at the northern reaches of the Golan and some 9,230 feet above sea level, is the site of the country's only ski resort—but it's also a great spring or summer destination, when it's abloom with flowers and herbs. The fertile volcanic soil of the region has helped make the Golan Heights Winery, in Katzrin, a world-class wine-making operation; wine tasting tours are available.

## EILAT AND THE NEGEV

The fascination of Bedouin life and the stunning geological treasures of the desert, not to mention luxurious hotels and spas in Eilat, are all high points of this region. In the north, the Bedouin market in Beersheva comes alive on Thursdays. Although these days there are goods made in Asia, arrive early and you may get lucky: a keen eye can lead to wonderful handmade textiles, beaded bags and jewelry, copperware, and other finds. The back country of the Negev Desert is a landscape of craters, valleys, gorges, and craggy mountains painted in gorgeous reds, browns, yellows, and greens. One of the best ways to experience it is to sign on for a camel trek tracing the fabled spice trade routes of the ancient Nabateans. Don't miss the phenomenal Makhtesh Ramon, where the primeval layers of rock are an open book of geological wonders. Farther south are the rugged Timna Mountains, where King Solomon and his predecessors mined copper. Thanks to erosion over the millennia, Timna Park has fantastic rock formations, including the mighty red piers known as Solomon's Pillars. At the southern tip of Israel are the resort town of Eilat and the Red Sea with its coral reefs and dazzling marine life. People come to scuba dive, snorkel, and relax at the fine hotels on the beach. Spa-going is another favorite pastime. The canyon city of Petra, nearby in Jordan, is an excellent side trip: its temples, tombs, monuments, and palaces, carved out of sandstone cliffs in the first century AD, have elaborate facades that change color dramatically as daylight waxes and wanes.

# QUINTESSENTIAL ISRAEL

## Falafel

Falafel sandwiches are a fast-food staple in Israel and stands are found from the busy streets of downtown Tel Aviv to the ultra-Orthodox areas of Jerusalem and the Eilat beach promenade; in some respects, falafel is a great social equalizer. At the most popular stands patrons might crowd three deep during the lunch rush. The cook wields a scoop that turns seasoned chickpea mash into small spheres that are quickly fried in oil, then thrust—six or so—into a pita. Patrons give a nod or a "no thanks" to the addition of a little hummus and/or *harif* (hot sauce), and to each of the colorful accompaniments: cubed cucumbers and tomatoes, pickled turnip and eggplant, shredded cabbage, parsley, pickles, and even French fries stuffed on top. Discerning diners then drizzle their creation with self-service sauces: *amba* (spicy pickled mango) and tahini. And about that drizzling—diners should have a few extra napkins ready, and assume the falafel position before taking their first bite: leaning forward well away from clothing and shoes.

## The Sabra Personality

Israelis are known to have prickly personalities. Although the most popular word in the country is *savlanut* (patience), natives don't seem to be blessed with an overabundance of that quality. An old saying tries to explain the character of Israelis, masters of the short retort, by comparing it to the pear cactus, known as a *sabra*, a fruit that has prickles all over the outside but is sweet on the inside. In fact, native-born Israelis are known as sabras. Fortunately, this national tendency toward abruptness is tempered with a dose of Mediterranean warmth. When asking directions, for example, you may find yourself personally escorted to your destination and given a

Israel is more than holy sites and turbulent politics; to get a sense of the country, familiarize yourself with some of the features of daily life.

great deal of mostly unsolicited advice. How should you respond to a perceived cold-shoulder? Persevere; a welcome thaw is likely to be close at hand.

## Markets & Bargaining

Shopping in Israel's open-air markets can be an exciting experience. The fresh produce and food markets are a feast for the eyes and palate, and cheaper than the supermarkets—just the place to soak up local culture while shopping for lunch fixings or fruit to stock your hotel room. Most produce markets also have stalls selling cheap clothing and other textiles—the 100% cotton socks and tablecloths made in Israel are often economical and high quality. Mahane Yehuda in Jerusalem, Tel Aviv's Carmel Market, and the Nazareth market are famous. For markets that sell decorative brass, ceramic and glass items, beads, embroidered dresses, and jackets or secondhand funky clothes—all make great souvenirs—head to Jerusalem's Old City or the Jaffa Flea Market.

Bargaining is the really fun part of any market experience but there are some useful ideas to remember: The vendors always seem to know by your body language how much you want the item. To combat this advantage never answer the question "how much do you want to pay?" And when the seller names a price, come back with about half. Probably the best advice is: Be prepared to walk out. They'll call you back if they want to make the sale. Give yourself plenty of time for market shopping. If you're in a hurry, the vendors will know it (see above) and they won't drop the price. Know, too, that not every vendor will be in the mood for the bargaining game: If you hear, "Come back when you have money," try your bargaining prowess elsewhere.

# IF YOU LIKE

## Beaches

One of Israel's nicknames is "land of the four seas"—the Med, the Dead, the Red, and the Sea of Galilee. And where there's sea, there are beaches.

On the Mediterranean, the sandy beaches of **Tel Aviv**'s waterfront are right on the doorstep of its most popular hotels. Farther up the coast, at **Caesarea**, are a public and a private beach, the latter with a dive club where qualified scuba divers lead underwater tours of sunken antiquities. Even farther north is **Achziv Beach**, beautifully maintained and great for kids.

The Dead Sea public relations people call the area "Jerusalem's beach" because it's less than an hour's drive from the capital—although the water is so salty you'll float rather than swim. Most hotels have private beaches, but if you're here for just an afternoon, there are a number of pay-beaches (about 25 to 60 NIS). The **public beach** has free access to the sea and basic changing facilities are NIS 8.

Eilat is Israel's sun-and-fun playground on the Red Sea and there are water sports galore, including scuba diving, snorkeling, and parasailing. **North Beach**, along the hotel strip, is well kept and pleasant.

As for the Sea of Galilee, the beaches are picturesque, but few outside hotel properties are suitable for more than a quick dip since most lack anything approaching basic amenities. Non-"official" beaches don't have lifeguards and, especially on the western coast when afternoon winds kick up, the swimming can be risky. You're better of in Tiberias, at the **Gai**, **Blue**, and **Sironit** beaches—all conveniently right in town.

## Desert Adventures

In antiquity, Israel's deserts were the stomping grounds for everyone from ancient prophets and hermits to traders. Today, there are several ways you can experience the rocky, spring-studded hills and dales of Israel's two deserts—the Judean and the Negev—and your excursion can be as short as a few hours or as long as a day, or several days. You can book tours through travel agents or through your hotel, but some tours don't operate in the summer, when it's very hot. Whatever you do, take plenty of water and a hat.

It's not advised to go off into the desert by yourself, but for a convenient, short exploration on foot, you can visit springs like **Ein Gedi** and the adjacent **Nahal Arugot** on the eastern edge of the Judean Desert southeast of Jerusalem. In the Negev, the trek to **Ein Avdat** is easy and begins at the end of a short drive from Ben-Gurion's tomb. Any of these is only a few minutes' walk from the road. If you're looking for something more intense, join an organized hike, like the ones led by guides from the **Society for the Protection of Nature in Israel.**

If you prefer to travel by other means than by foot, you can sign up to see the desert by jeep, with **Jeep See** in Eilat or **Israel Adventure Tours** in Jerusalem, or join a camel trip into the Negev mountains northwest of Eilat through the **Camel Ranch.** If horseback riding is your thing, **Texas Ranch,** also in Eilat, takes riders on trails through Wadi Shlomo (Solomon's Valley) and into the desert.

## A Chance to Dig

If you've ever been to a museum and wondered what it would be like to dig up one of those ancient artifacts, Israel has many options to feed the fantasy. Digs are under way all over the country, and volunteer programs range from a half-day to a week or longer. Most take place during spring or summer, and charge a fee to participants; some offer package deals that include accommodations. Current top options are listed below, and a list of digs looking for volunteers is updated on the Israel Ministry of Foreign Affairs Web site (www.mfa.gov.il) under "Our Bookmarks."

If getting your hands dirty for half a day sounds like fun, Archaeological Seminars has a year-round Dig-for-a-Day program, with three-hour excavations at **Bet Guvrin–Maresha National Park,** outside of Jerusalem. **Ramat Rachel,** almost *in* Jerusalem, is the site of a First Temple–era royal palace whose remains can be seen in the small archaeological park near the hotel; excavation has resumed and volunteers can sign up for one-week-long periods in the summer. A week is also the minimum to sign on with the ten-year-long project underway in **Tiberias** (for more information, visit www.tiberiasexcavation.com), which has the advantage of being right on the Sea of Galilee, a great location for free-time touring and water fun. If you can make a longer commitment, the excavation at **Megiddo,** the traditional Armageddon, in the Jezreel Valley, offers accommodations at a nearby kibbutz and has three- or four-week dig options.

## Sacred Places

This is the Holy Land and there are probably more sacred places per square mile here than anywhere else on earth. For many visitors, though, the look and feel of Israel's holy sites can be quite unexpected—even a shock—since sacred does not always mean a rarified, reverent atmosphere.

The hustle and bustle at the **Western Wall,** the **Temple Mount,** or the **Church of the Holy Sepulcher** in Jerusalem; at the **tomb of Rabbi Shimon Bar Yochai** in the Galilee; or at **Elijah's Cave** in Haifa may make it difficult to focus on matters of the spirit, but it does make it easy to appreciate the impact of places that have drawn believers, sometimes crossing the boundaries of faith, for millennia.

Those seeking quieter spiritual moments should not despair; these, too, can be found, even in Jerusalem: you can find a peaceful experience at the **Ethiopian Monastery,** tucked away behind the Church of the Holy Sepulcher, or visit the **Western Wall** at dawn, an entirely different scene than later in the day. Elsewhere, you can pull up a rock on the outskirts of Tzfat to contemplate the sweeping view of the Galilee Mountains, and in Akko it's worth a visit to the quiet corner of the flowering courtyard of the **El-Jazzar Mosque.** Tranquillity reigns, too, at the peaceful gardens at the **St. Gabriel Hotel,** in Nazareth, or at the open air altar at the **Church of the Multiplication** at Tabgha, beside the Sea of Galilee.

# GREAT ITINERARIES

## BEST OF ISRAEL, WITH THE NEGEV AND EILAT, 11–19 DAYS

Israel is a small but varied country. This itinerary lets you see the high points of Jerusalem and the northern half of the country; you can add the desert if you have the time and inclination.

### Jerusalem, 3–4 days

You could spend a lifetime in Jerusalem, but 3 days is probably a good minimum for the city and environs. First, spend a day getting an overview of the holy sites of Judaism, Christianity, and Islam by moving through the Jewish Quarter to the Western Wall, then seeing the mosques on the Temple Mount, the Via Dolorosa, and the Church of the Holy Sepulcher. Stop for a Middle Eastern–style lunch at one of the restaurants in the Old City's Jaffa Gate square.

On your second day, you can venture farther afield: many consider the Israel Museum and the Yad Vashem Holocaust Museum and Memorial essential if you're visiting Jerusalem, and Mt. Herzl National Memorial Park is also a pleasant excursion. (Note: the Israel Museum is closed Sunday; Yad Vashem and Mt. Herzl are closed Saturday.)

Your third day can be devoted to sites within an hour of Jerusalem: perhaps a wine tour in the Judean Hills. Or join a dig at Bet Guvrin–Maresha National Park with Archaeological Seminars—and on your way back, visit Mini Israel, with its hundreds of models of Israeli sites.

The 3 days suggested for Jerusalem are the bare minimum; a fourth day gives you time to relax and absorb the city—and shop.

### The Dead Sea region, 2 days

After getting an early start in your rental car, head east through the stark Judean desert to Qumran, where the Dead Sea Scrolls were discovered. You can spend an hour or so touring the ruins and seeing the audiovisual presentation. About 45 minutes south of Qumran on the road parallel to the Dead Sea is Ein Gedi, where a leisurely hike to the waterfall and back should take about two hours. End the day with a float in the Dead Sea, and spend the night at one of Ein Gedi's fine hotels or at the Kibbutz Ein Gedi Guest House. A highlight for many are the spa treatments featuring the famously curative Dead Sea mud.

In the morning, hike the Snake Path—or take the cable car—up Masada. The gate to the path opens at first light so you can catch the sunrise on the way up. Later, head back to Jerusalem to spend a night on your way to the Galilee, stopping a few miles north of the Dead Sea–Jerusalem highway at the oasis town of Jericho, the world's oldest city. It's almost worth a trip through this lush city—adorned with date palms, orange groves, banana plantations, bougainvillea, and papaya trees—just to be able to say "I was there," but there are also some significant archaeological sites at Tel Jericho, where you can stop for baklava and orange juice. Jericho is in the Palestinian Authority, so check the daily newspaper for political conditions and use common sense.

### The Galilee, 3 days

From Jerusalem, where you've spent the night, make an early start to allow time for all the sites on today's schedule. Take the Jordan Valley route (Route 90) to the

Galilee so you can stop at the springs of Gan Hashelosha for a swim, then visit the vast Roman-Byzantine ruins at Bet She'an, where you can have lunch in town or take a sandwich to the site. The Crusader castle of Belvoir will round out the day and then you can enjoy a lakeside fish dinner in Tiberias, where you'll spend the night.

The next day, spend an hour or two at the Dan Nature Reserve, with its rushing water and biblical archaeology. Spend the afternoon hiking, kayaking, or horseback riding at Bat Ya'ar (call ahead to reserve if you want to go trail riding), or kayak at Hagoshrim or Kfar Blum (no need to reserve). Overnight in Tiberias again, or better yet, farther north in a Hula Valley B&B.

On your third day, you can explore the treasures of Tzfat, with its beautiful vistas, old synagogues, and art and Judaica galleries. Depending on how you spend your day, you can also visit the Golan Heights Winery or do some hiking or bird-watching at Gamla. Overnight in Tiberias or at your Hula Valley B&B.

### The Mediterranean Coast and Tel Aviv, 3 days

From Tiberias or your Hula Valley B&B, head west to the coast. Your first stop can be the cable car ride to the white caverns of Rosh Hanikra. Then travel to Akko, with its Crusader halls and picturesque harbors. This is also an excellent place for a fish lunch. Then drive to Haifa for a view from the top of Mt. Carmel from the Panorama. Spend the night in Haifa.

The next day, visit Haifa's Baha'i Shrine and its magnificent gardens, then continue down

the coast to visit the city of Zichron Ya'akov and the Carmel Mizrachi Wine Cellars or the Bet Aaronson Museum. Have lunch and then head to Tel Aviv, stopping at the Roman ruins of Caesarea on the way. In Tel Aviv, you can enjoy a night on the town.

On your third day, take in Tel Aviv's museums, shop, and enjoy a dip in the Mediterranean. From here you can head to the airport if it's time to go home. If you're proceeding on to the desert, spend another night in Tel Aviv and get an early start in the morning.

### Add on: the desert
### The Negev, 2 days

From Tel Aviv, head south toward Beersheva and Road 40. If you're doing this on a Thursday, leave early enough to get to the Beersheva Bedouin market, which is most colorful in the morning (Beersheva is about a two-hour drive from Tel Aviv). Driving

# GREAT
# ITINERARIES

south, stop at Sde Boker, where you can have lunch and see David Ben-Gurion's house and gravesite overlooking the biblical Wilderness of Zin. Near Sde Boker is Ein Avdat, a wilderness oasis that has a trail with stone steps and ladders leading up the magnificent white chalk canyon. Drive on to Mitzpe Ramon, on the edge of the immense Ramon Crater. Stop at the Israel Nature and Parks Authority visitor center, where you can find out the best places to hike, or how to see the sites by car. Spend the night here, then enjoy the natural wonders of the Ramon Crater the next day. Spend a second night here as well.

## Eilat and environs, 2–5 days

Eilat is about a three-hour drive from Mitzpe Ramon. Drive south on Road 40 and continue south on the Arava Road to where it joins Road 90, which runs along the border with Jordan. Stop at Timna Park for a hike and a view of Solomon's Pillars, and at the Hai Bar Nature Reserve, arriving in Eilat in the late afternoon. A minimum of 2 days here allows you to see all the highlights; 3 to 5 days means you can have some serious beach or diving time, and take a side trip to Petra in Jordan. You'll probably want to pick one hotel in Eilat as a base.

The lunar-like red-rock canyons in the hills behind Eilat are great for hiking, and there are also plenty of options if you want to take to the water: you can snorkel, parasail, or arrange a boat trip to prime dive spots. To see Petra properly, plan on 2 full days, leaving Eilat early the first day and returning of the late afternoon of the second day. You can make the return drive from Eilat to Jerusalem via the Arava—leave yourself a full day to allow for stops along the way.

## TIPS

❶ In the summer, plan to do most of your walking and hiking by midday to avoid the heat.

❷ Make sure to take lots of water, and a hat, when hiking or walking.

❸ Consider flying back to Tel Aviv from Eilat—or fly round-trip to Eilat if you don't have the time or inclination to drive.

❹ Make your hotel/B&B reservations ahead of time, especially in summer and on weekends year round, when hotels and B&B's are crowded with vacationing Israelis.

❺ Most hotels in the Dead Sea area and Eilat have spas with a host of treatments; call ahead or book one when you arrive.

❻ You won't need a rental car in the Old City of Jerusalem; navigating and parking can be a challenge, so save the rental car for trips out of town.

# GREAT ITINERARIES

## IN THE FOOTSTEPS OF JESUS, 6 DAYS

Visit the Holy Land, they say, and you'll never read the Bible the same way; the landscapes and shrines that you'll see, and your encounters with local members of Christian communities at the landmarks of Jesus's life, will have a profound and lasting impact.

### Jerusalem and Bethlehem, 2 days

Spend your first day retracing the climax of the story of Jesus in Jerusalem, starting at the Mount of Olives. This is where Jesus taught, and wept over the city (Luke 19:41), and it is commemorated by the tear-shaped Dominus Flevit church. The walk down the Mount of Olives road, also known as the Palm Sunday road, leads to the ancient olive trees in the Garden of Gethsemane, where you can contemplate Jesus's arrest. Following the Via Dolorosa, walk the Stations of the Cross to the Church of the Holy Sepulcher, where most Christians believe Jesus was crucified, buried, and resurrected. The Garden Tomb—the site of Calvary for many Protestants—offers a spot of tranquillity. Take your time contemplating the sites; this will not be a rushed day.

The next day, you can explore the Southern Wall Excavation of the Ophel, adjacent to the Old City's Dung Gate. Scholars believe Jesus could have walked the stones of the ancient street here, and climbed the Southern Steps to the Temple—and if this is, as believed, the Gate Beautiful (Acts 3:10), Peter almost certainly did so. Down the hill in the City of David, excavations have revealed the steps of the pool of Siloam, where a blind man healed by Jesus washed (John 9:7–11). Add a visit to the Room of the Last Supper on Mt. Zion, up the hill from the Dung Gate, and then have lunch. In the afternoon, you can drive, political climate permitting (read the daily paper and use common sense), to Bethlehem, Jesus's birthplace, to visit the Church of the Nativity, one of the oldest churches in the world—or you can opt to stay in Jerusalem, checking out the Old Testament sites of the City of David, including Area G, Warren's Shaft, and Hezekiah's Tunnel. Bethlehem is in the Palestinian Authority so bring your passport, and even if you have a car, it's best to take a taxi to the border crossing south of Jerusalem's Gilo neighborhood. The crossing for tourists is usually uncomplicated, and there are Palestinian taxis waiting on the other side to take you to the church.

### On the way to the Galilee, 1 day

Making an early start, head east into the barren Judean Desert to Qumran, where the Dead Sea Scrolls were found. Some scholars believe John the Baptist may have passed through here, and a visit to the site—you can spend an hour here or longer—is an opportunity to learn about the desert in which Jesus (along with many Jews of that time) sought solitude, purity, and inspiration. Then head up the Jordan Valley (Route 90), passing through (depending on political conditions) or near Jericho, through which Jesus also passed when he healed a blind man (Mark 10:46) and had a meal with the tax collector Zaccheaus (Luke 19:1–5). If the security situation isn't favorable, the Israeli soldiers at the checkpoint at Jericho won't allow you in (again, read the newspaper and use common sense).

# GREAT ITINERARIES

If Jericho is a no-go or you decide to skip it, a detour allows you to bypass. In Jericho, though, a visit to Tel Jericho, the first conquest of the Israelites in the Holy Land (Joshua 6) is a must. You can have lunch at the restaurant next to the tell, or at a truck stop on the way north from Jericho. Then it's on to the ruins at Bet She'an, including the ancient main street, a bath house, and mosaics. Not only is this an important Old Testament site, it was also the capital of the Decapolis, the alliance of ten Roman cities, among which Jesus taught and healed (Mark 7:31). Farther north, pilgrims go to Yardenit to be baptized in the Jordan River, to remember the baptism of Jesus in these waters. Spend the night in Tiberias.

## Sea of Galilee, 1 day

Start the day heading north to the ancient wooden boat at Ginosar, which evokes Gospel descriptions of life on the lake—see, for example, Matthew 9:1. Then, after meditating on Jesus's famous sermon (Matthew 5) in the gardens of the Mount of Beatitudes and its chapel (off Route 90 north of the Sea of Galilee), descend to Tabgha to see the mosaics of the Church of the Multiplication of Loaves and Fishes. From a lakeshore perch at the nearby Church of the Primacy of St. Peter, where Jesus appeared to the disciples after the resurrection (John 21), you can marvel at how Scripture and landscape blend before your eyes. Farther east, the ruins of ancient Capernaum—the center of Jesus's local ministry—include a magnificent pillared synagogue and Peter's house. The massive ancient mound across the Jordan River, north of the Sea of Galilee, is believed to be Beth-

saida, where the Gospels say Jesus healed and taught (Luke 9:10, 10:13)—to get there, continue east of Capernaum, cross the Jordan River north of the Sea of Galilee, turn left onto Route 888, and follow the signs to Bethsaida in the Jordan River Park. From there, head back down to the lake and continue to Kursi National Park and the ruins of an ancient church where Jesus cast out demons into a herd of pigs that stampeded into the water (Matt. 8:28–30). A good idea for lunch is the fish restaurant at Kibbutz Ein Gev, after which you can join a cruise across the lake and back (the kibbutz also has a boat company). Spend the night in Tiberias, or at one of the kibbutz guesthouses or B&Bs in the Hula Valley.

## The Hula Valley and Banias (Caesarea Philippi), 1 day

The next day, drive through the Hula Valley; it's especially remarkable in the spring when the flowers bloom and bring alive Jesus's famed teaching from the Sermon on the Mount: "Consider the lilies of the field, how they grow" (Matt. 6:28). At the base of Mt. Hermon (which some scholars point out as an alternative identification for the site of the transfiguration, as described in Mark 9:2–8), northeast of the Hula Valley, is Banias (Caesarea Philippi), where Jesus asked the disciples, "Who do people say I am?" (Mark 8:27), and where the remains of Roman temples are a powerful backdrop for contemplation of that message. Dan, the capital of the biblical Northern Kingdom, has a beautiful nature reserve. Stay overnight at your B&B or kibbutz hotel in the Hula Valley.

## The Galilee Hills and the Coast, 1 day

Head for the hills, connecting to Route 77 and turning south onto Route 754 to Cana to see the church that marks the site where Jesus changed water into wine (John 2:1–11), on your way to Nazareth, Jesus's childhood town. Here, the massive modern Church of the Annunciation houses depictions of Mary from around the world, and the city's spring, now in the Greek Orthodox church, is believed to be where the Angel Gabriel appeared to her (Luke 1:26–38). A drive through the lush Jezreel Valley, via Route 60 then north on Route 65 (the New Testament Valley of Armageddon), brings you to Mt. Tabor, long identified as the Mount of Transfiguration. The valley is named Armageddon (Rev. 16:16) after the archaeological site of Megiddo, now a national park south of Afula on Route 65, with many sights to see. The drive back to Jerusalem from Megiddo is about two and a half hours, or you can spend the night in Haifa and return to Jerusalem the next day.

### TIPS

❶ First, and foremost, bring along your Bible; it will get a lot of use.

❷ You won't need a car in Jerusalem, but you will need one for the rest of this itinerary. Your best bet is to pick up a car on the afternoon of the day before you head out of Jerusalem, so that you can make an early start the next day (remember that rental agencies are normally not open on Saturday). The agency will provide you with a basic road map and advice.

❸ Gas stations are very frequent, some with convenience stores to stock up on snacks; some are closed on Saturday.

# WHEN TO GO

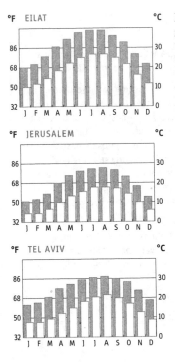

During school holidays, particularly in July and August, Israelis themselves take vacations; accommodations and attractions get very crowded, and surcharges are often added to hotel rates. Hotel prices also jump during the Passover and Sukkoth holiday periods (early April and late September–early October, respectively), and services and commerce are sharply curtailed; many Israelis simply go away for Passover. Reservations for this busy week should be booked at least four months in advance, and plane reservations six months to a year in advance. Some hotels require full board—paying for all meals as part of the room price—for the week of Passover.

## Climate

There is no bad time to visit Israel, in terms of weather. There are seldom any rainy days at all from May through September, but some travelers prefer to risk rain and come in the cooler, less expensive season of November through March. In winter, snow falls occasionally in the northern and central hills. In April, May, September, and October, the weather is generally sunny but not uncomfortably hot. March and April have the added attraction of a lush countryside painted with vivid wildflowers.

Jerusalem, Tzfat, the Dead Sea, Negev, and Eilat all have low humidity year-round. The coastal plain, center of the country, and Sea of Galilee experience high humidity levels during the long summer months. Temperatures at the Dead Sea and in Eilat soar during the day and stay high through the night; in the Negev Desert, on the other hand, the higher altitudes cause nighttime temperatures to drop sharply. The following are average daily maximum and minimum temperatures for Tel Aviv, Jerusalem, and Eilat.

**🗗 Forecasts Weather Channel** ⊕ www.weather.com.

# ON THE CALENDAR

| | |
|---|---|
| | New festivals appear on Israel's cultural calendar every year. Some, like the Israel Festival and the Red Sea Jazz Festival, are international in scope, with reliable dates. Some are permanent seasonal features, timed to coincide with the Jewish holidays in spring and fall. Still others are more local "occasionals," where scheduling is probable but not definite. Check with the Israel Government Tourist Office or the nearest Israeli consulate for details. Once in Israel, you can find information on upcoming festivals in the weekend editions of *The Jerusalem Post* and *Haaretz* both published in English. You can purchase tickets for major events in advance at ticket agencies in the major cities. |
| Dec. | Haifa reflects its mixed population as it hosts the **Hanukkah-Christmas-Ramadan Festival**, with arts and music. |
| Late Dec.– early Jan. | The **Liturgical Festival of Choral Music** (☎ 700/70–4000 ⊕ www.jso.co.il) sponsored by the Jerusalem Symphony Orchestra, runs from the end of December through the beginning of January. Also in Jerusalem is the **Classical Music Winter Festival**. |
| Jan. | The **International Marathon** is run in Tiberias in early January. |
| Mar. | The **Spring Migration Bird-watchers' Festival** is held in Eilat around the end of the third week. Mid-March brings the **Tel Aviv half-marathon**. The **Mt. Tabor Run**, in the Lower Galilee, is scheduled for the third week of the month. The **Artur Rubinstein Piano Master Competition** (☎ 03/685–6684 ⊕ www.arims.org.il) generates great interest among music lovers.<br><br>Many communities organize joyous street festivities to mark **Purim**. |
| Apr. | During **Passover**, when many Israelis go on vacation, the country hums with activities and events. Inquire at the local tourist office and watch newspapers for details. The **Ein Gev Festival**, on the Sea of Galilee, features Israeli music of various kinds. (☎ 06/758–027) **Haifa Festival of Children's Theater** appeals to families. The **National Parks Authority** (☎ 03/576–6834 in Tel Aviv) can update you on the various performances and activities (many of them great for kids) scheduled for this period in parks throughout the country. **Stone in the Galilee** is a sculpture symposium in the Upper Galilee town of Ma'alot held during Passover. A somber day during the week after Passover is **Holocaust Martyrs and Heroes Remembrance Day** (☎ 02/644–3400 ⊕ www.yadvashem.org.il) commemorated with ceremonies and performances all over the country. |

# ON THE CALENDAR

| | |
|---|---|
| Late Apr.–early June | The **International Book Fair** (☎ 02/629–7922 ⊕ www.jerusalembookfair.com) comes to Jerusalem, usually in April, alternating with the **International Judaica Fair** (books in 2007, Judaica in 2008). **Independence Day**, marking Israel's birthday, is the most widely celebrated national holiday, with celebrations taking place all over the country. The Roman amphitheater in Caesarea hosts the **International Opera Fest** at the end of May. |
| | The **Jacob's Ladder Folk Festival** (☎ 04/696–2231 ⊕ www.jlfestival.com) (mostly Anglo-American) takes place at Nof Ginossar on the Sea of Galilee in May. Israel's premier event, the international **Israel Festival** (☎ 02/561–1438), celebrates the performing arts and takes place in Jerusalem every year in late May or early June. Get tickets to major events well in advance. The village of Abu Ghosh, west of Jerusalem, hosts a **Vocal Music Festival** during Shavuot. Eat yourself silly at the **International Ethnic Food Fair**, in Jaffa's port. |
| | The popular **Food Trail**, in the Western Galilee, begins in late May and continues through early summer. Participating restaurants work up special menus, and guests work off the tasty food on guided nature walks between meals, accompanied by eclectic live music. |
| Late June–early July | The **International Folklore Festival**, much of which takes place in small villages, draws performers and artists from Israel and abroad. The **Israeli Folk-Dance Festival**, in Karmiel in early July, hosts ethnic-dance groups from around the world as well as community dancing. The late-June **Cherry Festival** at Kibbutz Kiryat Anavim, west of Jerusalem, features musical events in natural surroundings, and a cafeteria devoted to cherry-based delicacies. |
| | Film buffs should watch for the **International Student Film Festival** in Tel Aviv in early June. Jerusalem's prestigious **International Film Festival** (☎ 02/565-4350 ⊕ www.jff.org.il) is sponsored by the Cinematheque in mid-July. |
| Late July–Aug. | The **Voice of Music in the Upper Galilee**, on Kibbutz Kfar Blum, may be the high point of the year for chamber-music lovers. The **Klezmer Festival**, in Tzfat (Safed), showcases Jewish "soul music." The **Arts and Crafts Fair** outside Jerusalem's Jaffa Gate has a huge display of handmade items and nightly entertainment. (⊕ www.jerusalem.muni.il). Jerusalem hosts the **Zimriya** (⊕ www.zimriya.org.il), the triennial World Assembly of Choirs, next happening in 2007. |

| | |
|---|---|
| | Eilat's fine **Red Sea Jazz Festival** (☎ 03/695–9355 ⊕ www. redseajazz.com) has become an important date on the international jazz calendar. Israeli pop stars are in the limelight at the Negev's **Arad Festival. Nights of Love,** in Tzemach, at the southern end of the Sea of Galilee, brings in national pop stars. The **Jaffa Nights** festival offers music, theater, and general entertainment in the Old Jaffa square. |
| Sept. | The one-day **Wine and Vintage Festival** (☎ 04/813–6239), in Binyamina, features wine tasting and vocal and dance performances. Another event for wine lovers this month is **The Hilulim Wine Fest** (☎ 03/969–6701) in Rishon LeZion. The **Sea of Galilee Crossing** is a 4-km (2½-mi) swim from Kibbutz Ha'on to Tzemach. The YMCA hosts the weeklong **Jerusalem International Chamber Music Festival** (☎ 02/625–0444 ⊕ www.jcmf.org.il). |
| Oct. | The weeklong holiday **Sukkoth** brings almost as busy a calendar of events as Passover in the spring. Thousands of Christians from dozens of countries celebrate the **Feast of Tabernacles** and join in the **Jerusalem Parade** during the intermediate days of the Sukkoth festival. A different kind of parade takes place in Tel Aviv during October. It's the **Love Parade** (⊕ www.layla.co.il/loveparade/), which brings several hundred thousand Israelis out to celebrate love and peace in a huge dance party on the Tel Aviv beachfront. |
| | The **Israel Fringe Theater Festival** (☎ 04/955-2426 ⊕ www.galilee. gov.il), in Akko, features original Israeli plays, street theater, children's shows, and musicals. Rishon Lezion, south of Tel Aviv, and Zichron Ya'akov, on Mt. Carmel, both have festivals of **Wine and Song. Music in Tabgha,** on the Sea of Galilee, sponsors vocal and chamber music in the Church of the Loaves and Fishes. Haifa holds its **International Film Festival** (☎ 04/835-3570/1 ⊕ www. haifaff.co.il) in the fall. Yehiam, in the Western Galilee, is the site of the **Renaissance Festival.** |
| | As in late spring, Abu Ghosh, west of Jerusalem, hosts the **Vocal Music Festival** during the week of Sukkoth. To take a break from all the Sukkoth action, go to the Achziv Club Beach for the **Sagol Love and Meditation Festival** (☎ 08/993-3960 ⊕ www.sagol.org). |
| Nov. | Eilat hosts the **International Bridge Festival** (☎ 03/605–8355 ⊕ www. israbridge.com/ibf/Redsea). The **Olive Festival** features crafts, food, and folklore in celebration of the olive harvest. It's held in villages throughout the central and Western Galilee over a series of weekends from late October through November. |

# SMART TRAVEL TIPS

*Finding out about your destination before you leave home means you won't spend time organizing everyday minutiae once you've arrived. You'll be more streetwise when you hit the ground as well, better prepared to explore the aspects of Israel that drew you here in the first place. The organizations in this section can provide information to supplement this guide; contact them for up-to-the-minute details, and consult the Essentials sections that end each chapter for facts on the various topics as they relate to Israel's many regions. Happy landings!*

## ADDRESSES

In Israel there are no numbered streets. Streets are generally named after famous people or events throughout Jewish history, meaning that almost every city and town in Israel has a Herzl Street and a Six-Day War Street. Don't worry about the "boulevard" or "alley" attached to many street names— Israelis just use the proper name. You won't find a Jabotinsky Street and a Jabotinsky Alley in the same city. What you might encounter, because there are too many famous people and not enough streets, is a street that will change names after a couple of blocks. Street numbers follow the Western odd/even format. Larger apartment buildings often have several entrances marked by the first three or four letters of the Hebrew alphabet.

If you know history, you'll have an easier time finding your way around Jerusalem's neighborhoods. In Baka the streets are named after the biblical tribes, in Rehavia it's medieval Jewish scholars, and in Old Katamon the brigades who fought in Israel's War of Independence are honored with street names.

There are four towns in Israel that have functioning Old Cities dating from either biblical times (Jerusalem), the Crusader period (Akko and Jaffa), or the Middle Ages (Tzfat). Streets and alleyways in these Old Cities are named, but house numbers can be haphazard.

## AIR TRAVEL

Most travelers who come to Israel arrive at Ben Gurion Aiport, a few miles southeast of Tel Aviv. From North America, New York City offers the highest number of nonstop flights, with El Al Airlines, Continental, and Delta providing service. Direct flights via El Al are also available from Miami, Los Angeles, and Toronto. Israir is a charter airline with weekly flights between New York and Tel Aviv. Israir offers economy- and business-class only, with fares several hundred dollars less than on major carriers. If you're willing to stop over in Europe, fares can be even lower when flying from the United States. Major European carriers—including Air France, British Airways, Czech Airways, KLM, Lufthansa, Swissair, and Turkish Airways—have daily flights from the United States and on to Israel with stopovers in their domestic hub airports.

Charter airline traffic to Israel from several U.K cities fluctuates according to season and demand. It's best to check the local U.K newspapers for up-to-date information.

For the long haul from Australia and New Zealand, you can fly to Hong Kong, Bangkok, or Beijing, and then transfer to El Al, which has twice-weekly nonstop flights to Tel Aviv from all three cities.

Because Israel is only ⅟₁₆ the size of California, it's often more efficient to drive within the country than fly. The exception is traveling to the resort city of Eilat, which is 360 km (224 mi) south of Tel Aviv on the Gulf of Eilat. There are daily flights to Eilat from Haifa and Tel Aviv's Sde Dov and Ben Gurion airports.

A daily commuter flight runs between Sde Dov and the Galilee town of Rosh Pina. For the best prices on domestic travel, check the airline Web sites.

**BOOKING**
When you book, look for nonstop flights and remember that "direct" flights stop at least once. Try to avoid connecting flights, which require a change of plane. Two airlines may operate a connecting flight jointly, so ask whether your airline operates every segment of the trip; you may find that the carrier you prefer flies you only part of the way. To find more book-

ing tips and to check prices and make online flight reservations, log on to www.fodors.com.

**CARRIERS**
The national flag carrier of Israel, El Al Israel Airlines, is known for maintaining the strictest security standards. It is not necessarily the cheapest way to fly. Air Canada, Air France, British Airways, Continental, Delta, CSA/Czech Airlines, Lufthansa, Northwest/KLM, Swissair, and Turkish Air fly from the United States to Tel Aviv. Within Israel, Arkia Israeli Airlines has flights from Jerusalem and Tel Aviv (Sde Dov Airport) to Eilat and Rosh Pina. Children fly for half price. Tour packages sometimes offer better deals on Eilat flights. Israir Airlines has service from Eilat to Tel Aviv and Haifa.

🛫 **To & From Europe and North America** Air Canada ☎ 800/776-3000 in the U.S., 888/257-2262 in Canada ⊕ www.aircanada.ca. **Air France** ☎ 800/237-2747 ⊕ www.airfrance.com. **British Airways** ☎ 800/247-9297 ⊕ www.britishairways.com. **CSA/Czech Airlines** ☎ 800/223-2365 ⊕ www.czechairlines.com. **Continental** ☎ 800/231-0856 ⊕ www.continentalairlines.com. **Delta Airlines** ☎ 800/221-1212 ⊕ www.delta.com. **El Al Israel Airlines** ☎ 212/768-9200 or 800/223-6700 in the U.S., 800/361-6174 in Canada ⊕ www.elal.co.il. **Lufthansa** ☎ 800/399-5838 ⊕ www.lufthansa.com. **Northwest/KLM** ☎ 800/447-4747 ⊕ www.nwa.com. **Swiss Internatinal Airlines** ☎ 877/359-7947 ⊕ www.swiss.com. **Turkish Airlines** ☎ 800/874-8875 ⊕ www.turkishairlines.com.
🛫 **Within Israel Arkia Israeli Airlines** ☎ 03/690-3712 🖷 03/699-313 ⊕ www.arkia.co.il **Israir Airlines** ☎ 877/477-2471 ⊕ www.israirairlines.com.

**CHECK-IN & BOARDING**
Security checks on airlines flying to Israel are stringent. International passengers are asked to arrive three hours prior to flight time in order to allow for security checks. Be prepared for what might sound like personal questions about your itinerary, packing habits, and desire to travel to Israel. Remember that the staff is concerned with protecting you, and be patient.

Always **find out your carrier's check-in policy.** Plan to arrive at the airport about two hours before your scheduled departure time for domestic flights and three hours before international flights. You may need to arrive earlier if you're flying from one of the busier airports or during peak air-traffic times. To avoid delays at airport-security checkpoints, try not to wear any metal. Jewelry, belt and other buckles, steel-toe shoes, barrettes, and underwire bras are among the items that can set off detectors.

Assuming that not everyone with a ticket will show up, airlines routinely overbook planes. When everyone does, airlines ask for volunteers to give up their seats. In return, these volunteers usually get a several-hundred-dollar flight voucher, which can be used toward the purchase of another ticket, and are rebooked on the next available flight out. If there are not enough volunteers, the airline must choose who will be denied boarding. The first to get bumped are passengers who checked in late and those flying on discounted tickets, so get to the gate and check in as early as possible, especially during peak periods.

Always **bring a government-issued photo I.D.** to the airport; even when it's not required, a passport is best.

## CUTTING COSTS

The least expensive airfares to Israel are often priced for round-trip travel and must be purchased well in advance. Airlines generally allow you to change your return date for a fee; most low-fare tickets, however, are nonrefundable. It's smart to call a number of airlines and check the Internet; when you are quoted a good price, book it on the spot—the same fare may not be available the next day, or even the next hour. Always check different routings and look into using alternate airports. Also, price off-peak and red-eye flights, which may be significantly less expensive than others. Travel agents, especially low-fare specialists ( ⇨ Discounts & Deals), are helpful.

Flights to Israel tend to be least expensive from November through March, except for the holiday season at the end of December. Prices are also higher during the Jewish New Year's holidays (usually in September) and during Passover (usually in April).

Consolidators are another good source. They buy tickets for scheduled flights at reduced rates from the airlines, then sell them at prices that beat the best fare available directly from the airlines. (Many also offer reduced car-rental and hotel rates.) Sometimes you can even get your money back if you need to return the ticket. Carefully read the fine print detailing penalties for changes and cancellations, purchase the ticket with a credit card, and confirm your consolidator reservation with the airline.

**🔁 On-Line Consolidators AirlineConsolidator.com** ⊕ www.airlineconsolidator.com; for international tickets. **Best Fares** ☎ 800/880-1234 ⊕ www. bestfares.com; $59.90 annual membership. **Cheap Tickets** ⊕ www.cheaptickets.com. **Expedia** ⊕ www. expedia.com. **Hotwire** ⊕ www.hotwire.com. **last-minute.com** ⊕ www.lastminute.com specializes in last-minute travel; the main site is for the UK, but it has a link to a U.S. site. **Luxury Link** ⊕ www. luxurylink.com has auctions (surprisingly good deals) as well as offers at the high-end side of travel. **Onetravel.com** ⊕ www.onetravel.com. **Orbitz** ⊕ www.orbitz.com. **Priceline.com** ⊕ www. priceline.com. **Travelocity** ⊕ www.travelocity.com.

## ENJOYING THE FLIGHT

State your seat preference when purchasing your ticket, and then repeat it when you confirm and when you check in. For more legroom, you can request one of the few emergency-aisle seats at check-in, if you're capable of moving obstacles comparable in weight to an airplane exit door (usually between 35 pounds and 60 pounds)—a Federal Aviation Administration requirement of passengers in these seats. Seats behind a bulkhead also offer more legroom, but they don't have under-seat storage. Don't sit in the row in front of the emergency aisle or in front of a bulkhead, where seats may not recline. SeatGuru.com has more information about specific seat configurations, which vary by aircraft.

Ask the airline whether a snack or meal is served on the flight. If you have dietary concerns, request special meals when booking. These can be vegetarian, low-cholesterol, or kosher, for example. It's a good idea to pack some healthful snacks and a small (plastic) bottle of water in your carry-on bag. On long flights, try to maintain a normal routine, to fight jet lag. At night, get some sleep. By day, eat light meals, drink water (not alcohol), and **move around the cabin** to stretch your legs.

Smoking policies vary from carrier to carrier. Most airlines (including El Al) prohibit smoking on all of their flights; others allow smoking on certain routes or departures. Ask your carrier about its policy.

## FLYING TIMES

Flying time from New York to Israel is approximately 11 hours; from Los Angeles, it's about 18 hours (including the usual stopover in Europe or New York).

Flights from London to Israel take about 5 hours and from Sydney 22 hours.

## HOW TO COMPLAIN

If your baggage goes astray or your flight goes awry, complain right away. Most carriers require that you **file a claim immediately.** The Aviation Consumer Protection Division of the Department of Transportation publishes *Fly-Rights,* which discusses airlines and consumer issues and is available online. You can also find articles and information on mytravelrights.com, the Web site of the nonprofit Consumer Travel Rights Center.

**7** Airline Complaints **Aviation Consumer Protection Division** ✉ U.S. Department of Transportation, Office of Aviation Enforcement and Proceedings, C-75, Room 4107, 400 7th St. SW, Washington, DC 20590 ☎ 202/366-2220 ⊕ airconsumer.ost.dot.gov. **Federal Aviation Administration Consumer Hotline** ✉ for inquiries: FAA, 800 Independence Ave. SW, Washington, DC 20591 ☎ 866/835-5322 ⊕ www.faa.gov.

## RECONFIRMING

Check the status of your flight before you leave for the airport. You can do this on your carrier's Web site, by linking to a flight-status checker (many Web booking services offer these), or by calling your carrier or travel agent. Always confirm international flights at least 72 hours ahead of the scheduled departure time. Reconfirmation obligations differ from airline to airline (and change from time to time); be certain to check with your carrier for all legs of your journey.

## AIRPORTS

Israel's main airport, Ben Gurion International Airport (TLV) is a few miles southeast of Tel Aviv. For information about transfers to Jerusalem, Tel Aviv, and Haifa, *see* the Essentials section at the end of Chapters 1, 3, and 4. Charter flights from Europe sometimes land at Ovda Airport (which operates only late September through May) or Eilat Airport, in southern Israel. Sde Dov Airport in north Tel Aviv handles domestic flights.

**7** Airport Information **Ben Gurion International Airport** ☎ *6663 or 03/975-5555. **Eilat Airport** ☎ 08/636-3838 or 1700/705-022. **Ovda Airport** ☎ 08/637-5880. **Rosh Pina Airport** ☎ 04/693-6478. **Sde Dov Airport** ☎ 03/698-4500.

## DUTY-FREE SHOPPING

Ben Gurion Airport is a good place to buy Israeli wines and liquors, locally produced chocolates, spices, tea, and Dead Sea products. Prices are comparable if not necessarily much better than at off-airport locations, but making your purchases at the airport saves you from having to carry them around with you during your vacation. A good selection of coffee-table books in English about Israel is also available at the aiport branch of the Steimatzky bookstore. You'll also find CDs with a broad range of Israeli and Jewish music at good prices here.

## BEACHES

Israel's Mediterranean coastline has many public beaches, most of which offer beach chairs, changing facilities, and bathrooms for a modest fee. Every Israeli beach resounds with the sound of the national beach sport *matkot.* It's played with two wooden paddles and a small rubber ball. No points, just hit the ball as hard as you can.

Swim only in designated areas where lifeguards are on duty. Don't be alarmed by lifeguards shouting out instructions to bathers. A flag system indicates how dangerous the waves and undertow are: a black flag means that conditions are rough, and swimming is not allowed; a red flag means moderate waves, swim with discretion; a white flag indicates a calm sea.

Women sometimes sunbathe topless on the beaches in Eilat. At the other extreme, some beaches in Israel offer sections for women and men who prefer to bathe separately in the interest of modesty. Some Mediterranean beaches, and most beaches on the Dead Sea and the Sea of Galilee, are stony, so be sure to wear rubber beach shoes, especially amid the spiky coral reefs of the Red Sea.

## BIKE TRAVEL

With mountains, deserts, and rolling wooded hills—plus archaeological sites galore—all packed into a small country, Israel is ideal for bicycling. Off-road adventure tours take you places you'd only find on foot or bike. Keep in mind, though, that the riding can be difficult due to extreme heat much of the year, many winding and hilly roads, and aggressive drivers. Biking is best enjoyed from October to May. Trains don't accept bikes, but buses do. Mountain bikes are available for rental at Red Sea Sports Club in Eilat. In Tel Aviv you can rent bikes for the whole family next to the lake in Hayarkon Park or at the Hayarkon 48 Hostel.

🚲 Bike Rentals **Hayarkon Park** ☎ 03/642-0541. **Hayarkon 48 Hostel** ☎ 03/516-8989. **Red Sea Sports Club** ☎ 08/633-3666 ⊕ www. redseasports.co.il.

## BIKE TOURS

The Jerusalem Cyclists Club can give you advice about local conditions and recommend routes. They organize one-day tours from Jerusalem on occasional Saturdays. The Green Wheelers Mountain Biking Group offers Friday and Saturday tours in the Judean Hills, Carmel, and Galilee areas. For Saturday tours in Tel Aviv and Jaffa, try the Tel Aviv Bicycle Club. Walkways runs country-wide 7-, 10-, and 14-day trips with professional guides. These tours combine cycling and hiking along biblical paths around the Carmel area, the coastal plain, the Galilee, the Red Sea, the Sinai Desert, as well as Petra in Jordan. Walkways handles all logistics, including round-trip transfer to the airport.

🚲 Bike Tour Operators **Green Wheelers Mountain Biking Group** ☎ 054/944-539 ⊕ www. geocities.com/Ron5506. **Jerusalem Cyclists Club** ☎ 02/643-8386. **Tel Aviv Biker's Association** ☎ 03/566-9667. **Walkways** ☎ 02/534-4452 ⊕ www.inisrael.com/walkways/main.htm.

### BIKE MAPS

Biking maps in English are hard to find. Serious Israeli bikers use the Israel Hiking and Touring Maps with marked trails and tracks. At this writing, only one in this series (#20, Eilat mountains) has been published in English. It can be ordered from ⊕ www.a-zara.com.

### BIKES IN FLIGHT

Most airlines accommodate bikes as luggage, provided they are dismantled and boxed; check with individual airlines about packing requirements. Some airlines sell bike boxes, which are often free at bike shops, for about $20 (bike bags can be considerably more expensive). International travelers often can substitute a bike for a piece of checked luggage at no charge; otherwise, the cost is about $100. Most U.S. and Canadian airlines charge $40–$80 each way.

### BOAT TRAVEL

The ferries that used to provide a cheap way of traveling between Israel and Greece and Cyprus have all suspended operations as of this writing.

### BUS TRAVEL

You can get almost anywhere in Israel by bus, and the Central Bus Station is a fixture in most towns: ask for the *tahana merkazit*. The Egged bus cooperative handles all of the country's bus routes except those in metropolitan Tel Aviv, where the Dan company also operates. There's a no-smoking policy on all buses.

Be aware that buses are often overcrowded on Saturday nights (after Shabbat) and during rush hours. **Be prepared to assert yourself** getting on or off the bus.

### CLASSES

Buses in Israel are clean, comfortable, modern, and air-conditioned. Fares are a flat rate per journey, not based on distance. All intercity buses and most urban buses have upholstered seats, and city buses also have strong plastic straps for hanging on, since Israeli bus drivers tend to drive faster than drivers in many other countries. In the larger cities of Jerusalem, Tel Aviv, Haifa, and Beersheva, a security guard wearing either a khaki or dark blue short-sleeved jacket rides along at the front of most buses. He/she will get off at every stop, survey the surrounding area for suspicious objects or people, and ensure the safety of passengers entering and exiting the bus.

### CUTTING COSTS

For travel between major cities and within each city, Egged offers a multiride ticket, or *kartisia* (10% reduction of bulk tickets of 10 or 20 rides), and monthly tickets (unlimited service within the month) at any city bus station or on the bus. These are particularly good for children and senior citizens, who get large discounts. Children under age five ride free whether or not they occupy a separate seat; after that it's full fare.

### FARES & SCHEDULES

Both intercity and urban buses run from 5:30 AM to 12:30 AM Sunday–Thursday. On Fridays and the eve of Jewish holidays, service stops approximately two hours before sundown. Keep in mind that public transportation generally stops for Shabbat (the Jewish sabbath, which lasts from sundown Friday afternoon to sundown Saturday evening), although some lines run minibuses in Tel Aviv. Haifa, with a large Arab population, also has some Shabbat service. It's a good idea to reserve seats in advance on buses from the major cities to Eilat and the Dead Sea. Call the Egged or Dan information lines for specific scheduling questions—the Hebrew announcement is followed by an English one—or consult their Web sites. Bus drivers in the main cities will almost always speak enough English to sell you a ticket or tell you where to disembark.
🚩 **Dan** ☎ 03/639-4444 ⊕ www.dan.co.il/english/default.asp. **Egged** ☎ 03/694-8888 or *2800 ⊕ www.egged.co.il/Eng.

### PAYING

For both local and intercity travel, bus drivers accept payment for tickets (payable only in shekels). They do not make change for a bill over NIS 50. It's faster to buy tickets at the bus stations. You do not need exact change on city buses. If you get on a bus at a highway stop, you can pay the driver.

### RESERVATIONS

Reservations by phone are generally not accepted in Israel. It's best to buy tickets ahead at the bus stations if you plan to travel between cities on Thursday night or the weekend, including Saturday night and Sunday morning. The exception is for travelers going from either Tel Aviv or Jerusalem to Eilat: reservations can be made over the phone by credit card and should be placed as early as possible to ensure a seat; last-minute travelers may still get on the bus but may have to stand in the aisle.

### BUSINESS HOURS

For information on national and religious holidays in Israel and their effects on various businesses and services, *see* National and Religious Holidays *in* Understanding Israel. The weekly observance of Shabbat has a different impact on different parts of the country: businesses in Jewish Israel close, but many nonkosher restaurants stay open.

Sunday is a regular workday in Israel. All government offices and most private offices and travel agencies are closed on Fridays as well as for all Jewish religious holidays. Businesses are generally open by 8:30 AM in Israel.

### BANKS & OFFICES

Although hours can differ among banks, almost all open by 8:30 Sunday–Thursday. Most close at 12:30 and then reopen on Monday and Thursday from 4 to 7 PM. Banks are closed on Jewish religious holidays and on Friday and Saturday except in Muslim areas, where they're closed Friday only. In Christian areas they're open Saturday morning and closed Sunday.

### GAS STATIONS

City gas stations stay open into the evening, and quite a few are open around the clock. Many close for Shabbat and religious holidays, though many highway gas stations stay open through holidays and late into the night as well.

## MUSEUMS & SIGHTS

Museums don't have a fixed closing day, so although they're usually open 10–6, and often on Saturday mornings, **confirm the schedule** before you go.

## PHARMACIES

Most local pharmacies close at 7 PM. Large chain stores, such as Superpharm and Newpharm, are usually open until 10 PM. In most cities a few drugstores are open all night, on a rotating basis. Daily listings can be found in English- and Hebrew-language newspapers.

## SHOPS

Shops generally open at 9 or 9:30; neighborhood grocery stores usually open around 7. A few shops still close for a two- or three-hour siesta between 1 and 4. Most stores do not close before 7 PM; supermarkets are often open later, and in large cities, there are all-night supermarkets. Arab-owned stores usually open at 8 and close in late afternoon. Mall hours are 9:30–9:30 Sunday–Thursday. Friday, the malls that close for Shabbat (such as Jerusalem's Malcha Mall) shut down about two hours before sundown and reopen two hours after sunset on Saturday evening. Outside Jerusalem, some malls keep regular hours on Saturday, while others stay closed.

## CAMERAS & PHOTOGRAPHY

There are certain military and religious sites and neighborhoods where photography is forbidden, usually indicated by signs. Hasidic Jews and religious Muslims do not like having their picture taken, so try to show respect and resist the temptation. To really capture the local flavor, take snapshots of the spectacular Mediterranean sunsets, and within the Old City walls of Jerusalem.

The *Kodak Guide to Shooting Great Travel Pictures* (available at bookstores everywhere) is loaded with tips.
🔢 Photo Help **Kodak Information Center** ☎ 800/242-2424 ⊕ www.kodak.com.

## EQUIPMENT PRECAUTIONS

Come prepared to deal with the extremely bright and sometimes harsh sunlight in Israel, as well as sandy conditions in the Negev Desert and at the beach. Take resealable plastic bags to protect lenses and other camera equipment. **Don't pack film or equipment in checked luggage,** where it is much more susceptible to damage. X-ray machines used to view checked luggage are extremely powerful and therefore are likely to ruin your film. Try to ask for hand inspection of film, which becomes clouded after repeated exposure to airport X-ray machines, and keep videotapes and computer disks away from metal detectors. Always keep film, tape, and computer disks out of the sun. Carry an extra supply of batteries, and be prepared to turn on your camera, camcorder, or laptop to prove to airport security personnel that the device is real.

## FILM & DEVELOPING

There are camera stores everywhere in Israel, so purchasing and developing film or printing from your digital camera should not be a problem. But you may want to bring film and batteries with you, because they're somewhat expensive here. A roll of Fuji or Kodak 36-exposure color print film costs NIS 16–22 (it's about NIS 29 for a roll of Advantix film). One-hour film developing is widely offered at many photography stores in every city.

## CAR RENTAL

Rental rates in Israel start at around $50 per day and $200 per week for an economy car with unlimited mileage; there is no tax on car rentals in Israel.

Most rental companies in Israel offer European or Korean cars, such as Fiats, Fords, Hyundais, KIAs, and Opels. They're generally smaller than American models. Mazda or Hyundai minivans with 6–8 seats are very popular and should be reserved well in advance, especially during high season.
🔢 Major Agencies **Avis** ☎ 800/331-1084, 800/272-5871 in Canada, 0870/606-0100 in the U.K., 02/9353-9000 in Australia, 09/526-2847 in New Zealand ⊕ www.avis.com. **Budget** ☎ 800/472-3325, 800/268-8900 in Canada, 1300/794-344 in

Australia, 0800/283-438 in New Zealand ⊕ www.
budget.com. **Hertz** ☎ 800/654-3001, 800/263-
0600 in Canada, 0870/844-8844 in the U.K., 02/
9669-2444 in Australia, 09/256-8690 in New
Zealand ⊕ www.hertz.com.

## CUTTING COSTS

Prices are the same for airport or city
rental. There are no discount rental car
companies in Israel. Since car rental in Israel is relatively expensive, your best bet is
to reserve over the Internet and travel on a
weekly, unlimited-mileage basis. El Al passengers are offered special discounts on
rental cars. Eldan offers car rental/hotel
packages for its Jerusalem hotel. Avis and
Sixt both specialize in car rental packages
in Israel. For a good deal, book through a
travel agent who will shop around.

Do look into wholesalers, companies that
do not own fleets but rent in bulk from
those that do and often offer better rates
than traditional car-rental operations.
Prices are best during off-peak periods.
Rentals booked through wholesalers often
must be paid for before you leave home.
🛈 **Local Agencies Avis** ☎ 800/638-4016. **Eldan**
☎ 800/938-5000 ⊕ www.eldan.co.il. **Sixt** ☎ In Israel: 700/501-502 ⊕ www.sixt.co.il.
🛈 **Wholesalers Auto Europe** ☎ 207/842-2000 or
800/223-5555 🖷 207/842-2222 ⊕ www.
autoeurope.com.

## INSURANCE

When driving a rented car you are generally responsible for any damage to or loss
of the vehicle. You also may be liable for
any property damage or personal injury
that you may cause while driving. Before
you rent, see what coverage you already
have under the terms of your personal
auto-insurance policy and credit cards.

## REQUIREMENTS & RESTRICTIONS

Drivers must be at least 24 years old. Your
own driver's license is acceptable in Israel,
but an International Driver's Permit is still
a good idea; it's available from the American or Canadian Automobile Association,
and in the United Kingdom, from the
Automobile Association or Royal Automobile Club. This international permit is
universally recognized, so having one in
your wallet is extra insurance against

problems with the local authorities. The
insurance coverage does not extend to
areas outside the borders of Israel or in the
Palestinian Authority. Children ages seven
and under must be seated in age-appropriate car seats.

The local representative of AAA and of the
British AA in Israel is Memsi. Should anything happen to your rental car, call your
rental company for roadside repair or replacement of the vehicle.
🛈 **In Israel Memsi** ☎ 03/564-1111 in Tel Aviv, 02/
625-0661 in Jerusalem.

## SURCHARGES

Before you pick up a car in one city and
leave it in another, ask about drop-off
charges or one-way service fees, which can
be substantial. Also inquire about early-re-
turn policies; some rental agencies charge
extra if you return the car before the time
specified in your contract while others give
you a refund for the days not used. Most
agencies note the tank's fuel level on your
contract; to avoid a hefty refueling fee, return the car with the same tank level. If
the tank was full, refill it just before you
turn in the car, but be aware that gas stations near the rental outlet may overcharge. It's almost never a deal to buy a
tank of gas with the car when you rent it;
the understanding is that you'll return it
empty, but some fuel usually remains.

Car seats cost $3 per day, and each addi-
tional driver is charged another $2 per day.

## CAR TRAVEL

Driving in Israel can be unnerving at
times. Israeli drivers are notorious tail-
gaters and use their horn at the slightest
provocation, but driving is the only way to
get to some of the more remote parts of
the country.

## EMERGENCY SERVICES

In case of an accident or roadside emergency, call either the police or Shagrir, the
national breakdown service.
🛈 **Police** ☎ 100. **Shagrir** ☎ 03/557-8888.

## GASOLINE

Service stations are generally full service.
Attendants do not expect to be tipped.
Most rental cars take unleaded gas. As of

this writing, a liter of high-octane gasoline costs about NIS 5.20 per gallon. Gas is classified by numbers: 95, 96, and diesel, known locally as *solar*. Gas stations are abundant in all areas of the country except in the Negev Desert. Most stations accept international credit cards.

## ROAD CONDITIONS

Israeli highways are basically in good shape, except in some rural areas. Road signs are written in Hebrew, Arabic, and English. Try to avoid entering and leaving the main cities at rush hours (7:30 AM–8:30 AM and 4 PM–6 PM), when roads may be jammed. The trans-Israel highway, known as Route 6, is a toll road that starts in Gedera, 24 km (15 mi) southeast of Tel Aviv, and continues north for 85 km (53 mi) to Afula. There are no toll booths to slow you down—electronic sensors read your license plate number and a bill for NIS 18 is then sent to your rental car company. The highway was designed to avoid congestion in the central part of the country. The speed limit is 110 kph (68 mph). Israel's highways are numbered but most people still know them simply by the towns they connect: the Tiberias–Nazareth Road, for example. Intersections and turnoffs are similarly indicated, as in "the Eilat Junction." Orange arrow–shape signs indicate tourist sites; national parks signs are on brown wood.

Jerusalem, Haifa, and Tel Aviv are all clogged with traffic during the workday. Many of Jerusalem's streets were not built to accommodate 21st-century traffic volumes. Don't drive in the city center if you're not comfortable negotiating narrow spaces or parking in tight spots.

A flashing green traffic light indicates that the red stop light is about 3 seconds away and you should come to a halt.

If you're driving through the Negev, watch out for camels that can come loping out of the desert and onto the road. In the winter rainy season, sudden flash floods sometimes cascade through the wadis (streambeds that are usually dry) with little warning, washing out roads. It's best to postpone your desert trip if there's heavy rain in the forecast.

It's a good idea to carry extra water—both for yourself and for your car—while driving at any time of year.

The Hebrew word for a native-born Israeli is *sabra*, which literally refers to a prickly cactus with sweet fruit inside. You'll meet the sweet Israeli if you get lost or have automotive difficulties—helping hands are quick to arrive—but behind the wheel, Israelis are prickly, aggressive, and honk their horns far more than their Western counterparts. Try not to take it personally.

## ROAD MAPS

Good road maps in English are available at bookstores. The most comprehensive highway map is the spiral-bound *Carta Israel Road Atlas,* which costs NIS 60.

## RULES OF THE ROAD

Unfortunately, there have been more Israelis killed by car accidents than in all of the nation's wars combined. It's advised to **use extra caution when driving a car** in Israel. By law, drivers and all passengers (front and back seats) must wear seat belts at all times. **Don't drink and drive.** Police crack down on drunk driving; the legal-blood-alcohol limit is .05%. It's against the law (and this is vigilantly enforced) to use cell phones while driving. Speed limits vary little across Israel: motorways (represented with blue signs) have speed limits of either 90 or 100 kph (56 or 62 mph) except for Route 6, where the limit is 110 kph (68 mph); highways (green signs), 80 or 90 kph (50 or 56 mph); urban roads, 50 or 60 kph (31 or 37 mph). Parking meters in all Israeli cities are closely monitored. Fines for an expired meter are NIS 100. Parking in an unauthorized area carries a NIS 250 fine. Headlights must be turned on in daylight when driving on intercity roads from November through April 1.

Children ages seven and under must be seated in age-appropriate car seats, and children under 12 are not allowed in the front seat.

## CHILDREN IN ISRAEL

Israeli tourist attractions are all well equipped to accommodate families with children. No museum usher will shush your child, and some places, such as Jerusalem's Israel Museum, have separate youth areas with activities to engage your children while you browse. Israel is full of indoor and outdoor amusement parks as well as playgrounds of all sizes. All but the most exclusive restaurants cater to children with kid-size portions and booster seats. Baby supplies are readily available. Children travel at half price on domestic flights and on trains. Children under age five ride free on the buses; after that, it's full fare. There are, however, discounts on multiride bus tickets available to kids of all ages. The weekend edition of the *Jerusalem Post* and *Ha Aretz* newspapers list activities for children. If you are renting a car, don't forget to arrange for a car seat when you reserve. For general advice about traveling with children, consult *Fodor's FYI: Travel with Your Baby* (available in bookstores everywhere).

**FLYING**

If your children are two or older, ask about children's airfares. As a general rule, infants under two not occupying a seat fly at greatly reduced fares or even for free. But if you want to guarantee a seat for an infant, you have to pay full fare. Consider flying during off-peak days and times; most airlines will grant an infant a seat without a ticket if there are available seats. When booking, confirm carry-on allowances if you're traveling with infants. In general, for babies charged 10% to 50% of the adult fare you are allowed one carry-on bag and a collapsible stroller; if the flight is full, the stroller may have to be checked or you may be limited to less.

Experts agree that it's a good idea to use safety seats aloft for children weighing less than 40 pounds. Airlines set their own policies: if you use a safety seat, U.S. carriers usually require that the child be ticketed, even if he or she is young enough to ride free, because the seats must be strapped into regular seats. And even if you pay the full adult fare for the seat, it may be worth it, especially on longer trips. Do **check your airline's policy about using safety seats during takeoff and landing.** Safety seats are not allowed everywhere in the plane, so get your seat assignments as early as possible.

When reserving, request children's meals or a freestanding bassinet (not available at all airlines) if you need them. But note that bulkhead seats, where you must sit to use the bassinet, may lack an overhead bin or storage space on the floor.

**FOOD**

For familiar food, many American fast-food chains, including Burger King, McDonald's, Pizza Hut, and Sbarro are found in nearly every city and town in Israel. Local restaurants that serve plain meat kebabs with french fries always offer children's portions.

**LODGING**

Most hotels in Israel allow children under 18 to stay in their parents' room at no extra charge. Children's discounts are often less generous at kibbutz guest houses. Most mid- to higher-price hotels offer cribs and cots and can arrange babysitters. Some spa hotels do not allow children younger than their mid-teens.

Many hotels, especially in resorts such as Eilat, feature special entertainment and activities that appeal to children.

The Hilton hotels in Jerusalem and Tel Aviv offer a family plan, an organized youth camp during the summer months, and/or an all-day children's program. The Dan hotels offer the Danyland program, which includes supervised activities during vacation periods. Sheraton hotels also offer a family plan.
🏨 **Best Choices Dan** ☎ 800/223-7773, 00800/ 326-46835 in the U.K. ⊕ www.danhotels-israel. com. **Hilton** ☎ 800/445-8667, 0990/445-866 in the U.K. ⊕ www.hilton.com. **Sheraton Hotels** ☎ 800/ 598-1753 ⊕ www.starwoodhotels.com.

**PRECAUTIONS**

Children dehydrate faster than adults, so bring along a bottle of water for each child when you head out. Sunscreen, insect repellant, and sun hats are also essential.

**SIGHTS & ATTRACTIONS**

Places that are especially appealing to children are indicated by a rubber-duckie icon (🐤) in the margin.

**F** Children's Attractions: Jerusalem **Biblical Zoo/ Tisch Family Zoological Gardens** ⊠ Gan Hakhayot St., Malkah ☎ 02/675-0111. **Liberty Bell Garden** ⊠ Between King David and Jabotinsky sts.
**F** Children's Attractions: Tel Aviv and Environs **Kfar Daniel Monkey Park** ⊠ At Kfar Daniel, right near the airport ☎ 08/928-5888. **Lunar Park** ⊠ Rokach Blvd. ☎ 03/642-7080. **Mini Israel** ⊠ Latrun Junction ☎ 08/922-2444 ⊕ www. miniisrael.co.il.
**F** Children's Attractions: Eilat **Kings City Theme Park** ⊠ Opposite Herod's Palace Hotel ☎ 08/636-4200 ⊕ www.kingscity.co.il. **Texas Ranch** ⊠ Opposite the Eilat port ☎ 08/637-6663.

## SUPPLIES & EQUIPMENT

Major brands of baby foods, powdered as well as premixed formulas, and disposable diapers are available in supermarkets and pharmacies everywhere. American brands of diapers such as Huggies cost between NIS 50 and NIS 65 for a package of 70 newborn-size or 50 medium/large diapers. Local brands sell for about 10% less. Toys for older kids can be expensive, so parents might want to bring along a few from home.

## TOURS

If you'd rather have someone else do the planning, Kids' Jerusalem Adventures specializes in tours and activities for families with kids of all ages; or if the folks want time alone, the company will plan a fun-filled day just for the children. Bar/ Bat Mitzvah celebration packages are also available.
**F** Kids' Jerusalem Adventures ☎ 972/2536-3449.

## COMPUTERS ON THE ROAD

Many hotels in Israel have dataports for laptops, and the major chain hotels typically offer Wi-Fi access. You can also find Internet access at the Tel Aviv and Jerusalem central bus stations and in many cafés. Jerusalem has free Wi-Fi Internet access in the downtown area, on Emek Refaim Street, and at Safra Square. Ben Gurion Aiport and the Eilat Airport also offer free Wi-Fi.

## CONSUMER PROTECTION

Get receipts for your purchases, and check that the correct amount has been written in on credit-card receipts. It is helpful to carry a pocket calculator so you can convert to your home currency when checking prices.

Whether you're shopping for gifts or purchasing travel services, **pay with a major credit card** whenever possible, so you can cancel payment or get reimbursed if there's a problem (and you can provide documentation). If you're doing business with a particular company for the first time, contact your local Better Business Bureau and the attorney general's offices in your state and (for U.S. businesses) the company's home state as well. Have any complaints been filed? Finally, if you're buying a package or tour, always consider travel insurance that includes default coverage ( ⇨ Insurance).
**F** BBBs **Council of Better Business Bureaus** ⊠ 4200 Wilson Blvd., Suite 800, Arlington, VA 22203 ☎ 703/276-0100 🖷 703/525-8277 ⊕ www. bbb.org.

## CRUISE TRAVEL

Due to security concerns, cruise travel to Israel has been severely curtailed over the past few years. A few companies still offer a stop in Israel as part of a "Grand World Voyage" itinerary, and others are waiting to announce plans for eastern Mediterranean destinations for the 2007 season. Several Israeli companies offer three- to seven-night cruises leaving from and returning to Haifa and calling at Greece, Cyprus, and Rhodes.

To learn how to plan, choose, and book a cruise-ship voyage, consult *Fodor's FYI: Plan & Enjoy Your Cruise* (available in bookstores everywhere).
**F** Cruise Lines **Costa Cruise Lines** ⊠ 80 S.W. 8th St., Miami, FL 33130 ☎ 305/358-7325. **Holland America Lines-Westours** ⊠ 300 Elliott Ave., Seattle, WA 98119 ☎ 206/281-3535. **Royal Princess** ⊠ 1320 Kalani St., Suite 304, Honolulu, HI 96817 ☎ 877/835-1100. **Royal Olympic Cruises** ⊠ 805 3rd Ave., New York, NY 10022 ☎ 800/872-6400. **SilverSea Cruises** ⊠ 110 E. Broward Blvd., Fort Lauderdale, FL 33301 ☎ 800/722-9955.
**F** Local Cruise Agents **Caspi** ☎ 700/709-090 ⊕ www.caspi-cruise.co.il. **Mano** ☎ 700/700-666 ⊕ www.mano.co.il.

## CUSTOMS & DUTIES

When shopping abroad, keep receipts for all purchases. Upon reentering the country, **be ready to show customs officials what you've bought.** Pack purchases together in an easily accessible place. If you think a duty is incorrect, appeal the assessment. If you object to the way your clearance was handled, note the inspector's badge number. In either case, first ask to see a supervisor. If the problem isn't resolved, write to the appropriate authorities, beginning with the port director at your point of entry.

### IN AUSTRALIA

Australian residents who are 18 or older may bring home A$900 worth of souvenirs and gifts (including jewelry), 250 cigarettes or 250 grams of cigars or other tobacco products, and 2.25 liters of alcohol (including wine, beer, and spirits). Residents under 18 may bring back A$450 worth of goods. If any of these individual allowances are exceeded, you must pay duty for the entire amount (of the group of products in which the allowance was exceeded). Members of the same family traveling together may pool their allowances. Prohibited items include meat products. Seeds, plants, and fruits need to be declared upon arrival.

🇫 **Australian Customs Service** ⌖ Customs House, 10 Cooks River Dr., Sydney International Airport, Sydney, NSW 2020 ☎ 02/6275-6666 or 1300/363263, 02/8334-7444 or 1800/020-504 quarantine-inquiry line 🖷 02/8339-6714 ⊕ www.customs.gov.au.

### IN CANADA

Canadian residents who have been out of Canada for at least seven days may bring in C$750 worth of goods duty-free. If you've been away fewer than seven days but more than 48 hours, the duty-free allowance drops to C$200. If your trip lasts 24 to 48 hours, the allowance is C$50; if the goods are worth more than C$50, you must pay full duty on all of the goods. You may not pool allowances with family members. Goods claimed under the C$750 exemption may follow you by mail; those claimed under the lesser exemptions must accompany you. Alcohol and tobacco products may be included in the seven-day and 48-hour exemptions but not in the 24-hour exemption. If you meet the age requirements of the province or territory through which you reenter Canada, you may bring in, duty-free, 1.5 liters of wine or 1.14 liters (40 imperial ounces) of liquor or 24 12-ounce cans or bottles of beer or ale. Also, if you meet the local age requirement for tobacco products, you may bring in, duty-free, 200 cigarettes, 50 cigars or cigarillos, and 200 grams of tobacco. You may have to pay a minimum duty on tobacco products, regardless of whether or not you exceed your personal exemption. Check ahead of time with the Canada Border Services Agency or the Department of Agriculture for policies regarding meat products, seeds, plants, and fruits.

You may send an unlimited number of gifts (only one gift per recipient, however) worth up to C$60 each duty-free to Canada. Label the package UNSOLICITED GIFT—VALUE UNDER $60. Alcohol and tobacco are excluded.

🇫 **Canada Border Services Agency** ⌖ Customs Information Services, 191 Laurier Ave. W, 15th floor, Ottawa, Ontario K1A 0L5 ☎ 800/461-9999 in Canada, 204/983-3500, 506/636-5064 ⊕ www.cbsa.gc.ca.

### IN ISRAEL

For visitors with nothing to declare, clearing customs at Ben Gurion Airport requires simply walking through the clearly marked green line in the baggage claims hall. Lines are generally short with no more than a five-minute wait. Customs inspectors rarely examine tourists' luggage. The red line for those with items to declare is next to the green line. Those over 17 may import into Israel duty-free: 250 cigarettes or 250 grams of tobacco products; 2 liters of wine and 1 liter of spirits; ¼ liter of eau de cologne or perfume; and gifts totaling no more than $200 in value. You may also import up to 15 kg of food products, but no fresh meats.

Pets are not quarantined if you bring a certificate issued by a government veterinary officer in your country of origin issued within seven days prior to travel. The certificate must state that the animal has been vaccinated against rabies not more than a year and not less than one month prior to travel. Dogs and cats less than three months old will not be admitted. At least 48 hours prior to arrival, pet owners must send a fax to the Ramla Quarantine Section stating the name of the owner, animal species, age, flight number, and approximate arrival time.

🔲 **Ramla Quarantine Station** ☎ 03/968-8963
🖷 03/960-5194

## IN NEW ZEALAND

All homeward-bound residents may bring back NZ$700 worth of souvenirs and gifts; passengers may not pool their allowances, and children can claim only the concession on goods intended for their own use. For those 17 or older, the duty-free allowance also includes 4.5 liters of wine or beer; one 1,125-ml bottle of spirits; and either 200 cigarettes, 250 grams of tobacco, 50 cigars, *or* a combination of the three up to 250 grams. Meat products, seeds, plants, and fruits must be declared upon arrival to the Agricultural Services Department.

🔲 **New Zealand Customs** ✉ Head office: The Customhouse, 17-21 Whitmore St., Box 2218, Wellington ☎ 04/473-6099 or 0800/428-786 ⊕ www.customs.govt.nz.

## IN THE U.K.

From countries outside the European Union, including Israel, you may bring home, duty-free, 200 cigarettes, 50 cigars, 100 cigarillos, or 250 grams of tobacco; 1 liter of spirits or 2 liters of fortified or sparkling wine or liqueurs; 2 liters of still table wine; 60 ml of perfume; 250 ml of toilet water; plus £145 worth of other goods, including gifts and souvenirs. Prohibited items include meat and dairy products, seeds, plants, and fruits.

🔲 **HM Customs and Excise** ✉ Portcullis House, 21 Cowbridge Rd. E, Cardiff CF11 9SS ☎ 0845/010-9000 or 0208/929-0152 advice service, 0208/929-6731 or 0208/910-3602 complaints ⊕ www.hmce.gov.uk.

## IN THE U.S.

U.S. residents who have been out of the country for at least 48 hours may bring home, for personal use, $800 worth of foreign goods duty-free, as long as they haven't used the $800 allowance or any part of it in the past 30 days. This exemption may include 1 liter of alcohol (for travelers 21 and older), 200 cigarettes, and 100 non-Cuban cigars. Family members from the same household who are traveling together may pool their $800 personal exemptions. For fewer than 48 hours, the duty-free allowance drops to $200, which may include 50 cigarettes, 10 non-Cuban cigars, and 150 ml of alcohol (or 150 ml of perfume containing alcohol). The $200 allowance cannot be combined with other individuals' exemptions, and if you exceed it, the full value of all the goods will be taxed. Antiques, which U.S. Customs and Border Protection defines as objects more than 100 years old, enter duty-free, as do original works of art done entirely by hand, including paintings, drawings, and sculptures. This doesn't apply to folk art or handicrafts, which are in general dutiable.

You may also send packages home duty-free, with a limit of one parcel per addressee per day (except alcohol or tobacco products or perfume worth more than $5). You can mail up to $200 worth of goods for personal use; label the package PERSONAL USE and attach a list of its contents and their retail value. If the package contains your used personal belongings, mark it AMERICAN GOODS RETURNED to avoid paying duties. You may send up to $100 worth of goods as a gift; mark the package UNSOLICITED GIFT. Mailed items do not affect your duty-free allowance on your return.

To avoid paying duty on foreign-made high-ticket items you already own and will take on your trip, register them with a local customs office before you leave the country. Consider filing a Certificate of Registration for laptops, cameras, watches, and other digital devices identified with serial numbers or other permanent markings; you can keep the certificate for other trips. Otherwise, bring a sales receipt or insurance form to show that you owned the item before you left the United States.

For more about duties, restricted items, and other information about international travel, check out U.S. Customs and Border

Protection's online brochure, *Know Before You Go.* You can also file complaints on the U.S. Customs and Border Protection Web site, listed below.

🚩 **U.S. Customs and Border Protection** ⊠ for inquiries and complaints, 1300 Pennsylvania Ave. NW, Washington, DC 20229 ⊕ www.cbp.gov ☎ 877/227-5551, 202/354-1000.

## DISABILITIES & ACCESSIBILITY

Facilities for travelers with disabilities in Israel still lag behind those of many other countries. Crowded, hilly streets, uneven pavement, cobblestones, and steps can make it difficult to get around without a companion, and adapted minibuses and rental cars are hard to come by. However, several museums and other tourist sights are making improvements. There are several volunteer organizations that offer assistance to people with disabilities. From its 76 branches around the country, Yad Sarah provides free transportation for people who use wheelchairs and lends medical supplies and rehabilitation equipment at no charge. It's best to call at least two weeks ahead to book an airport pickup and to arrange for special needs.

Israel passed the Equal Rights Law for People with Disabilities in 1998, and an amendment strengthening the provisions of the Act was added in 2005.

For a listing of accessible sights and attractions in Israel, contact the Pauline Hephaistos Survey Projects. The Hymie Moross Community Center of the Jewish Quarter's Visitor's Center for People with Special Needs publishes a Wheelchair Friendly Tour of the Jewish Quarter in Jerusalem.

🚩 **Local Resources Hymie Moross Community Center** ☎ 02/628-3777 🖷 02/626-0194. **MILBAT—The Israeli Center for Technical Aids and Transportation** ⊠ Tel Hashomer, Tel Aviv 52621 ☎ 03/530-3739. **Pauline Hephaistos Survey Projects** ⊠ 39 Bradley Gardens, West Ealing, London W13 8HE, England ⊕ www.accessproject-phsp.org. **ILAN—The Israeli Foundation for Handicapped Children** ⊠ 9 Gordon St., Tel Aviv 63458 ☎ 03/524-8141. **Umbrella Association of Organizations of Persons with Disabilities** ⊠ 57 Frishman St., Tel Aviv 64383 ☎ 03/523-8799. **Yad Sarah** ⊠ 124 Herzl St., Jerusalem 96187 ☎ 02/644-4444 🖷 02/644-4508.

## LODGING

All new hotels in Israel are required to provide facilities for guests with disabilities. For a listing of accessible accommodations in Israel, contact the Pauline Hephaistos Survey Projects.

## RESERVATIONS

When discussing accessibility with an operator or reservations agent, ask hard questions. Are there any stairs, inside *or* out? Are there grab bars next to the toilet *and* in the shower/tub? How wide is the doorway to the room? To the bathroom? For the most extensive facilities meeting the latest legal specifications, opt for newer accommodations. If you reserve through a toll-free number, consider also calling the hotel's local number to confirm the information from the central reservations office. Get confirmation in writing when you can.

Before you arrive, notify your airline and hotel of any disability to ensure that proper accommodations will be arranged.

## SIGHTS & ATTRACTIONS

Accessibility at the major sights and attractions in Israel is a mixed bag. All the country's major museums are wheelchair accessible, but many of the historic churches and archaeological sites are not. The Jewish Quarter of Jerusalem's Old City, including the Western Wall and the Cardo, are accessible using the "Wheelchair Friendly Tour of the Jewish Quarter" guide. Two restrooms in the Jewish Quarter are designed for wheelchairs. Mini Israel near Latrun is completely accessible and rents electric carts to get around the site. Masada's wide cable car and plentiful wheelchair-accessible bathrooms make the Herodian mountaintop fortress a good choice for wheelchair users. The Ceasearea Roman amphitheater has wheelchair paths and ample accessible bathroom facilities. Agmon Hula, a nature reserve in the Hula Valley in northern Israel, was designed with special attention to accessibility. All pathways in this park—known as the best spot in Israel to observe migratory birds—are negotiable by wheelchairs, and lookout posts have low windows and accessible bathrooms.

Public restrooms in shopping malls, airports, bus stations, and newer gas stations can accommodate wheelchairs, but the facilities in many restaurants are too narrow. Telephones in public places are generally placed at a convenient height for wheelchair users.

## TRANSPORTATION

Ramps and elevators are available in the central bus stations in all the major cities. Newer-model buses in all the major cities are wheelchair accessible. The older models are gradually being phased out. Not all train stations are accessible, so it's advisable to contact the Israel Railway Authority in advance. All airports in Israel have ramps and elevators and accessible restrooms. Eldan rents automatic cars with left- or right-hand controls. Reserve at least 10 days in advance. The U.S. Department of Transportation Aviation Consumer Protection Division's online publication *New Horizons: Information for the Air Traveler with a Disability* offers advice for travellers with a disability, and outlines basic rights. Visit Disability-Info.gov for general information.

**🔼 Information and Complaints** Aviation Consumer Protection Division (⇨ Air Travel) for airline-related problems; ⊕ airconsumer.ost.dot.gov/publications/horizons.htm for airline travel advice and rights. **Departmental Office of Civil Rights** ✉ for general inquiries, U.S. Department of Transportation, S-30, 400 7th St. SW, Room 10215, Washington, DC 20590 ☎ 202/366-4648, 202/366-8538 TTY 🖥 202/366-9371 ⊕ www.dotcr.ost.dot.gov. **Disability Rights Section** ✉ NYAV, U.S. Department of Justice, Civil Rights Division, 950 Pennsylvania Ave. NW, Washington, DC 20530 ☎ ADA information line 202/514-0301, 800/514-0301, 202/514-0383 TTY, 800/514-0383 TTY ⊕ www.ada.gov. **U.S. Department of Transportation Hotline** ☎ for disability-related air-travel problems, 800/778-4838 or 800/455-9880 TTY.

## TRAVEL AGENCIES

In the United States, the Americans with Disabilities Act requires that travel firms serve the needs of all travelers. Some agencies specialize in working with people with disabilities.

**🔼 Travelers with Mobility Problems** Access Adventures/B. Roberts Travel ✉ 1876 East Ave.,

Rochester, NY 14610 ☎ 800/444-6540 ⊕ www.brobertstravel.com, run by a former physical-rehabilitation counselor. **Flying Wheels Travel** ✉ 143 W. Bridge St., Box 382, Owatonna, MN 55060 ☎ 507/451-5005 🖥 507/451-1685 ⊕ www.flyingwheelstravel.com.

## DISCOUNTS & DEALS

Discount coupons for accommodations, attractions, restaurants, and shops are available from the Israel Government Tourist Office Web site at ⊕ http://coupons.goisraelshop.com. Coupons for reductions at kosher restaurants all over the country may be found at ⊕ www.eluna.com.

Be a smart shopper and compare all your options before making decisions. A plane ticket bought with a promotional coupon from travel clubs, coupon books, and direct-mail offers or purchased on the Internet may not be cheaper than the least expensive fare from a discount ticket agency. And always keep in mind that what you get is just as important as what you save.

## DISCOUNT RESERVATIONS

To save money, look into discount reservations services with Web sites and toll-free numbers, which use their buying power to get a better price on hotels, airline tickets (⇨ Air Travel), even car rentals. When booking a room, always **call the hotel's local toll-free number** (if one is available) rather than the central reservations number—you'll often get a better price. Always ask about special packages or corporate rates.

When shopping for the best deal on hotels and car rentals, look for guaranteed exchange rates, which protect you against a falling dollar. With your rate locked in, you won't pay more, even if the price goes up in the local currency.

**🔼 Hotel Rooms** Accommodations Express ☎ 800/444-7666 or 800/277-1064. Hotels.com ☎ 800/219-4606 or 800/364-0291 ⊕ www.hotels.com. **IsraelDeal.com** ☎ 866/852-5906 ⊕ www.israeldeal.com. **Israel-Travel.net** ☎ 057/970-788 in Israel ⊕ www.israel-travel.net. **Steigenberger Reservation Service** ☎ 800/223-5652 ⊕ www.srs-worldhotels.com.

## PACKAGE DEALS

Don't confuse packages and guided tours. When you buy a package, you travel on your own, just as though you had planned the trip yourself. Fly/drive packages, which combine airfare and car rental, are often a good deal. In cities, ask the local visitor's bureau about hotel and local transportation packages that include tickets to major museum exhibits or other special events.

## EATING & DRINKING

In the past few years Israel has earned itself a name in the gastronomic world—the restaurants we list represent the cream of the crop in each price category. Properties indicated by ✕⌑ are lodging establishments whose restaurants warrant a special trip. Price-category information is given in each chapter.

Seafood is a specialty in many restaurants in Eilat, Haifa, and Tel Aviv. Mediterranean dishes such as grilled fish and plates of hummus and warmed pita bread are staples. A variety of skewered grilled meats accompanied by mounds of french fries and a salad of chopped tomatoes and cucumbers is served at neighborhood restaurants and known as a *steakiya*. But these days you can also sample just about any national cuisine you want—Thai, Italian, Indian, Chinese, French, Indonesian, Japanese, even American—at any price level you want. And whereas "kosher" once meant "uniform," kosher restaurants today have to compete with a growing number of nonkosher restaurants (which, among other differences, serve seafood, and milk and meat together), so the variety of kosher food is growing.

Restaurants certified as kosher by the local rabbinate in every city are required to display a dated and signed Hebrew certificate. The weekend editions of the *Jerusalem Post* and *Ha Aretz* newspapers both carry extensive restaurant listings and note kosher restaurants.

## MEALS & SPECIALTIES

Hotels serve a huge, buffet-style breakfast called *arukhat boker,* comprising a variety of breads and rolls, eggs, oatmeal, excellent yogurt, cheeses, vegetable and fish salads, and such American-style breakfast foods as pancakes and granola. You can find the same spread at many cafés. Outdoor coffee shops serving salads, sandwiches, cakes, and delicious coffee abound. Every city and small town has modestly priced restaurants that open in midmorning and serve soup, salad, and grilled meats.

Israelis do like Western-style fast food, such as hamburgers and pizza, but more traditional casual favorites are falafel served with salad and condiments in a pita pocket, *shawarma* (grilled meat), cheese, and *borekas* (phyllo turnovers filled with spinach, cheese, or potato). Many falafel stands have salad bars where you can fill the pita yourself. Juice bars serving fresh-pressed juices using every kind of seasonal fruit and vegetable are easy to find on main streets in larger towns. Supermarkets, particularly in the large cities, have long, eclectic counters of takeout food, with everything from fried eggplant to chocolate croissants. Familiar fast-food chains, including McDonald's, Pizza Hut, and Sbarro are scattered throughout Israel, especially in the big cities.

Unless otherwise noted, the restaurants listed in this guide are open daily for lunch (*arukhat tzohorayim*) and dinner (*arukhat erev*).

Many restaurants offer business lunch specials or fixed-price menus, but à la carte menus are most common. A service charge (*sherut*) of 10%–15% is sometimes levied and should be noted separately on your bill.

## MEALTIMES

Unless otherwise noted, the restaurants listed in this guide are open daily for lunch(*arukhat tzohorayim*) and dinner (*arukhat erev*). In Tel Aviv, Haifa, and Jerusalem, cafés are generally open Sunday–Thursday 8 AM–midnight. Kosher cafés close two hours before sundown on Friday and reopen after sundown Saturday night. Nonkosher places usually keep regular hours on Friday night and Saturday. Restaurants serving lunch and dinner usually open at noon and close around midnight or 1 AM. Israelis eat dinner fairly late, especially when dining out. It is not uncommon to wait in line at a restaurant for dinner at 10 PM; your best bet is to plan to eat around 8 PM. Because Friday is not a workday for most Israelis, Thursday night is the big night out at the start of the weekend, when cafés and restaurants fill up quickly.

## PAYING
Credit cards are widely accepted in restaurants, but always check first. Tips can be paid in cash only. If you are dining in a smaller town or village, make sure you have sufficient cash with you, as credit cards are sometimes not accepted.

## RESERVATIONS & DRESS
Reservations are always a good idea; we mention them only when they're essential or not accepted. Book as far ahead as you can, and reconfirm as soon as you arrive. (Large parties should always call ahead to check the reservations policy.) We mention dress only when men are required to wear a jacket or a jacket and tie.

Dress in Israeli restaurants is generally casual.

## WINE, BEER & SPIRITS
The local brews in Israel are Maccabi (lager) and Goldstar (bitter), while Carlsberg, Heineken, and Tuborg are popular imports. Beer is most commonly available by the bottle, but some bars serve it on draught.

Wine has deep roots in Israeli culture. Israel is one of the earliest wine-producing areas in the world, and the symbol of Israel's Ministry of Tourism is a cluster of grapes borne on a pole by two men. Wineries built during the 19th century are still producing wine today, and a plethora of boutique wineries have sprung up in the past five years. Some, like Domaine du Castel and Yatir, have won international recognition. Best readily available wine bets are from Dalton, Ben Ami, Golan, and Carmel's Rothschild Series, but ask locals for recommendations too. As for spirits, those with a taste for Greek *ouzo* may enjoy the comparable, local *arak*. Sabra is a locally produced chocolate- and orange-flavored liqueur.

You can purchase liquor at special liquor stores; most are open until midnight. In the major cities, you'll find some stores open all night. Wine is available in every supermarket as well as at specialty wine stores. The legal drinking age is 18 and is enforced.

Wine, beer, and liquor are served at bars, cafés, and restaurants during regular opening hours. There are no licensing laws limiting hours when liquor may be sold.

## ECOTOURISM
Given Israel's location at the junction of three continents, plant and animal life is rich and diversified, and Israel has enacted strict laws to protect the environment. Enforcement is spotty, but it is illegal to pick any wildflowers, even common roadside varieties.

Beerotayim Ecotourism Center is a leading ecotourism company that offers adventure tours in the Negev Desert. Take its Camel Caravan and Donkey Tours, which range from a three-hour introduction to the ecology of the Negev Desert to an eight-day trek following ancient caravan trails. Or cruise along the sand dunes in a 4-by-4 vehicle and design your own tours. Whatever tour you take, you're sure to enjoy the hospitality and splendid Bedouin meals against a desert backdrop.

The Jerusalem Bird Observatory houses the Israel national bird-ringing center and is a center for birdwatchers of the thousands of birds that migrate through the area every year. The observatory is between the Supreme Court building and Knesset.

🕖 **Ecotourism Information Beerotayim Ecotourism Center** ✉ Beerotayim Tours, D.N. Haluza, Ezuz 85513 ☎ 08/655-5788 🖷 08/655-4369 ⊕ www.beerotayim.co.il. **Jerusalem Bird Observatory** ✉ Jerusalem ☎ 052/386-9488 ⊕ www.jbo.org.il. **Society for the Protection of Nature in Israel (SPNI)** ✉ 4 HaShfela St., Tel Aviv ☎ 03/638-8666 🖷 03/688-3940 ✉ In the United States: ASPNI, 28 Arrandale Ave., Great Neck, NY ☎ 800/411-0966 ⊕ www.spni.org.il.

## ELECTRICITY
To use electric-powered equipment purchased in the United States or Canada, **bring a converter and adapter.** The elec-

trical current in Israel is 220 volts, 50 cycles alternating current (AC); wall outlets take Continental-type plugs, with two round prongs.

If your appliances are dual-voltage, you'll need only an adapter. Don't use 110-volt outlets marked FOR SHAVERS ONLY for high-wattage appliances such as blow-dryers. Most laptops operate equally well on 110 and 220 volts and so require only an adapter.

## EMBASSIES

🇫 Australia **Australian Embassy** ✉ Beit Europa, 37 Shaul Hamelech Blvd., Tel Aviv 64928 ☎ 03/695-0451 🖷 03/696-8404.

🇫 Canada **Canadian Embassy** ✉ 3 Nirim Beit Hasapanut, Tel Aviv 67060 ☎ 03/636-3300 🖷 03/636-3380.

🇫 New Zealand **New Zealand Honorary Consulate** ✉ 3 Daniel Frish St., Tel Aviv, 54731 ☎ 03/695-1869 🖷 03/695-0817; or **New Zealand Embassy in Turkey** (responsible for Israel) ✉ Level 4, Iran Caddefi 13, Kavaklidere, Ankara, Turkey 06700 ☎ 90/312467-9054 / 🖷 90/312467-9013 /.

🇫 United Kingdom **U.K. Embassy** ✉ 192 Hayarkon St., Tel Aviv 63405 ☎ 03/510-0160 🖷 03/510-1167.

🇫 United States **U.S. Embassy** ✉ 71 Hayarkon St., Tel Aviv 63903 ☎ 03/519-7575 🖷 03/510-2444.

## EMERGENCIES

To obtain police assistance at any time, dial 100.

For emergency ambulance service, dial 101; 24-hour first aid and ambulance service are provided in nearly every town by the Magen David Adom (Red Shield of David). Clinics in major cities offer treatment on Shabbat or at other times when regular treatment is unattainable.

To report a fire, dial 102.

Emergency calls are free at public phones; no tokens or telecards are necessary.

🇫 **Magen David Adom** ✉ 2 Alkalai St., Tel Aviv ☎ 03/546-0111.

## ENGLISH-LANGUAGE MEDIA

### BOOKS

Most stores carry a wide range of current and classic English titles at prices about 15% higher than the country where they were published. You can find some bar-gains in the many secondhand bookstores in Jerusalem, Tel Aviv, and Haifa.

## NEWSPAPERS & MAGAZINES

You can pick up a copy of the daily newspapers, *The International Herald Tribune* and the *Jerusalem Post,* or the semimonthly newsmagazine the *Jerusalem Report* at most newsstands. The *Jerusalem Post* is a centrist paper offering a mix of news, opinion, and features. The *International Herald Tribune* includes an English translation of the Israeli daily *Ha Aretz* which is a highbrow, left-of-center paper providing local and international news in one package.

## RADIO & TELEVISION

You can hear a 15-minute news broadcast in English on the Reka Network at 954 AM in the center of the country; 1575 AM in the north; and 88.2 FM in Jerusalem at 6:30 AM, 12:30 PM, and 8:30 PM. There's an English news broadcast on TV Channel One (Ha'arutz Harishon) Sunday through Thursday at 4:50 PM, Friday at 4:30 PM, and Saturday at 5 PM. There are seven local TV channels, including the government-run Channel One. Every channel runs dramatic series, films, and documentaries from the United States and United Kingdom. *Oprah* is carried on Channel 10, while American soap operas like *The Young and the Restless* and *Days of Our Lives* can be seen on Channel 3. Most cable systems carry CNN, BBC, and Sky News. Movies are almost always shown in their original language, with Hebrew subtitles.

## ETIQUETTE & BEHAVIOR

"Etiquette" is not a key word in the Israeli vocabulary. In this highly informal society, there are many traditions but few rules. That said, both Jewish and Arabic cultures have their own social customs and strictures. Visitors (particularly women) to ultra-Orthodox Jewish quarters, such as B'nei Brak, near Tel Aviv, and the Jerusalem neighborhood Mea She'arim, should wear modest dress. Local women keep their knees and elbows covered and do not wear pants; married women also keep their heads covered (keep a scarf handy). Tourists wandering the streets (especially in the Old City, where the major sites holy to Christianity, Islam, and Judaism are located) will feel more comfortable if they observe this dress code, and it becomes essential when you enter a synagogue or other important religious institution (again, women in particular, though head covering for men will also be appreciated). Very religious Jews of either gender, who wear black garb, do not shake hands or mingle socially with members of the opposite sex.

Guests in Muslim households insult their hosts if they decline a drink (strong coffee or a soft drink is usually offered). Muslims do not drink alcohol, so a gift of wine is inappropriate. Like religious Jews, Muslims do not eat pork. Remove your shoes upon entering a mosque; women should cover their hair. Note that shaking hands or picking up food with the left hand is considered impolite.

## BUSINESS ETIQUETTE

English is the language of Israeli business culture. Business cards are very important and should be in English, although you can have the reverse side printed in Hebrew. Israelis delight in debate (and may take a long time to arrive at a final decision). They have a tendency to come off as extremely opinionated: they are confrontational, emotional negotiators, and their speech will often be peppered by broad hand gestures. Don't take offense—it's all part of the culture. In a business setting, dress should be modest and conservative. The standard greeting is to extend a *shalom* and a handshake. Hasidic Jewish men will not shake hands with women. Women may want to wait for a man to extend his hand before offering a handshake. Business attire for both men and women working in the central Dan region of Tel Aviv and Herzlia tends toward the casual, particularly in the long, hot summer season. In Jerusalem, those working in government offices at the director or management level may be a little more formal. Ties are generally worn only in formal business meetings. A dark pants suit for women is always acceptable.

## GAY & LESBIAN TRAVEL

Outside of the ultrareligious sector there's a general atmosphere of tolerance toward gay and lesbian people. A law banning gay and lesbian relationships was abolished in 1988. Tel Aviv has a large, openly gay community and a thriving gay nightlife scene. The Hilton Beach in northern Tel Aviv is a favorite hangout. Tel Aviv's annual Gay Pride Parade takes place in mid-June and typically attracts about 100,000 people. In Jerusalem, gay and lesbian activities tend to be more low-key, with the Jerusalem Open House community center acting as a focal point. Same-sex couples generally won't have problems at hotel check-in desks. It is commonplace for men to be affectionate in Middle Eastern culture, but this should not to be mistaken as approval for same-sex couples to be openly affectionate. No matter your sexual orientation, you should refrain from public displays of affection in religious areas. The Society for Protection of Personal Rights has a gay and lesbian hotline.

🛂 Gay- & Lesbian-Friendly Travel Agencies **Different Roads Travel** ✉ 155 Palm Colony Palm Springs, CA 92264 ☎ 310/289–6000 or 800/429–8747 🖷 310/855–0323 ✍ lgernert@tzell.com. **Skylink Travel and Tour/Flying Dutchmen Travel** ✉ 1455 N. Dutton Ave., Suite A, Santa Rosa, CA 95401 ☎ 707/546–9888 or 800/225–5759 🖷 707/636–0951; serving lesbian travelers.

🛂 Local Resources **Association for Gay Men, Lesbians and Bisexuals in Israel** ✉ 28 Nahmani St., Tel Aviv 65794 ☎ 03/629–3681. **Community of Lesbian Feminists** 🖃 Box 22997, Tel Aviv 61228 ☎ 03/516–5606. **Jerusalem Open House for Gay Men and Lesbians** ✉ 7 Ben Yehuda, 3rd floor ☎ 02/625–3191 or 02/625–3192 ⊕ www.gay.org.il/joh. **The Society for Protection of Personal Rights** ☎ 03/629–3681.

## HEALTH

Most doctors at emergency clinics and hospitals in Israel speak English. Emergency and trauma care is among the best in the world.

## FOOD & DRINK

It is safe to drink tap water and eat fresh produce after it's been washed, but take care when buying cooked products from outdoor food stands; the food may have been sitting unrefrigerated for a long time. Immodium and Pepto-Bismol are available over the counter at every pharmacy.

**OVER-THE-COUNTER REMEDIES**
At the pharmacy (*beit mirkachat*) it is very easy to find many of the same over-the-counter remedies as you would at home. Everyday pain relievers such as Tylenol and Advil are widely available. Medication can be obtained from pharmacies, which are plentiful. Fluent English is spoken in the majority of pharmacies. Locally produced medication is fairly inexpensive, but expect to pay more for drugs that are imported. In most cities a few drugstores are open all night, on a rotating basis. Daily listings can be found in English- and Hebrew-language newspapers.

**PESTS & OTHER HAZARDS**
Heat stroke and dehydration are real dangers if you're going to be outdoors for any length of time: a sun hat and sunblock are musts, as is plenty of bottled water (available even in the most remote places) to guard against dehydration. Take at least 1 liter per person for every hour you plan to be outside. Use sunscreen with SPF 30 or higher. Most supermarkets and pharmacies carry sunscreen in a wide range of SPFs, but it is about 20% more expensive than in the United States.

U.S. brands of mosquito repellent with DEET are available in pharmacies and supermarkets. Wear light, long-sleeved clothing and long pants particularly at dusk when mosquitos like to attack.

**SHOTS & MEDICATIONS**
No vaccinations are required; Israel has one of the world's most advanced health care systems.

**HOLIDAYS**
*See* National and Religious Holidays *in* Understanding Israel.

**INSURANCE**
The most useful travel-insurance plan is a comprehensive policy that includes coverage for trip cancellation and interruption, default, trip delay, and medical expenses (with a waiver for preexisting conditions).

Without insurance you'll lose all or most of your money if you cancel your trip, regardless of the reason. Default insurance covers you if your tour operator, airline, or cruise line goes out of business—the chances of which have been increasing. Trip-delay covers expenses that arise because of bad weather or mechanical delays. Study the fine print when comparing policies.

If you're traveling internationally, a key component of travel insurance is coverage for medical bills incurred if you get sick on the road. Such expenses aren't generally covered by Medicare or private policies. U.K. residents can buy a travel-insurance policy valid for most vacations taken during the year in which it's purchased (but check preexisting-condition coverage). British and Australian citizens need extra medical coverage when traveling overseas.

Always **buy travel policies directly from the insurance company**; if you buy them from a cruise line, airline, or tour operator that goes out of business you probably won't be covered for the agency or operator's default, a major risk. Before making any purchase, review your existing health and home-owner's policies to find what they cover away from home.

**⋺ Travel Insurers** In the U.S.: **Access America** ✉ 2805 N. Parham Rd., Richmond, VA 23294 ☎ 800/729-6021 🖷 804/673-1469 or 800/346-9265 ⊕ www.accessamerica.com. **Travel Guard International** ✉ 1145 Clark St., Stevens Point, WI 54481 ☎ 715/345-1041 or 800/826-4919 🖷 800/955-8785 or 715/345-1990 ⊕ www.travelguard.com.
**⋺** In the U.K.: **Association of British Insurers** ✉ 51 Gresham St., London EC2V 7HQ ☎ 020/7600-3333 🖷 020/7696-8999 ⊕ www.abi.org.uk. In Canada: **RBC Insurance** ✉ 6880 Financial Dr., Mississauga, Ontario L5N 7Y5 ☎ 800/565-3129 ⊕ www.rbcinsurance.com. In Australia: **Insurance Council of Australia** ✉ Level 3, 56 Pitt St. Sydney, NSW 2000 ☎ 02/9253-5100 🖷 02/9253-5111 ⊕ www.ica.com.au. In New Zealand: **Insurance Council of New Zealand** ✉ Level 7, 111-115 Customhouse Quay, Box 474, Wellington ☎ 04/472-5230 🖷 04/473-3011 ⊕ www.icnz.org.nz.

**LANGUAGE**
Hebrew is the national language of Israel, but travelers can get by speaking English only. Virtually every hotel has English-

speaking staff; as do restuarants and shops in the major cities. In smaller towns and rural areas it might take a little longer to find someone who speaks English. If you have learned a few words of Hebrew, such as *toda* (thank you), *bevakasha* (please), and *shalom* (hello and goodbye), your efforts will be warmly appreciated. If you can progress to ask *Ayfo ha-sherutim?* (where are the restrooms?), you'll be considered a linguistic hero.

Hebrew has a unique history: the language of the Bible was long dormant as a spoken language, used only for reading the Holy Scriptures and prayers, writing religious works and poetry, and as the Jewish lingua franca for educated Jews to communicate with Jews in other regions of the world. The revival begun a century ago has given Hebrew a whole new life. If Abraham, Isaac, and Jacob came back today, they'd have to take *ulpan* (intensive language classes) just like other new immigrants. English has also had an impact on Hebrew, to the extent that you'll hear not only official words like *bank, telefon,* and *lefaksess* (to fax) but also slang such as *ledaskess* (to discuss) and *heppening* (happening, event).

Arabic is Israel's other official language, spoken by Arabs as well as many Jews (especially those with origins in Arab lands). Because Israel is a nation of immigrants, mistakes and various accents are tolerated cheerfully, and polyglot Israelis speak so many different languages that you might be able to try out French, Spanish, Italian, Yiddish, and Russian. All Israeli schoolchildren study English and speak it to varying degrees of fluency.

Israelis use a lot of hand gestures when they talk. A common gesture is to turn the palm outward and press the thumb and three fingers together to mean "wait a minute"; rest assured that this has no negative connotations. Just as harmless is the Israeli who says "I don't believe you" to express that something is unbelievably wonderful. Few Israelis differentiate between "bus stop" and "bus station" (because one Hebrew word covers both), so if you want the Central Bus Station, make

sure you ask for it (*tahana merkazit*). Different systems of transliteration have produced widely inconsistent spellings: so is that Golan town Katzrin or Qazrin?

*See* Hebrew and Palestinian Arabic vocabularies *in* Understanding Israel.

## LODGING

Nearly all hotel rooms in Israel have private bathrooms with a combined shower and tub. The best hotels have a swimming pool, a health club, and tennis courts; and with rare exceptions in major cities, most hotels have parking facilities.

The lodgings we list are the cream of the crop in each price category. We always list the facilities that are available—but we don't specify whether they cost extra: when pricing accommodations, always ask what's included and what costs extra. Price-category information is given in each chapter. Because paying bills at hotels (as well as at car-rental firms and special tourist shops) in foreign currency eliminates the Value-Added Tax (VAT), prices are in U.S. dollars. Unless otherwise noted, all lodgings have a private bathroom, air-conditioning, a room phone, and a television.

In times of political unrest, it's best to call ahead to make sure that hotels are open.

Assume that hotels operate on the European Plan (EP, with no meals) unless we specify that they use the Continental Plan (CP, with a Continental breakfast), Breakfast Plan (BP, with a full breakfast), Modified American Plan (MAP, with breakfast and dinner), or the Full American Plan (FAP, with all meals).

### APARTMENT & HOUSE RENTALS

If you want a home base that's roomy enough for a family and comes with cooking facilities, consider a furnished rental. These can save you money, especially if you're traveling with a group. Home-exchange directories sometimes list rentals as well as exchanges.

Short-term rentals are quite popular in Israel, particularly in Jerusalem and Tel Aviv. Options range from basic studios to magnificent private homes. Most are owned by private individuals. The cost of a studio is typically between $750 and $1,000 a month; one-bedroom apartments start at around $1,200. Agents can give you the biggest selection, but if you would rather do it yourself, it's possible to find listings on the Web site ⊕ www. flathunting.com or to reserve a flat through Israel Holiday Apartments or Good Morning Jerusalem. Or you can pick up a copy of the *Jerusalem Post* for its comprehensive classified section of apartment rentals.

🔃 **International Agents Hometours International** ✉ 1108 Scottie La., Knoxville, TN 37919 ☏ 865/690-8484 or 866/367-4668 ⊘ hometours@aol.com ⊕ thor.he.net/~hometour.

🔃 **Local Agents Good Morning Jerusalem** ☏ 02/623-3459 📠 02/625-9330 ⊕ www.accomodation.co.il. **Israel Holiday Apartments** ☏ 09/772-7163 ⊕ www.holidayapartments.co.il. **Kleiman Real Estate** ☏ 02/563-8403 ⊕ www.kleimanrealestate.com.

## BED & BREAKFASTS

Bed-and-breakfast lodgings have become increasingly popular in recent years, especially in northern Israel. They usually offer clean, pastoral accommodations and fresh country breakfasts that feature local cheeses, jams, and breads. Many of Israel's *kibbutzim* (communal settlements) have opened B&Bs. Private-home owners are also increasingly opening their doors to guests.

🔃 **Reservation Services Bed and Breakfast in Israel** ⊕ www.b-and-b.co.il. **Good Morning Jerusalem** ☏ 02/623-3459 📠 02/625-9330. **Home Accommodation Association of Jerusalem** ☏ 02/645-2198 ⊕ www.bnb.co.il.

## CAMPING

Campgrounds in Israel are more rustic than in the United States or United Kingdom. They're known as *Khenonyanei layla* (night parking) and may be found in national parks everywhere around the country except for the central region around Tel Aviv. It's illegal to set up camp outside of parks, but despite this, many hardy Israelis camp on the beaches overnight. Typical campers are the under-30 crowd as well as families with small children. Camping on the shores of the Sea of Galilee surrounded by palm trees

and bougainvillea is pleasant in late spring and fall.

## CHRISTIAN HOSPICES

Christian hospices (meaning hostelries, not facilities for the ill) provide lodging and sometimes meals; these are mainly in Jerusalem and the Galilee. Some are real bargains, while others are merely reasonable; facilities range from spare to luxurious. They give preference to pilgrimage groups, but almost all will accept secular travelers when space is available. A full list of hospices is available from the Israel Government Tourist Office.

## HOLIDAY VILLAGES

Holiday villages can range from the near primitive to quite luxurious but tend to be relatively inexpensive. Commonly they offer simple facilities, usually sleeping from four to six persons in a unit, with basic cooking facilities in each unit. Some villages have full kitchens and even TVs, and most have a grocery store on the grounds. The rooms vary from huts and trailers to little houses.

## HOSTELS

No matter what your age, you can save on lodging costs by staying at hostels. In some 4,500 locations in more than 70 countries around the world, Hostelling International (HI), the umbrella group for a number of national youth-hostel associations, offers single-sex, dorm-style beds and, at many hostels, rooms for couples and family accommodations. Membership in any HI national hostel association, open to travelers of all ages, allows you to stay in HI-affiliated hostels at member rates; one-year membership is about $28 for adults in the United States (C$35 for a two-year minimum membership in Canada, £15.50 in the U.K., A$52 in Australia, and NZ$40 in New Zealand); hostels charge about $10–$30 per night. Members have priority if the hostel is full; they're also eligible for discounts around the world, even on rail and bus travel in some countries.

Youth hostels in Israel have improved in recent years and now compete with hotels and guest houses. Many of Israel's hostels provide family rooms with private baths;

most are air-conditioned; some have communal cooking facilities; and all provide meals. It's worth coming equipped with a valid HI membership card—otherwise, the attractive, modern hostels charge guest-house prices. Even without a card, however, hostels are a good deal.

**◢ Organizations Hostelling International–USA** ✉ 8401 Colesville Rd., Suite 600, Silver Spring, MD 20910 ☎ 301/495-1240 🖷 301/495-6697 ⊕ www. hiusa.org. **Hostelling International–Canada** ✉ 205 Catherine St., Suite 500, Ottawa, Ontario K2P 1C3 ☎ 613/237-7884 or 800/663-5777 🖷 613/237-7868 ⊕ www.hihostels.ca. **Israel Youth Hostel Association** ✉ Binyenei Ha'Ooma, Congress Center, Box 6001, Jerusalem 91009 ☎ 02/655-8400 🖷 02/655-8432. **YHA England and Wales** ✉ Trevelyan House, Dimple Rd., Matlock, Derbyshire DE4 3YH, U.K. ☎ 0870/870-8808, 0870/770-8868, 01629/592-600 🖷 0870/770-6127 ⊕ www.yha.org.uk. **YHA Australia** ✉ 422 Kent St., Sydney, NSW 2001 ☎ 02/9261-1111 🖷 02/9261-1969 ⊕ www.yha.com.au. **YHA New Zealand** ✉ Level 1, Moorhouse City, 166 Moorhouse Ave., Box 436, Christchurch ☎ 03/379-9970 or 0800/278-299 🖷 03/365-4476 ⊕ www.yha.org.nz.

## HOTELS

Israel has no hotel star-rating system. All hotels listed have air-conditioning, private bath, and tubs with showers unless otherwise noted. Hotels belonging to local or international chains can typically accommodate your request for either double, queen, king, or twin beds pushed together. Smaller, local hotels may offer more limited choices. Be sure to book well in advance for hotel stays during the Jewish High Holy Days in September and October and during Passover. Travelers sensitive to noise should opt for multistory hotels and request an upper floor if staying in the center of Jerusalem and Haifa. Tel Aviv hotels almost all face the beach, where noise is not usually an issue.

### RESERVING A ROOM

**◢ Toll-Free Numbers Choice** ☎ 877/424-6423 ⊕ www.choicehotels.com. **Hilton** ☎ 800/445-8667 ⊕ www.hilton.com. **Holiday Inn** ☎ 800/465-4329 ⊕ www.ichotelsgroup.com. **Hyatt Hotels & Resorts** ☎ 800/233-1234 ⊕ www.hyatt.com. **InterContinental** ☎ 888/424-6835 ⊕ www.ichotelsgroup.com.

com. **Marriott** ☎ 800/236-2427 ⊕ www.marriott. com. **Le Meridien** ☎ 800/543-4300 ⊕ www. lemeridien.com. **Renaissance Hotels & Resorts** ☎ 800/468-3571 ⊕ www.marriott.com. **Sheraton** ☎ 800/325-3535 ⊕ www.starwood.com/sheraton.

## KIBBUTZ GUEST HOUSES

Kibbutz guest houses, popular in Israel for years, are similar to motels; guests are taken in as a source of extra income for the kibbutz and are not involved in its social life (with the possible exception of having meals in the communal dining room). Unlike motels, though, the kibbutz offers a rustic, quiet setting. Most kibbutzim have large lawns, swimming pools (usually open only in summer), and athletic facilities. Some offer lectures and tours of the settlement.

**◢ Kibbutz Hotels Chain** ✉ 90 Ben Yehuda St., Box 3193, Tel Aviv 61031, Israel ☎ 03/527-8085 🖷 03/523-0527 ⊕ www.kibbutz.co.il ✉ Israel Tourism Center, 114 Essex St., Rochelle Park, NJ 07662 ☎ 201/556-9669.

## MAIL & SHIPPING

It takes about 4–5 days for mail to reach the United Kingdom from Israel and 7–12 days to reach the United States. It takes about two weeks for mail to Australia and New Zealand. All overseas letters are sent airmail.

The post office handles regular and express letters, sends and receives faxes, accepts bill payments, sells phone cards and parking cards, handles money transfers, and offers quick-delivery service. Nearly every neighborhood has a post office, identified by a white racing deer on a red background, and English is almost always spoken. The main branches are usually open from 8 until 6 or 7, and small offices are usually open Sunday–Tuesday and Thursday 8–12:30 and 3:30–6, Wednesday 8–1:30, and Friday 8–noon. In Muslim cities the post office is closed Friday, in Christian towns it's closed Sunday, and in Jericho it's closed Saturday.

In mailing addresses, the abbreviation M. P. stands for Mobile Post (M.P. Gilboa, for example). You'll see this as part of the address in more rural areas.

## OVERNIGHT SERVICES

For overnight service within the country (or two-day express service internationally), you can either use the EMS service at any post office, or for international delivery to Australia, New Zealand, the United Kingdom and the United States, contact FedEx or UPS. Pickup is available in most parts of the country. Fedex and UPS guarantee delivery from Israel to Australia in four days; to the United Kingdom and United States in two days. Prices are about 20% higher than the post office service.
**◪ Major Services EMS Service** ☎ **03/538-5909 Fedex** ☎ **700/700-339. UPS** ☎ **800/834-834.**

## POSTAL RATES

If you bring a letter to the post office before 10 AM, same-day delivery is guaranteed for about NIS 12 within the city, NIS 20 out of town. An airmail postcard to anywhere in the world requires an NIS 1.40 stamp.

## RECEIVING MAIL

Tourists who want to receive mail at a local post office should have it addressed to "Poste Restante" along with the name of the town. Such mail will be held for pickup free of charge for up to three months. American Express offices in the major cities also receive and hold mail free for card members; for a list of foreign American Express offices, call 800/528-4800. Mail delivery from Israel is reliable.

## SHIPPING PARCELS

Most stores offer shipping to international destinations. If you choose to send your purchases home yourself, you'll find all the supplies you need at any local post office, but be prepared to wait in a long line for service. Be sure to bring picture ID with you. Boxes and labels are available in various sizes, and you may insure your package. Parcels are generally secure when mailed from Israel. Packages to Australia will take two–three weeks by airmail and up to three months by surface mail. To the United Kingdom, it's approximately 10–14 days by air and two months by surface mail. To Canada and the United States, it takes approximately two weeks by air and up to three months by surface mail.

Quicker, more expensive alternatives are FedEx and UPS.

## MONEY MATTERS

Israel is a moderately priced country compared to Western Europe, but it's more expensive than many of its Mediterranean neighbors. Tourist costs, calculated in dollars, are little affected by inflation. Prices are much the same throughout the country. To save money, try the excellent prepared food from supermarkets (buy local brands), take public transportation, eat your main meal at lunch, eat inexpensive local foods such as falafel, and stay at hotels with kitchen facilities and guest houses. Airfares are lowest in winter.

Sample prices: cup of coffee, NIS 10; falafel, NIS 10; beer at a bar, NIS 20; canned soft drink, NIS 8–NIS 10; hamburger at a fast-food restaurant, NIS 16; 2-km (1-mi) taxi ride, about NIS 20–NIS 25; movie, NIS 35.

Prices throughout this guide are given for adults. Substantially reduced fees are almost always available for children, students, and senior citizens. For information on taxes, *see* Taxes.

## ATMS

Automated teller machines are widespread in the major cities in Israel at banks and shopping malls and are known by the name *kaspomat*. Look for machines that have stickers stating that they accept foreign credit cards or that have a PLUS, NYCE, or CIRRUS sign.

With a debit card, the ATM machine will give you the desired amount of shekels and your home account will be debited at the current exchange rate. Note that there may be a limit on how much money you are allowed to withdraw each day and that service charges are usually applied. Make sure you have enough cash in rural areas, villages, and small towns where ATM machines may be harder to find.

The norm for Personal Identification Numbers (PINs) in Israel is four digits. If the PIN for your account has a different number of digits, you must change your number before you leave for Israel.

## CREDIT CARDS

All hotels, restaurants, and shops accept major credit cards. Israelis use credit cards even for $5 purchases. Plastic is also accepted at banks for cash advances, although some banks will accept one card but none of the others. For cash advances using a Visa card, go to the Israel Discount Bank or Bank Leumi; with a MasterCard go to Bank Hapoalim or the United Mizrahi Branch. All of the credit card companies give an exchange rate that can be up to 5% better than the rate commonly used by banks.

Before you leave home, you must have a Personal Identification Number (PIN) to withdraw cash while overseas. Even if you already have a PIN, check with your credit card company to make sure that it will work in Israel. Again, the norm for PINs in Israel is four digits. If the PIN for your account has a different number of digits, you must change your number before you leave for Israel. Most credit cards offer additional services, such as emergency assistance and insurance. Call and find out what additional coverage you have.

Throughout this guide, the following abbreviations are used: **AE**, American Express; **DC**, Diners Club; **MC**, MasterCard; and **V**, Visa.

**⑦ Reporting Lost Cards American Express** ☎ 03/777-8800. **Diners Club** ☎ 03/572-3666. **Master-Card** ☎ 800/307-7309. **Visa** ☎ 800/941-1605.

## CURRENCY

Israel's monetary unit is the New Israel Shekel, abbreviated NIS. There are 100 agorot to the shekel. The silver-color one-shekel coin is about the size of an American dime, but thicker. Smaller-value bronze coins are the half-shekel and the 10-agorot coin (both of which are larger than the shekel), and the less-used 5-agorot coin. There is also a 5-shekel coin (silver in color), about the size of an American quarter, and a similar-size 10-shekel coin (bronze center, silver-color rim). Paper bills come in 20-, 50-, 100-, and 200-shekel denominations.

## CURRENCY EXCHANGE

Dollars are widely accepted at hotels and shops—less so at restaurants. As of this writing, the exchange rate was about 4.7 shekels to the U.S dollar; 4.1 shekels to the Canadian dollar; 3.5 shekels to the Australian dollar; and 8.2 shekels to the pound sterling.

For the most favorable rates, **change money through banks.** Although ATM transaction fees may be higher abroad than at home, ATM rates are excellent because they're based on wholesale rates offered only by major banks. You won't do as well at exchange booths in airports or rail and bus stations, in hotels, in restaurants, or in stores. To avoid lines at airport exchange booths, get a bit of local currency before you leave home.

**⑦ Exchange Services International Currency Express** ✉ 427 N. Camden Dr., Suite F, Beverly Hills, CA 90210 ☎ 888/278-6628 orders 🖷 310/278-6410 ⊕ www.foreignmoney.com. **Travel Ex Currency Services** ☎ 800/287-7362 orders and retail locations ⊕ www.travelex.com.

## TRAVELER'S CHECKS

Do you need traveler's checks? It depends on where you're headed. If you're going to rural areas and small towns, go with cash; traveler's checks are best used in cities. Lost or stolen checks can usually be replaced within 24 hours. To ensure a speedy refund, buy your own traveler's checks—don't let someone else pay for them: irregularities like this can cause delays. The person who bought the checks should make the call to request a refund. Dollar-denomination checks are your best bet in Israel.

## NATURE PARKS & RESERVES

Israel has parks and nature reserves in every corner of the country. Obtain a full list of parks, including those with camping facilities, from the Jewish National Fund, which also runs summer camping programs for families. For information on nature reserves and national parks, contact the Israel Nature and National Parks Protection Authority, which also offers a pass for unlimited entry to all nature reserves and national parks around the country for one month.

**⑪ Jewish National Fund** (JNF) ✉ Corner of Keren Kayemet and Keren Hayesod Sts., Box 283, Jerusalem 91002 ☎ 02/670-7411 ⊕ www.jnf.org. **Israel Nature and National Parks Protection Authority** ✉ 3 Am ve Olamo St., Givat Shaul, Jerusalem 95463 ☎ 02/500-5444 ⊕ www.parks.org.il.

## PACKING

At the airport, free baggage carts are plentiful, but you'll be carrying your luggage through the bus and train stations where carts are nonexistent, so try to pack light. Israel is a very casual country, where comfort comes first. Rarely will you need more than an afternoon dress or sports jacket to feel adequately dressed. Even posh restaurants do not require a jacket and tie. For touring in the hot summer months, wear cool, easy-care clothing. If you're coming between May and September, you won't need a coat, but you should bring a sun hat that completely shades your face and neck. Take one sweater for cool nights, particularly in the hilly areas and the desert. Also take long pants to protect your legs and a spare pair of walking shoes for adventure travel. A raincoat with a zip-out lining is ideal for October to April, when the weather can get cold enough for snow (and is as likely to be warm enough in the south for outdoor swimming). Rain boots may also be a useful accessory in winter. Pack a bathing suit for all seasons. Note that many religious sites forbid shorts and sleeveless shirts for both sexes; and women should bring modest dress for general touring in religious neighborhoods.

Along with the sun hat, take plenty of sunscreen, insect repellent, and sunglasses in summer.

In your carry-on luggage, pack an extra pair of eyeglasses or contact lenses and enough of any medication you take to last a few days longer than the entire trip. You may also ask your doctor to write a spare prescription using the drug's generic name, as brand names may vary from country to country. In luggage to be checked, **never pack prescription drugs, valuables, or undeveloped film.** And don't forget to carry with you the addresses of offices that handle refunds of lost traveler's checks. Check

*Fodor's How to Pack* (available at online retailers and bookstores everywhere) for more tips.

To avoid customs and security delays, carry medications in their original packaging. Don't pack any sharp objects in your carry-on luggage, including knives of any size or material, scissors, nail clippers, and corkscrews, or anything else that might arouse suspicion.

To avoid having your checked luggage chosen for hand inspection, don't cram bags full. The U.S. Transportation Security Administration suggests packing shoes on top and placing personal items you don't want touched in clear plastic bags.

### CHECKING LUGGAGE

You're allowed to carry aboard one bag and one personal article, such as a purse or a laptop computer. Make sure what you carry on fits under your seat or in the overhead bin. Get to the gate early, so you can board as soon as possible, before the overhead bins fill up.

Baggage allowances vary by carrier, destination, and ticket class. On international flights from the U.S., as of September 2005, you're allowed to check two bags weighing up to 50 pounds (23 kilograms) each, although a few airlines allow checked bags of up to 88 pounds (40 kilograms) in first class. Some international carriers don't allow more than 66 pounds (30 kilograms) per bag in business class and 44 pounds (20 kilograms) in economy. If you're flying to or through the United Kingdom, your luggage cannot exceed 70 pounds (32 kilograms) per bag. On domestic flights, the limit is usually 50 to 70 pounds (23 to 32 kilograms) per bag. In general, carry-on bags shouldn't exceed 40 pounds (18 kilograms). Most airlines won't accept bags that weigh more than 100 pounds (45 kilograms) on domestic or international flights. Expect to pay a fee for baggage that exceeds weight limits. Check baggage restrictions with your carrier before you pack.

Airline liability for baggage is limited to $2,500 per person on flights within the United States. On international flights it amounts to $9.07 per pound or $20 per kilogram for checked baggage (roughly $540 per 50-pound bag), with a maximum of $634.90 per piece, and $400 per passenger for unchecked baggage. You can buy additional coverage at check-in for about $10 per $1,000 of coverage, but it often excludes a rather extensive list of items, shown on your airline ticket.

Before departure, itemize your bags' contents and their worth, and label the bags with your name, address, and phone number. (If you use your home address, cover it so potential thieves can't see it readily.) Include a label inside each bag and **pack a copy of your itinerary.** At check-in, make sure each bag is correctly tagged with the destination airport's three-letter code. Because some checked bags will be opened for hand inspection, the U.S. Transportation Security Administration recommends that you leave luggage unlocked or use the plastic locks offered at check-in. TSA screeners place an inspection notice inside searched bags, which are re-sealed with a special lock.

If your bag has been searched and contents are missing or damaged, file a claim with the TSA Consumer Response Center as soon as possible. If your bags arrive damaged or fail to arrive at all, file a written report with the airline before leaving the airport.

**🖪 Complaints U.S. Transportation Security Administration Contact Center** ☎ 866/289-9673 ⊕ www.tsa.gov.

## PASSPORTS & VISAS

When traveling internationally, carry your passport even if you don't need one. Not only is it the best form of I.D., but it's also being required more and more. As of December 31, 2005, for instance, Americans need a passport to reenter the country from Bermuda, the Caribbean, and Panama. Such requirements also affect reentry from Canada and Mexico by air and sea (as of December 31, 2006) and land (as of December 31, 2007). **Make two photocopies of the data page** (one for someone at home and another for you, carried separately from your passport). If you lose your passport,

promptly call the nearest embassy or consulate and the local police.

U.S. passport applications for children under age 14 require consent from both parents or legal guardians; both parents must appear together to sign the application. If only one parent appears, he or she must submit a written statement from the other parent authorizing passport issuance for the child. A parent with sole authority must present evidence of it when applying; acceptable documentation includes the child's certified birth certificate listing only the applying parent, a court order specifically permitting this parent's travel with the child, or a death certificate for the nonapplying parent. Application forms and instructions are available on the Web site of the U.S. State Department's Bureau of Consular Affairs (⊕ travel.state.gov).

### ENTERING ISRAEL

Australian, New Zealand, U.S., Canadian, and U.K. citizens, even infants, need only a valid passport to enter Israel for stays of up to 90 days. Make sure your passport is valid for at least six months after your travel date or you won't be permitted entry. No health certificate or innoculations are required.

Israel issues three-month tourist visas free of charge at the point of entry when a valid passport is presented. Some countries (particularly in the Middle East) refuse to admit travelers whose passports carry an Israeli visa entry stamp, so if you're concerned about regional mobility, you can ask the customs officer at your point of entry to issue a tourist visa on a separate piece of paper; or you can apply for a second passport and include a letter with the application explaining that you need the passport for travel to Israel. Be advised that it is not unheard of for Israeli customs officers to stamp passports despite requests not to do so; if you plan to travel repeatedly between Israel and those Arab states still hostile to Israel, a second passport is advisable.

### PASSPORT OFFICES

The best time to apply for a passport or to renew is in fall and winter. Before any trip, check your passport's expiration date, and, if necessary, renew it as soon as possible.

**⏹ Australian Citizens Passports Australia** Australian Department of Foreign Affairs and Trade ☎ 131–232 ⊕ www.passports.gov.au.

**⏹ Canadian Citizens Passport Office** ✉ to mail in applications: Foreign Affairs Canada, Gatineau, Québec K1A 0G3 ☎ 800/567–6868 ⊕ www.ppt.gc.ca.

**⏹ New Zealand Citizens New Zealand Passports Office** ☎ 0800/22–5050 or 04/474–8100 ⊕ www.passports.govt.nz.

**⏹ U.K. Citizens U.K. Passport Service** ☎ 0870/521–0410 ⊕ www.passport.gov.uk.

**⏹ U.S. Citizens National Passport Information Center** ☎ 877/487–2778, 888/874–7793 TDD/TTY ⊕ travel.state.gov.

## POLITICS

For information about the political unrest and safety in Israel, *see* Safety, *below.*

## RESTROOMS

Public restrooms are plentiful in Israel and similar in facilities and cleanliness to those in the United States. At gas stations and some parks, toilet paper is sometimes in short supply, so you might want to carry some with you. No public sinks, except those at hotels, have hot water, but most dispense liquid soap. Occasionally you may be asked to pay one shekel at some facilities.

## SAFETY

Traveling throughout much of Israel is safe for the most part. You should, of course, use common sense when driving or walking in isolated areas at night. Still, you'll find that the downtown areas of major cities are comfortable enough after dark, even if you're alone. Violent crime is not a serious problem in Israel, but thieves can easily prey on tourists, so be alert. Women should not leave handbags dangling off the back of a chair in restaurants or bars. Keep them on your lap or wind the strap around your leg under the middle of the table. Never leave valuables visible in a car, especially in parking lots of national parks or tourist sites. It's not uncommon for thieves to help themselves to the contents of car trunks even in the most remote areas.

Don't wear a money belt or a waist pack, both of which peg you as a tourist. Dis-

tribute your cash and any valuables (including your credit cards and passport) between a deep front pocket, an inside jacket or vest pocket, and a hidden money pouch. Do not reach for the money pouch once you're in public.

On the security front, Israel has been the subject of such intense media attention over the years that, ironically, many would-be visitors are more rather than less confused about where to go and what regions to avoid. Rest assured that security in Israel is priority number one and among the best in the world.

Despite the country's small size, trouble in one area does not necessarily influence travel in another. In Jerusalem, the Old City can be thronged during the day and relatively empty at night, when almost everything there is closed. Spend your evenings elsewhere. In times of particular political unrest, it is generally best to avoid shopping areas, public buses and bus stops, and other crowded areas. The Arab neighborhoods of East Jerusalem have become less hospitable of late, but unless there are general security problems at the time, the daytime wanderer should not encounter any problems. In the Palestinian autonomous areas, travel to Bethlehem, Jericho, and Ramallah is best undertaken on an organized tour or with a guide who knows the area well. The rest of the West Bank, including the city of Hebron, has been outside tourist itineraries for some years now. Do not drive your own car through these areas, and avoid Gaza entirely. There are standard security checks along the roads to the West Bank, but the routes are open except in periods of particular political tension.

Expect to have your handbags searched as a matter of course when you enter department stores, places of entertainment, museums, and public buildings. These checks are generally fast and courteous.

For the latest governmental travel advisories regarding travel to and within Israel, check with your consulate (⇨ Embassies, *above*) or with the U.S. State Department. The Israel Ministry of Tourism includes a section in its Web site with a nonalarmist perspective on visiting Israel during periods of unrest. For the latest local news, check the English-language papers *Ha Aretz* or the *Jerusalem Post,* available online.

## LOCAL SCAMS

You may encounter a taxi driver who refuses to turn on the meter and demands an exorbitant sum for a short ride. Get out and hail another cab. Merchants in the souk in Jerusalem's Old City will invite you into their store for tea or coffee. If you accept, you'll be expected to make a purchase. There are no fixed prices in the souk or the Jaffa flea market. Try to ask a local about the acceptable price for the item you want before you start bargaining. Watch your wallet in crowds, and keep valuables in the trunk of your (locked) car.

## WOMEN IN ISRAEL

If you carry a purse, choose one with a zipper and a thick strap that you can drape across your body; adjust the length so that the purse sits in front of you at or above hip level. (Don't wear a money belt or a waist pack.) Store only enough money in the purse to cover casual spending. Distribute the rest of your cash and any valuables between deep front pockets, inside jacket or vest pockets, and a concealed money pouch.

Women travelers feel at ease in Israel: dining alone is not uncomfortable, and even walking alone at night is safe (on the beaten paths). Young women, especially blondes and redheads, will get attention, but it's usually harmless. To avoid the hassles, don't wear short shorts or halter tops. Walk arm-in-arm with a woman friend to present a more formidable front. Men can be very forward, so if you're not interested, be very direct. Look them in the eye and say firmly, *lo* (no).

🚩 Israel Ministry of Tourism **Israel Ministry of Tourism** ⊕ www.goisrael.com.
🚩 On-line News *Ha Aretz* ⊕ www.haaretzdaily.com. *Jerusalem Post* ⊕ www.jpost.com.

## SENIOR-CITIZEN TRAVEL

In most cities, travelers over age 60 get reduced admission to museums, theaters, and other attractions. It is important to carry a form of identification that verifies your birth date, like a driver's license.

To qualify for age-related discounts, mention your senior-citizen status up front when booking hotel reservations (not when checking out) and before you're seated in restaurants (not when paying the bill). Be sure to have identification on hand. When renting a car, ask about promotional car-rental discounts, which can be cheaper than senior-citizen rates.

🚩 Educational Programs **Canadian-American Active Retirees in Israel** ☎ 888/563-0033, Ext. 239 ⊕ www.jnf.org. **The Mature Traveler** ✎ Box 50400, Reno, NV 89513 ☎ 800/460-6676.
🚩 Local Programs **Association of Americans and Canadians in Israel** ✉ 6 Mane St., Jerusalem ☎ 02/561-7151 📠 02/566-1186 ⊕ www.aaci.org.il.

## SHOPPING

The Ministry of Tourism publishes a guide to shopping in Israel, with frequent updates on special discounts for tourists; this is available at Israel Government Tourist Offices.

Israelis love to shop and there are malls, boutiques, and markets all over the country. Israeli clothing is not cheap, but many travelers find its high-fashion designs appealing, particularly in bathing suits and leather goods.

Jewelry, gems, and locally cut diamonds are considered good buys in Israel. The large cities have many reputable jewelry outlets. Ethnic items and crafts such as embroidered skullcaps (*kippot,* or yarmulkes), tie-dyed scarves, spice boxes, blown glass, Hanukkah lights, and the like are popular gifts.

If you're shopping in an outdoor market (except a food market), stall owners will expect you to bargain. You should expect to pay half of the original asking price.

## KEY DESTINATIONS

Tel Aviv is the fashion center of Israel, with dozens of boutiques ranging from stores that specialize in designer names clustered around the posh Kikar Hamedina circle and Dizengoff Street to the young, urban-chic shops of Sheinkin Street.

Jerusalem's Ben Yehuda Street and the Dizengoff Center in Tel Aviv both have army-surplus stores. The popular Naot footwear can be brought for about 20% cheaper here than in the United States, and even greater discounts are available if you make the trip to the Naot outlet store at Kibbutz Naot Mordechai in northern Israel.

Jerusalem is a good place to look for antiques and Judaica (Jewish religious items). The area known as Arts and Crafts Lane, the Cardo in the Jewish Quarter of the Old City, and the neighborhood called Mea She'arim have a large selection. Christian objects are also plentiful in Jerusalem, especially in the Old City.

Two of the largest retail malls are Ramat Aviv Mall in the northern Tel Aviv suburb and the Malcha Mall in the southern part of Jerusalem. The nation's first outlet mall is at Kibbutz Gaash, a few miles north of Tel Aviv.

### SMART SOUVENIRS

Attractive souvenirs from Israel include hand-painted decorative Armenian ceramic ware, handmade olive oil soaps, and the wooden Wissotzky Magic Tea Box, which includes a selection of 80 sachets of Israeli herbal teas. The best places to find quality Armenian ceramics are the small shops in the Armenian Quarter of Jerusalem's Old City. Prices vary depending on size and style, anywhere from $10–$60. The Magic Tea Box is available at the airport and larger supermarkets and costs around $25. The best-quality handmade olive oil soaps are made in the Galilee and sold in gift shops throughout the country.

### WATCH OUT

Antiquities trade is popular in Israel, but it is forbidden to export antiquities unless you are in possession of a written export permit. Such a permit can be obtained only through the Department of Antiquities and Museums of the Ministry of Education and Culture. If you have any trouble while shopping in Israel, submit consumer complaints to the Ministry of Industry and Trade's Consumer Protection Service.

**⚡ Consumer Complaints** Ministry of Industry and Trade's Consumer Protection Service ⊠ 76 Mazeh St., Tel Aviv ☎ 03/560-4671.

### SIGHTSEEING GUIDES

Guides are organized through tour companies and must be licensed by the Ministry of Tourism. Freelance guides may approach unaccompanied travelers near the Jaffa Gate in the Old City of Jerusalem. These guides are not licensed, so it's impossible to know whether the tour they're offering is worthwhile or if they're planning on taking you to the souvenir stall of their best friend. It's best to ignore them and walk on.

Advice and guiding service is available from Fodor's in-field writers, themselves qualified guides: Judy Balint (Jerusalem only), Judy Goldman, Mike Hollander, Mike Rogoff, and Miriam Feinberg Vamosh. **⚡ Judy Balint** ☎ 052/677-8804 ⎙ 02/566-2370 ✎ judy@jerusalemdiaries.com. **Judy Goldman** ☎ 02/624-5827 ⎙ 02/623-3834 ✎ judebob@netvision.net.il. **Mike Hollander** ☎ 052/640-6796 ⎙ 08/970-1506 ✎ mandmhollander@bezeqint.net. **Mike Rogoff** ☎☎ 02/679-0410 ✎ rogoff@netvision.net.il. **Miriam Feinberg Vamosh** ☎☎ 02/534-5071 ✎ mim@netvision.net.il.

### GUIDE-DRIVEN LIMOUSINES

Modern, air-conditioned limousines and minibuses driven by expert, licensed guides are not only a good value for a family or a group of five to seven but also an outstanding way to see the country for anyone whose budget can bear it. At this writing, the cost was $450 per day (nine hours) for up to seven passengers. Rates are based on 200 km (120 mi) of travel a day, averaged out over the entire tour, and nine hours a day of touring. An additional $100–$120 per night (depending on location) is charged for the driver's expenses if he or she sleeps away from home. Half-day tours are also available. **⚡ Limo Companies** Eshkolot Tours ⊠ 36 Keren Hayesod St., Jerusalem ☎ 02/563-5555 or 02/566-5555 ⎙ 02/563-2101. **Guided Limousine Tours** ☎ 03/642-1649 ⊕ www.glt.co.il. **Superb Limousine Services** ⊠ Ben Gurion Airport ☎ 03/973-1780 ⊕ www.superb.co.il.

## SPORTS & OUTDOORS

### GOLF

The Caesarea Golf Club, an 18-hole golf course on the northern coast, is open seven days a week. Tourists can obtain special memberships, and the club rents all equipment. The new, 9-hole Ga'ash Golf Club is 20 km (12 mi) north of Tel Aviv.

🏌 **Caesarea Golf Club** ✐ Box 4858, Caesarea 38900 ☎ 04/610-9600 ⊕ www.caesarea.org.il. **Ga'ash Golf Club** ✉ Kibbutz Ga'ash ☎ 09/951-5111 ⊕ www.gaashgolfclub.co.il.

### TENNIS

There are tennis centers throughout the country, with nominal court fees; reserve in advance. Ask for the National Tennis Center.

🏌 **National Tennis Center** ✐ Box 51, Ramat Hasharon 47100 ☎ 03/645-6666 ⊕ www.tennis.org.il.

### WATER SPORTS

Scuba diving and snorkeling are popular in Eilat and at various Mediterranean beaches. Dive trips to the Red Sea, home to some of the best diving sites in the world, leave from Eilat. Information is available from the Israeli Diving Federation. Divers must present an advanced open-water license or a junior scuba license, or take a course. Windsurfing and waterskiing are offered at various beaches and hotels in Eilat.

🏌 **Israeli Diving Federation** ✉ 94 Hayarkon St., Box 3404, Tel Aviv 61033 ☎ 03/523-6436.

### STUDENTS IN ISRAEL

The Israel Student Travel Association has 12 branches, in major cities and on university campuses throughout Israel. ISSTA offers discounted tours, car rentals, hotels, and flights. Students from abroad often take advantage of ISSTA's international travel programs.

🏌 **Local Resources** Israel Student Travel Association ✉ 50 Dizengoff St., Tel Aviv 64332 ☎ 03/621-6100 ✉ 31 Hanevi'im St., Jerusalem 95103 ☎ 02/621-3600 ✉ 2 Balfour St., Haifa 33121 ☎ 04/868-2222 ⊕ www.istc.org. 🏌 **I.D.s & Services** STA Travel ✉ 10 Downing St., New York, NY 10014 ☎ 212/627-3111, 800/781-4040 24-hr service center in the U.S. ⊕ www.sta.com.

**Travel Cuts** ✉ 187 College St., Toronto, Ontario M5T 1P7, Canada ☎ 800/592-2887 in the U.S., 416/979-2406, 888/359-2887 and 888/359-2887 in Canada ⊕ www.travelcuts.com.

### TAXES

As of this writing, Israel has no departure tax.

### VALUE-ADDED TAX

A Value-Added Tax (16.5% at this writing) is charged on all purchases and transactions except tourists' hotel bills and car rentals paid in foreign currency (cash, traveler's checks, or foreign credit cards). Upon departure, you are entitled to a refund of this tax on purchases made in foreign currency of more than $100 on one invoice; but the refund is not mandatory, and not all stores provide VAT return forms. Stores so organized display TAXVAT signs and give 5% discounts. If you charge meals and other services to your room at a hotel and pay with foreign currency, there is no VAT; the refund does not apply. Keep your receipts and ask for a cash refund at Ben Gurion Airport (Change Place Ltd. has a special desk for this purpose in the duty-free area); if you leave from another departure point, the VAT refund will be sent to your home address. You are expected to be able to produce the items on which you claim a VAT refund, so allow time and space for this procedure when you plan your departure. Tobacco, electrical, or photographic purchases are excluded from the refund. Eilat is a free trade zone; VAT is not charged on goods or services purchased there.

The Ministry of Tourism distributes a useful booklet, "Made in Israel," free of charge at Ben Gurion International Airport and at Israel Government Tourist Offices ( ⇨ Visitor Information, *below*).

### TAXIS

Taxis are plentiful and relatively inexpensive, and they can be hailed on the street or reached by phone. On the whole, drivers are cheerful. According to law, taxi drivers must use the meter (you need to be firm when you request this) unless you hire them for the day or for a trip out of town, for which there are set rates. If you're pressed to take the cab at a set price, you can ask your hotel staff for an estimate of the cost of your journey. In such a case, agree on the price before you begin the journey and assume that the driver has built in a tip. In the event of a serious problem with the driver, report his cab number (on the illuminated plastic sign on the roof) or license-plate number to the Ministry of Tourism or the Ministry of Transport. Note that official rates are 25% higher after 9 PM and any time public transportation is not running (on Shabbat, for example). Tipping a taxi driver is not the norm, but if your driver was extra helpful, a tip would be appreciated.

Certain shared taxis or minivans run fixed routes, such as from Tel Aviv to Haifa or from the airport to Jerusalem; such a taxi is called a *sherut* (as opposed to a "special," the term used for a private cab). These have fixed rates, which are generally slightly more expensive than bus rates; and they leave whenever they're full. Some sheruts can be booked in advance.

## TELEPHONES

Israel's phone company is called Bezek. It still has a monopoly on regular services within the country, but it now has competitors for international calls and cellular phone services, often with significantly cheaper prices. All phone numbers have seven digits, except for certain toll-free and other special numbers, that take four to six digits. Double-check the number if you don't get an answer.

It is significantly cheaper to rent a cell phone at Ben Gurion Airport than to use your cell phone from abroad. Rental booths are in the arrivals hall. You can also rent a cell phone that will be delivered to your home before your trip. Log on to TravelCell's Web site at www.travelcell. com. Most telephone cards purchased abroad have an Israeli toll-free access number. You can use this kind of card for local and international calls. Hotels will charge you for a local call for dialing this card's access number, but there's no charge for a toll-free call at public pay phones.

Toll-free numbers in Israel begin with 177, 1800, 1700, or 1888. When calling

an out-of-town number within Israel, be sure to dial the zero that begins every area code.

### AREA & COUNTRY CODES

The country code is 1 for the United States, 61 for Australia, 1 for Canada, 353 for Ireland, 64 for New Zealand, 27 for South Africa, and 44 for the United Kingdom. The country code for Israel is 972. When dialing an Israeli number from abroad, drop the initial 0 from the local area code.

### DIRECTORY & OPERATOR ASSISTANCE

Dial 144 for directory or operator assistance. Operators all speak English. You can ask for a *mefakahat* (supervisor) to help you. Dial 188 for an international operator.

### INTERNATIONAL CALLS

When calling internationally direct from Israel, first dial the international access code and then the country code. The international access code for the United States and Canada is 001; for Australia, 0011; Ireland, New Zealand, and the United Kingdom, 00; South Africa, 09.

You can make international calls using a telecard from a public phone. A call from Israel to most countries costs about 25¢ per minute.

By dialing Israel's toll-free numbers (1800 or 177) and the number of your long-distance service, you can link up directly to an operator in your home country. This service works from public phones without a telecard, and often from your hotel room (once you have an outside line).

### LOCAL CALLS

Making a local call in Israel is quite simple. All public telephones use phone cards. Pick up the receiver, insert the card in the slot, dial the number when you hear the tone, and the number of units remaining on the card will appear on the screen. One unit equals two minutes.

### LONG-DISTANCE CALLS

The area codes for dialing between cities within Israel are Jerusalem (02); Tel Aviv (03); Netanya and Hertzliya (09); Haifa,

Galilee, Tiberias, Zfat, and Nazareth (04); Eilat and the Negev (08).

## LONG-DISTANCE SERVICES

AT&T, MCI, and Sprint access codes make calling long-distance relatively convenient, but you may find the local access number blocked in many hotel rooms. First ask the hotel operator to connect you. If the hotel operator balks, ask for an international operator, or dial the international operator yourself. One way to improve your odds of getting connected to your long-distance carrier is to travel with more than one company's calling card (a hotel may block Sprint, for example, but not MCI). If all else fails, call from a pay phone. If you are traveling for a longer period of time, consider renting a cell phone from a local company.

🔢 **Access Codes AT&T Direct** ☏ 80/949-4949. **British Telecom** ☏ 80/943-2744. **Canada Direct** ☏ 800/949-4105. **MCI WorldPhone** ☏ 80/940-2727. **Sprint International Access** ☏ 800/938-7000.

## PHONE CARDS

Public phones operate only with a magnetic telephone card (telecard), available in units of 20 (NIS 20) or 50 (NIS 35) and sold at post offices, many newsstands and kiosks, some hotel reception desks, and the occasional special vending machine. One unit equals two minutes. Competing phone companies also sell international phone cards.

## PUBLIC PHONES

Pay phones are found in shopping malls, bus stations, gas stations, and at booths on main streets. On public phones, the number you're dialing appears on a digital readout; to its right is the number of units remaining on your card.

## TIME

Israel is 2 hours ahead of Greenwich Mean Time. Normally, New York and Montréal are 7 hours behind, California is 10 behind, London is 2 hours behind, and Sydney is 8 hours ahead. From late March until early September, Israel operates on Daylight Saving Time. When the Daylight Saving Times do not match, the time difference is reduced by one hour.

## TIPPING

There are no hard-and-fast rules for tipping in Israel. Taxi drivers do not expect tips, but a gratuity for good service is in order. If you have negotiated a price, assume the tip has been built in. If a restaurant bill does not include service, 10% is expected—round up if the service was particularly good, down if it was dismal. Hotel bellboys should be tipped a lump sum of NIS 10–NIS 20, not per bag. Tipping is customary for tour guides, tour-bus drivers, and chauffeurs. Bus groups normally tip their guide NIS 20–NIS 25 per person per day, and half that for the driver. Private guides normally get tipped NIS 82–102 a day from the whole party. A small tip is expected by both the person who washes your hair and the stylist—except if one of them owns the salon. Leave NIS 5 per day for your hotel's housekeeping staff.

## TOURS & PACKAGES

Because everything is prearranged on a prepackaged tour or independent vacation, you spend less time planning—and often get it all at a good price.

### BOOKING WITH AN AGENT

Travel agents are excellent resources. But it's a good idea to collect brochures from several agencies, as some agents' suggestions may be influenced by relationships with tour and package firms that reward them for volume sales. If you have a special interest, find an agent with expertise in that area. The American Society of Travel Agents (ASTA) has a database of specialists worldwide; you can log on to the group's Web site to find one near you.

Make sure your travel agent knows the accommodations and other services of the place being recommended. Ask about the hotel's location, room size, beds, and whether it has a pool, room service, or programs for children, if you care about these. Has your agent been there in person or sent others whom you can contact?

Do some homework on your own, too: local tourism boards can provide information about lesser-known and small-niche operators, some of which may sell only direct.

## BUYER BEWARE

Each year consumers are stranded or lose their money when tour operators—even large ones with excellent reputations—go out of business. So check out the operator. Ask several travel agents about its reputation, and try to **book with a company that has a consumer-protection program.** (Look for information in the company's brochure.) In the United States, members of the United States Tour Operators Association are required to set aside funds (up to $1 million) to help eligible customers cover payments and travel arrangements in the event that the company defaults. It's also a good idea to choose a company that participates in the American Society of Travel Agents' Tour Operator Program; ASTA will act as mediator in any disputes between you and your tour operator.

Remember that the more your package or tour includes, the better you can predict the ultimate cost of your vacation. Make sure you know exactly what is covered, and beware of hidden costs. Are taxes, tips, and transfers included? Entertainment and excursions? These can add up.

**⫟ Tour-Operator Recommendations American Society of Travel Agents** (⇨ Travel Agencies). **CrossSphere–The Global Association for Packaged Travel** ✉ 546 E. Main St., Lexington, KY 40508 ☎ 859/226-4444 or 800/682-8886 🖷 859/226-4414 ⊕ www.CrossSphere.com. **United States Tour Operators Association (USTOA)** ✉ 275 Madison Ave., Suite 2014, New York, NY 10016 ☎ 212/599-6599 🖷 212/599-6744 ⊕ www.ustoa.com.

## TRAIN TRAVEL

There's train service from Tel Aviv to Jerusalem, and the 75-minute journey is a scenic way to travel between the two cities. Other cities reached by train, but with service geared more toward commuters, include Ashkelon, Beersheva, Beit Shemesh, Ben Gurion Airport, Netanya, Haifa, Akko, and Nahariya. Trains are timely and changing trains takes between 5 and 15 minutes. Smoking is not permitted on any trains.

### CLASSES

There are no different classes of travel aboard the trains. All trains are less than five years old and are clean, spacious, and comfortable with well-upholstered seats. Sandwiches, snacks, and cold drinks are always available.

### FARES & SCHEDULES

All train stations post up-to-date schedules in English. Complete schedules are also available on the Web site of the Israel Railway Authority. Tickets may be purchased at the ticket office in the station. There's no train service on Saturdays or Jewish holidays.

**⫟ Train Information Israel Railways Authority** ☎ 03/577-4000 ⊕ www.israrail.org.il. **Bat Galim Station, Haifa** ☎ 04/856-4564. **Central Station, Tel Aviv** (also known as Arlosoroff) ☎ 03/577-4000. **Malcha Station, Jerusalem** ☎ 02/673-3764.

### PAYING

Purchase your train tickets with cash or credit card at the station ticketing booth before your board.

### RESERVATIONS

Reservations are not accepted for train travel.

## TRANSPORTATION AROUND ISRAEL

Apart from traveling by private automobile, buses are the most common form of transportation around Israel. They tend to be reliable and inexpensive. Trains are more scenic but less frequent. Another choice is the shared taxi service, *sherut*. Sheruts travel between most destinations and are up to 20% more expensive than buses, but still reasonable. For the quickest travel you can fly the inland air service, Arkia. There are daily flights (with the exception of Shabbat) connecting Eilat with Tel Aviv and Haifa, and flights between Rosh Pina (near Tiberias) and Tel Aviv.

## TRAVEL AGENCIES

A good travel agent puts your needs first. Look for an agency that has been in business at least five years, emphasizes customer service, and has someone on staff who specializes in your destination. In addition, **make sure the agency belongs to a**

**professional trade organization.** The American Society of Travel Agents (ASTA) has more than 10,000 members in some 140 countries, enforces a strict code of ethics, and will step in to mediate agent-client disputes involving ASTA members. ASTA also maintains a directory of agents on its Web site; ASTA's TravelSense.org, a trip planning and travel advice site, can also help to locate a travel agent who caters to your needs. (If a travel agency is also acting as your tour operator, *see* Buyer Beware *in* Tours & Packages.)

📌 Local Agent Referrals **American Society of Travel Agents (ASTA)** ✉ 1101 King St., Suite 200, Alexandria, VA 22314 ☎ 703/739–2782 or 800/965–2782 24-hr hotline 🖷 703/684–8319 ⊕ www. astanet.com and www.travelsense.org. **Association of British Travel Agents** ✉ 68–71 Newman St., London W1T 3AH ☎ 0901/201–5050 ⊕ www.abta. com. **Association of Canadian Travel Agencies** ✉ 350 Sparks St., Suite 510, Ottawa, Ontario K1R 7S8 ☎ 613/237–3657 🖷 613/237–7052 ⊕ www.acta. ca. **Australian Federation of Travel Agents** ✉ Level 3, 309 Pitt St., Sydney, NSW 2000 ☎ 02/9264–3299 or 1300/363–416 🖷 02/9264–1085 ⊕ www.afta.com.au. **Travel Agents' Association of New Zealand** ✉ Level 5, Tourism and Travel House, 79 Boulcott St., Box 1888, Wellington 6001 ☎ 04/499–0104 🖷 04/499–0786 ⊕ www.taanz.org.nz.

## VISITOR INFORMATION

Learn more about foreign destinations by checking government-issued travel advisories and country information. For a broader picture, consider information from more than one country. The Israel Ministry of Tourism also has a toll-free information line and Web site.

📌 Tourist Information **Israel Ministry of Tourism** ☎ 888/774–7723 ⊕ www.tourism.gov.il. **Israel Government Tourism Office** ⊕ www.goisrael.com. **In the U.S.:** ✉ 800 2nd Ave., 16th floor, New York, NY 10017 ☎ 212/499–5650 🖷 212/499–5655 ✉ 6380 Wilshire Blvd., Suite 1718, Los Angeles, CA

90048 ☎ 323/658–7463 🖷 323/658–6543. **In Canada:** ✉ 180 Bloor St. W, Toronto, Ontario M5S 2V6 ☎ 416/964–3784 🖷 416/964–2420. **In the U.K.:** ✉ UK House, 180 Oxford St., London W1N 0EL ☎ 020/7299–1111.

📌 Government Advisories **U.S. Department of State** ✉ Bureau of Consular Affairs, Overseas Citizens Services Office, 2201 C St. NW Washington, DC 20520 ☎ 888/407–4747 or 202/501–4444 from overseas ⊕ www.travel.state.gov. **Consular Affairs Bureau of Canada** ☎ 800/267–6788 or 613/944–6788 from overseas ⊕ www.voyage.gc.ca. **U.K. Foreign and Commonwealth Office** ✉ Travel Advice Unit, Consular Directorate, Old Admiralty Building, London SW1A 2PA ☎ 0845/850–2829 or 020/7008–1500 ⊕ www.fco.gov.uk/travel. **Australian Department of Foreign Affairs and Trade** ☎ 300/139–281 travel advisories, 02/6261–3305 Consular Travel Advice ⊕ www.smartraveller.gov.au. **New Zealand Ministry of Foreign Affairs and Trade** ☎ 04/439–8000 ⊕ www.mft.govt.nz.

## WEB SITES

Do check out the World Wide Web when planning your trip. You'll find everything from weather forecasts to virtual tours of famous cities. Be sure to visit Fodors.com (⊕ www.fodors.com), a complete travel-planning site. You can research prices and book plane tickets, hotel rooms, rental cars, vacation packages, and more. In addition, you can post your pressing questions in the Travel Talk section. Other planning tools include a currency converter and weather reports, and there are loads of links to travel resources.

📌 Israel-specific Sites **Focus Multimedia Online Magazine** ⊕ www.focusmm.com.au/israel/is anamn.htm. **Israel Embassy, London** ⊕ www.israel-embassy.org.uk. **Israel Ministry of Foreign Affairs** ⊕ www.mfa.gov.il. **Israel Tourism Guide** ⊕ www.index.co.il/tourism. **Knesset** ⊕ www.knesset.gov.il/index.html. **Society for the Protection of Nature in Israel (SPNI)** ⊕ www.spni.org.il.

# Jerusalem

## WORD OF MOUTH

"Jerusalem is like nowhere else. It's really three cities—the Old City, where the great religions jockey for position . . . ; the new (western) city, center of the Israeli state, great museums . . . beautiful neighborhoods built of golden stone (it's called Jerusalem of Gold and you'll see why); and the third city, East Jerusalem, center of Palestinian identity, home to great Islamic sites, [with] the Mount of Olives looking down on it."

—Gardyloo

"Jerusalem is the most amazing city I have ever been to. Walking in the Old City and seeing Hasidic Jews on their way to prayer, Armenian priests passing, and hearing the muezzin's call to prayer from the mosques at the same time is just unforgettable."

—Labatt

By Mike Rogoff   **THE WORD "UNIQUE" IS EASY** to throw around, but Jerusalem has a real claim on it. A mountainous walled city with a 5,000-year history, Jerusalem is sacred to more than one-third of the world's population.

For Jews, Jerusalem has always been the focal point of devotion and spiritual yearnings, and for many, the psychic center of their nationhood. "The world is like a human eye," wrote a Jewish sage in the 1st century AD: "the white is the ocean that girds the earth, the iris is the earth upon which we dwell, the pupil is Jerusalem, and the image therein is the Temple of the Lord."

For 2,000 years Christians have also venerated Jerusalem as the place where their faith was shaped—the site of the death, burial, and resurrection of Jesus of Nazareth. A famous Renaissance map shows the continents of Asia, Africa, and Europe as the leaves of a clover meeting in the holy city, a reality at once spiritual, historical, and (almost) geographically accurate.

Islamic tradition identifies Jerusalem as the *masjad el aqsa,* the "farthermost place," from which Muhammad ascended to Heaven for his portentous meeting with God. It is the third-holiest city for Muslims, after Mecca and Medina. A Muslim tradition claims that the great rock of Jerusalem's Mt. Moriah, site of the onetime Jewish Temple and present Dome of the Rock, is made of stones from the Garden of Eden.

The focal point of any visit to Jerusalem is the one-square-kilometer walled Old City, with its four residential quarters (Christian, Jewish, Armenian, and Muslim) and the enormous Temple Mount, or Noble Sanctuary. It is a sensual mix of exotic sights, sounds, and smells.

Step outside the Old City and you'll see a modern metropolis of 700,000—not as cosmopolitan as Tel Aviv, but with many good restaurants, concert halls, markets, and high-quality stores, as well as quaint neighborhoods that embody an earlier simplicity. The city prides itself on its historical continuity; a municipal bylaw makes it mandatory to face even high-rise commercial buildings with the golden "Jerusalem stone," the local limestone that has served Jerusalem's builders from time immemorial. Indeed, to see these limestone buildings glow golden in the sunset is to understand the mystical hold Jerusalem has had on so many minds and hearts for so many thousands of years.

### Top 5 Reasons to Go

- **The Old City:** For an astonishing combination of religions and cultures, the heart of Jerusalem—with the Church of the Holy Sepulcher, Arab bazaar, and Western Wall—is unmatched in the world.

- **City of David:** Explore Jerusalem's most ancient remains, and wade the 2,700-year-old water tunnel that once saved the besieged city.

- **Mt. of Olives:** This classic panorama puts the entire Old City, with the golden Dome of the Rock right in the foreground, squarely within your lens. Come in the morning when the sun's behind you.

*Numbers in the text correspond to numbers in the margin and on the Old City, East Jerusalem, and West Jerusalem & Center City maps.*

**If you have 1 day: highlights**

Catch the morning view from the **Mount of Olives Observation Point** ㉔. Enter the Old City through Jaffa Gate, and visit the **Church of the Holy Sepulcher** ⑨. Cut through the Arab bazaar to the Jewish Quarter to explore its fascinating archaeological treasures (and enjoy a good coffee). Head to the **Western Wall** ②, with a view en route of the Muslim shrines on the **Temple Mount** ④. Take a cab from Dung Gate to the **Israel Museum** ㊵ (Dead Sea Scrolls, archaeology, Judaica, and art) or **Yad Vashem** ㊱ (Holocaust museum).

**If you have 1 day: christian orientation**

Begin with an early view from the **Mount of Olives Observation Point** ㉔, and then walk down to the **Garden of Gethsemane** ㉘, with its ancient olive trees. If you're Catholic, add a visit to the **Pater Noster Convent** ㉕ and **Dominus Flevit** ㉖ church. Enter the Old City through the Lions' (St. Stephen's) Gates, and visit the **Pools of Bethesda and St. Anne's Church** ⑤ (the healing of the lame man). The street becomes the **Via Dolorosa** ⑦: follow the Stations of the Cross to the **Church of the Holy Sepulcher** ⑨. Have lunch in the Christian or Jewish Quarters, explore the archaeological finds of the Jewish Quarter, and end at the **Western Wall** ②. If you're Protestant, don't miss the **Garden Tomb** ㉛ on Nablus Road. If time allows, detour to Mt. Zion, with its **Room of the Last Supper** ⑰ and **Dormition Abbey** ⑯, before the Western Wall.

**If you have 3 days: highlights**

Begin with the view from the Haas Promenade; then explore the City of David. Enter the Old City at Dung Gate to visit the **Western Wall** ②, and perhaps the **Western Wall Tunnel** ③ or **Ophel Archaeological Garden** ①. Have lunch in the Jewish Quarter, poke around its sights and stores, and leave the Old City via the Arab market and Jaffa Gate. End the day at the vibrant **Machaneh Yehuda** (51) produce market. On the second day, visit the **Church of the Holy Sepulcher** ⑨. Head to Jaffa Gate for the tour of the **Tower of David Museum** ⑭, which covers Jerusalem's action-packed history with visuals, not artifacts. Cab over to the **Israel Museum** ㊵. If time allows, head to downtown **Ben Yehuda Street** ㊿ for coffee and people-watching. Begin the third day at **Yad Vashem** ㊱, the Holocaust museum. Visit the **Chagall Windows & Hadassah Hospital** ㉝. Have lunch in picturesque **Ein Kerem** ㉜ (with or without the **Church of the Visitation** ㉟). Take the rest of the afternoon off for a well-earned break at your hotel pool or in the stores.

---

- **Machaneh Yehuda:** You can munch a falafel or sip strong coffee as you watch shoppers swirl and eddy through West Jerusalem's outstanding produce market—or jump in and build a great lunch.
- **Israel Museum:** Follow your muse—from Dead Sea Scrolls and Impressionists to old synagogues and ancient glass in this justly renowned museum.

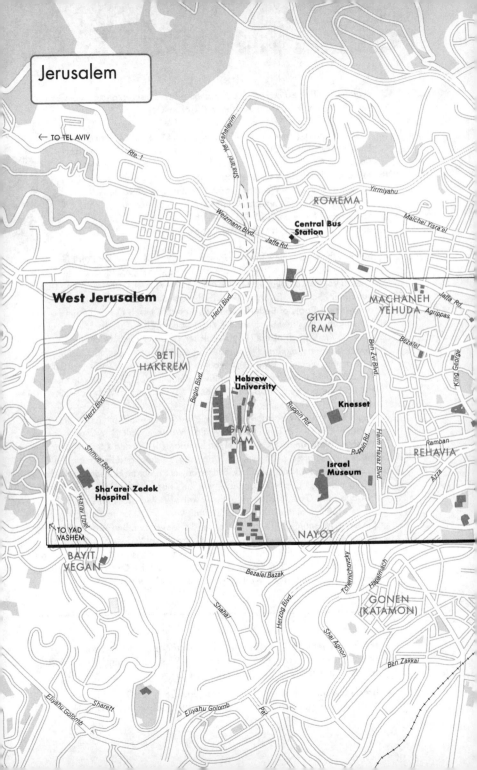

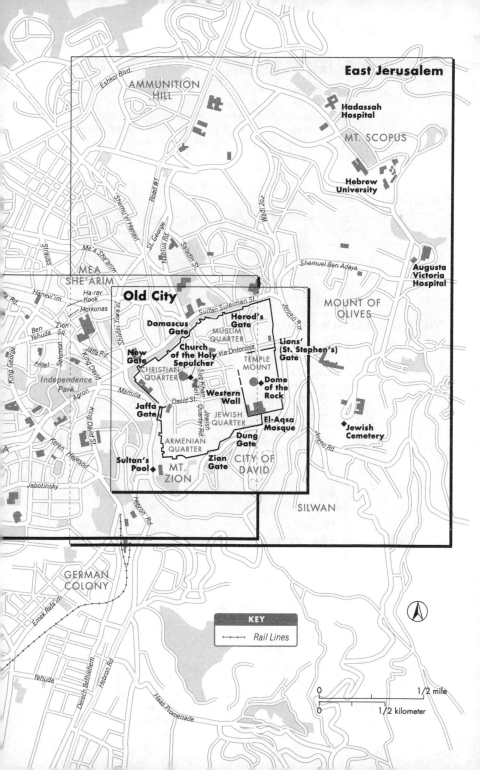

East Jerusalem

AMMUNITION HILL

Eshkol Blvd.

Hadassah Hospital

MT. SCOPUS

Hebrew University

Road #1

Shmu'el Hanavi

St. George

Nablus Rd.

Saladin St.

Me'a She'arim

Wadi Joz

Shemuel Ben Adaya

Augusta Victoria Hospital

MEA SHE'ARIM

Strauss

Hanevi'im

Ha-rav Kook

Horkonas

Ben Yehuda

Zion Sq.

Jaffa Rd.

King George

Hillel

Salomon

King David

Shivtei Israel / Tzanz

Independence Park

Agron

Mamilla

David St.

King David St.

Keren Hayesod

Jabotinsky

Old City

Sultan Suleiman St.

Damascus Gate

Herod's Gate

MUSLIM QUARTER

Via Dolorosa

New Gate

Church of the Holy Sepulcher

Lions' (St. Stephen's) Gate

TEMPLE MOUNT

CHRISTIAN QUARTER

Dome of the Rock

MOUNT OF OLIVES

Jericho Rd.

Suk Khan ez-Zeit

Jaffa Gate

Western Wall

JEWISH QUARTER

El-Aqsa Mosque

Jewish Quarter Rd.

ARMENIAN QUARTER

Dung Gate

Jericho Rd.

Jewish Cemetery

Sultan's Pool

MT. ZION

Zion Gate

CITY OF DAVID

SILWAN

Hebron Rd.

GERMAN COLONY

Emek Refa'im

Yehuda

Derech Bethlehem

Hebron Rd.

Haas Promenade

| KEY |
| --- |
| Rail Lines |

0        1/2 mile

0        1/2 kilometer

# EXPLORING JERUSALEM

Jerusalem is built on a series of hills, part of the country's north–south watershed. To the east, the Judean Desert tumbles down to the Dead Sea, less than an hour's drive away. The main highway to the west winds down through the pine-covered Judean Hills, toward the international airport and Tel Aviv. North and south of the city—Samaria and Judea, respectively—is what is known as the West Bank. Since 1967 this contested area has been administered largely by Israel, though the major concentrations of Arab population are currently under autonomous Palestinian control.

Jerusalem is a city with two centers of gravity—the downtown area of West Jerusalem (the "New City"), with its central triangle of Jaffa Road, King George Street, and Ben Yehuda Street; and the Old City, farther east, the natural focus for vistors. While it is a great town to see on foot, a car is useful for the outlying sights on the west side of town. On the east side, a rental car is sometimes more of a bother than a boon, and cabs are the way to go.

## Old City: The Classic Sights

Drink in the very essence of Jerusalem as you explore the city's primary religious sites and touch the different cultures that share it. The Old City's 30,000 inhabitants jostle in the cobblestone lanes with an air of ownership, at best merely tolerating the "intruders" from other quarters. Devout Jews in black and white scurry from their neighborhoods north and west of the Old City, through the Damascus Gate and the Muslim Quarter, toward the Western Wall. Arab women with baskets of fresh produce on their heads flow across the Western Wall plaza to Dung Gate and the village of Silwan beyond it. It is not unusual to stand at the Western Wall, surrounded by the burble of devotions, and hear the piercing call to prayer of the Muslim *muezzin* above you, with the more distant bells of the Christian Quarter providing a counterpoint. All the holy places demand modest dress: no shorts and no sleeveless tops.

### Main Attractions

★ ❾ **Church of the Holy Sepulcher.** Vast numbers of Christians, especially adherents of the older "mainstream" churches, believe this to be the place where Jesus was crucified by the Romans, was buried, and rose from the dead. Some claim that the very antiquity of the Holy Sepulcher tradition argues in favor of its authenticity, since the fiercely committed early Christian community would have striven to preserve the memory of such an important site. The church is outside the city walls *of Jesus's day*—a vital point, for no executions or burials took place within Jerusalem's sacred precincts.

The site was officially consecrated, and the first church built here, following the visit in AD 326 by Helena, mother of the Byzantine emperor Constantine the Great; it was destroyed and rebuilt three times over the centuries. The present great structure is 12th-century Crusader, and the Gothic plan is still clear despite the interior structures and decorations

Antiquities If you thrill to the thought of standing where the ancients once stood, you'll be in your element in this city of memories. From Old Testament walls and water systems to Second Temple streets and stones, the past calls to the attentive soul like a siren to a sailor. Scale models and outstanding local museums help give depth and perspective to the intense experience of exploring Jerusalem's past.

1

Arts & Crafts Handicrafts in Israel are worth seeking out, with jewelry and Judaica exceptional standouts in design and workmanship. Jerusalem offers good selections of these, as well as fine works in other specialties: paper cutting, ceramics, weaving, and harp making.

Holy Places Central to two faiths and holy to a third, Jerusalem is an almost bewildering collage of religious traditions and the shrines that have sanctified them. Pilgrims of one faith still tend to make time to view the shrines of the others. Sites such as the Western Wall, Calvary, Gethsemane, and the Haram esh-Sharif bring the thrill of recognition to ancient history. The devout cannot fail to be moved by the holy city, and its special, if sometimes dissonant, moods and modes of devotion tend to fascinate the nonbeliever as well.

Scenic Views Jerusalem is a city of hills—hard going for cyclists, but marvelous for the photographer and the romantic. Quite different views of the Old City unfold from Mt. Scopus and the Mount of Olives (you're facing west, so it's best to go in the morning) and the Haas Promenade, to the south. Mt. Scopus also looks east, to the Judean Desert and the Dead Sea; Mt. Herzl looks west; and Nebi Samwil, in the northwest, gives a commanding view in all directions.

---

added over the years by the several denominations that uncomfortably share it—an unusual arrangement that lends the church much of its color.

Just inside the entrance of the church is a rectangular pink stone slab called the **Stone of Unction,** where, it is said, the body of Jesus was cleansed and prepared for burial. Pilgrims often rub clothing or bits of fabric on the stone to absorb its sanctity, and take them home as mementos. Steep steps take you up to **Golgotha,** or Calvary, meaning "the place of the skull," as the site is described in the New Testament (Mark 15). The central chapel—all candlelight, oil lamps, and icons—is Greek Orthodox. Under the altar, and capping the rocky hillock on which you stand, is a bronze disc with a hole, purportedly the place where the cross actually stood. The chapel on the right is Roman Catholic and contains Stations X–XIV of the Via Dolorosa. The tomb itself (**Station XIV**) is encased in a pink marble edifice in the rotunda to the left of the entrance, under the great dome that dominates the Christian Quarter.

The 19th-century Status Quo Agreements—a list of possessions and privileges of each denomination—apply to this church. For example, each "shareholder" in the property—Greek Orthodox, Latin (Roman

The Old City

MOUNT OF OLIVES

Tomb of Jehosafat ◆
Absalom's Pillar ◆
Tomb of St. James ◆
Zechariah's Tomb ◆

Tomb of the Virgin ◆

Gethsemane ◆

Lions' (St. Stephen's) Gate

Golden Gate

El-Aqsa Mosque

Dome of the Rock

④

Bab al-Asbat

Bab al-Qattanin

Bab el Silsila

Bab el-Silsileh St. (St. of the Chain)

②

③ Western (Wailing) Wall Plaza

Ophel Rd.

Jericho Rd.

Rockefeller Museum

Sultan Suleiman Rd.

Pools of Bethesda

St. Anne's Church ⑤

Bab Hutta Rd.

El-Omari Rd.

Monastery of the Flagellation

Al Mujahideen Rd.

School Antonia

⑥

⑦ Via Dolorosa

Bab al-Ghawanmeh

Aqabat Shaddad

Aqabat el-Bistami

Aqabat el-Rahbat

Aqabat esh Sheikh Rihan

Aqabat el Mewlwiyeh

Ibn Al Jarrah Rd.

MUSLIM QUARTER

El-Wad Rd.

El-Wad Rd.

Suq Khan e-Zeit

Via Dolorosa

Aqabat el-Takiyeh (Khaski Sultan)

Aqabat el-Khalideh

El-Hakkari Rd.

Aqabat el-Saraya

Suq el'Attarin

Suq el Lahhamin

⑧

⑨

Deir el Habes

St. Francis Rd.

Christian Quarter Rd.

Muristan

Herod's Gate

Saladin St.

Damascus Gate

CHRISTIAN QUARTER

Nablus Rd.

Haranharim St.

Rd. 1

Notre Dame de France ◆

New Gate

Hospital St. Louis ◆

Custodia di Terra Santa

Greek Orthodox Patriarchate

Casa Nova Rd.

Greek Catholic Patriarchate Rd.

Casa Nova Hospice

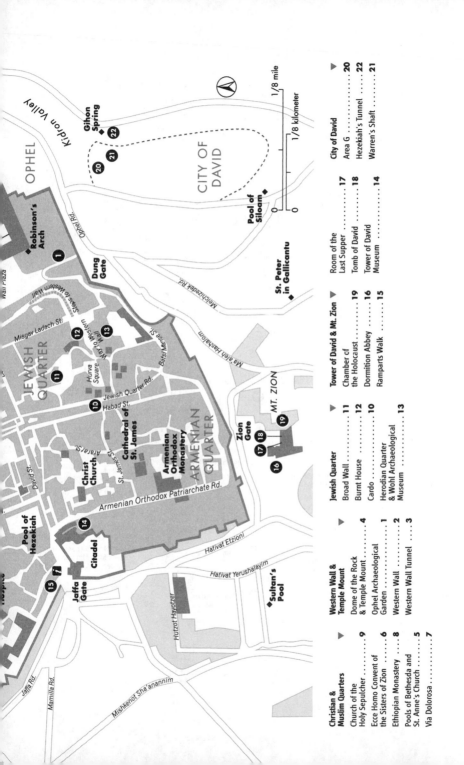

**Kidron Valley**

**OPHEL**

Gihon Spring **22**

**21**

**20**

CITY OF DAVID

Pool of Siloam

1/8 mile

1/8 kilometer

Robinson's Arch **1**

Ophel Rd.

Dung Gate

Stairs to Western Wall

Wall Plaza

Misgav Ladach St. **12** **13**

**11**

Hurva Square

Western Wall

Maalot to Western Wall

Batei Mahse St.

Melchizedek Rd.

St. Peter in Gallicantu

Ma'alen HaShalom

**JEWISH QUARTER**

**10** Habad St.

Jewish Quarter Rd.

David St.

**Christ Church**

St. James's St.

**Cathedral of St. James**

**Armenian Orthodox Monastery**

**ARMENIAN QUARTER**

Ararat St.

Armenian Orthodox Patriarchate Rd.

Zion Gate **17** **18** **19**

**MT. ZION**

**16**

**Citadel** **14**

Hativat Etzioni

Hativat Yerushalayim

Pool of Hezekiah

**15** **7**

**Jaffa Gate**

Hutzot Hatzfer

Sultan's Pool

Mishkenot Sha'anannim

Jaffa Rd.

Mamilla Rd.

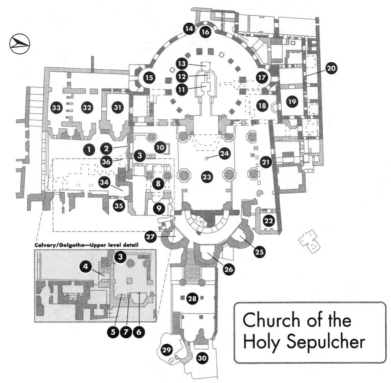

**Calvary/Golgotha—Upper level detail**

# Church of the Holy Sepulcher

Catholics), Armenian, and Copt (Egyptians)—exercises its daily right to a procession from Calvary to the tomb. A modern agreement among the Greeks, the Latins, and the Armenians on the interior restoration of the great dome was hailed as an almost miraculous breakthrough in ecumenical relations, and it was rededicated in 1996 in an unprecedented interdenominational service. The only hint of what the tomb must have been like 2,000 years ago is the ledge in the inner chamber (now covered with marble) on which Jesus's body would have been laid. You can see a more pristine example of a Jewish tomb of the period in the gloomy Chapel of St. Nicodemus, opposite the Coptic chapel in the back of the sepulcher. ✉ *Between Suq Khan e-Zeit and Christian Quarter Rd., Christian Quarter* ☎ *02/627–3314* ∰ *www.christusrex.org* 🌐 *Free* ☉ *Apr.–Sept., daily 5 AM–9 PM; Oct.–Mar., daily 4 AM–7 PM.*

★ **④ Dome of the Rock & Temple Mount.** Tall cypress trees create shady retreats from the glare of the white limestone pavement of the vast 35-acre Temple Mount, known to Muslims as Haram esh-Sharif (the Noble Sanctuary). Immediately in front of you as you enter the area from the Western Wall plaza (the only gate for non-Muslims) is the large, black-domed **El-Aqsa Mosque,** the third in holiness for Muslims everywhere. More historically significant, however—and incomparably more arresting—is the golden **Dome of the Rock,** 200 yards to the north.

The Temple Mount was one of the greatest religious enclosures of the ancient world. In the 1st century BC, the Jewish King Herod "the Great" had an immense wall constructed around the hill known as Mount Moriah, and filled the inside with rubble to level off the crest. At the center of the plaza stood his splendidly rebuilt Second Temple, the one Jesus knew, renowned as an architectural wonder of its day. The Romans reduced it to scorched ruins in the summer of AD 70.

Jewish tradition identifies the great **rock** at the summit of the hill—now under the gold dome—as the foundation stone of the world, and the place where Abraham bound and almost sacrificed his son Isaac (Genesis 22). More reliably, this was where the biblical King David made a repentance offering to the Lord (II Samuel 22), and where his son Solomon built "God's House" (the so-called First Temple). The Second Temple stood on the identical spot, but the precise location of its innermost Holy of Holies is a question that engages religious Jews and archaeologists to this day. In the absence of indisputable evidence, the devout will not approach the area for fear of desecrating the once-inviolable temple precincts.

The Haram today is a Muslim preserve. When the Arab caliph Omar Ibn-Khatib seized Jerusalem from the Byzantines in AD 638, he found the area covered with rubbish and had to clear the site to expose the rock. It is said that Omar asked his aide Ka'ab al'Akhbar, a Jewish convert to Islam, where he should build his mosque. Ka'ab recommended a spot north of the rock, hoping that the Muslims, praying south toward Mecca, would thus include the old temple site in their obeisance. "You dog, Ka'ab," bellowed the caliph. "In your heart you are still a Jew!" Omar's mosque, south of the rock, has not survived.

Jerusalem is not mentioned in the Koran, but Muhammad's Night Ride is. Awakened by the archangel Gabriel, he was taken on the fabulous winged horse el-Burak to the *masjad el-aqsa,* the "farthermost place" (hence the name "El-Aqsa" Mosque). From there he rose to heaven, met God face to face, received the teachings of Islam, and returned to Mecca the same night. Tradition has it that the masjad el-aqsa was none other than Jerusalem, and the great rock the very spot from which the prophet ascended. To be sure, Muhammad's triumphant successors venerated Jerusalem's biblical sanctity; but some modern scholars suggest they did not like the feeling of being Johnnies-come-lately in the holy city of rival faiths. The magnificent Dome of the Rock, completed in AD 691, was almost certainly intended to proclaim the ascendancy of the "true faith" and the new Muslim empire.

In the 12th century, the El-Aqsa Mosque became the headquarters of the Templars, a Crusader monastic order which took its name from the ancient site itself. The spot has been the setting for more recent dramas, though—most importantly the assassination of King Abdullah of Jordan (the present king's great-grandfather) in 1951.

At presstime, the Muslim shrines were closed to non-Muslims for an indefinite period, leaving the faithful alone to enjoy the wondrous interiors of stained-glass windows, granite columns, green-and-gold mosaics, arabesques, and superb medieval masonry. Even if you can't get inside, the vast plaza is both visually and historically interesting, and worth a visit. Take a look at the bright exterior tiles of the Dome of the Rock, and the remarkable jigsaws of fitted red, white, and black stone in the 14th- and 15th-century Mamluk buildings that line the western edge of the plaza. Overlooking the plaza at its northwestern corner is a long building, today an elementary school, built on the artificial scarp that once protected Herod's Antonia fortress. The Christian tradition, very possibly accurate, identifies the site as the *praetorium* where Jesus was tried. Security check lines to enter the area are long; it's best to come early. ⊠ *Access between the Western Wall and Dung Gate, Temple Mount* ☎ *02/628–3292 or 02/628–3313* ⊘ *Sun.–Thurs. 7:30 AM–10 AM and 12:30 PM–1:30 PM. Subject to change. Last entry 1 hr before closing.*

❶ **Ophel Archaeological Garden.** In several expeditions since 1968, Israeli archaeologists have dug deep and wide in the site many still refer to as the Western and Southern Wall Excavations. Interesting Byzantine and early Arab structures came to light, but by far the most dramatic—and monumental—finds were from the Herodian period, the late 1st century BC. Walk down to the high corner facing you. King Herod the Great rebuilt the Second Temple on the exact site of its predecessor, where the Dome of the Rock now stands. He expanded the sacred enclosure by constructing a massive, shoebox-shaped retaining wall on the slopes of the hill known as Mt. Moriah. Filling the inside with thousands of tons of rubble, his workmen created the huge plaza, the size of 21 football fields, still known today as the Temple Mount. The great stones near the corner, with their signature meticulous borders, are not held together with mortar; their sheer weight gives the structure its stability. The original wall would have been at least one-third higher than it is today.

# STATIONS OF THE CROSS

**THE 14 STATIONS** on the Via Dolorosa mark Jesus's route, from trial and condemnation to crucifixion and burial.

**Station I.** Jesus is tried and condemned by Pontius Pilate.

**Station II.** Jesus is scourged and given the cross.

**Station III.** Jesus falls for the first time. (The chapel was built after World War II by soldiers of the Free Polish Forces.)

**Station IV.** Mary embraces Jesus.

**Station V.** Simon of Cyrene picks up the cross.

**Station VI.** A woman wipes the face of Jesus, whose image remains on the cloth. (She is remembered as Veronica, apparently derived from the words vera and icon, meaning true image.)

**Station VII.** Jesus falls for the second time. (The chapel contains one of the columns of the Byzantine Cardo, the main street of 6th-century Jerusalem.)

**Station VIII.** Jesus addresses the women in the crowd.

**Station IX.** Jesus falls for the third time.

**Station X.** Jesus is stripped of his garments.

**Station XI.** Jesus is nailed to the cross.

**Station XII.** Jesus dies on the cross.

**Station XIII.** Jesus is taken down from the cross.

**Station XIV.** Jesus is buried.

---

Exposed to the left of the corner is the white pavement of an impressive main street and commercial area from the Second Temple period. The protrusion left of the corner and high above your head is known as **Robinson's Arch.** Named for a 19th-century American explorer, it is a remnant of a monumental bridge to the Temple Mount which was reached by a staircase from the street where you now stand: look for the ancient steps. On the street is a pile of square-cut building stones from the top of the original wall, left lying where they were found as dramatic evidence of the Roman destruction of AD 70.

Return to the higher level and turn left (east). Fifty yards over, a modern spiral staircase descends below present ground level to a partially reconstructed labyrinth of Byzantine dwellings, mosaics and all; from here you reemerge outside the present city walls. Alternatively, go straight, passing through the city wall by a small arched gate. The wide staircase to your left, a good part of it original, once brought hordes of pilgrims through the now-blocked gates of the southern wall of the Temple Mount. The rock-hewn Jewish ritual baths near the bottom of the steps are a visual reminder of the purification rites once demanded of Jews before they entered the sacred temple precincts.

The air-conditioned **Davidson Visitors Center** offers visual aids, some artifacts, two interesting videos (which continuously alternate between English and Hebrew), and toilet facilities. ✉ *Dung Gate, Western Wall* ☎ *02/627-7550* ⊕ *www.archpark.org.il* ☒ *NIS 30* ☉ *Sun.–Thurs. 8–5, Fri. and Jewish holiday eves 8–2.*

**❼ Via Dolorosa.** The Way of Suffering—or Way of the Cross, as it's more commonly called in English—is venerated as the route Jesus walked, carrying his cross from the place of his trial and condemnation by Pontius Pilate to the site of his crucifixion and burial. The present tradition is essentially 12th-century Crusader, but it draws on older Byzantine beliefs. Some of the incidents represented by the 14 Stations of the Cross are scriptural; others (III, IV, VI, VII, and IX) are not. Many stations are marked by tiny chapels; the last five are inside the Church of the Holy Sepulcher. The Via Dolorosa winds through the busy market streets of the Muslim and Christian quarters. The full pilgrim procession takes about an hour, with prayers and chants at each station. Some sites close for a few hours over lunch, and all day Sunday. Afternoons tend to be less crowded. ✉ *Muslim and Christian Quarters.*

**need a break?** Between the sixth and seventh stations of the Via Dolorosa is the very good **Holy Rock Café** (✉ Muslim Quarter). The name may be a little hokey, but there's nothing wrong with its freshly squeezed orange juice, Turkish coffee, mint tea, and superb bourma, a round Arab confection filled with whole pistachio nuts. An Internet café is only a few steps away.

**★ ❷ Western Wall.** Often just called "the Wall" (*Kotel* in Hebrew), the Western Wall is the most important *existing* Jewish shrine. It was not itself part of the actual Second Temple edifice, but of the massive retaining wall King Herod built to create the vast plaza known as the Temple Mount. After the destruction of Jerusalem by the Romans in AD 70, and especially after the dedication of a pagan town in its place 65 years later, the city became off-limits to Jews for generations. The memory of the precise location of the Temple—in the vicinity of today's Dome of the Rock—was lost. Even when access was eventually regained, Jews avoided entering the Temple Mount out of fear of unwittingly trespassing on the most sacred, and thus forbidden, areas of the ancient sanctuary. With time, the closest remnant of the period took on the aura of the temple itself, making the Western Wall a kind of holy place by proxy.

The Western Wall is in the southeast corner of the Old City, accessible from the Dung Gate, the Jewish Quarter, and the Muslim Quarter's El-Wad Street. It functions under the aegis of the rabbinic authorities, with all the trappings of an Orthodox synagogue. Modest dress is required (men must cover their heads in the prayer area), there is a segregation of men and women in prayer, and smoking and photography on the Sabbath and religious holidays are prohibited. The cracks between the massive stones are stuffed with slips of paper bearing prayers. The swaying and davening of the devout reveal the powerful hold this place still has on the minds and hearts of many Jews.

# WALKING THE STATIONS

**THE OLD CITY'S MAIN JEWISH AND MUSLIM SITES** *can be visited individually, but the primary Christian shrines—the Via Dolorosa (or "Way of the Cross") and the Holy Sepulcher—are best experienced in sequence. This walk will keep you oriented in the confusing marketplace through which the Via Dolorosa picks its way. (Beware of slick pickpockets along this route.) The route takes about an hour; plan additional time if you want to linger at the sights.*

*About 300 yards up the road from St. Anne's Church (near Lions' Gate), look for a ramp on your left leading to the blue metal door of a school. On Friday afternoons at 4 (April to September; at 3 from October to March), the brown-robed Franciscans begin their procession of the* **Via Dolorosa** *in the school courtyard. This is Station I; Station II is across the street. Just beyond it, on the right, is the entrance to the* **Ecce Homo Convent of the Sisters of Zion,** *with a basement of ancient pavements, a huge cistern, and a Roman arch in the chapel. The continuation of the arch crosses the street outside.*

*The Via Dolorosa runs down into El-Wad Road, one of the Old City's most important thoroughfares. To the right, the street climbs toward the Damascus Gate; to the left, it passes through the heart of the Muslim Quarter and reaches the Western Wall. Arab matrons in bright embroidered dresses sail by; black-hatted Hasidic Jews in beards and side curls hurry on divine missions; nimble local Muslim kids in the universal uniform of T-shirt, jeans, and sneakers play in the street; and earnest groups of Christian pilgrims, almost oblivious to the tumult, pace out ancient footsteps.*

*As you turn left onto El-Wad Road, Station III is on your left. A few steps beyond, also on the left, is Station IV and, on the corner, Station V. There the Via Dolorosa turns right and begins its ascent toward Calvary.*

*Halfway up the street, a brown wooden door on your left marks Station VI.*

*Facing you at the top of the stepped street, on the busy Suq Khan e-Zeit, is Station VII. The little chapel preserves one of the columns of the Byzantine Cardo, the main street of 6th-century Jerusalem, which lines up with the impressive remains excavated to the south, in today's Jewish Quarter. Step to the left, and walk 30 yards up the street facing you to Station VIII, marked by nothing more than an inscribed stone in the wall on the left. Return to the main street and turn right. (If you skip Station VIII, turn left as you reach Station VII from the stepped street.) One hundred yards along Suq Khan e-Zeit from Station VII, turn onto the ramp on your right that ascends parallel to the street. At the end of the lane is a column that represents Station IX.*

*Step through the open door to the left of the column into the courtyard of the* **Ethiopian Monastery** *known as Deir es-Sultan, an esoteric enclave of this poor but colorful sect. From the monastery's upper chapel, descend through a lower one and out a small wooden door to the court of the* **Church of the Holy Sepulcher.** *Most Christians venerate this site as that of the death, burial, and resurrection of Jesus—you'll find Stations X, XI, XII, XIII, and XIV within the church—but many Protestants are drawn to Skull Hill and the Garden Tomb, north of the Damascus Gate. A good time to be here is in the late afternoon, after 4 PM, when the different denominations in turn chant their way, amid billowing incense, between Calvary and the tomb.*

*For more information on the sights in bold, see the bulleted listings in the Old City.*

On Monday and Thursday mornings, the Wall bubbles with colorful bar-mitzvah ceremonies, when Jewish families celebrate the coming of age of their 13-year-old sons. The fervor is still greater on Friday evenings just after sunset, when the young men of a nearby yeshiva (Jewish seminary) come dancing and singing down to the Wall to welcome in the "Sabbath bride." But many people find that it's only when the crowds have gone (the Wall is floodlit at night and always open), and you share the warm, prayer-drenched stones with just a handful of bearded stalwarts or kerchiefed women, that the true spirituality of the Western Wall is palpable. (Expect a routine check of your bags—smaller is better—by security personnel at the plaza's entrance.) ⊠ *Near Dung Gate, Western Wall* ⊕ *http://english.thekotel.org* ⊘ *Daily 24 hrs.*

❸ **Western Wall Tunnel.** The long tunnel beyond the men's side (north of the plaza) is not a rediscovered ancient thoroughfare, but was deliberately dug in recent years with the purpose of exposing a strip of the Western Wall along its entire length. One course of the massive wall revealed two building stones estimated to weigh an incredible 400 and 570 tons, respectively. Local guided tours are available—one can visit the site only as part of an organized tour—but the times change from week to week (some include evening hours). The tour takes about 75 minutes, ending at the beginning of the Via Dolorosa, in the Muslim Quarter. At that point, you can be escorted back to the Western Wall plaza, or continue alone to explore the Via Dolorosa and the Arab souk. The ticket office is below the police station at the Western Wall plaza. Call for details. ⊠ *Western Wall* ☎ *02/627–1333* ⊕ *http://english.thekotel.org* ⊡ *NIS 15* ⊘ *Sun.–Thurs. 8 AM–late evening (changing schedules), Fri. and Jewish holiday eves 8–12:30. Call ahead for exact times.*

### Also Worth Seeing

❻ **Ecce Homo Convent of the Sisters of Zion.** The arch that crosses the Via Dolorosa continues into the present-day Ecce Homo Church. It was once thought to have been the gate of Herod's Antonia Fortress, and thus the spot where the Roman governor Pontius Pilate presented Jesus to the crowd with the words "*Ecce homo!*" ("Behold, the man!"; John 19). Recent scholarship, however, has declared it a triumphal arch built by the Roman emperor Hadrian in the 2nd century AD.

The basement of the convent has two points of interest: an impressive reservoir with a barrel-vault roof, apparently built by Hadrian in the moat of Herod's older Antonia Fortress, and the famous *lithostratos*, or stone pavement, etched with games played by Roman legionnaires. The origin of one such diversion—the notorious Game of the King—called for the execution of a mock king, a sequence tantalizingly reminiscent of the New Testament description of the treatment of Jesus by the Roman soldiers. Contrary to tradition, however, the pavement of large, foot-worn brown flagstones is apparently not from Jesus's day, but was laid down a century later. ⊠ *Via Dolorosa, Muslim Quarter* ☎ *02/627–7292* ⊕ *www.sion.org* ⊡ *NIS 7* ⊘ *Daily 8–5.*

❽ **Ethiopian Monastery.** Stand in the monastery's courtyard beneath the medieval bulge of the Church of the Holy Sepulcher, and look around. Views of the churches of Christendom crowd in. An Egyptian Coptic monastery is through a gate close by, and the skyline is broken by a Russian Orthodox gable, a Lutheran bell tower, and the crosses of Greek Orthodox, Armenian, and Roman Catholic churches.

The robed Ethiopian monks live in tiny cells in the rooftop monastery. One of the modern paintings in their small, dark church depicts the visit of the Queen of Sheba to King Solomon. Ethiopian tradition holds that more passed between the two than is related in the Bible—where it is said that she came to "prove" his wisdom "with hard questions" (I Kings 10)—and that their supposed union produced an heir to both royal houses, who eventually brought the precious Ark of the Covenant to Ethiopia. There (say the Ethiopians) it remains in a sealed crypt to this day. The script in the paintings is Gehz, the ecclesiastical language of the Ethiopian church. ⊠ *Roof of the Church of the Holy Sepulcher, access from Suq Khan e-Zeit, Christian Quarter* ⊡ *Free* ☉ *Daily during daylight.*

**❺ Pools of Bethesda and St. Anne's Church.** The transition is sudden and complete, from the raucous cobbled streets and persistent vendors to the drooping pepper trees, flower patches, and birdsong of this serene Catholic cloister. The Romanesque Crusader **St. Anne's Church,** built in 1140, was restored in the 19th century, and with its austere and unadorned stone interior and extraordinarily reverberant acoustics, it is one of the finest examples of medieval architecture in the country. According to local tradition, the Virgin Mary was born in the grotto over which the church is built, and the church is named for her mother.

In the same compound are the excavated **Pools of Bethesda,** a large, double public reservoir in use during the 1st century BC and 1st century AD. The New Testament speaks of Jesus miraculously curing a lame man by "a pool, which is called in the Hebrew tongue Bethesda" (John 5). The actual bathing pools were the small ones, east of the reservoir, but it was over the big pools that both the Byzantines and the Crusaders built churches, now ruined, to commemorate the miracle. ⊠ *Al-Mujahideen Rd., near Lions' Gates Muslim Quarter* ☎ *02/628-3285* ⊡ *NIS 7* ☉ *Apr.–Sep., Mon.–Sat. 8–12 and 2–6; Oct.–Mar., Mon.–Sat. 8–12 and 2–5.*

## Jewish Quarter

This is at once the Old City's oldest quarter and its newest neighborhood—archaeological finds date back 27 centuries; the Jewish Quarter, abandoned for a generation, was restored and resettled in the 1970s and '80s. If you have a photographer's eye, get off the main streets and stroll at random. The limestone houses and alleys—often counterpointed with a shock of bougainvillea or palm fronds and ficus trees—offer pleasing compositions.

If you like to people-watch, find a shaded café-table and sip a good latte while the world jitterbugs by. The population of the Jewish Quarter is almost entirely religious, roughly split between "modern" Orthodox (devout, but integrated into contemporary Israeli society at every level) and the more traditional ultra-Orthodox (men in black frock coats and black hats, in many ways a community apart). The locals, especially the

# CloseUp

## JERUSALEM: FOCUS OF FAITH

**THE FIRST KNOWN MENTION OF JERUSALEM** is in Egyptian "hate texts" of the 20th century BC, but archaeologists give the city a founding date of up to 1,000 years earlier. Abraham and the biblical Joshua may have been here, but it was King David, circa 1000 BC, who captured the city and made it his capital, thus propelling it onto the center stage of history. His son Solomon built the "First" Temple, giving the city a preeminence it enjoyed until its destruction by the Babylonians, and the exile of its population, in 586 BC.

They returned 50 years later, rebuilt the Temple (the "Second"), and began the slow process of revival. By the 2nd century BC, Jerusalem was again a vibrant Jewish capital, albeit one with a good dose of Hellenistic cultural influence. Herod the Great (who reigned 37 BC–4 BC) revamped the Temple on a magnificent scale and expanded the city into a cosmopolis of world renown. This was the Jerusalem Jesus knew, a city of monumental architecture, teeming— especially during the Jewish pilgrim festivals—with tens of thousands of visitors. It was here that the Romans crucified Jesus (circa AD 29), and here, too, that the Great Jewish Revolt against Rome erupted, ending in AD 70 with the total destruction (once again) of the city and the Temple.

The Roman emperor Hadrian redesigned Jerusalem as the pagan polis of Aelia Capitolina (AD 135), an urban plan that became the basis for the Old City of today. The Byzantines made it a Christian center, with a massive wave of church building (4th–6th centuries AD), until the Arab conquest of AD 638 brought the holy city under Muslim sway. Except during the golden age of the Ummayad dynasty, in the late 7th and early 8th centuries, Jerusalem was no more than a provincial town under the Muslim regimes of the early Middle Ages. The Crusaders stormed it in 1099 and made it the capital of their Latin Kingdom. With the reconquest of Jerusalem by the Muslims, the city again lapsed into a languid provincialism for 700 years under the Mamluk and Ottoman empires. The British conquest in 1917 thrust the city back into the world limelight as rising rival nationalisms vied to possess it.

Jerusalem was divided by the 1948 war: the much larger Jewish western sector became the capital of the State of Israel, while Jordan annexed the smaller, predominantly Arab eastern sector, which included the Old City. The Six-Day War of 1967 reunited the city under Israeli rule, but the concept of an Arab "East" Jerusalem and a Jewish "West" Jerusalem still remains, even though new Jewish neighborhoods in the northeastern and southeastern sections have rendered the distinction somewhat oversimplified. The holy city continues to engage the attention of devotees of Christianity, Islam, and Judaism. Between Jews and Arabs it remains the subject of passionate debate and occasional violence as rival visions clash for possession of the city's past and control of its future. It is widely recognized that any peace negotiations between Israel and the Palestinians will fail unless the thorny issue of sharing Jerusalem is resolved.

women, tend to dress very conservatively. Several religious study institutions attract a transient population of young students, many of them from abroad. Religious Jewish families tend to have lots of kids, and little ones here are given independence at an astonishingly early age. It's quite common to see 3- and 4-year-olds toddling home from preschool alone, or shepherded by a one-year-more-mature brother or sister. And if you see a big group of Israeli soldiers, don't assume the worst. The army maintains a center for its educational tours here, and the recruits are more likely than not boisterously kidding around with each other as they follow their guide. Shopping is good here—jewelry, Judaica, gift items—and there are decent fast-food options when the time comes.

## Main Attractions

**⑫ Burnt House.** The discovery here of stone weights inscribed with the name Bar Katros—a Jewish priestly family known from ancient sources—indicated that this may have been a basement industrial workshop, possibly for the manufacture of sacramental incense, during the Second Temple period, some 2,000 years ago. Charred cooking pots and debris give a vivid sense of the Roman devastation of the city in AD 70. Archaeologists were riveted by the discovery of the skeletal hand and arm of a woman clutching a scorched staircase in a futile attempt to escape the flames. A video presentation recreates the bitter civil rivalries of the period, and the city's tragic end. ⊠ *Tiferet Israel St., Jewish Quarter* ☏ *No phone* ⊠ *NIS 25; combined ticket with Herodian Quarter NIS 35* ☉ *Sun.–Thurs. 9–4:30, Fri. and Jewish holiday eves 9–12:30.*

★ **⑬ Herodian Quarter & Wohl Archaeological Museum.** Excavations in the 1970s exposed the Jewish Quarter's most visually arresting site: the remains of sumptuous mansions from the aristocratic Upper City of the Second Temple period. Preserved in the basement of a modern Jewish seminary, the geometrically patterned mosaic floors, faded frescoes, and costly glassware, stone objects, and ceramics provide a peek into domestic life of the richest families in the days of Herod and Jesus. Several small stone cisterns have been identified as private *mikva'ot,* (Jewish ritual baths); holograms depict their use. Large stone water jars are just like those described in the New Testament story of the wedding at Cana. Rare stone tables resemble the dining-room furniture depicted in Roman stone reliefs found in Europe.

On the last of the site's three distinct levels is a mansion with an estimated original floor area of some 6,000 square feet. None of the upper stories have survived, but the frescoes (half replaced by the later, more fashionable stucco) and the quality of the artifacts found here indicate an exceptional standard of living, leading some scholars to suggest this may have been the long-sought palace of the high priest. The charred ceiling beam and badly scorched mosaic floor and fresco at the southern end of the fine reception hall bear witness to the Roman torching of the neighborhood in the late summer of AD 70, exactly one month after the Second Temple itself had been destroyed. Precisely 19 centuries later, the victims' compatriots uncovered evidence of destruction so vivid, wrote chief archaeologist Nahman Avigad, "that we could almost smell the burning and feel the heat of the flames." ⊠ *Hakara'im Rd.,*

*Jewish Quarter* ☎ 02/628–3448 ☒ *NIS 15; combined ticket with Burnt House NIS 35* ⊙ *Sun.–Thurs. 9–5, Fri. and Jewish holiday eves 9:30–1 (last entry 30 mins before closing).*

## Also Worth Seeing

⑪ **Broad Wall.** The discovery in the 1970s of the rather unobtrusive 23-foot-thick foundations of an Old Testament city wall was hailed as one of the most important archaeological finds in the Jewish Quarter. The wall was built in 701 BC by Hezekiah, King of Judah and a contemporary of the prophet Isaiah, to protect the city against an impending Assyrian invasion. The unearthing of the Broad Wall—a biblical name—resolved a long-running scholarly debate about the size of Old Testament Jerusalem: a large on-site map shows that the ancient city was far larger than was once thought. ☒ *Jewish Quarter Rd., Jewish Quarter.*

⑩ **Cardo.** In AD 135, the Roman emperor Hadrian built his town of Aelia Capitolina on the ruins of Jerusalem, an urban plan essentially preserved in the Old City of today. The *cardo maximus* (the generic name for the city's main street) began at the strategic Damascus Gate, in the north, where sections of the road have been unearthed. With the Christianization of the Roman Empire in the 4th century, access to Mt. Zion and its important Christian sites became a priority, and the main street was eventually extended into today's Jewish Quarter. The original width—today you see only half—was 73 feet, about the width of an eight-lane highway. ☒ *Jewish Quarter Rd., Jewish Quarter.*

# Tower of David & Mt. Zion

Most of the walls that enclose the Old City (whose area is under ½ square-mi) were built in the 16th century by the Ottoman sultan Suleiman the Magnificent. According to legend, his two architects were executed by the sultan and buried just inside the imposing Jaffa Gate. One version relates that they angered Suleiman by not including Mt. Zion and the venerated Tomb of David within the walls. Another version has it that the satisfied sultan wanted to make sure they would never build anything grander for anyone else.

The gate got its name from its westerly orientation, toward the once-important Mediterranean harbor of Jaffa, now part of Tel Aviv. Its Arabic name of Bab el-Halil, Gate of the Beloved, refers to the biblical Abraham, the "Beloved of God" in Muslim tradition, because from here another road strikes south toward Hebron—El-Halil—where Abraham is buried. The vehicle entrance is newer, created by the Ottoman Turks in 1898 in honor of the visiting German emperor, Kaiser Wilhelm II. In December 1917, during the First World War, the victorious British general Allenby took a different approach: he and his staff dismounted from their horses to enter the holy city with befitting humility.

The huge stone tower on the right as you enter the gate is the last survivor of the strategic fortress built by King Herod 2,000 years ago. Today it is part of the so-called Citadel that houses the Tower of David Museum. Opposite the entrance (once a drawbridge) is the neo-Gothic Christ Church (Anglican), built in 1849 as the first Protestant church

# JEWS IN THE OLD CITY

**THE HISTORY OF JEWISH LIFE** in the Old City has been marked by the trials of conflict and the joys of creating and rebuilding community.

**1099.** Crusaders conquer Jerusalem, followed by wholesale massacre. Jews lived at the time in today's Muslim Quarter.

**1267.** Spanish rabbi Nachmanides ("Ramban") reestablishes Jewish community. (His synagogue is on Jewish Quarter Road)

**1517.** Ottoman Turks conquer Palestine and allow Sephardic Jews (expelled from Spain a generation earlier) to resettle the country. They develop four interlinked synagogues in the quarter.

**1700.** Large groups of Ashekenazi Jews from Eastern Europe settle in Jerusalem.

**1860.** The first neighborhood is established outside the walls (Mishkenot Sha'ananim). Initially, very few Old City Jews had the courage to move out.

**1948.** Israel's War of Independence. Jewish Quarter surrenders to Jordanian forces and is abandoned. By then, the residents of the quarter represent only a tiny percentage of Jerusalem's Jewish population.

**1967.** Six-Day War. The Jewish Quarter, much of it ruined, is recaptured. Archaeological excavations and restoration work begin side by side.

**1980s.** Section after section of the Quarter becomes active again as the restoration work progresses—apartments and educational institutions, synagogues and stores, restaurants and new archaeological sites.

in the Middle East. Directly ahead is the souk (Arab bazaar), a convenient route to the Christian and Jewish Quarters. To reach Mt. Zion, follow the vehicle road inside the walls to Zion Gate, or take the Ramparts Walk.

## Main Attractions

**15** **Ramparts Walk.** The narrow stone catwalks of the Old City walls provide an interesting perspective and an introduction to the area. It's an innocent bit of voyeurism as you look down into gardens and courtyards and become, for a moment, a more intimate partner in the secret domestic life of the different quarters you pass. Across the rooftops, the domes and spires of the three religions that call Jerusalem holy compete for the skyline, just as their adherents jealously guard their territory down below. Peer through the shooting niches—just like the long-ago watchmen—and take in the broad vistas beyond the walls: the hotels and highrises of the new city to the west and south, the bustle of East Jerusalem to the north, and the quiet churches and cemeteries of Mount of Olives to the east. There are many high steps on this route; the railings are secure, but small children should not walk alone.

The two sections of the walk are disconnected from each other (though the same ticket covers both). The shorter southern section is accessible only from the end of the seemingly dead-end terrace outside Jaffa Gate (near the exit of the Tower of David Museum). Descent is at Zion Gate. The longer and more varied walk begins at Jaffa Gate (up the stairs immediately on the left as you enter the Old City), with descent at New, Herod's, or Lions' Gates. ⊠ *Jaffa Gate* ☎ *02/625–4403* ⌨ *NIS 14; combined ticket with Ophel Archaeological Garden, Damascus Gate, and Hezekiah's Tunnel (on same day only) NIS 35* ۞ *Sat.–Thurs. 9–4, Fri. and Jewish holiday eves 9–2.*

⑰ **Room of the Last Supper.** Tradition has enshrined this spare, 14th-century second-story room as the location of the "upper room" referred to in the New Testament (Mark 14). Two thousand years ago, when Jesus and his disciples celebrated the Passover seder that would become known as "the Last Supper," the site would have been *inside* the city walls. Formally known as the Cenacle or the Coenaculum, the room is also venerated by a second tradition as the place where Jesus's disciples gathered on Pentecost, seven weeks after his death, were "filled with the Holy Spirit," and began to speak in foreign "tongues" (Acts 2).

A little incongruously, the chamber has the trappings of a mosque as well. There are restored stained-glass Arabic inscriptions in the Gothic windows. One window is blocked by an ornate mihrab (an alcove indicating the direction of Mecca). There are also two Arabic plaques in the wall and a Levantine dome. The Muslims were not concerned with the site's Christian traditions but with the supposed Tomb of King David—the "Prophet" David in Muslim tradition—on the level below. ⊠ *Mt. Zion* ⌨ *Free* ۞ *Sat.–Thurs. 8–5, Fri. 8–1.*

★ ⑭ **Tower of David Museum.** Housed in a series of medieval halls, known locally as the Citadel ("Hametzuda" in Hebrew), the museum tells the city's 5,000-year-old story through models, maps, holograms, and videos. The galleries are organized by historical period around the citadel's central courtyard, where the old stone walls and arches add an appropriately antique atmosphere. Walking on the ramparts often provides unexpected panoramas. Be sure to inquire about the next screening of the animated introductory film, which has English subtitles—and don't miss the spectacular view from the top of the big tower. ⊠ *Jaffa Gate* ☎ *02/626–5333, 02/626–5310 for recorded info* ⊕ *www.towerofdavid. org.il* ⌨ *NIS 30* ۞ *Apr.–Oct., Sun.–Thurs. 10–5, Fri. call ahead, Sat. 10–4; Nov.–Mar., Mon.–Thurs. 10–4, Sat. 10–2. Free guided tour in English with cost of admission, on weekdays at 11 (call ahead).*

### Also Worth Seeing

⑲ **Chamber of the Holocaust.** Not to be confused with Yad Vashem in West Jerusalem, this small museum is also dedicated to the memory of the six million European Jews annihilated by the Nazis in the Second World War. Among the artifacts salvaged from the Holocaust are items that the Nazis forced Jews to make out of sacred Torah scrolls (the biblical Five Books of Moses). With grim humor, one Jewish tailor fashioned the inscribed parchment into a jacket, choosing sections that contained the worst of the biblical curses. Plaques commemorate many of the five thousand Jewish communities destroyed from 1939 to 1945. ⌂ *Near Tomb of David, Mt. Zion* ☎ *02/671–5105* ⊕ *www.holocaustchamber. org* ▣ *NIS 12* ☉ *Sun.–Thurs. 9–3:45, Fri. 9–1:30.*

⓰ **Dormition Abbey.** This round, black-domed Roman Catholic church, distinctive in its ornamented turrets and landmark clock tower, was built on land given by the Turkish sultan to the German kaiser Wilhelm II during the latter's 1898 visit to Jerusalem. The echoing main church, with its Byzantine-style apse and mosaic floors, was dedicated in 1910 by the German Benedictines. The lower-level crypt houses a cenotaph with a carved-stone figure of Mary in repose ("dormitio"), reflecting the tradition that she fell into eternal sleep. Among the adjacent little chapels is one donated by the Ivory Coast, with wooden figures and motifs inlaid with ivory. The premises include a bookstore and a coffee shop. ⌂ *Near the Room of the Last Supper, Mt. Zion* ☎ *02/565–5330* ▣ *Free* ☉ *Mon., Tues., Wed., and Fri. 8:30–noon and 12:30–6; Thurs. 9:45–noon and 12:30–5:30; Sat. 8:30–noon and 12:30–5:30; Sun. 10:30–11:45 and 12:30–5:30.*

⓲ **Tomb of David.** According to the Bible, King David, the great Israelite king of the 10th century BC, was buried in "the City of David," or Jerusalem. The actual site has been identified and excavated on the small ridge east of here, but medieval Jewish pilgrims erroneously placed the ancient city on this hill, where they sought—and supposedly found— the royal tomb. Its authenticity may be questionable, but some nine centuries of tears and prayers have sanctified the place.

The tomb itself is capped by a cenotaph (a massive stone marker draped with velvet cloth that has been embroidered with symbols and Hebrew texts traditionally associated with David). Behind it is a stone alcove, which some scholars think may be the sole remnant of a synagogue from the 5th century AD, the oldest of its kind in Jerusalem. More stringent regulations by Jewish religious authorities have recently divided the shrine into a men's and a women's side. Modest dress is required; men must cover their heads. ⌂ *Mt. Zion* ☎ *02/671–9767* ▣ *Free* ☉ *Apr.–Sept., Sun.–Thurs. 8–6, Fri. and Jewish holiday eves 8–2; Oct.–Mar., Sun.–Thurs. 8–5, Fri. and Jewish holiday eves 8–1.*

## City of David

Ancient Jerusalem was originally built on this modest ridge over four millennia ago, primarily because of the precious spring at its foot. The Israelite king David captured it from the Jebusites around 1000 BC, and made it his capital (hence the biblical name "City of David"). David's son Solomon expanded the city northward and built the Temple of God on Mt. Moriah, where the Dome of the Rock now stands. In time, Jerusalem spread farther west and north, but in recent years the name "City of David" has been revived to describe the city's ancient core. If you're driving, there is paid parking in the lot outside the Old City walls, east of and below Dung Gate.

# CloseUp

## WALKING THROUGH TIME

**THIS ADVENTURE IS A HEADY COMBINATION** of mysterious tunnels and ancient remains. The climax is wading through the 2,700-year-old Hezekiah's Tunnel (water is knee-to thigh-deep; bring appropriate clothing, water shoes or sandals, and a flashlight; not recommended for very small children), though there is a dry exit from the site for nonwaders. Plan 1½ hours for the walk, and an additional 45 minutes to wade the tunnel.

A platform at the City of David Visitors Center gives a fine view of the Kidron Valley, which drops sharply to the east, and gave ancient Jerusalem its best protection. Steps descend to the excavation site **Area G**, and from there halfway down the hill to **Warren's Shaft** (small sign on the right). At the entrance to the shaft are enlargements of remarkable clay seals. A tunnel slopes down to the top of a shaft that drops 40 feet to the Gihon Spring. Conventional wisdom identifies this as the point where King David's commandos penetrated the city in 1000 BC, but recent excavations near the spring have suggested an alternative route.

A short flight of steps and a tunnel takes you down through a cavernous structure with the massive foundations of 18th-century BC towers that once guarded the Gihon Spring, the original water supply of ancient Jerusalem. **Hezekiah's Tunnel**, also known as the Shiloah or Siloam Tunnel, was cut through the hill to secure the city's water supply in the face of the Assyrian invasion of 701 BC. It emerges at a small pool long identified as the New Testament "Pool of Siloam" where a blind man had his sight restored (John 9). Nonwaders have an alternative dry exit from the site.

For more information on the sights in bold, see the bulleted listings in City of David.

### Main Attractions

**㉒ Hezekiah's Tunnel.** Wading through a 2,700-year-old tunnel that once
**Fodor'sChoice** supplied water to the city is a great adventure for those who like a lit-
★ tle exercise with their history. The Assyrians invaded Judah in 701 BC, 20 years after they had destroyed its sister-kingdom of Israel to the north. According to the Bible, King Hezekiah attempted to protect Jerusalem's precious water supply in order to meet the imminent assault on the capital. He instructed his men to "stop the water of the springs that were outside the city" (II Chronicles 32). Racing against time, they dug a water tunnel a third of a mile long through solid rock, one team starting from the Gihon Spring and another from a new inner-city reservoir. Miraculously, considering the serpentine course of the tunnel, the two teams met in the middle. The chisel marks, the ancient plaster, and the zigzags near the halfway point as each team sought each other by sound bear witness to the remarkable project. With the spring now diverted into the city, its original opening was blocked to deny enemy access. Hezekiah, says the same biblical chapter, "closed the upper outlet of the waters of Gihon and directed them down to the west side of the city of David."

In the 19th century, an inscription in ancient Hebrew was found chiseled into the tunnel wall near the exit (since removed). "This is the story of the boring through . . . " it began, echoing the biblical account; "the tunnelers hewed the rock, each man toward his fellow . . . And the water flowed from the spring toward the reservoir for 1,200 cubits [577 yards]."

If you don't want to get your feet wet, you can still view the spring and marvel at the ingenuity of the ancient engineers. If you do decide to enter the spring and wade through the long narrow tunnel, you can easily imagine the dull digging of the ancient teams, and relive the electric moment when the work was done, the water flowed, and the city saved. The tunnel emerges in the Pool of Siloam, mentioned in the New Testament as the place where a blind man had his sight restored (John 9). What you see today is a latter-day construction, but the original, impressive 1st-century reservoir has been discovered, and (at press time) was being excavated. ⊠ *Off Ophel Rd., Silwan* ☎ *02/626–2341* ⊕ *www.cityofdavid.org.il* ✉ *NIS 23, guided tour NIS 50 (includes admission)* ⊙ *Sun.–Thurs. 9–5, Fri. and Jewish holiday eves 9–1, last entrance 1½ hours before closing.*

★ ㉑ **Warren's Shaft.** Charles Warren was an inspired British army engineer who explored Jerusalem in 1867. In the City of David he discovered this spacious, sloping access tunnel—note the ancient chisel marks on the walls—which burrowed under the city wall to a point 40 feet above the Gihon Spring, in the valley. A narrow vertical shaft dropped into the spring, and conventional wisdom long maintained that this was the way water was hauled up into the city in ancient times. The presumption was that it was pre-Davidic, and perhaps the actual biblical *tzinnor* (gutter or water shaft) of II Samuel 5 through which David's warriors penetrated the city, ca. 1000 BC. Modern archaeologists believe that the space at the head of the shaft was only created in a later era; and a recent dig around the Gihon Spring at the bottom of the hill has uncovered a different access to the spring, protected by two huge towers that date back to the Middle Bronze Age, centuries before David. The biblical story remains intact for the moment, but the famous Warren's Shaft may not have been the exact place where it occurred. ⊠ *Off Ophel Rd., Silwan* ☎ *02/626-2341* ⊕ *www.cityofdavid.org.il* ✉ *NIS 23, guided tour NIS 50 (includes admission)* ⊙ *Sun.–Thurs. 9–5, Fri. and Jewish holiday eves 9–1, last entrance 1½ hours before closing.*

### Also Worth Seeing

⓴ **Area G.** Archaeologists have dug up bits of the City of David for well over a century—notably Charles Warren in the 1860s, and Kathleen Kenyon a hundred years later. The most thorough expedition, however, was led by Israeli archaeologist Yigal Shiloh from 1978 to 1985. In this locale, he confirmed that the angular pieces of the city wall, seen at the top, are indeed the 2nd century BC construction that the historian Josephus Flavius dubbed the First Wall. On the other hand, he redated the sloping "stepped structure" to at least the 10th century BC, the time of Israelite kings David and Solomon, when it apparently supported a palace or fortification on the crest of the ridge. In the 7th century BC, a house (now partially restored on a platform) was built against it.

The most intriguing artifacts are 51 bullae, clay seals used for documents, just as hot wax might be used today, with personal names impressed on them in ancient Hebrew script. All of the seals were found in one chamber, suggesting that it was used as an archive or a royal office. This idea was reinforced by the biblical name on one of the seals: Gemariah ben Shafan, the royal secretary in the days of Jeremiah. The clay seals were baked into pottery by a fire, apparently during the Babylonian destruction of Jerusalem in 586 BC. ⊠ *Off Ophel Rd., Silwan* ☎ *02/626-2341* ⊕ *www.cityofdavid.org.il* ⊠ *NIS 23, guided tour NIS 50 (includes admission)* ⊙ *Sun.–Thurs. 9–5, Fri. and Jewish holiday eves 9–1, last entrance 1½ hours before closing; tours in English.*

## Mount of Olives & East Jerusalem

The sights in this area are for the most part distinctly Christian. A few are a little off the beaten path, and the best way to explore them—if you're energetic enough—is on foot. If you're driving, however, you can find parking at the Seven Arches Hotel on the Mount of Olives, and at the American Colony Hotel; there are cabs. A word of caution: pickpockets continue to be a problem on the Mount of Olives lookout and on the road down to Gethsemane.

### Main Attractions

**28** **Garden of Gethsemane.** After the Last Supper, the New Testament relates, Jesus and his disciples came to a "place" called Gethsemane. There he agonized and prayed, and there, in the end, he was betrayed and arrested. Gethsemane derives from the Aramaic or Hebrew word for "oil press," referring to the precious olive that has always flourished here. The enormous, gnarled, and still-productive olive trees on the site may be older than Christianity itself, according to some botanists.

The **Church of All Nations** was built in the garden on the scanty remains of its Byzantine predecessor by the prolific architect Antonio Barluzzi, and dedicated in 1924. Within each of its interior domes are mosaic symbols of the Catholic communities that contributed to its construction. The seal of the United States is in the first dome on the right as you enter the church; Canada is two up in the same line; and the English dome is the first, nearest the door, in the middle line. The windows are glazed with translucent alabaster in somber browns and purples, creating a mystical feeling in the dim interior. The church was previously known as **the Basilica of the Agony** named for the so-called Rock of the Agony at the altar, where Jesus is said to have endured his Passion.

A popular approach to Gethsemane is walking down the steep road from the top of Mount of Olives, perhaps stopping in on the way at the Dominus Flevit church where, tradition has it, Jesus wept as he foretold the destruction of the city (Luke 19). The entrance to the well-tended garden at the foot of the hill is marked by a small platoon of vendors outside. ⊠ *Jericho Rd., Kidron Valley* ☎ *02/626–6444* ⊠ *Free* ⊙ *Apr.–Sept., daily 8–12 and 2–6; Oct.–Mar., daily 8–12 and 2–5.*

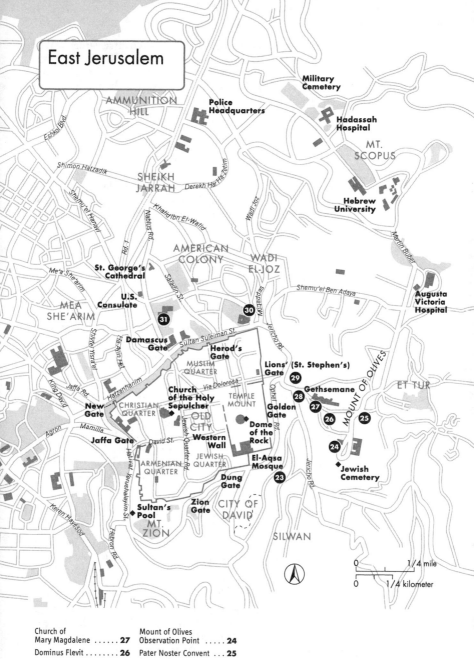

# East Jerusalem

Military Cemetery

Police Headquarters

Hadassah Hospital

AMMUNITION HILL

MT. SCOPUS

Eshkol Blvd.

Shimon Hatzadik

SHEIKH JARRAH

Derekh Har Ha-Tzofim

Hebrew University

Shemu'el Hanavi

Me'a She'arim

St. George's Cathedral

AMERICAN COLONY

WADI EL-JOZ

Augusta Victoria Hospital

Khalid Ibn El-Walid

Nablus Rd.

Rd. 1

Saladin St.

Wadi-Joz

Menihin Buber

MEA SHE'ARIM

U.S. Consulate

Shemu'el Ben Adaya

Ha-Ayin Het

Shirley Yisra'el

**31**

**30**

Damascus Gate

Sultan Suleiman St.

Herod's Gate

MUSLIM QUARTER

Lions' (St. Stephen's) Gate

**29**

MOUNT OF OLIVES

ET TUR

King David

Jaffa Rd.

Hatzanhanim

Via Dolorosa

Gethsemane

**28**

Agron

Mamilla

New Gate

CHRISTIAN QUARTER

Church of the Holy Sepulcher

TEMPLE MOUNT

Golden Gate

**27**

**26**

**25**

OLD CITY

Jewish Quarter Rd.

David St.

Ophel Rd.

Jaffa Gate

Western Wall

Dome of the Rock

**24**

HalVat. Yerushalayim St.

JEWISH QUARTER

ARMENIAN QUARTER

El-Aqsa Mosque

Jewish Cemetery

Keren Hayesod

Dung Gate

**23**

Sultan's Pool

Zion Gate

CITY OF DAVID

Jericho Rd.

Hebron Rd.

MT. ZION

SILWAN

0                1/4 mile

0                1/4 kilometer

★ ③ **Garden Tomb.** A beautifully tended English-style country garden makes this an island of tranquillity in the hurly-burly of East Jerusalem. What Christian pilgrims come for, however, is an empty ancient tomb, and a grand opportunity to ponder the Gospel account of the death and resurrection of Jesus. It is a favorite site for the many Protestant visitors who respond less or not at all to the ornamentation and ritual of the Holy Sepulcher.

The theory identifying this site with Calvary and Jesus's burial place goes back to 1883, when the British general Charles Gordon (of later Khartoum fame) spent several months in Jerusalem. From his window looking out over the Old City walls, Gordon was struck by the skull-like features of a cliff face north of the Damascus Gate. He was convinced that this, rather than the traditional Calvary in the Church of the Holy Sepulcher, was "the place of the skull" (Mark 15) where Jesus was crucified. His conviction was infectious, and after his death, a fundraising campaign in England resulted in the purchase of the adjacent site in 1894. An ancient rock-cut tomb had already been uncovered there, and subsequent excavations exposed cisterns and a wine press, features typical of an ancient garden.

All the elements of the Gospel account of Jesus's death and burial seemed to be in evidence, and the newly formed Garden Tomb Association was jubilant. According to the New Testament, Jesus was buried in the fresh tomb of the wealthy Joseph of Arimathea, in a garden close to the execution site, and archaeologists identified the tomb as an upper-class Jewish burial place of the Second Temple period. Recent research has challenged that conclusion, however. The tomb might be from the Old Testament period, making it too old to have been Jesus's, since his was freshly cut. The gentle guardians of the Garden Tomb do not insist on the identification of the site as that of Calvary and the tomb of Christ, but are keen to provide a contemplative setting for the pilgrim, in a place that just might have been historically significant. ⊠ *Conrad Schick St., East Jerusalem* ☎ *02/627–2745* ⊕ *www.gardentomb.com* ⊠ *Free* ☉ *Mon.–Sat. 2–5:30.*

**need a break?** The upscale **American Colony Hotel** (⊠ 23 Nablus Rd., American Colony ☎ 02/627–9777) is an elegant 19th-century limestone building with cane furniture, Armenian ceramic tiles, and a delightful courtyard. The food is generally very good, and a light lunch or afternoon tea in the cool lobby lounge, at the poolside restaurant, or on the patio under the trees can make for a well-earned break.

★ ㉔ **Mount of Olives Observation Point.** This is the classic panoramic view of the Old City: looking across the Kidron Valley over the gold Dome of the Rock. It's best in the early morning, with the sun at your back, or at sunset on days with some clouds, when the golden glow can compensate for the glare.

The Mount of Olives has been bathed in sanctity for millennia. On the slope beneath you, and off to your left, is the vast **Jewish cemetery,** reputedly the oldest cemetery still in use anywhere in the world. For more than 2,000 years, Jews have been buried here to await the coming of the Messiah and the resurrection to follow. The raised structures over the graves are merely tomb markers, not crypts; burial is below ground.

In the Old City wall facing you, and just to the right of the Dome of the Rock, is the blocked-up, double-arched Gates of Mercy, or Golden Gate. Jewish tradition holds that the Messiah will enter Jerusalem this way; Christian tradition says he already did, on Palm Sunday. To the south of the Dome of the Rock is the black-domed El-Aqsa Mosque, and behind it the stone arches of the Jewish Quarter. Some distance behind the Dome of the Rock is the large, gray dome of the Church of the Holy Sepulcher. To the left of the Old City, the cone-roof Dormition Abbey and its adjacent tower mark the top of Mt. Zion, today outside the walls but within the city of the Second Temple period. ⊠ *E-Sheikh St., opposite Seven Arches Hotel, Mt. of Olives.*

**㉚ Rockefeller Museum of Archaeology.** The Rockefeller's octagonal white stone tower is an East Jerusalem landmark. Built in the 1930s, its echoing stone halls and somewhat old-fashioned display techniques recall the British Mandate period, when it was in its prime. If you have only a passing interest in archaeology, the Israel Museum's finely presented collection will more than suffice; the Rockefeller branch is for the enthusiast.

The finds are all from this country, dating from prehistoric times to around AD 1700. Among the most important exhibits are cultic masks from Neolithic Jericho, ivories from Canaanite (Bronze Age) Megiddo, the famous Israelite "Lachish Letters" (6th century BC), Herodian inscriptions, and decorative reliefs from Hisham's Palace, in Jericho, and from the Church of the Holy Sepulcher. There is no parking available within the museum grounds. ⊠ *Sultan Suleiman St., East Jerusalem* ☎ *02/628–2251* ⊕ *imj.org.il/eng/branches/rockefeller* ⊠ *NIS 26; combined ticket with Israel Museum (good for 2 weeks) NIS 37* ⊙ *Sun., Mon., Wed., and Thurs. 10–3, Sat. 10–2.*

## Also Worth Seeing

**㉗ Church of Mary Magdalene.** Dedicated in 1888, this Russian Orthodox church, with its sculpted white turrets and gold onion domes, looks like something out of a fairytale. It has limited hours, but its icon-studded interior and tranquil garden are well worth a visit if your plans bring you to the area at the right time. ⊠ *Above Gethsemane, Mt. of Olives* ☎ *02/628–4371* ⊠ *Free* ⊙ *Tues., Thurs., and Sat. 10–noon.*

**㉖ Dominus Flevit.** Designed by Barluzzi in the 1950s, the tear-shape church—its name means "the Lord wept"—preserves the New Testament story of Jesus's sorrowful prophecy of the destruction of Jerusalem (Luke 19). The remarkable feature of its simple interior is a picture window facing west, the iron cross on the altar silhouetted against a superb view of the Old City. Many small archaeological items were found here, but the tradition that holds this as the site of the story is no older than the Crusader period. The courtyard is a good place to enjoy the view in peace between waves of pilgrim groups. (Equally worthy of mention are the rest rooms, rare in this area!) The church is about one-third of the way down the steep road that descends to Gethsemane from the Mount of Olives Observation Point. Beware of pickpockets on the street outside. ⊠ *Below Mount of Olives Observation Point, Mt. of Olives* ☎ *02/626–6455* ⊕ *www.christusrex.org* ⊠ *Free* ⊙ *Daily 8–5.*

**㉓ Kidron Valley.** The deep valley separates the Old City and the City of David from the high ridge of the Mount of Olives and the Arab neighborhood of Silwan. In the cliff face below the houses across the valley are the symmetrical openings of tombs from both the First Temple (Old Testament) and Second Temple (Hellenistic-Roman) periods. From the lookout terrace at the southeast corner of the Old City wall, down and to your left, you can see an impressive group of 2,200-year-old funerary monuments. The huge, square, stone structure with the conical roof is known as **Absalom's Pillar.** The one crowned by a pyramidal roof, a solid block of stone cut out of the mountain, is called **Zachariah's Tomb.** The association with those Old Testament personalities was a medieval mistake, and the structures more probably mark the tombs of wealthy Jerusalemites of the Second Temple period who wished to await in style the coming of the Messiah and the resurrection that would soon follow. ⊠ *Kidron Valley.*

**㉕ Pater Noster Convent.** The focal point of this Carmelite convent is a grotto, traditionally identified as the place where Jesus taught his disciples the so-called Lord's Prayer: "Our Father [*Pater Noster*], Who art in Heaven . . ." (Matthew 6). The site was purchased by the Princesse de la Tour d'Auvergne of France in 1868 and the convent was built on the site of earlier Byzantine and Crusader structures. The ambitious basilica, begun in the 1920s, was designed to follow the lines of a 4th-century church, but was never completed: its aisles, open to the sky, are now lined with pine trees. The real attractions of the site, however, are the many ceramic plaques adorning the cloister walls and the small church, with the Lord's Prayer in over 100 different languages. (Look for the high wall and metal door on a bend 200 yards before the Seven Arches Hotel.) ⊠ *E-Sheikh St., Mt. of Olives* ☎ *02/626–4904* ⊠ *Free* ⊙ *Mon.–Sat. 8:30–noon and 2:30–4:30.*

**㉙ Tomb of the Virgin.** The Gothic facade of the underground Church of the Assumption, which contains this shrine, clearly dates it to the Crusader era (12th century). However, tradition has it that this is where the Virgin Mary was interred and then "assumed" into heaven. In an otherwise gloomy church—hung with age-darkened icons and brass lamps—the marble sarcophagus, thought to date from the 12th century, remains illuminated. The Status Quo Agreement in force in the Church of the Holy Sepulcher and Bethlehem's Church of the Nativity pertains here, too: the Greek Orthodox, Armenian Orthodox, and Muslims control different parts of the property. The Roman Catholic Franciscans were expelled in 1757, a loss of privilege that rankles to this day. The shrine is a few steps away from the Garden of Gethsemane. ⊠ *Jericho Rd., adjacent to Gethsemane, Kidron Valley* ⊕ *www.christusrex.org* ⊠ *Free* ⊙ *Daily 6–noon and 2:30–5.*

## West Jerusalem

Visitors tend to focus, naturally enough, on the historical and religious sights on the eastern side of town, especially in the Old City; but West Jerusalem houses the nation's institutions, is the repository for its collective memory, and—together with the downtown—gives more insight into contemporary life in Israel's largest city. These attractions are most easily accessible by car or by a combination of buses and short cab rides.

Pay attention to the closing times of sites: several are not open on Saturdays and close early on Fridays. Some museums have evening hours on particular days—a time-efficient option. Avoid burn-out by staggering visits to the museums, and combining them with different kinds of experiences.

### Main Attractions

**39** **Bible Lands Museum.** This museum was the brainchild of Elie Borowski, whose personal collection of ancient artifacts forms its core. Most archaeological museums group artifacts according to their place of origin (Egyptian, Babylonian, and so on), but the curators here have abandoned this method in favor of a chronological display. This allows a comparison of objects of neighboring cultures of the same period, the better to explore cross-cultural interactions and influences. The exhibits cover a period of more than 6,000 years—from the prehistoric Neolithic period to that of the Byzantine Empire—and sweep geographically from Afghanistan to Nubia (present-day Sudan). Rare clay vessels, fertility idols, cylinder seals, ivories, and sarcophagi fill the soaring, naturally lighted galleries. Look for the ancient Egyptian wooden coffin, in a stunning state of preservation.

The concept of the museum is intriguing, but some have criticized its methodology. A concept was imposed on a largely preexisting collection, rather than a collection being created item by selected item to illustrate a concept. Join the guided tour to get the most out of the place. ✉ *25 Granot St., Givat Ram* ☎ *02/561–1066* ⊕ *www.blmj.org* ✉ *NIS 32* ⊙ *Sun.–Tues. and Thurs. 9:30–5:30, Wed. 9:30–9:30, Fri. and Jewish holiday eves 9:30–2. Guided tours in English Sun.–Fri. at 10:15 (Wed. at 5:30 in addition); call ahead to verify.*

**33** **Chagall Windows & Hadassah Hospital.** Hadassah is one of the leading general hospitals in the Middle East and the teaching hospital for Hebrew University's medical and dental schools. When the U.S.-based Hadassah women's organization approached the Russian-born Jewish artist Marc Chagall in 1959 about designing stained-glass windows for the synagogue at the new hospital, he was delighted and contributed his work for free. Taking his inspiration from the Bible—Jacob's deathbed blessings on his sons and, to a lesser extent, Moses's valediction to the tribes of Israel—the artist created 12 vibrant windows in primary colors, with an ark full of characteristically Chagallian beasts and a scattering of Jewish and esoteric symbols. The innovative techniques of the Reims glassmakers give the wafer-thin windows an astounding illusion

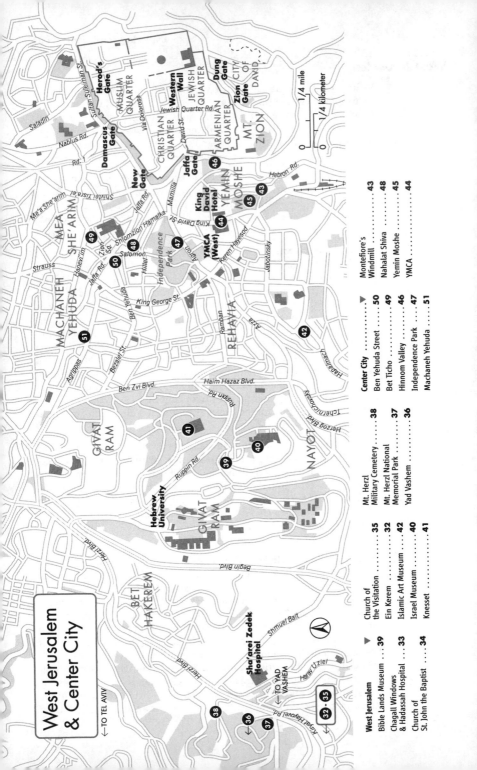

# West Jerusalem & Center City

←TO TEL AVIV

**West Jerusalem**

Bible Lands Museum ... **39**
Chagall Windows
& Hadassah Hospital ... **33**
Church of
St. John the Baptist .... **34**

Church of
the Visitation .......... **35**
Ein Kerem ........... **32**
Islamic Art Museum .... **42**
Israel Museum ......... **40**
Knesset ............. **41**

Mt. Herzl
Military Cemetery ...... **38**
Mt. Herzl National
Memorial Park ........ **37**
Yad Vashem ........... **36**

**Center City** ............. ▶
Ben Yehuda Street .... **50**
Bet Ticho ............ **49**
Hinnom Valley ........ **46**
Independence Park .... **47**
Machaneh Yehuda ..... **51**

Montefiore's
Windmill ............ **43**
Nahalat Shiva ........ **48**
Yemin Moshe ......... **45**
YMCA ............... **44**

of depth in many places. Buses 19 and 27 serve the hospital. ⊠ *Hadassah Hospital, Henrietta Szold Rd., Ein Kerem* ☎ *02/677–6271* ⊕ *www. hadassah.org.il/english* 🖾 *NIS 10* ☉ *Sun.–Thurs. 8–1:15, and 2–3:30.*

★ ㉜ **Ein Kerem.** The neighborhood of Ein Kerem (sometimes Ein "Karem") still retains much of its old village character. Tree-framed stone houses are strewn across its hillsides with a pleasing Mediterranean nonchalance. Many homes have been marvelously renovated by artists and professionals who have joined the older working-class population over the last 40 years. Back alleys provide an off-the-beaten-path feel, and occasionally a serendipitous art or craft studio. Though not mentioned by name in the New Testament, Ein Kerem is identified as the home of John the Baptist, and indeed the orange-roof **Church of St. John the Baptist** in the heart of the village, and the **Church of the Visitation** up the hillside above the Spring of the Virgin, are its most prominent landmarks. A few good eateries allow you to while away a bit more time here.

The road down to the valley begins at the big Mt. Herzl intersection. Alternatively, if you're driving and you've just visited the Chagall Windows, turn right as soon as you leave the hospital grounds, and descend to where the road joins Route 386. Turn right again, reentering Jerusalem through the bottom of Ein Kerem. ⊠ *Ein Kerem.*

☺ ㊵ **Israel Museum.** Put this eclectic treasure trove on your don't-miss list. Figure a couple of hours as a minimum, but museum buffs should certainly plan more. The three main thrusts of this exceptional museum are art, archaeology, and Judaica; although there are some fascinating exhibits of other world cultures. Check for changing exhibits, which are sometimes even more riveting than the permanent collections. If your time is limited, take 25 minutes for the Dead Sea Scrolls, and weigh the attractions of a new exhibit against your interest in one of the permanent wings.

Fodor'sChoice ★

The **Dead Sea Scrolls,** housed in the distinctive white, domelike Shrine of the Book, are certainly the Israel Museum's most famous—and most important—collection. The first of the 2,000-year-old scrolls were discovered by a Bedouin boy in 1947 in a Judean Desert cave, overlooking the Dead Sea. The adventures of these priceless artifacts before they found a permanent home here are the stuff of which Indiana Jones movies are made ( ⇨ *See* Dead Sea Region *in* Chapter 2). The shape of the pavilion was inspired by the lids of the clay jars in which the first scrolls were found.

The scrolls were written in the Second Temple period by a fundamentalist Jewish sect, conventionally identified as the Essenes, a group referred to by contemporary historians. All archaeological, laboratory, and textual evidence dates the earliest of the scrolls to the 2nd century BC; none could have been written later than AD 68, the year in which their home community, known today as Qumran, was destroyed by the Romans. Written on parchment, and still in an extraordinary state of preservation because of the exceptional dryness of the Dead Sea region, the scrolls contain the oldest Hebrew manuscripts of the Old Testament ever found, authenticating the almost identical Hebrew texts still in use today. Sectarian literature includes "The Rule of the Community," a constitution of this ascetic group, and "The War of the Sons of Light Against the Sons of Darkness," a blow-by-blow account of a final cataclysmic conflict that would, they believed, presage the messianic age.

The open-air **Billy Rose Sculpture Garden** was designed against a Judean Hills cityscape by the landscape architect Isamu Noguchi. Crunch over the gravel amid works by Daumier, Rodin, Moore, and Picasso. The main building houses a modest but high-quality collection of European art, including paintings by Rembrandt and Van Dyck, Monet, van Gogh, Pissarro, Renoir, and Gauguin. The adjacent **Cummings 20th-Century Art Building** is dedicated to modern and contemporary art, from Cézanne, Picasso, and Chagall, through Dubuffet, Rothko, and Lipchitz, to an interesting cross-section of Israeli artists still active today.

The **Judaica** section has perhaps the world's greatest collection of Jewish ceremonial art and artifacts, including medieval illuminated *haggadot* (Passover texts) and *ketubot* (wedding contracts); Sabbath spice boxes and Hanukkah menorahs; and the evocative interiors of synagogues, from 17th-century Venice, 19th-century Southern Germany, and the now-defunct community of Cochin, in India. Ethnographic exhibits include dazzling formal costumes and jewelry, as well as everyday objects from Jewish communities throughout the Middle East, North Africa, and Eastern Europe. Period rooms reflecting 18th- and 19th-century European design are an unexpected presence.

Look for the **archaeology wing's** lucid exhibit of artifacts, mostly discovered in Israel. The age and rarity of the prehistoric remains may surprise you, until you recall Israel's position as the only land bridge between Africa and Asia, and thus its attraction for migrants and settlers in the primeval past. For many visitors, the focal point of this wing is the biblical (Old Testament) period, illuminated by Canaanite idols, pots from the time of Abraham, a Solomonic gateway, and altars and inscriptions from the days of Isaiah and Jeremiah. A side hall holds a superb collection of glass, from rainbow-patinated Roman pieces to sleek Art Deco objects.

Once a year, the **youth wing** mounts an entirely new exhibition, delightfully interactive and often adult-friendly, designed to encourage children to appreciate the arts and the world around them, or be creative in a crafts workshop. Parents with restless kids will also be grateful for the outdoor play areas. A couple of cafeterias (closed Saturday) and two museum stores complete the site. A free shuttle bus for travelers with disabilities runs on request from the main gate to the main entrance at the top of the short hill. ⊠ *Ruppin Blvd., Givat Ram* ☎ *02/670–8811* ⊕ *www.imj.org.il* ⊠ *NIS 40 (includes audio-guide); half price for return visit within one month (keep your ticket)* ☉ *Mon., Wed., Sat. and, Jewish holidays 10–4; Tues. 4–9; Thurs. 10–9; Fri. and Jewish holiday eves 10–2. Free tours in English with cost of admission.*

**41** **Knesset.** Both the name of and the number of seats (120) in Israel's one-chamber parliament were taken from *Haknesset Hagedolah,* the Great Assembly of the Second Temple period. The 40-minute public tour held on Sunday and Thursday includes the session hall as well as three enor-

# ISRAEL'S ELECTORAL SYSTEM

**TAKE TWO ISRAELIS,"** runs the old quip, "and you've got three political parties!" The saying is not without truth in a nation where everyone has a strong opinion and usually will not hesitate to express it. The Knesset reflects this rambunctious spirit, sometimes to the point of paralyzing the parliamentary process and driving the public to distraction. Israel's electoral system, based on proportional representation, is a legacy of the dangerous but heady days of Israel's War of Independence, in 1948–49. To avoid an acrimonious and divisive election while the fledgling state was still fighting to stay alive, the founding fathers developed a one-body parliamentary system that gave representation to rival ideological factions in proportion to their comparative strength in the country's pre-State institutions.

Instead of the winner-takes-all approach of the constituency system, the Israeli system grants any party that wins 2% of the national vote its first seat in the Knesset. The good news is that even fringe parties can have their voices heard. The bad news is that the system spawns a plethora of political parties, making it virtually impossible for one party to get the majority needed to govern alone. Israeli governments have therefore always consisted of a coalition of parties, inevitably making them governments of compromise. The smaller parties—whose support is critical for the government to keep its ruling majority—have thus been able to extract major political and material concessions for their own party interests, which are often at odds with those of the nation at large.

mous, brilliantly colored tapestries designed by Marc Chagall on the subjects of the Creation, the Exodus, and Jerusalem. On other days, when in session, the Knesset is open to the public. (Call ahead to verify.) All the proceedings are conducted in Hebrew. Allow at least 1½ hours for the visit (perhaps more in summer, when the lines are longer), arrive at least 30 minutes before the tour, and be sure to bring your passport.

Across the road from the Knesset main gate is a 15-foot-high bronze menorah, based on the one that once graced the ancient temple in Jerusalem. The seven-branch candelabra was adopted soon after independence as the official symbol of the modern State of Israel. This one, designed by artist Bruno Elkin, and given as a gift of the British Parliament to the Knesset in 1956, is decorated with bas-relief depictions of events and personages in Jewish history, from biblical times to the modern day. Behind the menorah is the Wohl Rose Garden (enter from outside the Knesset security barrier), which has hundreds of varieties of roses, many lawns for children to romp on, and adult-friendly nooks in its upper section. ⊠ Kiryat Ben Gurion, Givat Ram ☎ 02/675–3416 ⊕ www.knesset.gov.il ☑ Free ☉ Guided tours Sun. and Thurs. 8:30–2. Call ahead to verify specific tour times in English.

**③⑦ Mt. Herzl National Memorial Park.** Cedars of Lebanon and native pine and cypress trees surround the entrance to the memorial and cemetery. Immediately to the left is the **Herzl Museum** (✉ Mt. Herzl ☎ 02/643–3266 ☉ Sun.–Thurs. 9–3:30, Fri. 9–12:30), a new interactive introduction to the life, times, and legacy of Israel's spiritual forebear. Tours take an hour and cost NIS 20. Call ahead to verify times of tours in English.

In 1894 the Budapest-born Theodor Herzl was the Paris correspondent for a Vienna newspaper when the Dreyfus treason trial hit the headlines. The anti-Semitic outbursts that Herzl encountered in cosmopolitan Paris shocked him. Dreyfus, a Jewish officer in the French army, had actually been framed and was later exonerated. Herzl devoted himself to the problem of Jewish vulnerability in "foreign" host countries and to the need for a Jewish state. The result of his activities was the first World Zionist Congress, held in Basel, Switzerland, in 1897. That year Herzl wrote in his diary: "If not in five years, then in 50, [a Jewish state] will become reality." True to his prediction, the United Nations approved the idea 50 years later, in November 1947. Herzl died in 1904, and his remains were brought to Israel in 1949. His simple grave marker, inscribed in Hebrew with just his last name, caps the hill.

To the left (west) of the grave site, a gravel path leads down to a section containing the graves of Israeli national leaders, among them prime ministers Levi Eshkol, Golda Meir, and Yitzhak Rabin, and presidents Zalman Shazar and Chaim Herzog. Bear down and right through the military cemetery, exiting back on Herzl Blvd., about 250 yards below the parking lot where you entered. ✉ *Herzl Blvd., Mt. Herzl ☎ 02/643–3266 ▣ Free ☉ Apr.–Sep., Sun.–Thurs. 8–6:45, Fri. and Jewish holiday eves 8–12:45; Oct.–Mar., Sun.–Thurs. 8–4:45, Fri. and Jewish holiday eves 8–12:45.*

**★ ③⑥ Yad Vashem.** The experience of the Holocaust—the annihilation of six million Jews by the Nazis during World War II—is so deeply seared into the Jewish national psyche that understanding it goes a long way toward understanding Israelis themselves. The institution of Yad Vashem, created in 1953 by an act of the Knesset, was charged with preserving a record of those times. The name "Yad Vashem"—"a memorial and a name (a memory)"—comes from the biblical book of Isaiah (56:5). The Israeli government has made a tradition of bringing almost all high-ranking official foreign guests to visit the place.

The riveting new **Historical Museum** (opened March 2005)—a 200-yard-long triangular concrete prism—is the centerpiece of the site. Powerful visual and audiovisual techniques in a series of galleries document Jewish life in Europe before the catastrophe and follow the escalation of persecution and internment to the hideous climax of the Nazi's "Final Solution." Video interviews and personal artifacts individualize the experience.

The small **Children's Memorial** is dedicated to the 1.5 million Jewish children murdered by the Nazis. Architect Moshe Safdie wanted to convey the enormity of the crime without numbing the visitor's emo-

Worshipper at Western Wall, Jerusalem.

(top left) Baha'i Shrine and Gardens, Haifa. (top right) Bedouin market, Beersheva. (bottom) Remains of the Roman theater at Bet She'an.

(top) Church of the Holy Sepulcher, Jerusalem. (bottom) Floating in the Dead Sea.

(top) A walk in a *wadi* (dry riverbed) in the Negev Desert. (bottom left) Beach at Herzliya, near Tel Aviv. (bottom right) Bethlehem.

The *souk* (market) in the Old City, Jerusalem.

(top) Flowers in the Lower Galilee. (bottom left) Ruins of the hot baths at Masada. (Bottom right) Statue at Yad Vashem, Holocaust national memorial and museum.

(top) Remains of synagogue at Capernaum. (bottom) Outdoor dining on Ben Yehuda Street, Jerusalem.

(top) Waterfront at Jaffa, near Tel Aviv. (bottom) Excavating at Tel Maresha, west of Jerusalem.

tions or losing sight of the victims' individuality. The result is a single dark room, lit by five candles infinitely reflected in some 500 mirrors. Recorded narrators intone the names, ages, and nationalities of the known victims. The effect is electrifying. There are no steps, and guide rails are provided throughout.

Elsewhere on the site is the **Art Museum,** with an ongoing exhibition of children at play in the Holocaust.

The **Avenue of the Righteous** encircles Yad Vashem with several thousand trees marked with the names of Gentiles in Europe who risked and sometimes lost their lives trying to save Jews from the Nazis. Raoul Wallenberg, King Christian X of Denmark, Corrie ten Boom, and Oskar Schindler are among the more famous honorees. The **Hall of Remembrance** is a heavy basalt-and-concrete building that houses an eternal flame, with the names of the death and concentration camps in relief on the floor.

At the bottom of the hill, large rough-hewn limestone boulders divide the **Valley of the Communities** into a series of small, man-made canyons. Each clearing represents a region of Nazi Europe, laid out geographically. The names of some 5,000 destroyed Jewish communities are inscribed in the stone walls, with very large letters highlighting those that were particularly important in prewar Europe.

There is an information booth (be sure to pick up a map of the site), a bookstore, and a cafeteria at the entrance to Yad Vashem. Photography is not permitted within the exhibition areas. Egged's Line 99 is the only public transportation into Yad Vashem; the site is a 10-minute walk from the Mt. Herzl intersection, which is served by many city bus lines. ⊠ *Hazikaron St., near Herzl Blvd., Mt. Herzl* ☎ *02/644-3565* ⊕ *www. yadvashem.org* 🎫 *Free* ☉ *Sun.–Thurs. 9–5, Fri. and Jewish holiday eves 9–2. Last entrance 1 hr before closing.*

**off the beaten path**

**THE BIBLICAL ZOO** – Apart from the usual entertaining species of most zoos—like monkeys, snakes, and birds—the 62-acre Biblical Zoo (known officially as the Tisch Family Zoo) focuses on two groups of wildlife. The first is creatures mentioned in the Bible that have become locally extinct, some as late as the 20th century. Among these are lions, bears, cheetahs, the Nile crocodile, and certain deer and horned animals. Cage plaques with biblical references tell more. The second focus is on endangered species worldwide, among them the Asian elephant and rare macaws and cockatoos. This is a wonderful place to let kids expend some energy. Early morning or late afternoon are the best hours in summer. ⊠ *Near the Jerusalem (Malcha) Mall, Malcha* ☎ *02/675-0111* ⊕ *www.jerusalemzoo.org.il* 🎫 *NIS 40* ☉ *June–Aug., Sun.–Thurs. 9–7, Fri. 9–4:30, Sat. 10–6; Sept., Apr., and May, Sun.–Thurs. 9–6, Fri. and Jewish holiday eves 9–4:30, Sat. 10–6; Oct.–Mar., Sun.–Thurs. 9–5, Fri. and Jewish holiday eves 9–4:30, Sat. 10–5. Call ahead to verify closing times and possible guided tours. Last entrance 1 hr before closing.*

### Also Worth Seeing

**34 Church of St. John the Baptist.** The orange tile roof of this large, late-17th-century Franciscan church is a landmark in Ein Kerem. Though not mentioned by name in the New Testament, the village has long been identified as the birthplace of John the Baptist, a tradition that apparently goes back to the Byzantine period (5th century AD). Apart from the grotto where John the Baptist is said to have been born, the church's old paintings and glazed tiles alone make it worth a visit. ⊠ *Ein Kerem St., Ein Kerem* ☎ *02/641-3639* ⌨ *Free* ⊙ *Apr.–Sept., daily 8–noon and 2:30–6; Oct.–Mar. 8–noon and 2:30–5.*

**35 Church of the Visitation.** Built over what is thought to have been the home of John the Baptist's parents, Zechariah and Elizabeth, this church sits high up the hillside in Ein Kerem, with a wonderful view of the valley and the surrounding wooded hills. When Mary, pregnant with Jesus, came to visit her pregnant cousin, the aging Elizabeth, "the babe leaped in [Elizabeth's] womb" with joy at recognizing the unborn Jesus, and Mary pronounced the paean to God known as the Magnificat ("My soul doth magnify the Lord . . ." [Luke 1]). One wall of the church courtyard is covered with ceramic tiles quoting the Magnificat in 41 languages. The upper church is adorned with large wall paintings depicting the mantles with which Mary has been endowed—Mother of God, Refuge of Sinners, Dispenser of All Grace, Help of Christians—and the Immaculate Conception. Other frescoes depict Hebrew women of the Bible also known for their "hymns and canticles," as the Franciscan guide puts it. ⊠ *Above the Spring of Virgin, Ein Kerem* ☎ *02/641-7291* ⌨ *Free* ⊙ *Apr.–Sept., daily 8–noon and 2:30–6; Oct.–Mar., daily 8–noon and 2:30–5. Gates closed Sat., ring bell to be let in.*

**42 Islamic Art Museum.** The institution prides itself on being a private Jewish initiative (opened 1974) to showcase the considerable and diverse artistic achievements of Islamic culture worldwide. Its rich collections—ceramics, glass, carpets, fabrics, jewelry, metal-work, and painting—reflect a creativity that spanned half a hemisphere, from Spain to India, and from the 7th century to modern times. Unconnected to the main theme is a unique collection of European clocks, the pride of the founder's family. ⊠ *2 Hapalmach St., Hapalmach* ☎ *02/566-1291* ⊕ *www. islamicart.co.il* ⌨ *NIS 20 (free on Sat.)* ⊙ *Sun., Mon., Wed., Thurs. 10–3; Tues. 10–6; Fri., Sat. 10–2.*

**38 Mt. Herzl Military Cemetery.** The tranquillity and well-tended greenery of Israel's largest military cemetery almost belie its somber purpose. Different sections are reserved for the casualties of the wars the nation has fought. The large number of headstones, all identical, is a sobering reminder of the price Israel has paid for its national independence and security. Note that officers and privates are buried alongside one another—lost lives are mourned equally, regardless of rank. ⊠ *Herzl Blvd., Mt. Herzl* ☎ *02/643-7257* ⌨ *Free* ⊙ *Daily.*

## Center City

West Jerusalem's downtown and near-downtown areas are a mix of old neighborhoods, new limestone edifices, monuments, and markets.

## Main Attractions

**50 Ben Yehuda Street.** Named after Eliezer Ben Yehuda, who in the late 19th century almost single-handedly revived Hebrew as a modern spoken language, the street is the heart of the downtown triangle formed with King George Street and Jaffa Road. It's an open-air pedestrian mall, known in Hebrew as the Midrachov, a combination of *midracha* (sidewalk) and *rechov* (street). Cafés have tables out on the cobblestones; vendors display cheap, arty items like funky jewelry and prints; and buskers are usually out in good weather, playing tunes old and new. It's a great place to sip coffee or munch falafel and watch the passing crowd. ⊠ *Downtown* ☉ *Many establishments closed Sat. and Jewish holidays.*

**51 Machaneh Yehuda.** This block-long alley is filled with the brilliant colors of the city's best-quality and lowest-price fruit, vegetables, cheeses, confection stalls, falafel stands, fresh fish, and poultry. It's riotously busy, especially on Thursday and Friday, when Jewish Jerusalem shops for the Sabbath. Look for the excellent new coffee shop, "Hakol leofeh Ve'gam Kafeh," on Shazif Street, third lane on the left as you enter from the Agrippas Street end. ⊠ *Machaneh Yehuda* ☉ *Sun.–Thurs. 8 AM–sunset, Fri. and Jewish holiday eves 8 AM–2 hrs before sunset.*

FodorśChoice

★

**43 Montefiore's Windmill.** Sir Moses Montefiore was prominent in the financial circles of mid-19th-century London—a rare phenomenon for a Jew at the time. He devoted much of his long life, and his wealth, to aiding fellow Jews in distress, wherever they might be. To this end he visited Palestine, as this district of the Ottoman Empire was then known, seven times. He had the limestone windmill built in 1857 to provide a source of income for his planned neighborhood of Mishkenot Sha'ananim, but the prevailing winds were insufficient, and it was soon superseded by its newfangled steam-driven rivals. The narrow interior of the windmill has a small photographic exhibit on Montefiore's life and works (closed at press time). The restored carriage in which Montefiore once traveled the country was on display until torched by vandals a few years ago; the one you see now is an exact replica. ⊠ *Yemin Moshe St., Yemin Moshe.*

**★ 48 Nahalat Shiva.** This small downtown neighborhood has a funky feel with worn flagstones, wrought-iron banisters, and defunct water cisterns. Its name translates roughly as "the Estate of the Seven," in honor of the seven Jewish families that founded the neighborhood, only the second to be established outside the Old City walls, in 1869. Salomon Street, Rivlin Street, and their in-between alleys and courtyards have been refashioned as a pedestrian district, offering equal opportunities to the keen photographer, the eager shopper, and the gastronome. ⊠ *Nahalat Shiva* ☉ *Many establishments closed Sat. and Jewish holidays.*

**44 YMCA.** The palatial white-limestone facade and high dome bell tower of the YMCA often surprise visitors who associate that international organization with modest buildings and sports facilities. The Y has those, too, as well as an auditorium with excellent acoustics, built with a Levantine-inspired dome and decorative motifs. The whole complex was planned by the same architects who designed New York's Empire State Building.

# CloseUp
## A GOOD WALK IN CENTER CITY

**JERUSALEM IS A GOOD CITY TO STROLL.**
Beyond its famous shrines and antiquities,
the limestone buildings, shaded
courtyards, and colorful peoplescapes of
the center city make for an absorbing
backstreet experience. The first part of the
walk—up to the YMCA—is good anytime;
avoid the rest late Friday and on Saturday,
when the downtown area is closed for the
Jewish Sabbath. The route will take
approximately 1½ hrs to walk.

Begin at the landmark **Montefiore's
Windmill,** across the valley from Mount
Zion. Immediately below the adjacent
patio is the long crenelated roof of
**Mishkenot Sha'ananim,** the first
neighborhood outside the walls of
Jerusalem, built by Sir Moses (Moshe)
Montefiore in 1860 as a more benign
alternative to the wretched conditions of
the Jewish Quarter at the time. Today it's a
prestigious guest house for visiting artists,
writers, and musicians.

Separating you from Mt. Zion and the Old
City is the deep **Hinnom Valley,** the
biblical border between the Israelite tribes
of Judah (to the south) and Benjamin (to
the north), and the site of human sacrificial
rites in the 7th century BC. A few hundred
yards off to your right (as you face the
valley) is the fortress-like St. Andrew's
Scots Church, right above the bend in the
valley known as Ketef Hinnom (the
Hinnom Shoulder). An excavation in the
late 1970s on the rock scarp below the
church uncovered a series of rock-hewn
tombs and a treasure trove of
archaeological finds.

Stroll through the attractive cobblestone
streets and greenery of the **Yemin Moshe**
neighborhood, abutting the windmill, and
up through the small park that separates it
from King David Street. The landmark
King David Hotel is a handsome,
rectangular limestone building with a back
terrace overlooking well-kept gardens and

the Old City walls. Drinks or dessert are
not cheap here, but the location and the
Hollywood echoes (Paul Newman and
Eva Marie Saint in Exodus) count for
something. Across the street is the
imposing **YMCA**: take the elevator to the
top of its tower for stunning panoramas.

Turn onto Abraham Lincoln Street,
alongside the YMCA and opposite the gas
station. From the small intersection 70
yards beyond it, a narrow pedestrian lane
(George Eliot Street) continues in the same
direction, emerging at Agron Street, next
to the U.S. Consulate-General. Cross
Agron and walk over the lawns of
**Independence Park.** The park's crossroad,
50 yards to your right, emerges at Hillel
Street, where there are several excellent
coffee shops.

Across Hillel is Yoel Moshe Salomon
Street, and to the right and parallel to it is
Yosef Rivlin Street, named after two of the
seven founders of **Nahalat Shiva,** the
second neighborhood built outside the city
walls, in 1869. Hidden courtyards and
funky stores and eateries make this a fun
time-out option. At the other end of
Salomon Street is Zion Square, where
Jaffa Road, Jerusalem's main
thoroughfare, is met by **Ben Yehuda Street,**
a pedestrians-only commercial street.

At the top of Ben Yehuda Street, cross
King George Street, turn right, and take
your first left onto Agrippas Street. (The
falafel stand on the corner is your
landmark.) A five-minute walk up the
street, on your right, is the entrance to the
colorful, often raucous, always interesting
**Machaneh Yehuda** produce market. It
extends for one city block, to Jaffa Road.

For more information on the sights in bold,
see the bulleted listings in Center City.

The tower, served by a small elevator, is 150 feet high, giving superb, long-range views in all directions. For NIS 5, you can ride up (minimum two people) Monday through Thursday between 8 AM and 8 PM, Friday between 8 and 5, and Saturday between 8 and noon. To the east, look across the roof of the King David Hotel toward the Old City. In 1946 the hotel served the British administration in Jerusalem, and was thus targeted by the Irgun, a radical Jewish underground group. The south wing was blown up, with considerable loss of life. ⊠ *26 King David St., King David St.* ☎ *02/569–2692* ⊕ *www.ymca3arch.co.il.*

## Also Worth Seeing

**49** **Bet Ticho** (Ticho House). Dr. A. A. Ticho was a renowned ophthalmologist who immigrated to Jerusalem from Austria in 1912. His cousin, Anna, a trained nurse, followed the same year, to assist him in his pioneering struggle against the endemic scourge of trachoma. They were soon married, and in 1924 bought and renovated this fine, large stone 19th-century house. Anna's artistic talent gradually earned her a reputation as a brilliant chronicler—in charcoal, pen, and brush—of the landscape around Jerusalem. Set among pine trees, just a few steps off the busy downtown streets, Bet Ticho houses a permanent exhibit of Anna Ticho's works and a very good nonmeat restaurant. ⊠ *Ticho La., at 7 Harav Kook St., Downtown* ☎ *02/624–5068* ⊕ *www.imj.org.il* 🏷 *Free* ⊙ *Sun., Mon., Wed., Thurs. 10–5; Tues. 10–10; Fri. and Jewish holiday eves 10–2; Sat. dusk–11 PM.*

**46** **Hinnom Valley.** The Hinnom Valley achieved notoriety in the 7th century BC during the long reign of the biblical king Menasseh (697–640 BC). He was an idolater, the Bible relates, who supported a cult of child sacrifice by fire in the Valley of the Son of Hinnom. Its very name in Hebrew—Gei Ben Hinnom, contracted to Gehennom or Gehenna—became a synonym for hell in both Hebrew and New Testament Greek.

In the late 1970s, Israeli archaeologist Gabriel Barkai discovered a series of Old Testament–period rock tombs at the bend in the valley, below the fortresslike St. Andrew's Scots Church. A miraculously unplundered pit yielded "grave goods" like clay vessels and jewelry; the most spectacular finds, however, were two tiny rolled strips of silver designed to be worn around the neck as amulets. When unrolled, the fragile pieces revealed a slightly condensed and damaged version of the biblical priestly benediction, inscribed in the ancient Hebrew script. (The original, in Numbers 6, reads: "The Lord bless you and keep you; the Lord make his face to shine upon you and be gracious to you; the Lord lift up his countenance upon you and give you peace.") The 7th–century BC text is the oldest biblical passage ever found. The tombs are an open site, to the left and behind the new Menachem Begin Heritage Center. ⊠ *Hinnom Valley.*

**47** **Independence Park.** This is a great area for lounging around, throwing Frisbees, or eating a picnic lunch in warm weather. Some of the Muslim graves at the bottom of the park date from the 13th century. The large defunct reservoir nearby, known as the Mamilla Pool, is probably medieval, though it may have much earlier origins. ⊠ *Between Agron and Hillel sts., Downtown* ⊙ *Daily.*

★ ㊺ **Yemin Moshe.** This now-affluent neighborhood, with its attractive old stone buildings and well-kept cobblestone streets, grew up a century ago alongside the older Mishkenot Sha'ananim, and was named for that project's founder, Sir Moses (Moshe in Hebrew) Montefiore. In the 1950s and '60s, the area was on the nervous armistice line that gashed through the city, and dangerously exposed to Jordanian sniper positions on the nearby Old City walls. Most families sought safer lodgings elsewhere, leaving only those who couldn't afford to move, and the neighborhood ran to seed. The reunification of Jerusalem under Israeli rule after the Six-Day War in 1967 changed all that. Developers bought up the area, renovated old buildings, and built new and spacious homes in a compatible style. Yemin Moshe is now a place to wander at random, and that offers joy to photographers. A few artists' galleries and a couple of restaurants are added bonuses. ⊠ *Yemin Moshe.*

**off the beaten path**

A great way to get your bearings in Jerusalem is to absorb the panorama from the **HAAS PROMENADE,** an attractive 1-km (⅔-mi) promenade ("tayelet" in Hebrew) along one of the city's highest ridges. Hidden behind a grove of trees to the east (your right as you pan the view) is a turreted limestone building, the residence of the British High Commissioner for Palestine in the 1930s and '40s. In Hebrew, the whole ridge is known as Armon Hanatziv, the Commissioner's Palace. The building became the headquarters of the U.N. Truce Supervision Organization (UNTSO), specially formed to monitor the 1949 armistice line that divided the city. It remained a neutral enclave between Israeli West Jerusalem and Jordanian-controlled East Jerusalem until the reunification of the city in the Six-Day War of 1967. West Jerusalem is off to your left, its downtown area easily distinguishable by the high-rises. The walls of the Old City and the golden Dome of the Rock are directly in front of you. To the right of it is the ridge of Mt. Scopus–Mt. of Olives, with its three towers (from left to right, Hebrew University, Augusta Victoria Hospital, and Russian Church of the Ascension), separated from the Old City by the deep Kidron Valley. Between that valley and the shallow Cheesemakers' Valley to the west of it (now just an asphalt road) is a blade-shape strip of land—the City of David—which was the nucleus of ancient Jerusalem four or even five thousand years ago. You can reach the promenade from Hebron Road: consult a map, and look for signs to East Talpiot and the Haas Promenade. ⊠ *Daniel Yanovsky St., East Talpiot.*

# WHERE TO EAT

Jerusalem is less chic and cosmopolitan than Tel Aviv—no question about it—but you can still eat very well in the Holy City. Some cuisine designations are self-explanatory, but other terms may be less so. A restaurant advertising itself as "dairy" will serve meals without meat; many such places do fish, in addition to pasta, soup, and salads. "Oriental" on a sign is usually a literal translation of *mizrachi,* suggesting Middle Eastern (in contrast to Western). "Kosher" does not imply a particular style of cooking, only that certain religious restrictions are adhered to in the selection and preparation of the food. Remember that kosher restaurants are closed for Friday dinner and Saturday lunch in observation of the Jewish Sabbath.

Dress codes are pretty much nonexistent in Jerusalem's restaurants (as in the rest of Israel). People tend to dress very casually—jeans are perfectly appropriate almost everywhere anytime. A modicum of neatness and modesty (trousers instead of jeans, a button-down shirt instead of a T-shirt) might be expected in a hotel dining room on the Sabbath, for example. Still, if you've taken the trouble to bring your dressy duds, you won't be out of place in a more exclusive establishment.

| WHAT IT COSTS In Israeli shekels | | | | | |
|---|---|---|---|---|---|
| | **$$$$** | **$$$** | **$$** | **$** | **¢** |
| AT DINNER | over NIS 100 | NIS 76–NIS 100 | NIS 50–NIS 75 | NIS 32–NIS 49 | under NIS 32 |

Prices are for a main course at dinner.

## Downtown & Nahalat Shiva

### Eclectic

**¢–$$**  ✕ **Focaccetta.** This animated, downtown bar-restaurant is where locals come to meet friends and have fun. Focaccetta has a particularly broad menu with both Italian and French influences. The focaccia choices are great, but there's far more on offer for carnivores, piscavores, and vegetarians. The service is attentive without being intrusive, but the smokiness and noise, particularly in the evening, may not be everyone's idea of a good time. ⊠ *4 Shlomzion Hamalka, Downtown* ☎ *02/624–3222* ⌕ *Reservations essential for dinner and weekends* ⊟ *AE, DC, MC, V.*

### Ethiopian

**¢–$**  ✕ **Ansara.** Neither the family-centered culture nor the economic difficulties of Israel's sizable Ethiopian immigrant community has encouraged restaurant enterprises. This modest exception is simply decorated with the Ethiopian national colors, a few native artifacts, and some red-and-green-jewel embroidered fabrics. Video clips of traditional Ethiopian song and dance add color. The charming owner-chefs have created a short menu of dishes to be eaten with bite-size pieces of *enjera* (pancake-like spongy bread). Try the excellent *menchet abish* (finely chopped beef, fried with ginger, cardamom, and white pepper) and "special tibs" (lamb chunks cooked in onion, garlic, and tomato). Friday night's patrons dance until dawn, despite the cramped quarters. ⊠ *17 Jaffa Rd., Downtown* ☎ *054/698–6664* ⌕ *Dinner reservations essential* ⊟ *No credit cards* ⊘ *No lunch Sat.*

### French

**$$$–$$$$**  ✕ **Cavalier.** The view of stone balconies overhung with wisteria, gently lit yellow and cream walls, wood ceiling beams, and alcoves filled with racks of wine offer a warm welcome. The predominantly French menu is modified by Mediterranean influences and even a few Japanese touches. Among the many starters, the sashimi tuna in sesame oil and

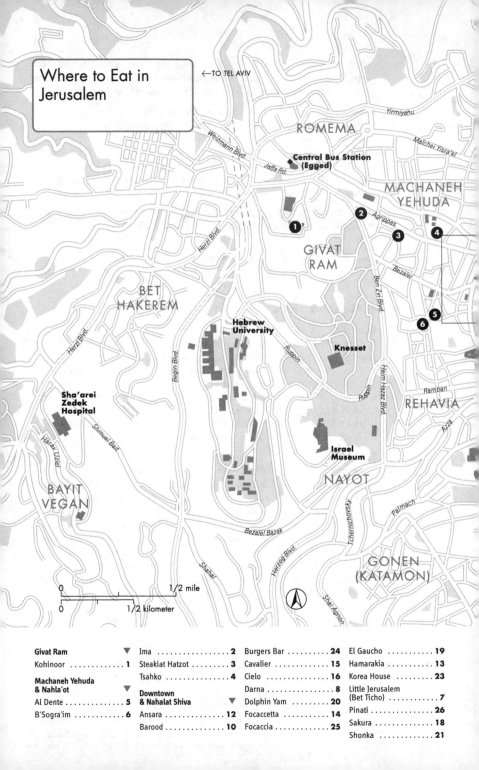

# Where to Eat in Jerusalem

←TO TEL AVIV

ROMEMA

Central Bus Station (Egged)

MACHANEH YEHUDA

GIVAT RAM

BET HAKEREM

Hebrew University

Knesset

Sha'arei Zedek Hospital

REHAVIA

Israel Museum

BAYIT VEGAN

NAYOT

GONEN (KATAMON)

0          1/2 mile
0          1/2 kilometer

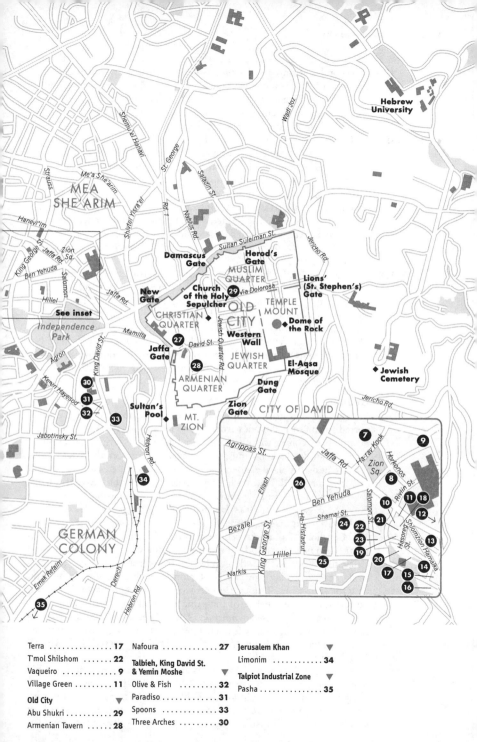

wasabi and the goose liver are particularly fine. For entrées try the delicate combination of red drum fish (known locally as *moussa*) and shrimp with fragrant citrus oil and fettuccine. Don't miss the excellent desserts, including a traditional Provençal lemon tart and a couple of death-by-chocolate choices. ☒ *1 Ben Sira St., Downtown* ☎ *02/624–2945* ☒ *Reservations essential* ☐ *AE, MC, DC, V.*

★ $$$–$$$$ ✕ **Shonka.** The restful colors and lighting, impeccable service, and impressive wine list are barely preparation for the celebration of flavors in this sophisticated bar-restaurant. Chef Ginedi Nazia is a true artist. The many seafood or meat options are all of a consistently high standard, but the ravioli filled with eggplant, goat cheese, and basil flowers is ravishing. Scallops with roquefort and lamb chops in garlic and ginger melt in the mouth. The limited dessert menu includes a delicious take on *crème catalan* with a cardamom and coffee sauce. ☒ *1 Hasoreg St. (off Jaffa Rd.), Downtown* ☎ *02/625–7033* ☒ *Reservations essential* ☐ *AE, DC, MC, V.*

$–$$$ ✕ **Terra.** A tasteful combination of Jerusalem stone, gentle lighting, unobtrusive music, and soothing modern fabrics sets the mood. Attentive service and an impressive wine list complete the picture. The creative menu tempts with a tomato-based interpretation of bouillabaisse, seared foie gras with mango sauce, and scallops in a subtle roquefort sauce. The crème brûlée is excellent, though the unusual touch of grilled bananas threatens to overwhelm its delicate flavor. It's not cheap, but it's worth a bit of a splurge. ☒ *3 Ben Shetach, Downtown* ☎ *02/623–5001* ☒ *Reservations essential* ☐ *AE, DC, MC, V.*

## Grills

$$$$ ✕ **Vaqueiro.** The stone arches of a restored old house frame an unexpected fusion of grill styles from opposite sides of the South Atlantic. From Brazil comes the all-you-can-eat ("churrascuria") selection of skewered steak, chicken wings, roast beef, and more. South African–born Stanley adds his native *boerewors* (beef sausage), *potjie* (stew), and *bobotee* (meat and fruit, with Asian spices). It's hard to leave this place (best enjoyed with four or more diners) hungry. Salads are included in the price; dessert is not. ☒ *54 Haneviim St., Downtown* ☎ *02/624–7432* ☒ *Reservations essential* ☐ *AE, DC, MC, V* ☉ *Closed Fri. and Sat.*

$$–$$$$ ✕ **El Gaucho.** It's all about red meat at this Argentinian grill in the Nahalat Shiva neighborhood. The stone building with interior arches and a flagstone floor has wooden tables, lattice screens, and some artifacts from the Argentinian pampas. Nibble on great chicken wings while you wait for your steak. Best are the entrecôte and the chorizo (a sirloin cut; no relation to the sausage of the same name, though that's also available) with a parsley-based *chimichurri* sauce. There are several kid-friendly items, a fish dish, and a few cheaper pasta and vegetarian options. ☒ *22 Rivlin St., Nahalat Shiva* ☎ *02/624–2227* ☐ *AE, DC, MC, V* ☉ *Closed Fri. No lunch Sat.*

¢–$ ✕ **Burgers Bar.** The menu bears a passing resemblance to that of the big hamburger chains, but the product is a different creature altogether. Hamburgers of different weight are more like cakes than patties, come with good sauces, and all are made to order. Chicken offerings and robust salads reflect Israeli tastes. Even those who generally oppose the fast-food experience have been happy here. ⊠ *12 Shammai St., Downtown* ☎ *02/622–1555* ▭ *No credit cards* ☉ *No dinner Fri. No lunch Sat.*

## Israeli

★ **$–$$$** ✕ **Little Jerusalem** (Bet Ticho). This imposing old stone building, in a tranquil rustic setting, was once the home of artist Anna Ticho, whose evocative drawings of Jerusalem adorn its walls. House specialties include excellent salmon blintzes, onion soup served inside a crusty loaf of bread, and fish in fresh ginger sauce. The generous portions are large enough to share. Apple strudel and ice cream cake topped with hot fudge are among the indulgent desserts. On Tuesday night, there is a wine-and-cheese buffet accompanied by jazz music. Friday morning you can hear a chamber music concert in the upstairs gallery for a separate fee. Jewish soul music and a light buffet are featured on Saturday night. Angle for a table on the patio in good weather. ⊠ *7 Harav Kook St., Downtown* ☎ *02/624–4186* ⌂ *Dinner reservations essential* ▭ *AE, DC, MC, V* ☉ *No dinner Fri. No lunch Sat.*

**$–$$** ✕ **T'mol Shilshom.** The name—a Hebrew literary phrase that translates roughly as "days of yore"—is a clue to this restaurant's character. The funky café-restaurant and used bookstore are in two separate rooms on the upper floor of a mid-19th-century house. Hosting Hebrew poetry readings, modest book-launches, and occasional intimate concerts, it's long been a popular spot with the intellectual population in the city. The food covers both vegetarian and fish options, from simple sandwiches and salads to more sophisticated fare. (Desserts are not universally successful.) It's a good family choice, and a very comfortable place to linger over breakfast with a good book. ⊠ *Off 5 Yoel Solomon St., Nahalat Shiva* ☎ *02/623–2758* ▭ *AE, DC, MC, V.* ☉ *No dinner Fri. No lunch Sat.*

**¢** ✕ **Hamarakia.** Housed in a slightly dilapidated old building, this is a funky hang-out for young, impecunious students. The name means "soup pot," and a changing menu of hearty soups served with half-loaves of crusty bread and butter make it a satisfying alternative to the conventional three-course meal. There's a piano in the corner, a box of old records, and even a cluttered backyard. ⊠ *4 Koresh St., Downtown* ☎ *02/625–7797* ☉ *Dinner only. Closed Fri.*

## Italian

**$$$** ✕ **Cielo.** Chef Adi maintains his family's tradition of good Italian fare. The soft lighting is easy on the eye, and the neutral colors of the molded walls, fine linen tablecloths, and porcelain complete the sense of taste without fuss. Service is professional but friendly. Great traditional dishes include the ravioli (the stuffings change: look for zucchini and truffles), the cannelloni, and a succulent veal marsala. There are also creative tangents such as lamb with fresh herbs and olive oil. Seasonal produce inspires the daily specials and some desserts (like an exquisite summer prickly-pear spumone). ⊠ *18 Ben Sira St., Downtown* ☎ *02/625–1132* ⌂ *Reservations essential* ▭ *AE, DC, MC, V* ☉ *No lunch Fri.*

**$–$$** ✕ **Focaccia.** The smallish interior in an old stone building is pleasant enough, but the spacious patio just off the street is much livelier. A popular haunt for those in their twenties, this "focaccia bar" offers good value. There are many toppings (don't miss the black olive spread), and some tasty starters (try the fried mushrooms stuffed with sheep cheese). Chicken liver stir-fried with apples, shallots, and nuts is delicious. There are great sandwich options, like sirloin strips, and several pasta dishes. Tarte tatin makes an excellent dessert. ☒ *4 Rabbi Akiva St., Downtown* ☏ *02/625–6428* ▤ *AE, DC, MC, V.*

### Japanese

**$$–$$$** ✕ **Sakura.** Many consider Jerusalem's veteran Japanese restaurant the best of its kind in the country. The standard of food and presentation appears to be unshakable. Sitting upstairs in the minimalistic room with Japanese decorative accents, or outside in the courtyard, you can choose from combinations of sushi and sashimi, or try salmon teriyaki, tempura, or *donburi.* The miso soup is delicious and satisfying. Vegetarian options are available. ☒ *31 Jaffa Rd. (Finegold Court), Downtown* ☏ *02/623–5464, 02/623–5244* ☖ *Reservations essential* ▤ *AE, DC, MC, V.*

### Korean

**$–$$** ✕ **Korea House.** Tucked into a corner of a restored 135-year-old neighborhood, the restaurant combines charming decor (including murals of ancient Korean and Chinese texts) with gracious service. Set menus and lunch specials are good values. If you order à la carte, start with the sushi-like *modeum kim bab,* or the *goo jul pan,* assemble-your-own paper-thin crêpes with meat and raw vegetables. Recommended entrées include the delicate *saeng sun zim* (stewed Nile perch) or the dishes of chopped roast beef, chicken, or shrimp in a special brown sauce. Vegetarians will find several tempting alternatives. ☒ *7 Ma'alot Nahalat Shiva St., Nahalat Shiva* ☏ *02/625–4756* ☖ *Reservations essential on weekends* ▤ *AE, DC, MC, V* ☻ *Closed Sat.*

### Middle Eastern

**$–$$$** ✕ **Barood.** Tenth-generation Jerusalemite Daniella Lerer fiercely preserves her family's Sephardic culinary traditions. Try the fixed-price sampler's menu or order à la carte. The rich, homemade *labaneh*—by itself or with filling large falafel balls—is particularly tasty. Daily specials, some seasonal, supplement the permanent menu. Red meat predominates. For dessert, look for the traditional *sutlach,* a cold rice pudding topped with cinnamon, nuts, and jam. Barood's other face is its well-stocked bar, with more familiar fare like spareribs and sausages. Very smoker-friendly. There is often live jazz Saturday evening. ☒ *In courtyard off 31 Jaffa Rd., Downtown* ☏ *02/625–9081* ☖ *Reservations essential on weekends* ▤ *AE, DC, MC, V* ☻ *Closed Sun.*

**¢–$** ✕ **Pinati.** When aficionados of local standards like hummus, skewered shish kebab, and bean soup argue hotly about the merits of *their* favorite eateries, Pinati comes up as a leading contender. In the very heart of the downtown, it's a convenient place to take the weight off your feet and rub shoulders with the locals. Not for long, though: your table will soon be in demand. ☒ *13 King George St., Downtown* ☏ *02/625–4540* ☖ *Reservations not accepted.* ▤ *No credit cards* ☻ *No dinner Fri. Closed Sat.*

# MIDDLE EASTERN FAST FOODS

**Baba ghanoush** is a dip made from roasted eggplant blended with tahini. There's also an untraditional mayonnaise-based look-alike that is a concession to perceived Western tastes.

**Falafel,** the region's fast-food snack, consists of deep-fried chickpea balls. The name also refers to the whole production of the balls served in pita pockets with salads and sauces. It's filling, nutritious, and cheap.

**Hummus,** a ubiquitous dish in this region, is a creamy paste made from chickpeas, moistened with olive oil and tahini, and scooped up with pieces of flat pita bread. Eat hummus at a Middle Eastern specialty place; many "Western" establishments serve poor imitations.

**Kibbeh,** a popular Kurdish-Iraqi specialty, is seasoned ground meat formed into small torpedo shapes and deep-fried in a jacket of bulgur (cracked wheat).

**Labaneh,** derived from the Hebrew word for white, is somewhere between tart yogurt and cream cheese. It's typically dressed with olive oil, garnished with herbs, and scooped up with chunks of pita bread.

**Me'oorav yerushalmi** (Jerusalem mixed grill) is a specialty of the grills on Agrippas Street, near the market. It's a deliciously seasoned meal of grilled chicken hearts and other organ meats in pita.

**Shawarma** is grilled meat (lamb or turkey), also served in pita bread with salads and sauces. It's sold at stands in the Ben Yehuda Street open-air mall, and near the Machaneh Yehuda produce market.

**Tahini** is a slightly runny white sauce made from sesame seeds and sometimes thickened with cornstarch. The delicious green variety has parsley blended into it.

## Moroccan

★ $$$–$$$$   ✕ **Darna.** A vaulted tunnel deposits you in a corner of Morocco, complete with imported floor tiles and decorative artifacts. The pricey set menu is a veritable banquet; ordering à la carte, though, offers more flexibility. The excellent salads are quite different from the local Arab meze, but don't miss the *harira* soup, meat, chickpeas, and lentils, flavored with cumin, or the *pastilla fassia,* phyllo pastry stuffed with almonds, cinnamon, and Cornish hen (nonmeat versions usually available). The *tagines,* or Moroccan stews, are very good entrées. Finish with refreshing mint tea (served with fine ceremony) and the wonderful *toubkal* delight, sweet phyllo layers in cinnamon and (nondairy) almond milk. ✉ *3 Horkonos St., Downtown* ☎ *02/624–5406* ▭ *AE, DC, MC, V* ☉ *Closed Fri. No lunch Sat.*

## Seafood

$$–$$$   ✕ **Dolphin Yam.** This is the city's best seafood. You can start with a meze of refillable dishes; the green salad and the eggplant in tomato sauce are excellent. Try the shrimp in cream and mushroom sauce or the *musar baladi* (drum fish) with ginger and black olives. There are also beef, poultry, and pasta options. ✉ *9 Ben Shetach St., Downtown* ☎ *02/623–2272* ⚑ *Reservations essential* ▭ *AE, DC, MC, V.*

### Vegetarian

**$–$$** ✕ **Village Green.** Right near Zion Square, this airy vegetarian restaurant prides itself on the quality of its offerings. There's a good variety of soups, quiches, and wonderfully fresh vegetable salads with a choice of tasty dressings. Salads and the hot buffet are self-service (charged by weight). Vegans will be happy with the tofu-and-organic-vegetable pies made with wholewheat flour. Every meal comes with homemade whole wheat or sourdough bread. The home-baked cakes and pies are great. ✉ *33 Jaffa Rd., Downtown* ☎ *02/625–3065* ▭ *AE, DC, MC, V* ◔ *No dinner Fri. Closed Sat.*

## Givat Ram

### Indian

★ **$$** ✕ **Kohinoor.** The aroma of spices greets you at the door. Gracious service, Moghul-influenced decor, and Indian music set a tone of quiet, informal elegance. The specialty is the less-spicy northern Indian cuisine. *Naan* breads, piquant dips, deep-fried samosas, and *pakoras* are great starters. Avoid the untraditional and disappointing fresh salad. The mulligatawny soup is excellent. For entrées choose superb *rogan gosht* lamb, subtle chicken tikka masala, or *kastoori,* chicken meatballs. Vegetable curries and *tadka plal,* delicious yellow lentils, will tempt even meat-eaters. Finish with fragrant *kulfi* ice cream or a sorbet. The lunch buffet is an excellent value. ✉ *Crowne Plaza Hotel, 1 Ha'aliyah St., Givat Ram* ☎ *02/658–8867* ⬥ *Reservations essential* ▭ *AE, DC, MC, V* ◔ *No dinner Fri. No lunch Sat.*

## Jerusalem Khan

### Eclectic

**$$** ✕ **Limonim.** A meal of flavorful mallard in pear and red wine sauce or salmon with port wine and figs might conclude with a simple but satisfying dessert such as fruits baked with spices. Overlooking a typical Jerusalem stone courtyard, the restaurant is decorated with spare, primary-color accents: the lemon-tree lithographs on the wall reflect the name of the place ("lemons"). Service is charming and the background music is relaxing. Check ahead for scheduled events in the courtyard, when the noise level can become intrusive. There are good value and family options. ✉ *2 David Remez St., Jerusalem Khan* ☎ *02/671–9602* ⬥ *Reservations essential* ▭ *AE, DC, MC, V* ◔ *Closed Fri. and Sat.*

## Machaneh Yehuda & Nahla'ot

### Eclectic

**$$$** ✕ **Tsahko.** The food here is always made from the highest-quality produce. No wonder: the chefs can choose from the market one minute away. Creative appetizers such as succulent lamb kebabs, eggplant in tahini, and sashimi on slices of beet are particularly fine. Meat and fish entrées are the mainstays of the menu; desserts are less interesting. On warm evenings the restaurant spills out beyond its patio into the neighborhood courtyard. The high stools, bench tops, ochre walls, and soft lights in the small inner sanctum provide warm intimacy. ✉ *Off 4 Eshkol St., Shuk Iraki, Machaneh Yehuda* ☎ *02/623-4916* ⚹ *Reservations essential* ▤ *AE, DC, MC, V* ☉ *No dinner Fri. Closed Sat.*

### Israeli

**$–$$$** ✗ **B'Sogra'im.** In nice weather, you can sit outside at this homey, stone house. There's no lack of choices (except perhaps for unrepentant carnivores): wholesome soups, delicious pies, quiches, pastas, generous salads, and excellent fish. A short walk from the downtown area makes this an attractive business lunch option. ✉ *45 Ussishkin St., Nahla'ot* ☎ *02/624–5353* ⚹ *Dinner reservations essential* ▤ *AE, DC, MC, V* ☉ *No dinner Fri. No lunch Sat.*

### Italian

**¢–$** ✗ **Al Dente.** This restaurant seems at first glance like a small neighbor-
**Fodor'sChoice** hood eatery, but it's much more. The reasonably priced food is simply
**★** delicious. Although you sit close to the street, the vines twining around the porch soften the effect, and awareness of traffic disappears with the first mouthful. Classic Italian dishes with homemade pasta vie with creative ideas such as sweet potato soup flavored with orange, ginger, and pepper; pumpkin ravioli; and rotolo (pasta stuffed with a teasing combination of spinach, mushrooms, cheese, and nuts). The thin, crisp pizza crust is the best you can buy. Be sure to leave room for dessert. ✉ *50 Ussishkin St., Nahla'ot* ☎ *02/625–1479* ▤ *AE, MC* ☉ *No dinner Fri. Closed Sat.*

### Middle Eastern

**★ $–$$$** ✗ **Ima.** It's pronounced "*ee*-mah," means "mom," and is named for Miriam, the owner's Kurdish-Jewish mother, who still does some of the cooking. This restaurant, at the bottom of the Nahla'ot neighborhood, opposite Sacher Park, serves very good traditional Middle Eastern food. First courses include a modest but quality meze of some half-dozen salads, such as hummus and baba ghanoush (eggplant dip), as well as the excellent *kibbeh* and stuffed grape leaves. Try the tangy kibbeh soup, full of dumplings—it's almost a meal in itself. Entrées, like shashlik or a Jerusalem mixed grill, are accompanied by *majadra* (rice and lentils). ✉ *189 Agrippas St., Nahla'ot* ☎ *02/624–6860* ▤ *AE, DC, MC, V* ☉ *No dinner Fri. Closed Sat.*

**$–$$** ✗ **Steakiat Hatzot.** Agrippas Street, down the street from the Machaneh Yehuda produce market, has some of Jerusalem's best-known blue-collar "mizrahi" (Middle Eastern) diners. Loyalists claim that Steakiat Hatzot (which means "midnight grill," though nobody uses the translation) actually pioneered the *me'oorav yerushalmi*—Jerusalem mixed grill—a substantial and delicious meal-in-a-pita of cumin-flavor bits of chicken hearts and other organ meats. Certainly that's its specialty; though for other traditional Middle Eastern dishes, you might prefer the better conditions of the competition across the street. Make sure of prices before you order to avoid unasked-for side dishes. ✉ *123 Agrippas St., Machaneh Yehuda* ☎ *02/624–4014* ⚹ *Reservations not accepted.* ▤ *No credit cards* ☉ *Closed Fri. and Sat.*

# Old City

The Old City includes the Armenian Quarter, the Christian Quarter, the Jewish Quarter, and the Muslim Quarter.

## Middle Eastern

**$$–$$$** ✕ **Nafoura.** Just inside the Jaffa Gate, Nafoura offers an attractive tranquil courtyard for alfresco dining, where your table might lean against the Old City's 16th-century wall. Start with the traditional meze, an array of salads: the smaller version is enough for two people. Insist on the excellent local dishes only (hummus, eggplant dip, tahini, carrots, etc.) and skip the mushrooms and corn. Ask particularly for the *kibbeh,* delicacies of cracked wheat and ground beef, or the *lahmajun,* the meat-topped "Armenian pizza." From the typical selection of entrées, try the lamb cutlets or the sea bream (called "denise"). ✉ *18 Latin Patriarch Rd., Christian Quarter* ☎ *02/626–0034* ▭ *AE, DC, MC, V.*

**$–$$** ✕ **Abu Shukri.** In the heart of the Old City, right at the fifth Station on the Via Dolorosa, Abu Shukri has an extraordinary, and well-deserved, reputation for the best hummus in town. A look at the clientele—local Palestinian Arabs and Jewish Israeli insiders—confirms that you have gone native. Enjoy the excellent fresh falafel balls, labaneh, baba ghanoush, tahini, and fresh vegetable salad. Eat family-style, and don't over-order: you can get additional portions on the spot. ✉ *63 El-Wad (Hagai) St., Muslim Quarter* ☎ *02/627–1538* ⌕ *No reservations accepted* ▭ *No credit cards* ☽ *Open for lunch only.*

**$** ✕ **Armenian Tavern.** Below street level, and with a small, active fountain and exposed stone walls, this is a cool summer haven. Armenian ceramics and jewelry (some of it for sale) give the place character. Try the mixed platter, or order the individual simple but tasty dishes, such as *lahmajun* ("Armenian pizza"), kibbeh, and *soujuk* (spicy sausages). Also delicious is the traditional stew *khaghoghi derev,* consisting of ground beef in grape leaves with spicy yogurt. Wash it down with draught beer, and finish with local coffee and the excellent *paklava* (baklava). ✉ *79 Armenian Orthodox Patriarchate Rd., Armenian Quarter* ☎ *02/627–3854* ▭ *AE, DC, MC, V.*

# Talbieh, King David St. & Yemin Moshe

## Eclectic

★ **$$–$$$** ✕ **Olive & Fish.** The location, near major hotels, is part of its success, but Olive & Fish has pleased locals on its own merits. Starters and salads are excellent, and both meat and fish offerings are well worth trying. Try the tender chicken livers with figs and red wine, perfectly cooked sea bass, and salmon fillet in tarragon and anise sauce. The pistachio and cherry pie is a happy creation. Sit on the patio in fine weather. "Olive," its partner restaurant in the German Colony, has a large garden for outdoor dining, a more carnivorous bent, and a neighborhood character. ✉ *2 Jabotinsky St., Talbieh* ☎ *02/566–5020* ✉ *36 Emek Refaim St., German Colony* ☎ *02/561–1102* ⌕ *Reservations essential* ▭ *AE, DC, MC, V* ☽ *Closed Fri. No lunch Sat.*

**$$–$$$** ✕ **Three Arches.** In good weather, the wide, flagstone patio and stone arches make this restaurant at the YMCA one of Jerusalem's most relaxing spots.

(Move indoors when it's cold.) The extensive menu—with kid-friendly options—is a good family choice, especially for Saturday lunch when most West Jerusalem eateries are closed. People-watch over a sigh-of-satisfaction draught beer while you wait for your first-rate first courses: baba ghanoush, hummus, green tahini, fried cauliflower, and kibbeh. Try shrimp in an exquisite anise sauce or the excellent steak fillets. Desserts are less memorable. ⊠ *26 King David St., King David St.* ☎ *02/569–2692* 🖃 *AE, DC, MC, V.*

**$–$$** ✕ **Paradiso.** You may be suspicious of the strategic location near major hotels, but the food is excellent and the clientele mostly local. Still a great cake-and-coffee place, Paradiso has evolved. You can eat light—breakfasts, sandwiches, salads, soup—but its reasonably priced main menu and daily specials will tempt you with grilled meats and spareribs, delicious chicken combinations, pasta and seafood risotto, and the occasional fresh fish. Save space for dessert. For fine-weather dining, there is a small outdoor patio, near the street but surrounded by greenery. ⊠ *36 Keren Hayesod St., Talbieh* ☎ *02/563–4805* ⚛ *Reservations essential* 🖃 *AE, DC, MC, V.*

### Mediterranean

**★ $$$$** ✕ **Spoons.** Chef Hila Solomon hosts custom-crafted gourmet dinners in her own stone house, in the historic Yemin Moshe neighborhood. Superb Old City views come with the aperitif; the soft tones and old-fashioned grace of the salon (think vaulted ceilings and arched windows) augur well for the rest. Kosher and fine dining are clearly not contradictory. The inspiration is part French, but meals are primarily a happy encounter between culinary imagination and superior seasonal produce. A single reservation per evening (from 4 to 20 guests) ensures privacy, though multiple reservations are accepted one night a week in the winter. The cost is commensurate: leisurely five-course meals run NIS 300 per person. Although no credit cards are accepted, you don't have to bring a huge amount of cash: Spoons will accept personal checks. ⊠ *27 Tura St., Yemin Moshe* ☎ *02/623-5778* 🖃 *No credit cards* ⚛ *Reservations essential.*

## Talpiot Industrial Zone

### Middle Eastern

**¢–$$** ✕ **Pasha.** In a busy commercial district, this favorite local lunch spot has no pretensions to style and designer ambience—guests come only for the food. You may be familiar with the names of some dishes from other Middle Eastern restaurants, but there are differences which reflect the Turkish influence. The lamb kebabs with pine nuts, spring chicken stuffed with pistachios and cashews, and *kibbeh* are all worth trying. Beyond the usual hummus, tahini and so on, vegetarians will also find options like stuffed vegetables. The soups are filling on a winter's day. If you need dessert, you'll find more choices elsewhere. ⊠ *28 Pierre Koenig St., Talpiot Industrial Zone* ☎ *02/648-2220* ⚛ *Reservations essential for dinner* 🖃 *AE, DC, MC, V* ⊘ *No dinner Fri. Closed Sat.*

## Cafés

Sitting down for coffee and cake in one of Jerusalem's fine cafés is something of a tradition. The selection of sweets includes the gooey, cream-filled pastries many Israelis favor; more sophisticated cheesecakes and pies; and yeast cakes and strudels, a Central European legacy.

The downtown Midrachov, the open-air mall of Ben Yehuda Street and its side lanes, has several venerable hangouts from an earlier era, but a new generation of cafés offers a more sophisticated menu and better coffee. Two neighborhood arteries—Azza Street, in Rehavia, and Emek Refa'im Street, in the German Colony—are well stocked with popular watering holes, a few of which serve decent light meals as well. On summer evenings in particular, these places teem with the young set; arrive by early evening to beat the after-show crowd from the nearby movie theater.

**Hillel** (✉ 8 Hillel St., Downtown ☎ 02/624–7775 ✉ 1 Helene Hamalka St., Downtown ☎ 02/625–6552 ✉ Jerusalem Mall, Malcha ☎ 02/679–3225 ✉ 50 Emek Refai'm, German Colony ☎ 02/566–7187) is a popular chain. This is a favorite with locals for breakfast, with its good food (some healthy, some indulgent) and good prices.

**Modus** (✉ 31 King George St., Downtown ☎ 02/624–4215) has a loyal following among the locals due to the homemade sandwiches, apple strudel, and the sometimes-quirky behavior of the owner/chef (who has been known to burst unaccountably into song). Good for breakfast or a light lunch. **Shamai-12** (✉ 12 Shamai St., Downtown ☎ 02/623–2421) offers good coffee, the usual pastries, and generous sandwiches. You can ask for a half, or share with a companion. While you're enjoying the produce market, stop at **Hakol La'ofeh Ve'gam Cafe** (✉ 12 Hashezif St., Machaneh Yehuda ☎ 02/624–2105), which serves some of the best coffee around. They also stock fancy (imported) utensils and accessories for enthusiastic cooks and bakers.

**Coffee Mill** (✉ 23 Emek Refa'im, German Colony ☎ 02/566-1665) is a must for coffee devotees, with its dizzying selection of blends and flavors. **Paradiso** (✉ 36 Keren Hayesod St., Talbieh ☎ 02/563–4805) does delicious meals, coffee, and exceptional cakes. **Jan's** (✉ 20 Marcus St., Talbieh ☎ 02/561–2054), under the plaza of the Sherover (Jerusalem) Theater, is a special place. The pillows and rugs, low lights, and Asian ornaments enhance enjoyment of the food which, while not cheap, is very good. It's better for intimate whispers than clubby conversation.

# WHERE TO STAY

Some travelers insist on a hotel in a central location; others prefer to retreat to a haven at the end of the day, with ambience more important than accessibility. Jerusalem has more of the first option than the second, and even hotels once considered remote are really no more than 10 minutes by cab from the city center. With only a few exceptions, most hotels are modern, with little claim to old-world charm.

Hotels in Arab East Jerusalem, most in the less-expensive categories, were seriously affected by Palestinian street violence in the late 1980s and early '90s, and again in the early 2000s. Unfortunately, the ensuing shrinkage of hotel occupancy there has led to a widespread decline in standards as well. Exceptions are the American Colony, the Addar, and the Ambassador.

High season is typically from a week to a month around the Jewish holiday of Passover (March–April), a similar period over the Jewish holidays in September and October (High Holy Days and Sukkoth), a good part of the summer, and for some hotels, the Christmas season. Because of variations in what different hotels consider high season, and because the dates of Jewish holidays shift annually in accordance with the Jewish calendar, the difference in room rates can be significant. Shop around, and check online or with a good travel agent for the best deals.

| WHAT IT COSTS In U.S. Dollars | | | | |
|---|---|---|---|---|
| | **$$$$** | **$$$** | **$$** | **$** | **¢** |
| FOR 2 PEOPLE | over $250 | $175–$250 | $111–$174 | $65–$110 | under $65 |

Prices are for two people in a standard double room in high season. Non-Israeli citizens paying in foreign currency are exempt from the 16.5% VAT tax on hotel rooms.

## Rehavia, Talbieh & King David St.

★ **$$$$**  David Citadel. Stonework and arches make a powerful first impression. The lobby—a monument to the architect—is somewhat cold, though offset by the bright lounge and terrace one floor above. Views of the Old City walls from many rooms and public areas remind you that this is more than a good business and events hotel. The aesthetics are carried over into the spacious guest rooms, with furnishings in soft tones of beige and cream, decorative old-style mosaic wall-pieces, and well-appointed bathrooms. The location—5 minutes' walk from Jaffa Gate and 10 minutes from downtown—is unbeatable. ⊠ *7 King David St., King David St. 94101* ☎ *02/ 621–1111* ⊟ *02/621–1000* ⊕ *www.thedavidcitadel.com* ⇄ *381 rooms* ♧ *Restaurant, dining room, room service, in-room safes, minibars, cable TV, in-room broadband, Wi-Fi, pool, gym, hair salon, spa, bar, lobby lounge, shops, babysitting, children's programs (holidays), dry cleaning, laundry service, concierge, business services, convention center, car rental, parking (fee), no-smoking rooms* ⊟ *AE, DC, MC, V* ⊙ *BP.*

**$$$$**  King David. The grande dame of Israeli luxury hotels opened in 1931
**Fodor'sChoice** and has successfully (and self-importantly) defended its title ever since.
★ The ceilings, columns, and walls of the bustling lobby-lounge are decorated in "ancient Mesopotamian" geometrics. Spacious guest rooms are elegantly orchestrated in cream and gold, with old-fashioned writing tables a gracious addition. Pricier rooms have views of the Old City, and the suites have balconies in the same direction. The beautifully landscaped pool area is a winner. An in-house French-style restaurant, La Régence, completes the picture. ⊠ *23 King David St., King David St.*

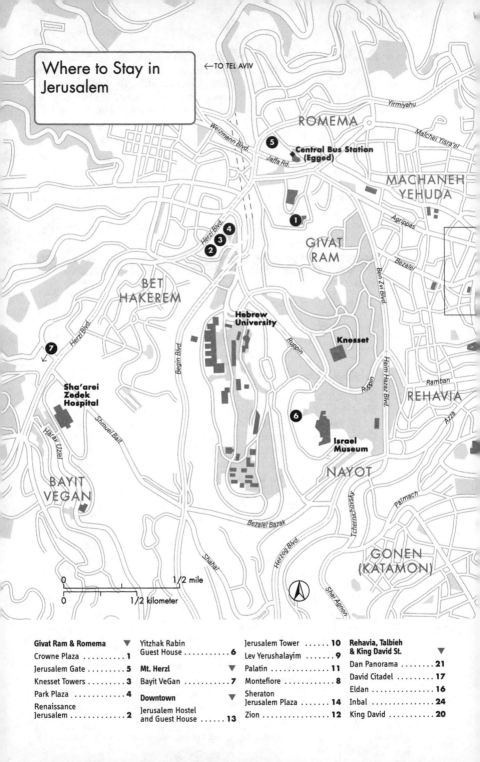

# Where to Stay in Jerusalem

← TO TEL AVIV

**ROMEMA**

Yirmiyahu

Malchei Yisra'el

Weizmann Blvd.

Jaffa Rd.

**5** Central Bus Station
(Egged)

**MACHANEH
YEHUDA**

Agrippas

**1**

Herzl Blvd.

Bezalel

**4**
**3**
**2**

**GIVAT
RAM**

Ben Zvi Blvd.

**BET
HAKEREM**

Begin Blvd.

**Hebrew
University**

Ruppin

**Knesset**

Haim Hazaz Blvd.

Ramban

**REHAVIA**

Herzl Blvd.

**7**

Ruppin

Azza

**Sha'arei
Zedek
Hospital**

Shmuel Bait

**6**

**Israel
Museum**

Har av Uziel

**NAYOT**

**BAYIT
VEGAN**

Bezalel Bazak

Tchernichovsky

Palmach

Shahal

Herzog Blvd.

**GONEN
(KATAMON)**

0 _____ 1/2 mile

0 _____ 1/2 kilometer

Shai Agnon

| | |
|---|---|
| **Givat Ram & Romema** ▼ | |
| Crowne Plaza ........... **1** | Yitzhak Rabin Guest House .......... **6** |
| Jerusalem Gate ......... **5** | **Mt. Herzl** ▼ |
| Knesset Towers ........ **3** | Bayit VeGan ......... **7** |
| Park Plaza ............ **4** | **Downtown** ▼ |
| Renaissance Jerusalem ............ **2** | Jerusalem Hostel and Guest House ...... **13** |

| | |
|---|---|
| Jerusalem Tower ...... **10** | **Rehavia, Talbieh & King David St.** ▼ |
| Lev Yerushalayim ...... **9** | Dan Panorama ........ **21** |
| Palatin .............. **11** | David Citadel ......... **17** |
| Montefiore ........... **8** | Eldan ............... **16** |
| Sheraton Jerusalem Plaza ....... **14** | Inbal ............... **24** |
| Zion ............... **12** | King David .......... **20** |

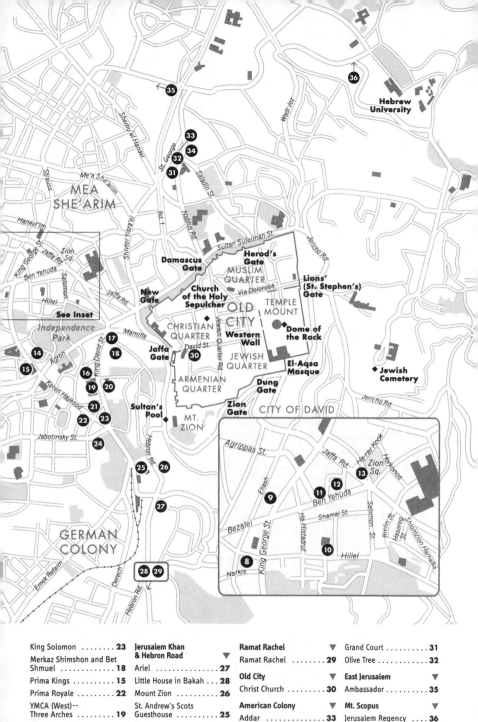

*94101* ☎ *02/620–8888* 🖷 *02/620–8882* ⊕ *www.danhotels.com* ⇴ *202 rooms, 35 suites* ⚴ *2 restaurants, dining room, snack bar, room service, in-room safes, minibars, cable TV, in-room broadband, Wi-Fi, tennis court, pool, wading pool, gym, hair salon, massage, Ping-Pong, bar, lobby lounge, shops, babysitting, children's programs (holidays), dry cleaning, laundry service, concierge, business services, meeting rooms, some free parking, no-smoking rooms* ▤ *AE, DC, MC, V* ¶◎¶ *BP.*

**$$$$** 🏨 **King Solomon.** The centerpiece of the lobby is a huge, spherical sculpture of Jerusalem by Frank Meisler. A split-level atrium reveals shops half a floor down and restaurants a floor below that. The standard guest rooms are not overly spacious, but the more deluxe ones are quite large. The decor is attractive, with matching floral-on-beige drapes and bedcovers, dark wood, translucent glass tabletops, and prints above the beds. The small pool offers a stunning view of southeast Jerusalem. High-season rates are steep, but regular rates are a very good value. ✉ *32 King David St., Talbieh 94101* ☎ *02/569–5555* 🖷 *02/624–1774* ⊕ *www. kingsolomon-hotel.com* ⇴ *142 rooms, 6 suites* ⚴ *Coffee shop, dining room, room service, in-room safes, minibars, cable TV, in-room data ports, Wi-Fi, pool, hair salon, bar, shops, babysitting, dry cleaning, laundry service, Internet room, meeting rooms, free parking, no-smoking floor* ▤ *AE, DC, MC, V* ¶◎¶ *BP.*

**$$$** 🏨 **Dan Panorama.** The copper ceiling, palm-tree planters, and dark polished-stone floors and columns enhance the pleasantly muted feel of the reception area. The newer guest rooms are a bit compact (good lighting and interesting old prints on the wall make a difference); the similarly smallish bathrooms are tiled with pleasing sand-colored ceramics. Rooms in the older wing are larger but less well appointed: the front desk is usually happy to accommodate your preference when available. Advantages are the excellent location (convenient to downtown and the Old City), the pleasant setting, and a friendly staff. ✉ *39 Keren Hayesod St., Talbieh 94188* ☎ *02/569–5695* 🖷 *02/623–2411* ⊕ *www.danhotels. com* ⇴ *283 rooms, 8 suites* ⚴ *Coffee shop, dining room, room service, in-room safes, minibars, cable TV, Wi-Fi, pool, health club, hair salon, bar, shops, business services* ▤ *AE, DC, MC, V* ¶◎¶ *BP.*

**★ $$$** 🏨 **Inbal.** A low-rise building of Jerusalem stone wrapped around a central courtyard and atrium, the Inbal is more appealing for its architecture and friendly, energetic spirit than for its decor. In warm weather, an outdoor breakfast in the courtyard makes a great start to the day. The guest rooms, decorated in shades of brown and beige, are comfortable if unremarkable; bathrooms are small. Many deluxe rooms have balconies and fine views. The pool is covered and heated in winter. Its location next to the playgrounds of Liberty Bell Garden is a plus for families. ✉ *3 Jabotinsky St., Talbieh 92145* ☎ *02/675–6666* 🖷 *02/675– 6777* ⊕ *www.inbal-hotel.co.il* ⇴ *278 rooms, 16 suites* ⚴ *Restaurant, coffee shop, dining room, room service, in-room safes, minibars, cable TV, pool, gym, hair salon, spa, bar, shops, babysitting, children's programs (summer), business services* ▤ *AE, DC, MC, V* ¶◎¶ *BP.*

**$$$** 🏨 **Prima Kings.** The Kings—the name by which it's still known—is on a busy intersection (but insulated from the noise) less than 10 minutes' walk from the city center. Cane furniture and deep sofas create comfortable, if not particularly intimate, public areas. Most of the guest rooms are fairly spacious, the deluxe ones offering new burgundy and green decor, with touches of leather. If your budget allows, upgrade to a junior suite with a balcony. Especially large family rooms are also available. ⊠ *60 King George St. (entrance on Ramban St.), Rehavia 94262* ☎ *02/620–1201* 🖷 *02/620–1211* ⊕ *www.prima.co.il/eng* ⟿ *217 rooms* ♨ *Coffee shop, dining room, minibars, cable TV, Wi-Fi, bar, lobby lounge, shop, babysitting, dry cleaning, laundry service, Internet room, parking (fee)* ☰ *AE, DC, MC, V* ⊺⊚⊺ *BP.*

**$$$** 🏨 **Prima Royale.** Cabbies will know this as the old Windmill Hotel, but the structure is almost all that's left of its former life: the hotel has been completely renovated down to the fine details. The well-lighted, golden marble lobby—with potted palms, brightly colored armchairs and cushions, and touches of leather—augurs well. The good taste is reflected in the guest rooms' burgundy drapes and cushions, and the soft earth-colored tiles and colorful accents in the bathrooms. Ask for a room with a view. The location is good, too: a 15–20 minute walk from the city center or the Old City. ⊠ *3 Mendele St., off Keren Hayesod, Talbieh 92147* ☎ *02/560–7111* 🖷 *02/561–0964* ⊕ *www.prima.co.il/eng* ⟿ *126 rooms, 7 suites* ♨ *Restaurant, minibars, Wi-Fi, gym, sauna, lobby lounge, shop, laundry service, Internet room, free parking, no-smoking floor* ☰ *AE, DC, MC, V* ⊺⊚⊺ *BP.*

**$$** 🏨 **Eldan.** Its central location in the heart of a prestigious hotel district—just 10 minutes walk from downtown or from Jaffa Gate—is a major draw. Rooms are bright and decorated in cheerful colors. Those over the side-street main entrance are smaller but quieter. Rooms facing King David Street (from some you can see the Old City) are more spacious; but expect traffic noise when the double-glazed windows are open. There is a restaurant for lunch, but no dinner. The car-hire company that owns the property often offers good deals on rentals. ⊠ *24 King David St., King David St.* ☎ *02/567–9777* 🖷 *02/624–9525* ⊕ *www. eldan.co.il* ⟿ *76 rooms* ♨ *Restaurant, café, in-room safes, refrigerators, cable TV, Wi-Fi, babysitting, dry cleaning, laundry service, Internet room, car rental, free parking* ☰ *AE, DC, MC, V* ⊺⊚⊺ *BP.*

**$–$$** 🏨 **Merkaz Shimshon and Beit Shmuel.** The stone complex, with its cool inner courtyards and fabulous Old City views from the roof, is the center of the World Union for Progressive Judaism. The new wing has better-grade hotel rooms: ask for one facing the private inner courtyard and lawn; the "Old City view" is very partial. The "guest house" (superior hostel) rooms are bright and pleasant, if utilitarian. They can sleep six when bunk beds are lowered from the walls. Request a street-facing room to avoid the noise of fine-weather evening events in the inner courtyard. The location is excellent: only 5 minutes' walk to Jaffa Gate, 10 minutes to downtown. ⊠ *13 King David St. (entrance on Sham'a St.), King David St. 94101* ☎ *02/620–3456* 🖷 *02/620–3467* ⊕ *www.beitshmuel. com* ⟿ *41 rooms* ♨ *Coffee shop, dining room, cable TV in some rooms, Wi-Fi, Internet room, free parking; no TV in some rooms* ☰ *AE, DC, MC, V* ⊺⊚⊺ *BP.*

**$** 🏨 **YMCA (West)–Three Arches.** Built in 1933, this limestone building with its famous domed bell tower is a Jerusalem landmark. Stone arches, exotic murals, latticed cupboards, and Armenian tiles give it charm and character. The guest rooms are not large, but they're comfortable and attractively fitted in beige and burgundy, with Anna Ticho prints on the walls. There is a library and a good patio adjacent to the Three Arches restaurant. These, the excellent sports facilities, and a great location make the Y a very attractive deal. ⊠ *26 King David St., Box 294, King David St. 91002* ☎ *02/569–2692* 🖷 *02/623–5192* ⊕ *www.ymca3arch.co.il* 🛏 *52 rooms, 4 suites* ☙ *Restaurant, café, some refrigerators, cable TV, Wi-Fi, indoor pool, gym, sauna, basketball, squash, babysitting, playground, laundry facilities, Internet room, free parking* ⊟ *AE, DC, MC, V* ⦿❙ *BP.*

## Downtown

**$$$$** 🖭 **Sheraton Jerusalem Plaza.** Near the lively downtown area, the 22-story Sheraton looks like a big business hotel anywhere. Some rooms have matching pastel curtains and bedcovers, color-compatible carpets, and a pale orange stucco effect. Balcony views are impressive. The Ninth Gate Lounge and Bar in the lobby is comfortably inviting, and the nonmeat Italian restaurant, Primavera, has won kudos locally for its good food and elegance. The pool, surrounded by unaesthetic concrete, encourages quick dips, not long relaxation. ⊠ *47 King George St., Box 7686, Downtown 91076* ☎ *02/629–8666* 🖷 *02/623–1667* ⊕ *www. sheraton.com* 🛏 *300 rooms* ☙ *Restaurant, coffee shop, dining room, room service, in-room safes, minibars, cable TV, Wi-Fi, pool, hair salon, sauna, bar, shops, babysitting, children's programs (holidays), dry cleaning, laundry service, concierge, business services, meeting rooms, parking (fee), no-smoking floors* ⊟ *AE, DC, MC, V* ⦿❙ *BP.*

**$$** 🖭 **Lev Yerushalayim.** This all-suite hotel is in the heart of the city center, but you leave the heat and noise behind as you enter the stone-walled, plant-filled lobby. Suites are decorated in pleasing blues and pastels. A great deal for families, bigger suites have an additional room with sofa beds—easily worth the extra charge. The kitchenettes include refrigerators and microwaves, and can be equipped fully for an extra fee. ⊠ *18 King George St., Downtown 91079* ☎ *02/530–0333* 🖷 *02/623–2432* ⊕ *www.levyerushalayim.com* 🛏 *86 suites* ☙ *Restaurant, kitchenettes, microwaves, refrigerators, cable TV, dry cleaning, laundry facilities, parking (fee); no smoking* ⊟ *AE, DC, MC, V* ⦿❙ *BP.*

**$** 🖭 **Montefiore.** Reopened in October 2005 under new ownership and a new name (it was previously Hanagid), this small hotel enjoys a side-street location smack in the center of town. Shops and restaurants abound within blocks—yards, even—of the front door. The aesthetic remodeling has added rough limestone edges in the lobby; and off-white bedcovers and large mirrors to enhance light and space in the guest rooms. Windows are double-glazed. After breakfast, the dining room is transformed into La Carossa, a nonmeat Italian restaurant, with access from the street. ⊠ *1 Shatz St., Downtown* ☎ *02/622–1111* 🖷 *02/624–8420* ⊕ *www.montefiorehotel.com* 🛏 *47 rooms, 1 suite* ☙ *2 restaurants, dining room* ⊟ *AE, DC, MC, V* ⦿❙ *BP.*

**$** 🖭 **Jerusalem Tower.** This hotel is in a choice location: smack in the center of downtown. The stone floor of the lobby is studded with replicas of ancient mosaics. Guest rooms are small, but have large wall mirrors above the wood-panel headboards to enhance the sense of space. Ask for a room above the sixth floor to guarantee a view. ⊠ *23 Hillel St., Downtown* ☎ *02/620–9209* 🖶 *02/625–2167* ⊕ *www.inisrael.com/jth/jerusalem* ⇨ *120 rooms* ⟜ *Café, dining room, in-room safes, minibars, cable TV, in-room data ports, bar, dry cleaning, laundry service, Internet room, meeting rooms, parking (fee)* ⊟ *AE, DC, MC, V* ⎟⊙⎜ *BP.*

$ 🏨 **Palatin.** It's unpretentious, the rooms aren't large, and there's no elevator; but the selling points of this veteran family-run hotel are its downtown location (on a small, picturesque pedestrians-only square) and the personal service. ⊠ *4 Agrippas St., Downtown 94301* ☎ *02/623-1141* 🖶 *02/625-9323* ⊕ *www.hotel-palatin.co.il* ⇨ *28 rooms* ⟜ *Dining room, Wi-Fi, parking (fee)* ⊟ *AE, DC, MC, V* ⎟⊙⎜ *BP.*

¢ 🏨 **Jerusalem Hostel and Guest House.** Overlooking Zion Square, this is as downtown as you can get. Don't look for frills—this is for the budget traveler—but it is surprisingly well appointed for what it is: double-glazed windows in the rooms facing Zion Square, for example, and wall-to-wall carpet. Dormitory beds (8 in a room) are just $12 a night; larger private rooms sleep parents and two kids; children under 12 are free. ⊠ *44 Jaffa Rd., Downtown* ☎ *02/623–6102* 🖶 *02/623–6092* ⊕ *www.jerusalem-hostel.com* ⇨ *20 rooms, 2 dormitories* ⟜ *Fans, kitchen, Internet room; no a/c in some rooms, no room TVs* ⊟ *AE, DC, MC, V* ⎟⊙⎜ *BP.*

¢ 🏨 **Zion.** With little balconies overlooking a pedestrian street off the downtown Ben Yehuda mall, this 19th-century stone building has an Old World feel to it. Front rooms get some street noise until late hours, though air-conditioning has eased the problem. Furnishings are simple and pleasant, but several hard years have clearly left their mark. Ten rooms have showers only. There is no elevator. The lobby, reception area, and a few rooms are up a single flight of stairs (other rooms are up farther still). Guests can opt for a room-only arrangement, or take an included breakfast in the adjacent restaurant. The manager/receptionist speaks five languages, but English isn't one of them. ⊠ *10 Dorot Rishonim St., Downtown 94625* ☎ *02/623-2367* 🖶 *02/625-7585* ⇨ *25 rooms* ⟜ *Cable TV* ⊟ *DC, MC, V.*

## Givat Ram & Romema

$$$$ 🏨 **Crowne Plaza.** This classic business and convention hotel is very comfortable for the vacationer as well. The landmark tall building gives sweeping city views from most rooms. Guest rooms are light and airy, with conventional carpets newly replaced by blond parquet in some. Bathrooms are small. The lobby-level bar–coffee shop is well laid out, with semiprivate alcoves; there is an excellent business lounge; and the Kohinoor Indian restaurant is a real treat. The pool, and its adjacent lawns and playground, provide good downtime for all ages at the end of a hot day. (The pool is covered and heated in winter.) ⊠ *1 Ha'aliyah St., Givat Ram 91130* ☎ *02/658–8888* 🖶 *02/651–4555* ⊕ *www.ichotelsgroup.com* ⇨ *379 rooms, 18 suites* ⟜ *Restaurant, coffee shop, dining room, room service, some in-room safes, minibars, cable TV, some in-room*

broadband, Wi-Fi, 2 tennis courts, pool, gym, health club, hot tub, sauna, bar, playground, Internet room, business services, convention center, meeting rooms ☰ AE, DC, MC, V ⑩ BP.

**$$** 🏨 **Jerusalem Gate.** The hotel attracts individual tourists, budget-minded families, businessmen, and tour groups. Its location next to the Central Bus Station makes transportation simple. Guest rooms have solid-wood furniture (a rarity) and duvets; ask for a high floor with a view. The lobby has a copper ceiling, and an attractive bar on the mezzanine overlooking it. The rooftop sundeck offers great panoramas while you work on your tan. The hotel has direct access to a small mall with stores and fast-food options. ✉ 43 Yirmiyahu St., Romema 94467 ☎ 02/500–8500 🖷 02/500–2121 ➘ 294 rooms, 4 suites ♨ Coffee shop, dining room, room service, minibars, cable TV, Wi-Fi, bar, dry cleaning, laundry service, business services, meeting rooms, parking (fee), no-smoking rooms ☰ AE, DC, MC, V ⑩ BP.

**$$** 🏨 **Park Plaza.** This West Jerusalem hotel has a good local reputation. The bar-lounge offers comfortable sofas, deeply upholstered in burgundy or bottle green. Guest rooms are better than adequate, with pastel duvets and dark carpets. Breakfast is served in a roofed stone courtyard. ✉ 2 Vilnai St., Box 3835, Givat Ram 95435 ☎ 02/658–2222 🖷 02/658–2211 ⊕ www.parkplaza.com ➘ 210 rooms, 7 suites ♨ Coffee shop, dining room, room service, cable TV, Wi-Fi, lobby lounge, shop, babysitting, dry cleaning, laundry service, business services, meeting rooms, free parking, no-smoking rooms ☰ AE, DC, MC, V ⑩ BP.

**$$** 🏨 **Renaissance Jerusalem.** Part of the Marriott chain, this hotel offers good facilities at a surprisingly low rate. The marble lobby, with its reflecting copper ceiling and potted palms, is at once spacious and elegant. Rooms are comfortably large and warmly designed with quilted bedcovers. Most have fine views—insist on one. The big pool area is a green haven on a hot day. ✉ Ruppin Bridge at Herzl Blvd., Givat Ram 91033 ☎ 02/659-9999 🖷 02/651-1976 ⊕ http://marriott.com/JRSRN ➘ 350 rooms, 10 suites ♨ 2 restaurants, dining room, room service, some in-room safes, cable TV, in-room broadband, Wi-Fi, tennis court, 2 pools (1 indoors), health club, massage, lobby lounge, shops, babysitting, children's programs (holidays; to age 10), dry cleaning, laundry service, business services, convention center, free parking, no-smoking floors ☰ AE, DC, MC, V ⑩ BP.

**$** 🏨 **Knesset Towers.** This hotel is a standout in its price category, with fairly spacious guest rooms (ask for one with a view), larger family rooms (with a little kitchenette and a refrigerator on request), and good recreational facilities. The indoor pool, saunas, and whirlpool bath are free to guests; the gym is extra. Gardens and an outdoor pool area provide delightful, relaxing environments at the end of an intense day of summertime sightseeing. The bright, open lobby-lounge is comfortable and inviting. ✉ 4 Vilnai St., Givat Ram 91036 ☎ 02/655–8888 🖷 02/651–2266 ⊕ www.knessettowers.com ➘ 172 rooms, 8 suites ♨ Coffee shop, dining room, room service, in-room safes, some kitchenettes, some refrigerators, cable TV, Wi-Fi, 3 pools (1 indoors), health club, bar, shop, dry cleaning, laundry service, Internet room, some free parking, no-smoking rooms ☰ AE, DC, MC, V ⑩ BP.

★ ¢  🏨 **Yitzhak Rabin Guest House.** Part of the official Youth Hostel Association, this facility, opened in 1999, is an example of how good budget accomodations can be. The large, airy, stone-and-aluminum lobby is a gathering place that opens out to flower-bedecked patios, with a view of Hebrew University's abundantly green Givat Ram campus. Guest rooms are spacious enough (they sleep from two to five, two in fold-up bunks), with private showers and toilets; furnishings are functional. The Israel Museum is a short walk away; there is a bus route to the downtown and the Central Bus Station; and guests get discounts to both the museum and the campus pool and gym. ⊠ *1 Nahman Avigad St., Givat Ram 91390* ☎ *02/678–0101* 🖷 *02/679–6566* ⊕ *www.youth-hostels. org.il/english.html* 🛏 *77 rooms* ⚇ *Dining room, snack bar, laundry facilities, meeting rooms, free parking; no room phones* ☰ *AE, DC, MC, V* ⎰⎱ *BP.*

## Mt. Herzl

¢  🏨 **Bayit VeGan.** The setting, opposite Mt. Herzl in West Jerusalem, has sweeping views of the Judean Hills, yet is only a 10-minute cab ride (there's a taxi stand next door) or a 20-minute bus ride from downtown. Upgraded from a youth hostel to a guesthouse, this large facility offers two grades of accommodations. The new wing is essentially an economy hotel: 62 spacious, well-laid-out rooms (light wood furnishings; some with tubs, others shower only) that sleep four. The 84 older hostel rooms (some sleep six) are simpler, though still with carpets and en-suite bathrooms. Always ask for a view. Meals are substantial and cheap. ⊠ *8 Hapisgah St., Bayit Vegan, Box 16350, Mt. Herzl 91162* ☎ *02/642–0990* 🖷 *02/ 642–3362* ⊕ *www.youth-hostels.org.il/english.html* 🛏 *146 rooms* ⚇ *Café, dining room, convention center, free parking; no room TVs* ☰ *AE, DC, MC, V* ⎰⎱ *BP.*

## Jerusalem Khan & Hebron Road

★ $$$  🏨 **Mount Zion.** Columns, arched doorways, and windows in Jerusalem stone all frame ethereal views of Mt. Zion and create attractive nooks filled with wall hangings, Armenian tiles, and plants. The core of the hotel is a 19th-century building that once served as a British hospital. A new wing was added in the 1970s, but the older "Citadel" rooms are more interesting and spacious. Suites have attractive, antique-style, wrought-iron furniture frames. The swimming pool and children's pool enjoy views over the Hinnom Valley; the Turkish steam bath, complete with traditional blue tiles, is a fun addition. ⊠ *17 Hebron Rd., Hebron Rd. 93546* ☎ *02/568–9555* 🖷 *02/673–1425* ⊕ *www.mountzion.co.il* 🛏 *116 rooms, 14 suites* ⚇ *Coffee shop, dining room, room service, in-room safes, cable TV, Wi-Fi, pool, outdoor hot tub, sauna, Turkish bath, bar, shop, babysitting, dry cleaning, laundry service, Internet room, some free parking* ☰ *AE, DC, MC, V* ⎰⎱ *BP.*

$  🏨 **Ariel.** The Ariel was originally conceived as an apartment hotel, but an early change in plans left it with a good number of spacious guest rooms and sizable bathrooms (aesthetically done in beige tiles). About a third of the rooms have excellent views of Mt. Zion: reception assigns them on a first-come first-serve basis, but don't hesitate to pay the extra $10 per night to secure such a room ahead of time. The public areas—lobby, bar, and dining room—balance marble with copious subtropical plants. ⊠ *31 Hebron Rd., Hebron Rd. 93546* ☎ *02/568–9999* 🖷 *02/673–4066* ⊕ *www.atlas.co.il/en* ⟿ *119 rooms, 6 suites* ⟐ *Coffee shop, dining room, cable TV, bar, shop, dry cleaning, laundry service, Internet room, free parking* ☰ *AE, DC, MC, V* ⦿| *BP.*

$ ▦ **Little House in Bakah.** The intimate hotel occupies an attractive, stone-arched building on the edge of a residential neighborhood, with good bus lines, and many eateries and shops just a few minutes away by foot. Some rooms are a little cramped, others quite spacious: ask for an upper floor if stairs don't bother you. Decor is cheerful, with primary colors, tasteful terracotta-hued bathroom tiles, and headboards imprinted with old Jerusalem images. A sunken room with vaulted ceiling and wooden floor serves as an inviting bar and coffee shop, spilling out into a fine courtyard. ⊠ *1 Yehuda St., corner of 80 Hebron Rd., Hebron Rd. 93627* ☎ *02/673–7944* 🖷 *02/673–7955* ⊕ *www.o-niv.com/bakah* ⟿ *28 rooms, 4 suites* ⟐ *Coffee shop, dining room, cable TV, Wi-Fi, bar, dry cleaning, laundry service, Internet room, free parking, no-smoking rooms* ☰ *AE, DC, MC, V* ⦿| *BP.*

★ $ ▦ **St. Andrew's Scots Guesthouse.** Built in the early 1930s as part of the St. Andrew's (Presbyterian) Church complex, the guesthouse is as much a retreat as a place to stay overnight. The comfortable library, the garden, and the lounge with cane furniture and stone arches framing Old City views define the character of the place. (The lounge also serves as a coffee shop and à la carte restaurant, with convenient hours.) Some of the guest rooms—tiled floors, matching green-patterned bedcovers and curtains, no TV—have tubs, others showers only. Bigger rooms have less of a view; some rooms have balconies. ⊠ *1 David Remez St., Box 8619, Jerusalem Khan 91086* ☎ *02/673–2401* 🖷 *02/673–1711* ⊕ *www.scotsguesthouse.com* ⟿ *16 rooms, 1 suite* ⟐ *Restaurant, in-room broadband, Wi-Fi, shop, Internet room, free parking; no room TVs* ☰ *AE, DC, MC, V* ⦿| *BP.*

## Mt. Scopus

$$ ▦ **Jerusalem Regency.** Cascading down Mt. Scopus, the Regency has a dramatic setting, bold design, and qualities that place it well above its price range. The lobby is a stylish combination of stone and greenery; the spacious guest rooms (one-third with Old City views) are decorated in soft colors, blond wood panels, and royal blue upholstery; and the pool area, with an adjacent playground, is a cool enclave of palms and plants. The large, sophisticated spa, popular among Jerusalemites, includes an authentic marble Turkish bath, imported piece by piece. The in-house Valentino's restaurant (nonmeat Italian and fish) is very good. ⊠ *32 Lehi St., Mt. Scopus 97856* ☎ *02/533–1234* 🖷 *02/581–5947* ⊕ *www.regency.co.il* ⟿ *502 rooms* ⟐ *Restaurant, coffee shop, dining room, snack bar, room service, in-room safes, minibars, cable TV, in-room broadband, Wi-Fi, tennis court, 2 pools (1 indoors), health club, hair salon, spa, Ping-Pong, bar, shops, babysitting, children's programs*

*(holidays, to age 10), playground, dry cleaning, laundry service, Inter-
net room, convention center, free parking, no-smoking rooms* ▭ *AE,
DC, MC, V* ⦿ *BP.*

## Old City

The Old City includes the Armenian Quarter, the Christian Quarter, the
Jewish Quarter, and the Muslim Quarter.

**$** 🏨 **Christ Church.** This is the guesthouse of the adjacent Anglican church,
the oldest Protestant church (1849) in the Middle East. The pinkish limestone floors and pastel furnishings in the guest rooms produce a pleasing aesthetic. Rooms in the newer Nicolayson Block are air-conditioned.
The courtyard makes a good retreat, and there is a comfortable common room with cane chairs and cable TV. The location, in the Old City
just inside Jaffa Gate, is excellent for sightseeing, though some people
feel more at ease in modern West Jerusalem. ⊠ *Jaffa Gate, Box 14037,
Jaffa Gate 91140* ☎ *02/627–7727 or 02/627–7729* 🖨 *02/628–2999*
✐ *christch@netvision.net.il* ⇌ *32 rooms* ⚹ *Coffee shop, dining room,
Ping-Pong, shop, free parking; no room TVs, no a/c in some rooms*
▭ *MC, V* ⦿ *BP.*

## East Jerusalem

**$$** 🏨 **Ambassador.** One of East Jerusalem's veteran hotels, the Ambassador
has been transformed by thorough and tasteful renovations, with the
use throughout of Jerusalem limestone and beige-and-cream decor.
Rooms are spacious and well appointed; for extra space, upgrade to a
junior guest room, and ask for an Old City view. In fine weather, the
very eclectic à la carte restaurant—Middle Eastern, Italian, French, and
Mexican—expands to the patio on the edge of the inviting gardens.
⊠ *Nablus Rd., East Jerusalem* ☎ *02/541–2222* 🖨 *02/582–8202*
⇌ *120 rooms* ⚹ *Restaurant, dining room, room service, in-room
safes, minibars, cable TV, Wi-Fi, gym, bar, lobby lounge, babysitting,
dry cleaning, laundry service, Internet room, meeting rooms* ▭ *AE, DC,
MC, V* ⦿ *BP.*

## American Colony

**★ $$$$** 🏨 **American Colony Hotel.** Once a pasha's palace, this cool limestone oasis
with its flower-bedecked inner courtyard has been a hotel for more than
a century. It's a 10-minute walk from the Damascus Gate, in East
Jerusalem, but worlds away from the hubbub of the Old City. A favorite
haunt of American and British expats, foreign journalists, and diplo-
mats, the hotel (Swiss-run and affiliated with Relais & Châteaux) is noted
for its service and ambience: turquoise-and-blue tilework, Damascene
wood inlay, potted palms. The best, enormously spacious rooms breathe
elegance, with rug-strewn flagstone floors and vaulted or antique painted-
wood ceilings. The in-house Arabesque restaurant has a good local rep-
utation. ⊠ *23 Nablus Rd., Box 19215, American Colony 97200* ☎ *02/
627–9777* 🖨 *02/627–9779* ⊕ *www.americancolony.com* ⇌ *73 rooms,
11 suites* ⚹ *Restaurant, cafeteria, coffee shop, room service, cable TV,*

in-room broadband, Wi-Fi, pool, gym, sauna, bar, shops, concierge, business center ▤ AE, DC, MC, V ⦿ BP.

**$$$** ▦ **Olive Tree.** Aesthetics are the strong point of this property. Stone arches, wood latticework, and bronze ornaments in the reception area, old flagstones in the skylit atrium, and polished floorboards in the comfortable lounge all combine to create a distinctly regional ambience. Guest rooms are not huge, but spacious enough for comfort. Black and gold touches, and framed old prints, give them some class. ⊠ 23 St. George St., American Colony ☎ 02/541–0410 ⊟ 02/541–0411 ⊕ www. olivetreehotel.com ⇌ 300 rooms, 4 suites ⚬ Coffee shop, dining room, room service, cable TV, Wi-Fi, lounge, Internet room, no-smoking rooms ▤ AE, DC, MC, V ⦿ BP.

★ **$$** ▦ **Addar.** On the "seam" between East and West Jerusalem, the Addar was originally designed as a boutique all-suite hotel. It has retained its elegant intimacy, but created some regular guest rooms as well. The red marble floor, gilded columns, wooden lattices, wrought-iron work, and plush burgundy upholstery of the lobby could have been gaudy, but manage to be stylish instead. The suites are furnished in antique style and upholstered in deep blue and beige: in-room whirlpool baths are standard. ⊠ 10 St. George Rd., American Colony ☎02/626–3111 ⊟02/626–0791 ⊕www. addar-hotel.com ⇌7 rooms, 23 suites ⚬ Restaurant, in-room safes, some kitchenettes, minibars, refrigerators, cable TV, some in-room VCRs, in-room broadband, Wi-Fi, dry cleaning, laundry service, Internet room, business services, some free parking ▤ AE, DC, MC, V ⦿ BP.

**$$** ▦ **Grand Court.** This huge hotel opened in 2005 near the American Colony and abutting Road No. 1. It's a celebration of light and space: from the large, airy lobby, with its limestone walls and marble arches, to the well-lighted, comfortable guest rooms, with their soft-color décor and light-tile bathrooms. The suites are impressively large. At press time, the opening of the sauna, gym, and roof pool was imminent. ⊠ 15 St. George St., American Colony ☎02/591–7777 ⊟02/591–7788 ⊕www.grandcourt. co.il ⇌ 427 rooms, 15 suites ⚬ Coffee shop, dining room, room service, in-room safes, minibars, cable TV, in-room broadband, Wi-Fi, bar, shop, Internet room, convention center, free parking, no-smoking rooms ▤ AE, DC, MC, V ⦿ BP.

# Ramat Rachel

★ **$$$** ▦ **Ramat Rachel.** As a country kibbutz hotel less than 15 minutes drive from downtown Jerusalem, Ramat Rachel enjoys the best of both worlds. Rooms in the older South Wing have balconies with stunning views of Bethlehem and the Judean Desert. The pleasant if unexceptional decor is offset by the brilliant colors of Calman Shemi quilted "soft art" originals above each headboard. Bathrooms are very small. West Wing guest rooms are decorated in tasteful aquamarines: no balconies, but great views toward Jerusalem. With its free pool (including a giant waterslide) and other sports facilities, all free to guests, Ramat Rachel feels like an isolated resort. Cheaper hostel rooms are also available. ⊠ Kibbutz Ramat Rachel, Ramat Rachel 90900 ☎ 02/670–2555 ⊟ 02/673–3155 ⊕ www.ramatrachel.co.il ⇌ 164 rooms ⚬ Restaurant, coffee shop, some refrigerators, cable TV, 3 tennis courts, pool, gym, hair salon, hot tub, sauna, bar, shop, babysitting (summer), playground, dry cleaning, laundry service, Internet room, convention center, free parking, no-smoking floor ☰ AE, DC, MC, V ⦿❘ BP.

# NIGHTLIFE & THE ARTS

## Nightlife

Jerusalem's nightlife is a great deal more limited than Tel Aviv's—seeming almost provincial by comparison—but some lively spots do keep late hours. Thursday to Saturday, Rivlin Street and the lower half of Hillel Street are packed with noisy teenagers doing nothing in particular. Azza Street, in the Rehavia neighborhood, has become an alternative hangout for students.

### Bars & Lounges

Bars and pubs are not as common in Jerusalem as they are in cosmopolitan Tel Aviv. All the major hotels have bars, but none of them are particularly distinctive. A few restaurants incorporate a bar setting for their patrons. A popular development is the area of Shlomzion Hamalka Street, downtown, where many establishments have sprung up in the last few years. All serve food, some indifferent and some very good.

**Sol** (⊠ 15 Shlomzion Hamalka St., Downtown ☎ 02/624–6938) is a well-respected bar with good tapas. **Mona** (⊠ 12 Shmuel Hanagid St., Downtown ☎ 02/622–2283), in the Artists' House, is the place for 20- to 30-year-olds to see and be seen. The bar and the food are excellent.

### Dance Clubs

Primarily the preserve of the 17- to 25-year-old crowd (Israel's drinking age is 18), Jerusalem dance clubs come alive on Thursday, Friday, and Saturday nights. Don't even *think* about going before midnight. Admission ranges from NIS 40 to NIS 70.

The Talpiot Industrial Zone, 4 km (2½ mi) south of city center, may seem an unlikely place to find a clutch of discos, but it makes sense in a city where the Jewish Sabbath is sacrosanct to so many. Nothing much happens before midnight, but by then parking is tight on Yad Harutzim Street and the adjacent side streets, and the snack bars are crowded. Most places are geared to the college-age set, a few to a slightly older crowd. Individual clubs appear and disappear with bewildering speed, so ask your hotel staff for recommendations.

**Yellow Submarine** (⊠ 13 Harechavim St., Talpiot Industrial Zone ☎ 02/570–4646) is one of the longer-lasting clubs. Order tickets in advance for the performances of local groups. Rock predominates in this small, intimate space, but there are also salsa evenings and nights for different age groups. **Ha'Oman-17** (⊠ 17 HaOman St., Talpiot Industrial Zone ☎ 02/678–1658) is an enormous, internationally known club specializing in electronic music (mostly trance and house). The best DJs from both Israel and abroad take turns here.

### Folk-Music Clubs

Jerusalem has a modest folk scene, with performances by local artists and occasional visits by international performers. Watch for listings, usually under "Entertainment" in the *Jerusalem Post, Ha'aretz,* and elsewhere. You can also call folk singer Jill Rogoff (☎ 02/679–0410) for connections with the local folk community.

### Jazz Clubs

Apart from performances in more conservative venues, you can sometimes find jazz at smaller places around town.

**Barood** (✉ 31 Jaffa Rd., Downtown ☎ 02/625–9081) features live jazz on many a Saturday night. Check ahead of time. Both international and local musicians play at **The Lab** (The Jerusalem Performing Arts Laboratory or, in Hebrew, Hama'abada) (✉ 28 Hebron Rd., Hebron Rd. ☎ 02/629–2000, 02/629–2001). You can sit at the bar and just enjoy the DJ's offerings, or pay extra for a specific performance. Check listings ahead of time.

### Pubs

A half-dozen nondescript pubs populate a courtyard off 31 Jaffa Road, where a drink is just a drink, not a celebration. There's another cluster of pubs in and around the Russian Compound. A new generation of establishments has arisen, however, along Shlomzion Hamalka Street, with good food and a wide liquor selection.

**Shot** (✉ 22 Shlomo Hamelech St., Downtown ☎ 02/624–4995) is the main pub for college students. It offers an excellent bar, good snacks, and music in a modern, stylish setting. There's a room upstairs where large groups can sit and talk together. **Stardust** (✉ Rivlin St., Nahalat Shiva ☎ 02/622–2196) is as close as Jerusalem gets to the hippie scene. A favorite hangout of young locals, it offers good rock and alternative music in an intimate space.

## The Arts

For schedules of performances and other cultural events, consult the Friday weekend section of the *Jerusalem Post* and its insert *In Jerusalem*; Friday's "The Guide" of *Ha'aretz*'s English edition; the Ministry of Tourism's monthly bulletin, *Events in Jerusalem*; and the free weekly booklets *This Week in Jerusalem* and *Hello Israel*; all in English.

There are three **main ticket agencies** for performances in Jerusalem. Student discounts are sometimes available; present your card at the ticket office: **Ben-Naim** (✉ 38 Jaffa Rd., Downtown ☎ 02/623–1273), **Bimot** (✉ 8 Shammai St., Downtown ☎ 02/623–7000), and **Kla'im** (✉ 12 Shammai St., Downtown ☎ 02/622–2333).

### Dance

The Tel-Aviv based **Israel National Ballet** and the modern **Bat-Dor** have a varied performance record. The better-known **Batsheva** modern-dance troupe is the one to look out for. Performances in Jerusalem are rare; check local listings.

## Festivals

Top Israeli and international orchestras, choirs, singers, theater companies, dance troupes, and street entertainers participate in the **Israel Festival** (☎ 02/ 566–3198 or 02/561–1438 ☒ 02/566–9850 ⊕ www.israel-festival.org. il), usually held in May or early June. All of the performing arts are represented, and offerings range from the classical to the avant-garde.

## Film

The usual Hollywood fare is available at the comfortable modern cinemas clustered in the center of town, in the Jerusalem Mall, and south of the city in the Talpiot Industrial Zone. Some of these places now stay open on Friday night and Saturday during the day. Check newspaper listings. Movies are subtitled in Hebrew and, when appropriate, English. The **Jerusalem Cinemateque** (☒ Hebron Rd., Hinnom Valley ☎ 02/565– 4333 ⊕ www.jer.cine.org.il) specializes in old, rare, and art films, but its many programs often include current offerings. Its monthly series focuses on specific directors, actors, or subjects, and its annual **Jerusalem Film Festival,** held in July, is a must for film buffs. The theater is open Friday night.

## Music

Classical music abounds in Jerusalem, with Israeli orchestras and chamber ensembles performing year-round and a trickle of international artists passing through. The **International Convention Center,** or ICC (☒ Givat Ram ☎ 02/655–8558), still known locally by its old name, Binyanei Ha'ooma, is opposite the Central Bus Station and is the local venue for the subscription series of the world-renowned **Israel Philharmonic Orchestra** (☎ 1700/703–030 ⊕ www.ipo.co.il) in Tel Aviv. For tickets, contact the orchestra's office or one of the local ticket agencies.

The **Jerusalem Center for the Performing Arts** (☒ 20 Marcus St., Talbieh ☎ 02/560–5755 or 02/560–5757), still commonly known as the Jerusalem Theater, houses the Jerusalem Sherover Theater, the Henry Crown Auditorium, and the more intimate Rebecca Crown Theater. This is Jerusalem's most active venue for classical music and live theater. They also screen movies.

**Bet Ticho** (Ticho House) (☒ 9 Harav Kook St., near Zion Sq., Downtown ☎ 02/624–4186) holds intimate recitals on Friday mornings in a serene setting. The **Targ Music Center** (☒ 29 Hama'ayan St., Ein Kerem ☎ 02/641–4250), 7 km (4½ mi) from the city center, often holds noontime chamber-music performances on Fridays and Saturdays. The surroundings have a rustic charm. **Etnachta** (☒ 20 Marcus St., Talbieh ☎ 02/560–5757) is a popular (and free) series of concerts produced by Israel Radio's classics station and broadcast live. This takes place Monday at 5 PM, generally from October through June, at the Henry Crown Auditorium. Check by phone first.

Hearing music in one of Jerusalem's many churches can be a moving experience. The **Church of the Redeemer** (☒ Muristan, Christian Quarter ☎ 02/627–6111) is a favorite venue. **Dormition Abbey** (☒ Mt. Zion, Mt. Zion ☎ 02/565–5330) also offers concerts. Watch the listings for concerts of Russian Orthodox music by a local choir.

The **Jerusalem International YMCA (West)** (✉ 26 King David St., King David St. ☎ 02/569–2692) presents a rousing concert of Israeli folklore—mostly singing and folk dancing—usually on Monday, Tuesday, Thursday, and Saturday evenings. Call ahead to confirm. Reservations are advised, but as the 500-seat hall is generally inundated by tour groups and seats are unmarked, it's recommended that you arrive early. The cost is NIS 81.

The **Bible Lands Museum** (✉ 25 Granot St., Givat Ram, next to the Israel Museum ☎ 02/561–1066) hosts Saturday-evening concerts for most of the year. The programs presented include chamber music, jazz, gospel, folk music, and country-and-western. Each concert is preceded by cheese and wine in the foyer; and the museum's galleries are open to concertgoers for half an hour before and after the concert.

A Friday-night Oneg Shabbat series is presented at **Beit Shmuel** (✉ Eliyahu Shama'a St., off King David St., King David St. ☎ 02/620–3455 or 02/620–3456 ⊕ www.beitshmuel.com), which typically hosts some of the most popular Israeli pop performers. The evening will be in Hebrew, catering to the predominantly local audience, but the music may speak to you in an international language.

### Theater

The Israel Festival (in May and June) is your best bet for quality non-Hebrew productions. English theater in Jerusalem throughout the rest of the year is too rare to predict: check listings.

**The Lab** (The Jerusalem Performing Arts Laboratory or, in Hebrew, Hama'abada) (✉ 28 Hebron Rd., Hebron Rd. ☎ 02/629–2000 or 02/629–2001) offers a mixture of food, drink (they have a bar), live theater, music, and dance. The presentations are all in Hebrew and cost extra.

# SPORTS & THE OUTDOORS

## Biking

The **Jerusalem Bicycling Club** (☎ 02/561–9416) leads rides on Saturday morning at 7 AM starting from the International Convention Center, Binyanei Ha'ooma (opposite the Central Bus Station). This informal club is a good source for information on bike rentals and can recommend routes within the city.

## Bowling

The **Jerusalem Bowling Center** (✉ Achim Yisrael Mall "Kenyon Talpiot," 18 Yad Harutzim St., Talpiot Industrial Zone ☎ 02/673–2195) has 10 lanes, a small cafeteria, and billiard tables. The center is open Sunday to Friday 10 AM–2 AM and Saturday from 11 AM–2 AM. From Sunday through Thursday, the cost per game (including shoe rental) is NIS 22 from 10 AM–6 PM, and NIS 27 from 6 PM–2 AM; from Friday evening through Saturday night the cost is NIS 30. If you play two games, you get the third free.

## Health Clubs

The best health clubs in Jerusalem are in hotels; a few are privately run concessions. All welcome health seekers who are not hotel guests.

The **Crowne Plaza Hotel** (✉ 1 Ha'aliyah St., Givat Ram ☎ 02/658–8888) has the most comprehensive facilities. The cost is NIS 70 Monday to Friday, NIS 90 on Saturday. The sophisticated complex at the **Jerusalem Regency Hotel** (✉ 32 Lehi St., Mt. Scopus ☎ 02/533–1204) is much admired. NIS 235 gets you a day of activities, including breakfast. Daily charges are NIS 75 at the **Renaissance Jerusalem** (✉ 6 Wolfson St., Givat Ram ☎ 02/659–9999), which includes access to the swimming pool.

## Horseback Riding

Stables offer lessons and trail rides, including ones suitable for children, as well as longer (and more interesting) trails. Rates vary, so call ahead.

**King David's Riding Stables** (✉ Shoresh ☎ 057/739–8866), in the wooded Judean Hills, is 16 km (10 mi) west of Jerusalem. The basic rate is NIS 90 for a 45-minute session. The **Riding Club** (✉ behind Angel's Bakery, Kiryat Moshe ☎ 02/651–3585) breeds Arabians. A 50-minute session costs NIS 110.

## Squash

The **YMCA (West)** (✉ 26 King David St., King David St. ☎ 02/569–2692, 02/569–2684) has three squash courts for rental. They're available for NIS 65 for 45 minutes, 6 AM–9 PM, Monday–Saturday. The price includes use of the gym, sauna, and swimming pool. To book a court, call at least two hours ahead of time. The **Hebrew University** (✉ Ruppin Blvd., Givat Ram ☎ 02/658–4358 or 02/658–4287) has two courts in its on-campus Cosell Center (opposite the Science Museum), open Sunday–Thursday 7 AM–10 PM, Friday 7–5, and Saturday 8–5. Reservations can be made by phone from 7 AM–noon and 3 PM–9:30 PM. The cost is NIS 30 per session, and rackets can be rented for NIS 10 each.

## Swimming

The enthusiast can swim year-round at several pools. (Those at hotels welcome nonguests.) Check opening hours, as some pools provide specific hours for mixed or single-sex swimming. In addition to outdoor pools, the following hotels provide winter swimming as well.

Swimming at the **Renaissance Jerusalem Hotel** (✉ 6 Wolfson St., Givat Ram ☎ 02/659–9999) costs NIS 75, including access to the health club. The **Inbal Hotel** (✉ 3 Jabotinsky St., Talbieh ☎ 02/675–6666) has an outdoor pool that is covered and heated in winter. The fee is NIS 80 Monday through Friday; NIS 100 on Saturday. There are beautifully landscaped facilities at the **Crowne Plaza Hotel** (✉ 1 Ha'aliyah St., Givat Ram ☎ 02/658–8888), which asks NIS 70 Monday through Friday; NIS 90 on Saturday. It costs NIS 80 to swim at the **Jerusalem Regency Hotel**

(⊠ 32 Lehi St., Mt. Scopus ☎ 02/533–1234). The **King David Hotel** (⊠ 23 King David St., King David St. ☎ 02/620–8888) has the loveliest of pool settings in Jerusalem, and the highest rates: NIS 90 Monday through Thursday; NIS 130 on Friday and Saturday. The **Knesset Towers Hotel** (⊠ 4 Wolfson St., Givat Ram ☎ 02/655–8888) has attractive facilities that are NIS 50 for the day, including access to the health club.

Public pools provided a more colorful local experience, at a lower price. **Bet Hano'ar Ha'ivri** or YMWHA (⊠ 105 Herzog Blvd., Pat Junction ☎ 02/649–4111) charges NIS 40 Monday through Friday, NIS 47 Saturday. **Djanogly** (⊠ Bet Avraham Community Center, 6 Recanati St., Ramot Allon ☎ 02/586–8055, 02/586–7662) charges NIS 35 per session. The **Jerusalem Pool** (⊠ 43 Emek Refa'im St., German Colony ☎ 02/563–2092) has a public pool that is covered in winter. It gets very crowded in July and August, but it's one of the most reasonable places around, at NIS 50 for the day.

## Tennis

Tennis has become increasingly popular in Israel. Advance reservations are always required.

The **Hebrew University at Mt. Scopus** (⊠ 1 Churchill St., Mt. Scopus ☎ 02/588–2796 or 02/582–6960) has 10 lighted courts and rental equipment. Courts go for NIS 35 an hour in daylight and NIS 45 an hour in evenings, and are open Sunday 11 AM–10 PM, Monday–Thursday 6:30 AM–10 PM, Friday 7–4, and Saturday 8–4. You can rent a racket for NIS 20, and buy three balls for NIS 30. Call ahead to book, especially during campus recess.

The **Israel Tennis Center** (⊠ 5 Almaliach St., Katamon Tet ☎ 02/679–1866 or 02/679–2726) has 18 lighted courts, available for NIS 40 per hour, Sunday–Thursday, 6 AM–4 PM; NIS 50 per hour Sunday–Thursday, 7 PM–10 PM, Friday 6 AM–6 PM (Oct.–Mar. until 5 PM), and Saturday 7 AM–noon. Equipment rental is sometimes available; call ahead. The **YMCA (West)** (⊠ 26 King David St., King David St. ☎ 02/569–2692) has four courts that rent for NIS 40 per hour; they're open Monday–Saturday 8–8. A few major hotels have their own courts, but may restrict usage to guests or club members. Ask your concierge to make inquiries if you want to play at a particular hotel.

# SHOPPING

Jerusalem offers distinctive ideas for gifts—for yourself or others—from jewelry and art to traditional crafts and souvenirs. The several shopping areas make it easy to plan expeditions. Prices are generally fixed in the city center and the Jewish Quarter of the Old City, though you can sometimes negotiate for significant discounts on expensive art and jewelry. Shopping in the Old City's colorful Arab bazaar, or souk (pronounced "shook" in Israel—rhymes with "book"), is fascinating but can be a trap for the unwary. Unless you know how much it's really worth, avoid buying gold, silver, or gem-studded jewelry here.

Stores generally open by 8:30 AM or 9 AM, and some close between 1 PM and 4 PM. Some also close on Tuesday afternoon, a traditional but less and less observed half day. Jewish-owned stores (that is, all of West Jerusalem—the "New City"—and the Old City's Jewish Quarter) close on Friday afternoon at 1 PM or 2 PM, depending on the kind of store and the season (food and souvenir stores tend to stay open later), and reopen on Sunday morning. Some stores geared to the tourist trade, particularly downtown, reopen on Saturday night after the Jewish Sabbath ends, especially in summer. Arab-owned stores in the Old City and East Jerusalem are busiest on Saturday and quietest on Sunday, when many (but not all) Christian storekeepers close for the day.

## Shopping Streets & Malls

**Arts and Crafts Lane** (✉ Yemin Moshe) (known in Hebrew as Hutzot Hayotzer), opposite and downhill from the Jaffa Gate, is home to goldsmiths and silversmiths specializing in Judaica, generally done in an ultramodern, minimalist style. The work is extremely high quality and priced accordingly. Most exquisite among them is **Sari Srulovitch** (✉ Hutzot Hayotzer, Hinnom Valley ☎ 02/628–6699). You can also find excellent jewelry and fine art here.

The **Cardo** (✉ Jewish Quarter Rd., Jewish Quarter), in the Old City's Jewish Quarter, began life as the main thoroughfare of Byzantine Jerusalem, was a street during the Crusader era, and has now been converted into an attractive shopping area. Beyond discovering souvenirs and Judaica, you'll find good-quality jewelry and art here.

**Emek Refai'm** (✉ German Colony), in the German Colony, has become the funkiest area in which to shop, eat, and people-watch from early morning to late at night. There's plenty of variety, from cheap takeaway eateries to mid-price restaurants and bars. Gifts and jewelry are easy to find in a rainbow of styles and tastes. The place is hopping with a fascinating spectrum of Israelis on Thursday through Saturday nights.

The **Jerusalem Mall** (✉ Malcha ☎ 02/679–1333), known locally as Kenyon Malcha, is—at 500,000 square feet, not counting parking—one of the largest in the Middle East. It includes a department store, a supermarket, eight cinemas, and almost 200 shops and eateries (Pizza Hut and Burger King among them). The interior is an attractive mix of arched skylights and wrought-iron banisters in a quasi–art deco style. The mall is clearly signposted from the Begin Boulevard, via Eliyahu Golomb Street, and from the Pat Junction–Gilo Road. It's open Sunday to Thursday from 9:30 AM–9:30 PM, Friday from 9:30–2:30, and Saturday dusk–11 PM.

The pedestrian-only **Midrachov** (✉ Downtown) is simply downtown Ben Yehuda Street, the heartbeat of West Jerusalem (the New City). The selection of clothing, shoes, jewelry, souvenirs, T-shirts, and street food here makes for a fun shopping experience. Street musicians serenade the passersby, and the human parade is best appreciated from one of the many outdoor cafés. Summer evenings are lively, as the mall fills with peddlers of cheap jewelry and crafts, and young admiring shoppers.

King David Street (✉ King David St.) is lined with prestigious stores, most with an emphasis on art, Judaica, antiquities, or interesting jewelry.

Salomon Street (✉ Nahalat Shiva), in the old neighborhood of Nahalat Shiva, just off Zion Square, has also been developed as a pedestrian mall. Between the many eateries, you'll find several crafts galleries and arty jewelry and clothing shops, both on the main drag and in the adjacent alleys and courtyards.

## Specialty Stores

### Art Galleries

Several galleries representing Israeli artists are close to the city's premier hotels, on King David Street.

Udi Merioz, the artist and owner of **Blue and White Art Gallery** (✉ Cardo, Jewish Quarter ☎ 02/628–8464), does "soft painting," a special appliqué technique that uses cloth on cloth. The gallery also represents Israeli artist Yaacov Agam. **Motke Blum** (✉ Hutzot Hayotzer [Arts and Crafts Lane], Hinnom Valley ☎ 02/623–4002) does fine soft-colored oils and minimalist landscapes.

### Clothing

Clothing tends to be expensive in Israel, and in Jerusalem you have to search for really fashionable clothes. Furthermore, what's available for the female population, in larger stores or trendy boutiques, tends to be either for impossibly thin teenagers or women with full figures; there are no petite sizes here.

**A.B.C.** (✉ 25 King George St., Downtown ☎ 050/849-2029) is a home-grown label that has proved popular. **Kedem Sasson** (✉ 21 King George St., Downtown ☎ 02/625–2602), an Israeli fashion designer, caters to the fuller figure with clothes in soft fabrics, some of them in decidedly quirky styles. **Tashtari** (✉ 25 King George St., Downtown, ☎ 02/625–3282) is an exclusive boutique offering unique, handmade evening bags by artists from other lands. Owner Amos Sadan is delighted to share the story of each item with you. Also featured in this tiny store are his own outstanding, original clothes—"wearable art"—many of them heavily influenced by Japanese aesthetics. This is high-end merchandise.

SWIMWEAR Israeli swimsuits and beach accessories have revolutionized the market overseas with their dazzling designs and colors. **Hamashbir** (✉ 28 King George St., Downtown ☎ 02/624–0511), essentially Jerusalem's only department store, stocks both Gottex and Gideon Oberson swimwear.

### Crafts

The **Jerusalem House of Quality** (✉ 12 Hebron Rd., Hebron Rd. ☎ 02/671–7430) showcases the work of some excellent Israeli craftspeople in the media of ceramics, glass, jewelry, sculpture, wooden ornaments, and ritual objects. You can often see them at work in their studios on the second floor.

Armenian hand-painted pottery—geometric or stylized natural motifs, predominantly blue and white, with non-Western brown and yellow accents—is a good idea for gifts. **Jerusalem Pottery** (✉ Via Dolorosa, Muslim Quarter ☎ 02/626–1587), at the VI Station of the Cross, is the store of one of the best artisans: Stefan Karakashian. His particularly high-quality work includes plates, bowls, tiles, and plaques. **Hagop Antreassian** (✉ near Zion Gate, Armenian Quarter ☎ 02/627–2584) also makes fine Armenian pottery, and focuses on practical items for the home. You can often catch him painting or firing his clay creations in his studio just inside Zion Gate. **Sandrouni** (✉ Armenian Orthodox Patriarchate Rd., Armenian Quarter ☎ 02/628–3567) stocks pieces in many colors and styles.

**Ruth Havilio** (✉ Ein Kerem 4/d, Ein Kerem ☎ 02/641–7912) produces tiles with a more modern feel, for both decorative and practical purposes. Her sense of color and fun (whimsical clay animals, for instance) play alongside more traditional styles. You can have tiles personalized, but keep in mind that this cannot be done on the spot. To get there, take the alley to the left of St. John's Church. Part of the charm of the gallery is its evocative setting in a courtyard.

Whether you like the unpredictable shapes of contemporary ceramics or more conservative items, local artists present a rich choice at three cooperative stores, all on the same street. **Cadim** (✉ 4 Salomon St., Nahalat Shiva ☎ 02/623–4869) presents a decidedly contemporary selection. **Shemonah Beyachad** (✉ 11 Salomon St., Nahalat Shiva ☎ 02/624–7250) displays the work of its eight members, some of whom you may find on duty in the store. The **Guild of Ceramicists** (✉ 27 Salomon St., Nahalat Shiva ☎ 02/624–4065) beckons you in with its delightful serendipity of colorful tiled steps, though the decorated pottery on sale inside, both functional and ornamental, is entirely different.

**Danny Azoulay** (✉ 5 Salomon St., Nahalat Shiva ☎ 02/623–3918) offers delicate items in fine porcelain, all hand-painted in rich shades of blue, red, and gold. Many are traditional Jewish ritual objects—some pricey—but you can also find less expensive items, such as napkin rings and bottle stoppers.

**Klein** (✉ 3 Ziv St., off Bar Ilan St., Tel Arza ☎ 02/538–8784) produces some of the highest-quality olive-wood objects in Israel. This is the factory showroom; it stocks everything they make, from bowls and yo-yos to attractive trays of Armenian pottery tiles set in olive wood, picture frames, boxes, and desktop paraphernalia.

Paper-cutting is a traditional and well-established Jewish art form. These pieces make unusual gifts—to say nothing of being both light and easy to pack. **Archie Granot** (✉ 1 Agron St., Downtown ☎ 02/625–2210, 054/528–7399 for appointment) has evolved his own complex, multilayered style of paper-cut Judaica inspired by traditional motifs. Some of his high-end creations are displayed in museum collections around the world. Call ahead; the store is by appointment only. **Judaicut** (✉ 21 Yoel Salomon St., Nahalat Shiva ☎ 02/623–3634) sells more traditional and affordable papercuts, which can be customized with your name.

**Sunbula** (✉ St. Andrew's Scots Guesthouse, 1 David Remez St., Jerusalem Khan ☎ 02/673–2401) sells high-quality, traditional Palestinian embroidery. Colorful cushion covers and decorative cloths are particularly good value for the money, but there are smaller items and gift ideas for limited budgets as well.

**Charlotte** (✉ 4 Coresh St., Downtown ☎ 02/625–1632) carries colorful items of high quality: ceramics, weavings, painted silks, jewelry, and fashion accessories. **Gans** (✉ 8 Rivlin St., Nahalat Shiva ☎ 02/625–1159) proudly sells art and crafts made only in Israel. Choose from good-quality Judaica, glassware, weaving, jewelry, painted silk, wood, and ceramic ornaments. **Ann Kippot,** (✉ 6 Ben Yehuda St., Downtown ☎ 02/625–8280) sells a fine selection of colorfully designed, hand-crocheted skullcaps.

**Jerusalem Experience** (✉ 17 Jaffa St., opposite Safra Square, Downtown ☎ 02/622–3030) is the place for items of Christian interest. The friendly staff are happy to show you Israeli perfumes, skincare products, ceramics, glassware, and textiles, but also books about Jerusalem and other aspects of the Holy Land.

**Hoshen** (✉ 32 Emek Refa'im, German Colony ☎ 02/563-0966) offers attractive items in wood, ceramics, fabric, and jewelry. **Set** (✉ 34 Emek Refa'im, German Colony ☎ 02/566–3366) can solve your gift problems with an array of different objects in both traditional and modern styles.

## Harps

The **House of Harrari** (✉ Ramat Raziel ☎☎ 02/570–9075) is in the village of Ramat Raziel, a 25-minute drive from downtown Jerusalem, west of Ein Kerem. The small decorative door harps and graceful 10- and 22-string folk instruments are inspired (the makers say) by the Bible. The workshop displays the instruments in different stages of production. There are many kinds of ornamentation, and the door harps can be decorated with an inscription. The gallery will ship your purchase home. Call for directions.

## Jewelry

Jewelry in Israel is of a high international standard. You can choose between conservative styles; sleek, modern pieces inspired by different ethnicities; and the increasingly popular bead jewelry of Michal Negrin and other current Israeli stars of both the local and international scene.

★ **Stav** (✉ 35 Emek Refa'im, German Colony ☎ 02/561–0843) is the standout, offering exquisite (and expensive) pieces in a graceful mix of both ethnic and modern influences. **Sheshet** (✉ 34 Emek Refa'im, German Colony ☎ 02/566–2261) has high-quality merchandise at accessible prices. **Keo** (✉ 25 Emek Refa'im, German Colony ☎ 02/563–7026) specializes in delicate, modern pieces at reasonable prices. The **Michal Negrin** store (✉ 2 HaMelitz St., on the corner of Emek Refa'im, German Colony ☎ 02/563–3080), offers other gift items decorated with beads. **Shani Culiner** (✉ P.O. Box 28345 91283 ☎ 050/522–1484) creates stylishly modern gold and silver designs, based on motifs from both Jewish and Christian tradition. Call for an appointment; she will bring her collection (pendants are her most popular pieces) to your hotel room.

**Daniel Alsberg** (✉ Hinnom Valley ☎ 02/627–1430), in the Arts and Crafts Lane (Hutzot Hayotzer), outside the Jaffa Gate, is a particularly outstanding and original craftsman of modern pieces, mostly in gold and silver. **Idit** (✉ 23 King George St., Downtown ☎ 02/622–1911) stocks formal jewelry. **Hedya** (✉ 7 Ma'alot St., Nahalat Shiva ☎ 02/622-1151) has the collections of both Ze'ev Tammuz and Sarah Einstein: necklaces and earrings made from antique silver, amber, and other materials that have retained a feel of the past.

**H. Stern** has its main store at the **David's Citadel Hotel** (✉ 7 King David St., King David St. ☎ 02/624–3606), with branches at many of the other major hotels in town. The international company offers high-quality, expensive pieces. **Adipaz** (✉ 20 Pierre Koenig St., Talpiot Industrial Zone ☎ 02/678–3887) cuts diamonds and makes its own jewelry, much of it without precious stones.

### T-Shirts

Tourist shops all stock the same range of machine-stamped merchandise, but many stores will also custom-decorate shirts from a selection of designs. There are several around the Ben Yehuda pedestrian mall. **Sweet** (✉ 2 Ben-Yehuda St., Downtown ☎ 04/625–4835) has a good selection of T-shirts ready for custom-decoration. **Lord Kitsch** (✉ 42 Jaffa Rd., Downtown ☎ 02/625–2595 ✉ Jerusalem Mall, Malcha ☎ 02/678–0576 ✉ Achim Yisrael Mall, 18 Yad Harutzim, Talpiot Industrial Zone ☎ 02/673–3106) stocks a range of casual clothes, including T-shirts in a full range of colors.

### Beauty Products

The **Dead Sea Gallery** (✉ 17 Jaffa Rd., corner of King Solomon St., Downtown ☎ 02/622–1451) stocks Ahava skincare products, based on Dead Sea minerals. Their Dermud line is particularly worth trying. The helpful staff makes this visit a particular pleasure. Mail-order service is also available. The **Ahava Center** (✉ 5 Ben Yehuda St., Downtown ☎ 02/625–2592) also stocks all the Ahava products, but at less attractive prices.

## Street Markets

Jerusalem's main market is the **souk** (✉ Christian and Muslim Quarters) in the Old City, spread over a warren of intersecting streets. This is where much of Arab Jerusalem shops. It's awash with color and redolent with the clashing scents of exotic spices. Village women's baskets of produce vie for attention with hanging shanks of lamb, fresh fish on ice, and fresh-baked delicacies. Food stalls are interspersed with purveyors of fabrics and shoes. The baubles and trinkets of the tourist trade often seem secondary, except along the well-trodden paths of the Via Dolorosa, David Street, and Christian Quarter Road.

Haggling with merchants in the Arab market—a time-honored tradition—is not always the good-natured experience it once was. Unless you know what you want, know how much it's *really* worth, and enjoy the sometimes aggressive give-and-take of bargaining, you're better off just enjoying the local color (stick to the main streets, and watch your wallet or purse) and doing your shopping in the more modern and familiar New City.

**Fodor'sChoice**   Off Jaffa Road, near the commercial Clal Center, is the **Machaneh Yehuda**
★   produce market (✉ Machaneh Yehuda), a block-long alleyway that be-
comes a blur of brilliant primary colors as the city's best-quality fruit
and vegetables, pickles and cheeses, fresh fish and poultry, confections,
and falafel await inspection. The busiest days are Thursday and Friday,
when Jews shop for the Sabbath; the market is closed on Saturday along
with the rest of Jewish West Jerusalem.

# JERUSALEM ESSENTIALS

## Transportation

### BY AIR

Jerusalem's tiny domestic airport has been closed since October 2000.
Most visitors entering Israel fly into Ben Gurion International Airport
outside Tel Aviv, which is 50 km (31 mi) and a 35-minute drive west of
Jerusalem.

Taking the bus from the airport to Jerusalem has become a more te-
dious experience since the opening of Terminal 3 in November 2004.
You need to board the Egged local shuttle for a 10-minute ride to the
Airport City commercial complex, and wait there for the Jerusalem-
bound bus (number 947, and occasionally 423 or 943). It runs to
Jerusalem's Central Bus Station approximately every 30 minutes dur-
ing the day, a little less frequently in the evening. The cost is NIS 20,
payable on the shuttle. You need Israeli currency, but not exact change.
There is no bus service from Friday afternoon to Saturday night, or on
Jewish religious holidays.

Eight- or ten-seat *sherut* taxis (limo-vans) depart when they fill up and
drop passengers off at any Jerusalem address for NIS 45. To get to Ben
Gurion Airport from Jerusalem the same way, call Nesher to book a place,
preferably a day in advance. A "special" taxi (as opposed to a shared
sherut) should cost about NIS 190, and NIS 230 after 9 PM and on Saturday and holidays.
**🚩Ben Gurion International Airport** ☎ *6663 or 03/975–5555 ⊕ www.iaa.gov.il. **Egged**
☎ 03/694–8888 ⊕ www.egged.co.il/Eng. **Nesher** ☎ 02/625-3233 or 02/623-1231.

### BY BUS

Egged, the nationwide bus cooperative, serves Jerusalem's Central Bus
Station with comfortable, air-conditioned buses from all major cities in
Israel. Egged buses in and out of Jerusalem stop running about a half
hour before sunset on Friday and Jewish religious holiday eves and resume after dark on Saturday or religious holidays. The East Jerusalem
Bus Station is the terminus for private Arab-run lines serving West Bank
towns such as Bethlehem and Jericho.

Egged enjoys a monopoly on the extensive bus service within Jerusalem.
Service begins at 5:30 AM and ends around midnight, depending on the
route. Service stops half an hour before sunset on Friday (or on the eve
of a religious holiday) and resumes after dark on Saturday. The fare on
all routes is NIS 5.50; you need local currency, but not exact change.

There are no transfers. Buses do not automatically stop at every bus stop; you need to signal the driver. Bus schedules are available at the Central Bus Station, on Jaffa Road in West Jerusalem, and some commercial maps show the bus routes. Inquire at your hotel or ask the locals for advice.

The two small, Arab-run bus stations in East Jerusalem primarily serve routes to towns in the West Bank ( ⇨ *see* Side Trips from Jerusalem Essentials *in* Chapter 2).

Egged operates Route 99, a 2-hour circle tour of Jerusalem for visitors. Its distinctive red double-decker buses are equipped with audio explanations in several languages. The route begins at the Central Bus Station at the city's western entrance, and its 25 stops include Machaneh Yehuda, the edge of the downtown, Mea She'arim, the Jerusalem Regency Hotel, Mt. Scopus, Novotel Hotel, Jaffa Gate, City Hall, the King David Hotel, the Haas Promenade, the Jerusalem (Malcha) Mall, the railway station at the Biblical Zoo, Mt. Herzl, Yad Vashem, Israel Museum, the Knesset, and the Supreme Court. Departures are Sun.–Thurs. at 9 AM, 11 AM, 1 PM, 3 PM, and 5 PM. On Friday and the eves of Jewish holidays, the last bus leaves at 1 PM. There is no service on Saturday or Jewish religious holidays. The cost is NIS 45 for a one-day ticket, with unlimited transfers on this route.

🚌 **Central Bus Station** ✉ 224 Jaffa Rd., Romema ☎ 03/694–8888 or *2800. **East Jerusalem Bus Station** ✉ Sultan Suleiman St., opposite Damascus Gate, East Jerusalem ☎ 054/449–3088. **Egged** ☎ 03/694–8888 for local information or *2800.

## BY CAR

Route 1 is the chief route to Jerusalem from both the west (Tel Aviv, Ben Gurion Airport, Mediterranean Coast) and the east (Galilee via Jordan Valley, Dead Sea area, Eilat). The road from Tel Aviv is a divided highway that presents no problems except at morning rush hour (7:30–9), when traffic backs up at the entrance to the city. Some drivers prefer Route 443 for this reason—it leaves Route 1 just east of the Ben Gurion Airport and enters Jerusalem from the north. Once it enters Jerusalem, Route 1 becomes Jaffa Road, which runs into the city center but is reserved for public transportation; private cars need to use parallel streets.

Navigating a rental car through unfamiliar territory and looking for legal parking make driving in Israel's big cities a dubious pleasure. A combination of walking and taking cabs or a guide-driven tourist limo-van is often more time-effective—and sometimes more cost-effective as well. In Jerusalem, the only sights that may be easier to reach by car are West Jerusalem and the out-of-the-way panoramic overlooks.

There are a fair number of paid parking lots and garages in the downtown area. Note that curbs painted with alternate bands of blue and white indicate legal parking, but only by feeding a meter, or the use of pay-and-display tickets (there is usually a machine within sight of your parking place: make sure you have Israeli coins). Parking attendants are fairly zealous, and illegally parked cars that actually hinder traffic are likely to be towed.

Gas stations are easy to find, and some never close, but gasoline is expensive in Israel. At press time, a liter cost NIS 6.30 (about NIS 24 a U.S. gallon)—and the number is rising. Drive defensively: many local drivers take hair-raising risks on the road.

## BY TAXI

Seven- to ten-seat sheruts (stretch cabs or minivans) ply the same routes as the Egged buses to and from Tel Aviv and Haifa, and charge a similar fare (25% more on Saturday and holidays, when the buses don't run). From Jerusalem, Ha'ooma/Habira goes to Tel Aviv. Sheruts from Tel Aviv to Jerusalem congregate at Tel Aviv's New Central Bus Station. Sheruts to Jerusalem from Haifa leave from the Hadar district.

Taxis can be flagged on the street, ordered by phone, or picked up at a taxi stand or at major hotels. There are usually taxis waiting outside the Israel Museum and Yad Vashem. The law requires taxi drivers to turn on their meters, but it's mysterious how many meters fail to function the moment a tourist enters the cab. You can insist on it; but if you want the cab badly enough, you may need to compromise. Negotiating the fare puts you at a disadvantage unless you're familiar with the distance involved. A 10- to 15-minute ride (day rates until 9 PM) should cost between NIS 25 and NIS 30. The fare is 25% higher after 9 PM and on Saturday and holidays. Any serious problem with the cabbie can be reported to the Ministry of Tourism: be sure to note the number emblazoned on the front doors of the taxi or on the illuminated roof sign. Among the 24/7 cab companies are Hapalmach and Rehavia. Hapisgah is closed on the Sabbath. Ha'ooma/Habira runs a sherut service to and from Tel Aviv.

🚖 **Hapalmach** ☎ 02/679-2333 or 02/679-3333. **Hapisgah** ☎ 02/642-1111, 02/642-3333 except on Sat. **Ha'ooma/Habira** ✉ 1 Harav Kook St., near Zion Sq., Downtown ✉ Central Bus Station, Romema ☎ 02/538-9999 **Rehavia** ☎ 02/625-4444 or 02/622-2444.

## BY TRAIN

Suspended in 1998, the train service between Jerusalem and the coast was revived in the spring of 2005. The comfortable ride takes about an hour and 20 minutes—a good alternative at rush hour, but almost half an hour slower than the bus at other times. Many just do it for fun, or for the attractive scenery. The train leaves the Malcha Station (near the big Jerusalem Mall) almost every hour, with a first stop very close by at the Biblical Zoo. It terminates at Tel Aviv Hashalom Station, with connections to Haifa and the north. Service ends midafternoon on Friday (because of the Sabbath), and resumes after dark on Saturday. (A similar schedule applies to Jewish religious holidays.) The fare to or from Tel Aviv is NIS 19 one-way, and NIS 34.50 return, for any passenger over 10 years old.

🚆 **Hashalom Station** ✉ Derech Hashalom Tel Aviv ☎ 03/577-4000 or *5770 from any phone in Israel. **Israel Railways** ☎ 03/577-4000 or *5770 from any phone in Israel ⊕ www.israrail.org.il/english. **Malcha Station** ✉ Yitzhak Modai St. Malcha ☎ 03/577-4000 or *5770 from any phone in Israel.

## Contacts & Resources

### BANKS & EXCHANGING SERVICES

The main branches of all the banks—Hapoalim, Leumi, Discount, First International—are in the downtown area, but they are arguably the last resort for changing money. Several times a week they have morning hours only (different banks, different days), they give relatively low rates of exchange, and it usually involves waiting in line and having the clerk fill out paperwork. Best are the private currency-exchange operations (typically marked "Change") that have proliferated around Zion Square and the Ben Yehuda Street open mall, inside Jaffa Gate, and at a few strategic locations elsewhere in the city (Jerusalem Mall, German Colony neighborhood, Jewish Quarter). The banks and the exchange bureaus in the downtown and Jewish neighborhoods close early on Friday, and only reopen on Sunday morning. There are many ATMs across town: most accept foreign credit cards and give Israeli shekels, a few give U.S. dollars. And then there are hotel cashiers, which offer lower rates but great convenience.

### EMERGENCIES

The privately run, 24-hour Terem Emergency Care Center offers first aid and other medical attention. Yad Sarah is a voluntary organization that lends medical equipment and accessories such as wheelchairs, crutches, and canes. There is no charge, but a contribution is expected. It's open Sunday–Thursday 8–7 and Friday 8–noon.

A private dental clinic offers emergency service Sunday and Tuesday–Thursday 8 AM–8 PM, Monday 8 AM–6 PM, and Friday 8–1. Call first: when the office is closed, the call is automatically transferred to an on-call dentist.

The ambulance service, Magen David Adom, is the Israeli version of the Red Cross.

Emergency rooms in major hospitals are on duty 24 hours a day in rotation; the schedule is published in the daily press. In an emergency, call Magen David Adom to find out which hospital is on duty that day for your specific need (orthopedic or gastric, for example). Be sure to take your passport with you. There will be a fee. The major hospitals in Jerusalem are Bikur Holim downtown, Hadassah Ein Kerem, Sha'arei Zedek near Mt. Herzl, and Hadassah Mt. Scopus.

The daily press publishes the addresses of pharmacies on duty at night, on Saturday, and on holidays. This information is also available from Magen David Adom.

SuperPharm Nayot is open Sunday–Thursday 8:30 AM–midnight, Friday 8:30 AM–3 PM, and Saturday one hour after the Sabbath ends until midnight. Its downtown location opens at 8 AM.

🚑 **Ambulance/Magen David Adom** ☎ 101 or 02/652-3133. **Bikur Holim** ✉ Strauss St., Downtown ☎ 02/646-4111, 02/646-4113 emergency room. **Dental clinic** ✉ 1 Mendele St., at 24 Keren Hayesod St., opposite Dan Panorama Hotel, Talbieh ☎ 02/563-2303. **Fire** ☎ 102. **Hadassah Ein Kerem** ✉ Ein Kerem ☎ 02/677-7111, 02/677-7222 emergency room, 02/677-7444 children's emergency room. **Hadassah Mt. Scopus** ☎ 02/684-4111. **Police** ☎ 100. **Sha'arei Zedek** ✉ Mt. Herzl ☎ 02/655-5111, 02/655-5509 emergency room. **SuperPharm** ✉ 5 Burla St., Nayot ☎ 02/649-7555 ✉ 3 Hahistadrut St., Downtown ☎ 02/624-6244. **Terem Emergency Care Center** ✉ 7 Hamag St., Romema ☎ 02/652-1748. **Yad Sarah** ✉ 124 Herzl Blvd., Bet Hakerem ☎ 02/644-4444.

### INTERNET, MAIL & SHIPPING

Israel is very much on-line. Most hotels offer Internet terminals; many have Wi-Fi. Internet cafés are popular. The city has created numerous "hot" areas with permanent free wireless access: check out the Jerusalem Municipality Web site for details.

The Postal Authority not only sells stamps: its post offices throughout the city provide a fast international courier service (EMS) as well. The big names of package shipping—FedEx, DHL and UPS—are all well established in Israel.

**📠 Café Net** ✉ 3rd floor, Central Bus Station, Romema ☎ 02/537-9192. **DHL** ☎ 03/557-3557 ⊕ www.dhl.com. **FedEx** ☎ 02/651-2693 ⊕ www.fedex.com. **Freeline Internet Cafe** ✉ 8th Station, Via Dolorosa, Christian Quarter ☎ 02/627-1959. **Game Zone** ✉ 15 Shammai St., Downtown ☎ 02/624-1606. **Israel Postal Authority** ☎ 03/538-5909 ⊕ www.postil.com. **Jerusalem Municipality** ⊕ www.jerusalem.muni.il. **UPS** ☎ 02/654-1880 ⊕ www.ups.com.

### MEDIA

For better or for worse, Israel is a world leader when it comes to breaking news; by extension, Israelis are avid consumers of media. Newspaper readership and TV and radio news program ratings are among the highest in the world. That's in Hebrew; but English-speakers have no shortage of sources either. The liberal Hebrew daily, *Ha'aretz,* puts out an English edition, which is sold together with the Europe-based *International Herald Tribune.* The veteran and more conservative *Jerusalem Post* also appears every morning. Friday is the weekend edition, since there is no paper on Saturday (the Sabbath), but both return on Sunday, the first day of the Israeli business week. *The Jerusalem Report* is a biweekly magazine, well respected for its analyses of current affairs. All have online editions.

The Israel Broadcasting Authority (IBA) has a 15-minute TV newscast in English every afternoon at 4:50 PM (Fridays and Saturdays at 6 PM) on Israel Channel 3 (not always available on hotel cable packages). Its Voice of Israel radio network carries English news on the "Reka" station at 6:30 AM, 12:30 PM, and 8:30 PM. The Jerusalem frequency is 88.2 or 101.3 FM. The website gives more details, as well as real time and recorded broadcasts. Your hotel TV will quite likely pull in cable news stations like CNN, Fox, BBC World, and Sky.

**📠 Ha'aretz** ⊕ www.haaretzdaily.com. **International Herald Tribune** ⊕ www.iht.com. **Israel Broadcasting Authority** ⊕ www.iba.org.il. **Jerusalem Post** ⊕ www.jpost.com. **Jerusalem Report** ⊕ www.jrep.com.

### TOUR OPTIONS

ORIENTATION Several years of low-volume tourism in the early 2000s froze most programs of even well-established tour operators, like Egged Tours and United

Tours. The revival has brought them back into action, but so far (at press time) with just a single orientation itinerary. Prices are usually quoted in U.S. dollars so that tourists are exempt from the VAT. A half-day Old City highlights tour costs about $26. The full-day option typically adds Yad Vashem and Ein Kerem (or Mount of Olives) in the afternoon, and costs about $48. The price includes pickup and drop-off at your hotel. You can reserve directly or through your hotel concierge.

🚗 **Egged Tours** ☎ 03/694-8888 or *2800 ⊕ www.egged.co.il. **United Tours** ☎ 02/625-2187 ⊕ www.inisrael.com/united.

**PERSONAL GUIDES** At press time the daily rate for a private guide with an air-conditioned car or limousine was $350–$400, depending on the size of the vehicle. Many guides will offer their services without a car for about $180–$200. The customary rate for a half day is 60% of the full-day rate. For private guiding, approach Eshcolot Tours; or contact the Fodor's writers ( ⇨ *See* Sightseeing Guides *in* Smart Travel Tips).

🚗 **Eshcolot Tours** ✉ 36 Keren Hayesod St., Talbieh ☎ 02/563-5555.

**SPECIAL-INTEREST TOURS** The Society for the Protection of Nature in Israel, or SPNI, emphasizes nature, often trekking off the beaten path. Tours in English have been discontinued, however. There is little point for a non-Hebrew-speaker to join SPNI's city walking tours; but for nature hikes, where the experience and the camaraderie often matter more than the explanations, you might want to consider it. Many such tours are family-oriented, but require you to have your own vehicle.

The Sonia and Marco Nadler Institute of Archeology in Tel Aviv University runs week-long programs in the summer for volunteers who want to join the excavations of the First Temple era royal palace near Ramat Rachel.

🚗 **Ramat Rachel** ⊕ www.ramatrachel.co.il/archeology/VolunteerPrograms.htm **Society for the Protection of Nature in Israel** ☎ 03/638-8666 ⊕ www.spni.org.il.

**WALKING TOURS** Zion Walking Tours offers both classic and off-the-beaten-path itineraries. Tours last about three-and-a-half hours and cost $15–$29, depending on the sites visited. Both Egged Tours and United Tours do half-day walking tours of Old City highlights.

🚗 **Egged Tours** ☎ 03/694-8888 or *2800 ⊕ www.egged.co.il. **United Tours** ☎ 02/625-2187 ⊕ www.inisrael.com/united. **Zion Walking Tours** ✉ Inside Jaffa Gate, opposite police station, Jaffa Gate ☎ 02/628-7866 ⊕ http://zionwt.dsites1.co.il.

## VISITOR INFORMATION

The Tourist Information Office is open Sunday–Thursday 8:30–5. The Christian Information Center is open Monday–Saturday 8:30 AM–1 PM, except Christmas, New Year's Day, and Good Friday.

🚗 **Christian Information Center** ✉ Jaffa Gate ☎ 02/627-2692 ⊕ www.christusrex.org/www1/ofm/cic/CICmenu.html. **Tourist Information Office** ✉ Jaffa Gate ☎ 02/627-1422 ⊕ http://tour.jerusalem.muni.il.

# Side Trips from Jerusalem

## INCLUDING BETHLEHEM, MASADA, AND THE DEAD SEA

**WORD OF MOUTH**

"A day trip to the Dead Sea (the lowest point on earth and one of the most healing places on earth, thanks to the mineral richness of the extremely heavy water), including climbing Masada (lots of history), is a real experience."

—Mamamia

"[Our] local guide . . . showed us from a distance some of the landmark mountains and fields just outside of Bethlehem, and of course the Church of the Nativity. . . . I was so surprised to realize that [the distance] between the town limits of Jerusalem and Bethlehem is barely two miles."

—elaine

By Mike Rogoff

Updated by
Mike
Hollander

**JERUSALEM IS THE PHYSICAL AND SPIRITUAL CENTER OF ISRAEL,** and also serves as an excellent base for day trips to some of the most interesting and variegated landscapes in the country. For a break from the intensity of Jerusalem, this area provides a number of short excursions.

The most dramatic sights are in the Judean Desert–Dead Sea area, just beyond the edge of Jerusalem. The barren, desert landscapes contrast sharply with the lush greenery of the oases of Ein Gedi, Ain Fashka, and the town of Jericho. The route along the Dead Sea shore is hemmed in by awesome, fractured brown cliffs over 1,600 feet high, and is often cut by (mostly dry) riverbeds. Ein Gedi has two of the most spectacular of these riverbeds, Nahal David and Nahal Arugot. The region also surprises visitors with its unusual water courses, flora, and fauna—including the ibex (wild goat) and hyrax (rock coney).

The Dead Sea—actually a lake—is the lowest point on Earth. The therapeutic qualities of the saltiest body of water in the world are well documented. Visitors can relax while floating on the waters, spread mineral-rich mud over their bodies, and enjoy varied treatments in the well-equipped spas in the Ein Bokek hotel district, at the southern end of the Dead Sea ( ⇨ *See* Chapter 7).

Masada, King Herod's mountaintop palace-fortress built over 2,000 years ago, became a UNESCO World Heritage Site in 2001. Overlooking the Dead Sea, the king's extravagant architectural feat has ingenious water systems, wall frescoes, mosaic floors, bath houses, and a fresh-water swimming pool. Its remote location and almost unassailable position are evidence of his paranoia. Add the human drama of the last Jewish defense against Rome during the Great Revolt, and it is easy to understand why this is one of the most visited sights in Israel.

Adjacent to Jerusalem, Bethlehem is a major site of Christian pilgrimage. The Church of the Nativity, the oldest church in the country, is built over the grotto where Christian tradition believes that Jesus was born. The West Bank Arab city of almost 40,000 sits on the ancient highway through the rocky, olive groved Judean Hills.

Still on the trail of the Bible, you'll find echoes of Joshua (though not his walls) at the oasis of Jericho, to the east and the Ella Valley to the west, the dueling ground of David and Goliath.

The reforested hills west of Jerusalem in the Judean Lowlands (Shefela) are full of delightful views, picnic spots, and a few nature reserves. Don't miss the Sorek Cave, a fantastic cavern of stalagmites and stalactites; or the extraordinary ancient man-made caves of Bet Guvrin and Maresha. The area has become more inviting and popular with Israelis as well as tourists, with its thriving new wineries and cheese producers.

## Top 5 Reasons to Go

- **The desert fortress of Masada:** This UNESCO World Heritage site was built by King Herod as a palace. A century later it was the site of the last battle in the Great Revolt against Rome.

- **Bethlehem, the birthplace of Jesus:** The traditional site of the manger is in the Church of the Nativity, the oldest standing church in Israel.

- **Dead Sea:** The lowest place on Earth is also the most mineral-rich body of water in the world. Float on the water or apply some mud to fully experience the wonders of this natural phenonemon.

- **Desert oases:** In the heart of the dry Judean Desert, the stunning oasis of Ein Gedi is rich in flora, fauna, and archaeological remains. While trekking one of the most popular hiking sites in the country look out for local ibex (desert mountain goats) and hyrax (rock coney).

- **Flavors of Israel:** A stone's throw from where David slew Goliath, the Judean Hills Wine Route has over two dozen wineries, which produce some of the country's finest cabernet sauvignons, merlots, and chardonnays. A number of local goat and sheep cheese farms allow visitors to fully appreciate the flavors of this fertile area.

## Exploring Outside Jerusalem

This area offers three day-trip options. The Dead Sea has the richest fare and takes the most time, but some of its sights can be visited en route to the Galilee via the Jordan Valley. The area west of Jerusalem and Bethlehem can be combined with Jerusalem sights or with each other.

### About the Restaurants & Hotels

There are some passable lunch cafeterias in this area, but no tempting restaurants for dinner. If you don't want to grab a quick bite at one of the cafeterias, either take a packed lunch or have a picnic west of Jerusalem with wine and cheese. Most tours return to Jerusalem or Tel Aviv by nightfall, where the options are plenty ( ⇨ *See* Where to Eat *in* Chapters 1 *and* 3).

The lodgings in the Dead Sea region are heavily used by visitors, both local and international, who come to "take the waters." Many enjoy the quiet scenery of cliffs and coastline. Others just make this a convenient base from which to explore the Judean Desert. Facilities range from youth hostels to the luxury hotels of the nearby Ein Bokek area ( ⇨ *See* Chapter 7).

People typically explore the area west of Jerusalem as a day trip from Jerusalem or Tel Aviv. The only decent lodgings here are some fine guest houses 15–20 minutes outside the capital. Bethlehem, now governed by the Palestinian Authority, has a few unprepossessing hotels; Jerusalem, only 10 minutes away, is a far more convenient and congenial base. Try to book as much in advance as possible, as it may be difficult to find accommodation during the peak seasons (typically from the end of December to the beginning of January, in the spring around Passover and Easter, and from the end of June through July).

# GREAT ITINERARIES AROUND JERUSALEM

To explore the **Dead Sea region,** drive east through the arid Judean Desert to Qumran, where the Dead Sea Scrolls were found; the salty Dead Sea, the lowest point on Earth; the canyons and waterfalls of Ein Gedi; and the ancient palace-fortress of Masada. With an early start, most of these sights can be visited in one day. Masada (with its dramatic history and archaeological remains), the relaxation of the Dead Sea, and the nature reserve at Ein Gedi make a good combination. From April to October, later closing times allow a visit to Qumran as well. Visit the oasis town of Jericho (political climate permitting) on the way to an overnight trip along the Dead Sea or en route to the Jordan Valley and Galilee.

The area **west of Jerusalem** encompasses part of the Judean Hills and the lowland area known as the Shefelah. Highlights include the Sorek stalactite cave, the Ella Valley (where David and Goliath clashed),

and the man-made caves of Bet Guvrin and Maresha. Don't miss the local wine and cheese on the Judean Hills Wine Route. It's a full but comfortable day trip from Jerusalem.

**Bethlehem,** with its famous Church of the Nativity, is no more than a 10-minute drive south of Jerusalem (make sure to check the political climate before visiting). At press time, continuing deeper into the West Bank was not recommended.

| WHAT IT COSTS | | | | | |
|---|---|---|---|---|---|
| | **$$$$** | **$$$** | **$$** | **$** | **¢** |
| RESTAURANTS | over NIS 100 | NIS 76–NIS 100 | NIS 50–NIS 75 | NIS 32–NIS 49 | under NIS 32 |
| HOTELS | over $250 | $175–$250 | $111–$174 | $65–$110 | under $65 |

Restaurant prices are per person for a main course at dinner in NIS. Hotel prices are in US dollars, for two people in a standard double room in high season. Non-Israeli citizens paying in foreign currency are exempt from the 16.5% VAT tax on hotel rooms.

### Timing

The Dead Sea region is pleasant in the cool season (October–April) but often very hot the rest of the year. Getting a very early start and beginning the day with Masada can help beat the heat and the crowds. Ending the day with Masada often achieves the same result, but be aware of closing times. Bethlehem is best first thing in the morning or late in the afternoon (to avoid the crowds), but do note the hours for the Grotto of the Nativity. The area west of Jerusalem is good anytime, although the Sorek Cave has limited hours and no guided tour on Friday.

# DEAD SEA REGION

The almost 4,000-foot descent from Jerusalem's Mt. Scopus and Mount of Olives through the barren Judean Desert to the Dead Sea is only 24 km (15 mi). Clouds from the Mediterranean disperse as they descend from Jerusalem, creating a rain shadow. The average annual rainfall drops from 22 inches in Jerusalem to a mere 2 inches at the Dead Sea. The desert's proximity to Jerusalem has always made it part of that city's consciousness. Refugees fled to it; hermits sought its solitude; and in ancient times, before the Jewish Day of Atonement, the scapegoat symbolically bearing the sins of the people was driven into oblivion among its stark precipices.

It is vital to wear a hat and drink plenty of water here in hot weather. Do not attempt unfamiliar trails without expert guidance.

Route 1 leaves Jerusalem through a newly opened tunnel under Mt. Scopus, which emerges into the Judean Desert. The steep descent to the Dead Sea passes beneath the city of Ma'aleh Adumim, built in the 1970s as a bedroom suburb of Jerusalem. This and the handful of small Jewish villages in the desert are some of the West Bank settlements. Because of their isolation, however, they have been spared the friction with Palestinian Arab neighbors typical of settlements in the mountain region.

Tent-dwelling Bedouins (Arab nomads) still cling to their ancestors' way of life along the road, eking out a livelihood by herding sheep and goats. They have made some concessions to modernity: cars, water tanks and tractors, synthetic fabrics flapping on clotheslines, and even TV antennas sprouting from tents bear witness to a culture in flux.

*Numbers in the text correspond to numbers on the Side Trips from Jerusalem map.*

## Inn of the Good Samaritan

❶ *20 km (13 mi) east of Jerusalem on Rte. 1, 500 yards east of the junction with Rte. 458.*

This lone one-story building sits on the strategic spot which marks the halfway point between Jerusalem and Jericho, as well as the border between the biblical Israelite tribes of Benjamin, to the north, and Judah, to the south (Joshua 15). Although no 1st-century remains have been found, the Turkish-period structure could very well sit in the same place as the inn mentioned in the New Testament (Luke 10) parable of a man ambushed on the Jericho road and helped only by a Samaritan who lodged him at a nearby inn.

If you're energetic, turn away from the "inn," cross the highway *very, very* carefully, and climb the dirt track to the top of the hill opposite. Amid the scanty ruins of the small 12th-century Crusader fort of Maldoim—from which the outskirts of Jerusalem and Jericho are visible—the Gospel passage comes alive.

**2**

## Dead Sea Beaches, Spas & Mineral Pools
You cannot actually swim in the briny Dead Sea; you simply float in it. The incredible density of its water—about 10 times that of the ocean—makes it impossible to sink. The Dead Sea area is one of the world's primary health retreats for sufferers of psoriasis and rheumatic and arthritic ailments. Anyone can enjoy the benefits of the incredible mineral concentration in the Dead Sea water and mud, the natural warm mineral springs, and the oxygen-rich atmosphere at the lowest point on Earth. There are several places to swim along the Dead Sea and at the Ein Gedi Spa. ( ⇨ For spas in Ein Bokek see Chapter 7.)

Doctors recommend remaining in the water for no more than 15 minutes at a time because of the enervating effect of the brine; travelers with heart conditions or high blood pressure should not bathe here at all. Avoid getting the salt water in your eyes and mouth. Rinse off at the outdoor showers and faucets found at recognized beaches. It's imperative to drink a lot of fresh water, especially in the hot season (April to October). Many beaches are rocky (and hot in summer), so it's a good idea to wear protective rubber sandals, shoes, or sneakers. Don't leave possessions unguarded on the beach.

## Hiking
The Judean Desert has some excellent hiking trails. Ein Gedi's two nature reserves, Nahal David and Nahal Arugot, are the best for beginners. Serious hikers can seek out more challenging walks in spectacular canyons but should pursue these only with expert local guidance. The combination of heat and dryness can be dangerous, so bring a hat and lots of water when hiking in this region.

### Jericho

★ 35 km (22 mi) east of Jerusalem on Rte. 1, and north 5 km (3 mi) on Rte. 90.

The oasis town of Jericho, immortalized as the place where "the walls came tumblin' down" at the sound of Joshua's trumpets, is the oldest city in the world, and at 850 feet below sea level, it's also the lowest. It may be worth a trip through the lush town—adorned with date palms, orange groves, banana plantations, bougainvillea, and papaya trees—just to be able to say "I was there," but the town does have some significant archaeological sites. The Arab population of about 20,000 is mostly Muslim, with a tiny Christian minority.

Jericho has been under autonomous Palestinian control since 1994. Check the current situation before visiting. Be sure to ask about any restrictions on tourists in private cars visiting the town.

Entering the town from the south, take the left fork at the traffic island. A few hundred yards farther, the road swings sharply to the left. To the right of the bend and one block down a no-entry street is a huge, fenced-

## Side Trips from Jerusalem

- Hisham's Palace
- **3** Tel Jericho
- **2** Jericho
- Qarantal ◆
- Monastery of St. George ◆
- Mukhmas
- **1** Inn of the Good Samaritan
- Kalia
- **4** Qumran
- Almog
- Einot Zukim (Ain Fashkha) ◆
- Ma'aleh Adumim
- El-Azariya
- Jerusalem ★
- Bira
- Ramallah
- Airport ✈
- Atarot
- Givat Ze'ev
- Ramot
- Bet Horon
- Kubeibe
- Ein Hemed
- Herodion ■
- Bethlehem ◆
- Rachel's Tomb ◆
- **24**
- Solomon's Pools ◆
- Beit Jala
- Efrat
- WEST BANK BORDER
- Horon Junction
- Ma'aleh Hahamisha
- Kiryat Anavim
- Abu Ghosh
- Neve Ilan
- Zova
- Mevo Betar
- Elazar
- Alon Shevut
- Kfar Etzion
- Neot Kedumim
- Modi'in
- Emmaus **16**
- Mini Israel **19**
- Sha'ar Hagai
- Shoresh
- Kesalon
- Nes Harim
- Sorek Cave **15**
- Ya'aran Farm **12**
- Ella Valley Vineyard **10**
- WEST BANK BORDER
- Latrun **17**
- Trappist Abbey of Latrun **18**
- Nachshon Winery **14**
- Latrun Armored Corps Museum
- Nahshon
- Neve Shalom
- Hulda
- Mony Wines **13**
- Kibbutz Tzora **11**
- Tel Bet Shemesh **20**
- Bet Shemesh
- Beit Jimal
- Ella Valley **21**
- Tzuk Farm **9**
- Eshta'ol
- Ayalon Valley
- TO TEL AVIV
- SHEFELAH

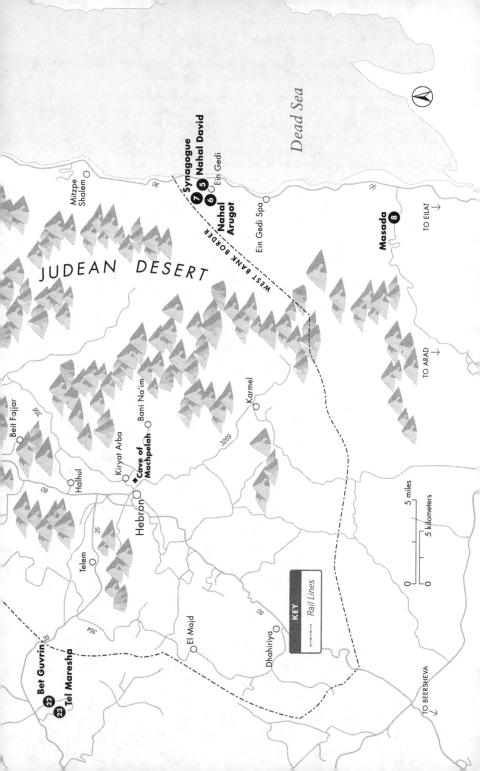

off sycamore tree, which tradition (and the postcard vendors) identifies as the very one Zacchaeus climbed to watch Jesus pass by (Luke 19).

**②** **Tel Jericho** is the mound of accumulated earth that entombs the legendary ancient city. Although it's been extensively excavated, archaeologists have not found the walls that fell to the blast of Israelite rams' horns when Joshua stormed the city in the mid-13th century BC. The most impressive ruins that have been unearthed are a massive tower and a wall, remains of the world's oldest walled city, which predates the invention of pottery. Carbon-14 tests have placed human skulls and bones found here in the Neolithic period (Late Stone Age) between 7800 and 6500 BC. Little is known about these early urbanites, or why they needed such fortifications thousands of years before they became common in the region, but a wealth of artifacts, displayed in the Israel and Rockefeller museums in Jerusalem (⇨ *See* Exploring Jerusalem *in* Chapter 1), helps us imagine their domestic life and customs.

From the top of the tell, there is a sweeping view of Jericho, the biblical "City of Palms." The generous spring that was always its source of life, is across the road, capped by a pump house. It is known as **Ain es-Sultan,** the Sultan's Spring, or Elisha's Spring, in recognition of the prophet's miracle of sweetening the water with a bowl of salt (II Kings 2). To the east in Jordan are the mountains of the biblical kingdoms of Ammon and Moab, among them the peak of Mt. Nebo, from which Moses viewed the Promised Land.

To the south, among the banana trees some 3 km (2 mi) away, is a small but distinctive mound of earth. This is **Tel Abu Alaik,** where the remains of the royal palace of the Hasmonean dynasty (2nd–1st centuries BC) have been uncovered. In the 1st century BC, Mark Antony gave the valuable oasis of Jericho to his beloved Cleopatra; the humiliated King Herod, Antony's local vassal, was then forced to lease the property back from the Egyptian queen. Herod expanded and improved the palace, turning it into his winter retreat. He died there in 4 BC.

To the west is the **Mount of Temptation,** identified by tradition as the "exceedingly high mountain" from which Satan tempted Jesus with dominion over "all the kingdoms of the world" (Matthew 4). Halfway down the mountain sits the remarkable Greek Orthodox monastery of Qarantal, the name being a corruption of *quarantena*—a period of 40 days (the source of the English word "quarantine")—the period of Jesus's temptation. Built into the cliff face on Byzantine remains, it is flanked by many caves, which once housed hermits. From a station opposite the tell, a **cable car** (cost is NIS 45) transports passengers to the foot of the stairs leading up to the monastery. The upper station is served by a restaurant with a spectacular view. ⊠ *Turn left at sharp bend in the main road through town; enter the parking lot of the tell from the west* ☎ *02/232–1590, 02/232–2240* 🎫 *NIS 10* 🕙 *Oct.–Mar., daily 8:30–5; Apr.–Sept., daily 8:30–6; subject to change.*

**need a break?**

The **Temptation Restaurant,** next to the Tel Jericho parking lot, has excellent *bourma,* a honey-rolled pastry filled with whole pistachio nuts. The lunches are a good value, with tasty *mezes* (Middle Eastern salads) and meats. The nearby fruit stands tend to overcharge, but try the pomelo (related to the grapefruit), in season from December to March.

**❸** The remains of **Hisham's Palace** (Hirbet el-Mafjar, in Arabic) have interesting stonework and a spectacular mosaic floor. Hisham was a scion of the Ummayad dynasty, which built the Dome of the Rock and El-Aqsa Mosque in Jerusalem. Although the palace was badly damaged by the great earthquake of AD 749 while under construction and was never completed, the high quality of the surviving mosaics and stone and plaster reliefs is evidence of its splendor.

To get here from Tel Jericho, go north for 2 km (1 mi) and turn right at the sign to Hisham's Palace/Hirbet el-Mafjar. After that, the left turn toward the site itself is another kilometer (½ mi) down the road but is marked only by a low stone pillar on the right. Before going, check at the tell to see if this site is open.

A small gatehouse leads into a wide plaza dominated by a large, star-shape stone window that once graced an upper-floor. Several sections of the fine geometric mosaics have been left exposed; others are covered by sand. The most impressive part of the complex is the reception room, off the plaza. Its intricate mosaic floor, depicting a lion hunting a stag, is one of the most beautiful in the country, the tiny colored tesserae producing an astonishing realism. Fragments of ornate stucco reliefs are still visible on some of the walls, but the best examples that were found here are now in Jerusalem's Rockefeller Museum ( ⇨ *See* Exploring Jerusalem *in* Chapter 1). The balustrade of an ornamental pool reflects the artistic influences of both East and West. ⊠ *Jericho* ☎ *02/232–2522* ⊡ *NIS 10* ⊗ *Daily 8–6; subject to change.*

en route | Route 90 south heads back toward the **Dead Sea.** A milestone by the side of the road just before the gas station (at the Kalia Junction) announces that you have reached the bottom of the world. The Dead Sea is shrinking, and the shore at this point is a kilometer (over ½ mi) away. To the left, sometimes there are heaps of white potash, the primary product of the Dead Sea, though most extraction of potash, bromine, and magnesium takes place at the huge plant at Sodom, at the southern end of the lake.

## Qumran

**❹** *6 km (4 mi) south of the Kalia Junction on Rte. 90, 20 km (13 mi) south of Jericho, 50 km (31 mi) east of Jerusalem.*

Although the remains of Qumran are not especially impressive, caves in the cliffs west of the site yielded the most significant archaeological find ever made in Israel: the **Dead Sea Scrolls.** They were found under extraordinary circumstances in 1947 when a young Bedouin goatherd stumbled on a cave containing parchment scrolls in earthen jars. Because the scrolls were made from animal hide, he went to a Bethlehem shoemaker to turn them into sandals! The shoemaker alerted a local antiquities dealer, who brought them to the attention of Professor Eliezer Sukenik of the Hebrew University of Jerusalem. Six other major scrolls and hundreds of fragments have since been discovered.

Most scholars believe that the scrolls were written by the Essenes, a Jewish sect which set up a monastic community here in the late 2nd century BC. During the Great (Jewish) Revolt against Rome (AD 66–73), they apparently hid their precious scrolls in the caves in the cliffs before the town was destroyed in AD 68.

Almost all books of the Hebrew Bible were discovered here, many of them virtually identical to the texts still used in Jewish communities. Sectarian texts were also found, including the constitution or "Community Rule;" a description of an end-of-days battle ("The War of the Sons of Light Against the Sons of Darkness"); and the "Thanksgiving Scroll," containing hymns reminiscent of biblical psalms.

The scrolls are tremendously significant for Bible scholars and students of ancient Hebrew, and gave researchers rare insights into this previously shadowy Jewish sect. Christian scholars have long been intrigued by the suggestion that John the Baptist, whose lifestyle seems to have paralleled that of the Essenes, may have been a member of this community. Several scrolls are on display in the Israel Museum in Jerusalem ( ⇨ See Exploring Jerusalem in Chapter 1).

A short film at the entrance introduces the mysterious sect that once lived here. Climb the tower for a good view, and note the unusual number of water channels and cisterns that gathered floodwater from the cliffs. Just below the tower (looking toward the Dead Sea) is a long room identified as the **scriptorium.** A plaster writing table and bronze and ceramic inkwells found here confirm that this was where the scrolls were written. A good air-conditioned cafeteria and gift store serve the site. ✣ *Rte. 90, 13 km (8 mi) south of Almog Junction* ☎ *02/994–2235* ⊕ *www. parks.org.il* 🎫 *NIS 18* ☷ *Apr.–Sept., daily 8–5; Oct.–Mar., daily 8–4.*

### Beaches & Pools

**Kalia Beach,** on the Dead Sea, has free mud, showers, and beach chairs, as well as towel rental, a gift shop, and a snack shop. ⊠ *3 km (2 mi) north of Qumran off Rte. 90* ☎ *02/994–2391* 🎫 *NIS 25* ☷ *Oct.–Mar., daily 8–5; Apr.–Sept., daily 8–6.*

**Biankini and Siesta Beach** has the most facilities in this area. As well as a beach, there is free mud, showers, towels for rent or purchase, changing rooms, a spa offering Dead Sea mineral treatments and massages, and a Moroccan-style restaurant. This beach has the only fresh-water swimming pool in the northern Dead Sea area, an attraction for those who prefer not to swim in the sea. There are fourteen bed-and-breakfast huts (approximately $100 per couple per night). Backpackers can pitch their own tents for 70 NIS per person per night. ⊠ *3 km (2 mi) north of Qumran off Rte. 90* ☎ *02/940–0266, 02/940–0033* ⊕ *www. biankini.co.il* 🎫 *NIS 30* ☷ *Oct.–Mar., daily 8–5; Apr.–Sept., daily 8–6.*

**Einot Zukim (Ain Fashkha)** is a nature reserve, with fresh (though brackish) springs, and many species of trees and reeds rare in the arid Judean

Desert. The most beautiful part of the reserve is closed to the general public to preserve its fragile ecosystem, but you can swim in the springs and a pool. Picnic and changing facilities are also available. ⊠ *3 km (2 mi) south of Qumran on Rte. 90* ☎ *02/994–2355* ⊕ *www.parks.org. il* ⊡ *NIS 23* ⊙ *Apr.–Sept., daily 8–5; Oct.–Mar., daily 8–4.*

**Mineral Beach** has easy sea access, sulfur pools, mud, showers, a freshwater wading pool for kids, and a snack shop. It also offers massage (reserve a few days in advance). ⊠ *20 km, or 12 ½ mi, south of Qumran on Rte. 90* ☎ *02/994–4888* ⊕ *www.dead-sea.co.il* ⊡ *Sun.–Thurs. NIS 36; Fri. and Sat. NIS 43* ⊙ *Sun.–Thurs. 9–5; Fri. and Sat. 8–5.*

### Shopping

**Kibbutz Mitzpe Shalem** (⊠ 20 km, or 12½ mi, south of Qumran on Rte. 90 ☎ 02/994–5117) manufactures the excellent Ahava skin- and hair-care products based on (but not smelling like) the Dead Sea minerals. The factory outlet here is open Sunday–Thursday from 8–5; Friday and Jewish holiday eves from 8–4; and Saturday from 8:30–5. The products are also sold elsewhere (at Masada, Qumran, and the Ein Gedi Spa, for example) and at pharmacies in major cities.

## Ein Gedi

★ *33 km (21 mi) south of Qumran, 20 km (12½ mi) north of Masada, 83 km (52 mi) southeast of Jerusalem.*

After miles of burnt brown and beige desert rock, the green lushness of the Ein Gedi oasis provides a vivid and welcome contrast. This is one of the most beautiful places in Israel—with everything from hiking trails to ancient ruins. Settled for thousands of years, it inspired the writer of the *Song of Songs* to describe his beloved "as a cluster of henna in the vineyards of Ein-Gedi."

**❺** A major attraction of the Ein Gedi Nature Reserve, **Nahal David** (David's Stream), is believed to be the place where David hid from the wrath of King Saul (I Samuel 24) 3,000 years ago. The clearly marked trail goes past several pools and small waterfalls to the beautiful top waterfall. There are many steps, but it's not too daunting. Allow at least 1¼ hours to include a refreshing dip under one of the lower waterfalls. Look out for ibex (wild goat), especially in the afternoon, and for the small, furry hyrax, often seen on tree branches. Leopards were rediscovered in this area some years ago but face extinction again because of breeding problems; they're seldom seen nowadays.

If you're a more serious hiker who is interested in further adventure, don't miss the trail that breaks off to the right 50 yards down the return path from the top waterfall. It passes the remains of Byzantine irrigation systems and offers breathtaking views of the Dead Sea. The trail doubles back on itself toward the source of Nahal David. Near the top, a short side path climbs to the remains of a 4th-millennium BC Chalcolithic Period temple. The main path leads on to the streambed, again turns east, and reaches Dudim (Lovers') Cave, formed by boulders and filled with crystal-clear spring water. You are directly above the waterfall of Nahal David (don't throw stones—there are people below). Since this trail involves a considerable climb (and hikers invariably take time to bathe in the "cave"), access to the trail is permitted only up to 3½ hours before closing time. Reaching Ein Gedi from the north, the first turnoff to the right is the parking lot at the entrance to Nahal David. ⊠ *Ein Gedi* ☎ *08/658–4285* ⊕ *www.parks.org.il* ⊠ *NIS 23 (includes admission to Nahal Arugot); combined day ticket for Nahal David, Nahal Arugot, and synagogue: NIS 26* ☉ *Sat.–Thurs. 8–4, Fri. 8–3; last admission 1 hr before closing.*

**❻** Although not quite as green as Nahal David, the deep canyon of **Nahal Arugot** is perhaps more spectacular. Enormous boulders and slabs of stone on the opposite cliff face seem poised in mid-cataclysm. The hour-long hike to the **Hidden Waterfall** (many steps, but not especially steep) goes by beautiful spots where the stream bubbles over rock shelves and shallow pools offer relief from the heat. If you're adventurous and have water shoes, you can return through the greenery of the streambed, leaping the boulders and wading the pools. ⊹ *From Nahal David parking lot, continue south through the date orchards of the kibbutz, follow signs to Nahal Arugot (no entrance from Rte. 90),* ⊠ *Ein Gedi* ☎ *08/658–4285* ⊕ *www. parks.org.il* ⊠ *NIS 23 (includes admission to Nahal David); combined day ticket for Nahal David, Nahal Arugot, and synagogue: NIS 26* ☉ *Sat.–Thurs. 8–4, Fri. 8–3; last admission 2 hrs before closing.*

**❼** Nestled between Nahal David and Nahal Arugot are the remains of a Jewish settlement from the late Roman and Byzantine periods (3rd to 6th centuries AD), including a **synagogue** and ritual purification bath. On the floor of the synagogue is an incription in Hebrew and Aramaic written into the mosaic tiles. The text invokes the wrath of heaven on various troublemakers, including "whoever reveals the secret of the town." The secret is believed to refer to a method of cultivating the balsam tree, which was used to make the prized perfume for which the town was once famous. ⊠ *From Nahal David parking lot, continue south a few hundred yards though the date orchards Ein Gedi* ☎ *08/658–4285* ⊕ *www.parks.org.il* ⊠ *NIS 12; combined day ticket with Nahal David and Nahal Arugot: NIS 26* ☉ *Sat.–Thurs. 8–4, Fri. 8–3.*

## Beaches & Pools

**Ein Gedi Spa** offers good facilities (indoor showers and changing rooms with lockers), access to the Dead Sea, a freshwater pool, free Dead Sea mud, and relaxing, warm indoor sulfur pools. Massages and treatments are available; advance reservation recommended. ⊠ *3 km (2 mi) south of Ein Gedi gas station* ☎ *08/659–4813* ⊕ *www.ein-gedi.co.il* ⊠ *Sun.–Fri. NIS 60, Sat. NIS 65, NIS 40 if accompanied by licensed guide* ☉ *Apr.–Sept., daily 8–6; Oct.–Mar., daily 8–5.*

A somewhat rocky **public beach,** 200 yards south of Nahal David behind the gas station, has free access to the Dead Sea. Freshwater showers (absolutely essential) by the water's edge and basic changing facilities are NIS 8. There is also an air-conditioned restaurant, gift shop, and 24-hr outdoor kiosk. Don't leave valuables unguarded. ⊹ *200 yards south of Nahal David parking lot, behind the Paz Gas station on Rte. 90* ☎ *08/659–4761* ⊠ *Free (shower NIS 8)* ☉ *Oct.–Mar., daily 8–5; Apr.–Sept., daily 8–6.*

## Where to Stay & Eat

**$$** ✕ **Pundak Ein Gedi.** The nondescript entrance to the restaurant can be somewhat misleading. In addition to offering a cool respite from the hot desert sun, this self-service restaurant has a large salad bar, as well as assorted cooked entrées. It's nothing fancy, but the food is good and wholesome. The outdoor kiosk is open 24 hours a day and has sandwiches, ice cream, snacks, and espresso. ✉ *Rte. 90, 200 yards south of Nahal David parking lot, behind the Paz Gas station* ☎ *08/659–4761* ▤ *AE, MC, V* ⊗ *No dinner.*

**$–$$** ▦ **Kibbutz Ein Gedi.** A country hotel on the kibbutz grounds is set between 1,600-ft-high cliffs and the Dead Sea and is surrounded by subtropical landscaping. A range of accommodations—from simple self-catering country-lodging units to deluxe rooms overlooking Nahal David—are available. Rates for all rooms (except the country lodging) include breakfast, another full meal, and unlimited entry to the nearby Ein Gedi Spa, to which there's a free shuttle throughout the day. ✛ *5 km (3 mi) south of the kibbutz on Rte. 90,* ✉ *M.P. Dead Sea 86980* ☎ *08/659–4220, 08/659–4221* ㅂ *08/658–4328* ⊕ *www.ein-gedi.co.il* ❧ *175 rooms* ⚭ *Kitchenettes, 2 tennis courts, pool; no room phones in some rooms* ▤ *AE, DC, MC, V* ⊗❙ *MAP.*

**¢** ▦ **Ein Gedi Youth Hostel.** This newly renovated lodging belongs to the YHA network. It has 280 beds in either dormitory or (far better) guest-house configurations, all with facilities en suite. ✛ *From Ein Gedi turnoff on Rte. 90, take an immediate right up the hill,* ✉ *M.P. Dead Sea 86980* ☎ *08/658–4165* ㅂ *08/658–4445* ⊕ *www.youth-hostels.org.il* ❧ *255 beds* ⚭ *Cafeteria; no room phones* ▤ *AE, DC, MC, V* ⊗❙ *BP.*

## Sports & the Outdoors

There is no problem hiking the area alone, on well-marked trails. In addition to the stunning landscape, this is one of the most popular, easily accessible, and well-serviced hiking areas in the country. It offers all types of easy hikes, from the short climb to the David Spring to many hours of steeper climbing. For advice on more serious trails and information on organized hikes, contact the **Society for the Protection of Nature in Israel** (✉ From Ein Gedi turnoff on Rte. 90, take an immediate right up the hill, field school, Ein Gedi ☎ 08/658–4350). They also offer accommodation.

# Masada

❽ *19 km (12 mi) south of Ein Gedi on Rte. 90, 103 km (64 mi) east and*
**Fodor'sChoice** *south of Jerusalem, 20 km (12½ mi) north of Ein Bokek.*
★
The isolated flattop rock of Masada is visible to the west of the highway from the approach. Its unusual, natural form forebodes its historical significance, famous as one of the opulent desert escape palaces of King Herod and the last stand of the less than 1,000 Jewish rebels in the Great Revolt against Rome. In recognition of its historical significance, it was the first site in Israel to be added to the UNESCO World Heritage List in 2001.

Most visitors take the **cable car** (three minutes) up Masada. Starting at 8 AM, it runs every half hour, with intermediate runs depending on demand. The intrepid climb the **Snake Path** (up to one hour of steep walking), some even going before dawn to watch the sunrise. Others take the easier, western Roman Ramp path, accessible only from Arad ( ⇨ *See* Exploring Eilat and the Negev *in* Chapter 7). It is imperative to drink lots of water and wear a hat. Water fountains (but no other refreshments) are available on Masada itself, so save bottles for refilling. Allow 1½ to 2 hours to explore the site. The most popular route heads counterclockwise, along the eastern side to the north, and comes back along the western side. If time allows, be sure to visit the southern area as well (especially the huge cistern and echo wall). Maps, a detailed brochure, and a very useful audio guide are available at the top entrance.

The entire mountaintop—less than 20 acres—is surrounded by a 4,250-ft-long **casemate,** a double wall that included living quarters and guardrooms. Most of the important buildings are concentrated in the high northern area. Walk through long storerooms where broken jars, seeds of grain, and dried fruit pits were found, bearing out Josephus's story that the Jews burned their possessions but spared their food supply to show the Romans that they did not die of want.

The **Northern Palace** is an extraordinary three-tiered structure that seems to hang off the highest and most northerly point of the mountain. The panoramic effect is awesome: baked brown precipices and bleached valleys shimmer in the midday glare. The lowest level is adorned with colorful wall frescoes and a private bathhouse. Perhaps the king's private residence, the palace was protected—from inside the fortress—by a plastered wall.

Clearly visible from the upper terrace are the Roman camps and "runner's path" (used for communication between the camps), as well as the Ein Gedi oasis, 16 km (10 mi) to the north, from which the Romans had to haul their water. The Jewish defenders used Herod's old system of channeling winter floodwaters from streams west of the mountain into huge cisterns in the slope of the mountain, and then hauled the water to the top by hand. By the time the Romans came, they had their supply "on tap."

The **bathhouse** (upon return from the upper terrace) was a state-of-the-art facility in Herod's time, with its *apodyterium* (changing room), *frigidarium, tepidarium,* and *caldarium* (cold, lukewarm, and hot rooms, respectively). Frescoes and floor tiles are evidence of the Herodian opulence; intrusive benches and a pool represent alterations by the later occupants. The caldarium was once a closed room, heated, sauna-style, from below, and through wall pipes by hot air pumped in from an outside furnace.

Two **mikvahs** (Jewish ritual baths) from the time of the revolt were found on Masada, creating a sensation after rabbis confirmed that the mikvahs had been built in accordance with Jewish law. They were astounded that even when under siege, the Jewish rebels had undertaken the difficult task of building mikvahs (which require "living," i.e. rain or spring, water) to ensure their ritual purity.

The **synagogue,** one of only four that have been uncovered from the Second Temple period, can be seen in the western casemate. The building's orientation toward Jerusalem suggested its function, but the stone benches (synagogue means "place of assembly") and the man-made pit for damaged scrolls (a genizah) confirmed it. It was likely here, in the community's spiritual center, that the leaders of the revolt against Rome made their fateful decision. In the summer of 2005, the rear genizah was renovated to house a permanent Torah scroll, which is used for bar and bat mitzvah (coming-of-age) ceremonies.

At an opening in the walls on the western edge, stand where the Roman legionnaires broke into Masada. The original wedge-shape **ramp** is below, though its upper part has since collapsed. The Western Gate leads to a modern trail down this side of the mountain (access via Arad only).

The small 5th-century **Byzantine chapel,** with mosaic floor and wall designs, is what remains of a small community of devout monks who sought solitude in the Judean Desert during the Byzantine Period. South of the chapel is the **Western Palace,** the largest structure on Masada and originally its residential and administrative center. Its most interesting features are two colorful Herodian mosaics, with meticulous geometric and fruit motifs.

If time and energy allow, explore the sparser, southern part of Masada, with its huge water cistern and spectacular view from the southern citadel. Test the echoes here while facing the great canyon to the south.

The new visitor center, alongside the lower cable-car station, offers a short movie, a model of Masada, some of the discovered artifacts, a photo gallery of the archaeological dig, and a store.

A fine summer-night diversion is the **sound-and-light show** (☎ 08/995-9333 ✉ NIS 41), accessible only from Arad at Masada's western base. Call ahead to verify show times. ⊠ *Off Rte. 90* ☎ *08/658–4207, 08/658–4208* ⊕ *www.parks.org.il* ✉ *Site and cable car (round-trip) NIS 61; site and cable car (1-way) NIS 45; site only (for walkers) NIS 23* ☉ *Apr.–Sept., Sat.–Thurs. 8–5 (last car up at 4, last down at 5), Fri. and Jewish holiday eves 8–3 (last car up at 2, last down at 3); Oct.–Mar., Sat.–Thurs. 8–4 (last car up at 3, last down at 4), Fri. and Jewish holiday eves 8–2 (last car up at 1, last down at 2).*

## Beaches & Pools

The **Ein Bokek** hotel district, about 10 minutes' drive south of Masada, has a free public beach with showers (between Kapulsky's and Hordos restaurants). Nonguests can pay to use the beaches and freshwater pools at the Lot, Tsell Harim, Caesar Premier, Crowne Plaza, Magic Nirvana, Hod, Le Meridien, and Sheraton Moriah. ⇨ *For more information on Ein Bokek, see* Chapter 7.

# CloseUp

# THE LAST STAND OF JEWISH FREEDOM AGAINST ROME

**MASADA WAS BUILT** in the 1st century BC by Herod the Great—King of the Jews by the grace of Rome. It was an impregnable yet palatial refuge, to which he could escape from his hostile subjects or from the military threats of Cleopatra, Queen of Egypt. Nowhere are both Herod's paranoia and sense of grandeur more evident.

The fortress was later the site of the dramatic last stand of Jewish rebels against Rome. With Herod's death in 4 BC and the exile of his son, Archelaus, 10 years later, the central part of the country came under direct Roman control. Decades of oppression and misrule precipitated the Great Revolt of the Jews in AD 66. After the Roman reconquest of the country and the fall of Jerusalem in AD 70, Masada became the last refuge for almost a thousand men, women, and children.

Roman Governor Silva came with thousands of troops and slaves to crush the last vestige of resistance. The Roman siege wall at the foot of the mountain and the eight Roman camps in strategic locations on all sides attest to the thoroughness of the siege. These are the most complete Roman siege works surviving in the world.

The 1st-century Jewish historian Josephus Flavius sets the final scene. Despite the Jews' vigorous defense, the Romans succeeded in constructing a massive earth assault ramp from the high western plateau to the summit of the mountain. Seeing that the battle was lost, the rebel leader, Elazar Ben Yair, assembled his warriors and exhorted them to "at once choose death with honor, and do the kindest thing we can for ourselves, our wives and children" rather than face the brutal consequences of capture. The decision was not easy, relates Josephus,

but once taken, each man had to "carry out his terrible resolve" without delay. Having dispatched their own families, the men then drew lots to select 10 executioners for the rest; the 10 similarly chose the last man, who would kill them all and afterward take his own life.

Josephus' melodramatic account has been suspect in the eyes of some historians, not least of all because he had gone over to the Romans during the revolt. Archaeologists and historians are still arguing over whether the artifacts discovered—including human skeletal remains and inscribed potsherds (the lots, perhaps?)—prove the veracity of his account.

The message of the Jews' last stand on Masada was not lost on Jews fighting for independence in the 1930s and '40s, or on the modern Israel they created. "Masada shall not fall again!" became a rallying cry and a state of mind, reflecting the resolve of many Jews (made more poignant by the Nazi Holocaust) for self-determination. The legacy of Masada is still hotly debated within contemporary Israel, as the society continues to define its identity.

### Where to Stay

Lodging at Masada itself is fairly limited, however about 15 km (9 mi) south of Masada are the excellent hotels of Ein Bokek ( ⇨ *See* Beersheva to Ein Bokek *in* Chapter 7).

**$** 🖼 **Masada Guest House.** This new 280-bed hostel is an inexpensive option at the foot of Masada. Part of the YHA network, it has single, double, and family rooms, each with their own en-suite facilities. There is also a swimming pool. ⊠ *Off Rte. 90 at the entrance to Masada* 🕾 *08/ 995–3222* 🖨 *08/658–4650* ⊕ *www.youth-hostels.org.il* ♿ *Refrigerators, pool* ❘⊙❘ *BP.*

# WEST OF JERUSALEM

The rugged and reforested Judean Hills tumble down to the west, eventually easing into the gentler terrain of the Shefelah lowlands. This is a region of forested landscapes, biblical ghosts, and ancient fingerprints. It's also the fastest-growing wine-producing area in the country. Its new wine route includes over two dozen vineyards. A number of local farmers also produce goat and sheep cheese.

There are many approaches from Jerusalem (though all sites are accessible from Tel Aviv as well). The most scenic takes in the exquisite Sorek stalactite cave in the Avshalom Nature Reserve, before heading down to Bet Shemesh and points south. From Mt. Herzl, in West Jerusalem, descend through Ein Kerem. One kilometer (½ mile) beyond the neighborhood is the Kerem Junction. Continue straight (left fork) on Route 386. On the hills to the left is the Hadassah Hospital complex ( ⇨ *See* West Jerusalem *in* Chapter 1). Most of these hillsides have the terraced effect of the natural strata of sedimentary limestone; many were laboriously widened by farmers over the centuries by enclosing them with drystone walls. One of the landscape's dominant features is the reforestation of the hills, an attempt to reverse the decimation of ancient woodlands, provide recreation areas, and restore the habitat of animals such as the gazelle.

The road crosses the Jerusalem–Tel Aviv railway line, where the Refaim Valley merges with Nahal Sorek, and at once begins climbing, offering fine views of the deep gorge below. At the Bar Giora Junction (a T-junction) turn right onto Route 3866 and follow the signs to the cave. Back up the road, just before the turn down Route 3855 to Bet Shemesh, is the Ya'aran Farm on the left, which produces some of the finest local goat cheese. Continue on to join Route 38 south.

An alternative is to take Route 1, the main Jerusalem–Tel Aviv highway. Ten kilometers (6 miles) west of Jerusalem, Route 425 turns off to the Arab village of Abu Ghosh with its fine guest houses. Abu Ghosh also has several excellent Middle Eastern restaurants on its main street. A very popular music festival is held in local churches during the spring Shavuot and fall Sukkot festivals. Farther down Route 1, in several places by the roadside, are trucks and armored cars preserved as memorials to those who died in the 1948 War of Independence. Many supply convoys attempting to relieve the siege on the Jewish side of Jerusalem were ambushed on the steep and winding road.

Twenty kilometers (13 miles) west of Jerusalem is the Sha'ar Hagai Interchange, where the rugged Judean Hills suddenly give way to the low hills of the Shefelah. There is a gas station on the right. To the left of the road are two restored old buildings, once the overnight caravansary or inn for the two-day journey from Jaffa to Jerusalem.

## Judean Hills Wine Route

Halfway between Tel Aviv and Jerusalem is the fastest-growing wine-producing region in Israel. There's significant archaeological evidence—including dozens of ancient wine presses—that people have made wine here for millennia. The diversity of soil, climate, and altitude allows for a wide range of wine to be produced in the relatively small area between the Mediterranean Sea and the Judean Mountains.

Until recently good Israeli wine was an oxymoron. Traditionally, Israeli wine was a sweet beverage (affectionately described as "cough syrup") used for sacramental purposes. No more than a handful of vineyards were in production. There's been tremendous growth in the past twenty years—primarily as a result of the international success of vineyards from the Golan Heights and Upper Galilee, the most modern technology, internationally trained winemakers, and the discerning preferences of well-travelled Israelis familiar with the wonders of cabernet, merlot, chardonnay, and muscat. Today, one can go into a good wine store and be faced with the wonderful quandry of trying to choose the most appropriate wine from a wide selection of over 75 vineyards. Welcome to the Israeli viniculture revolution!

The Judean Hills Wine Route includes over two dozen vineyards. A few have produced wine for decades, but most have opened in the past several years. The majority are close to Route 38, north and south of Bet Shemesh. Since most vineyards are "boutique"—producing less than 100,000 bottles per year—few have visitors' centers that encourage drop-in visits and offer regularly scheduled tours. It's important to call in advance.

The best way to experience the viniculture of this area is to visit a few vineyards, buy some wine and local goat and sheep cheese, and find a picnic area to enjoy the wonderful flavors of Israel. There are many well-marked and easily accessible reforested picnic spots maintained by the Jewish National Fund throughout the region.

**⑪** One of the first vineyards in the area, **Kibbutz Tzora,** produces some excellent red wines. Be sure to taste some of their homemade olive oil and honey, interesting deli items, and goat and sheep cheeses. Breakfast and a light lunch are served in the outdoor garden. You can also buy a picnic basket—complete with tablecloth, plates, wine, cheeses, and salad—and explore one of the picnic spots in the area. ✛ *300 yds south of Bet Shemesh on Rte. 38, take western turn off toward Kibbutz Tzora (Zora on the sign). Follow signs to wine store.* ☎ *02/990–8261, 02/990–8278*

🖳 *02/991–5479* ⊕ *www.tzorawines.com* ◷ *Sun.–Thurs. 10–5, Fri. and Jewish holiday eves 10–2; call ahead to verify.*

⑬ Next to the Deir Raffat monastery is **Mony Wines,** one of the more interesting vineyards in the area. The Arab Christian Artul family moved here from the Galilee to farm olives on land leased from the adjacent Catholic monastery, later planting vineyards too. Still a family-run business, the vineyard became kosher (manufactured by orthodox Jews and under rabbinic supervision) in 2004 to allow it to sell wine to religious Jews. The shop sells their wines, mostly reds, but also chardonnay and muscat, as well as olives and olive oil. ⊹ *4 km (2½mi) west of Kibbutz Tzora, near Deir Raffat Monastery* 🕾 *02/991–6629* 🖳 *02/991–0366* ◷ *Daily 9:30–5:30; call ahead to verify.*

★ ⑩ The largest wine producer in the area is **Ella Valley Vineyards,** a "stone's throw" away from where David slew Goliath. Although this young winery produced its first harvest in 2002, ancient winepresses from the Byzantine Period attest to the region's historical importance for the production of wine. It offers a number of outstanding, top-quality wines including cabernet, merlot, chardonnay, and muscat. Don't miss the changing art exhibit of Israeli artists in the visitor's center. ⊹ *10 km (6½ mi) south of Bet Shemesh on Rte. 38, turn left into Kibbutz Netiv Ha Lamed Hey, immediate left toward industrial zone, look for signs* 🕾 *02/999–4885* 🖳 *02/999–4876* ⊕ *www.ellavalley.com* ◷ *Sun.–Thurs. 8:30–4:30, Fri. and Jewish holiday eves. 8:30–12:30; by appointment only.*

⑭ Close to Latrun, **Nachshon Winery** is run by a kibbutz that also produces very tasty hard and soft sheep cheese. The shop sells wine (only reds) and close to a dozen cheeses, including feta, haloumi, brie, and camembert. The outdoor garden is a great spot to enjoy a glass of wine and a cheese plate. Drop in to the shop or call in advance to arrange a tour of the winery, vineyard, and ancient winepress. ⊹ *Kibbutz Nachshon, 2 km (1¼ mi) south of Latrun, off Rte. 3* 🕾 *08/927–8641* 🖳 *08/927–8607* ◷ *Sun.–Thurs. 9–4, Fri. 9–3, Sat. 10–5.*

⑫ The popular but small **Ya'aran Farm,** run by the Ya'aran family, produces over 10 varieties of hard and soft goat cheese as well as yogurt. It's best to come on a Saturday, when they also bake their own bread. ⊹ *On Rte. 3866 en route to the Sorek Cave* 🕾 *02/999–7811* ◷ *Call for hours.*

★ ⑨ The **Tzuk Farm,** nestled in the hills south of the Ella Valley, offers a rich culinary experience. Two brothers have created a tranquil farm that produces fabulous goat cheese, wine, olives, olive oil, and pomegranates. Reservations are essential for meals, which include a platter of cheeses, fresh bread, and seasonal salads. Be sure to try the fennel root salad sprinkled with pomegranates, the beet root in sour *labaneh,* and the spicy roasted eggplant. Picnic baskets with wine, tablecloth, cheese, and salads are also available. ⊹ *Take eastern turn off south of Ella Valley Junction (Rtes 38 and 375), 2 km (1¼ mi) down dirt road* 🕾 *054/523–9117, 054/523–9118* ◷ *Call for hours.*

## Sorek Cave

★ ⑮   *25 km (17 mi) southwest of Jerusalem on Rtes. 386 and 3866, 12 km (7 ½ mi) east of Bet Shemesh on Rte. 3855.*

The Sorek Cave, within the Avshalom Reserve, contains every type of stalactite formation currently known. It was discovered when a routine blast in the nearby quarry tore away the rock face, revealing a subterranean wonderland.

Colored lights are used to highlight the stones' natural whites and honey browns. Local guides have given the stalactite forms nicknames like "macaroni," "curtains," and "sombreros." In a series of "interfaith" images, some find rocky evocations of Moses, the Madonna and Child, Buddha, and the Ayatollah Khomeini. Photography is allowed only on Friday morning, when there are no guided tours. Despite the almost 100% humidity, the temperature in the cave is comfortable year-round.

A set of steps winds down to the cave entrance—visitors with mobility concerns should bear in mind the climb back to the parking lot. Local guides take groups as they arrive into the cave every 15 minutes for a 30-minute tour (English tours on request and dependent on demand). A video in an acclimatization room (English version available) explains how the cave was formed. ⊠ *Avshalom Reserve, Rte. 3866* ☎ *02/991–1117* ⊕ *www.parks.org.il* ✍ *NIS 23* ⊙ *Apr.–Sept., Sat.–Thurs. 8–5, Fri. 8–3; Oct.–Mar., Sat.–Thurs. 8–4, Fri. 8–1; last entry 1¼ hour before closing.*

### Where to Stay

There are four very good kibbutz guest houses in wooded enclaves of the Judean Hills, 15–20 minutes' drive west of Jerusalem. All have commanding hilltop views, quiet surroundings, very comfortable if not luxurious accommodations, and good swimming pools.

$$   🏨 **Belmot at Kibbutz Tzuba.** This all-suites kibbutz hotel offers fun family activities. There is a children's entertainment park (one of the country's most popular), tennis courts, a swimming pool, and a cycling sports center. Hikes to historical and archaeolgical sites in the area are also available. Suites can accommodate up to five people and include two rooms, a porch with a magnificent view of the Judean Hills, and a kitchenette. Try to come on a Friday to sample cheeses, fish, and salads as part of the hotel's unique Friday brunch. ⊠ *12 km (7½ mi) west of Jerusalem, Rte. 395 M.P. Judean Hills 90870* ☎ *02/534–7090* 🖶 *02/534–7091* ⊕ *www.belmont.co.il* ✍ *64 suites* ⅋ *Tennis courts, pool, bicycles* ⊟ *AE, DC, MC, V* ⑩ *BP.*

$$   🏨 **Ma'aleh Hahamisha.** This large guesthouse, spread over beautiful landscaped gardens, has a health club, including an indoor heated pool, gym, saunas, and whirlpool baths. Some rooms lead to a garden patio. A few have a shower only. ⊠ *14 km (9 mi) west of Jerusalem, north of Rte. 1, M.P. Judean Hills 90835* ☎ *02/533–1331* 🖶 *02/533–1330* ⊕ *www.inisrael.com/maale5* ✍ *239 rooms* ⅋ *Indoor pool, gym, health club, hot tub, sauna* ⊟ *AE, DC, MC, V* ⑩ *BP.*

$–$$   🏨 **Shoresh.** This guesthouse has a diversity of offerings, including simple country lodging units (similar to a motel), hotel rooms in a central building, and more luxurious suites. The swimming pool (open in summer months only) also has a very attractive children's pool with slides and fountains. ⊠ *15 km (8½ mi) west of Jerusalem, south of Rte. 1, 88 M.P. Judean Hills 90860* ☎ *02/533–8338* ⊞ *02/534–0262* ⊕ *www. shoresh.co.il* ⇙ *20 country lodging units, 70 rooms, 40 suites* ⚐ *Pool, wading pool* ⊟ *AE, DC, MC, V* ⑩ *BP.*

★ $ ⌸ **Neve Ilan.** A cut above its neighbors, this hotel has larger and better-furnished rooms. Superior-grade rooms and minisuites with their own whirlpool baths are available. The pool is covered year-round and heated in winter, and there is a well-equipped exercise room. ⊠ *15 km (10 mi) west of Jerusalem, north of Rte. 1, M.P. Judean Hills 90850* ☎ *02/ 533–9339* ⊞ *02/533–9335* ⊕ *www.shalomplaza.co.il/neve-ilan* ⇙ *160 rooms* ⚐ *Some in-room hot tubs, pool, gym* ⊟ *AE, DC, MC, V* ⑩ *BP.*

## Latrun

*25 km (16 mi) west of Jerusalem on Rte. 1.*

Latrun is the high ground that projects into and dominates the western side of the Ayalon Valley. A natural passage between the coastal plain and the Judean Hills, the valley has been a battleground throughout history, from the conquests of the biblical Israelite leader Joshua in the 13th century BC, through the Maccabean campaigns of the 2nd century BC, to the conflicts of modern times.

Coming from Jerusalem on Route 1, exit onto Route 3 (the Modi'in and Ashkelon–Beersheba road), about 5 km (3 mi) west of the Sha'ar Hagai gas station. At the T-junction, turn right for Emmaus and Canada Park, left for the Trappist Monastery of Latrun, the Latrun Armored Corps Museum, and Mini Israel.

The New Testament (Luke 24) records one of Jesus's appearances after ⑯ his resurrection on the road to **Emmaus.** The traditional text places the site "60 stadia" (about 11 km or 7 mi) from Jerusalem, but other ancient sources talk of "160 stadia" (about 29 km or 18 mi), a confusion that has spawned several rival sites. The enduring Arabic name of this place—Imwas—seems to echo the ancient name and may strengthen its claims of authenticity. Within the remains of Byzantine mosaic floors and a 5th-century basilica is the ruined but better-preserved Crusader church of the 12th century. ⊠ *Rte. 3, 100 yards toward Modi'in from the junction with Rte. 1* ☎ *08/925–6940* ⚑ *3 NIS* ☉ *Mon.–Fri. 8:30–noon and 2:30–5:30, Sat. 8:30–5.*

The name "Latrun" is thought to derive from "La Toron de Chevaliers" (the Tower of the Knights), the French name of the Crusader castle that occupied the crest of the hill (behind the present Trappist monastery) in the 12th century. Eight centuries later, the British erected a concrete fortress for much the same reason: to secure the road to Jerusalem. Jordanian troops took the site in the 1948 war but lost it to Israel in 1967. ⑰ Today it is the flag-bedecked national memorial site of the **Latrun Armored Corps Museum,** offering visitors grand views, a movie (call to inquire about English showtimes), and an outside exhibit of some 100 varieties of tanks that have fought in the region. The site is about 1 km (½ mi) south of Route 1, on Route 3 (the Ashkelon–Beersheba highway). A decent restaurant, offering salads and hot meals, serves the site. ⊠ *Yad La'Shiryon, M.P. Shimshon* ☎ *08/925-5268 or 08/924-6722* ⊕ *www. arcm-latrun.org.il* ⎙ *NIS 30* ۞ *Sun.–Thurs. 8:30–4:30, Fri. and Jewish holiday eves 8:30 AM–12:30 PM, Sat. and Jewish holidays 9–4.*

⑱ In dramatic contrast to the angular raw concrete of the fortress are the graceful facade and soft green groves and vineyards of the **Trappist Abbey of Latrun,** built in the early 20th century. The interior of the church (access only to the entrance) is an odd mix of round neo-Byzantine arches and apses and the soaring ceiling that seems Gothic in inspiration. Survivors of the Cistercian Order suppressed in the French Revolution, the Trappists keep a vow of silence, with exceptions made for the monks who run the monastery's wine and olive oil operation. ⊠ *Rte. 3 South, 2 km (1.5 mi) off Rte. 1* ☎ *08/922–0065* ۞ *Church: Apr.–Sept., Mon.–Sat. 8:30–noon and 3:30–5; Oct.–Mar., Mon.–Sat. 8:30–11 and 2:30–4. Wine shop: Apr.–Sept., Mon.–Sat. 8:30–6; Oct.–Mar., Mon.–Sat. 8:30–5:30.*

🍴 ⑲ **Mini Israel,** 1 km (⅔ mi) south of Latrun on Route 424, is one of the newest and most popular attractions in Israel. Designed in the shape of the Star of David, the world's largest miniature city is spread over 13 acres and contains over 350 exact replica models of the most important historical, national, religious, and natural sites in the country. The thousands of miniature "residents" have been meticulously created to present not just the physical, but also the cultural, religious, and social aspects of contemporary Israel. A walk through the park allows visitors to see and hear the people of different faiths and cultures that make up the human landscape of the country. Looking out of the park, you can even see a few of the neighboring real sites while examining their replicas. Mini Israel is an excellent way to start off or wrap up a visit to Israel. ⊠ *99762 Mobile Post Shimshon* ☎ *08/922–2444* 🖷 *08/920–4546* ⊕ *www.minisrael.co.il* ⎙ *NIS 56, audio guide NIS 10* ۞ *Nov.–Mar., Sun.–Thurs. and Sat. 10–6, Fri. and Jewish holiday eves 10–2; Apr.–Oct., Sun.–Thurs. and Sat. 10–8, Fri. and Jewish holiday eves 10–2.*

**off the beaten path**

Halfway between Jerusalem and Tel Aviv is the 625-acre "Biblical landscape reserve" of **NEOT KEDUMIM** (Oasis of Antiquity) – The country's biblical landscape has been re-created here to help visitors understand and visualize how the Bible uses the imagery of the native flora to convey its messages and values. Ancient terraces and wine and oil presses were excavated and restored, thousands of trees and shrubs were planted, and pools and cisterns were dug. A network of roads and walking paths (most of them paved and wheelchair-accessible) allows for a leisurely exploration of the site. Take one of the self-guided tours (brochures and maps in English provided) or inquire ahead of time about guided tours in English. Allow two hours minimum for the visit. ⊠ *40 km (25 mi) west of Jerusalem on Rte. 443* ☎ *08/977–0777* ⊕ *www.n-k.org.il* ⎙ *NIS 25* ۞ *Sun.–Thurs. 8:30–4, Fri. and Jewish holiday eves 8:30–1.*

### Where to Eat

**$$ ✕ Nof Latroun.** This self-service Kosher cafeteria has both indoor seating as well as outdoor picnic tables. Inside, indulge in one of the main hot meals (fish or meat), or partake of the cold salad bar. This is a good place to try the staple Israeli food, "shnitzel and chips" (breaded and fried chicken or turkey breast served with french fries). Sandwiches and ice cream are available at the outdoor window. ✉ *Across the parking lot from the Latrun Armored Corps Museum* ☎ *08/920–1670* ▭ *AE, MC, V* ⊘ *No dinner Fri. Closed Sat.*

## Bet Shemesh

*12 km (7½ mi) west of Sorek Cave on Rtes. 3855 and 38, 35 km (22 mi) west of Jerusalem.*

The modern town of Bet Shemesh takes its name from its ancient predecessor, now entombed by the tell on a rise on Route 38, 2 km (1 mi) south of the town's main entrance. This is Samson country. Samson, one of the judges of Old Testament Israel, is better known for his physical prowess and lust for Philistine women than for his shining spiritual qualities, but it was here, "between Zorah and Eshta'ol," that "the Spirit of the Lord began to stir him" (Judges 13). Today, Eshta'ol is a moshav (a cooperative settlement composed of individual farms) a few minutes' drive north, and Tzora (Zorah) is the kibbutz immediately to the west.

**㉕** On Route 38 south, and under 2 km (1 mi) from the Tzora turnoff, the road rises over the low-profile **Tel Bet Shemesh.** There is a clearing to pull off the road on the right (only southbound). From the top of the tell there is a fine view of the fields of Nahal Sorek, where Samson dallied with Delilah (Judges 16). When the Philistines captured the Israelite Ark of the Covenant in battle (11th century BC), they found that their prize brought divine retribution with it, destroying their idol Dagon and afflicting their bodies with tumors and their cities with rats (I Samuel 5). In consternation and awe, the Philistines rid themselves of the jinxed ark by sending it back to the Israelites at Bet Shemesh. ✛ *Rte. 38, 2 km (1 mi) from Tzora turnoff.*

## Ella Valley

**㉑** *10 km (6 mi) south of Bet Shemesh, 42 km (26 mi) west of Jerusalem.*

The Ella Valley is one of those delightful places—not uncommon in Israel—where you can relate the scenery to a specific biblical text and confirm the maxim that once you've visited this country, you'll never read the Bible the same way again.

Just beyond the junction of Route 38 with Route 383, and up to the right above the pine-wood slopes, is a distinctively bald flattop hill, **Tel Azekah,** the site of an ancient Israelite city. The hills are especially delightful in spring when the wildflowers are out.

In the Ella Valley, the road crosses a usually dry streambed; 200 yards beyond it is a place to pull off and park. If you have a Bible, open it to

I Samuel 17 and read about the dramatic duel between David and the giant Philistine champion Goliath. The battle probably took place close to where you're standing. Skeptical? Review the following passage:

*Now the Philistines gathered their armies for battle; and they were gathered at Socoh, which belongs to Judah* [identified by a mound 800 yards east of the junction ahead of you], *and encamped between Socoh and Azekah* [your location] . . . *And Saul and the men of Israel were gathered, and encamped in the valley of Ella, and drew up in line of battle against the Philistines. And the Philistines stood on the mountain on the one side, and Israel stood on the mountain on the other side, with a valley between them.*

Look east up the valley (across the road) to the mountains of Judah in the distance and the road from Bethlehem—the same road by which David reached the battlefield. The white northern ridge, a spur of the mountains of Judah, may have been the camp of the Israelite army. The southern ridge (where the gas station is today)—including Tel Socoh, where the Philistines gathered—ascends from the Philistine territory to the west. The creek is the only one in the valley: "And David . . . chose five smooth stones from the brook . . . ; his sling was in his hand, and he drew near to the Philistine." The rest, as they say, is history: Goliath was slain, the Philistines were routed, and David went on to become the darling of the nation and eventually its king.

en route

Between the Ella Junction (Routes 38 and 375) and Bet Guvrin, some 10 km (6 mi) to the south, the sharp eye can pick out evidence of the 2nd–3rd century AD Roman road that ran from coastal Ashkelon through the Ella Valley to Bethlehem and Jerusalem. Look for small standing milestones above the road to the right, about 1½ km (1 mi) south of the Ella Junction, and another group of stones and long sections of the terrace where the road once ran, to the left of the road farther south.

## Tel Maresha & Bet Guvrin

*21 km (13 mi) south of Bet Shemesh, 52 km (33 mi) southwest of Jerusalem.*

★ ❷ The flattop mound of ancient Maresha, known today as **Tel Maresha**, was already the site of an important city in the Israelite period (early 1st millennium BC); but it was during the Hellenistic period (4th–2nd centuries BC) that the endless complexes of chalk caves were excavated. Maresha was finally destroyed by the Parthians in 40 BC, and replaced by the nearby Roman city of Bet Guvrin.

The Bet Guvrin-Maresha national park is a wonderland, both under the ground and above it. The antiquities sprawl around the kibbutz of Bet Guvrin, just beyond the junction of Routes 30 and 35. These are bits and pieces of the 2nd- to 3rd-century AD Bet Guvrin, renamed (around the year 200) Eleuthropolis, "the city of free men." The amphitheater— an arena for blood sports—is one of only a few discovered in Israel, and the only one visitors can enter (via the parking lot of the gas station).

The ruins of a 12th-century church are virtually the only evidence of the Crusader town of Bethgibelin.

After entering the park, drive toward the tell, where remains from the Old Testament period are visible at the corner of the mound. The view from the tell is worth the short climb.

Ancient Mareshans excavated thousands of underground chambers around the tell to extract soft chalk bricks, with which they built their homes aboveground. Residents then turned their "basement" quarries into industrial complexes, including water cisterns, olive oil presses, and **columbarium** (derived from the Latin word *columba,* meaning dove or pigeon). The birds were used in ritual sacrifice, and as food, producers of fertilizer, and message carriers.

The most interesting and extensive **cave system** is just off the road on the opposite side of the tell (at a parking lot, the trail begins through the posts, and down to the left). It includes water cisterns, storerooms, and a restored ancient olive press. The excitement of exploration makes this sight a must for kids (with close parental supervision, though the safety features are good), but the many steps are physically demanding.

After leaving this system, make sure to continue walking down the hill to visit the **Sidonian Burial Caves.** These magnificent 3rd- to 2nd-century BC tombs—adorned with colorful, restored frescoes and inscriptions—give insight and important archaeological evidence as to the nature of the town's ancient residents.

On a ridge to the north of Tel Maresha, look for a large **apse** standing in splendid isolation. Known as Santahanna in Arabic, it has been identified by scholars as a remnant of the Crusader Church of St. Anne. Other fascinating but undeveloped complexes of caves near the tell have dangerous pits and are off-limits to visitors. Keep to the marked sites only. The brochure at the entrance has a good map of the site.

Archaeological Seminars, in Jerusalem, runs a program at the park called **Dig for a Day** (☎ 02/586–2011 ⊕ www.archesem.com ✉ US$25, not including park admission fee). The three-hour activity includes supervised digging in a real excavation inside a cave, into which local inhabitants dumped earth and artifacts 21 centuries ago. Participants then sift the buckets of dirt they have hauled out of the cave, looking for finds. Some museum-quality artifacts of the 3rd–2nd centuries BC (Hellenistic Period) have been uncovered here. (No, you can't take home what you find!) The participants are then led on a fun 30-minute exploration through unexcavated caves not yet open to the public. This involves some crawling, because some spaces are too tight or too low to do anything else. Those who prefer to pass on that experience can just wait for the last component—a short talk in the pottery shed about how clay vessels are restored from sherds. Individuals can join this program on Fridays by prior reservation, though groups are sometimes organized on other days if there is a demand. ✉ *Off Rte. 35, 21 km (13 mi) south of Bet Shemesh* ☎ *08/681–1020* ⊕ *www.parks.org.il* ✉ *NIS 23 (includes entrance to Bet Guvrin)* ☉ *Apr.–Sept., Sat.–Thurs. 8–5, Fri.*

# THE WEST BANK

**THE WEST BANK** is that part of the onetime British Mandate of Palestine, west of the Jordan River, that was occupied by the Kingdom of Transjordan in its war with Israel in 1948 and annexed shortly afterward. That country then changed its name to the Hashemite Kingdom of Jordan to reflect its new territorial reality. The territory was lost to Israel in the Six-Day War of 1967 and, with the exception of recently autonomous areas (mostly urban), has remained under Israeli military administration ever since. In Israel itself, the region is often referred to as "the territories," "over the Green Line" (a term denoting the pre-1967 border between the West Bank and Israel), or by its biblical names Yehuda (or Judea, the area south of Jerusalem), and Shomron (or Samaria, the much larger area north of Jerusalem).

The West Bank is a kidney-shape area, a bit larger than the U.S. state of Delaware and almost half the size of Northern Ireland. The large majority of the approximately two million Arabs is Muslim, with the Christian minority living mostly in the greater Bethlehem area and Ramallah.

In the mid- and late-1990s, the Oslo Accords—a series of negotiated agreements between Israel and the Palestinians—transferred most of the Gaza Strip, all the West Bank Arab towns, and some hinterland to Palestinian control. A much-sought-after final status agreement proved elusive, however, as there were seemingly irreconcilable rival stands on the thorny questions of land, refugees, and Jerusalem. In 2000 the simmering crisis exploded with lethal ferocity as young Palestinian Arabs took to the streets. In the summer of 2005, Israel unilaterally withdrew from all of the Gaza Strip and from four of the northern settlements in Samaria. Although violence has subsided significantly, security for visitors to the West Bank and the future of the peace process were uncertain at press time.

The Jewish population in the West Bank is approximately 225,000, dispersed in a handful of small towns and more than 125 village communities. Although some of the towns are really suburbs of Jerusalem and Tel Aviv, other settlements were set up by nationalist Israelis who see the region as an integral and inalienable part of their ancient homeland. They consider the almost miraculous "homecoming" of 1967 as a first rumble of the messianic age. With its prime location—within 14 km (9 mi) of the Mediterranean Sea—and its mountain heights—dominating Israel's main population centers—the West Bank has a strategic value that has convinced even many moderate Israelis that it would be folly to relinquish it to potentially hostile Arab control. A person's attitude toward the questions of continuing settlement in the West Bank and the ultimate status of the region is an important touchstone of political affiliation in Israel. The country is completely divided on these issues.

Tourists can travel to Bethlehem and Jericho as political and security conditions permit. At press time, Israeli citizens were instructed by the Israel Defense Forces not to visit areas under Palestinian Authority control. In the fall of 2005, the IDF opened a new terminal between Jerusalem and Bethlehem; final passage arrangements were not worked out, but have your passport ready. If taking a taxi, sherut (shared taxi), or bus from Arab East Jerusalem, you must take a local bus or taxi from the Bethlehem side of the terminal to Manger Square. Because of some unrest, it's best to avoid other Arab parts of the West Bank entirely. Please check your government's travel advisory before visiting these areas, and always exercise caution.

and Jewish holiday eves 8–4; Oct.–Mar., Sat.–Thurs. 8–4, Fri. and Jewish holiday eves 8–3.

**22** The great "bell caves" of **Bet Guvrin** date from the Late Roman, Byzantine, and even Early Arab periods (2nd–7th century AD), when the locals created a quarry to extract lime for cement. At the top of each bell-shaped space is a hole through the 4-ft-thick stone crust of the ground. When the ancient diggers reached the soft chalk below, they began reaming out their quarry in the structurally secure bell shape, each bell eventually cutting into the one adjacent to it. Although not built to be inhabited, the caves may have been used as refuges by early Christians. In the North Cave, a cross high on the wall, at the same level as an Arabic inscription, suggests a degree of coexistence even after the Arab conquest of the area in AD 636. ⊠ *Off Rte. 35, 21 km (13 mi) south of Bet Shemesh* ☎ *08/681–1020* ⊕ *www.parks.org.il* ⊡ *NIS 23* ☉ *Apr.–Sept., Sat.–Thurs. 8–5, Fri. and Jewish holiday eves 8–4; Oct.–Mar., Sat.–Thurs. 8–4, Fri. and Jewish holiday eves 8–3.*

An attractive alternative route back to Jerusalem is Route 375 through the Ella Valley, past Israel's main satellite communications receiver, and up through wooded hill country to Tzur Hadassah (look out for the rock-hewn Roman road on the right). Route 386 heads off to the left and runs north to Jerusalem through rugged mountain scenery, emerging in the Ein Kerem neighborhood on the city's western edge. Continuing on Route 375 takes you to Bethlehem, or on to Jerusalem along the faster "tunnels" route, entering the city at the southern Gilo neighborhood. Use this route only if the Bethlehem area itself is peaceful. For security reasons, avoid Route 35 from Bet Guvrin to Hebron.

# BETHLEHEM

**24** The birthplace of Jesus is a mere 10 minutes' drive from Jerusalem. Upon
Fodor'sChoice leaving Jerusalem, look for the large buildings of Kibbutz Ramat Rahel
★ on the hill to the left. This was an important Israeli position in the War of Independence of 1948, and then a border outpost in the years that followed. The next ridge is capped by the Greek Orthodox monastery of Mar Elias (St. Elijah) and immediately beyond it is the first view of Bethlehem. Even from a distance, the town is easily identified by the minarets and church steeples that struggle for control of its skyline. On the eastern horizon is a prominent flattop hill. This is Herodion, one of Herod's great palace-fortresses, later used by the Zealots in the Great Revolt against Rome (AD 66–73) and by Bar Kochba's fighters in the 2nd century AD. Note that Bethlehem is now an autonomous Palestinian enclave, with all security and tourism matters in the hands of the Palestinian Authority.

**Rachel's Tomb,** the only Israeli enclave in a Palestinian area, is on the right shortly after passing the Israeli army roadblock. Its once-landmark white dome is now invisible behind a security wall. The Bible relates that the matriarch Rachel, second and favorite wife of Jacob, died in childbirth on the outskirts of Bethlehem, "and Jacob set up a pillar upon her grave" (Genesis 35).

The present building, behind the security wall, is probably medieval, with 19th-century additions. There is no vestige of Jacob's original pillar, but the large, velvet-draped cenotaph inside the building has been hallowed by observant Jews for centuries as the site of Rachel's tomb. People come to pray here for good health and fertility. Some pilgrims wind a red thread seven times around the tomb, and give away snippets of it as talismans to cure all ills. Many beggars offer it for sale for a charitable contribution near the Western Wall in Jerusalem.

Rachel is venerated by Islam as well. Next to the tomb is a Muslim cemetery, reflecting the Middle Eastern tradition that it is a special privilege to be buried near a great personage. ⊠ *Rte. 60, a few hundred yards past the Israeli checkpoint* ☒ *Free* ☉ *Sun.–Thurs. 8–5, Fri. and Jewish holiday eves 8–1.*

Immediately beyond the checkpoint, take a local taxi or bus along Manger Street to **Manger Square.** Manger Street winds past gift shops and religious institutions. To the east are occasional panoramas of what geographers call "marginal land"—still more or less arable, but very close to the desert. The fields of the adjacent town of Beit Sahour are traditionally identified with the biblical story of Ruth the Moabite, daughter-in-law of Naomi, who "gleaned in the field" of Boaz, Naomi's kinsman. Boaz eventually "took Ruth and she became his wife" (Ruth 4); it was in Bethlehem that their great-grandson, King David, was born. The same fields are identified by Christian tradition as those where shepherds "keeping watch over their flock by night" received word of the birth of Jesus in Bethlehem (Luke 2). Several denominations maintain sites in the valley, which they venerate as the authentic "Shepherds' Fields."

Manger Square, Bethlehem's central plaza and the site of the Church of the Nativity, is built over the grotto thought to be the birthplace of Jesus. The square has a tourist-information office (inside the Peace Center), a few restaurants, and some shops. It's brilliant with lights and bursting with life on Christmas Eve (December 24; the Greek Orthodox celebrate Christmas Eve on January 6, the Armenian Orthodox on January 18). Traditionally, choirs from around the world perform carols and sacred music in the square between 8:30 PM and 11:30 PM, and at midnight the **Roman Catholic mass** (☎ 02/627–2692) from the Franciscan Church of St. Catherine is simultaneously relayed on closed-circuit television onto a large outside screen and, via satellite, to all parts of the globe. At press time, foreign tourists had started to return to Bethlehem, taking in the Church of the Nativity and avoiding the souk (market) and narrow alleys beyond Manger Square.

★ The stone exterior of the **Church of the Nativity** is crowned by the crosses of the three denominations sharing it: the Greek Orthodox, the Latins (Roman Catholic, represented by the Franciscan order), and the Armenian Orthodox. The blocked square entranceway dates from the time of the Byzantine emperor Justinian (6th century AD), the arched entrance (also blocked) within the Byzantine one is 12th-century Crusader, and the current low entrance was designed in the 16th century to protect the worshipers from attack by hostile Muslim neighbors.

The church interior is vast and gloomy. In the central nave, a wooden trapdoor reveals a remnant of a mosaic floor from the original church, built in the 4th century by Helena, mother of Constantine the Great, the Roman emperor who first embraced Christianity. Emperor Justinian's rebuilding two centuries later enlarged the church, creating its present-day plan and structure, including the high columns that run the length of the nave in two paired lines.

This is the oldest standing church in the country. When the Persians invaded in AD 614, they destroyed every Christian church and monastery in the land except this one. The story holds that the church was adorned with a wall-painting depicting the Nativity tale, including the visit to the infant Jesus by the Three Wise Men of the East. For the local artist, "east" meant Persia, and he dressed his wise men in Persian garb. The Persian conquerors did not understand the picture's significance, but they "recognized" themselves in the painting and spared the church. In the eighth century the church was pillaged by the Muslims, and was later renovated by the Crusaders. Patches of 12th-century mosaics high on the walls, the medieval English oak ceiling beams, and the burned-wax figures of saints on the Corinthian pillars hint at its medieval splendor.

The elaborately ornamented front of the church serves as the parish church of Bethlehem's Greek Orthodox community. The right transept is theirs, too, but the left transept belongs to the Armenian Orthodox. For centuries, all three "shareholders" in the church have vied for control of the holiest Christian sites in the Holy Land. The 19th-century Status Quo Agreement that froze their respective rights and privileges in Jerusalem's Church of the Holy Sepulcher and the Tomb of the Virgin pertains here, too: ownership, the timing of ceremonies, the number of oil lamps, and so on are all clearly defined.

From the right transept at the front of the church, descend to the **Grotto of the Nativity.** Once a cave—precisely the kind of place that might have been used as a barn—the grotto has been reamed, plastered, and decorated beyond recognition. Immediately on the right is a small altar, and on the floor below it is the focal point of the entire site: a 14-point **bronze star** with the Latin inscription HIC DE VIRGINE MARIA JESUS CHRISTUS NATUS EST (Here of the Virgin Mary, Jesus Christ was born). The original star was placed here in 1717 by the Latins, who lost control of the altar 40 years later to the more influential Greek Orthodox. In 1847 the star mysteriously disappeared, and pressure from the Turkish sultan compelled the Greeks to allow the present Latin replacement to be installed in 1853. The Franciscan guardians do have possession, however, of the little alcove a few steps down on the left at the entrance to the grotto, said to be the manger where the infant Jesus was laid. There is clear evidence of the fire that gutted the grotto in the 19th century; the asbestos wall hangings were a French gift to prevent a recurrence.
✉ *Manger Sq.* ☎ *02/274–1020* ✉ *Free* ☉ *Church: Apr.–Sept., daily 6:30 AM–7:30 PM; Oct.–Mar., daily 5:30–5:30. Grotto: Apr.–Sept., Mon.–Sat. 9–7:30, Sun. noon–7:30 PM; Oct.–Mar., Mon.–Sat. 9–5:30, Sun. noon–5:30.*

The **Church of St. Catherine,** adjacent to the Church of the Nativity and accessible by a passage from its Armenian chapel, is Bethlehem's Roman Catholic parish church. Completed in 1882, and renovated in 1999, the church incorporates remnants of its 12th-century Crusader predecessor. It has fine acoustics but is otherwise unexceptional. From this church the midnight Catholic Christmas mass is broadcast around the world. Steps descend from within the church to a series of dim grottoes, clearly once used as living quarters. Chapels here are dedicated to Joseph; to the Innocents killed by Herod; and to the 4th-century St. Jerome, who wrote the Vulgate, the Latin translation of the Bible, supposedly right here. At the end of a narrow passage, a small wooden door (kept locked) connects the complex with the Grotto of the Nativity. ✉ *Manger Sq.* ☎ *02/274-2425* ✆ *Apr.–Sept., daily 6–noon and 2–7; Oct.–Mar., daily 5:30–5:30.*

## Shopping

Bethlehem craftspeople make carved olive-wood and mother-of-pearl objects, mostly of a religious nature, but the many stores along the tourist route in town sell jewelry and trinkets. For quality and reliability, most of the large establishments on Manger Street, where the tour buses stop, are worth investigating, but some of the merchants near the Church of the Nativity, on Manger Square, have good-quality items as well.

# SIDE TRIPS FROM JERUSALEM ESSENTIALS

## Transportation

### BY AIR

The points of departure for the three areas explored in this chapter are Jerusalem and Tel Aviv. ⇨ *For information about arriving and departing, see* Jerusalem Essentials *and* Tel Aviv Essentials *in* Chapters 1 *and* 3, *respectively.*

### BY BUS

The Egged Bus Cooperative has a nationwide monopoly on intercity bus routes. Buses are modern, comfortable, air-conditioned, and reasonably priced. Service is dependable on main routes but infrequent to outlying rural districts.

Jerusalem's Central Bus Station (a midsized mall with many shops) is in the city's northwestern corner, on Jaffa Road. Allow ample time to buy a ticket and get in line for the often crowded Dead Sea routes.

Since Jericho became autonomous under the Palestinian Authority, Egged no longer serves it. For the Dead Sea area (Qumran, Ein Gedi, Masada, and Ein Bokek), take Bus 421 or 486 (or 487 only as far as Ein Gedi). Service is approximately six times a day. The crowded Bus 444 to Eilat (which does not drive into Masada) runs four times a day. Only one bus departs daily from Tel Aviv to the Dead Sea area—Bus 421, currently at 8:40 AM.

To get to Rachel's Tomb (when politics permit), take the infrequent Bus 163 from Jerusalem's Central Bus Station, or pick it up near downtown Jerusalem, on Keren Hayesod Street opposite the Dan Panorama Hotel. From the East Jerusalem Bus Station, on Sultan Suleiman Street near the Damascus Gate take Bus 22 to the IDF checkpoint at the entrance to Bethlehem. From there, take a local bus or taxi to Manger Square. There is no direct bus service from Tel Aviv to Bethlehem.

The sights west of Jerusalem are difficult to reach by public transportation. There are almost hourly buses between Jerusalem and Bet Shemesh, but little else is easily accessible by bus in this area. The only bus going to Bet Guvrin (Bus 011) leaves at 8 AM from the town of Kiryat Gat. There are frequent buses to Kiryat Gat: Bus 446 from Jerusalem and Bus 369 from Tel Aviv.

🚍 **Central Bus Station** ✉ 224 Jaffa Rd., Romema, Jerusalem ☎ 03/694-8888 or *2800. **East Jerusalem Bus Station** ✉ Sultan Suleiman St., opposite Damascus Gate, East Jerusalem, Jerusalem ☎ 054/449-3088. **Egged** ☎ 03/694-8888 or *2800.

### BY CAR

Driving is much better than relying on public transportation here, as many of the sights are on secondary roads, where bus service is infrequent or in some cases nonexistent. Road conditions are fair to excellent, and most destinations are clearly marked. Drive defensively—many Israeli drivers are frustrated fighter pilots. Be cautious of Israeli drivers who overtake on winding roads, and make sure not to pass another car on a road with a solid line. (It's illegal and dangerous.) Stick to the intercity speed of 80 kmh (unless otherwise posted on some roads). Budget extra time for leaving and entering Jerusalem during rush hour (7:30–9 AM, and 4–6 PM). Gas stations are plentiful, and some are open 24 hours a day. Still, it's wise to play it safe and keep the tank at least half full at all times. Pay special attention to keeping the radiator topped off in the hot Israeli summer. In times of political unrest, check with local authorities to confirm safety of roads that pass through the West Bank.

Masada, the farthest of the Dead Sea sites in this chapter, is 100 km (62 mi) from Jerusalem, about 1½ hours' drive, on Routes 1 and 90 south; add one hour from Tel Aviv. Jericho, which is 40 km (25 mi) from Jerusalem, can be reached in 35 minutes via Routes 1 and 90 north. Heading southwest from Jerusalem, it takes 40 minutes to get to the Sorek Cave via Route 386 (about 24 km, or 15 mi) and another 30 minutes' driving time (about 30 km, or 19 mi) to Bet Guvrin via Route 38. Latrun, on Route 1, is 20 minutes from Jerusalem (25 km, or 16 mi); Bet Guvrin, via Bet Shemesh, is another 35 minutes on Routes 3, 44, and 38 (40 km, or 25 mi). From Tel Aviv (east on Route 1, south on Route 38), Bet Shemesh is about 40 minutes. Bethlehem is a mere 8 km (5 mi) from downtown Jerusalem, a 15-minute drive (depending on how long it takes to cross the IDF check-point). Driving your own car in other areas of the West Bank is not recommended.

### BY TAXI

A *sherut* is a shared taxi (seating up to seven passengers) that runs along a set route. Usually it follows a major bus route and charges a comparable fare. Arab sheruts to Bethlehem and Jericho are available from Arab East Jerusalem. This provides some local flavor—and sometimes a hair-raising driving experience. An Arab taxi is likely to be delayed at military checkpoints, however.

Using a regular taxi to tour is not cheap. Define the itinerary, get a quote from one of the main West Jerusalem taxi companies, and use that as a starting point for negotiating a better deal with an individual cabbie (outside hotels, or the Arab cabbies at the Jaffa Gate). Hiring a taxi for seven hours to Ein Gedi, the Dead Sea, and Masada, for example, costs about NIS 900. Hiring a qualified tour guide with an air-conditioned vehicle for the same trip is a far better value for the money.

**BY TRAIN**
Israel Railways provides regular train service between Jerusalem and Tel Aviv via Bet Shemesh on an almost hourly basis from 6 AM to 9 PM. Trains depart from the southern neighborhood of Malcha, opposite the Jerusalem mall. There are also occasional departures from the Jerusalem Biblical Zoo. Many people take the beautiful 40-minute ride through the forested hills to the Judean Lowlands merely for the journey.
🚆 Israel Railways ☎ 03/577-4000 or *5770 ⊕ www.israrail.org.il/english ✉ NIS 14 for one-way ticket from Jerusalem to Bet Shemesh.

## Contacts & Resources

**BANKS & EXCHANGING RESOURCES**
This is a largely rural area, so visitors would be best advised to exchange foreign currency in Jerusalem or Tel Aviv before setting out on a day trip. Note that many sites allow payment of entrance fees with credit cards (especially National Parks). Most hotels will offer a currency-changing service, but generally better rates are available from change point counters in the major cities.

**EMERGENCIES**
There are no hospitals, emergency dental services, or pharmacies in this largely rural area. Visitors should use one of the major hospitals in Jerusalem: Bikur Holim, Hadassah Ein Kerem, Hadassah Mt. Scopus, and Sha'arei Tzedek. ⇨ See Emergencies in Jerusalem Essentials for more details on emergency dental services or pharmacies.
🚑 Bikur Holim ✉ Strauss St., Downtown, Jerusalem ☎ 02/646-4111, 02/646-4113 emergency room. Hadassah Ein Kerem ✉ Ein Kerem, Jerusalem ☎ 02/677-7111, 02/677-7222 emergency room, 02/677-7444 children's emergency room. Hadassah Mt. Scopus ☎ 02/684-4111. Sha'arei Zedek ✉ Mt. Herzl, Jerusalem ☎ 02/655-5111, 02/655-5509 emergency room.

**INTERNET, MAIL & SHIPPING**
These services are best accessed from Jerusalem. ⇨ See Internet, Mail & Shipping in Jerusalem Essentials.

**TOUR OPTIONS**

"Regular" bus tours, as they're known locally, pick travelers up at their hotel and return them there at the end of the tour. Guided bus tours departing from Tel Aviv offer the same itineraries as those leaving Jerusalem.

There are discounts for children. The two operators are Egged Tours and United Tours. Most hotels carry the tour companies' brochures and can book tours. Both companies offer full-day tours of Masada, the Dead Sea, and Ein Gedi. Tours depart daily and cost $70 per person from Jerusalem (slightly more from Tel Aviv), not including lunch.

Touring in a private guide-driven limo or van is comfortable and convenient, and for four or more people, it's cost effective as well. With a private licensed guide in a limousine or minivan, you determine the tour's character and pace. Current recommended rates are $350–$400 per day depending on the vechicle size. Rates include all guiding and car expenses (up to 200 km [120 mi] per day, averaged out over the days of the tour). There is a charge for the guide's expenses for overnights away from the home base.

Some guides have organized into cooperatives, but all are essentially freelancers. In Jerusalem, try Eshcolot Tours. In Tel Aviv, call Twelve Tribes or Tar-Hemed. Advice and guiding service info is also available from Fodor's writers ( ⇨ *See* Sightseeing Guides *in* Smart Travel Tips). Hotel concierges can usually recommend guides as well.

🚌 **Egged Tours** ☎ 03/694-8888 or *2800 ⊕ www.egged.co.il/eng. **Eshcolot Tours** ✉ 36 Keren Hayesod St., Talbieh, Jerusalem ☎ 02/563-5555 🖷 02/563-2101. **Tar-Hemed** ✉ 59 Hayarkon St., Tel Aviv ☎ 03/517-6101 🖷 03/510-0165. **Twelve Tribes** ✉ 29 Hamered St., Tel Aviv ☎ 03/510-1911 🖷 03/510-1943. **United Tours** ☎ 02/625-2187, 03/616-2656 or 03/693-3412 ⊕ www.unitedtours.co.il.

JEEP TOURS    Israel Adventure Tours offers Jeep day tours to the Judean Desert. Each vehicle can take up to seven passengers and costs $350. A roughly five-hour moonlight tour costs $260.

🚌 **Israel Adventure Tours** ✉ 10 Ben Tabai St., Jerusalem ☎ 02/678-4635.

SPECIAL-
INTEREST TOURS    Archaeological Seminars in Jerusalem offers a Dig-for-a-Day program, a three-hour excavation at Bet Guvrin-Maresha National Park, outside of Jerusalem. The cost is $25 per person, not counting the entrance fee to the park itself (23 NIS per person).

🚌 **Archaeological Seminars** ☎ 02/586-2011 ⊕ www.archesem.com.

### VISITOR INFORMATION
The only tourist office in the area is in Bethlehem.

🚌 **Tourist Information Offices** (TIOs) ✉ Peace Center, Manger Sq., Bethlehem ☎ 02/276-6677 🖷 02/274-1057 ⊕ www.visit-palestine.com ✉ Jaffa Gate, Jerusalem ☎ 02/627-1422 🖷 02/627-1362 ⊕ www.goisrael.com.

# Tel Aviv

**WORD OF MOUTH**

"Shopping? Music? Food? Tel Aviv is your place. You can find the most fantastic deals in European-style women's clothing there. . . Visit the Nahalat Binyamin pedestrian mall in Tel Aviv (next to the colorful Carmel open market) on Friday (open till sundown), for original arts and crafts (great jewelry). Good place for souvenirs and gifts."
—Mamamia

"If you find yourself in Tel Aviv, check out Jaffa."
—Weezie

By Lisa Perlman

Updated
by Miriam
Feinberg
Vamosh

**PROUD RESIDENTS CALL IT** the city that never stops, and if you don't believe them, just come around 4 AM, when you may find yourself waiting in line for a table at a café or stuck in a traffic jam on Hayarkon Street.

The first impression Tel Aviv makes depends on the direction from which visitors enter. Glass office towers along the Ayalon Freeway, the city's ring road, showcase the latest trends in high-rise architecture. A dose of Israeli urban sprawl circa 1960 awaits those who come in via the neighborhoods northeast of Old Jaffa along Kibbutz Galuyot Street, eventually easing into the area's own funky charm. Tel Aviv's Bauhaus and art deco masterpieces, which can be seen from the Ayalon Freeway and Yizhak Sade Street, are the pride of Center City. Whatever the route, one thing is clear: Tel Aviv is the heart of Israeli commerce and culture, and its restaurants, art galleries, museums, and beaches are unmatched anywhere in the country.

Having risen from empty sand dunes less than a century ago, Tel Aviv could never hope for the ancient aura of Jerusalem. Still, the city's southern border, the port of Jaffa, is as old as they come: Jonah set sail from here for what turned out to be his journey to the belly of a whale. The cedars of Lebanon used to build Solomon's Temple arrived in Jaffa before being transported to Jerusalem.

According to archaeologists, Jaffa was founded in the Middle Canaanite period, around 1600 BC. For the next thousand years it was dominated by one ancient people after another: Egyptians, Philistines, Israelites, Phoenicians, and Greeks. After being taken by Crusaders twice, in the 11th and 12th centuries, Jaffa was recaptured by the Muslims and remained largely under Arab control until the 20th century. During much of this time it was abandoned; it did not regain its importance as a port until the 19th century.

In the second half of the 19th century, Jewish pioneers began immigrating here in numbers that strained the small port's capacity. By the late 1880s, Jaffa was overcrowded, rife with disease, and stricken with poverty. A group of Jewish families moved to the empty sands north of Jaffa to found Neveh Tzedek, now a beautifully restored cultural district. This was followed by Ahuzat Bayit (literally, "housing estate"), an area to the north of Neveh Tzedek that became the precursor of Tel Aviv. The city was named Tel Aviv in 1909; Arab riots in Jaffa in the 1920s then drove more Jews to Ahuzat Bayit, spurring further growth. These Jews were joined by immigrants from Europe, mostly Poland, and a decade later by an influx of German Jews fleeing the Nazis. These new, urban arrivals—unlike the pioneers from earlier immigrant waves—brought with them an appreciation for the arts and a penchant for sidewalk cafés, making the strongest social and cultural impact Tel Aviv had seen.

Tel Aviv's beginning as a string of separate neighborhoods helps to explain its eclectic (some would say discordant) appearance. Mediterranean-style buildings jostle each other in the shadow of towering skyscrapers. In the 1930s and '40s, Tel Aviv was named "white city," the world's only city dominated by the International Style of Le Corbusier and Mies van der Rohe—an aesthetic of functional forms, flat roofs, and whitewashed exteriors that became known as Bauhaus. By the 1950s, many of these buildings fell into disrepair or were demolished. But Tel Aviv still has the largest collection of Bauhaus buildings in the world, which won it a place on UNESCO's World Heritage List.

Tel Aviv has come a long way in its short life. Today, the white city area homes are undergoing renovation and reemerging as gentrified residences. The old charm of Neveh Tzedek—a neighborhood that had long been forgotten as the city spread north and west—has recently been reborn as the city's cultural center thanks to the Suzanne Dellal Center for Dance and Theater, with its surrounding area a wonderful place to wander among galleries, boutiques, and eateries. The working-class neighborhood of Florintine is still rather drab during the day, but after dark it comes alive with pubs and dance clubs that are favorites with the 20s to 30s crowd. It's hard to imagine the scene just 90 years ago, when this teeming metropolis was nothing but sand.

## Top 5 Reasons to Go

- **Eretz Israel Museum:** This is an excellent place for visitors of all ages to get to know Israelite culture, from its ancient pottery to its exhibit on the postal service, which turns out to be a fascinating way of looking at the country's modern history and includes a colorful display of stamps from various periods. The ground's beautiful landscaping makes for pleasant strolling. Don't miss the excellent museum shop.

- **Nahalat Binyamin Pedestrian Mall:** Stalls of this twice-weekly street fair show off a wealth of handmade jewelry and other crafts at very reasonable prices; street performers add a fun accent, and it's close to both the Carmel Market and trendy Sheinkin Street.

- **Neveh Tzedek:** Restoration has meant a renaissance for this dilapidated old area of Tel Aviv, with shops, museums, restaurants, and the Suzanne Dellal Center with its orange-tree-studded square. A must-see destination day or night.

- **Old Port:** New life has been brought to the abandoned old warehouses here, transforming this area into Tel Aviv's toniest place to be. It begins in its southern section with a row of four or five fish restaurants interspersed with a couple of cafés facing a promenade parallel to the water, and ends where the pavement gives way to a wavy wooden walkway and a small mall with eclectic fashion shops. A number of outlets here are also popular with locals.

- **Yehoshua Gardens (Hayarkon Park):** Give tired touring feet a rest and kick back with the locals here, where you can also go boating or scamper up a rock-climbing wall.

# EXPLORING TEL AVIV

The beachfront Tayelet (promenade) running from north Tel Aviv to Jaffa, some 4 km (2½ mi) to the south, is great to walk along, especially at sunset and on Saturdays. The city's main north–south thoroughfares of Hayarkon, Ben Yehuda (which becomes Allenby), Dizengoff (the once but no longer central shopping district), and Ibn Gvirol

Spending two to four days in Tel Aviv is ideal. You'll be able to explore a variety of neighborhoods and museums and still have time left over to cool off on the beach. A shorter stay will require a lot of action, though you'll still be able to catch the highlights.

**If you have**
**2 days**

Begin in Old Jaffa, wandering around the restored section and delving into the small galleries and shops. Enjoy a meal of fresh fish on the waterfront at the port, and walk along the coastal Tayelet (promenade) back to central Tel Aviv. Head for the trendy Sheinkin Street area to get a feel for the contemporary Israeli lifestyle, and if it's a Tuesday or Friday, walk over to the street fair created by local artisans along the Nahalat Binyamin Pedestrian Mall. Nearby, Rothschild Boulevard has good examples of the city's various architectural styles and periods, from Middle East–influenced to Bauhaus to latter-day steel and glass, and some of the city's best restaurants and cafés.

**3**

On the second day, take in a museum on a subject that interests you: the Tel Aviv Museum of Art; the Eretz Israel Museum, with its excellent archaeological exhibits; or Beth Hatefutsoth (Diaspora Museum), which depicts Jewish life around the world throughout the ages; or the Palmach Museum. You may want to squeeze in some shopping after that, then spend a few hours doing what Tel Avivians do best— *beten-gav* (tummy-back, in Hebrew)—cooling off on the beach.

**If you have**
**3 days**

The Nahalat Binyamin Pedestrian Mall street fair (on Tuesday and Friday) and the Carmel Market are good places to start. From there, it's a hop, skip, and a jump to Sheinkin Street for a coffee break or lunch, window shopping, and people watching. Get in some beach time today and go out for a late dinner in the Old Port in north Tel Aviv. Spend the morning of the second day walking through Old Jaffa, including the flea market, and afternoon or early evening strolling around and shopping in Neveh Tzedek. If there's a performance at the Suzanne Dellal Center in Neveh Tzedek, make an evening of dinner and a show. Save browsing and shopping around the city center for the last day, and make sure to stroll the Tayelet along the beach front. Hit the museums then spend the latter part of the day in Jaffa; the atmosphere is very different at night. Try one of the Rothschild Boulevard restaurants tonight.

---

streets run more or less parallel to the shore. Most hotels are on the seafront, along lively Hayarkon Street. At the northern end of Hayarkon is the Old Port (not to be confused with the Jaffa Port), the city's hottest new shopping and restaurant district. Visitors can easily spend several hours at the Nahalat Binyamin Pedestrian Mall and on Sheinkin Street (both off Allenby), as well as at Carmel Market, a real junction of East-meets-West and old-meets-new. Kikar Hamedina (Hamedina Square) has some of the city's highest-end retail stores. The residential area continues north to Hayarkon Park, which is a welcome ribbon of greenery in an otherwise urban setting.

## Center City

Think of central Tel Aviv as the hub on the wheel whose spokes lead to all the great sites the city has to offer. Swirling around you might be surfers heading up from the beach crossing paths with ladies doing lunch, or 30-somethings after work huddled around a tiny table at a café on Sheinkin, or families enjoying the play areas and paths along Rothschild, or tour groups checking out architectural treasures around Montefiori and Ahad Ha'am.

### Main Attractions

**㉕ Independence Hall Museum.** This impressive structure was originally the home of the city's first mayor, Meir Dizengoff; he donated it to the city in 1930 for use as the first Tel Aviv museum. More significantly, the country's leaders assembled here in May 14, 1948, to announce to the world the establishment of the State of Israel. Today the museum's **Hall of Declaration** stands as it did on that dramatic day, with the original microphones on the long table where the dignitaries sat. Behind the table is a portrait of the Zionist leader Theodor Herzl. ⊠ *16 Rothschild Blvd.* ☎ *03/517–3942* ⊠ *NIS 17* ⊙ *Sun.–Thurs. 9–2.*

**❺ Nahalat Binyamin Pedestrian Mall.** The selection at this street market, open
**Fodor's**Choice Tuesday and Friday, is broad—ranging from plastic trinkets to sophis-
★ ticated crafts such as hand-carved wooden boxes, attractive glassware, and handmade silver jewelry. Nahalat Binyamin is further enlivened with a profusion of buskers. For a finishing touch of local color, cafés serving cakes and light meals line the street. At the end of the fair is a large
• Bedouin tent, where you can treat yourself to a *laffa* with *labaneh* and *za'atar* (large pita bread with tangy sour cream, sprinkled with hyssop, a mintlike herb). ⊠ *Nahalat Binyamin St., off Allenby St.* ⊙ *Tues. and Fri. until sundown.*

**⑮ Tel Aviv Museum of Art.** The TAM houses a fine collection of Israeli and international art, including works by Israeli artist Reuven Rubin and a Roy Lichtenstein mural commissioned for the museum in 1989. There's also an impressive French Impressionist collection and many sculptures by Aleksandr Archipenko. ⊠ *27 Shaul Hamelech Blvd.* ☎ *03/696–1297* ⊕ *www.tamuseum.com* ⊠ *NIS 40* ⊙ *Mon., Wed., and Sat. 10–4; Tues., Thurs. 10–10; Fri. 10–2.*

### Also Worth Seeing

**⑯ Azrieli Towers.** A spectacular 360-degree view of Tel Aviv and beyond awaits on the 49th-floor observatory of this office building and mall complex, which consists of three buildings—one triangular, one circular, and one square. The observatory is sometimes closed for private events; it's advised to call ahead to check availablilty. Visitors can also watch a 15-minute 3D film about Tel Aviv, with the help of those strange red and blue cardboard glasses. ⊠ *Hashalom exit west, Ayalon Fwy.* ☎ *03/608–1179* ⊠ *NIS 38 for observatory entrance, audio-guide, and film.*

★ **❷ Bet Bialik.** Set to reopen in early 2007, Bialik House is the charmingly restored two-story house of Chaim Nachman Bialik (1873–1934), the national poet who is considered the father of Hebrew poetry. Bialik was

**3**

## Beaches

Tel Aviv's western border, an idyllic stretch of Mediterranean sand, has miles of beaches and a beachfront promenade. Sunsets here are spectacular. Still, the Med can be moody; the lapping of gentle waves offers respite and relaxation for most of the year, but jellyfish are out in force in July and August, and an air-conditioned café with a view of the sea might be a more pleasurable place to be. There's a strong undertow on these beaches, so exercise caution.

## Cultural Activities

As Israel's undisputed cultural capital, Tel Aviv puts on a great show, even at the street level. There's a stimulating range of museums; dance and music of all kinds are popular; opera is budding; and theater (almost all in Hebrew) is prolific. As for pop culture—well, it's all around you.

## Water Sports

Tel Aviv has no shortage of water-sport opportunities, and even some that may come as a surprise. In addition to enjoying the more obvious swimming, sailing, and windsurfing, you can rent pleasure boats on the Hayarkon River and water-ski on the artificial lake at the Yehoshua Gardens.

---

already a respected poet and publisher by the time he moved to Tel Aviv from Russia in 1924; in the remaining 10 years of his life, his house, built in 1927, became the intellectual center of Tel Aviv. ⊠ *22 Bialik St.* ☎ *03/525–3403.*

**①** **Bialik Street.** This area has been more successful than many other Tel Aviv neighborhoods in maintaining its charming older buildings. Bialik has long been a popular address with many of the city's artists and literati, so it's not surprising that some of the houses have been converted into small museums. Next to the Bialik house is a **mosaic,** designed by artist Nahum Gutman, which depicts the history of the city from the ancient days of Jaffa to the rise of Tel Aviv. Gutman was among the elite group of Tel Aviv's first artists.

★ **④** **Carmel Market.** The first section of Carmel Market (commonly referred to as the *shuk*) consists of cheap clothing, but a little farther down, in the fruit and vegetable section, is where the real local color begins. Vendors loudly hawk their fresh produce, and crowded aisles reveal Israel's incredible ethnic mix. ⊠ *Along Hacarmel St.*

**need a break?**

The Carmel Market borders the **Yemenite Quarter,** which hides several cheap and satisfying little eateries (closed Friday night and Saturday) offering *shawarma* and barbecued skewered meats, all kosher. Visitors can dig into any that catch their fancy, and wash them down with a cold beer.

**㉔** **Founders' Monument and Fountain.** Dedicated in 1949, the Founders' Monument names those who founded Tel Aviv. This large slab of stone

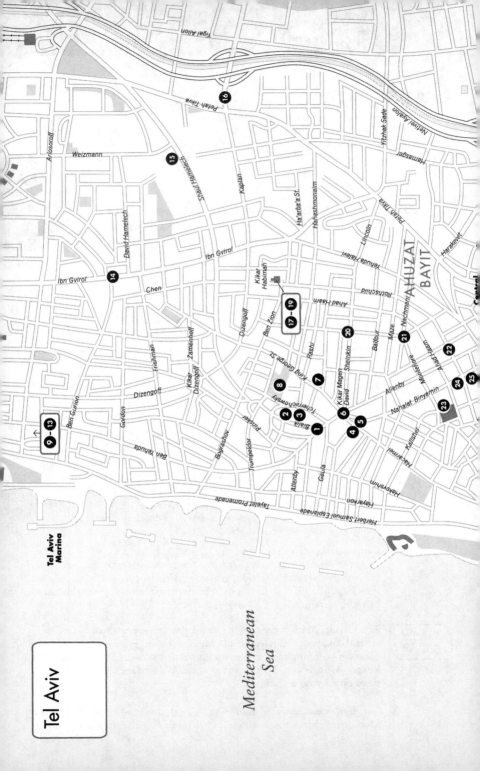

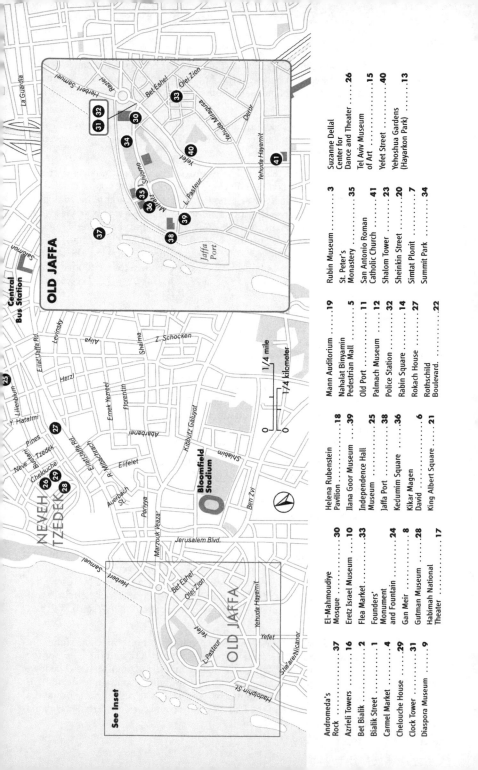

also encapsulates the city's past in three copper bas-relief panels representing the earliest pioneer days of planting and building as well as modern structures and houses. ⊠ *Rothschild Blvd., on the traffic divider at Nahalat Binyamin St.*

**⑧ Gan Meir.** In this park you can rest on one of the benches and take in a free performance given by city birds. It's something of a green haven in muggy Tel Aviv.

**⑰ Habimah National Theater.** The origins of Israel's national theater are rooted in the Russian Revolution, when a group of young Jewish actors and artists in Russia established a theater company that performed in Hebrew—this at a time when Hebrew was barely a living language. Subsequent tours through Europe and the United States in the 1920s won wide acclaim. In the late 1920s and '30s, many of the group's members moved to Israel and helped to establish the theater. The cornerstone was laid in 1935; the current large, rounded glass-front building dates from 1970. ⊠ *Kikar Habimah* ☎ *03/526–6666* ⊕ *www.habima.org.il.*

**⑱ Helena Rubinstein Pavilion.** This annex of the Tel Aviv Museum of Art houses changing contemporary art exhibitions. ⊠ *6 Tarsat St.* ☎ *03/528-7196* ⊕ *www.tamuseum.com* ⊠ *Free* ☉ *Sat.–Mon. and Wed. 10–4, Tues. and Thurs. 10–10.*

**⑥ Kikar Magen David.** This meeting point of six streets is named for the six-point Magen David, or Star of David. It's also an intersection of cultures, surrounded by some of old Tel Aviv's historic buildings on one side and Sheinkin, the ultimate in trendiness, on the other. The intersection gives you an all-too-close look at the Israelis' hair-raising driving style; if you need to cross the street here, use the underpass.

**㉑ King Albert Square.** Named after the Belgian monarch who was a personal friend of Mayor Dizengoff, the square, reached from Rothschild Boulevard past the restored buildings on Nahmani Street, is in the heart of Tel Aviv's restored architectural area and has some interesting monuments of its own. Pagoda House, a recently completed makeover, was built in 1924 at the height of the Bauhaus period as a private home. It is very ornamental, topped with the Japanese element that gave it its name. Its architect, Alexander Levy, came to Palestine in the '20s, and designed a number of buildings. However he never felt at home here, and eventually returned to Germany, where he was killed in Auschwitz. Inside the elegant stairwell of the Shifrin House at 2 Melchett Street off the square, are crumbling remnants of frescoes of the Western Wall and Rachel's Tomb.

**⑲ Mann Auditorium.** One of the several cultural centers on Kikar Habimah, Mann Auditorium is Israel's premier concert hall and the home of the Israel Philharmonic Orchestra, led by maestro Zubin Mehta. The low-slung gray building, among the most distinguished and sophisticated cultural buildings in the country of its time, has excellent acoustics and a seating capacity of 3,000. It also hosts pop and rock concerts. ⊠ *Habima Sq.* ⊕ *www.hatarbut.co.il.*

**⑭ Rabin Square.** The square fronting the nondescript Tel Aviv municipality building was renamed for prime minister Yitzhak Rabin after he was assassinated here on November 4, 1995. Passersby often stop at the small monument of black stones rippled and uneven as if after an earthquake, the work of Israeli artist Danny Karavan. On the wall under glass are copies of the ad-hoc commemoration graffiti that covered the area in the months following the assassination. ⊠ *Ibn Gvirol St.*

**㉒ Rothschild Boulevard.** Half a century ago, this magnificent tree-lined boulevard was and is once again one of the most exclusive streets in the city. Many of the original buildings in the Bauhaus or Art Deco style were allowed to deteriorate; most have now been restored.

**❸ Rubin Museum.** Recognized as one of Israel's major painters, Rubin (1893–1974) bequeathed his house to Tel Aviv along with 45 of his works, which make up the permanent collection here. The house is now an art gallery, with changing exhibits by Israeli artists in addition to the great Rubin's work. Upstairs, there is a small but well-stocked art library where you can pore over press clippings and browse through art books. An audiovisual presentation tells the story of the artist's life, and his original studio can still be seen on the third floor. ⊠ *14 Bialik St.* ☎ *03/ 525–5961* ⊕ *www.rubinmuseum.org.il* ⊡ *NIS 20* ☉ *Mon., Wed., Thurs. 10–3; Tues. 10–8; Sat. 11–2.*

**㉓ Shalom Tower.** Israel's first skyscraper stands on the site of the first high school ever to hold its classes entirely in Hebrew: the Herzliya Gymnasium (named, like the street, for the founder of the Zionist movement, Theodor Herzl). The building is your basic office block, but there is a photograph exhibit and models of old and new Tel Aviv in the lobby. The rooftop observatory is well worth a visit for its magnificent city and sea views. ⊠ *Herzl St.* ☎ *03/517–0991* ⊡ *NIS 15* ☉ *Sun.–Thurs. 10–6, Fri. 10–2, Sat. 11–4.*

**⑳ Sheinkin Street.** This street off Allenby across from Nahalat Binyamin recalls New York's Greenwich Village, with its artists and would-be artists, trendoids and wanna-bes, cafés and restaurants. Shopping here is fun, too, especially for teens and young adults. Street performances in good weather add to the boisterous fun (though it's hard to see much through the crowds).

**❼ Simtat Plonit.** It's worth a wander down this alley to see old Tel Aviv decorative architecture at its best. Note the stucco lion in front of **Number 7**, which used to have glowing eyes fitted with lightbulbs. The tract of land that incorporates Simtat Plonit was bought in the 1920s by an outspoken builder from Detroit named Meir Getzel Shapira. (He established what is still known as the Shapira Quarter, just south of the Central Bus Station and now one of the city's seedier neighborhoods.) After buying the land, Shapira insisted that this pint-size street be named after him, and the story goes that he fought furiously with Tel Aviv's first mayor, Meir Dizengoff, to get his way. (Dizengoff had already planned to name another street Shapira, after a different Shapira.) The mayor emerged victorious and named the alley Plonit, meaning "What's-His-Name."

# CloseUp

# A FOCUS ON THE ARTS

**FOR A TINY NATION,** *Israel has a thriving and abundant arts scene. The country is home to thousands of classical musicians—many of whom immigrated from the former Soviet states—and the Israel Philharmonic Orchestra has a world-class reputation.*

*A number of music festivals are held annually, drawing international crowds—from the Red Sea Jazz Festival, in the south, to the Voice of Music chamber music event and Jacob's Ladder folk festival, in the north.*

*Israeli theater, too, enjoys a significant following. There are six professional repertory theaters—including the Habmiah and the Cameri in Tel Aviv—and dozens of regional and amateur companies performing throughout the country. They perform almost exclusively in Hebrew.*

*Professional dance companies are also abounding in Israel today. The Suzanne Dellal Center for Dance and Theater in Tel Aviv is the primary venue.*

*Folk dancing has always been unusually popular in Israel, where it is, in fact, an evolving art form. As well as "Israeli" folk dancing (really a blend of Jewish and non-Jewish folk dance forms from around the world), some of Israel's different ethnic groups have preserved their traditional dances.Enthusiasm for the visual arts can be seen in all walks of Israeli life. A wide range of Israeli art can be seen at both the Israel Museum (in Jerusalem), the Tel Aviv Museum, and for modern Israeli art, the Ramat Gan Art Museum.*

## Jaffa

The origin of Jaffa's name is unclear: some say it derives from the Hebrew *yafeh* (beautiful); others claim the town was named after its founder, Japhet, son of Noah. What is certain is its status as one of the oldest ports in the world—perhaps the oldest. The Bible mentions Jaffa in connection with a number of significant events: the cedars used in the construction of the Temple passed through Jaffa on their way to Jerusalem; the prophet Jonah set off from Jaffa before being swallowed by the whale; and St. Peter raised Tabitha from the dead here. Napoléon was but one of a succession of invaders who brought the city walls down; these walls were rebuilt for the last time in the early 19th century by the Turks and torn down yet again as recently as 1888.

By the 19th century Christian and Jewish pilgrims on their way to Jerusalem were a familiar sight in what became a thriving town. Jews and Arabs lived peacefully here until the1920s, when discord brought about the establishment of Jewish Tel Aviv to the north. Now part of the municipality of Tel Aviv, Jaffa is a mosaic of Jews, Christians, and Muslims, accented by communities of foreign guest-workers mainly from Asia and Africa.

The restored section, Old Jaffa, is only a small part of this fascinating port; it caters primarily to tourists and fishermen. Beyond the restored section, visit the Jaffa flea market where trading, bargaining, and arguing are as much a part of life as ever.

## Main Attractions

**36 Kedumim Square.** This is Old Jaffa's central plaza. The square is chockablock with excavation sites, restaurants, expensive gift and souvenir shops, and galleries. The artists who live here complain that there's too much noise on summer nights; some visitors say it's too touristy. But Old Jaffa is indisputably charming and should not be missed. The labyrinthine network of tiny alleys snakes in all directions from Kedumim Square down to the fishing port; a good selection of galleries and jewelry stores can be found along Mazal Dagim Street and its offshoots, south of the square. The focus of Kedumim Square is an archaeological site that exposes 3rd-century BC catacombs; the site has been converted into an underground visitor center with large, vivid, illustrated descriptions of Jaffa's history. Admission is free.

**35 St. Peter's Monastery.** Established by Franciscans in the 1890s, St. Peter's was built over the ruins of a citadel that dates from the Seventh Crusade, which was led by King Louis IX of France. It remained Jaffa's principal Roman Catholic church until the church of San Antonio was built in 1932. A monument to King Louis stands today at the entrance to the friary. Napoléon is rumored to have stayed here during his Jaffa campaign of 1799. To enter, ring the bell by pulling the string on the right side of the door; you will probably be greeted by one of the custodians, most of whom speak Spanish and some English. ⊠ *Kedumim Sq.* ☎ *03/ 682–2871.*

**34 Summit Park.** It's fun to watch the newlyweds who come here to be photographed in their wedding garb at sunset against the backdrop of the sea and the old buildings before heading to the ceremony. Seven archaeological layers have been unearthed in a section of the park called Ramses II Garden. The oldest sections of wall (20 feet thick) have been identified as part of a 17th-century BC Hyksos city. Other remains include part of a 13th-century BC city gate inscribed with the name of Ramses II; a Canaanite city; a Jewish city from the time of Ezra and Nehemiah; Hasmonean ruins from the 2nd century BC; and traces of Roman occupation. At the summit is a stone sculpture called *Faith*, in the shape of a gateway, which depicts biblical stories.

## Also Worth Seeing

**37 Andromeda's Rock.** From Kedumim Square, a number of large boulders can be seen out at sea not far from shore. Greek mythology says one of these (pick your own, everyone does) is where the people of Jaffa tied the virgin Andromeda to sacrifice her to a sea monster to appease Poseidon, god of the sea. But Perseus, riding the winged horse Pegasus, soared down from the sky to behead the monster, rescue Andromeda, and promptly marry her.

**31 Clock Tower.** The tower is the focus of Jaffa's central square and stands at the center of town, with restored Old Jaffa to the west and the flea market to the east. The clock tower was completed in 1906, in time to mark the 30th anniversary of the reign of Sultan Abdul Hamid II; similar clock towers were built for the same occasion in Akko and in Jerusalem. The four clock faces stood still for many years until 1965, when the city renovated the tower and set them in motion again; the renovation also added stained-glass windows depicting events in Jaffa's history. ⊠ *Clock Tower Square, Yefet St.*

**need a break?**

There's always a line outside **Abulafia Bakery** (⊠ 7 Yefet St.), south of the clock tower. The Middle East's answer to pizza goes like hot cakes here—literally. For a simple snack with an exquisite flavor, order a pita topped with the herb *za'atar* (hyssop), or stuffed with salty cheese, calzone-style. Abulafia is a good place to try *sachlab*, a warm drink sprinkled with coconut and cinnamon.

**30 El-Mahmoudiye Mosque.** When the fountain here was built by Turkish governor Mohammed Abu Najat Aja in the early 19th century, it had six pillars and an arched roof, providing shade as well as water. The archway just beyond formed the entrance to the *hamam*, or old Turkish baths. In the late 19th century a separate entrance was built into the east wall to save the governor and other dignitaries the bother of having to push through the market-square crowds at the main entrance, on the south wall. The mosque managed to escape the fate of other sites in Jaffa that were destroyed during the War of Independence. With a minaret and two colorful domes, this is one of the local Muslim community's most important mosques and is not usually open to the general public. ⊠ *Yefet St.*

★ **33 Flea Market.** The flea market actually began as one of many small bazaars that surrounded the clock tower in the mid-19th century, and it's now the only survivor of that era. The market's main street is **Olei Zion,** but there are a number of smaller streets and arcades to explore at your leisure, so take your time. Today there's more junk than there are treasures, and bargaining is not as vigorous as it once was; but it's still important to play the game, so don't agree to the first price the seller demands.

**39 Ilana Goor Museum.** The veteran Israeli artist Ilana Goor, who works and resides in this restored 18th-century house with its romantic stone arches and high ceilings, has turned part of it into a museum of her sculptures in wood, stone, and metal, some reminiscent of the "found-art" genre, and of local crafts. A gift shop also occupies part of the complex. ⊠ *4 Mazal Dagim St., Jaffa* ☎ *03/683–7676* 🎫 *NIS 24* ☉ *Sun.–Fri. 10–4, Sat. and Jewish holidays 10–6.*

★ **38 Jaffa Port.** A great many fishing boats line this small marina, as well as a handful of houseboats. Along the waterfront are a number of restaurants; the view the main attraction of most of them.

**32 Police Station.** This building has the original Ottoman-designed arch above its entrance. The design over the door is the seal of Turkish sultan Abdul Hamid II. During the British Mandate, the British used the building to intern both Arabs and members of the Zionist group Irgun. ⊠ *Clocktower Sq.*

**㊶ San Antonio Roman Catholic Church.** Although it looks quite new with its clean white-stone bricks, this church actually dates from 1932, when it was built to accommodate the growing needs of Jaffa's Roman Catholic Church. (St. Peter's was in a heavily populated Muslim area and was unable to expand due to lack of land.) The church is named for St. Antonius of Padua, friend and disciple of St. Francis of Assisi. ✉ *51 Yefet St.* ☎ *03/682–2667.*

**㊵ Yefet Street.** Think of Yefet as a sort of thread between eras: beneath it is the old market area, while all around you stand the Christian and Western schools and churches of the 19th and 20th centuries. Numbers 21, 23, and 25 deserve mention. The first is the **Tabitha School**, established by the Presbyterian Church of Scotland in 1863. Behind the school is a small cemetery where some fairly prominent figures are buried, including Dr. Thomas Hodgkin, the personal physician to Sir Moses Montefiore and the first to define Hodgkin's disease; he died in Jaffa in 1866. **Number 23** was a French Catholic school (it still carries the sign COL-LÈGE DES FRÈRES) from 1882 but has long since been used by the French Embassy for administrative purposes. And next door, the neo-Tudor, fortresslike **Urim School,** with its round tower, was set up as a girls' school in 1882 by nuns of the same order that built the St. Louis French Hospital. It's now a local school.

## Neveh Tzedek

In 1887 a small group of Jewish families concentrated their efforts to get out of crowded, poverty-stricken Jaffa and began creating a community on the sand to the north of the mainly Arab port town. Building at a rate of 10 houses a year, they laid the cornerstone for Neveh Tzedek (Dwellings of Justice) in 1890. This was the forebear of Tel Aviv. The area is off the beaten path for most tourists, but as time and money are invested in its restoration, it attracts renewed interest.

Today, Neveh Tzedek is the home of many of Tel Aviv's artists, rich and poor; it also has a splendid dance and arts complex (the Suzanne Dellal Center) and a growing number of small trendy galleries, gift stores, and restaurants. Though bordered on three sides by major thoroughfares (Eilat Road to the south, Herzl Street to the west, and Kaufman Street along the sea), this little quarter is very tranquil. Made up of only about a dozen tiny streets stuffed with one- and two-story dwellings in various stages of either depressing disrepair or enthusiastic renovation, Neveh Tzedek is rich with tales of 100 years ago.

### Main Attractions

**㉖ Suzanne Dellal Center for Dance and Theater.** The two large whitewashed buildings that make up this attractive complex started as schools, one built in 1892 and the other in 1908. Both were used for education until the 1970s, though they also served as headquarters for the political force Etzel and the underground military group Haganah, which marched on Arab Jaffa in the 1940s, when Arab residents terrorized Jewish neighborhoods. The square, designed by foremost landscape designer Shlomo Aronson, has hints of a medieval Middle Eastern courtyard in its scattering of orange trees connected by water channels. The complex was always something of a meeting place for theater folk, and it opened as a dance center after extensive renovations in 1990. The halls are open only for performances, but you can walk around the attractive grounds. There are two cafés—Belini's, an Italian restaurant, and an ice cream shop. ✉ *6 Yehieli St.* ☎ *03/510–5656* ⊕ *www.suzannedellal.org.il.*

**28** **Gutman Museum.** A number of Tel Aviv's most famous writers lived in this building during the 1920s, but extensive renovation has somewhat obscured its original look. One of the first houses in Neveh Tzedek, the premises now display the art of Nahum Gutman, colorful chronicler of early Tel Aviv. ✉ *21 Rokach St.* ☎ *03/510–8554* ⊕ *www.gutmanmuseum. co.il* ✍ *NIS 20* ⊙ *Sun., Mon., Wed., Thurs. 10–4; Tues. 10–7, Fri. and Jewish holiday eves 10–2, Sat. 10–5.*

**27** **Rokach House.** This mansion was built by and was home to the founder of Neveh Tzedek, Shimon Rokach and his wife Hannah, and like other homes in the quarter, it fell into disrepair. Its restoration is the "baby" of the Rokachs' daughter, the artist Leah Majaro-Mintz. It now houses Majaro-Mintz's art and an exhibit of items from the quarter's early days. Guided tours in English are by prearrangement. A dramatization (in Hebrew) of Neveh Tzedek's history, preceded by culinary tastings of the period, is put on most weekend evenings at 9:30. ✉ *36 Rokach St., Neveh Tzedek* ☎ *03/516–8042* ⊕ *www.rokach-house.co.il* ✍ *NIS 10* ⊙ *Sun.–Thurs., Fri.–Sat. 10–2.*

### Also Worth Seeing

**29** **Chelouche House.** Drawn to this quarter like so many other Israeli literati and artists, writer S. Y. Agnon lived here from 1909 to 1912. At the time, the young Agnon was working as a literary assistant to the more senior writer Simcha Ben Zion, the namesake of the boulevard leading from King George Street to Habimah Square; his first story was published in literary journals produced by Ben Zion. Much of Agnon's writings reflects these very surroundings. Unfortunately, this is closed to the public now, but even the outside of the building is very impressive. ✉ *36 Chelouche St.*

## Northern Tel Aviv

Among the sights north of the Yarkon River are three important museums. The Eretz Israel Museum is close to Tel Aviv University; the Palmach Museum is next door to it; and the Diaspora Museum is farther north, on the university campus. The museums are about 8 km (5 mi) from the downtown hotels; Buses 24, 25, 27, 45, and 49 will take you to both. Allow at least two hours for each.

### Main Attractions

★ **9** **Diaspora Museum.** Presented here are 2,500 years of Jewish life in the Diaspora (the settling of Jews outside Israel), beginning with the destruction of the First Temple in Jerusalem and chronicling such major events as the exile to Babylon and the expulsion from Spain in 1492. Also covered is Eastern Europe before the Holocaust. Photographs and text labels provide the narrative, and films and music enhance the experience. One highlight is a replica collection of miniature synagogues throughout the world, both those destroyed and those still functioning. Another is the computerized genealogy section, where it's possible to look up Jewish family names to determine their origins. ✉ *Tel Aviv University Campus (Gate 2) Klausner St., Ramat Aviv* ☎ *03/640–8000* ⊕ *www.bh.org.il* ✉ *NIS 34* ☉ *Sun.–Thurs. 10–4, Wed. 10–6, Fri. 9–1.*

★ ⑩ **Eretz Israel Museum.** This national museum comprises eight pavilions that present such facets of Israeli life as ethnography and folklore, ceramics and other handicrafts, and coinage; the displays span 3,000 years of history. In the center of the complex is the ancient site of Tel Kassile, where archaeological digs have so far uncovered 12 layers of settlements. There is also a daily sound-and-light show in the adjacent planetarium with Hebrew narration (call to verify hours). ✉ *2 Levanon (University) St.* ☎ *03/641–5244* ⊕ *www.eretzmuseum.org.il* ✉ *Museum NIS 35, planetarium NIS 58* ☉ *Sun.–Thurs. 9–3, Fri.–Sat. 10–2.*

⑪ **Old Port.** The old "hangars," as the warehouses are called here, are quickly being transformed into Tel Aviv's toniest place to eat, shop and stroll. It begins in its southern section with a row of four or five fish restaurants with outdoor tables interspersed with a couple of cafes facing a promenade parallel to the water, constructed over the old breakwater. It ends where the pavement gives way to a wooden platform designed with moderate dips and curves that are pleasing to the eye and fun for the roller-skaters, and a small mall, called Bayit Banamal, with eclectic fashion shops. A number of outlets in the area of the Old Port are also popular with the locals. Saturday it's particularly busy, with the restaurants full by 1 PM, and a small swap meet at the northern end with some hand-made jewelry on offer, old books, and circa-1950s Israeli crafts and memorabilia.

⑫ **Palmach Museum.** This museum makes its visitors feel as if they were back in the days of the Palmach, the prestate underground, with a group of young defenders. Visitors are led through rooms, each of which encompasses one part of the Palmach experience. There's the "forest," which has real-looking trees, a room with a falling bridge and faux-explosions, and a chilling mock-up of an illegal immigrants' ship. ✉ *10 Haim Levanon St., Ramat Aviv* ☎ *03/643–6393* 🖷 *03/643–6964* ⊕ *www.palmach.org.il* ☉ *Sun.–Thurs. 9–2; by reservation only.*

⑬ **Yehoshua Gardens** (Hayarkon Park). This park is a strip of emerald tranquility in the midst of the hustle-bustle. Located in the northern part of town, it's the place where Tel Avivians go to stretch out on the grass for a picnic or a nap in the shade. For those seeking more activity, a long walk on one of its paths to renting a pedal boat, or rowboat (NIS 60per hour) and motorboats (NIS 80, per half-hour) to ply the Yarkon Stream or the park's artificial lake. There's even a pleasure boats, which take up to 100 people for 20-minute rides (NIS 12, per person). Bicycles or tandems that take up to six people (NIS 45 per half-hour) are great for family fun, as are the kids' play areas, that are a great place to meet young Israeli families. ✉ *Rokach Blvd.* ☎ *03/642–0541*

# WHERE TO EAT

The city's cosmopolitan character is now happily represented in its food, although stands selling Middle Eastern fast food for which this part of the world is famous—such as falafel and *shawarma* (spit-grilled meat)—still occupy countless street corners. But beyond these are restaurants serving everything from American burgers to Chinese dim sum. In contrast to Jerusalem, diners who keep kosher really have to search for a kosher restaurant outside the hotels.

Tel Aviv is also very much a café society. The murmur of varied languages and the range of exotic coffees at the scores of cafés across town will convince you as nothing else will that you are in a world-class cosmopolitan city.

Most Tel Aviv restaurants are open throughout the day and well into the night year-round, except on Yom Kippur. Many serve business lunches at reasonable prices, making them less-expensive options than the price categories suggest. Like elsewhere in the Mediterranean, Israelis dine late; chances are there will be no trouble getting a table at 7 PM, whereas past 10, diners may face a long line. Casual attire is always acceptable in Tel Aviv, even in the poshest restaurants.

Tel Aviv's restaurants are concentrated in several areas: Sheinkin and Rothschild streets, Basel, Ibn Gvirol Street, and the Old Port. In addition, in Herzliya Pituach, a suburb north of Tel Aviv, the best restaurants are now located at the upscale Arena Mall in the Marina.

| WHAT IT COSTS In Israeli shekels | | | | |
| --- | --- | --- | --- | --- |
| $$$$ | $$$ | $$ | $ | ¢ |
| AT DINNER over NIS 100 | NIS 76–NIS 100 | NIS 50–NIS 75 | NIS 32–NIS 49 | under NIS 32 |

Prices are for a main course at dinner.

## American

**$$–$$$$** ✕ **Dixie.** This bar and grill is west of central Tel Aviv, and mostly serves the surrounding offices and commercial centers. But it's open 24 hours a day, and there's no place like Dixie for a hearty American-style breakfast of eggs Benedict or a stack of pancakes. The dinner menu includes prime ribs, Cajun chicken, Norwegian salmon, and a selection of burgers. There is a minimum charge to sit at the comfortable leather couches in the main dining area, but feel free to sit at the bar with an order of spicy chicken wings, the house specialty. ⊠ *120 Yigal Allon, corner of Tozeret Haaretz St., California House, near the Azrieli Center* ☎ *03/ 696–6123* ☲ *AE, DC, MC, V.*

**$$–$$$** ✕ **Moses.** This bar and grill, located on the western end of tony Rothschild Boulevard, has an extensive menu. It's good for the whole family, with kids' dishes like the Moses hamburger and, for the adults, an interesting selection of cocktails. The ribs in molasses are a real treat. ⊠ *35 Rothschild Blvd.* ☎ *03/566–4949* ☲ *AE, DC, MC, V.*

## Barbecue

**$–$$** ✕ **Brewhouse.** One of Rothschild Boulevard's original mansions, the brewhouse has been restored to house a working boutique brewery. Copper vats and pipes add an interesting accent to the décor and the beer is a highlight of the menu. The focus is grilled meat, but lunchtime specials sometimes include an Asian buffet. Service is excellent and prices are moderate for this area. ⊠ *11 Rothschild Blvd.* ☎ *03/516–8666* ▭ *AE, DC, MC, V.*

## Cafés

**$$–$$$** ✕ **Badulina.** This unassuming establishment in Tel Aviv's Old Port is squeezed in along a row of splashier neon-lit restaurants. The menu is in Hebrew only but the friendly staff will translate quickly. The main dishes (mostly fish) come with a choice of two sides: including salad, home-fried potatoes with a sweet Thai chili sauce, and rice. This is a good stop for coffee, prepared with care and flourish, and dessert, appetizingly displayed in a refrigerator up front. There are several kinds of beer on tap. ⊠ *2 Yordi Hasira St., Old Port* ☎ *03/544–9449* ▭ *AE, DC, MC, V.*

**$–$$** ✕ **Café Metzada.** A varied menu—including steak, generous salads, sandwiches, and pasta—makes this a great place for supper after a day at the beach or for a cup of coffee at sunset. There's a fabulous Mediterranean view and the option of indoor or outdoor seating. ⊠ *83 Hayarkon St., Basel* ☎ *03/510–3353* ▭ *AE, DC, MC, V.*

**¢–$** ✕ **Ashtor.** A popular hangout among locals, this small corner café in the heart of the upscale Basel area is a great place "to see and be seen," a favorite Tel Aviv pastime. The coffee is good, the sandwich and salad menu appealing, and the service is helpful. ⊠ *37 Basel St., Basel* ☎ *03/546–5318* ▭ *AE, DC, MC, V.*

**¢–$** ✕ **Café Basel.** Diagonally across the street from Ashtor, this café lacks the neighborhood feel of its competition, but offers a more varied menu. ⊠ *42 Basel St., Basel* ☎ *03/546–1875* ▭ *AE, DC, MC, V.*

**¢–$** ✕ **Ilan's Coffee Shop.** The exclusively developed "Angelo Mio" is considered the best espresso in town. But this café, as well as Ilan's other 12 Tel Aviv locations, also offers 20 other blends of coffee, a selection of teas, and specialty sandwiches. Don't leave without trying a dessert. Especially recommended is the heated *jocolada*—a doughy cake that oozes melted white chocolate from the center. ⊠ *90 Ibn Gvirol St.* ☎ *03/523–5334* ▭ *AE, DC, MC, V.*

**¢–$** ✕ **Siakh Café ("coffee talk").** There's no English menu, and the décor in this small place is spare, but it's a constantly busy local neighborhood favorite. There's a moderately priced selection of sandwiches, salads and quiches, and coffee to linger over with a newspaper at one of the small tables. ⊠ *50 Sheinkin St.* ☎ *03/528–6352* ▭ *AE, DC, MC, V.*

**¢–$** ✕ **Sus Etz.** Lacking an English sign, hungry Sheinkin shoppers will have to be on the lookout for this eatery's logo—an old-fashioned wooden horse. The menu is extensive, including a tempting array of sandwiches served alongside a generous salad as a main dish, pastas, and desserts.

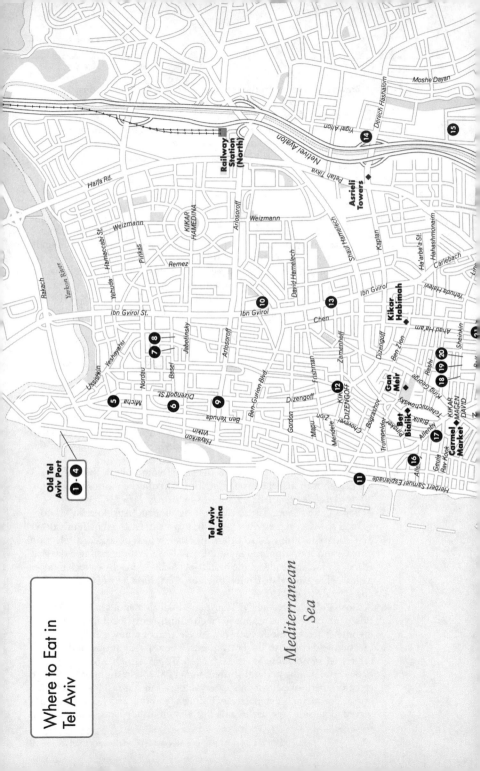

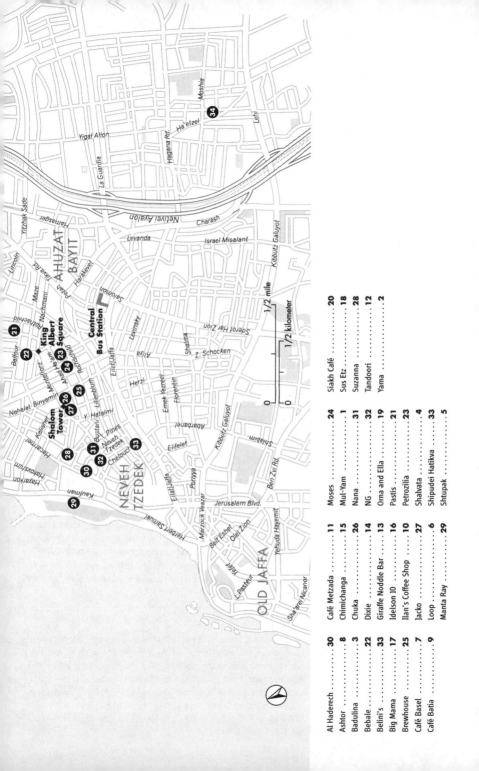

OLD JAFFA

NEVEH TZEDEK

AHUZAT BAYIT

Central Bus Station

King Albert Square

Shalom Tower

1/2 mile
1/2 kilometer

A typical day brings patrons from average folks to lunching ladies, so the people-watching inside and from streetside tables is part of the fun. ⊠ *20 Sheinkin St.* ☏ *03/528–7955* ⊟ *AE, DC, MC, V.*

¢   ✕ **Idelson 10.** Unlike most establishments that bill themselves as "cafés," this neighborhood favorite really does serve only baked goods, coffee, and tea. Service is inside or outside, in a courtyard a few steps down from the street. The courtyard shuts out some of the hustle of nearby Ben Yehuda Street and—along with some retro background music—makes for a tranquil and fun place to stop and sit. The almond croissant, beautifully presented with a few little vanilla-cream-filled petit fours, is delicious. ⊠ *10 Idelson St., Basel* ☏ *03/516–6518* ⊟ *AE, DC, MC, V.*

## Contemporary

$$$–$$$$   ✕ **NG.** Tucked away in a quiet corner of the city, where downtown Tel Aviv becomes Neveh Tzedek, this small, elegant eatery specializes in fine cuts of meat expertly prepared. It's purported to be the only place in Israel to enjoy a real porterhouse steak. Desserts? That depends on the time of year. Tangy strawberry-vanilla pie is a winter specialty, and fig-vanilla pie is a summer favorite. The décor is in warm tones, with Santa Fe–style terra-cotta stucco walls complementing Mediterranean tile floors. ⊠ *6 Ahad Ha'am St.* ☏ *03/516–7888* ⚘ *Reservations essential* ⊟ *AE, DC, MC, V* ☺ *No lunch Sun.–Mon., Wed., Thurs.*

$$–$$$   ✕ **Nana.** Beautifully designed inside and out, this restaurant has an exposed brick exterior and a dark-wood interior, with colorful glass chandeliers and unique stone floors. ⊠ *1 Ahad Ha'am St., Neveh Tzedek* ☏ *03/516–1915* ⚘ *Reservations essential* ⊟ *AE, DC, MC, V.*

$$–$$$   ✕ **Shtupak.** The later in the evening, the longer the line at this unadorned eatery. Locals agree the food is good, reasonably priced, and always fresh. For the main course, there's a daily selection of fresh "catches of the day," which may include whole trout, fried calamari, or oysters in cream sauce. Fish entrées come with an assortment of salads and spreads for starters. ⊠ *256 Ben Yehuda St.* ☏ *03/544–1973* ⊟ *AE, MC, V.*

$–$$   ✕ **Orna and Ella.** As loyal clientele from the greater Tel Aviv area will
Fodor'sChoice   attest, Orna and Ella is worth several trips. The restaurant styles itself
★   as "home-cooked gourmet;" it's also an excellent stop for cakes and desserts. The day's highlight might be anything from moussaka to pasta in butternut squash sauce. Desserts include a scrumptious tarte tatin (apple tart) and pear pie. There is often a long wait for tables, especially Friday afternoon and after 8 PM on weekdays. Call ahead to be put "in the line." ⊠ *33 Sheinkin St.* ☏ *03/620–4753* ⊟ *AE, DC, MC, V.*

## Eastern European

$   ✕ **Bebale.** Old-style Jewish food and plain surroundings are unusual on Israel's restaurant scene, especially in Tel Aviv. Visitors with a yen for inexpensive Eastern European fare should give it a try. Specialties include gefilte fish, chopped liver, meatballs in tomato sauce, and borscht. When Bebale is closed to diners because of take-out activity, Vienna, a few doors away at 62 Ben Yehuda, has similar fare and prices; it's only open until 4. ⊠ *64 Ben Yehuda St.* ☏ *03/560–2228* ⊟ *AE, DC, MC, V* ☺ *Open from 3 PM–6 PM.*

**$**  ✕ **Café Batia.** The simple decor of this Dizengoff Street institution hasn't been changed in years and the menu is similarly filled with old-fashioned Eastern European favorites. Try a bowl of matzoh-ball soup or stuffed cabbage for a nostalgic reminder of the kind of meal that Grandma used to prepare. Eating outside while people-watching is a perk. ⊠ *197 Dizengoff St.* ☎ *03/522–1335* ▤ *AE, DC, MC, V.*

## Indian

★ **$–$$**  ✕ **Tandoori.** This veteran restaurant—the oldest of the Tandoori chain, which introduced Israelis to fine Indian cuisine—has maintained the high quality of its food and service over the years, a noteworthy accomplishment in Tel Aviv. The curries come in three strengths, but tandoori chicken is the specialty: it comes to the table sizzling hot, and finger bowls of rose water mean you can dig in with abandon. ⊠ *2 Zamenhoff St., Dizengoff Circle* ☎ *03/629–6185* ▤ *AE, DC, MC, V.*

## Italian

**$$–$$$**  ✕ **Belini's.** With indoor and outdoor seating, this Tuscan-style establishment facing the open square across from the Suzanne Dellal Center is perfect for a before-theater dinner. The fine wide pasta with hunter's sauce—a brown sauce with mushrooms and white wine—is an unusual blend of flavors for the local scene. The service is friendly and helpful and the Italian house wine is a break from the usual. ⊠ *6 Yechieli St, Neveh Tzedek* ☎ *03/517–8486* ⌲ *Reservations essential* ▤ *AE, DC, MC, V.*

**$$–$$$**  ✕ **Pastis.** In addition to a wide selection of pastas, this bistro offers a selection of seafood and meat dishes. You can eat indoors at dark-wood tables, wine glasses at the ready, or for a more casual experience, try the patio facing the street. ⊠ *73 Rothschild Blvd.* ☎ *03/525–0773* ▤ *AE, DC, MC, V.*

★ **¢–$**  ✕ **Big Mama.** This spot, near the Carmel Market, is a great place to soothe a pasta yen. Try the delicious pumpkin ravioli in cream sauce. The thin-crust pizza is excellent, and the owners use only the freshest ingredients. Toppings range from the traditional basil to more unusual ideas, such as zucchini or prosciutto and egg. ⊠ *13 Nagara St.* ☎ *03/517–5096* ▤ *AE, DC, MC, V.*

## Mediterranean

**$$**  ✕ **Suzanna.** This restaurant, inside a century-old building, bustles day and night. There's something for everyone: from Iraqi *kibbeh* (meat-filled semolina dumplings) and pumpkin soup to a thick Moroccan soup, Kharira, with chickpeas, veal, and coriander. The dessert menu is equally expansive, with home-style sorbet, pear-and-apple tart, and chocolate fudge cake. It's especially nice to sit on the leafy terrace. ⊠ *9 Shabazi St., Neveh Tzedek* ☎ *03/517–7580* ▤ *AE, DC, MC, V.*

## Mexican

**$$**  ✕ **Chimichanga.** Located in a light-industrial area near the Yad Eliyahu stadium, this large and cheerful restaurant is a good place to join celebrating sports fans after a game. Start with a margarita, then tuck into chef Avi Conforti's personal favorite—red sea bream with pepper salsa and red lime sauce. ⊠ *6 Kriminitzky St., Bizzaron* ☎ *03/561–3232* ⊟ *AE, DC, MC, V.*

## Middle Eastern

$ ✕ **Al Haderech.** The name means "on the road" and the location is excellent at this restaurant, sandwiched between the parking lots abutting Neveh Tzedek and across the street from the Dan Panorama Hotel. The food—including falafel, breaded chicken breast, and a selection of salads—is fresh and filling; and the service is friendly and fast. ⊠ *22 Hamered St.* ☎ *03/510–1213* ⊟ *No credit cards* ⊙ *No dinner Fri. Closed Sat.*

$ ✕ **Shipudei Hatikva.** This family-owned restaurant chain is the best known of the many grills along Ha'etzel Street, the bustling main drag of the working-class Hatikva Quarter. The Formica tables and fluorescent lighting are no impediment to the "who's who" of society when they're in the mood for good Middle Eastern fare. There's a selection of salads and spreads to begin, including eggplant in mayonnaise and hot Turkish salad, as well as hummus and pita. For the main course, diners can pick from a range of sumptuous skewered meats grilled over hot coals. The specialty is barbecued goose liver. ⊠ *37 Ha'etzel St., Hatikva* ☎ *03/687–8014* ⊟ *AE, DC, MC, V* ⊙ *No dinner Fri. Closed Sat.*

¢–$ ✕ **Petrozilia.** One of the few kosher restaurants on Rothschild Boulevard, this eatery has a good selection of Israeli favorites, including the ubiquitous schnitzel (breaded chicken breast), and a typical array of Middle Eastern salads. Food is prepared by the garrulous chefs at a front-and-center counter. ⊠ *47 Rothschild Blvd.* ☎ *03/516–2468* ⊟ *AE, DC, MC, V* ⊙ *No dinner Fri. No lunch Sat.*

$–$$ ✕ **Shalvata.** The food is unremarkable, but Shalvata does unusual double-duty: by day it's where trendy Tel Aviv moms take their kids to run around on the lawn while they sip coffee, and there's access to the beach via a flight of steps. By night it's one of the city's better known watering holes, with live performances and room for an audience of 3,000. ⊠ *Old Port* ☎ *03/544–1279, 546–8536* ⊟ *AE, DC, MC, V* ⊙ *Daily 9 AM–late-night.*

## Pan-Asian

$–$$ ✕ **Chuka.** The location is perfect for a bite after an afternoon of shopping at Nahalat Binyamin open-air market. The pleasant, roomy restaurant serves colorful dishes from Burma and Vietnam, along with a variety of sushi. A great sushi platter (for two people) is a house specialty. Locally caught shark, which has been marinated in milk for two days before cooking, is a mainstay of the menu. ⊠ *37 Nahalat Binyamin St., Nahalat Binyamin* ☎ *03/560–5500* ⊟ *AE, DC, MC, V.*

¢–$$ ✕ **Loop.** What this restaurant lacks in atmosphere it more than makes up for with its varied menu of Thai and other Asian dishes. The focus is noodles; try the cold noodles in sesame sauce topped with black cumin and coriander. This is a great place for a filling bowl of miso soup. ⊠ *177 Ben Yehuda St.* ☎ *03/544–9833* ⊟ *AE, DC, MC, V.*

$ ✕ **Giraffe Noodle Bar.** Generous portions of noodles in a variety of Japanese, Thai, and other Asian styles attract a loyal clientele to this crowded, lively restaurant. There's a selection of soups and sushi for starters. Save room for the meringue-based, berry-topped pavlova. Lunch is a particularly good bargain. ⊠ *49 Ibn Gvirol St.* ☎ *03/691–6294* ☷ *AE, DC, MC, V.*

## Seafood

$$–$$$$   ✕ **Mul-Yam.** This high-end eatery is Israel's first true-to-life oyster and
**Fodor'sChoice**  seafood bar. Everything is flown in fresh from abroad—including Nova
★   Scotia lobsters, Forbidden Black Rice from China, red snapper from New Zealand, turbid from the North Sea, and clams from Bretagne—so the prices are not low. Still, it's a true pleasure. Dishes are tasty and well presented; and the great location, in the trendy Old Port by the Mediterranean, adds to the flavor. ⊠ *Hangar 24, Old Port* ☎ *03/546–9920* ⌕ *Reservations essential* ☷ *AE, DC, MC, V.*

$$–$$$   ✕ **Yama.** This brasserie-restaurant serves a good selection of carefully prepared dishes including a selection of steaks, hamburgers, black oysters, and Mediterranean fish and shrimp. Like other restaurants along this strip at the Old Port, Yama has outdoor tables overlooking the water; but the food, service, and décor (with copper and wood accents and cheerful Israeli art) make it one of the area's better eateries. ⊠ *1 Yordei Hasira, Old Port* ☎ *03/546–9093.*

$–$$$   ✕ **Manta Ray.** This large restaurant has a relaxed, if noisy, atmosphere, a great beach view, and indoor and outdoor dining. It appeals to a cross-section of diners from families to couples looking for romance, and attracts a loyal clientele from as far away as Jerusalem. Filling appetizers and beautifully presented, seasoned main dishes and desserts make this a good choice. ⊠ *Alma Beach, near the Dolphinarium* ☎ *03/517–4773* ⌕ *Reservations essential* ☷ *AE, DC, MC, V.*

$$   ✕ **Jacko.** This branch of the Jacko chain is located opposite the Shalom Tower, in one of the most successfully restored houses in old Tel Aviv. The menu features a selection of Mediterranean seafood, grilled trout, and St. Peter's fish (tilapia). It's a good place to try sea bream, a mild-tasting fish raised in the Gulf of Eilat. A filling array of appetizers is included in the price. ⊠ *2 Herzl St.* ☎ *03/516–9325* ⌕ *Reservations essential* ☷ *AE, DC, MC, V.*

# WHERE TO STAY

Nothing stands between Tel Aviv's luxury hotels and the Mediterranean Sea except the golden beach and the Tayelet (promenade), outfitted with chairs and gazebos. Even the small hotels are only a short walk from the water. Tel Aviv's hotel row is on Hayarkon Street, which becomes Herbert Samuel Esplanade as you proceed south between Little Tel Aviv (the Old Port area) and Jaffa. This means that no matter where you stay, you're never far from the main thoroughfares of Ben Yehuda and Dizengoff streets, with their shops and outdoor cafés, or the city's major concert hall, museums, art galleries, and open-air Carmel Market.

Hotel reservations are essential during all Jewish holidays and are advised throughout the year. In winter, Tel Aviv hotels close their outdoor pools, and the lifeguards at the public beaches take a break as well. Hotel health clubs are open to anyone over age 18 but often charge an entrance fee. Keep in mind that most hotels include breakfast in the price: fresh vegetables, salads, and fruit; cereals and pastries; and eggs and cheeses are usually among the options.

Tel Aviv is not known for an overabundance of budget hotels, but those that exist are generally clean and comfortable, with friendly employees who create a warm atmosphere.

| WHAT IT COSTS In U.S. Dollars | | | | |
|---|---|---|---|---|
| $$$$ | $$$ | $$ | $ | ¢ |
| over $250 | $175–$250 | $111–$174 | $65–$110 | under $65 |

Prices are for two people in a standard double room in high season. Non-Israeli citizens paying in foreign currency are exempt from the 16.5% VAT tax on hotel rooms.

## Center City

★ $$$$ 🏨 **Carlton.** The Carlton fancies itself a boutique hotel, and with good reason. The lobby is made up of several intimate sitting areas, each of which features the works of a different artist. Fresh flowers and bowls of fruit can be found on every floor. Wake-up calls are accompanied by fresh juice and newspapers, and milk and cookies are delivered in the evening upon request. The rooms are elegantly designed in muted colors with dark wood furniture. The hotel also has a rooftop pool, a glass-enclosed gym, and two conference rooms with state-of-the art equipment. Service is efficient and personal. ☒ *10 Eliezer Peri St., 61064* ☎ *03/520–1818* 🖳 *03/527–1043* ⊕ *www.carlton.co.il* ⟿ *284 rooms* ⚇ *Restaurant, coffee shop, minibars, Wi-Fi, pool, bar, parking (fee)* ⊟ *AE, DC, MC, V* ⧴ *BP.*

★ $$$$ 🏨 **Dan Tel Aviv.** Despite its reputation for exclusivity, this landmark hotel has a warm, congenial atmosphere. The bathrooms have hair dryers, phones, and radios. Rooms in the luxurious King David wing are larger, have panoramic sea views, and double-glazed windows to muffle city noise. Locals favor the hotel's restaurant for elegant dining. A public beach is across the street. ☒ *99 Hayarkon St., 63903* ☎ *03/520–2525* 🖳 *03/524–9755* ⊕ *www.danhotels.com* ⟿ *49 rooms, 37 suites* ⚇ *3 restaurants, café, minibars, Wi-Fi, 2 pools, health club, sauna, bar, parking (fee)* ⊟ *AE, DC, MC, V* ⧴ *BP.*

$$$$ 🏨 **David InterContinental.** At the southern end of the Tel Aviv coastline, this luxurious hotel is quickly becoming the preferred place to stay for many business travelers, vacationers, and celebrities. The atrium lobby—a massive and elegant room with high ceilings and marble floors—has three restaurants, including Aubergine, which specializes in French and Italian cuisine, and Café Connect, where guests can surf the Net as they face the water. Most rooms overlook the sea. The hotel's top floors are reserved for club-room guests, who have use of a private lounge. ☒ *12 Kaufman St., 68012* ☎ *03/795–1111* 🖳 *03/795–1112* ⊕ *www.interconti.*

*com* ⇗ *516 rooms, 39 suites* ⛲ *2 restaurants, café, 2 pools, spa, bar, shops, children's programs (ages 3–12), business services, Internet room, parking (fee)* ⊟ *AE, DC, MC, V* ⏩ *BP.*

**$$$$** 🏨 **Hilton.** Overlooking the Old Port and bordered on three sides by Independence Park, the Hilton is a luxury hotel that caters directly to business travelers. It offers a state-of-the-art business center, meeting rooms, and Japanese-language services. The hotel's large seawater pool is the best in town and, together with the spa and all the guest rooms, recently has been fully renovated. In addition to enjoying the excellent, eclectic cuisine at the intimate King Solomon Grill, you can grab a bite at the Café Med or at the sushi bar that has a seaside view. ⊠ *Hayarkon St., Independence Park, 63405* ☎ *03/520–2222* 🖷 *03/527–2711* ⊕ *www. hilton.com* ⇗ *582 rooms* ⛲ *2 restaurants, saltwater pool, health club, beach, 2 bars, parking (fee)* ⊟ *AE, DC, MC, V* ⏩ *BP.*

★ **$$$$** 🏨 **Sheraton Tel Aviv Hotel and Towers.** Combining a personal touch with the efficiency and experience of an international chain, this hotel is one of the most attractive lodging options in Tel Aviv. An excellent lobby design allows for private areas within the public space, and there's a lounge bar with a view of the sea. The rooms are decorated in soft hues and color-coordinated fabrics. The well-run executive Sheraton Towers floors have their own check-in and private lounge, which serves refreshments throughout the day. The Olive Leaf restaurant offers Mediterranean-inspired cuisine with a French accent. ⊠ *115 Hayarkon St., 61032* ☎ *03/521–1111* 🖷 *03/523–3322* ⊕ *www.sheraton-telaviv. com* ⇗ *345 rooms* ⛲ *2 restaurants, minibars, Wi-Fi, 2 pools, health club, bar, nightclub, business services, parking (fee)* ⊟ *AE, DC, MC, V* ⏩ *BP.*

**$$$** 🏨 **Dan Panorama.** This high-rise hotel is located at the southern end of the Tel Aviv beachfront, adjacent to the new business district and a short walk to Jaffa and Neveh Tzedek. Each of the attractive rooms has a balcony; north- and south-facing rooms overlook the sea. Poolside barbecues in the summer are a plus. ⊠ *10 Y. Kaufman St., 68012* ☎ *03/519–0190* 🖷 *03/517–1777* ⊕ *www.danhotels.com* ⇗ *500 rooms* ⛲ *Restaurant, coffee shop, Wi-Fi, pool, gym, health club, massage, sauna, bar, parking (fee)* ⊟ *AE, DC, MC, V* ⏩ *BP.*

**$$$** 🏨 **Renaissance Tel Aviv.** All rooms have balconies with sea views at this comfortably informal luxury hotel. Club-floor guests enjoy a private lounge that offers refreshments throughout the day. Restaurants include the Jaffa Terrace, which serves a selection of dairy dishes and pastas, as well as sandwiches and beverages, and the Sabres Brasserie, an eclectic buffet that is open for lunch and dinner. The hotel has direct access to the beach and one of the few indoor heated swimming pools in Tel Aviv. ⊠ *121 Hayarkon St., 63453* ☎ *03/521–5555* 🖷 *03/521–5588* ⊕ *www.marriott.com* ⇗ *342 rooms, 4 suites* ⛲ *2 restaurants, coffee shop, minibars, Wi-Fi, indoor pool, gym, hot tub, sauna, Turkish bath, sun deck, beach, bar, parking (fee)* ⊟ *AE, DC, MC, V* ⏩ *BP.*

**$$$** 🏨 **Sheraton Moriah Tel Aviv.** In this 18-floor hotel all rooms have Mediterranean views from their balconies. Public areas are decorated in earth tones and rooms have Mediterranean color schemes. The outdoor saltwater pool overlooks the beach. ⊠ *155 Hayarkon St., 63453* ☎ *03/*

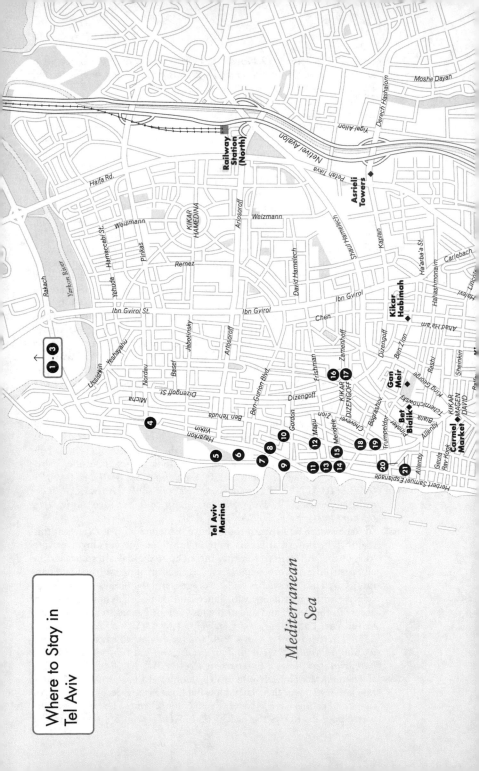

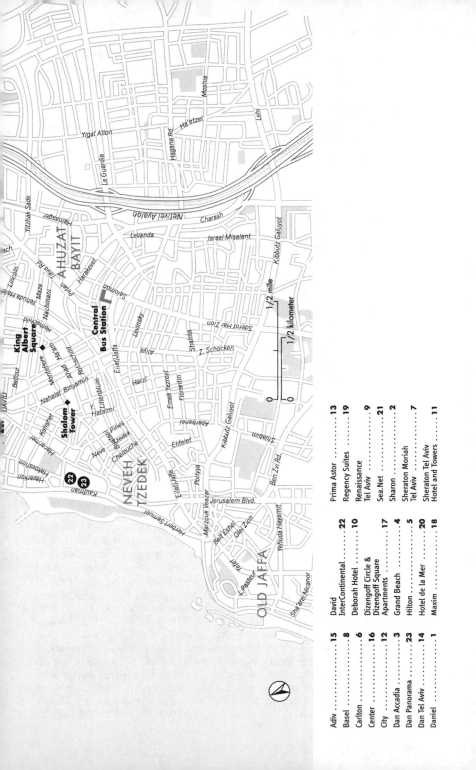

*521–6666* 🖷 *03/527–1065* ⊕ *www.sheraton.co.il* ➷ *335 rooms* ⚲ *2 restaurants, patisserie, in-room safes, minibars, saltwater pool, health club, hair salon, bar, business services, meeting rooms, parking (fee)* ▤ *AE, DC, MC, V* †❍| *BP.*

**$$** ▥ **Adiv.** This amiable five-story hotel is on a side street off Hayarkon Street. Rooms have pleasing modern furnishings and pastel-print bedspreads and curtains. Most rooms have no sea view. The fifth floor has four suites, all with kitchen facilities. ⊠ *5 Mendele St., 63907* ☎ *03/522–9141* 🖷 *03/522–9144* ⊕ *www.adivhotel.com* ➷ *79 rooms* ⚲ *Café, room service, some kitchenettes, Wi-Fi, Internet room* ▤ *AE, DC, MC, V* †❍| *BP.*

**$$** ▥ **Basel.** It's not on the beach side of Hayarkon Street, but this seven-story hotel, one minute's walk from the beach and recently renovated, lives up to its reputation as a good deal. All but five rooms on each floor have sea views. The décor includes well-designed wooden furniture and patchwork-style fabrics. Expect personalized service—probably the legacy of the original Swiss owners. The lobby, with a corner bar, overlooks the small swimming pool. ⊠ *156 Hayarkon St., 63451* ☎ *03/520–7711* 🖷 *03/527–0005* ⊕ *www.inisrael.com/atlas/basel* ➷ *120 rooms* ⚲ *Coffee shop, room service, pool, bar, parking (fee)* ▤ *AE, DC, MC, V* †❍| *BP.*

**$$** ▥ **Deborah Hotel.** The bar and the lobby share a relatively small space, so you can have a drink as you check in. Pleasant guest rooms are decorated with warm colors and wood trim. The location, with easy access to the city center and the beach, is a plus. ⊠ *87 Ben Yehuda St., 63437* ☎ *03/527–8282* 🖷 *03/527–8304* ⊕ *www.deborah-hotel.co.il* ➷ *63 rooms* ⚲ *Lobby lounge, Internet room, free parking* ▤ *AE, DC, MC, V* †❍| *BP.*

**$$** ▥ **Grand Beach.** This basic hotel is a good value for its location: near the northern entance to the city, a 10-minute walk from the Old Port, and a short drive from the museums in Ramat Aviv. The restaurant has a view of city streets; and there's a pool on the rooftop. The beach is a five-minute walk away. ⊠ *250 Hayarkon St., 63113* ☎ *03/543–3333* 🖷 *03/546–6589* ⊕ *www.grandbeach.co.il* ➷ *212 rooms* ⚲ *In-room safes, pool, lobby lounge* ▤ *AE, DC, MC, V* †❍| *BP.*

**$$** ▥ **Hotel de la Mer.** This boutique hotel is in a historic 1930s Bauhaus building a block from the beach. The establishment prides itself on its personalized service and adherence to the design principles of Feng Shui—both in color scheme and furnishings. Its intimate lobby is graced with works by Israeli artist Amos Aricha. There are several varieties of breakfast served either in the tiny dining room; the lobby; guest rooms; or best of all, the rooftop terrace overlooking the beach. ⊠ *62 Hayarkon, off Nes Tziona St., 63904* ☎ *03/510–0011* 🖷 *03/516–7575* ⊕ *www.delamer.co.il* ➷ *26 rooms* ▤ *AE, DC, MC, V* †❍| *BP.*

**$$** ▥ **Prima Astor.** Built on a rise on the corner of Frishman and Hayarkon streets, the Astor has an excellent view of the sea. The rooms in this 30-year-old hotel have recently been enlarged, and many face the Mediterranean. The restaurant, Shangri-La, serves kosher Thai cuisine and sushi and has a beautiful canopied terrace that faces seaward. There's also a coffee bar. ⊠ *105 Hayarkon St., 63903* ☎ *03/520–6666* 🖷 *03/*

*523–7247* ⊕ *www.prima.co.il* ⟿ *50 rooms* ♿ *Restaurant, Wi-Fi, bar, business services, free parking* ▤ *AE, DC, MC, V.*

**$$** ⊞ **Regency Suites.** This Best Western hotel is made up entirely of well-equipped one-bedroom suites, each of which comes with a small living area and kitchenette. The decor is tasteful and the atmosphere is homey. Suites can accommodate up to four people. There's also a lovely breakfast room, but breakfast isn't included. Full, daily cleaning services are provided. ✉ *80 Hayarkon St., 63432* ☎ *03/517–3939* 🖷 *03/516–3276* ⊕ *www.bestwestern.co.il* ⟿ *30 suites* ♿ *Kitchenettes, Wi-Fi, free parking* ▤ *AE, DC, MC, V.*

**$$** ⊞ **Sea.Net.** Offering compact but sparkling and well-appointed rooms with coffee corners, and refrigerators available at an extra charge, this hotel has the informal atmosphere hoped for in a smaller establishment, and a Mediterranean view from the roof terrace a block from the real thing. ✉ *6 Nes Tsiona St. 63904* ☎ *03/517–1655* 🖷 *03/517–1656* ⊕ *www.seanethotel.co.il* ⟿ *70 rooms* ♿ *Café, in-room safes, some refrigerators* ▤ *AE, DC, MC, V* ⛷ *BP.*

**$** ⊞ **Center.** This hotel has simple rooms, warm but basic service, and a good location, only a 15-minute walk from the beach and just off Dizengoff Circle. There's a pleasant sitting area in the lobby and a small dining area where breakfast is served. Rooms are small and tasteful. Many have balconies facing the square, though there is no Mediterranean view. ✉ *2 Zamenhoff St., Dizengoff Circle* ☎ *03/629–6181* 🖷 *03/629–6751* ⊕ *www.atlashotels.co.il* ⟿ *56 rooms* ▤ *AE, DC, MC, V* ⛷ *BP.*

**$** ⊞ **City.** On a quiet street near the beach, this inexpensive six-story hotel has a light, airy lobby with a small sitting area on one side and a cozy restaurant on the other. Basic but pleasant café service is provided on a balcony which faces the neighbor's hedge and offers a glimpse of the sea. ✉ *9 Mapu St., 63577* ☎ *03/524–6253* 🖷 *03/524–6250* ⊕ *www. atlashotels.co.il* ⟿ *96 rooms* ♿ *Restaurant, café, room service, Internet room, free parking* ▤ *AE, DC, MC, V* ⛷ *BP.*

**$** ⊞ **Dizengoff Circle Apartments.** These two apartment complexes—on opposite sides of the Agam Fountain in the heart of Dizengoff Square—provide a comfortable, reasonably priced alternative to Tel Aviv's more expensive hotels. The homey studios, rooms, and suites all have kitchenettes and come in a variety of sizes and prices. The amiable owner will take the time to personally offer travel advice. ✉ *4 Dizengoff Circle, Dizengoff Circle 61111* ☎ *03/524–1151* 🖷 *03/523–5614* ⊕ *www. hotel-apt.com/dsa* ⟿ *51 studio units, 4 suites* ♿ *Kitchenettes with refrigerator, microwave, and electric range, TV/Cable, Wi-Fi in some units* ▤ *AE, DC, MC, V.*

**$** ⊞ **Maxim.** This hotel is a good value, especially considering the location: just across the street from the luxury hotel strip and the beach. The rooms are basic, but most have sea views. Europeans like to stay here, and there is a Continental feel about the place, owing in part to the many languages heard in the lobby. The lobby café is a popular place to relax. Coffee and cake in the afternoon are included in the room price. ✉ *86 Hayarkon St., 63903* ☎ *03/517–3721* 🖷 *03/517–3726* ⊕ *www.maxim-htl-ta.co.il* ⟿ *60 rooms* ♿ *Café, Wi-Fi* ▤ *AE, DC, MC, V* ⛷ *BP.*

## Herzliya Pituach

Herzliya Pituach is a resort area 12 km (7½ mi) up the coast from Tel Aviv. It has a number of beachfront hotels, a wide range of dining options (some on the beach but most a short distance inland), public squares with outdoor cafés and shops, and the marina and adjacent Arena Mall with its selection of high-end shops. Affluent suburbanites live here, as do diplomats and foreign journalists; there's a cosmopolitan, holiday air to the place.

**$$$$** 🏨 **Dan Accadia.** The two buildings of this veteran seaside hotel are surrounded by plant-filled lawns, which in turn surround a pool overlooking the sea. Sixty rooms face the pool, with direct access to the beach; others face the marina. The rooms are not huge, but they have balconies with sea views; interior decor includes quilted bedspreads and matching blue-and-pink drapes. Organized activities help keep children and teenagers amused on Friday and Saturday. Guests have access to the adjacent tennis courts, to the nine-hole executive Ga'ash golf course (a 10-minute drive), and to the golf course at the Dan Caesarea, farther north. ⊠ *22 Ramat Yam St., Herzliya Pituach, 46851* 🕾 *09/959–7070* 🖷 *09/959–7091* ⊕ *www.danhotels.com* 🖙 *185 rooms* ⚸ *2 restaurants, coffee shop, 6 tennis courts, pool, gym, hair salon, massage, sauna, bar, children's programs (ages 5–12), free parking* ▤ *AE, DC, MC, V* ⍾ *BP.*

**$$$$** 🏨 **Daniel.** One of the bonuses of the seaside Daniel is the fine spa, whose facilities include an indoor pool, wet and dry sauna, and single and double treatment rooms. All rooms look onto the Mediterranean; the deluxe rooms have balconies. The décor is a tasteful mix of sea-blue and mustard hues. Business-club floors offer office services and access to a plush lounge that serves light refreshments. There is a movie theater adjacent to the hotel. ⊠ *60 Ramot Yam, Herzliya Pituach, 46851* 🕾 *09/952–8282* 🖷 *09/952–8500* ⊕ *www.danielhotel.com* 🖙 *200 rooms* ⚸ *2 restaurants, room service, 2 tennis courts, 2 pools (1 indoor), saunas, spa, bar, shops, business services, parking (fee)* ▤ *AE, DC, MC, V* ⍾ *BP.*

**$$$** 🏨 **Sharon.** Most of the renovated rooms have balconies overlooking the sea. Garden rooms are near the outdoor seawater pool. The Sharon's health club has a heated indoor pool, a workout room, dry and wet saunas, massage, and Dead Sea mineral baths. The Sharon Kiddy Club runs during the summer months, on holidays, and weekends. ⊠ *5 Ramat Yam, Herzliya Pituach 46748* 🕾 *09/957–5777* 🖷 *09/956–8741* ⊕ *www.sharon.co.il* 🖙 *170 rooms* ⚸ *Restaurant, room service, tennis court, indoor pool, saltwater pool, health club, hair salon, bar, children's programs (ages 5–10), free parking* ▤ *AE, DC, MC, V* ⍾ *BP.*

# NIGHTLIFE & THE ARTS

## Nightlife

Peak hours on Hayarkon Street on a Friday or Saturday night continue until about 3 AM, when things finally begin to wind down. On Allenby

Street and Florentine, the clubs are still crowded at 5 AM. Partygoers are not daunted by the fact that nightspots come and go about as quickly as the tides.

Bars and nightspots in Tel Aviv usually open long before the night owls descend; typically, they offer either full dinners, beer and fries, or at the very least, the coffee and cake they've been serving throughout the afternoon.

## Bars, Pubs & Nightclubs

**Cafe Noga** (⊠ 4 Pinsker St. ☎ 03/629–6457) is a bar that doubles as a pool hall. The music ranges from oldies to ambient, with a hint of local sound tossed in the mix.

**Gorky** (⊠ 16 Elipelet St. Florintine Quarter ☎ 03/683–0202) has a loyal cadre of youngish regulars go for a wide range of live music and a good bar.

**Lola** (⊠ 54 Allenby St. ☎ 03/516–7803) features alternative and electronic music, and a crowd to match.

**Mike's Place** (⊠ 81 Hayarkon ☎ 03/516–8619) is small and has a well-stocked bar, with a variety of music that attracts an over-30 crowd (unlike many other Tel Aviv nightspots). It sometimes organizes parties, especially to coincide with sporting events, which patrons can watch on a big-screen TV and rejoice or cry into their beer over the fate of their team until the wee hours.

**Mishmish** (⊠ 17 Lilienblum St. ☎ 03/516–8178) is a classy and retro cocktail bar with:great service.

**My Coffee Cup/Bar 39** (⊠ 39 Allenby St.) is an outdoor café by day and a bar by night. It's a great place to check out the fervor of Allenby Street's nightlife scene while being able to hold a conversation.

**Nanutchka** (⊠ 28 Lilienblum St. ☎ 03/516–2254) is a bistro-bar, with an ornate Georgian (of the former Soviet Union) design occupying a number of rooms in an old building, and a Georgian menu to match.

**Scene** (⊠ 56 Allenby St.) is a bar–dance club specializing in house and techno. The long, dimly lit bar separates the lounge in the front from the dance area in the back. Monday is Gay Night, and on Wednesday internationally known DJs are featured. It's closed on Sunday and Tuesday.

**Shoshana Johnson** (⊠ 94 Allenby St. ☎ 03/560–7443) has a well-stocked and roomy bar, with a quiet tangerine-tree garden and a Mediterranean menu that makes this place popular with a youngish local crowd.

**Yoezar** (⊠ 2 Yuazar Ish Habira, near clock tower, Jaffa ☎ 03/683–9115), is a posh wine bar with a good Provençal French menu, owned and operated by one of Israel's best-known gourmets.

## Gay Bars

Tel Aviv's thriving gay scene is part of its cosmopolitan image. Gay bars come and go even faster than other bars and restaurants, though a few seem to be standing the test of time.

**Evita** (✉ 31 Yavne St ☎ 03/566–9559) is a small, classy place with good food. It's often marked by the long line outside in the later hours, attesting to its popularity.

**Carpe Diem** (✉ 17 Montefiori ☎ 03/560–2006) has the same crowd as Evita, with the added advantage of a garden area.

**Minerva** (✉ 20 Beit Hamoshava St. ☎ 03/566–6051) is a fashionable bar with its own art gallery and a decent menu, and a men's night once a week.

## The Arts

Tel Aviv is Israel's cultural capital, and it fulfills this role with relish. Like New York, the city is full of people who devote their lives to the arts without necessarily getting paid for it. It's entirely likely that your waitress, taxi driver, or salesperson is also a struggling actor, painter, or musician.

The Friday editions of the English-language *Jerusalem Post* and *Ha'aretz* contain extensive entertainment listings for the entire country.

There are three **main ticket agencies** for performances in Tel Aviv. All accept major credit cards. You must pick up your tickets in person and have your credit card with you: **Hadran** (✉ 90 Ibn Gvirol St ☎ 03/527–9955), **Castel** (✉ 153 Ibn Gvirol St. ☎ 03/604–5000), and **Le'an** (✉ 101 Dizengoff St. ☎ 03/524–7373, 03/523–0898).

### Dance

Most of Israel's dance groups, including the contemporary Bat Sheva Dance Company, perform in the **Suzanne Dellal Center for Dance and Theater** (✉ 6 Yeheli St., Neveh Tzedek ☎ 03/510–5656), and Neveh Tzedek itself is home to artists and a growing number of tony galleries and gift shops. A visit here is a cultural experience, as the complex itself is an example of new Israeli architectural styles used to restore some of the oldest buildings in Tel Aviv.

### Music

**Mayumana** (✉ 15 Louis Pasteur St., Jaffa ☎ 03/681–1787) is Israel's answer to Stomp, a troupe of drummers who bang in perfect synchronicity on anything from garbage pails to the floor. Performances are held on some Thursdays, and weekends; tickets cost NIS 145.

The **Enav Cultural Center** (✉ Gan Ha'Ir [roof level], 71 Ibn Gvirol St. ☎ 03/521–7766, 03/521–7763) is a more intimate venue, also with eclectic fare.

The **Mann Auditorium** (✉ 1 Huberman St. ☎ 03/621–7777), Israel's largest concert hall, is home to the Israel Philharmonic Orchestra from the end of October through the end of July. It is also possible to catch an occasional rock, pop, or jazz concert here.

**Hayarkon Park** (☎ 03/642–2828) is where large outdoor concerts are held at the Wohl Amphitheater.

**Shablul** (✉ Hangar 13, Old Port ☎ 03/546–1891) is located in the reborn Old Port. This intimate club offers jazz performances Monday through Saturday nights spanning the scale from mainstream, hip-hop, bee-bop, Latin, and ethno-jazz, to avant-garde and free jazz. Performers include veteran jazz artists and up-and-coming young talents; open stage every Monday night.

### Opera

The **Tel Aviv Performing Arts Center** (✉ 28 Leonardo da Vinci St. ☎ 03/692–7700, 03/692–7777 for box office) is home to the budding New Israeli Opera during the November-to-June season. Tickets are available at the box office.

### Theater

Performances are almost always in Hebrew.

Most of the plays at **Bet Leissin** (✉ 101 Dizengoff St. ☎ 03/725–5333) are by Israeli playwrights.

The **Cameri Theater** (✉ 30 da Vinci St. ☎ 03/606–1900) sometimes offers screened English translations.

**Habimah** (✉ Habimah Sq. ☎ 03/629–5555) is the national theater; plays here are all in Hebrew, but some have simultaneous translation.

**Hasimta Theater** (✉ 8 Mazal Dagim St. ☎ 03/681–2126), in Old Jaffa, features avant-garde and fringe performances.

# SPORTS & THE OUTDOORS

## Beaches

Tel Aviv alone has eight distinct beach areas, each with its own personality. Tel Baruch Beach at Namir Road and Propes Street has lawns and a boardwalk, making it the city's top family beach, while the Aviv Beach at the southern tip of Hayarkon Street attracts a youthful singles crowd. At sunset on Fridays, musicians gather and form drumming circles.

Beaches in the heart of the city are free. Hatzuk, on the northern edge of Tel Aviv, charges an entrance fee, as do the beaches in Herzliya (except Sidni Ali).

Beaches are generally named after something nearby—a street or a hotel, for example. Thus, you have Hilton Beach in front of the hotel of that name, Gordon Beach at the end of Gordon Street, and likewise Bograshov Beach. Sometimes, however, this gets a bit confusing: Sheraton Beach is at the site of the first Sheraton Hotel in Tel Aviv, about 1 km (½ mi) north of today's Sheraton; and Jerusalem Beach, at the bottom of Allenby Road, is named after the city, not after something in Tel Aviv.

When choosing a beach, look for one with timber lifeguard huts, where first aid is available. Lifeguards are on duty from roughly May to October, from 7 AM until between 4 PM and 7 PM, depending on the month (check with your hotel's concierge). Be forewarned: Tel Aviv's lifeguards are fond of yelling commands over the loudspeakers if they think swimmers are misbehaving. Most beaches have public amenities, including bathrooms and changing rooms. If you sit in a chaise lounge or under an umbrella, a municipal worker will come by to charge you a small fee and give you a receipt.

## Participant Sports

### Boating

**Yehoshua Gardens (Hayarkon Park)** (☎ 03/642–0541), along Rokach Boulevard in the northern part of the city, rents out pedal boats and rowboats (NIS 60 per hour) and motorboats (NIS 80 per half hour). You can also opt for pleasure boats, which take up to 100 people for 20-minute rides (NIS 12 per person); bicycles; or tandems that take up to six people (NIS 45 per half hour).

### Health Clubs

Most of the city's luxury hotels have health clubs, normally free for guests.

The Cybex Spa at the **Hilton** (✉ Hayarkon St. ☎ 03/520–2222) has the largest gym but is open only to guests and members. The club is open Sun.–Thurs. 6 AM–10 PM, Fri. 6 AM–7 PM, Sat. 9 AM–7 PM.

### Sailing

All sailboats require an Israeli license to operate. However, you can charter a sailboat or a yacht with a skipper at the **Old Port** (☎ 03/527–2596).

### Scuba Diving

The **Dugit Diving Center** (✉ 250 Ben-Yehuda St. ☎ 03/604–5034) serves as a popular meeting place for veteran divers. Although the view beneath the surface of the Mediterranean Sea doesn't offer as breathtaking an array of fish and coral as the Red Sea, it's a good place to start. Diving courses are available Dugit holds diving courses for all levels. Diving equipment is available for sale, and for rent on a daily basis to licensed divers.

### Swimming

The **Gordon Pool** (✉ Eliezer Peri 14, near the end of Gordon St. ☎ 03/527–1555), a Tel Aviv institution since the 1950s, at present open only during July and August, includes an outdoor Olympic-size pool of saline groundwater changed daily. Entrance to the pool costs NIS 50. It's open daily 6 AM–7 PM.

### Waterskiing

**Park Darom** (☎ 03/739–1168), in southern Tel Aviv, runs waterskiing without boats: cables attached to a revolving crane pull you around an artificial lake, a system that holds no appeal for some but is particularly good for beginners. Costs are around NIS 70 for half an hour, including instruction, on weekdays, and NIS 81 on Saturdays. It's open daily from April through October, but hours vary, so call in advance.

## Spectator Sports

**Yad Eliyahu (Nokia) Stadium** (✉ 51 Yigal Alon St. ☎ 03/537–6376) is the place to go for basketball games.

**Bloomfield Stadium** (✉ 1 Hatehiya St., Jaffa ☎ 03/681–7115) hosts soccer matches.

The **Ramat Gan Football Stadium** (✉ Abba Hillel Rd., Ramat Gan ☎ 03/617–1500) is another venue for soccer.

# SHOPPING

Tel Aviv's shopping scene has made rapid advances in recent years, as prosperous Israelis have begun demanding higher-quality goods.

## Department Stores

**Hamashbir** (✉ Dizengoff Center, Dizengoff and King George sts. ☎ 03/528–5136) carries, for the most part, a rather banal selection of goods, often at prices a little higher than those in smaller stores. On the second floor, however, its Designer Avenue features women's clothing by local designers, who also have boutiques at the northern end of Dizengoff Street or in the surrounding area—sample the range here, and then ask for the address if you'd like to see more of a particular designer's line. It's open 10 AM–9:30 PM, Mon.–Thurs.; Friday until 2 PM.

## Shopping Districts & Malls

Shopping malls are generally open from 9:30 AM to 9:30 PM Mon.–Thurs., and Friday 9:30 AM to 2 PM.

The **Azrieli Center** (✉ Hashalom Rd., above the railway station) is a sparkling new mall with the added attraction of the view from the top floor.

**Gan Ha'Ir** (✉ 71 Ibn Gvirol St., north Tel Aviv) is a small, quiet, upscale mall centrally located off Rabin Square.

The **Dizengoff Center** (✉ Dizengoff and King George sts.) is Israel's first shopping mall and can no longer be considered its most lustrous. It's multileveled and somewhat confusing to navigate. Stores sell everything from air conditioners to camping equipment, with many fashion boutiques in between.

**Kikar Hamedina,** in northern Tel Aviv, is arguably the most expensive real estate in the country; this is where the wealthy shop. Hit the shops on this circular street for, say, a Sonia Rykiel or Chanel suit, perhaps a Kenzo creation, or a pound of Godiva chocolates. The middle of the square is an unkempt plaza that, alas, is the perfect foil to the luxury surrounding it but does nothing to bring prices down.

The **Opera Tower** (✉ 1 Allenby St.) is near the sea and has a small but eclectic range of stores. It's particularly good for jewelry. The Tower Records on the ground floor is a great place to find local music.

The **Ramat Aviv Mall** (✉ 40 Einstein St. Ramat Aviv) is a good place to shop and have lunch if you're visiting the Ramat Aviv museums.

## Specialty Stores

### Jewelry, Judaica & Ethnic Crafts

**Ayala Bar** (✉ 36 Shabazi St. ☎ 03/510–0082 ☉ Sun.–Thurs. 10:15–7, Fri. 10:15–4) is the sparkling multicolored creation of Israeli designer

Ayala Bar. Her bracelets, earrings, and necklaces are now famous and popular around the world.

**The Bauhaus Center** (✉ 99 Dizengoff St. ☎ 03/522–2049 ⊙ Sun.–Thurs. 10–7:30, Fri. 10–2:30), with its display of books, maps, posters, furnishings, dishes, and even Judaica, all inspired by Bauhaus design, reminds visitors that this school of design embraced more than buildings. At the center, you can book Friday morning tours (often in English) of Tel Aviv's Bauhaus buildings, which are on the prestigious UNESCO World Heritage List.

**Ben Yehuda Street** has a few mostly hole-in-the-wall gift shops that specialize in Judaica, especially between Gordon and Bograshov streets, but you will find some bargains. For silver and hand-crafted items, hit the **Nahalat Binyamin Pedestrian Mall** street fair on Tuesday or Friday. Shop for sophisticated gems and jewels at **H. Stern**, with branches in the David InterContinental, Daniel, Sheraton Tel Aviv, Hilton, and Dan hotels.

Visitors wandering Neveh Tzedek shouldn't miss the **Ceramics Gallery** (✉ 27 Shabazi St., Neveh Tzedek ☎ 03/516–6229 ⊙ Sun.–Thurs. 10–8, Fri. 10–5), which houses a collection of several of Tel Aviv's most creative ceramicists. A pleasingly eclectic group of both decorative and practical items in a variety of colors, shapes, and textures grace the shelves here, at a variety of prices, and small, relatively inexpensive items that travel well, such as tea-bag stands and spoon rests, are on offer.

**comme il faut** (✉ Bait Banamal, Hangar 26, Old Port ☎ 03/544–9211 ⊙ Sun.–Thurs. 9–9, Sat. 11–9) is a cluster of contemporary port shops run by a company whose products and vision highlight elements of women's lifestyle, including fashions, housewares, and gifts, both practical and whimsical. A changing gallery of photographs and other artwork adorn the walls of the mall.

### Swimwear

For a bargain, visit Tel Aviv's three **bathing-suit factory outlets,** in Yad Eliyahu near the Cinerama arena: **Gottex** (✉ 62 Anilvich St. ☎ 03/537–3879 ⊙ Mon.–Thurs. 9–5:45, Fri. 9–2), **Oberson** (✉ 8 Nirim St. ☎ 03/639–6151 ⊙ Mon.–Thurs. 9:30–5:30, Fri. 9:30–1 PM),and **Pilpel** (✉ 3 Nirim St. ☎ 03/537–5784 ⊙ Mon.–Thurs. 9:30–5:30, Fri. 9:30–1).

## Street Markets

At the **Nahalat Binyamin** street fair, held Tuesday and Friday, local crafts ranging from handmade puppets to olive-wood sculptures and silver jewelry attract throngs of shoppers and browsers. The **flea market** in Jaffa is mostly full of junk these days, but you can still find a bargain, even if it's not an authentic antique. The flea market has a wide selection of reasonably priced Middle Eastern–style jewelry that uses chains of small silver coins and imitation stones.

# TEL AVIV ESSENTIALS

## Transportation

### BY AIR

All international flights land at Ben Gurion International Airport, which is 16 km (10 mi) southeast of Tel Aviv, except charter flights to Eilat. The airport is modern and efficient and is served by most major American and European carriers, with frequent and convenient connections to major cities around the world.

From Sde Dov Airport, about 4 km (2½ mi) north of the city center, the domestic airline Arkia flies to Eilat (some 10 flights per day), Haifa (3 flights).

The train to Ben Gurion International from central Tel Aviv is a convenient way to go. When departing for the airport from central Tel Aviv by car or taxi at rush hour (7–9 AM, 5–7 PM), the roads can get clogged so allow 45 minutes for a trip that would otherwise take only about 20 minutes.

🚹 **Arkia Airlines** ☎ 1800/444-8888 **Ben Gurion International Airport** ☎ *6663, 03/975-5555 ⊕ www.iaa.gov.il. **Sde Dov Airport** ☎ 03/698-4500.

### BY BUS

Bus travel in Israel is generally very convenient. The main interurban bus company operates primarily from Tel Aviv's **Central Bus Station** but also from the **Central Railway Station.** Buses leave for Jerusalem every 15 minutes throughout most of the day. Travelers purchase their tickets at the central ticket booth or, if the booth is closed, from the driver on the bus. Only the Eilat line requires advance reservations—particularly necessary in peak season.

The city bus system is well developed, with lines run primarily by the Dan bus cooperative, as well as by Egged. The fare is a fixed NIS 5.30 within the city center, and you buy your tickets on the bus. There is a small discount for a 10-ride card, and travelers who think they might use the buses extensively in the city can buy a monthly pass at the Central Bus Station good on Egged or Dan busses in the greater metropolitan area of Tel Aviv for NIS 149.

Two of the major lines, Bus 4 (Ben Yehuda and Allenby streets) and Bus 5 (Dizengoff Street and Rothschild Boulevard), are also serviced by privately run red minibuses. You can flag these down and ask to get off at any point along their routes; the fare is the same as on regular buses. Minibuses also run on Saturday, when regular buses do not.

🚹 **Central Bus Station** ⊠ Levinsky St. **Central Railway Station** ⊠ Arlosoroff St. **Dan Bus Services** ☎ 03/639-4444. **Egged** ☎ 03/694-8888.

### BY CAR

Driving in Tel Aviv is not for the faint-hearted. Aside from the aggressive tactics of other drivers, Tel Aviv's no-turns and no U-turns can be daunting. Moreover, many of Tel Aviv's main streets are only accessible to taxis and public transportation vehicles during the day. Some street names may not be marked in English—or, indeed, at all—which makes getting to your destination nothing short of a headache, and parking is a major problem, including the clamping or towing of illegally parked cars. In central Tel Aviv, much of the parking is for residents only, who have the appropriate stickers for their areas. Cars without stickers are either towed or clamped. Yellow signs indicating public parking are displayed in English (along with Hebrew and Arabic) where this is permitted; there is either a meter or, at short intervals on the nearby sidewalks, ticket dispensers which you punch in the time you will be using the space (some spaces are limited to two or three hours). Good navigators, armed with a good map should take advantage of Tel Aviv's belt road, the Ayalon Freeway, to access various parts of the city, though not during rush hour (7–9 AM and 3–7 PM). Gas costs approximately NIS 6 per liter. Gas stations are very frequent; some close for the Sabbath (from Friday around sundown to Saturday after sundown).

Thankfully, central Tel Aviv is more fun on foot. Most attractions and sights are in the heart of the city within walking distance of one another; and when you get tired, a bus or taxi is never far away.

### BY TAXI

*Sherut* taxis are a fleet of stretch Mercedes-Benzes or vans at the Central Bus Station that run the same routes as the buses, at comparable one-way prices (unlike buses, sheruts do not offer round-trip tickets). Arrivals and departures are determined by how long it takes to fill all seven seats of each car. Sheruts can be found at various points (depending on destination) in front of the bus platforms; you can usually hear someone yelling the destination before you even approach. (If you don't, try yelling yourself—someone is sure to point you in the right direction.) Sheruts do run on Saturday at a higher charge.

Taxis here can be any car model or color; they're identified by lighted signs on top. Cabs are plentiful, even in bad weather; drivers will honk their horns to catch your attention, even if you're not trying to catch theirs. If you're traveling within the metropolitan area, make sure the driver turns the meter on when you get into the car. Rates are NIS 7.70 for the first 18 seconds and 30 agorot in increments thereafter. For interurban trips, there is a fixed tariff; if you think you're being quoted a price that's too high, ask to see the tariff in the booklet each driver carries. Expect night rates to be about 25 percent higher than day rates.

### BY TRAIN

The train is an excellent way to travel between Tel Aviv and cities and towns to the north, such as Netanya, Hadera, Haifa, and Nahariya. Trains run frequently from Ben Gurion's Terminal 3 directly to and from Tel Aviv. The northbound train leaves from the Central Railway Station and the Azrieli station. The information office is open Sunday to Thursday 6 AM–11 PM and Friday 6–3. Trains run roughly every hour on weekdays from 5–6 AM to 10–11 PM depending on destination; there are fewer trains on Friday and Jewish holiday eves and no service on Saturday or on holidays. There is also a line to and from Beersheva. The Tel Aviv–Jerusalem train runs to the new station in south Jerusalem near the Malkha Mall.

🚉 **Central Railway Station** ⊠ Arlosoroff St. ☎ 03/577–4000.

## Contacts & Resources

### ATMS

ATMs are located at almost every bank, and they usually accept U.S. credit cards (although not always debit cards). When you insert your bank card, the screen will automatically switch to English.

### BANKS & EXCHANGING SERVICES

**Change Place** (⊠ Ben Gurion Airport Lod ☎ 03/973–0348 ⊕ www.cpl. co.il ⊗ 24 hours) **Change Spot** (⊠ 140 Dizengoff ☎ 03/524–3393 ⊕ www.changespot.co.il ⊗ Sun.–Thurs. 9–7, Fri. 9–2).

**Hapoalim Bank, Ben Yehuda Branch** (⊠ 25 Ben-Yehuda Tel Aviv ☎ 03/ 567–3333 ⊕ www.bankhapoalim.co.il ⊗ Sun., Tues., and Wed. 8:30–2, Mon. and Thurs. 8:30–2, 4–5).

**Discount Bank, Main Branch** (⊠ 27–31 Yehuda Halevy ☎ 03/514–5555 ⊕ www.discountbank.co.il ⊗ Sun. 8:30–2, Mon.–Thurs. 8:30–3, Fri. 8:30–1).

### DENTISTS

Ichilov Hospital has dental service Sunday, Monday, and Wednesday 8–7, Tuesday and Thursday 8–1. The dental clinic is open daily from 8 AM to 10 PM.

🚉 **Dental clinic** ⊠ 18 Reines St., Dizengoff Center ☎ 03/522-1226.

### EMERGENCIES

Ichilov Hospital, which is in north Tel Aviv, is about a 10-minute drive (depending on traffic) from the heart of downtown. They have a 24-hour emergency room that is the best place to go for emergency medical care. Be sure to bring your passport with you. You will be provided with all records in English for your insurance providers at home. If you need an ambulance, you can call 101 to reach Magen David Adom.

Emergency calls are free at public phones; no tokens or telecards are necessary.

Pharmacies take turns keeping late hours, and the duty roster changes daily. Check the *Jerusalem Post* or *Ha'aretz* for those currently on call.

🚉 **Ambulance/Magen David Adom** ⊠ 2 Alkalai St. ☎ 101 for emergencies, 03/546-0111. **Fire** ☎ 102. **Ichilov Hospital** ⊠ Weizmann St., Dizengoff Center ☎ 03/697-4444. **Police** ☎ 100. **Police Stations** ⊠ 14 Harakevet St., near the Central Bus Station ☎ 03/564-4444 ⊠ 221 Dizengoff St. ☎ 03/545-4444.

### INTERNET, MAIL & SHIPPING

The major hotels have Wi-Fi connections in guest rooms or data ports and full-service business centers. There are post office branches throughout the city. Federal Express and DHL will pick up packages from any Tel Aviv address.

🛈 **DHL** ✉ 5 Hapardes St.  ☎ 1700/707-345. **Federal Express** ✉ 90 Jabotinsky St., Petah Tikvah ☎ 03/920-2211, 1700/700-378. **Post Office** ✉ Industrialists House, 29 Hamered St., near Neveh Tzedek ☎ 03/510-3735 ⓥ Sun.-Thurs. 8-3, Fri. 8-noon ✉ Habima, 17 Tarsat St. ☎ 03/620-4858 ⓥ Sun., Mon., Wed., Thurs., 8-12:30 and 4-6, Tues. 8-1:30, Fri. 8-noon ✉ 61 Hayarkon St. ☎ 03/510-0218 ⓥ Sun.-Thurs. 8-6, Fri. 8-12.

## MEDIA

There are two local English newspapers, the same as in the rest of the country; they are the *Jerusalem Post* and *Ha'aretz,* which comes inside the *Herald Tribune.*

ENGLISH-LANGUAGE BOOKSTORES

Steimatzky is Israel's best-known chain, with several Tel Aviv locations and a large selection of books in English.

🛈 **Steimatzky** ✉ 107 Allenby St.  ☎ 03/566-4277 ✉ 109 Dizengoff St. ☎ 03/522-1513.

## TOUR OPTIONS

BOAT TOURS

Kefand runs a half-hour boat tour on Saturdays year-round, from the Jaffa Port along the Tel Aviv water front and back. The fare is NIS 20.

PERSONAL GUIDES

Twelve Tribes provides personal guides, usually with a car, who will take you anywhere in the city and even around the country. Personal guides can also be arranged through most hotels.

WALKING TOURS

The Tel Aviv–Jaffa municipality has laid out four self-guided tours of the city called the Tapuz (Orange) Routes; these take in both historic and current cultural sites. Maps are available from the Tel Aviv Tourist Information Office. Free, city-sponsored walking tours of Old Jaffa begin at the clock tower on Wednesday at 9 AM; no prior registration is required.

🛈 **Kefand** ✉ Jaffa Port ☎ 03/682-9070. **Twelve Tribes** ✉ 29 Hamered St. ☎ 03/510-1911 🖷 03/510-1943.

## VISITOR INFORMATION

The tourist bureau at Ben Gurion Airport is open 24 hours. You'll find the latest local information at the Tel Aviv Tourist Information Office, open Sunday to Thursday 9–5, Friday 9–1. They can also provide a list, albeit not comprehensive, of *zimmerim* (bed-and-breakfast-type accommodations) and youth hostels.

🛈 **Tel Aviv Tourist Information Office** ✉ 46 Herbert Samuel St. ☎ 03/516-6188 ⓥ Sun.-Thurs. 9:30-4, Fri. 9:30-1:00 ✉ City Hall Lobby, 69 Ibn Gvirol St. ☎ 03/521-8500 ⓥ Sun.-Thurs. 9-2.

# Haifa &
# the Northern
# Coast

## INCLUDING CAESAREA, AKKO & WESTERN GALILEE

**4**

### WORD OF MOUTH

"Haifa [is] a really beautiful city with a mixed population. . . . The view from [Mt. Carmel] is stunning and the beaches are nice. You can see the German Colony (street with artists and their work), Arab areas, Jewish areas, and there are great restaurants to boot! Near Haifa I would say to take a day trip to the artists' colony of Ein Hod. This is a wonderful little town that only lets artists live in the community . . . The artists open their studios (often inside their homes) and show and sell their work. In Ein Hod there is an INCREDIBLE Argentinian restaurant."

—littlerandi

Updated by
Judy Stacey
Goldman

**STRETCHED TAUT ON A NARROW COASTAL STRIP** between Tel Aviv and the chalky cliffs of the Lebanese border, this region offers more than just balmy Mediterranean beaches. Sand and sea meet archaeology here—historical sights line the shore along with the gently undulating dunes, fields, and citrus groves of the Sharon Plain. This fertile swath encompasses Netanya and Caesarea, and gives way to the Shomron wine region. Today, Caesarea is a panoply of restored Roman, Byzantine, and Crusader bathhouses; mosaic floors; and columned streets, with a theater and a frescoed forum. A moat surrounds the ancient Crusader city, set beside the azure Mediterranean. The arches of an ancient aqueduct disappear into the sand, and Israeli children splash in the cove in summer, heedless of the feats of King Herod's engineers.

It was in the softly contoured foothills and valleys at the base of Mt. Carmel that the philanthropic Baron Edmond de Rothschild came to the Jews' aid in helping Israel create a wine industry, now one of the region's most successful enterprises. The Carmel range rises dramatically to its pine-covered heights over the coast of Haifa, a friendly, hardworking, and thoroughly modern port city. North of Haifa is the Western Galilee, which runs along a fertile plain up to the Lebanese border. Just across the sweeping arc of Haifa Bay lies Akko, a jewel of a Crusader city that combines Romanesque ruins, Muslim domes and minarets, and swaying palms. To the north, the resort town of Nahariya draws droves of vacationing Israelis. And just south of the Lebanese border, don't miss the amazing seaside caves at Rosh Hanikra, which have been scooped from the cliffs by the pounding surf.

As the scenery changes, so does the ethnic mix of the residents and their ancestors: Druze, Carmelite monks, Ottomans, Baha'is, Christian and Muslim Arabs, and Jews. Paleontologists continue to study on-site the artifacts of the most ancient natives of all, the prehistoric people of the caves of Nahal Me'arot, on Mt. Carmel. The Baha'is, whose universalist religion embraces the teachings of many others, dominate Haifa's mountainside. Their golden-dome shrine gleams, and the terraced gardens spill down the slope like bright jewels. Robed Carmelite monks preside quietly over their monasteries in Haifa and in Mukhraka, on Mt. Carmel, next door to the Druze villages. Although the north-coast Druze consider themselves an integral part of Israeli society, they maintain a unique cultural and religious enclave on Mt. Carmel, with the secret rites and rituals of their faith and the distinctive handlebar moustaches and white head scarves favored by the older men. Arabs and Jews live side by side in Akko, whose dilapidated, cramped, and dusty old quarter belies its pristine, picture-postcard reputation. Yet Akko's vast subterranean Crusader vaults and halls, Ottoman skyline of domes and minarets, and outdoor *shuk* (market) can still enchant.

As you drive north, you'll enjoy long stretches of unimpeded views of the sparkling blue Mediterranean. Beautiful beaches lie beside Netanya, Haifa, and Achziv, replete with soft sand, no-frills hummus joints, and elegant seaside restaurants. You can learn to scuba dive or explore underwater shipwrecks, and then vist ancient Caesarea and Akko, listening to the roar of the surf all the while. Other great pleasures of the region

Remember to allow time for swimming, hiking, or golfing if you're so inclined. Here the Mediterranean coast is lined with beaches, the land is packed with scenic trails, and Caesarea has Israel's only 18-hole golf course. Less-conventional sporting options include paragliding and underwater diving to shipwrecks.

*Numbers in the text correspond to numbers in the margin and on the Northern Coast & Western Galilee, Haifa, and Akko–Old City maps.*

**4**

**If you have
2 days**

For a quick tour of the highlights, start with King Herod's port city, **Caesarea ❷**, bursting with Roman, Byzantine, and Crusader ruins. Then travel through Rothschild wine country, in the rolling Carmel Hills, and **Binyamina ⓳**, one of the area's first settlements. Set aside several hours to half a day for the pioneer village of **Zichron Ya'akov ㉑** and the picturesque Druze villages of **Daliyat el Carmel ㉔** and **Isfiya ㉕**. Stay overnight in modern 🔲 **Haifa ❺–⓲**, atop Mt. Carmel. The next day, get an early start so you can see the Baha'i Shrine and Gardens on your way down the hill and out of Haifa. Head north to the walled Crusader city of **Akko ㉘–㊱**, and after a late lunch, head up to the Lebanese border and watch the waves crash through the caves at **Rosh Hanikra ㊵**.

**If you have
3 days**

Start with a visit to the Carmel Wine Cellars (reserve a tour in advance) and **Zichron Ya'akov ㉑**; then head through the hilly wine country to see the Carmelite Monastery at **Mukhraka ㉓**. Stop at **Daliyat el Carmel ㉔** en route to 🔲 **Haifa ❺–⓲**. Bright and early the next morning, visit the Baha'i Shrine and Gardens; then head north to **Akko ㉘–㊱** and zip up the coast to **Rosh Hanikra ㊵**. Return to Haifa for the night. On the third day, explore the artists' village of **Ein Hod ㉖** and **Caesarea ❷**.

**If you have
5 days**

On a hot summer's day, stop at **Netanya ❶** for a swim beneath the cliffs. Then drive through Rothschild wine country to the restored Roman theater and Ottoman fortress at **Shuni ⓴**, and continue on to the Carmel Wine Cellars and the pioneer town of **Zichron Ya'akov ㉑**. Travel through the foothills of Mt. Carmel to the Carmelite Monastery at **Mukhraka ㉓** and the Druze villages of **Daliyat el Carmel ㉔** and **Isfiya ㉕**. Spend the night in 🔲 **Haifa ❺–⓲**, and devote the next day to exploring the city. On day three, leave Haifa early for the walled Crusader city of **Akko ㉘–㊱**, the Holocaust memorial museum at **Lochamei Hageta'ot ㊳**, and the seaside town of **Nahariya ㊴**. Now that you're almost at the Lebanese border, a short drive north brings you to the incredible sea caves at **Rosh Hanikra ㊵**. You can spend the night in Haifa, but you may want to move on to tomorrow's stomping ground, **Caesarea ❷**. After exploring the myriad ruins, head south to **Nahsholim-Dor ❸** to see the intriguing Underwater Museum. From here you'll zigzag between Route 2 and Route 4 to see the reconstructed British detention camp at **Atlit ❹** and the artists' village of **Ein Hod ㉖**. The prehistoric Carmel Caves are near the entrance to the **Nahal Me'arot Nature Reserve ㉗**, where you might want to set aside a few hours for a hike on the wooded slopes of Mt. Carmel.

include hiking the slopes of pine-scented Mt. Carmel, treading the winding lanes of Ein Hod artists' village, and tasting local wines and tangy cheeses at some of the region's excellent wineries.

## Top 5 Reasons to Go

- **Caesarea:** The ruins of Roman structures built by King Herod, mosaic-floored Byzantine bathhouses, Crusader moats, crumbling walls, and gatehouses sit beside the sea, along with a tempting selection of restaurants.

- **Baha'i Gardens:** In the middle of Haifa, tumbling down from the mountaintop, 18 stunning, jewel-like terraces enclose a shimmering gold-dome shrine.

- **Underground Akko:** At this fascinating site, you can marvel at how the Crusaders built numerous halls with huge pillars. There's also a secret tunnel and a Turkish bathhouse where the "attendant" tells his story.

- **Glorious beaches:** The coast means beaches, and this is Israel's stretch of golden sand on the deep-blue Mediterranean. Whether you're into scuba diving in old shipwrecks or windsurfing on the rippling waves, there's plenty to keep you busy here.

- **Great wine:** Taste and toast internationally known wines at the Shomrom appellation wineries, set in the hillsides of the northern coast.

# Exploring the Northern Coast & Western Galilee

Starting from Tel Aviv, Route 2 (the Coastal Road) hugs the coast, introducing travelers to the northern coast via Netanya, Caesarea, and Haifa, with archaeological sites Nahsholim-Dor and Atlit in between. It's about an hour's drive from Tel Aviv to Haifa. Zigzagging along to the east, parallel to Route 2 (at the most about 10 km, or 6 mi, away), is Route 4, also known as the Old Haifa Road. Just off Route 4 is the Rothschild wine country—the scenic back-door route to Haifa—which meanders through the foothills and up the spine of Mt. Carmel, taking in Shuni, Zichron Ya'akov, the Carmel Park, the Carmelite monastery at Mukhraka, and two Druze villages near Haifa. (A branch of Route 4, going north and then inland, winds through the huge Carmel National Park and later connects with Route 672, leading to the Druze villages.) Haifa is Israel's third-largest city and is a good base for two other sights to the south, Ein Hod and the Carmel Caves. The Western Galilee is the area north of Haifa, including Akko, Nahariya, and Rosh Hanikra, with several sights along the way and inland. All sights in this region are within easy driving distance of Caesarea and Haifa, the former a quiet overnight spot and the latter a thriving city.

## About the Restaurants

You won't have to look hard in this region for a restaurant with either a striking view of the Mediterranean or good fresh fish, or both. These range in style from fishing-shack to upscale chic. The fish you'll most often find on your menu—served grilled or baked, with a variety of sauces—are *locus* (grouper), *mulit* (red mullet), *churi* (red snapper), and *farida* (sea bream). Also fresh, but hailing from commercial fishponds and the Sea of Galilee, are *buri* (gray mullet) and the ubiquitous tilapia,

## Archaeology
It's said that wherever you put down a shovel in Israel, you'll find ancient ruins. Even onetime visitors to Caesarea have found old coins after a rainfall, when the surface earth is washed away (keep an eye out when you visit!). Archaeologists continue to uncover history, while restorers lovingly assemble shards and patch up ancient buildings. Caesarea and Akko are two of Israel's star archaeological sites, where even repeat visitors are amazed to find new and stunning discoveries each time. Such museums as the underwater archaeology museum at Nahsholim-Dor and the Hecht Museum at Haifa University display finds in unusually engaging style. And Herod's fabulous port, which subsided beneath the Caesarea waters 2,000 years ago, beckons scuba divers to an underwater tour.

**4**

## Beaches
Between Tel Aviv and the Lebanese border are miles of beautiful sandy beaches, most of them public and attended by lifeguards from early May to mid-October. Many Israeli beaches are left untended off-season and get pretty grubby, but they're generally cleaned up and well maintained once warm weather returns. *Never* swim in the absence of a lifeguard, as the currents and undertows can be dangerous.

## Hiking & Walking
Lovely parks and nature reserves grace the coastal area, both along the Mediterranean shore and in the hilly areas to the east. The best known of these is the flourishing Carmel Park, which comprises 20,000 hilly acres and covers the top of Mt. Carmel. Several parks and reserves have visitor centers, where staff can explain maps and trails, and all have parking lots, restrooms, and picnic areas. Though parks and reserves are generally not sign-posted from the road in English, you can spot the entrances by looking for the distinctive dark wooden boards with white or yellow letters.

## Performing Arts
On many a balmy summer night in towns up and down the coast, you're bound to find an outdoor concert or dance performance. In summer, the events held under the stars on the reconstructed stage of Caesarea's are particularly memorable; in other seasons, catch chamber music in the artists' village of Ein Hod. For printed listings, check the Friday issue of the *Jerusalem Post* or *HaAretz* (with the *Herald Tribune*) or pick up a copy of the brochure "Haifa-Israel," available at hotels and the Tourist Board in Haifa.

## Wine
Wine lovers, take note: this is one of the country's prime wine-growing areas (its classification is Shomron). Though wine has been produced in Israel for thousands of years, and the Rothschilds updated viniculture around Zichron Ya'akov some 120 years ago, truly high-quality wines have appeared on the market only in the last decade or so. Not only can visitors tour the cavernous old barrel rooms of the Carmel Wine Cellars, the very first winery established in Israel, but a couple of wineries now have charming restaurants. After a tour of the winery it is delightful to sit under the grapevines and sample the vintages along with fresh salad, warm bread, and good local cheese.

as well as the hybrid *iltit* (salmon-trout). Fresh seafood, such as shrimp and calamari, is also found in restaurants along the coast. Many casual restaurants serve french fries and shnitzel (breaded and fried chicken cutlets), which kids often love.

Until recently, coastal restaurants weren't as refined as those in Tel Aviv, with a few exceptions. Not so any longer. Hilly Haifa, now firmly on the tourist track with the opening of the Baha'i Garden terraces and the newly restored German Colony, has several interesting restaurants with creative chefs and good wine lists. The hilltop artists' village of Ein Hod presents sumptuous Argentinian dining in the village square. Breakfasts at local country B&Bs are nothing short of delicious. Eating ethnic food is always a pleasure: you can sample the locally famous falafel in the Druze village of Daliyat el Carmel or try hearty dishes at family-run Eastern European restaurants in Haifa. Netanya has the region's highest concentration of kosher establishments—and a French-owned creperie.

Even at the most expensive restaurants in this region, dress is informal (but tasteful). Ties are never required.

| WHAT IT COSTS in Israeli shekels | | | | |
|---|---|---|---|---|
| **$$$$** | **$$$** | **$$** | **$** | **¢** |
| AT DINNER | over NIS 100 | NIS 76–NIS 100 | NIS 50–NIS 75 | NIS 32–NIS 49 | Under NIS 32 |

Prices are for a main course at dinner.

## About the Hotels

Options range from small and spare to luxury hotels, though you won't find nearly the selection and quality of deluxe accommodations comparable to those in, say, Tel Aviv. However, gracious and attractive B&Bs are tucked into the trees along the coast, mostly north of Nahariya. As well, the splendid spa hotel in the Carmel forest near Haifa warrants its great reputation, and a small and charming spa lodging sits in a rural coastal settlement not far from Akko. In some places, such as Zichron Ya'acov, the pickings are slim but because this region is so compact, you can cover many coastal sights from one base.

The chart below lists peak-season prices, which normally kick in for July and August; Passover, Rosh Hashanah, Yom Kippur; and Hanukkah. Many hotels are considerably less expensive—sometimes 40% less—during low season, from November through February.

Camping facilities, including some bungalows and cabins, dot the coastline north of Netanya. Note that the wooded slopes of Carmel National Park, however inviting, do not have facilities. Contact the tourist office in Tel Aviv ( ⇨ *see* Visitor Information *in* Chapter 3) or Haifa.

| WHAT IT COSTS In U.S. Dollars | | | | |
|---|---|---|---|---|
| **$$$$** | **$$$** | **$$** | **$** | **¢** |
| FOR 2 PEOPLE | over $250 | $175–$250 | $111–$174 | $65–$110 | Under $65 |

Prices are for two people in a standard double room in high season. Non-Israeli citizens paying in foreign currency are exempt from the 16.5% VAT tax on hotel rooms.

### Timing

Summer (June–September) is hot, but there's no humidity, and soft sea and mountain breezes cool things down. Spring (April–May) and fall (October–November) are balmy and crisp. Winter (late December, January, February, and into March) brings cold weather (sun interspersed with rain), while the sea makes the wind chilly. If you have warm clothes, you can wander in comfort.

As in the rest of Israel, hotels and other lodgings fill up on weekends. On Saturdays and national holidays, Israelis themselves hit the road, so it's best to avoid north-to-south travel out of Tel Aviv or Jerusalem altogether, or prepare for big crowds at beaches and sights. If you're taking a two-day trip, and if you have the option, the weekdays (Sunday to Thursday) will give you peace and quiet at hotels and sites. If you can only go on Friday and Saturday, make reservations well in advance.

Summer brings theater and dance to Caesarea's Roman theater and a blues festival to Haifa, usually in July.

# THE NORTHERN COAST

## Netanya

❶ *30 km (18 mi) north of Tel Aviv, off Rte. 2; take second exit (Central Netanya).*

Netanya, the geographic hub of the Sharon Plain, is a seaside resort, with cliffs rising above a pristine beach. Once a sleepy town of farms and orange groves, Netanya—named after Jewish philanthropist Nathan Strauss—has steadily burgeoned from a few settlers in 1929 to some 200,000 residents today.

Though citrus farming is still evident on Netanya's outskirts, there are few traces of small-town charm and few sights to see in the rambling clusters of apartment buildings, some built on the coast itself. Travelers revel in consistently sunny days, the sandy public beaches just below the cliffs—ideal for swimming, sunbathing, windsurfing, and paragliding—and the pleasant outdoor cafés on the pedestrian mall.

*need a break?* Cool off at **Tony's Ice** (Ha'atzmaut Square near Dizengoff St.) with divine authentic Italian ice cream (*gelatti*) in a huge array of flavors, home-produced by a family of immigrants from Italy. Tony's also has a coffee bar, milkshakes, and pastries.

Lively **Ha'atzmaut Square,** near the beach, is the city's heart, along with the adjoining pedestrian mall. Both are packed with open-air cafés and restaurants that are crowded late into the night, often in the mornings, and all day Friday. Benches sit among the flower beds and palm trees; a tourist information office is nearby. Saturday nights are enlivened by folk dancing, and the amphitheater hosts free concerts in summer and an arts-and-crafts fair on Friday mornings. Netanya attracts droves of French visitors, and in summer their lilting tones float above the café au lait and croissants served in the outdoor cafés. To get to your hotel

The Northern Coast & Western Galilee

LEBANON

GOLAN HEIGHTS

Sea of Galilee (Lake Kinneret)

Jordan R.

Mediterranean Sea

Rosh Hanikra **40**

Nahariya **39**

Lochamei Hageta'ot **38**

Baha'i Founder's Shrine and Garden **37**

Achziv National Park

Montfort

Yehiam

8833

Yehiam

Hazor HaGelilit

Zfat

Meron

Karmi'el

Sakhnin

Arraba

Tamra

Shefar'am

Kiryat Ata

Nesher

Kiryat Bialik

Akko **28 – 35** see detail map

Haifa **5 – 18** see detail map

Mt. Carmel

Carmel National Park

Tirat Carmel

Atlit **4**

Nahshalim-Dor

Nahal Me'arot Nature Reserve **27**

Ein Hod **26**

Isfiya **25**

Daliyat el Carmel **24**

Mukhraka **23**

South Bar Shlomo **22**

Zichron Ya'akov **3**

Nazareth

Afula

Tiberias

Degania

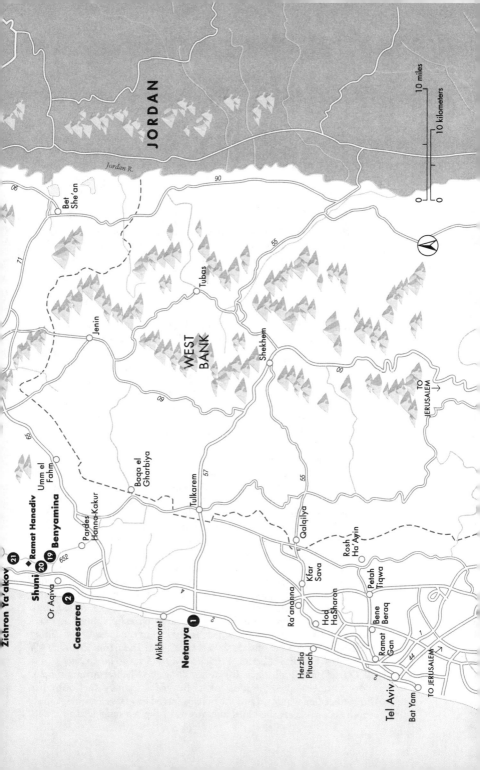

or the beach, drive down the town's main artery, Herzl Street, which ends at the pedestrian mall and Ha'atzmaut Square; access to the (free) beaches is south and north of the mall.

★ ☾ Netanya's **Oved Ben Ami Promenade** (also known as "the Boulevard") is a beautifully landscaped walkway that winds around the contours of the cliffs overlooking the sea; at every angle there's a different gorgeous view. It's dotted with pergola-shaded benches, colorful playground areas on soft groundcover, and waving palm trees. You can pick up about a mile of it, going north, three blocks north of the Carmel hotel, on Gad Machness Street, where you enter just after the Blauweiss hotel; it ends at Shaul Hamelech Boulevard.

**off the beaten path**

**FIELDS OF FLOWERS** – In February and March, detour a few kilometers south of the city to see fields carpeted with a rare, exotic variety of deep-indigo wild iris that is indigenous to this area. Marked paths lead the way, and there's a parking lot on Ben Gurion Boulevard.

## Where to Stay & Eat

**$$$** ✕ **El Gaucho.** Tucked into the Carmel Hotel, El Gaucho is one of Israel's top-quality (and kosher) steak houses. Decorated in a rustic style, the restaurant is dominated by a dramatic view of the sea, with a picturesque garden below. South American–style meat specialties are cooked over embers on a giant grill that forms part of the restaurant. Juicy steaks, grilled chicken, and fish are highlights, and the wine list is extensive. Eating here during daylight hours or at sunset is recommended because of the breathtaking view of sea and sky. ✉ *Carmel Hotel, Jabotinsky St.* ☎ *09/884–1264* ⚓ *Reservations essential* ▭ *AE, DC, MC, V* ☾ *No lunch Sat., no dinner Fri.*

**$$$** ✕ **Rosemarine.** This unpretentious place is fish heaven, offering plenty of great people-watching, too. Sample fresh and tasty fare as you sit either indoors or on the terrace overlooking the famous Netanya promenade. The kitchen serves a wide range of fish dishes, such as tilapia and gray mullet, which are prepared grilled, baked, or sautéed. Entrées come with a choice of salad or roasted potatoes. ✉ *8 Nice St.* ☎ *09/832–3322* ▭ *AE, DC, MC, V* ☾ *Closed Sat. No dinner Fri.*

★ ☾ ¢ ✕ **Bat Ha'ikar.** The locally beloved "Farmer's Daughter" is worth a visit despite its setting amid workshops, garages, and warehouses in an industrial zone. Spacious, busy, noisy, and totally informal, it's a venue for bustling family celebrations. The cooking is strictly Middle Eastern, including an endless array of fresh salads and skewers of grilled lamb and chicken. It's fun to roll the various foods in fresh, piping-hot, oversize *laffas* (large, thin pitas), which are baked in full view of the dining area inside massive ovens. ✉ *8 Pinkas St., Old Industrial Zone* ☎ *09/884–4474* ▭ *AE, DC, MC, V* ☾ *No dinner Fri., no lunch Sat.*

**$$$** ▦ **Carmel Hotel.** Built on a cliff overlooking the Mediterranean, the 20-story Carmel makes the most of its beautiful setting—the lobby has floor-to-ceiling windows and the hotel is served by glass elevators. Guest-room decor reflects the blues and greens of the sea outside, and all accommodations have sea views. Most also have kitchenettes (dishes, pots, and utensils furnished upon request). The pool is open from May to October; there's a well-equipped fitness center. It's fun to sit on the lawn and watch the paragliders, who use the grass as their springboard into the blue. ✉ *Jabotinsky St., south of Ha'atzmaut Sq.* ☎ *09/860–1111* 🖷 *09/887–6060* ⊕ *www.carmel-hotel.co.il* ⇥ *77 rooms, 13 suites* ⌂ *Restaurant, refrigerators, cable TV, pool, children's pool, sauna, massage, gym, lobby lounge, pub, free parking* ⊟ *AE, DC, MC, V.*

★ **$$$** ⌨ **Seasons Netanya.** Attractive and well established, the Seasons provides consistently good service. The bedrooms are spacious, with private terraces and sea views; they are decorated in restful pastels, and the baths are luxurious. Eight "garden" rooms are beside the pool. The pool overlooks the sea and is surrounded by flower beds and yellow chaises (it's open, though unheated in winter). The dining room also has a view of the water. ✉ *1 Nice Blvd., 42269* ☎ *09/860–1555* 🖷 *09/862–3022* ⊕ *www.seasons.co.il* ⇥ *97 rooms, 45 suites* ⌂ *2 restaurants, room service, minibars, tennis court, pool, children's pool, gym, massage, sauna, lobby lounge, children's programs (ages 3–11), laundry service, business services, internet room* ⊟ *AE, DC, MC, V.*

**$** ⌨ **Mizpe Yam.** Don't expect luxury at this relatively small family-owned hotel. What you can count on is a great value and warm, personal service. This is a fine option if you're passing through and need a clean and basic accommodation for an evening or two; there's no pool, though the beach is a few minutes away. There's a sundeck on the roof, and self-service coffee machines are in the hallways. ✉ *1 Jabotinsky St., 42112* ☎🖷 *09/862–3730* ⊕ *www.mizpe-yam.co.il* ⇥ *32 rooms* ⌂ *Restaurant, refrigerators, in-room safes, Wi-Fi* ⊟ *AE, DC, MC, V* ⏏ *BP.*

## Sports & the Outdoors

BEACHES   Standard facilities, including lifeguards, first-aid station, showers, toilets, and changing rooms, are available free at all of Netanya's beaches, which cover 12 km (7 mi) of soft, sandy coastline. Most beaches also

★ rent beach chairs and umbrellas. The main section, **Sironit,** is open year-round; the parking lot is on the beach, just off Jabotinsky Street south of the main square, and costs NIS 12 per car. An elevator at Gad Machness Street, just south of Ha'atzmaut Square, takes pedestrians down the seaside cliff to this beach. There are volleyball nets and snack bars along the sand. North of town is the Orthodox beach **Kiryat Sanz,** where men and women have different bathing days and hours. There's a beach near the **Seasons Hotel,** with a restaurant and refreshment stand as well as standard facilities. **Herzl** is right in front of Ha'atzmaut Square and has a water slide, restaurant, and refreshment stand. **Argamon** has a refreshment stand but no chair or umbrella rentals.

There's a lovely **private beach** (☎ 09/866–6230) 5 km (3 mi) north of Netanya, next to Moshav Bet Yannai. Amenities include grills, picnic tables, a lifeguard in season, toilets, cold showers, and chair and umbrella rentals. There is no entrance fee, but parking costs NIS 25. Because this beach is only 2,400 feet long and cannot comfortably accommodate crowds, it's wise to come on a weekday.

The beach at **Mikhmoret,** 7½ km (4½ mi) north of Netanya, is very popular. The huge dirt parking lot, which charges NIS 30 per car, is 1 km (½ mi) after the turnoff from Route 2. There are three lifeguard stations, a restaurant, a café, and chair and umbrella rentals.

HORSEBACK RIDING   The **Ranch** (✉ HaMelachim St. ☎ 09/866–3525) is in northern Netanya, 2 km (1 mi) up the road from the Blue Bay Hotel. It's wise to reserve well ahead for Saturday or for moonlight rides on the beach. (You'll need at least eight people to make a reservation.) The stables are open daily 9–6; the cost is NIS 100 per hour.

PARAGLIDING   Netanya's cliffs offer great paragliding. Under the guidance of experienced instructors, you take off from a specially designed field by the Promenade. **Air Taxi** (☎ 050/576–1259) offers paragliding instruction. **Dvir Paragliding** (☎ 09/899–0277 or 050/833–3103) is an established company that offers thrilling adventures. **Shahaf** (☎ 052/280–5944 or 050/833–3093) takes two passengers on a tandem motorized flight.

## Shopping

Netanya is known for quality diamonds. **Caprice** (✉ 90 Herzl St. ☎ 09/862–4770) is a reliable shop that also sells watches and semiprecious stones. One store worth visiting is **Inbal Jewelry** (✉ 1 Ussishkin St. ☎ 09/882–2233), known for its special in-house designs. Prices are competitive.

# Caesarea

❷   *16 km (10 mi) north of Netanya, 49 km (29½ mi) south of Haifa.*

Fodor'sChoice
★   By turns ancient Roman port city, Byzantine capital, and Crusader stronghold, Caesarea marks the northern tip of the Sharon Plain. Chockfull of Roman, Byzantine, and Crusader ruins, it's a delightful place to spend a day of leisurely sightseeing, and you can also visit the innovative Time Tower (especially fun for children), discover great shopping, and swim at the beach. Stretched out over 3 km (2 mi) are a Roman theater, a Crusader city, and Roman-Byzantine remains that include a mosaic-floored bathhouse, a Herodian amphitheater, parts of Herod's port, and, in the sand dunes themselves, an ancient aqueduct.

There are two entrances to this intriguing site. A good strategy is to start at the Roman Theater, at the southern entrance to the site (not far from the Caesarea Museum), and then end up by the Time Tower, restaurant, and shopping area. You can then leave through the northeast medieval Crusader gate and come out the northern entrance. (If you're short of time, you can enter through the northern entrance, visit part of the site and the Time Tower, and eat at one of the restaurants on the water.) At either entrance, pick up the free brochure and map. Always lock your car and keep valuables hidden. ☎ 04/636–1010 ⊕ www.parks.org.il 🎫 NIS 23 *without the Time Tower; NIS 40 with the Time Tower* ☉ *Oct.–Mar., daily 8–4; Apr.–Sept., daily 8–5. Arrive well before closing time.*

Caesarea is distinguished by well-marked signs in English. Entry to the **Roman theater** is through one of the vomitoria (arched tunnels that led the public into Roman theaters). Herod's theaters—here and elsewhere in Israel—were the first of their kind in the ancient Near East. The theater today seats 3,600 and is a spectacular venue for summer concerts and performances. What you see today is predominantly a reconstruction. Only a few of the seats of the *cavea* (where the audience sat) near the orchestra are original, in addition to some of the stairs and the decorative wall at the front of the stage.

Behind the theater in the large area of ongoing excavations along the shore, you'll see the **promontory palace**. The **Herodian amphitheater** is a huge, elongated, horseshoe-shape entertainment area, its sloping sides filled with rows of stone seats (most likely the one mentioned by 1st-century AD historian Josephus Flavius in *The Jewish War*). Here some 10,000 spectators watched horse and chariot races and various sporting events some 2,000 years ago. Up the wooden steps, you'll see the the street's beautiful and imaginative mosaic floors in the bathhouse complex of the Roman-Byzantine administrative area.

The walls that surround the **Crusader city** were built by King Louis IX of France. They enclose both the remains of the Herodian port and the Crusader city itself, which was actually only one-third the size of Herod's original city. The bulk of what you see today—the moat, escarpment, citadel, and walls, which once contained 16 towers—dates from 1251, when the French king actually spent a year pitching in with his own two hands to help restore the existing fortifications. The Crusaders first besieged and conquered Caesarea in 1101 after it had been ruled for nearly five centuries by Arabs, who had allowed the port to silt up.

You enter the Crusader city over a dry moat. Note the sloping glacis against the outer wall, the shooting niches, and the groined vaults of the gatehouse. Once inside, signs direct you on a walking tour. You'll soon arrive at the high area containing the remains of the unfinished Crusader cathedral; the three graceful curves of its apses stand out. At the observation point looking seaward, there's a lookout over the ancient port, now underwater. The port was devastated by an earthquake in AD 130. The Crusaders utilized only a small section of the harbor when they conquered Caesarea in 1101. You can actually see the shadowy outlines of these submerged harbor constructions from the top of the tower, which is now the Citadel restaurant. The diving center in Caesarea's port offers underwater tours with marked maps of the port area.

Even today, **Herod's port** can be regarded as an awesome achievement. Josephus Flavius described the wonders of the port in glowing terms, comparing it to Athens's port of Piraeus. Once archaeologists explored the underwater ruins, beginning in the 1960s and continuing sporadically into the 1990s, it became clear that what had been long dismissed by many historians as hyperbole was exactly as Josephus described it.

Don't miss the **Time Tower** (☎ 04/617–4444) in the squarish stone building with glass windows, on the jetty sticking out into the harbor. Climbing the stairs brings you to an intriguing three-dimensional animation on giant screens that explains the amazing construction of Herod's port. You can meet Caesarea's fascinating historic figures—among them

# CloseUp

## BUILDING HEROD'S PORT

The port's construction at Caesarea was an unprecedented challenge—there was no artificial harbor of this size anywhere in the world. There were no islands or bays to provide natural protection, and the work itself was hindered by bad weather. During preliminary underwater digs in 1978, archaeologists were stunned to discover concrete blocks near the breakwater offshore, indicating the highly sophisticated use of hydraulic concrete (which hardens underwater). Historians knew that the Romans had developed such techniques, but before the discoveries at Caesarea, they never knew hydraulic concrete to have been used on such a massive scale. The main ingredient in the concrete, volcanic ash, was probably imported from Mt. Vesuvius, in Italy, as were the wooden forms. Teams of professional divers actually did much of the trickiest work, laying the foundations hundreds of yards offshore. To inhibit the natural process of silting, engineers designed sluice channels to cut through the breakwaters and flush out the harbor. Herod's engineers also devised underwater structures to break the impact of waves.

Once finished, two massive breakwaters—one stretching west and then north from the Citadel restaurant some 1,800 feet and the other 600 feet long, both now submerged—sheltered an area of about 3½ acres from the waves and tides. Two towers, each mounted by three colossal statues, marked the entrance to the port; and although neither the towers nor the statues have been found, a tiny medal bearing their image was discovered in the first underwater excavations here, in 1960. The finished harbor also contained the dominating temple to Augustus and cavernous storage facilities along the shore.

King Herod, Rabbi Akiva, and St. Paul. These realistic-looking figures can answer all kinds of questions you might have.

East of the northern entrance to the site (across the road), a small, sunken, fenced-in area encloses Caesarea's **Byzantine street.** It was during the Byzantine period and in late Roman times that Caesarea thrived as a center of Christian scholarship and as an episcopal see; in the 7th century, Caesarea had a famous library of some 30,000 volumes that originated with the collection of the Christian philosopher Origen (185–254), who lived in Caesarea for two decades. Towering over the street are two monumental marble statues that face each other, both probably carted here from nearby Roman temples. The provenance of the milky white one is unknown; the red porphyry figure might have been commissioned by the Emperor Hadrian when he visited Caesarea.

★ The excellent **Caesarea Museum** houses many of the artifacts found by kibbutz members as they plowed their fields in the 1940s. The small museum has arguably the best collection of late-Roman sculpture in Israel; impressive holdings of rare Roman and Byzantine gemstones; and a large variety of coins minted in Caesarea over the ages, as well as oil lamps, urns excavated from the sea floor, and fragments of jewelry. ⊠ *On grounds* *of Kibbutz Sdot Yam, about 600 feet south of entrance to theater* ☎ *04/ 636–4367* ⊕ *www.parks.org.il* ✉ *NIS 12* ☉ *Sat.–Thurs. 10–4, Fri. 10–1.*

A wonderful finale to your trip to Caesarea (especially at sunset) is the **Roman aqueduct** on the beach. The chain of arches tumbling north toward the horizon, where they disappear beneath the sand, is a captivating sight and forms a unique backdrop for a great photo. During Roman times, the demand for a steady water supply was considerable, but the source was a spring about 13 km (8 mi) away in the foothills of Mt. Carmel. Workers had to cut a channel approximately 6½ km (4 mi) long through solid rock before the water was piped into the aqueduct, whose arches spanned that entire length. In the 2nd century, Hadrian doubled its capacity by adding a new channel. Today you can walk along the sea side of the aqueduct and see marble plaques dedicated to the support troops of various legions who toiled here. On your way back to the road, you might want to drive around the villa area and admire some of Israel's tonier homes, some brand new and many covered with swaths of brilliant bougainvillea. ⊠ *Villa area, north of Crusader city.*

## Where to Stay & Eat

★ ☾ **$$$** ✕ **Crusaders' Restaurant.** You can depend on satisfying, tasty fare at this cavernous, open, bustling restaurant named for the nearby Crusader city. Expect to find fresh seafood on the menu, caught right from the sea, which the restaurant overlooks. An excellent starter salad is grilled eggplant, hummus, and fried cauliflower—crunchy pita rounds toasted with olive oil and za'atar (a local spice) are served alongside. House specialties include grilled fish (served with roasted potatoes), but don't overlook the baked red snapper fillet topped with chopped vegetables, or the zingy seafood platter (shrimp, calamari, and crab). Still hungry? Hot-chocolate soufflé or apple pie with ice cream does the trick. ⊠ *At the northern end of the port* ☎ *04/636–1679* ▭ *AE, DC, MC, V.*

★ **$$$** ✕ **Helena.** Two of Israel's best-known culinary personalities opened this restaurant, aiming to create a first-rate yet affordable dining experience. It's definitely a success. The multilevel restaurant occupies a beautifully restored stone building on the water, in the ancient port, with large windows everywhere to maximize the view. The chef specializes in the Mediterranean style, with Italian and French touches, turning out such tantalizing appetizers as hearty focaccia breads, crab bisque infused with lavender, and Caesar salad. Main dishes include aromatic fish stew, juicy lamb kebabs with puree of eggplant, and *barbuni* (tiny, grilled sardine-like fish). Israeli wines are served. A children's menu is available. ⊠ *At the southern end of the port* ☎ *04/610–1018* ▭ *AE, DC, MC, V.*

**$$** ✕ **Minato.** Convenient to Caesarea's entrances, Minato, which means "port" in Japanese, is perfect for beachgoers craving sushi—the restaurant does a brisk takeout business, serving sashimi and nigiri sushi as well as a variety of tempura dishes. Or you can eat in at the long, black sushi bar, watching the chefs' knives flash in front of you. ⊠ *At the Paz gas station by the entrance to Caesarea* ☎ *04/636–0812* ☉ *No dinner Fri., no lunch Sat.* ▭ *AE, DC, MC, V.*

☾ **¢–$** ✕ **Agenda.** In the same building as the Japanese restaurant Minato, this 24-hour restaurant serves breakfast, sandwiches, salads, pasta, lasagna,

# CloseUp
## FROM HEROD TO RABBI AKIVA

**HEROD THE GREAT** *gave Caesarea its name, dedicating the magnificent Roman city he built to his patron, Augustus Caesar. It was the Roman emperor who had crowned Herod—born to an Idumean family that had converted to Judaism— King of the Jews around 30 BC. Construction began in 22 BC; Herod spared nothing in his elaborate designs for the port and the city itself, which included palaces, temples, a theater, a marketplace, a hippodrome, and water and sewage systems. When Caesarea was completed 12 years later, only Jerusalem outshined it. Its population under Herod grew to around 100,000, and the city covered some 164 acres. In AD 6, a decade after Herod died, Caesarea became the seat of the Roman procurators, one of whom was Pontius Pilate, governor of Judea when Jesus was crucified. With Jerusalem predominantly Jewish, the Romans preferred the*

*Hellenistic Caesarea, with its Jewish minority, as the seat of their administration.*

*Religious harmony did not prevail. The mixed population of Jews and Gentiles (mainly Greeks and Syrians) repeatedly clashed, with hostilities exploding during the Jewish revolt of AD 66. The first Jewish rebellion was squelched by Vespasian, proclaimed emperor by his legions in AD 69. A year later, his son and co-ruler, Titus, captured and razed Jerusalem and celebrated his suppression of the Jewish revolt. Henceforth Caesarea was a Roman colony and the local Roman capital of Palestine for nearly 600 years. It was here that Peter converted the Roman centurion Cornelius to Christianity—a milestone in the spread of the new faith—and Paul preached and was imprisoned for two years. In the 2nd century, Rabbi Akiva, the spiritual mentor of the Bar Kochba revolt, was tortured to death here.*

and great homemade cakes. The staff is friendly, the ambience casual. ⊠ *At the Paz gas station at the entrance to Caesarea* ☎ 04/626–2092 ☽ *No dinner Fri., no lunch Sat.* ⊟ *AE, DC, MC, V.*

★ **$$$** ⊞ **Dan Caesarea.** Quiet comfort is combined here with accessibility to a range of sports facilities, the beach, and the famed site of ancient Caesarea. Adjacent to the hotel's 15-acre gardens lies Israel's only 18-hole golf course, which offers Dan guests a discount. The four-story hotel, built in 1958, is set unobtrusively in attractively landscaped grounds and is halfway between Tel Aviv and Haifa. All the rooms have balconies, overlooking either the sea or the open countryside. Especially recommended are the comfortable deluxe doubles, with marble bathrooms and modern decor in cheerful hues. ⊠ *North of Crusader city (opposite entrance to villa area), Caesarea 30600* ☎ 04/626–9111 🖶 04/626–9122 ⊕ *www.danhotels.com* ⊴ *111 rooms, 3 suites* ⟐ *Restaurant, room service, in-room safes, refrigerators, cable TV, 18-hole golf course, 2 tennis courts, pool, children's pool, spa, gym, hot tub, lobby lounge, bar, Internet room, free parking* ⊟ *AE, DC, MC.*

### Nightlife & the Arts

At **Caesarea's Roman theater** you can watch occasional evening performances of the highest caliber, by both local and international artists and troupes, May to mid-October; the box office is open on performance days. Check the Friday editions of major newspapers for schedule information. For tickets, contact **Le'an** (✉ 101 Dizengoff St., Tel Aviv ☎ 03/ 524–7373).

## Sports & the Outdoors

BEACHES  Bathers have three choices here. In the Old City, in a sandy cove in Herod's
★  ancient harbor, is the small **Caesarea Beach Club,** where the admission charge of NIS 35 includes chairs, umbrellas, and the use of hot showers. The beach has a diving platform, and you can also rent kayaks. The largest and most popular beach in the area is **Hof Shonit** (☎ 04/636–2927), just south of Caesarea—from Route 2, turn left instead of right toward the Old City. The parking lot here accommodates 400 vehicles and charges NIS 15. There are lifeguards in season, a refreshment stand, and a restaurant, as well as toilets and cold showers.

At the **Roman aqueduct,** just north of the Crusader city in the residential area, is a spacious beach with the dramatic backdrop of Roman arches disappearing into the sand. The amenities, however, are few: toilets, and a lifeguard in season. There is no entrance fee, and there's plenty of parking. The beach and swimming area have been cleared of rocks and debris, but swimming outside the designated, guarded area is prohibited (never swim at all unless the guard is on duty).

GOLF  Golfers flock to **Caesarea Golf Club** (☎ 04/610–9600), the only 18-hole layout in Israel. Adjacent to the Dan Caesarea hotel, the club is open from sunrise to sunset; the course is built on sandy soil so you can even play after heavy rainfall. Reservations are advisable. The greens fee is NIS 400 from Sunday to Thursday and NIS 470 on Friday and Saturday. After noon, the "twilight" fee is NIS 210 on weekdays and NIS 260 on Friday and Saturday. Golf-club rentals run NIS 120; cart rental costs NIS 155. There's a French bistro on the premises.

It's an easy 10-km (6-m) drive north of Tel Aviv to reach the 9-hole **Ga'ash Golf Club** (☎ 09/951–5111 ⊕ www.gaashgolfclub.co.il), which you can play a second time from alternative tees to make for an 18-hole golfing experience. Greens fees are NIS 225 on weekdays and NIS 300 on weekends; clubs can be rented for NIS 50, electric cart is NIS 85 (NIS 100 on weekends); there's a shop and a restaurant here, too.

SCUBA DIVING  The **Old Caesarea Diving Center** (✉ on the jetty in the harbor ☎ 04/626–
★  5898) runs a full range of diving courses for novices, experts, and those in between. Licensed divers can explore the submerged port built by King Herod 2,000 years ago.

# Nahsholim-Dor

❸  *20 km (12 mi) north of Caesarea. Travel east at Zichron Ya'akov turnoff until the Fureidis Junction (marked "to Haifa"), turn south, and travel 1 km (½ mi) to sign for Nahsholim-Dor. Turn west and drive 3 km (2 mi).*

Founded 3,500 years ago, biblical Dor was once the maritime capital of the Carmel coast. Its small bay made it the best harbor between Jaffa and Akko and thus a target for many imperial ambitions, from the ancient Egyptians and the "Sea Peoples" through King Solomon and on down. It was renowned in antiquity for its precious purple dye, called Tyrian purple; reserved for royalty, this hue was extracted from a mollusk that was abundant along the coast. During the Arab period, the town was renamed Tantura, which is also the name of the town's popular beach today.

★ ☺ Well worth a visit is the **Nahsholim-Dor Museum** (or Hamizgaga Museum); turn in at the sign for the Nahsholim Guest House, which is also the Center for Nautical and Regional Archaeology. It's in the partly restored former glass factory opened by Baron Rothschild in 1893 to serve the wineries of nearby Zichron Ya'akov. The museum is a rich trove of finds from both local nautical digs and excavations at nearby Tel Dor. The sequence of peoples who settled, conquered, or passed through Dor— from the Phoenicians to Napoléon—can be traced through these artifacts. Of particular interest is the bronze cannon that Napoléon's vanquished troops dumped into the sea during their retreat from Akko to Egypt in May 1799. An interesting film in English illuminates the history of the ancient city of Dor. ⊠ *Kibbutz Nahsholim, Rd. 7011 off Road 4* ☎ *04/639–0950* ⊠ *NIS 12* ☉ *Sun.–Thurs. 8:30–2, Fri. 8:30–1, Sat. and Jewish holidays 10:30–3.*

> **need a break?** The decor is fishing-shack and the music is loud at **Lagoona** (☎ 052/ 375–0830). Children run and play freely, and the restaurant is right on the beach. It's a great pitstop for hummus, fresh fish, steaks, ice-cold beer, or chocolate ice cream, and it's just about 100 yards to the right of the Dor Beach entrance.

## Where to Stay

¢–$ ⊞ **Nahsholim.** You'd have to travel a great distance to find a prettier beach than the one outside this motel-like accommodation facing the blue sea. Single-story buildings contain standard rooms (24 have sea views) and family apartments, each with a bedroom, living-room sofa bed, and room for up to five guests. All units have refrigerators, kettles, and cups. In summer, you can rent water-sports equipment on the beach, and small islets just off the coast attract nesting birds and give nature watchers plenty to see in spring and fall. ⊠ *Off the main highway; take the Zikron Ya'akov exit, turn left after 1 km, and turn right (toward the sea) at "Nahsholim-Dor" 30815* ☎ *04/639–9533* 🖷 *04/639–7614* ⊕ *www.nahsholim.co.il* ⌁ *41 rooms, 48 apartments* ⚇ *Restaurant, café, tennis court, basketball, billiards* ⊟ *AE, DC, MC, V.*

## Sports & the Outdoors

BEACHES **Dor Beach** (☎ 04/630–7180), also known as Tantura Beach, is one of ★ the most popular in Israel thanks to the fine sand lining its 1½ km (1 mi) of coastline. It's right beside Kibbutz Nahsholim. Amenities are ample: parking, lifeguards in season, a snack bar and restaurant, a first-aid station, a trampoline (fee), and chair and umbrella rentals, as well as changing rooms and showers. At the time of this writing, the changing rooms and other facilities were in need of renovation.

DIVING Kurt Raveh, a diver-archaeologist and resident of Kibbutz Nahsholim,
★ runs the **Underwater Archaeological Center** (☎ 052/279–6695). Kurt conducts underwater expeditions and "dives into history" where divers (even those without experience) get to tour ancient shipwrecks under his experienced eye.

## Atlit

❹ *9 km (6 mi) north of Nahsholim-Dor, 15 km (9 mi) south of Haifa.*

Atlit is a peninsula with the jagged remains of an important Crusader castle. Of more recent vintage, to the west (about 1,500 feet from the highway), is the **Atlit detention camp,** used by the British to house refugees smuggled in during and after World War II. The reconstructed barracks, fences, and watchtowers stand as reminders of how Jewish immigration was practically outlawed under the British Mandate after the publication of the infamous White Paper in 1939. More than a third of the 120,000 illegal immigrants to Palestine passed through the camp from 1934 to 1948. The authenticity of the exhibit is striking: it was re-created from accounts of actual detainees and their contemporaries; you'll see the living quarters, complete with laundry hanging from the rafters. Call ahead to make sure it's open. ⌂ *Rte. 2* ☎ *04/984–1980* ✉ *NIS 17* ☉ *Sun.–Thurs. 9–4, Fri. 9–12:30.*

# HAIFA

Spilling down from the pine-covered heights of Mt. Carmel to the blue Mediterranean is Haifa, a city with a vertiginous setting that has led to perhaps hyperbolic comparisons with San Francisco. Israel's largest port and third-largest city, Haifa was ruled for four centuries by the Ottomans and gradually grew up the mountainside into a cosmopolitan city whose port served the entire Middle East. In 1902, Theodor Herzl enthusiastically dubbed it "the city of the future."

Today, the metropolis is divided into three main levels that run parallel to the harbor, crisscrossed by parks and gardens. The downtown port encompasses the largely uninhabited Old City; the midtown area, called Hadar HaCarmel (Hadar for short), was one of the early Jewish neighborhoods and is now a bustling shopping area; and Central Carmel, or Mercaz HaCarmel, on top, includes upscale residential developments and the posher hotels. The most striking landmark on the mountainside is the gleaming golden dome of the Baha'i Shrine. The city is the world center for the Baha'i faith.

Haifa was already a center for science and technology by 1924, when the Technion Institute opened. The Turks' construction at the turn of the 20th century of the Hijaz Railway—which stretched from Constantinople via Damascus to Mecca and Medina—proved a boon to Haifa, which had its own branch of the new line to Damascus. Under the British Mandate, a deep-water port was dug and opened to world traffic in 1933, and Haifa was linked to Iraq by an oil pipeline the following year. After Israel's independence, Haifa's links with neighboring Arab states were broken, but today cruise ships from abroad ply its waters, and the Technion is still the nation's citadel of scientific research.

## Exploring Haifa

Haifa is a city of fairly steep slopes, which reward the visitor not only with sites to see amid pine trees and blossoming foliage but vistas of the Mediterranean at every turn, all accompanied by hillside breezes. And thanks to the beneficence of the Baha'is, you can enjoy two different walks that take you through the stunning terraces that lie like multicolored jewels from the crest of the city at Mt. Carmel to the German Colony below.

### Main Attractions

**13** **Baha'i Shrine and Gardens.** The most striking feature of the stunning gardens that form the centerpeice of Haifa is the Shrine of the Bab, whose brilliantly gilded dome dominates as well as illuminates the city's skyline. Haifa is the world center for the Baha'i faith, founded in Iran in the 19th century. It holds as its central belief the unity of mankind. Religious truth for Baha'is is not doctrinaire; rather, it consists of progressive revelations of a universal faith. Thus the Baha'is teach that great prophets have appeared throughout history to reveal divine truths, among them Moses, Zoroaster, Buddha, Jesus, Mohammed, and most recently, the founder of the Baha'i faith, Mirza Husayn Ali, known as Baha'u'llah—the Glory of God. Baha'u'llah (1817–1892) was exiled from his native Persia by the Shah and then by the Ottomans to Akko, where he lived as a prisoner for almost 25 years. The Baha'is' holiest shrine is on the grounds of Baha'u'llah's home, where he lived after his release from prison and where he is now buried, just north of Akko.

FodorśChoice
★

Here in Haifa, at the center of the shrine's pristinely manicured gardens, is the mausoleum built for the Bab (literally, the "Gate"), the forerunner of this religion, who heralded the coming of a new faith to be revealed by Baha'u'llah. The Bab was martyred by the Persian authorities in 1850. The gardens and shrine were built by Baha'u'llah's son and successor, who had the Bab's remains reburied here in 1909. The building, made of Italian-cut stone and rising 128 feet, gracefully combines the canons of classical European architecture with elements of Eastern design and also houses the remains of Baha'u'llah's son. The dome glistens with some 12,000 gilded tiles imported from the Netherlands. Inside, the floor is covered with rich Oriental carpets, and a filigree veil divides visitors from the inner shrine.

The magnificent gardens are a sight to behold: 18 stunningly landscaped circular terraces extend from Yefe Nof Street for 1 km (½ mi) down the hillside to Ben Gurion Boulevard, at the German Colony. The terraces are a harmony of color and form—pale pink–and gray-stone staircases and carved urns overflowing with red geraniums delineate perfect cutouts of emerald green grass and floral borders, dark green trees, and wildflowers, with not a leaf out of place anywhere.

Three areas are open to the public year-round (except on Baha'i holidays): the Shrine and surrounding gardens (from Hatziyonut Avenue);

# HAIFA FROM THE TALMUD TO NAPOLÉON

**FIRST MENTIONED IN THE TALMUD,** *the area around Haifa had two settlements in ancient times. To the east, in what is today a congested industrial zone in the port, lay Zalmona, and 5 km (3 mi) west around the cape was Shiqmona. The Crusaders conquered Haifa while it was an important Arab town and maintained it as a fortress along the coastal road to Akko for 200 years; it was lost and repeatedly regained by the Christians. During this period, in 1154, the Order of Our Lady of Mount Carmel (the Carmelite order) was founded on the slopes of Mt. Carmel by a group of hermits following the principles of the prophet Elijah and the rules of poverty, vegetarianism, and solitude. After Akko and Haifa succumbed to the Mamluk Sultan Baybars in 1265, Haifa was destroyed and left derelict. It was a sleepy fishing village for centuries.*

*The city reawakened under the rule of Bedouin sheikh Dahr el-Omar, who had rebelled against direct Ottoman rule in the mid-18th century and independently governed Akko and the Galilee. In 1761 Dahr ordered the city to be demolished and moved about 3 km (2 mi) to the south. The new town was fortified by walls and protected by a castle, and its port began to compete with that of Akko across the bay.*

*Napoléon, too, came to Haifa, though only briefly, and en route to ignominious defeat at Akko during his Eastern Campaign. Napoléon left his wounded at the Carmelite Monastery when he beat a retreat in 1799, but the French soldiers there were killed and the monks driven out by Ahmed el-Jazzar, the victorious pasha of Akko.*

the upper terrace and observation point (Yefe Nof Street); and the entry at the lower terrace (Hagefen Square, at the end of Ben Gurion Boulevard). You can visit the gardens only by guided tour; these take place daily and must be reserved at least three days in advance by phone, Sunday–Thursday 9–5. The Shrine of the Bab (along with the Shrine of Baha'u'llah, north of Akko) is a pilgrimage site for the worldwide Baha'i community; visitors to the shrine are asked to dress modestly (no shorts). ✉ *Entrance to the Shrine: 65 Sderot Hatziyonut, Merkaz Carmel* ☎ *04/ 835–8358, 04/831–3131 for garden tour* ⊕ *www.bahai.org* 🎫 *Free* ☉ *Shrine daily 9–noon; gardens daily 9–5.*

**⓯ German Colony.** Ben Gurion Boulevard, ruler-straight, was the heart of **Fodor'sChoice** a late-19th-century colony established by the German Templer religious
★ reform movement. Neglected for years, the German Colony is a prime example of meticulous renovation that makes for Haifa's loveliest (and flattest) stroll. Ben Gurion runs between Yaffo Street, in downtown Haifa, and the bottom of the magnificent Baha'i Gardens. It's only one street— actually a broad boulevard—but it packs in history (with explanations on boards), interesting architecture, coffeehouses and restaurants, shaded benches for people-watching, and Haifa's tourism office. Along either side, note the robust one- and two-story stone houses, with pointed red-

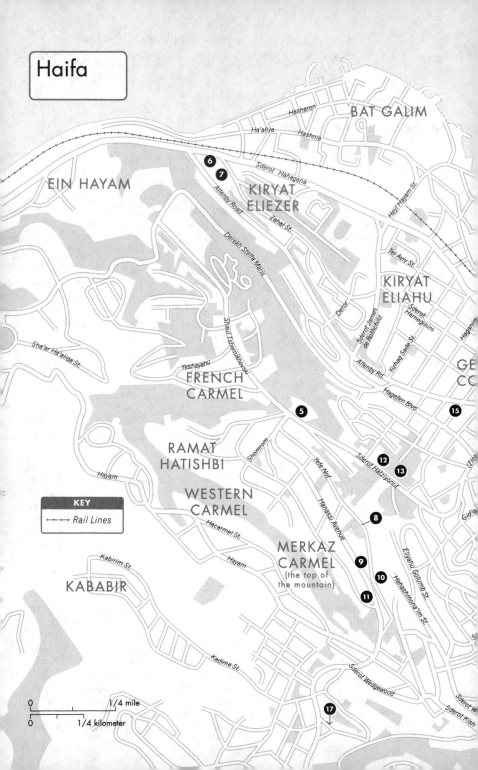

Mediterranean Sea

Harbor

GERMAN
COLONY

DOWNTOWN

HADAR

TEL AMAL

tile roofs typical of the neighborhood; many bear German names, dates from the 1800s, biblical inscriptions above the doors, and old wooden shutters on the narrow windows. It's best to start your walk at Yaffo Street (at the City Centre Mall) and walk toward the Baha'i Gardens, so their beauty lies ahead of you the entire walk.

The Templers' colony in Haifa was one of five in the Holy Land. The early settlers formed a self-sufficient community; by 1883 they had built nearly 100 houses and filled them with as many families. Industrious workers, they introduced the horse-drawn wagon—unknown until their arrival—to Haifa; They also built with their own funds a pilgrimage road from Haifa to Nazareth. The Germans' labors gave rise to modern workshops and warehouses, and it was under their influence that Haifa began to resemble a modern city, with well-laid-out streets, gardens, and attractive homes.

Haifa's importance to Germany was highlighted in 1898, when Kaiser Wilhelm II sailed into the bay, on the first official visit to the Holy Land by a German emperor in more than 600 years. During World War II the Germans who lived in the colony were expelled, suspected of being Nazis. ⊠ *German Colony.*

## Also Worth Seeing

**❺ Carmelite Monastery and Stella Maris Church.** During the Crusader period, certain hermits emulating the ascetic life of the prophet Elijah lived in caves on this steep mountain slope. In the early 13th century they united under the leadership of the Italian pilgrim (later saint) Berthold, who petitioned the patriarch of Jerusalem for a charter. Thus was born the Carmelite order, which spread across Europe; it esteems the prophet Elijah, the order's patron. The Carmelite monks were forced to leave their settlements on Mt. Carmel at the end of the 13th century, and they did not return until nearly four centuries later. When they found Elijah's cave inhabited by Muslim dervishes, they set up a monastery nearby.

The church of the present monastery dates from 1836 and was built with the munificence of the French monarchy, hence the name of the surrounding neighborhood: French Carmel. The French connection is explained by a small pyramid, topped with an iron cross, that stands outside. The monument commemorates those French who were slaughtered here by the Turks in 1799 after the retreating Napoléon left his ailing troops behind to be treated at the monastery. Inside, the academic paintings in the dome depict Elijah in the chariot of fire in which he ascended to heaven, and other biblical prophets. The small cave a few steps down at the end of the nave is traditionally associated with Elijah and his pupil, Elisha. ⊠ *Carmelite Monastery, Stella Maris Rd., French Carmel* ☎ *04/833–7758* ☞ *Free* ⊙ *Daily 6:30–1 and 3–6.*

**❻ Clandestine Immigration and Naval Museum.** The rather dull name of this museum belies the dramatic nature of what's inside. The museum tells the story of the often heroic efforts to bring Jewish immigrants to Palestine from war-torn Europe in defiance of British policy.

Emigration to Palestine was well nigh impossible after the British imposed a naval blockade, bowing to pressure by Arabs opposed to Jewish immigration. In 1939, on the eve of World War II, the British issued the so-called White Paper, which effectively strangled Jewish immigration to Palestine. Small boats sometimes managed to elude the vigilant British warships and unload their human cargoes at secret landing beaches, but for bigger ships the odds were daunting. Out of 63 clandestine ships that tried to run the blockade after the war's end, all but five were intercepted, and their passengers were deported to Cyprus.

The museum is full of moving stories of courage, tenacity, and disaster. A photomural of the celebrated ship the *Exodus* recalls the story of the 4,530 refugees aboard who were forcibly transferred back to Germany in 1947, but not before the British forces opened fire on the rebellious ship. Another tragic episode befell the *Struma*, a leaky vessel that was forced to anchor in Istanbul for repairs in 1941. The Turks refused to assist the ship after warnings from the British; the boat wallowed in Istanbul harbor for two months and finally sank a few miles offshore. Of the 767 on board, one person survived.

One of the blockade runners was an old American tank-landing craft renamed *Af-al-pi-chen* ("Nevertheless," in Hebrew), which serves as the museum's centerpiece. This ship left Italy in 1947 for Palestine and was intercepted by the British, at which point its 434 passengers, all survivors of the Holocaust, were sent to internment camps in Cyprus. ⊠ *204 Allenby Rd. Kiryat Eliezer* ☎ *04/853–6249* ⊕ *www.amutayam.org.il* 🗺 *NIS 10* ⊗ *Sun.–Thurs. 8:30–4, Jewish holiday eves 8:30–1.*

**Elijah's Cave.** This site is considered sacred by Jews, Christians, and Muslims; an early Byzantine tradition identified it as the cave in which Elijah found refuge from the wrath of Ahab, king of Israel from 871 to 853 BC. Graffiti from pilgrims of various faiths and different centuries are scrawled on the right wall, and written prayers are often stuffed into crevices. Modest dress is requested. The cave is a 20-minute walk down the fairly steep path across from the entrance to the Carmelite Monastery and church. ⊠ *French Carmel* 🗺 *Free* ⊗ *Sun.–Thurs. 8–5, Fri. and Jewish holiday eves 8–1.*

**⑭ Haifa Museum of Art** (Museum of Modern Art). This is one of three museums under the aegis of Haifa Museums. The others are the Maritime Museum and the Tikotin Museum of Japanese Art, and one admission ticket is good for all three. The Museum of Modern Art displays work from all over the world, dating from the mid-18th century to the present. It's an excellent venue to learn about contemporary Israeli art: included are 20th-century graphics and contemporary paintings, sculptures, and photographs. The print collection is of special note. ⊠ *26 Shabbtai Levy St., Hadar* ☎ *04/852–3255* ⊕ *www.hms.org.il* 🗺 *NIS 24 includes all 3 museums* ⊗ *Mon., Wed., Thurs. 10–4; Tues. 4–8; Fri. 10–1; Sat. and Jewish holidays 10–3.*

**need a break?**

In a city known for great falafel, check out the **falafel joints** called Michel and Haskenim at 18 and 21 Wadi Street, on the circular street in the Wadi Nisnas market. You'll get plenty of fresh steaming chickpea balls, warm pita bread and toppings, and a choice a cold drinks.

★ ☾ ❾   **Haifa Zoo.** Down past the play equipment in Gan Ha'Em, across from the Dan Panorama hotel, amid masses of trees and foliage, is a seemingly happy collection of roaring lions, two tigers, big brown bears, chattering monkeys, stripe-tailed lemurs, a placid camel, lots of snakes, one croc, and fierce-eyed eagles and owls—plus a bat cave and a water-bird pond. It's a hilly place, but there's a tram to take visitors up the steepest terrain. ⊠ *Hanassi Blvd. (opposite the Dan Panorama) Merkaz Carmel* ☎ *04/837–2886* ⊕ *www.ethos.co.il* ⊠ *NIS 30.*

★ ⓱   **Hecht Museum.** It's worth the trip to Haifa University, where this museum is located, to see the fine archaeological holdings. At the summit of Mt. Carmel, in the main campus tower (designed by noted Brazilian architect Oscar Niemeyer), the collection spans the millennia from the Chalcolithic era to the Roman and Byzantine periods, concentrating on "The People of Israel in Eretz Israel." (The roof observation deck, on the 27th floor, affords spectacular views.) The artifacts range from religious altars and lamps to two coffins and figurines from the Early Bronze Age. Featured prominently are finds from the excavations of Jerusalem's Temple Mount. A separate wing displays a small collection of paintings, mostly Impressionist and Jewish School of Paris, with works of Monet, Soutine, and Pissarro, among others. To get here, take Bus 37 from the Nof Hotel. ⊠ *Abu Hushi St., Mt. Carmel (Har Carmel)* ☎ *04/824–0577* ⊠ *Free* ☾ *Sun., Mon., Wed., Thurs. 10–4; Tues. 10–7; Fri. and Jewish holiday eves 10–1; Sat. 10–2.*

❿   **Mané Katz Museum.** This is the house and studio where the Expressionist painter Emmanuel Katz (1894–1962) lived and worked for the last four years of his life. Katz spent the 1920s in Paris, where he exhibited with a group of Jewish artists from the École de Paris; as in the canvases of fellow members Marc Chagall and Chaim Soutine, a recurring theme in his work is the village life of Jews in Eastern Europe. A whitewashed building, it contains Katz's paintings, drawings, and sculptures. You'll also find the Ukrainian-born artist's legacy to the city plus his collection of rugs, 17th-century antiques from Spain and Germany, and Judaica. ⊠ *89 Yefe Nof St., Merkaz Carmel* ☎ *04/838–3482* ⊠ *Free* ☾ *Sun.–Thurs. 10–4; Tues. 2–6; Fri. 10–1; Sat. 10–2.*

❼   **National Maritime Museum.** Here 5,000 years of maritime history are told (and made more interesting than you might imagine) with model ships, archaeological finds, coins minted with nautical symbols, navigational instruments, and other artifacts. There are also intriguing underwater finds from nearby excavations and shipwrecks. The ancient-art collection is one of the finest in the country; it comprises mostly Greek and Roman stone and marble sculpture, Egyptian textiles, Greek pottery, and encaustic grave portraits from Fayyum, in Lower Egypt. Particularly rare are the figures of fishermen from the Hellenistic period. Among numerous terra-cotta figurines from Syria and Egypt are several curious animal-shape vessels—once used as playthings, incense burners, or funerary gifts—from Haifa's nearby Shiqmona excavation. ⊠ *198 Allenby Rd., Kiryat*

*Eliezer* ☎ *04/853–6622* ⊕ *www.hms.org.il* ✉ *NIS 24, including Museum of Modern Art and Tikotin Museum of Japanese Art* ☉ *Mon., Wed., Thurs. 10–4; Tues. 4-8; Fri. 10–1; Sat. and Jewish holidays 10–3.*

**⟲ ⑯ National Museum of Science and Technology (Techmoda).** Both children and adults are captivated by the hands-on chemistry and physics exhibits in this beautifully designed building, the original home of the Technion. ✉ *Balfour St., Hadar* ☎ *04/862–8111* ⊕ *www.mustsee.org.il* ✉ *NIS 24* ☉ *Sun., Mon., Wed., Thurs. 9–6; Tues. 9–7; Fri. and Jewish holiday eves 10–3; Sat. 10–5.*

**⑱ Technion.** Israel's foremost center for applied research, the 300-acre Technion City is highly fertile ground for Israel's scientific innovations: two-thirds of the nation's university research in such fields as science, technology, engineering, medicine, architecture, and town planning takes place here. Visitors can get an idea of the vast scope of these studies, plus the goals for the future, at the Coler-California Center, housed in a concrete-and-glass building. A 20-minute English-language film called "Vision" is an introduction to the multimedia touch screens and Internet stations available in the comfortable lounge. Laser-disc videos describe the various Technion departments. To get here, take Bus 31 from the Nof Hotel or the Dan Panorama Hotel. ✉ *Kiryat Ha-Technion (Technion City), Neveh Sha'anan, Neveh Sha'anan* ☎ *04/832–0664* ⊕ *www. technion.ac.il* ✉ *Free* ☉ *Sun.–Thurs. 8:30–3.*

**★ ⑪ Tikotin Museum of Japanese Art.** Established in 1957 by Felix Tikotin, of Holland, this graceful venue adheres to the Japanese tradition of displaying beautiful objects that are in harmony with the season, so exhibits change frequently. The Japanese atmosphere, created in part by sliding doors and partitions made of wood and paper, enhances a display of scrolls, screens, pottery and porcelain, lacquer and metalwork, paintings from several schools, netsuke (small objects used as toggles), and fresh-flower arrangements. ✉ *88 Hanassi Blvd., Merkaz Carmel* ☎ *04/838–3554* ⊕ *www.hms.org.il* ✉ *NIS 24, including Museum of Modern Art and National Maritime Museum* ☉ *Mon., Wed., Thurs. 10–4; Tues. 4–8; Fri. 10–1; Sat. and Jewish holidays 10–3.*

**⑫ Vista of Peace Sculpture Garden.** You can contemplate the life-size bronzes of people and animals from a bench on the winding path through this garden, which affords views of Haifa Bay beyond. Sculptor Ursula Malbin, who came to Israel as a refugee from Nazi Germany, created this oasis. The garden opens at sunrise and closes at 6. ✉ *Just west of Baha'i Shrine, Bahai* ⊕ *www.malbin-sculpture.com.*

**★ ⑧ Yefe Nof Street.** Also known as Panorama Road, this curving street high above the city skirts the backs of Haifa's biggest hotels, providing superlative views. Part of the walk (through the black iron gate) takes you past two magnificent terraces of the Baha'i Gardens. Enjoy the beauty of the lushly planted Louis Promenade, with shaded benches along the way, beginning behind the Dan Carmel Hotel. On a clear day, from any of several lookouts, you can see the port below; Akko, across the bay; and the cliffs of Rosh Hanikra, with Lebanon in the distance. Panorama Road is beautiful during the day and at night. ✉ *Merkaz Carmel.*

## Where to Eat

**$$$** ✕ **1872 Restaurant.** Known as "Hashmura" ("preservation" in Hebrew), this handsome restaurant occupies the beautifully renovated old Templer building. Entering the two-story white-stone building with three arches, you find yourself on a glass floor with a wine cellar underneath. Wood-beam ceilings slant over many small rooms, and old architectrual drawings adorn the walls. There's also a sunroom with a wall of glass, a bar fashioned out of an old cistern, and a palm-shaded patio. Alas, the stunning setting overshadows the somewhat unsophisticated food. But you can still sample a decent starter of goose liver and such entrées as ravioli, a shrimp and squid combo, and sea bass fillet. Israeli and international wines are served. ⊠ *15 Ben Gurion Blvd. German Colony* ☎ *04/855–1872* ⌲ *Reservations essential* ⊟ *AE, D, MC, V.*

**$$** ✕ **Isabella.** With tiny lights in the ceiling, walls and curving surfaces in muted gray tones, dark-wood tables with sleek leather chairs, and a brushed-cement floor, Isabella is a suitable setting for modern Italian cuisine. Try an appetizer of eggplant carpaccio in garlic-lemon tahini sauce; excellent "stuffed" pizza (filled with, among other choices, mushrooms, mozzarella, arugula, and marinated zucchini); veal scallopini; or a seafood mix in champagne and saffron sauce. Grilled steak is a specialty here—try the veal or beef T-bone with rosemary and lemon sauce. An extensive wine list is available. ⊠ *6 Ben Gurion Blvd., City Center Mall, German Colony* ☎ *04/855–2201* ⌲ *Reservations essential* ⊟ *AE, D, MC, V.*

★ **$$** ✕ **Jacko.** If ever there was a beloved eating place in Haifa, Jacko is it. Say the name to your taxi driver, and he'll nod approvingly and gun the motor; you'll be dropped at a nondescript building with a Hebrew sign, in a crowded, downtown area. Since 1976, this family-run restaurant has been serving up delicious food in a rowdy, informal setting with shared tables. The specialties here are fish and seafood (grilled or fried); there's seafood pasta, and piles of crab, mussels, or calamari with sauces, as well as large shrimp grilled in their shells, and Mediterranean lobster (in summer). For dessert try the Turkish cookies or semolina and coconut cake. Wine and draft beer are available. There's a second Jacko in the hotel area that's similarly popular. ⊠ *12 Hadekalim St., Downtown* ☎ *04/866–8813* ⊠ *11 Moriah St., Merkaz Carmel* ☎ *04/810–2355* ⌲ *Reservations essential* ⊟ *AE, D, MC, V* ⊘ *No dinner Sat.*

★ **$$** ✕ **Mayan Habira.** If you're a vegetarian, forget it. But if you're looking for meat with a capital "M," you've found the place. Like its neighbor, Jacko, this restaurant is in the traffic-ridden downtown area, with a sign in Hebrew only outside. It's a highly esteemed Haifa institution with shared tables. The decor is informal: beer kegs are piled up in a corner; the walls are covered with photos of politicians, glowing restaurant reviews, and a mural of the customers painted by an art student in 1989. The family's been in business since 1962; today, son, Reuven, his children, and his Romanian mother do the excellent cooking. To start, savor meat kreplach, chopped liver, jellied calf's foot, gefilte fish, or oxtail soup. Then go to work on delectable spareribs or goose or beef pastrami, which they smoke themselves. Grilled rabbit is also a good choice. ⊠ *4 Nathanson St., Downtown* ☏ *04/862–3193* ▤ *AE, D, MC, V* ◷ *Closed Sat. No dinner.*

**$$** ✕ **Douzan.** Douzan occupies an old German Templer building. Metal lamps with cut-out apertures cast a lacy design on the walls, tasseled cushions rest on velvet and wooden chairs, and books sit atop the half wall near the bar. The food, prepared by the owner's mother, is an intriguing combination of French and local Arabic cuisines. You might try chicken cordon bleu with mustard cream sauce, or onion, bacon, and thyme quiche among the French dishes. Also consider such Arabic fare as *sfeeha* (a puff pastry topped with delicately spiced minced beef, onions, and pine nuts), and *tarweeka* (thick, cheeselike yogurt, feta cheese, olive oil, and za'atar on thin, crispy pitas. ⊠ *35 Ben Gurion Blvd. German Colony* ☏ *04/852–5444* ▤ *AE, DC, MC, V.*

**$** ✕ **Fattoush.** Olive trees hung with blue and olive lights and a patterned rug on the sidewalk set the tone for the elaborate interior of Fattoush, which contains several rooms. One is a "cave" with Arabic script on the walls, low banquettes, wooden stools, and filigree lamps; another is modern with leather seats, appliquéd cushions, and a changing art exhibit set against burnt-orange walls. And now for the food: Fattoush salad is a favorite, consisting of chopped tomato, cucumber, onion, and mint and sprinkled with crisp toasted pita pieces. You might follow with *emsakhan,* roast chicken topped with pieces of sumac and served on oven-baked pita. Steak and fish are also served, and there's a refreshing dessert of ice cream draped with espresso. ⊠ *40 Ben Gurion Blvd. German Colony* ☏ *04/852–4930* ▤ *AE, DC, MC, V.*

★ **$** ✕ **Giraffe.** Here's a welcome combination of jolly atmosphere and tasty food—and there's some culinary combining going on here, too: Asian cuisine is followed by French desserts. It's sort of a New York lounge–style hangout: stainless-steel open kitchen, black tables and chairs, black bar and stools, silver photography-studio ceiling lights, and a waitstaff in bright white T's, jeans, and long black aprons. Noodles are the specialty, and most dishes are prepared in a wok. You might start with a crispy Thai salad in peanut sauce; then feast on spicy Philippine egg noodles with chicken, roast goose, and chopped shrimp in a hot chili sauce. There's a Giraffe in Tel Aviv, too. ⊠ *131 Hanassi Blvd. Merkaz Carmel* ☏ *04/ 810-4012* ▤ *AE, D, MC, V.*

## Where to Stay

**$$$$** ⌂ **Carmel Forest Spa Resort.** Set off by itself in the Carmel Forest, this
**Fodor'sChoice** spa-resort lies 25 km (15 mi) from Haifa. It's the ultimate escape: a hand-
★ some, top-of-the-line spa with a tastefully appointed lodging designed to pamper guests in a calm and healthful setting (no cell phones or children under 16). The hotel is on a hillside, with stunning views of pine trees and the Mediterranean. Some 25 treatment rooms offer a variety of massages, from aromatherapy to shiatsu; facials; body peels; seaweed

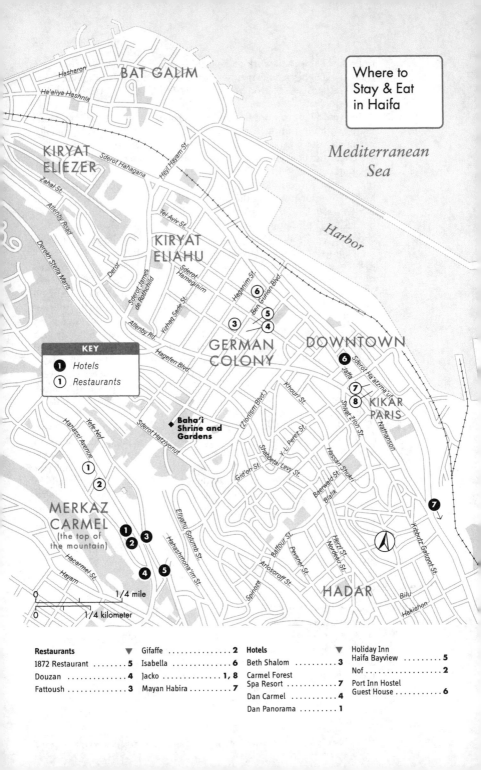

# Where to Stay & Eat in Haifa

Mediterranean Sea

BAT GALIM

KIRYAT ELIEZER

KIRYAT ELIAHU

Harbor

GERMAN COLONY

DOWNTOWN

KIKAR PARIS

Baha'i Shrine and Gardens

MERKAZ CARMEL
(the top of the mountain)

HADAR

### KEY
- **1** Hotels
- ① Restaurants

0 ___ 1/4 mile
0 ___ 1/4 kilometer

**Streets:**
Hasharon, Ha'aliya Hashnia, Sderot Hahagana, Zahal St., Allenby Road, Derekh Stella Maris, Sderot James de Rothschild, Tel Aviv St., Sderot Hameginim, Yizhak Sade St., Allenby Rd., Hagefen Blvd, Hanassi Avenue, Yefe Nof, Sderot Hatzyonut, Hacarmel St., Hayam, Eliyahu Golumb St., Hahashmona'im St., Hameginim St., Ben Gurion Blvd., Heyl Hayam St., Defor, (Zionism Blvd.), Khouri St., Gid'on St., Shabetai Levy St., Y. L. Perez St., Hassan Shukri, Baerwald St., Bialik, Balfour St., Pevsner St., Spinoza, Arlosoroff St., Herzl St., Mordeau St., Sderot Ha'atzma'ut, Jaffa, Shivat Zion St., Nathanson, Kibbutz Galuyot St., Bilu, Hakishon

wraps; and such treatments as hydrotherapy, mind-body harmony, reflexology, and body sculpture. Green wicker chaises face the forest and the Mediterranean coast through the solarium windows. A sample day? Consult the nutritionist, strike out on a forest walk, have a sesame-oil massage, and then sit down to a meal prepared with all-natural ingredients. Day guests are welcome. ✉ *Carmel Forest, Box 90000, Haifa 31900* ☎ *04/832–3111* 🖶 *04/832–3988* ⊕ *www.isrotel.co.il* ⬦ *126 rooms* ⚭ *Restaurant, cable TV, in-room safes, 2 pools, gym, hair salon, hot tub, spa, lobby lounge, tennis, mountain biking, free parking; no kids under 16* ▭ *AE, D, MC, V* ⦿ *FAP.*

**$$$** ▦ **Dan Carmel.** The Dan is beautifully situated on the heights of the Carmel. One of Haifa's first hotels, this 1970s institution still has charm, and the staff is devoted. The premises could use a renovator's touch, but the deluxe rooms on the upper floors are nicely furnished, with wooden bureaus and satin bedspreads. Other rooms are less luxurious, but they're cheerfully decorated in pastels. All guest rooms have balconies with stunning views over the city or the bay below. The large garden around the pool, with potted geraniums and many trees, is always breezy and pleasant. ✉ *85–87 Hanassi Blvd., Merkaz Carmel, 31060* ☎ *04/830–6211* 🖶 *04/838–7504* ⊕ *www.danhotels.co.il* ⬦ *204 rooms, 18 suites* ⚭ *Restaurant, room service, some in-room safes, minibars, cable TV, Wi-Fi, pool, wading pool, gym, massage, sauna, lobby lounge, shop, laundry service, parking (fee), no-smoking rooms* ▭ *AE, DC, MC, V.*

**$$** ▦ **Dan Panorama.** Another member of the Dan hotel chain, this one is somewhat glitzier than its sister down the road. The winding Louis Promenade, overlooking the city, is a few minutes' walk from the entrance. The rooms are spacious with blue-and-yellow color schemes and light-wood furnishings. Some rooms look out onto the gold-topped Baha'i Shrine and the bay; the rest have lovely city views, though none have balconies. The hotel is connected to the Panorama Center shopping mall, with casual eateries and boutiques. ✉ *107 Hanassi Blvd., Merkaz Carmel, 31060* ☎ *04/835–2222* 🖶 *04/835–2235* ⊕ *www.danhotels.co.il* ⬦ *266 rooms* ⚭ *Restaurant, room service, in-room safes, minibars, cable TV, some Wi-Fi, pool, wading pool, fitness classes, gym, massage, sauna, lobby lounge, laundry service, Internet room, parking (fee), no-smoking rooms* ▭ *AE, DC, MC, V.*

**$$** ▦ **Holiday Inn Haifa Bayview.** On the Carmel heights, in the hotel neighborhood, this well-designed and comfortable hotel is built into a pine-shaded slope (guests enter at the ninth floor). The glass-domed lobby has tawny gold-and-green sofas, set off by floral arrangements in clay pots. The business floor has a fully equipped business center. Executive rooms are equipped with Internet and fax machines, plus a trouser press to keep you looking spiffy. Views from the guest rooms are gorgeous, and 10 rooms on the sixth floor have balconies. ✉ *111 Yefe Nof St., Merkaz Carmel, 31061* ☎ *04/835–0835* 🖶 *04/835–0836* ⊕ *www.holiday-inn.com/haifaisrael* ⬦ *100 rooms* ⚭ *Restaurant, room service, in-room safes, minibars, cable TV, Wi-Fi, indoor pool, gym, 2 saunas, lobby lounge, laundry service, internet room, parking (fee), no-smoking rooms* ▭ *AE, D, MC, V.*

**$$** ▦ **Nof.** This is a smaller lodging, but it holds its own with the fancier hotels because it's alongside them in appealing Carmel Heights. The modest guest rooms (ask for one above the fourth floor) take full advantage of the setting, with large windows facing the sea. They're done up in turquoise and are perfectly comfortable. The lobby lounge, which opens onto the promenade, also has superb views. A friendly front-desk staff lends a welcome touch; the on-site (kosher) Chinese restaurant makes for a convenient, and rewarding dining experience. ⊠ *101 Hanassi Blvd., Merkaz Carmel, 34642* ☎ *04/835–4311* 🖷 *04/838–8810* ⊕ *www. inisrael.com/nof* ⇨ *80 rooms, 6 suites* �ᗉ *Restaurant, room service, refrigerators, some Wi-Fi, lobby lounge, laundry service, Internet room, parking (fee)* ⊟ *AE, DC, MC, V.*

$ 🏨 **Beth Shalom.** Plain but pleasant, clean, and comfortable, this Christian-run lodging has three floors of small rooms (there's an elevator), each with wicker furniture, beds with white blanket covers, and good reading lights. A healthy breakfast is served cafeteria-style, and you can enjoy it on the patio. Beth Shalom is on a busy street, but the front rooms are quiet thanks to the double-glazed windows. There's a coffee and hot drinks machine in the lobby, and beverages are complimentary for guests of the hotel. ⊠ *110 Hanassi Blvd., Merkaz Carmel, 31061* ☎ *04/837–3480* 🖷 *04/837–2443* ⊕ *www.beth-shalom.co.il* ⇨ *30 rooms* ᗉ *Lounge, free parking; no smoking* ⊟ *AE, DC, MC, V* ⫶◯⫶ *CP.*

★ ¢ 🏨 **Port Inn Hostel Guest House.** In lower Haifa, two bus stops from the beach and near the train station, this haven for budget travelers opened in the late '90s. In one of Haifa's earliest neighborhoods, which buzzes with interesting shops, the inn occupies an older house beautifully renovated in quiet shades of pale yellow, with plants and decorative bric-a-brac. The dormitories mainly interest backpackers (one is for women, one for men, and two are co-ed), but there are 10 double rooms with private bath, and one that has a shared bath. Reserve early for this good value, which comes with a small outside patio, kitchen facilities, a tasty breakfast, and a helpful staff. ⊠ *34 Yaffo St., Downtown, Haifa 33261* ☎ *04/852–4401* ⊕ *www.portinn.co.il* ⇨ *10 doubles, 9 with bath* ᗉ *Kitchen, lounge, in-room data ports, laundry service, Internet room* ⊟ *AE, DC, MC, V* ⫶◯⫶ *CP.*

## Nightlife & the Arts

For the latest information on performances, festivals, and other special events in and around Haifa, check Friday's *Jerusalem Post* or the *Ha Aretz* newspaper; both have weekend entertainment guides. In balmy weather, a stroll along the Louis Promenade and then along Panorama Road, with the lovely views of nighttime Haifa, is a relaxing way to end the day. For a guided hour-long evening walk, which ends with wine and cheese, call **G.U.Y. tours** (☎ 04/810–0999 or 050/532–1169). For a more festive evening, try the restaurants and café-cum-pubs in the German Colony. Nightspots in Haifa come and go, and some open only on certain evenings, so call ahead if possible.

BARS   The bar at **Barbarossa** (⊠ 8 Pica St., Merkaz Carmel ☎ 04/811–4010) is on the balcony, where you can enjoy happy hour while soaking up the great view from 6:30 to 9. Then stick around for a dinner of steak and entrecôte.

In the warm and cheery space at **Brown (a.k.a. "Baron")** (✉ 131 Moriah Blvd., Merkaz Carmel ☎ 04/811–2391), you can choose from 15 kinds of beer served to go with a complement of Italian food.

The lovely **Duke** (✉ 107 Moriah Blvd., Merkaz Carmel ☎ 04/834–7282) has an old-world European ambience and entertainment from noon on.

In the Haifa tradition, **Mydlar's** (✉ 126 Moriah Blvd., Merkaz Carmel ☎ 04/824–8754) serves food at the bar, and it's particularly tasty fare. This is a warm and inviting place for a drink, too.

★ One of Haifa's oldest and most reliable bars, **Pundak Ha Dov** (✉ 135 Hanassi Blvd., Merkaz Carmel ☎ 04/838–1703) has live music weekly and tends to fill with enthusiastic revelers.

DANCE CLUBS In the basement of the Dan Panorama hotel, the disco **Chaplin Club** (✉ 107 Hanassi Blvd., Merkaz Carmel ☎ 04/835–2206) caters to the thirtysomething crowd. There's no cover charge and no minimum on weekdays; on Friday the minimum per person is NIS 80 plus a 10% service charge. The club is open from 10:30 PM to 2 AM daily. On Friday, call for reservations.

FILM Around the Sukkot holiday (end of September, start of October), Haifa hosts an international film festival. Contact the **Haifa Cinemateque** (☎ 04/835–3521 ⊕ www.haifaff.co.il) for schedules and venues.

MUSIC A **blues festival** (☎ 04/853–5606) takes place in July in Haifa's port; for information call the tourist office.

**Israel Philharmonic Orchestra** (✉ 138 Hanassi Blvd., Merkaz Carmel ☎ 04/835–3506) gives approximately 30 concerts at the Haifa Auditorium from October through July. Tickets are generally sold only at Philharmonic box offices in Jerusalem, Tel Aviv, and Haifa (In Haifa ✉ 16 Herzl St. Hadar ☎ 04/866–4167). Concerts start at 8:30 PM or 9 PM, and the box office opens one hour before performances.

The **New Haifa Symphony Orchestra** (✉ 6 Eliyahu Hakim St., French Carmel ☎ 04/859–9499) performs at the Haifa Auditorium three times a month from October through July. For ticket and performance information, contact the box office.

## Sports & the Outdoors

BEACHES Haifa's coastline is one fine, sandy public beach after another. Note: never swim without a lifeguard on duty. From south to north, **Dado, Zamir, Carmel, and Bat Galim beaches** (☎ 04/852–4231) cover 5 km (3 mi) of coast, with many lifeguard stations among them. Entrance and parking are free as of this writing (parking fees may be assessed in the future). The beaches have sports areas, changing rooms, showers, toilets, refreshment stands, restaurants, and a winding stone promenade. On Saturday afternoon (morning in winter) at Dado Beach (near the Hof HaCarmel bus and train station at the city's entrance), Israelis of all ages come and folk dance, to the delight of onlookers. **Hof HaShaket,** just north of Rambam Hospital, offers separate gender days: Sunday, Tuesday, and Thursday for women; Monday, Wednesday, and Friday for men; Saturday for both.

BOWLING   It's hardly the national sport, but bowling at **Haifa Mall**, (⊠ 4 Flieman St., 3rd floor, Tel Amal ☎ 04/850–0130) is good fun. It's open daily from 10 AM til 1 AM (even later Friday night). One game costs NIS 24, including shoe rental.

DIVING   Learn to dive at the **Val Tal diving club** (⊠ 2 Hubert Humphrey St., Bat Galim ☎ 04/851–1523), or—if you already know how and would like to explore 20th-century wrecks, reefs, and an Italian submarine sunk by the British—look for Val Tal at the bottom station of the cable car, near the Yotvata restaurant. Rental equipment is available, and it's open daily 9 to 5.

## Shopping

Haifa is studded with modern shopping malls with boutiques, eateries, and movie theaters plus drugstores, photography stores, and money exchange desks. Convenient to the hotels on the Carmel is the **Panorama Center,** next to the Dan Panorama hotel. The huge, upscale **Grand Canyon,** a bit out of the way in Neveh Sha'anan, has more than 100 shops. At the southern entrance to the city are both the **Haifa Mall** and **Castra.** The latter, with large decorative murals, sells local art. Next door, Haifa Mall has gifts shops among many other boutiques.

**Amira's IOS Gallery** (⊠ 55 Ben Gurion Blvd., opposite the tourism office, German Colony ☎ 04/850–7504 ⊕ www.ios-g.com) has lovely glass art, jewelery, and souvenirs; Amira's workshop is behind the shop.

★ **Sara's Gift Shop** (⊠ Dan Carmel hotel, 85–87 Hanassi Blvd., Merkaz Carmel ☎ 04/830–6238 ⊕ www.sarapapo.com) stocks particularly interesting gifts for everyone at reasonable prices. It's crammed with jewelry made exclusively for these displays; the silver and Roman glass pieces are unique. Other choices are Judaica and gifts for Baha'i visitors.

# THE WINE COUNTRY & MT. CARMEL

This is the back-door route to Haifa, one that wanders through the foothills and up the spine of Mt. Carmel through Druze villages. Route 4 is smooth sailing, with the Carmel looming to the east beyond cultivated fields and banana plantations (though you may not see the bananas, as they're usually bagged in blue or gray plastic). The road leads through undulating countryside dotted with cypresses, palms, and vineyards.

## Benyamina

⑲ *55 km (34 mi) north of Tel Aviv on Rte. 652.*

Coming from the south, you'll drive through Benyamina, the youngest settlement in the area. Founded in 1922, it was named after Baron Edmond de Rothschild (1845–1934), the head of the French branch of the famous family, who took a keen interest in the welfare of his fellow Jews in Palestine. (His Hebrew name was Benyamin.) With his prestige, vision, and financial contributions, Rothschild laid the foundations in the late 19th century for Zichron Ya'akov and Bat Shlomo, as well as other towns along the coastal plain and in the Upper Galilee.

The advice of the viniculture experts Rothschild hired in the 1880s paid off handsomely, at least in this region—the fruit of the vines flourished in the 1890s. Rothschild's paternalistic system was not without its pitfalls, however; some of his administrators ruled his colonies like petty despots, trying, for instance, to impose use of the French language on the local settlers, who wished to speak Hebrew. Note that in Benyamina, as in other Rothschild towns, the signs of early settlement are respectfully preserved: rows of lofty, willowy Washingtonian palms introduced to the area by the local hero and agronomist Aaron Aaronson, of neighboring Zichron Ya'akov; and modest, one-story stucco homes capped with terra-cotta roofs, inspired by towns in Provence.

## Shuni

**20** *At railroad tracks in Benyamina, turn left onto Rte. 652, then drive 1 km (½ mi) north.*

This stone fortress was built by effendis in the 18th and 19th centuries, on the site of existing ruins, because of its sweeping command over the surrounding lands, some planted with grain (*shuni* is Arabic for granary). It is now part of the landscaped **Jabotinsky Park,** which includes Shuni (the Ottoman fortress) and the Roman theater. You can also dine in the fortress. The spring at present-day Shuni was also the source of the spring water that was tapped for the aqueducts of ancient Caesarea. In the 1930s and '40s, the site was chosen for its remote location as a training ground for members of self-organized units inspired by Ze'ev Jabotinsky (1880–1940), the right-wing Zionist leader who was the spiritual head of the Jewish underground organization Irgun Zvai Leumi. Armed Irgun units later launched attacks from here.

Excavations of the well-preserved, 2nd-century **Roman theater** (which you enter through the fortress) have revealed the remains of bathing pools lined with 2nd-century Roman mosaics and a marble statue of the Greek god of medicine, Aesculapius, both now in storage at the Rockefeller Museum, in Jerusalem. These finds support the theory that this was once a sacred spa whose waters had healing powers—indeed, an early-4th-century pilgrim mentioned in his writings that women who bathed here always became pregnant, like it or not. The theater also contains an ancient olive press, carved lintels, and fragments of columns. On the right, before you enter the fortress, you can still see part of a mosaic floor. Call ahead to arrange a guided tour of the site. ✉ *Rte. 652* ☎ *04/638–9730* ⊕ *www.shuni.co.il* ✉ *NIS 12* ☉ *Sun.–Thurs. 9–4, Fri. and Jewish holiday eves 9–12:30, Sat. 9–4.*

> **need a break?**
>
> Shortly after passing Shuni, turn left past the olive trees and into the **Tishbi Estate Winery** (✉ *Rte. 652* ☎ *04/638–0434* ⊕ *www.tishbi. com*) for a look at one of the country's most esteemed wineries, and a delicious breakfast or lunch. Tishbi Estate is the premier label (the sauvignon blanc and chardonnay are among the best in Israel). Under the grapevines, travelers enjoy local cheeses, salads, soups, pastas, and fish. Call ahead to reserve a wine tasting and a tour of the old buildings—the Tishbi family's great-grandfather planted the first

vineyards in the area almost 120 years ago. Tishbi's is open Sunday to Thursday 8–4 and Friday 8–3.

## Where to Eat

★ $$$ ✕ **Bracha b'Shuni.** What a lovely way to spend an evening: dine on the rooftop of a stone fortress enjoying delightful views of a Roman theater and vineyards. Then take in a jazz concert—under the stars if it's summertime. Bracha is the chef in this family-run business. Her menu celebrates the tastes of Provence and Tuscany, making use of local herbs, wines, and cheeses. Tempting starters are veal meatballs with pomegranate sauce and grilled chicken livers with grapes. Entrée choices include roast chicken with local dates and market-fresh fish with a sauce of butter, lemon, and Jerusalem artichokes. Pear tarte tatin makes a grand finale. ⊠ *In the fortress, in Jabotinsky Park* ☏ *04/638–8760* ⌂ *Reservations essential* ➾ *AE, DC, MC, V* ☯ *Closed Sun.*

## Nightlife & the Arts

The hip **Milestone Jazz Club** (⊠ In the fortress, in Jabotinsky Park ☏ 04/638–8760), in the fortress where Bracha b'Shuni's restaurant is located, offers gigs by some of Israel's best jazz musicians on Thursday, Friday, and Saturday nights. It's best to reserve ahead for a table.

# Zichron Ya'akov

★ ㉑ *61 km (40 mi) north of Tel Aviv.*

The planted roundabout marks the main entrance to Zichron Ya'akov, a town named by its original settlers in honor of Rothschild's father, James. Pick up a town map in the tourist office just opposite, next to the Founders' Monument and near the old cemetery. You can visit Zichron Ya'akov in a few hours en route to other places, and it also makes a nice day trip from Tel Aviv or Haifa. Allow time for a relaxing lunch at one of the town's relatively new restaurants (reserve ahead if you're coming on Saturday or if it's a holiday).

A visit to this old-world town starts at the white stone arch with the red-tile roof, just past the Founders' Monument, and continues along the main street, **Hameyasdim.** Residents have made every effort to maintain the original appearance of this short thoroughfare, and the cobblestone street is lined, for the most part, with small, restored, red-roof 19th-century homes. In those days, people needed courtyards behind their homes to house animals, carts, and farm equipment; several of these have been restored exactly to their original appearance. These days, upscale restaurants, historic sites, and offbeat shops fill the courtyards and are interspersed with the old houses along the main street.

About halfway down the street is **Bet Aaronson** (Aaronson's House), whose late-19th-century architecture successfully combines Art Nouveau and Middle Eastern traditions. This museum was once the home of the agronomist Aaron Aaronson (1876–1919), who gained international fame for his discovery of an ancestor of modern wheat. The house remains as it looked after World War I, with family photographs and French and Turkish furniture, as well as Aaronson's library, diaries, and letters.

Aaronson and his sisters became local heroes as leaders of the spy ring called the NILI (an acronym for a quotation from the Book of Samuel: "The Eternal One of Israel will not prove false")—a militant group dedicated to ousting the Turks from Palestine by collaborating with the British during World War I. Both sisters, Sarah and Rebecca, were in love with Aaron's assistant, Absalom Feinberg. A double agent was disrupting NILI's communications with the British, so Feinberg set off to cross the Sinai desert to make contact. He was killed in an ambush in the Gaza Strip. His remains were recovered some 50 years later from a grave marked simply by a palm tree, the tree having sprouted from some dates in Feinberg's pockets. (After the Six-Day War, Feinberg's body was reburied in Jerusalem.) Sarah Aaronson was captured by the Turks and committed suicide in her brother's house (now part of the museum) after being tortured. Other NILI leaders were executed by the Turks upon discovery. Aaron returned to Zichron Ya'akov with the victorious British in 1918, but the following year his plane mysteriously vanished en route from London to the Paris Peace Conference. A tour in English is provided; the last one takes place at 1:30 PM. ⊠ *40 Hameyasdim St.* ☎ *04/639–0120* ▣ *NIS 15* ⊙ *Sun.–Thurs. 8:30–2:15 (last tour at 1:30), Tues. 8:30–3, Fri. 8:30–noon.*

A few doors up the street is **Binyamin Pool,** a misnomer because it's actually the town's original water tower, built in 1891. Zichron was the first village in Israel to have water piped to its houses; Meir Dizengoff, the first mayor of Tel Aviv, even came to town to see how it was done. The facade resembles that of an ancient synagogue.

At the corner of Hanadiv and Hameyasdim streets stands the old synagogue, **Ohel Ya'akov,** built by Rothschild in 1886 to satisfy the settlers' first request.

Turn left onto Hanadiv Street, at the end of which stands the **First Aliya Museum,** located in the former Administration House. Commissioned by Baron de Rothschild, it is a fine example of late-19th-century Ottoman-style architecture, built of white stone with a central pediment capped by a tile roof. The museum is dedicated to the lives of immigrants who came to Israel with the First Aliya (a period of settlement from 1882 until 1904). Life-size model displays of local immigrants (like Zachariya, the seed vendor, and Izer, the cobbler) help illustrate how life was lived at that time. One film, among others, traces a family who came from Europe to follow a vision and describes the struggle encountered in a difficult, not-so-dreamlike period of Israel's modern history. ⊠ *2 Hanadiv St.* ☎ *04/629–4777* ▣ *NIS 15* ⊙ *Weekdays 9–2.*

**need a break?**  An inviting place to relax and watch the action in this still-rural town is the sweet little **park** on Hanadiv Street, opposite the old synagogue and the First Aliya Museum. In the spring it's filled with multicolored roses and all year round flowers blossom vibrantly.

 Founded in 1882 by Romanian pioneers, this settlement nearly foundered until rescued by Edmond de Rothschild. A decade later, however, the town's winery took off, the same **Carmel Wine Cellars** that you can see at the southern end of Zichron (in the direction of Binyamina). Today the winery is Israel's largest, producing more than 160 different wines and spirits. The old wooden buildings house a wine shop, and a homey restaurant where local cheeses and pasta are served on weekdays. The original storage vats and oak barrels are still on view, though wine is now stored mostly in stainless-steel vats and concrete tanks. A guided one-hour tour outlines the stages of local wine production. Included in the tour are a tasting of some four varieties, and a seven-minute audiovisual presentation screened in a 100-year-old wine cellar. Tours leave between 9 AM and 4 PM, and it's a good idea to reserve ahead. The finest Carmel wines are the Rothschild vintages: merlot, chardonnay, cabernet sauvignon, sauvignon blanc, and the single vineyard series. An autumn wine festival takes place around the time of the Sukkoth holiday. ☎ 04/629-0977 ⊕ www.carmelwines.co.il ⊠ NIS 15 ⊙ Sun.–Thurs. 9–4, Fri. 9–1.

## Where to Stay & Eat

**$$$** ✕ **Il Bacio (Ha Neshika).** Walk in off the main street until you spy an old one-story farmhouse with a large garden, usually packed with diners. Inside, the place is small and cozy—there's a little upstairs section as well. The food is delicious and creative. You might start with mozzarella gnocci with sautéed mushrooms, or a zucchini and feta cheese terrine; served with your meal is homemade bread, with lentils in balsamic vinegar. Main courses include baked crabs in sweet-and-hot chili sauce, lamb casserole with eggplant and pine nuts, and seafood and fennel salad. Two types of sea fish are always available. A hearty breakfast is served on Fridays and Saturdays. ⊠ 37 Hameyasdim St. ☎ 04/639-0133 ⚱ Reservations essential ⊟ AE, D, MC, V ⊙ Closed Sun.

★ **$$$** ✕ **Picciotto.** Not so long ago, Zichron was a sleepy village, and many of its old houses sat shuttered and closed. One of these, on the main street, retains its original wood shutters and warm clay color but has been lovingly restored inside. The ceiling is the original wood, and settlers peer out sternly from photos on the vanilla-colored walls; there's a woodburning stove in the middle. The chef's calamari on grilled eggplant and the seafood soup merit mention. Each makes a fine introduction to main courses such as sea bream cooked in fish stock and lemon juice and grilled fillet of pork with balsamic vinegar and olive oil. For dessert, try the chocolate terrine with coffee sauce. ⊠ 41 Hameyasdim St. ☎ 04/629-0646 ⚱ Reservations essential ⊟ AE, D, MC, V.

**$$** ✕ **Hatemaniya shel Santo.** Settle down on this wooden porch, in a courtyard well off the main street, for a tasty and authentic Yemenite meal. There's no menu—the waiter brings you soft pita bread, country black bread, and a large, fresh vegetable salad along with a rugged hummus dripped with olive oil. You can order stuffed vegetables or chicken, but make sure you also try the potato cakes and a plate of the small meat patties flavored with cilantro. It's all delicious, and nicely washed down by Yemenite coffee or cold water with lemon and mint. ⊠ 52 Hameyasdim St. ☎ 04/639-8762 ⊟ AE, DC, MC, V ⊙ Closed Sat.

**$** ▦ **Bet Maimon.** This unassuming family-run hotel on the western slopes of Zichron Ya'akov has a spectacular view of the coastal valley and the sea. The terrace restaurant serves both Middle Eastern and Eastern European meals. Inquire about the special health-vacation packages. The rooms are decorated in a gentle pastel yellow; there's a pretty garden. Guests who are less than fit will feel the climb to the sundeck on the roof; the three-story building has no elevator. There's Wi-Fi in the public areas. ✉ *4 Zahal St., 30900* ☎ *04/639–0212* 🖶 *04/639–6517* ⊕ *www.maimon.com* 💤 *25 rooms* 🍴 *Restaurant, Wi-Fi, pool, hot tub, sauna, free parking* 🖃 *AE, DC, MC, V.*

## South Bat Shlomo

❷❷ *5 km (3 mi) northeast of Zichron Ya'akov on Rte. 4, then Rte. 70 (toward Yokneam).*

Bat Shlomo was established in 1889 and named after the Baron de Rothschild's mother, Betty, daughter of Solomon ("bat Shlomo" in Hebrew). Established for the children of Zichron Ya'akov's farmers, this tiny hamlet failed to grow, and the town remains virtually unchanged. The oldest part of the village (south Bat Shlomo) comprises just one street; it's a charming stroll past small, square houses with red-tile roofs, the spaces between each of them leaving just enough room for a farmer's horse and wagon. The old synagogue is in the middle of the block. A few of the owners still cultivate the land and sell cheese, olive oil, and honey, much like their forebears. The short walk ends with a dramatic view of vineyards below and, opposite, the lushly forested hill of a nature reserve established by the British in 1941.

Along the street, behind a giant ficus tree, you'll find **Gallerina** (☎ 04/639–9735), an art gallery with café that's open on Thursday, Friday, and Saturday. The owners change the exhibition according to the season and the food suits the show; for instance, in winter they'll have ceramic soup bowls on sale and soup in the café. Other art objects for sale are photographs, paintings, and jaunty papier-mâché figures; on the menu are cheese plates, quiches, cake, and good hot coffee, served from 9:30 to 5. At twilight on summer Friday afternoons there's jazz in the garden.

## Mukhraka

★ ❷❸ *18 km (11 mi) northeast of Bat Shlomo, on Rte. 70, then Rte. 672. Drive 3 km (2 mi) east on 672, turn at sign for Mukhraka.*

Past open, uncultivated fields and a goatherd's rickety shack is the **Carmelite Monastery** at Mukhraka. The monastery stands on the spur of the Carmel range, at an altitude of 1,580 feet, on or near the site where the struggle between Elijah and the priests of Ba'al is believed to have taken place. *Mukhraka* is the Arabic word for a place of burning, referring to the fire that consumed the offering on Elijah's altar. The conflict developed because the people of Israel had been seduced by the pagan cults introduced by King Ahab's wife, Jezebel. Elijah demanded a contest with the priests of Ba'al in which each would erect an altar with a butchered ox as an offering and see which divinity sent down fire. Elijah drenched his altar with water, yet it burst into flames.

On his orders, the priests were taken down to the Brook of Kishon and executed.

The stark stone monastery was built in 1883 over Byzantine ruins. Records show that the site was revered as early as the 6th century, when hermits dwelled here. The Carmelites, a Roman Catholic monastic order established in the 13th century, look to Elijah as their role model. The courtyard contains a statue of a fearless Elijah brandishing a knife. The monks who live here have no telephones and only a generator for power. Climb to the roof for an unforgettable panorama: to the east stretches the Jezreel Valley and the hills of Nazareth, Moreh, and Gilboa. On a clear day you can even see Jordan's Gilead Mountains beyond the Jordan River and Mt. Hermon. ☎ *No phone* ✉ *NIS 4* ☉ *Mon.–Sat. 8–1:30 and 2:30–5.*

## Daliyat el Carmel

㉔ *2 km (1⅓ mi) west of Mukhraka (at junction with Rte. 672).*

Daliyat el Carmel is Israel's largest Druze village. The Druze are a close-knit, Arabic-speaking people who practice a secret religion; they form one of the most intriguing entities in the mosaic of Israel's population (of which they number 2%). So exclusive is this sect that only around 6% of the community is initiated into its religious doctrine, one tenet of which is a belief in reincarnation. The Druze broke away from Islam about 1,000 years ago, believing in the divinity of their founder, al Hakim bi Amir Allah, the Caliph of the Egyptian Fatimid dynasty from AD 996 to 1021. The Druze who live in the two existing villages on Mt. Carmel (the other is Isfiya) serve in the Israeli Army, a sign of their loyalty to Israel. Though many of the younger generation wear jeans and T-shirts, some older men and women are easily recognizable in their traditional garb. Head coverings indicate the degree of religious belief, from high white turban (resembling a fez) to white kerchief covering the head and shoulders. Many men sport a bushy moustache, a hallmark of the Druze, and some older ones wear dark robes and black pantaloons. Although many women wear Western garments, they retain the white headdress, often worn with an embroidered dress.

About 1 km (½ mi) inside town, take a right turn into the marketplace, a colorful jumble of shops lining the street. You can be assured of eating excellent falafel at any of the roadside stands or restaurants.

### Where to Eat

$$ ✕ **House of Druze Heritage.** The Druze are famous for their hospitality. Here you get not only a warm welcome and a good, solid meal but a look at the accoutrements of the Druze way of life. The traditional meal begins with appetizers such as hot-pepper salad, pickles, tahini (sesame paste), and hummus with big, flat Druze pita bread. The main course consists of skewers of grilled lamb or steak; baklava and Turkish coffee provide the finishing touch. The museum in the back displays Druze clothing and farm implements, household objects, handicrafts, and photos. ✉ *4 Ahat St.* ☎ *04/839–3242* ▭ *AE, D, MC, V.*

## Shopping

Along a brief stretch of the main road that winds through Daliyat el Carmel are shops selling lightweight throw rugs, handwoven baskets, brightly colored pottery, brass dishes, characteristic woven wall hangings, and embroidered skullcaps (for men). Bargaining is expected. Some shops close on Friday; the strip is crowded on Saturday.

# Isfiya

**㉕** *1 km (½ mi) north of Daliyat el Carmel on Rte. 672.*

Isfiya is very similar to neighboring Daliyat el Carmel, with flat-roof homes built closely together into the hillside, many of them raised on pillars and cut with arched windows. Hospitality is second nature to the Druze; you may be able to visit a village home and watch as the woman of the house bakes crispy-thin pita bread in the courtyard, then eat it with yogurt cheese and spices while hearing about Druze life from an ornate sofa in the living room. As you leave the village, at the top of the hill, note the vista of the Jezreel Valley opening suddenly on your right. The final approach to Haifa also affords a magnificent view of the coast stretching up to Akko, across the bay.

## Where to Eat

**★ $** ✕ **Nof Carmel.** To find this very good Druze restaurant, drive to the northern edge of the village. It's on your left; look for a red RESTAURANT sign, two tables outside under trees, and a Pepsi sign. People come from all over for the fine Middle Eastern fare, especially the homemade hummus with pine nuts, olive oil, garlic, and lemon juice, and the well-seasoned kebab on skewers. Those with a sweet tooth should sample the *sahlab* (a warm, custardlike pudding of crushed orchid bulb with thickened milk and sugar), or the scale-bending baklava. ⊠ *Rte. 672* ☎ *04/ 839–1718* ⚓ *Reservations not accepted* ▤ *AE, MC, V.*

# Ein Hod

**★ ㉖** *5 km (3 mi) west of Isfiya.*

To get to the artists' village of Ein Hod, head east straight from the coastal highway to Route 4, where you turn right. The exit ramp, climbing through olive trees and scrub, is on your left. Today, Ein Hod is home to around 135 families of sculptors, painters, and other artists. The setting is an idyllic one, with rough-hewn stone houses built on the hillside with sweeping views down to the Mediterranean. The Dadaist painter Marcel Janco (1895–1984) wrote upon his first visit in 1950: "The beauty of the place was staggering."

Parking is across the road, opposite the entrance to the village. Climbing up the hill, you soon come to a winding street on the left that starts a lovely walk through the small village. Signs indicate studios and workshops where artists paint, sculpt, and make jewelry, pottery, silkscreen prints, and clothing. You can continue straight to the town square, bordered by a restaurant and a large gallery where works by Ein Hod artists are exhibited.

Village artist Dan Ben-Arye has created an excellent Web site, (⊕ www. ein-hod.israel.net), an online guide that describes the resident artists and what they do as well as recommending trail workshops, art demonstrations, and village sights. The site also lists accommodations in private homes, known as "zimmers" around here. Most of the places take cash or travelers' checks only. At Ben-Arye's shop, **Art and Wear** (☎ 04/ 984–1126), near the village square, you can pick up an Ein Hod tour map, and Ben-Arye also happily dispenses advice over the phone.

By the square is the **Janco-Dada Museum.** As one of the founders of the Dada movement, the Romanian-born Marcel Janco had already established considerable professional acclaim by the time he emigrated to Israel (then Palestine) in 1941. The museum, which opened in 1983, houses a permanent collection of the artist's works in various media, reflecting Janco's 70-year output both in Europe and Israel. A 20-minute slide show chronicles the life of the artist and the Dada movement. Also exhibited are works by other Israeli modern artists. Don't miss the view from the rooftop before leaving. ☎ 04/984–2350 ⊕ www. jancodada-museum.israel.net ⊠ NIS 14 ☉ Sun.–Thurs. and Sat. 9:30–5, Fri. and Jewish holiday eves 9:30–4.

## Where to Stay & Eat

★ $$ ✕ **Dona Rosa.** If you can't read the restaurant's sign in Hebrew, just follow the tantalizing aroma up the steps of this wooden building on the town square. Dona Rosa's grandsons, Uri and Doron, import meat and special charcoal from Argentina and prepare the food in the true Argentinian style, by slow grilling. A bar is decorated with a drawing of a hefty cow, illustrating each cut of meat. Highlights include pork spareribs marinated all night, then grilled; the Dona version of paella (seafood simmered with fragrant yellow rice), and *assado,* delicious, chunky ribs (available only on Saturday or by special order). There's beer and mostly Chilean and Argentinian wine, too. Dine on the balcony in warm weather. ⊠ On the village Sq. ☎ 04/954–3777 ⊕ www. dona-rosa.israel.net ⊟ AE, DC, MC, V ☉ Closed Sun.

$ ✕ **Abu Yakov.** You reach Abu's by climbing the stone seats of Ein Hod's amphitheater, or you can walk through nearby Melanie's café. There are a few Formica tables inside—most of the seating is outside, overlooking the "amphi," enclosed beneath a ragged plastic cover. It feels a bit makeshift, but the fresh food counts for everything. Dine on what's often called "Oriental" food in Israel: hummus, fluffy pitas, red-hot sauce, chopped vegetable salad, and grilled meat on skewers. On Saturdays when there's a crowd, they prepare french fries, too. ⊠ At the top of the amphitheater, near village Sq. ☎ 04/984–3377 ⊟ No credit cards.

¢ ✕ **Melanie's.** To reach this funky café, climb up the stone steps to the right of Dona Rosa restaurant and watch for the CAFE GALLERY sign, keeping an eye out on your left for a two-level collection of mismatched chairs and odd tables surrounded by small trees and potted plants—there's often a cat sunning himself on a stool. Inside the funky stone building, under the arches, handmade handbags and clothes are for sale. Guests sit outside to drink coffee; eat delectable homemade cheesecake, apple pie, and other seasonal fruit tarts, or nosh on grilled cheese sandwiches with salad.

You can stop for a beer or glass of wine, too. ✉ *Near village Sq.* ☎ *04/ 954–1383* ⊙ *Closed Wed.* ⊟ *No credit cards.*

**$** 🏠 **Jancourt B& B.** Looking for pine and maple Canadiana? Not only is the furniture here just that, but it's featured in the on-premises antique shop. Batia and Claude's bed-and-breakfast is quiet and private, hidden behind hot pink bougainvillea. The accommodation consists of a living/dining room, bedroom, and kitchenette, all decked with such comfy antiques as stuffed armchairs, art deco lamps, kilim rugs, and '50s-era side tables. Modernity is the vibe, however, in the fully equipped kitchenette and the contemporary bathroom with its jet-stream shower. Olives from the yard and homemade bread and jam come with a breakfast of eggs, vegetables, and local cheeses. ✉ *Second part of Ein Hod, 30890* ☎ *04/984–1648* 🖶 *04/984–3056* ⊕ *www.ein-hod.israel.net* ↪ *1 room* ♻ *Kitchenette, cable TV* ⊟ *No credit cards* ⏍ *BP.*

### Nightlife & the Arts

**Gertrud Kraus House** (☎ 04/984–1058 or 04/984–2018), a café just off the main square, features chamber music on occasional Saturday evenings at 6:30. Admission is NIS 40, which includes complimentary coffee and cakes. Performances are held from June to October; call for details.

### Shopping

Many of the artists who live in the winding lanes of Ein Hod throw open their workshops to visitors, who are welcome to browse and buy. Between the olive trees and behind painted gates, look for signs on homes that indicate the sale of jewelery, gold metalwork, sculptures, paintings, ceramics, stained glass, hand-painted clothing, and artistic photography. Start either at the entrance to the village where signs point to the left, or head for the village square straight ahead.

★ **The Gallery** (☎ 04/984–2548) carries a large selection of handicrafts and art is shown at this space on Ein Hod's main square. Displayed in the front room are silver, enamel, and gold jewelry; ceramics; and Judaica. Three other rooms are devoted to paintings, watercolors, sculptures, and graphic works by resident artists, some of them internationally known. The gallery is open Sunday–Thursday and Saturday 11–4, Friday and Jewish holiday eves 10–5.

**Silver Print** (☎ 04/954-1673), a gallery run by Vivienne Silver-Brody, is devoted to 19th- and 20th-century Israeli photography. Ask to see these lovely old photos, many taken by Vivienne's grandfather; she loves to share with potential collectors her wide knowledge of local photography. It's best to call ahead for an appointment.

## Nahal Me'arot Nature Reserve

★ ㉗ *3 km (2 mi) south of Ein Hod, 1 km (½ mi) east of Rte. 4.*

The prehistoric **Carmel Caves** are in the Nahal Me'arot Nature Reserve. The three excavated caves are up a steep flight of stairs, on a fossil reef that was covered by the sea 100 million years ago. The first discoveries of prehistoric remains were made when this area was being scoured for stones to build the Haifa port. In the late 1920s, the first archaeological expedition was headed by Dorothy Garrod of England, who received assistance from a British feminist group on condition that the dig be carried out exclusively by women. It was. In the Tannur cave, the first on the tour, the strata Garrod's team excavated are clearly marked, spanning about 150,000 years in the life of early man. The most exciting discovery made in the area was the existence of both Homo sapiens and Neanderthal skeletons; evidence that both lived here has raised fascinating questions about the relationship between the two and whether they lived side by side. A display on the daily life of early man as hunter and food gatherer occupies the Gamal cave. The last cave you'll visit, called the Nahal, is the largest—it cuts deep into the mountain—and was actually the first discovered. A burial place with 84 skeletons was found outside the mouth of the cave.

The bone artifacts and stone tools discovered in the Nahal cave suggest that people who settled here, about 12,000 years ago, were the forebears of early farmers with a modified social structure more developed than that of hunters and gatherers. There is also evidence that the Crusaders once used the cave to guard the coastal road. Inside, an audiovisual show sheds light on how early man lived here. There's a snack bar and parking lot at this site. ☎ 04/984–1750 or 04/984–1752 ⊕ www.parks.org.il 🖃 NIS 23 ⊙ Oct.–Mar., Sat.–Thurs. and Jewish holidays 8–4, Fri. and Jewish holiday eves 8–1; Apr.–Sept., Sat.–Thurs. and Jewish holidays 8–5, Fri. and Jewish holiday eves 8–2.

### Sports & the Outdoors
At the entrance to the Carmel Caves is the stone office of the **Nature Reserves Authority** (☎ 04/984–1750), where trained staff provide maps and information about two well-marked nature walks that leave from this point. The route of the Botanical Path takes two hours, while the Geological Path takes 40 minutes; both include lookout points.

# FROM AKKO TO ROSH HANIKRA

## Akko

FodorsChoice  *22 km (13½ mi) north of Haifa.*
★
The walled Old City of Akko (also known as Acre), in the modern town of Akko, is an enchanting mix of mosques, markets, khans (Ottoman inns), and vaulted Crusader ruins (many of which are underground) at the northern tip of Haifa Bay. Plan on spending the better part of a day if you want to see everything, which would include time to see the excellent presentation in the Turkish Bath House; the day can include a good lunch as well.

You can approach Akko from Haifa on Route 4. A much slower but far prettier inland route takes you north on Route 70, a scenic drive that runs roughly parallel to Route 4 about 7 km (4½ mi) to the east, through rolling hills, avoiding the drab satellite towns of Haifa. Continue north past a small jog in the road that you'll encounter 10 km (6 mi) ahead. Take Route 85 west some 14 km (9 mi) later to reach Akko's walled Old City, where you'll start your visit.

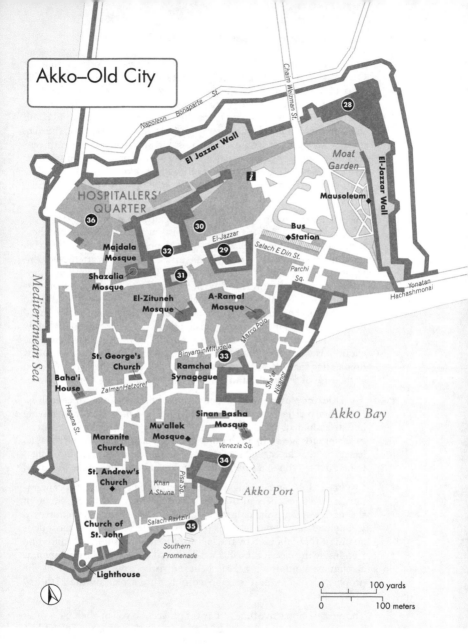

# Akko–Old City

**HOSPITALLERS' QUARTER**

El Jazzar Wall

Napoleon Bonaparte St.

Chaim Weizman St.

Moat Garden

El-Jazzar Wall

Mausoleum

Majdala Mosque

Shazalia Mosque

El-Zituneh Mosque

El-Jazzar

A-Ramal Mosque

Bus Station

Salach E Din St.

Parchi Sq.

Yonatan Hachashmonai

Mediterranean Sea

St. George's Church

Ramchal Synagogue

Binyamin Mitudela

Marco Polo

Baha'i House

Zalman Hatzoref

Hagana St.

Maronite Church

Mu'allek Mosque

Sinan Basha Mosque

Venezia Sq.

Sha'ar Nikanor

Akko Bay

St. Andrew's Church

Khan A-Shuna

Pisa Sq.

Akko Port

Church of St. John

Salach Raytziri

Southern Promenade

Lighthouse

0          100 yards
0          100 meters

You approach the Old City on Weizman Street (watch for signs that say OLD AKKO), proceeding through a breach in the surrounding walls. Once inside, park at the Knights parking lot, where you start a (lengthy) walking tour (the circular route brings you back to your car). Double back a few steps to the entrance to the Old City at the walls and climb **㉘** the signposted blue-railing stairway on your right for a stroll on the **ramparts.** Walking right, you can see the stunted remains of the 12th-century walls built by the Crusaders, under whose brief rule—just under two centuries—Akko flourished as never before or since. The indelible signs of the Crusaders, who made Akko the main port of their Christian empire, are much more evident inside the Old City itself.

The wide wall you are walking on, which girds the northern part of the town, was built by Ahmed el-Jazzar, the Pasha of Akko, who added these fortifications following his victory over Napoléon's army in 1799. With the help of the British fleet, el-Jazzar turned Napoléon's attempted conquest into a humiliating rout. Napoléon had dreamed of founding a new Eastern empire, thrusting northward from Akko to Turkey and then seizing India from Great Britain. His defeat at Akko hastened his retreat to France, thus changing the course of history. Walk around to the guard towers and up an incline just opposite; there's a view of the moat below and Haifa across the bay. Turn around and let your gaze settle on the exotic skyline of Old Akko, the sea-green dome of the great mosque its dominating feature. Walk down the ramp, crossing the Moat Garden at the base of the walls, and walk straight ahead to see the mosque.

★ **㉙** The **El-Jazzar Mosque** is considered one of the most magnificent in Israel. Ahmed el-Jazzar, who succeeded Dahr el-Omar simply by having him assassinated, ruled Akko from 1775 to 1804. During his reign he built this mosque along with other public structures. His cruelty was so legendary that he earned the epithet "the Butcher." (He is buried next to his adopted son in a small white building to the right of the mosque.)

Just beyond the entrance is a pedestal engraved with graceful calligraphy; it re-creates the seal of a 19th-century Ottoman sultan. Some of the marble and granite columns that adorn the mosque and courtyard were plundered from the ruins of Caesarea. In front of the mosque is an ornate fountain used by the faithful for ritual washings of hands and feet. Inside the mosque, enshrined in the gallery reserved for women, is a reliquary containing a hair believed to be from the beard of the prophet Muhammad; it is removed only once a year, on the 27th day of Ramadan.

The mosque closes five times a day for prayers, so you might have a short wait. Dress modestly. ⊠ *Off El-Jazzar St., on the left of the Sq.* ☏ *NIS 6* ☉ *Sat.–Thurs. 8–5, Fri. 8–11 and 1–5.*

**need a break?** In the plaza outside the El-Jazzar Mosque are **outdoor restaurants** where you can enjoy a falafel, fresh-squeezed orange juice (or pomegranate in season), or coffee while watching the world go by.

To visit the intriguing **underground Crusader city,** return to the parking lot (around the corner to your left), where you will find the entrance to the visitor center. There's a short film, and a model of Akko to help you get your bearings. Your admission ticket gives entrance to the Turkish Bath, so hang on to it. You can pick up the headphones for a guided tour here (price is included in admission), as well as brochures and maps.

★ ㉚ Crossing the grassy lawn, you begin a tour of the 12th-century subterranean city, **Crusader Vaults and Halls,** which unfolds beneath the 18th- and 19th-century buildings you see today. Deep inside is a series of barrel-vaulted rooms known as the Crusader Vaults and Halls (one of which is sometimes used for chamber-music concerts). Six such halls have been discovered thus far. Arrows point the way through dimly lit vast rooms filled with ongoing reconstruction work, huge marble columns, and myriad archaeological pieces from the past. Above this part of the Crusader city stands the Ottoman citadel, which you can glimpse from the courtyard. Raised by Dahr el-Omar in the 18th century on the rubble-filled Crusader ruins, the citadel was the highest structure in Akko. It was later converted by the British into a prison (now a museum), and in order to unearth the Crusaders Halls, the former prison courtyard was completely dug out. Archaeologists are always busy delving into the mysteries of Akko, but signs keep you on a safe path.

The seeds of the Crusaders' downfall in Akko were probably sown by the divisive factions within its walls. The Hospitallers and Templars, the so-called fighting monks, also had separate quarters (the Templars, also French, lived near the lighthouse by the western Crusader sea wall). By the mid-13th century, open fighting had broken out between the Venetians and Genoese. When the Mamluks attacked with a vengeance in 1291, the Crusaders' resistance quickly crumbled, and the city's devastation was complete. It subdued the city for centuries, and even today Akko retains a medieval cast. ☒ *Parking lot at 1 Weizman St.* ☎ *04/ 991-1764* ⊕ *www.akko.org.il* ✉ *Refectory with Crusader Vaults and Halls, NIS 25; Bathhouse with Crusader Vaults and Halls, NIS 44* ☉ *Nov.–Mar., Sun.–Thurs. 9–4:15, Fri. and Jewish holiday eves 9–1:15, Sat. 9–4:15; Apr.–Oct., Sun.–Thurs. 9–5, Fri. and Jewish holiday eves 9–2:15, Sat. 9–5.*

★ ㉛ Akko's remarkable **Turkish Bathhouse,** built for Pasha el-Jazzar in 1781, was in use until 1947. Don't miss the sound-and-light show called "The Story of the Last Bath Attendant," set in the beautiful bathhouse itself. You follow the story, with visual and audio effects, from the dressing room decorated with Turkish tiles and topped with a cupola, through the rooms with colored-glass bubbles protruding from the roof domes, sending a filtered green light to the steam rooms below. ☒ *Parking lot at 1 Weizman St.* ☎ *04/991-1764* ⊕ *www.akko.org.il* ✉ *Bathhouse with Crusader Vaults and Halls, NIS 44* ☉ *Nov.–Mar., Sun.–Thurs. 9–4:15, Fri. and Jewish holiday eves 9–1:15, Sat. 9–4:15; Apr.–Oct., Sun.–Thurs. 9–5, Fri. and Jewish holiday eves 9–2:15, Sat. 9–5.*

㉜ The **Refectory** was once known as the Crypt of St. John—before excavation it was erroneously thought to have been an underground chamber (diggers thought the high-up windows were the doors). The dimensions of the colossal pillars that support the roof (they're girdled with metal bands for extra support) make this one of Israel's most monumental ex-

## AKKO'S HISTORY

**HISTORY CLINGS TO THE STONES** *of old Akko, with each twist and turn along its streets telling another tale. The city's history begins 4,000 years ago, when Akko was first mentioned in Egyptian writings that refer to the mound, northeast of its walls. The Old Testament describes in Judges 1 that after the death of Joshua the tribe of Asher was unable to drive the Canaanites from Akko, so he lived among them. Akko has always been worth fighting for. It had a well-protected harbor, fertile hinterland, and a strategic position that linked Egypt and Phoenicia. Alexander the Great had such regard for Akko that he set up a mint here. Akko was Phoenician for long periods, but when the Hellenistic king Ptolemy II gained control in the 2nd century BC, he renamed it Ptolemais.*

*The Crusaders who conquered Akko in 1104 were led by King Baldwin I. The port city, which the victorious French*

*Hospitallers renamed for their patron saint—Jeanne d'Arc—was the Crusaders' principal link to home. Commerce thrived, and the European maritime powers Genoa, Pisa, Venice, and Marseilles developed separate quarters here. After the disastrous defeat of the Crusader armies in 1187, Akko surrendered to Saladin, but Richard the Lionheart soon recaptured the European stronghold. In its Crusader heyday, Akko had about 40 churches and monasteries and a population of 50,000. In the 13th century, after the conquest of Jerusalem by the Muslims, Akko became the effective capital of a shrunken Latin kingdom. Dahr el-Omar, the Bedouin sheikh, moved his capital from Tiberias to Akko in 1749 and rebuilt the walls of the city.*

 amples of Crusader architecture. It's also one of the oldest Gothic structures in the world. In the right-hand corner opposite the entrance is a fleur-de-lis carved in stone—the crest of the French House of Bourbon—which has led some scholars to postulate that this was the chamber in which Louis VII convened the knights of the realm.

Just outside this room is an entrance to an extremely narrow subterranean passageway. Cut from stone, this was a secret tunnel that the Crusaders probably used to reach the harbor when besieged by Muslim forces. (Those who are claustrophobic can take an alternate route, which goes back to the entrance of the Turkish Bathhouse and continues straight.) You'll emerge to find yourself in the cavernous vaulted halls of the fortress guardpost, with a 13th-century marble Crusader tombstone at the exit. Go up the stairs to the left and turn right into the covered market, where artisans beat pieces of copper into bas-relief plates and bowls and sell other handcrafted items. Exit to the left. ⊠ *Parking lot at 1 Weizman St.* ☎ *04/991-1764* ⊕ *www.akko.org.il* 🏛 *Refectory with Crusader Vaults and Halls, NIS 25; Bathhouse with Crusader Vaults and Halls, NIS 44* ☉ *Nov.–Mar., Sun.–Thurs. 9–4:15, Fri. and Jewish holiday eves 9–1:15, Sat. 9–4:15; Apr.–Oct., Sun.–Thurs. 9–5, Fri. and Jewish holiday eves 9–2:15, Sat. 9–5.*

**③③** At the local **souk** (market), stalls heaped with fresh produce alternate with specialty stores: a pastry shop with an astonishing variety of exotic Middle Eastern delicacies; a spice shop filled with the aromas of the East; a bakery with steaming-fresh pita. You'll often see fishermen sitting on doorsteps, intently repairing their lines and nets to the sounds of Arabic music blaring from the open windows above.

**need a break?** In the souk, duck into the **Oudah Brothers Cafe** (✉ Khan ha Frankim St. ☎ 04/991–2013) and enjoy a coffee, hummus, or kebab in the courtyard of the 16th-century Khan el-Faranj, or Franks' Inn. Note the 18th-century Franciscan monastery and tower to your left.

**③④** In Venezia Square, in front of the port, is the **Khan el-Umdan,** or Inn of the Pillars. Before you visit this Ottoman *khan*—the largest of the four in Akko—and the Pisan Quarter beyond, take a stroll around the port, with its small flotilla of fishing boats, yachts, and sailboats. Then walk through the khan's gate beneath a square clock tower, built at the turn of the 20th century. The khan served vast numbers of merchants and travelers during Akko's golden age of commerce, in the 18th century. The 32 pink-and-gray granite pillars that give it its name are compliments of Ahmed el-Jazzar's raids on Roman Caesarea. There was once a market at the center of the colonnaded courtyard.

**③⑤** You can walk along the sea walls at **Pisan Harbor.** Start at the café perched on high—a great lookout—and head west in the direction of the 18th-century Church of St. John. You'll end up at the southwestern extremity of Akko, next to the lighthouse. The Templers once occupied this area. Head north along Haganah Street, which runs parallel to the crenellated western sea wall. After five minutes you'll reach the whitewashed, blue-trimmed Baha'i house (not open to the public), where the prophet of the Baha'i religion, Baha'u'llah, spent 12 years of his exile. His burial site is just north of Akko.

**③⑥** The **Museum of the Underground Prisoners** is in several wings of the citadel built by Dahr el-Omar and then amended by Ahmed el-Jazzar in 1785. It became a British prison during the Mandate. On the way in, you pass the citadel's outside wall; the difference between the large Crusader building stones and the smaller Turkish ones above is easy to spot. Prison life is illustrated by the original cells and their meager contents, supplemented by photographs and documents that reconstruct the history of the Jewish resistance to British rule in the 1930s and '40s. During the Mandate, the citadel became a high-security prison whose inmates included top members of Jewish resistance organizations, among them Ze'ev Jabotinsky. In 1947 a dramatic prison breakout by leaders of the Irgun captured headlines around the world and provided Leon Uris's novel *Exodus* with one of its most dramatic moments.

As you leave the museum, turn right after 60 feet and follow the massive walls around the northern part of town to the breach at Weizman Street and the parking lot where you entered the Old City. ✉ *Haganah St. (a few mins north of the lighthouse)* ☎ *04/991–8264* ✎ *NIS 10* ⊙ *Sun.–Thurs. 9–3, Fri. 9–1.*

## Where to Stay & Eat

★ $$$ ✕ **Uri Buri.** Uri's famous fish and seafood restaurant is housed in an old stone, arched Turkish building; one room is furnished with sofas, copper dishes, and *nargillas* ("water pipes"). Everything on the menu is seasonal (i.e., very fresh), and the fish is steamed, baked, or grilled. Allow time to linger here–it's not your everyday fish fry. Two house specialties are gravlax and Thai-style fish; seafood soup is another fixture. Or have a go at baby calamari with kumquats and pink grapefruit, or anchovy fillets in lemon, oil, and hot pepper. It's near the lighthouse, on one edge of the coast-side parking lot. ⊠ *93 Haganah St.* ☎ *04/955–2212* ⚠ *Reservations essential* ☱ *AE, D, MC, V* ☉ *Closed Tues.*

$$ ✕ **Abu Christo.** This popular waterfront fish restaurant at the northern edge of the Crusader port actually stands at one of the original 18th-century gates built by Pasha Ahmed el-Jazzar when he fortified the city after his victory over Napoléon. At this family business, opened in 1948 and passed from father to son, Abu Christo serves up the daily catch—often grouper, red snapper, or sea bass—prepared simply, either grilled or deep fried. Shellfish and grilled meats are also available. The covered patio on the water is idyllic in summer. ⊠ *Crusader Port* ☎ *04/991–0065* ⚠ *Reservations essential July–Sept.* ☱ *AE, DC, MC, V.*

$$ ✕ **Galileo.** Here you can sit on a terrace alongside the Old City's ancient walls and eat fresh fish, grilled meats, or Middle Eastern salads. You'll be right on the water in the Pisan Harbor, with nothing but a few ruins and an expanse of blue before you. The view compensates for the undistinguished fare. ⊠ *Crusader Port* ☎ *04/991–4610* ☱ *AE, DC, MC, V.*

$$$$ ▥ **Ahuzat Gaya.** This very special B&B occupies a gorgeous house in
**Fodor'sChoice** Moshav Shavei Zion, an aging beachside communal settlement 8 km (5
★ mi) north of Akko. It's a large, two-story peach-colored building: there's a welcoming fireplace in the entryway; wood-framed windows looking out at the Med, and flowers gracing the large wooden dining table. A winding staircase leads to the spacious guest rooms with white billowing curtains, huge beds, and stereos. A gourmet breakfast is served on the patio, beside the turquoise pool. Alternative massage treatments are offered in the tranquil downstairs salons. Lunch is available on request. ⊠ *1 Hof St., turn off Rte. 4 onto Moshav Shavei Zion and make a left onto Hof St.* ☎ *04/952–5656* ☱ *04/952–4442* ⊕ *www.ahuzatgaya. co.il* ⇆ *4 rooms* ⚠ *Pool, refrigerators, DVDs, massage; no room phones, no kids under 18* ☱ *AE, DC, MC, V* ⊙ *BP.*

$ ▥ **Nes Ammim Guest House.** Founded in 1964, Nes Ammim is an ecumenical Christian settlement of about 40 people, where life and studies center on the furthering of mutual respect and tolerance. Guests are invited to chat with members of the community, who can take you around the grounds. Lodging options are either standard rooms or family apartments with fully equipped kitchens. The furnishings are basic; the setting, 10 km (6 mi) north of Akko, is picturesque and rural, once you get past the dismal approach road. A friendly and welcoming staff are a nice plus. In summer, classical music is performed in the serene chapel, or near the large pool (drawing local music lovers as well as guests), often after a barbecue meal. To get here, drive north from Akko on Route 4. ⊠ *D. N. Western Galilee, 25225* ☎ *04/995–0000* ☱ *04/995–0098*

⌐⇁ *48 rooms, 13 apartments* ⌂ *Restaurant, grocery, pool, lounge* ☰ *AE, D, MC, V.*

**$** ⌷ **Palm Beach.** The Palm Beach is on Route 4 just south of Akko—right on the beach, with fine views of Haifa Bay and the rooftops of the Old City. Rooms are outfitted with blond-wood furniture with gold and brick curtains, bedspread, and carpets; all face the sea. The comprehensive relaxation and entertainment facilities are in the country club adjacent to the hotel, a few steps away. ⊠ *Rte. 4* ☎ *04/987–7777* 🖷 *04/991– 0434* ⊕ *www.palmbeach.co.il* ⌐⇁ *98 rooms, 27 suites* ⌂ *2 restaurants, room service, in-room safes, some minibars, cable TV, 2 tennis courts, 2 pools, wading pool, hot tub, gym, spa, basketball, Ping-Pong, free parking, no-smoking rooms* ☰ *AE, MC, V.*

## Sports & the Outdoors

BEACHES Just south of the Old City on the Haifa–Akko road is a sandy stretch of municipal beach in Akko Bay, with parking, showers, toilets, and chair rentals. Admission is NIS 8.

## Shopping

**Nili's** (⊠ 1 Weitzman St., at the entrance to Old Akko, at the parking lot ☎ 04/955-3439) sells a whole range of Israeli-made products. The jewelry that combines silver and gold is especially interesting; some incorporates Roman glass, some uses turquoise Eilat stone, and there's also hand-worked copperware.

# Baha'i Founder's Shrine & Gardens

★ ③⑦ *Rte. 4, 1 km (⅔ mi) north of gas station at northern edge of Akko.*

For the Baha'is, this is the holiest place on earth, the site of the tomb of the faith's prophet and founder, Baha'u'llah. First you'll pass the west gate of the gardens, open only to Baha'is. Take the first right (no sign) and continue to the unobtrusive turn, 500 yards up, to the north and main gate. Baha'u'llah lived in the red-tile mansion here after he was released from jail in Akko and was buried in the small building next door, now the Shrine of Baha'u'llah. Visitors to the shrine are asked to dress modestly. The gardens and terrace are exquisitely landscaped. ▦ *Free* ⊙ *Gardens daily 9–4; tomb Fri.–Mon., 9–noon.*

( **en route** ) To the west of the highway, as you travel north, stands a segment of the multitiered aqueduct built by Ahmed el-Jazzar in the late 18th century to carry the sweet waters of the Kabri springs to Akko.

# Lochamei Hageta'ot

③⑧ *2 km (1 mi) north of Akko, 6 km (4 mi) south of Nahariya.*

Kibbutz Lochamei Hageta'ot ("Ghetto Fighters") was founded in 1949 by survivors of the German, Polish, and Lithuanian Jewish ghettos and veterans of the ghetto uprisings against the Nazis. To commemorate their compatriots who perished in the Holocaust, and to perpetuate the memory thereof, the kibbutz members set up a **museum**, which you enter to the right of the main gate. Exhibits include photographs documenting the Warsaw Ghetto and the famous uprising, and halls devoted to different themes, among them Jewish communities before their destruction in the Holocaust; the death camps; and deportations at the hands of the Nazis. You can also see the actual booth in which Adolf Eichmann, architect of the "Final Solution," sat during his Jerusalem trial.

Opened in 1996, **Yad Layeled** (Children's Memorial), a white, cone-shape building, is dedicated to the memory of the 1½ million children who perished in the Holocaust. It's designed for young visitors, who can begin to comprehend the events of the Holocaust through a series of tableaux and images accompanied by recorded voices, allowing them to identify with individual victims without seeing shocking details. There is a small restaurant on the premises. ☎ *04/995–8080* ✉ *Free; donation appreciated* ⊙ *Sun.–Thurs. 9–4, Fri. 9–1, Sat. 10–5.*

## Nahariya

**㊴** *8 km (5 mi) north of Akko.*

The first Jewish settlement in the Western Galilee, Nahariya was founded in 1934 by German Jews who had fled the Nazis and come to farm in what was then termed a communal village for agricultural settlement. Eventually these pioneers turned from the soil to what they realized was their greatest natural resource—some of the country's best beaches—for a more lucrative livelihood. Thus a popular seaside resort was born. The *yekke* (Jews of German origin) spirit lingers on in the clean and orderly boulevards and streets. Nahariya's main thoroughfare, Haga'a-ton Boulevard, was built along the banks of a river, now dried up, lined with shady eucalyptus trees; the town's name comes from *nahar,* the Hebrew word for "river."

Although German was once the language here, you're now just as likely to hear Russian or Amharic (spoken by Ethiopians), and blue-bereted U.N. soldiers from bases to the north are frequent visitors. In July and August, there's dancing in the amphitheater at the mouth of the river, and Israeli stars perform on the beach and in the town square.

The **Byzantine church** has an elaborate, 17-color mosaic floor, discovered in 1964, that depicts peacocks, other birds, hunting scenes, and plants. It was part of what experts consider one of the largest and most beautiful Byzantine churches in the Western Galilee, where Christianity rapidly spread from the 4th to the 7th century. Call the tourist office (☎ 04/987–9800) to arrange a visit, as the church is not always open. To get here, head east on Haga'aton to Route 4, making a left at the stoplight and then the first right onto Yechi'am Street. From here take the third left and then an immediate right onto Bielefeld Street. The church is next to the Katzenelson school. ⊠ *Bielefeld St.* ✆ *NIS 2.*

### Where to Stay & Eat

★ **$$$** ✕ **Adelina.** When dining at this stellar restaurant, you may wonder how you got so lucky. There's the knockout view of the Mediterranean, the tree-shaded setting, and the wonderful Spanish-accented dishes prepared by kibbutz member and chef Adelina. Dining options include light tapas, a fixed business lunch, à la carte main dishes, and Friday brunch. Cooking is done in the huge silver *taboon* (oven)—Spanish music drifts across the dark wooden tables. Try the paella marina ra (shellfish, fish, rice, and saffron), pork chorizo wrapped in a crepe, or the day's fish catch grilled with lemongrass, herbs, and cream. Then onward to *knafe* (a local pastry) with pistachio ice cream. ⊠ *Off Rte. 4, turn into Kibbutz Kabri on Rte. 89 and follow the signs* ☎ *04/995–2707, Ext. 1* ▤ *AE, DC, MC, V* ☻ *Closed Sun.*

**$** ✕ **La Crepe Jacob.** There's nothing like tasting an authentic Bretagne-style crepe in a northern town. Owner and *maître crepier* Jacques has created a space reminiscent of a small restaurant in rural France; he imports his flour directly from the French, which gives his crepes that unmistakably authentic flavor. They're hefty, too—a single crepe makes an entire meal. As you listen to French *chansons* in the background, try a crepe with feta cheese, ham, and mushrooms; smoked salmon and cheese; or tomato, onion, olives, cheese, and mushrooms. The sweet specialty is flambéed apple slices with cinnamon and ice cream. Wine is available. ⊠ *66 Weitzman St.* ☎ *04/992–5593* ▤ *AE, D, MC, V.*

**$** ✕ **Penguin.** This casual, main-street institution opened its doors in 1940. Three generations of the same family work here, and the walls carry enlarged photographs of how the place looked when it was just a hut. Stop off for coffee and cake, or make a meal of spinach blintzes with melted cheese; pasta; hamburger platters; or Chinese dishes. The management swears that the schnitzel gets accolades from Viennese visitors. All main dishes come with salad, rice, french fries, and vegetables. Finish off with a frozen yogurt from the adjacent stand, under the same venerable ownership. ⊠ *31 Haga'aton Blvd.* ☎ *04/992–8855* ▤ *V.*

**$$$$** ▥ **Pinhas & Avraham.** To enter this compound, you park beside an orange grove, walk in through an arboretum, and stand before a fairy-tale garden, densely shaded with every color of green and crammed with flowers and plants. Accommodations are in eight small, unusually shaped, pale beige units with two bikes beside each entryway. This place offers over-the-top, luxurious extravagance: the large rooms have carved-wood beds, soft-white down quilts, and plasma swivel TVs with DVD players that you can see from bed, the hot tub, or the kitchenette dining nook. The showers double as saunas, and bathrooms come with white robes. A dark rose sofa with Moroccan pillows and espresso machines in the kitchenettes complete the experience. A covered stone patio with white roses climbs along one side of the property. ⊠ *Off Rte. 4, turn into Moshav Liman and make an immediate left* ☎ *057/728–2828 or 04/982–2356* ↝ *8 units* ⚴ *Kitchenettes, cable TV, DVDs, in-room hot tubs, saunas, bicycles* ▤ *AE, DC, MC, V* ▥ *BP.*

**$$** ▥ **Aromantica.** In the rural farming settlement of moshav Ben Ami, the comfortable country cottage–inspired cabins are operated by owner Varda, who makes every effort to make a stay here comfortable and relaxing. Her touches include chocolates left bedside, and complimentary wine, microwavable popcorn, lemonade, and ice cream. A tiny rock fountain burbles outside the door of each wooden, red-tile-roofed cabin, and wind chimes provide soothing sounds. Inside, each unit has clay-hued sofas, bright white pillows and coverlets, woodburning stoves, and corner hot tubs. Outside there are mini–herb gardens beside the private, shaded front porches of each cabin.  ⊠ *Off Rte. 4, turn into Moshav Ben Ami on Rte. 89, 25240* ☎ *054/498–2302 or 04/982–0484* 🖷 *04/ 982–3023* ⊕ *www.aromantica.co.il* ⌁ *3 cabins* ♿ *Kitchenettes, in-room hot tubs; no kids under 18 (except infants)* ☰ *AE, DC, MC, V* †◎| *BP.*

★ $$ ⊡ **Pivko Village.** Nestled among the trees on the grounds of a kibbutz, this B&B with a most unusual design offers private cabin accommodations. Pairs of cabins are divided by sliding walls, so guests can mingle if they'd like during the day and then enjoy privacy later on. The stunning view from the wide windows and patios (each with a hot tub) sweeps from Haifa across the sea to the cliffs of Rosh Hanikra. The beautiful interiors are quite lovely to look at, too. Each cabin has a seating area with two sofas, a comfy bedroom, a computer (with Internet), two TVs, and a barbecue grill. Udi, the owner, is an expert on local hiking trails. You can enjoy lunch in the kibbutz dining room, and the excellent restaurant Adelina is right on the grounds. ⊠ *Off Rte. 4, turn into Kibbutz Kabri on Rte. 89 and follow the signs, 25120* ☎ *04/995–2711 or 050/724–7086* ⊕ *www.pivko-village.co.il* ⌁ *6 cabins* ♿ *Restaurant, kitchenettes, cable TV, hot tubs, Internet* ☰ *AE, DC, MC, V* †◎| *BP.*

$ ⊡ **Carlton.** The best lodging option in town, this centrally located, six-story 1970 hotel is popular with Israelis and is blessed with a staff that goes the extra mile. The public rooms are rather drab, but the pool is in good shape. You can walk straight down the street to the wonderful beach. The guest rooms are tasteful with taupe curtains and one wall in darker taupe, white duvet covers, and black-and-taupe carpets. Some rooms have balconies overlooking the sea or the mountain range to the north. La Scala dance club attracts revelers from all over the north with live music in the summer. ⊠ *23 Haga'aton* ☎ *04/900–5555* 🖷 *04/ 982–3771* ⌁ *192 rooms, 8 suites* ♿ *Restaurant, room service, refrigerators, cable TV, pool, hot tub, sauna, lobby lounge, nightclub, babysitting, Internet room, free parking* ☰ *AE, D, MC, V.*

## Nightlife & the Arts

**La Scala** (☎ 04/900–5555), Nahariya's flashiest disco, draws the over-30 crowd for standard dance tunes with a throbbing beat. It's in the passageway just west of the Carlton. The cover charge on Friday is NIS 50; doors open at 10 PM.

## Sports & the Outdoors

BEACHES   Nahariya's public bathing facilities, at **Galei Galil Beach,** just north of
🐾 Haga'aton Boulevard, are ideal for families. Apart from the lovely beach, facilities include an Olympic-size pool, a wading pool, a playground for children, changing rooms and showers, plus a snack bar. In peak season, the beach offers exercise classes early in the morning. The entrance fee is NIS 12 for children.

★ 🐾 Beautifully maintained because it's in the Achziv National Park just north of Nahariya, **Akhziv Beach** is great for kids, with a protected man-made lagoon, lifeguards, and playground facilities. You can picnic on the grassy slopes or make use of the restaurant. Enter at the second sign for

Akhziv Beach, not the first. Admission, which is NIS 25, includes the use of showers and toilets. **Betzet Beach,** a bit farther north, is part of a nature reserve and offers abundant vegetation, trees, and the ruins of an ancient olive press. There's a lifeguard on duty in season.

SCUBA DIVING **Trek Yam Ltd** (Sea Treks) (☎ 04/982–3671) takes scuba divers to explore
★ the Achziv Canyon (NIS 190, including tank and weight belt) and the caves at Rosh Hanikra (NIS 140, including tank and weight belt) along the northern coast. The outfit also offers Jeep tours from two hours to a full day, costing from NIS 700 to NIS 2,100. It's best to reserve several days in advance.

## Rosh Hanikra

★ ☺ ⓐ *7 km (4½ mi) north of Nahariya.*

The dramatic white cliffs on the coast signal both Israel's border with Lebanon and the sea **grottoes** of Rosh Hanikra. Even before you get in line for the two-minute cable-car ride down to the grottoes, take a moment to absorb the stunning view back down the coast. Still clearly visible is the route of the railway line, now mostly a dirt road, built by the British through the hillside in 1943 to extend the Cairo–Tel Aviv–Haifa line to Beirut. After the descent, you can see the 12-minute audiovisual presentation called *The Sea and the Cliff.* The incredible caves beneath the cliff have been carved out by relentless waves pounding away at the white chalky rock for countless years. Footpaths inside the cliff itself lead from one huge cave to another, while the sound of waves echoes among the water-sprayed rocky walls. Huge bursts of seawater plunge into pools at your feet (behind protective rails). It's slippery, so hang on to the children. ☎ 04/985-7109 ⊕ *www.rosh-hanikra.com* 🖃 NIS 38 ☺ *Nov.–Mar., Sat.–Thurs. 8:30–4, Fri. and Jewish holiday eves 8:30–4; Apr.–June, Sat.–Thurs. 8:30–6, Fri. and Jewish holiday eves 8:30–4; July–Aug., Sat.–Thurs. 8:30 AM–11 PM, Fri. and Jewish holiday eves 8:30–4. Call to verify hours.*

┌─────────┐
│ need a  │ The **cafeteria** on top of the Rosh Hanikra cliff may not be a
│ break?  │ gourmet's dream, but you'd be hard pressed to find a more fabulous
└─────────┘ view. It's bright and breezy, with snacks, drinks, and ice cream as well as hot meals. It's fun to take a photo outside at the sign on the cafeteria wall, which indicates the distance from there to Beirut.

┌─────────┐
│ off the │ **YEHIAM** – This kibbutz, set in a wooded area, has an unusual
│ beaten  │ attraction, the ruins of the medieval **Castle Judin.** The **memorial**
│ path    │ that you pass on the way commemorates the convoy that set out to
└─────────┘ bring fresh supplies and reinforcements to the besieged kibbutz in Israel's War of Independence, in 1948. Apparently built by the Templars in the late 12th century, Castle Judin was destroyed by the Mamluk sultan Baybars in the 13th century, but its ruins so impressed the 18th-century Bedouin sheikh Dahr el-Omar that he transformed it into a palatial citadel 500 years later. You can see the remains of a large reception hall and mosque, as well as a tower and

bathhouse. There are picnic facilities on-site. The site is 12 km (8 mi) east of Nahariya: at Hanita Junction, turn south onto Route 70; then at Kabri Junction, head east 7 km (4½ mi) on Route 89. ☎ *04/985–6004* ⊕ *www.parks.org.il* ✉ *NIS 12* ☉ *Daily 8–4.*

# HAIFA & THE NORTHERN COAST ESSENTIALS

## Transportation

### BY AIR

Most travelers from abroad arrive at Ben Gurion International Airport, at Lod on the outskirts of Tel Aviv. The airport is 105 km (65 mi) south of Haifa, about a 90-minute drive. At the airport you can catch Bus 945 or 947 (on Saturday only after 9 PM) to Haifa. Or share a sherut taxi, which costs NIS 30.

🚩 **Ben Gurion International Airport** ☎ 03/971-0111.

### BY BOAT & FERRY

Many cruise ships that tour the Mediterranean stop at Haifa. You'll exit the docks area through either Gate 5 or the Passenger and Customs Terminal, depending on whether or not you're required to go through customs. Taxis are usually waiting at the exits. You can catch buses nearby for the central bus station, the Hadar district, and Mt. Carmel.

### BY BUS

The Egged bus cooperative serves the coastal area from Ben Gurion Airport and from the Jerusalem Central Bus station as well as from Tel Aviv central (Merkaz, also called Tzafon). Service to Netanya, Hadera, Zichron Ya'akov, and Haifa from both cities starts before 8 AM and usually ends around 8 PM. A bus leaves Tel Aviv for Haifa every 20 minutes between 5:20 AM and 11 PM. Travel to Caesarea requires a change at Hadera; service from Hadera to Caesarea runs only until 12:30 PM. You must change buses at Haifa to get to Akko and Nahariya. Egged buses do not operate between late Friday afternoon and Saturday evening (sometimes Sunday morning). One exception is Haifa, where some buses do run on Saturday. There are heavy crowds at major bus stations on Sunday morning and Thursday night. Ask for an "express" bus to Haifa; it travels directly and takes two hours from Jerusalem and one hour from Tel Aviv. Some bus lines allow bicycles on board. The Egged Information Centre provides advice and contacts for the entire region. It's open Monday–Thursday 6:30 AM–9 PM; Friday and Jewish holiday eves 7:30 AM–3 PM; and Saturday 1 hour after sunset–11 PM.

🚩 **Egged Information Center** ☎ 03/624-8888 or *2800 ⊕ www.egged.co.il.

### BY CAR

You can take Route 2 or Route 4 north along the coast from Tel Aviv to Haifa, continuing on Route 4 up to the Lebanese border. From Jerusalem follow Route 1 to Tel Aviv and then connect through the Ayalon Highway to Herzliya, where you can pick up Route 2.

Driving is the most comfortable and convenient way to tour this region, and it allows you to explore some of the more scenic back roads. The distances are short: for example, 29 km (18 mi) from Tel Aviv to Netanya, 22 km (15 mi) from Haifa to Akko, 37 km (23 mi) from Haifa to Zichron Ya'akov.

Traffic gets particularly snarled along the coast at rush hour, especially entering and exiting major cities. The worst times are in the morning between 7:30 and 8:30, weekdays after 4 PM, and Saturday evenings, also after 4 PM. Expect gridlock in Haifa's port area during morning and evening rush hours. Even at the best of times, Haifa traffic is heavy, and streets zigzag up the slope and are difficult to negotiate. Pay attention to Haifa's street signs indicating which streets close on Saturday.

### BY TAXI

Taxis can be hailed on the street day or night. Restaurants will call one for you. Be sure to ask the driver to turn on the meter (*moneh*) and ask for a receipt (*kaballa*). Drivers usually charge a few shekels for luggage. **⁊Akko Zafon** ☎ 04/981-6666. **Carmel-Ahuza (Haifa)** ☎ 04/838-2727. **Hasharon (Netanya)** ☎ 09/833-3338. **Kefarim (Nehariya)** ☎ 04/992-3333. **Mercaz Mitzpe(Haifa)** ☎ 04/866-2525.

### BY TRAIN

The Northern Coast is one part of Israel where train travel is truly practical (except on Friday night, Saturday until after 8 PM or so, the eve of Jewish holidays, and holidays themselves). Israel Railways is the region's only railway company. Trains from Jerusalem and Tel Aviv travel at least twice a day to Netanya (there are two stations there, one in south Netanya called Bet Yehoshua, and one in north Netanya called Netanya Station), Binyamina, Caesarea-Pardes Hanna, Haifa, Atlit, Akko, and Nahariya. You might have to change trains in Tel Aviv when coming from Jerusalem. The train line from Ben Gurion Airport travels to Tel Aviv, Binyamina, Atlit, Haifa, Akko, and Nahariya.

The trip from Tel Aviv to Haifa takes 60 minutes and costs NIS 25. Trains depart every half hour from 6 AM until 10:30 PM; on Friday from 6 AM until 3:20. During the day on Saturdays trains do not run, but there are four departures after 9:30 PM. There is also a fast (one-hour) direct train that runs twice a day from Tel Aviv to Haifa. Timetables in English are available at all stations, and on the Israel Railways Information Centre Web site. The information center is open Monday to Thursday 6 AM–11 PM; Friday and Jewish holiday eves 6 AM–3 PM; and Saturday 1 hour after sunset till 11 PM.

Haifa has Israel's only subway system: the six-station Carmelit subway runs from Gan Ha'em Park on Hanassi Boulevard (opposite the Dan Panorama) in Central Carmel down to Kikar Paris in the port area in six minutes. The fare is NIS 6, and the train operates Sunday–Thursday 6 AM–10 PM, Friday 6–3, and Saturday 7 PM–midnight. Though the Carmelit doesn't serve the tourist sites, children enjoy this ride (it's so short you just travel both ways). **⁊ Israel Railways Information Centre** ☎ 03/577-4000 ⊕ www.israrail.org.il.

# Contacts & Resources

### BANKS & EXCHANGE SERVICES

There's a bank on every corner in the Merkaz Carmel area of Haifa, where the hotels are located. Banks are usually open Sunday–Thursday 8:30–12:30 and sometimes in the afternoons—hours vary from city to city and even among neighborhoods. Currency exchange offices are usually open Sunday–Thursday 8–5 and closed Friday afternoon, Saturdays, and on Jewish holidays. **⊠ Change Po Money Ltd.** ⊠ Kikar Ha'atzmaut Sq. ☎ 09/884-4966. **Change Spot** ⊠ Haga'aton Blvd., Hehariya ☎ 04/951-3350. **First International Bank** ⊠ 1 Elchanan St., Haifa ☎ 04/835-0200. **Super Change** ⊠ 113 Hanassi Blvd., Haifa ☎ 04/810-7141.

### EMERGENCIES

Magen David Adom is Israel's health, medical, blood, and disaster service; both they and the police force are always on call, and English is spoken. Magen David may be contacted for assistance with emergency prescriptions (bring your prescriptions with you to Israel). The major hospital serving Haifa and the north is the Rambam Medical Center. **⊠ Ambulance, Akko** ⊠ 101 Magen David Adom ☎ 04/991-2333. **Ambulance, Haifa** ☎ 101. **Ambulance, Nahariya** ☎ 101 or 04/823-332. **Ambulance, Netanya** ☎ 101. **Hospital, Carmel** ☎ 04/825-0211. **Rambam Medical Center (Haifa)** ☎ 04/854-3111 ⊕ www.rambam.org.il. **Western Galilee Regional Hospital(Nahariya)** ☎ 04/985-0766. **Laniado Hospital (Netanya)** ☎ 09/860-4666. **Police Akko** ☎ 100. **Police Haifa** ☎ 100. **Police Nahariya** ☎ 100 or 04/992-0344. **Police Netanya** ☎ 100.

### INTERNET, MAIL & SHIPPING

You can log on to the Web in Haifa at NorEm Internet Cafe. The Israel Postal Authority offers Express Mail Service, a guaranteed worldwide courier service at the above branches. **⊠ Israel Postal Authority** ☎ 1700/500-171 ⊕ www.postil.com. **NorEm Internet Cafe** ⊠ 27-29 Nordeau St., Hadar, Haifa ☎ 04/866-5656

### MEDIA

The daily (except Saturday) *Jerusalem Post* and *Ha Aretz* newspaper (published with the *Herald Tribune*) each have weekend magazines—*Billboard* in the *Post* and *The Guide* in *Ha Aretz*—that include information about events in the north (along with the rest of the country). There are no English-language newspapers published in the western coast area.

Steimatzky's, a chain bookshop that sells English-language books, magazines, and newspapers, is located inside Haifa Mall, at the southern entrance to the city. **⊠ Steimatzky's** ⊠ Haifa Mall ☎ 04/850-1538 ⊕ www.ibooks.co.il.

### TOUR OPTIONS

GENERAL-
INTEREST
You can arrange to be picked up at your Jerusalem or Tel Aviv hotel on Sunday, Tuesday, and Friday for a one-day trip that heads north to visit the ancient port cities of Caesarea and Akko, and farther to Rosh Hanikra, with its cliffside caves pounded by waves. Two well-known

companies, Egged Tours and Unitours, operate these excursions, which cost between NIS 310 and NIS 330.

The Haifa Tourist Board conducts a free Saturday morning 1½-hour walking tour that departs at 10 AM from 89 Yefe Nof (Panorama Road), behind the Nof hotel and near the Mane Katz museum. On this tour you take a leisurely stroll along the Promenade, see entrancing views, step into one of the Baha'i terraces, and visit the Sculpture Garden.

ARCHAEOLOGY If you'd like to learn about Israel's ancient past, two local archaeologists fill the bill: Haim at Isratour, in Haifa, can take you to Caesarea and Akko, and guide you through their fascinating archaeology. From Dor, on the coast, underwater expert Kurt Raveh guides visitors around sites with a nautical heritage.

BOAT TOURS Carmelit offers boat tours of Haifa Bay from Magan Hadayag, beside the airport. The ride lasts one hour and costs NIS 30. Call ahead (tours are seasonal) for departure times. From Akko's Crusader port, the *Queen of Akko* ferry makes a 40-minute jaunt around the bay, setting out when the boat fills up, year-round. The cost is NIS 20. From a location 5 km (3 mi) north of Nahariya, Trek Yam takes you on an exciting 30-minute ride up the coast in a high-speed motorboat, the *Tornado,* for NIS 60.

DRUZE HOSPITALITY For an ethnic adventure in Isfiya village in the Carmel (minimum of 6 people), call El Carmel. Avi will arrange for a visit to a private home, where you can enjoy a delicious traditional meat meal at noon (NIS 120), or tea, coffee, hummus, and fresh-baked pita at 5 P.M. (NIS 85), while a villager discusses the distinctive life of the Druze.

🖪 **Carmelit** 🕾 04/841-8765. **Egged Tours** 🕾 03/920-3919 for all reservations ⊕ www. eggedtours.co.il. **El Carmel** 🕾 052/453-5100. **G.U.Y.** 🕾 050/532-1169. **Haifa Tourist Board** 🕾 04/853-5606 ⊕ www.tour-haifa.co.il. **Isratour** 🕾 04/824-7911 or 050/567-7994 ⊕ www.isratour.com. **Mitzpe Tours** 🕾 04/867-4341. *Queen of Akko* 🕾 050/555-1136. **Kurt Raveh** 🕾 052/279-6695. **Society for the Protection of Nature (SPNI)** 🕾 03/638-8666 ⊕ www.spni.org.il. **Trek Yam** 🕾 04/982-3671. **United Tours** 🕾 03/693-3412 or 03/522-2008 for reservations ⊕ www.inisrael.com/united/index.html.

### VISITOR INFORMATION

In Haifa, pick up the excellent city map (NIS 4), and the "Haifa-Israel" booklet; both in English (most other tourist information is in Hebrew). At the Akko Visitor Center, there's a model of the Old City, and a seven-minute film showing sights to see. The following towns and cities have tourist offices (most information is in Hebrew).

The Akko Visitor Center is open Sunday–Thursday and Saturday 8:30–4, Friday 8:30–1. The Haifa Tourist Board is open Sunday–Thursday 9–4:30, Friday 9–1:30; some Saturdays 10–3. The Nahariya Tourist Information Office is open Sunday–Thursday 8–1 (and also 4–6 Sunday and Wednesday). The Netanya Tourist Information Office is open Sunday–Thursday 8:30–6 (8:30–4 in winter), Friday 9–noon. The Zichron Ya'akov Tourist Office is open Sunday–Thursday 8:30–1.

🚺Akko Tourist Information Office ✉at the entrance to the site ☎04/995–6727 ⊕www. akko.org.il. **Haifa Tourist Board** ✉48 Ben Gurion Blvd., German Colony ☎04/853–5606 ⊕ www.tour-haifa.co.il. **Nahariya Tourist Information Office** ✉19 Ga'aton Blvd. ☎04/987–9830 ⊕ www.nahariya.muni.il. **Netanya Tourist Information Office** ✉12 Ha'atzmaut Sq. ☎09/882–7286. **Zichron Ya'akov Tourist Office** ✉southern entrance to town, opposite the cemetery ☎04/639–8811.

# Lower Galilee

INCLUDING NAZARETH, TIBERIAS, AND
THE SEA OF GALILEE

**WORD OF MOUTH**

"We drove to Bet She'an to see the magnificent ruins of what was a very important city with its . . . Roman amphitheater [and] main street. . . . We continued on to the Bet Alpha Synagogue with its beautiful zodiac mosaic floor, [and] Megiddo, the ruins of a city 7,000 years old with 25 layers of different periods and cultures."
—paulfr

"My absolute favorite was the Nazareth Village. It had a fully re-created village from biblical times. They have houses, shops, people in period attire, donkeys, a threshing floor, and much more."
—JackieSun

By Mike Rogoff **TO MOST ISRAELIS, THE GALILEE IS SYNONYMOUS WITH "THE NORTH"**, a land of mountains and fertile valleys, nature reserves and national parks. In short, they would claim, it's a great place to visit, but they wouldn't want to live there: it's provincial, rustic, and remote. Although much of the wild scenery associated with the north—rugged highlands, waterfalls, and endless panoramas—is in the Upper Galilee, the Lower Galilee has its own quiet beauty, varied landscape, and more than anything else, rich history.

Whatever your agenda—spiritual, historical, recreational, or restful—take time to savor the region. Follow a hiking trail above the Sea of Galilee or drive up to the Belvoir castle. Wade through fields of rare irises in the spring. Bathe in a warm mineral spa or a spring-fed pool. Buy some good goat cheese.

Farming and tourism form the economic base. The region's *kibbutzim* and a smaller number of *moshavim* (Jewish family-farm villages) are concentrated in the Jezreel and Jordan valleys and around the Sea of Galilee. The rockier hill country is predominantly Arab (*Israeli* Arab; this is not disputed territory), and for the last half-century it has been a challenge for the two communities—Jewish and Arab—to cultivate neighborly relations despite the ethnic tensions that swirl around them. By and large, they have succeeded.

Culture and entertainment are not this region's strong suits. A number of annual festivals and other events are the highlights. Tiberias's pubs and restaurants probably come closest to providing lively nightlife, but there are worse ways to spend an evening than sitting by a moonlit lake washing down a good St. Peter's fish or a lamb shashlik (chunks of meat grilled on a skewer) with an excellent Israeli wine.

## Top 5 Reasons to Go

- **Sunset on the Sea of Galilee:** The lake at sundown is always evocative, often beautiful, and occasionally spectacular. Walk a beach, sip a drink, or sail a boat as dusk slowly settles.

- **Zippori National Park:** The distant past is palpable at this site, with flagstones grooved by ancient wheels and the loveliest old mosaics in the land.

- **Nazareth:** Tradition and modernity collide in this town suspended between East and West—a town of baklava and BMWs, new politics and ancient passions. Talk to a local as you sample excellent Middle Eastern delicacies.

- **Mt. Gilboa:** This undervisited region offers local beauty and grand views for the independent traveler with a bit of time and no checklist of must-see famous sites.

- **A spiritual source:** Tune your ear to the Galilee's spiritual reverberations. Listen as pilgrims chant a mass at Beatitudes, read scripture by the lake, or sit meditatively on Tabgha's pebbly shore.

It's possible to get a feeling for this region in a few days, but you may want to expand your trip to include some highlights of the Upper Galilee and the Golan including Tzfat (Safed) (⇨ Chapter 6).

*Numbers in the text correspond to numbers in the margin and on the Lower Galilee map.*

**If you have**
**2 days**

Use 🏨 **Tiberias** ⓯ or the Sea of Galilee region as a base. Explore the archaeological excavations of **Megiddo** ❷ and **Bet She'an** ❽ on the way into or out of the area. In hot weather, take a dip at **Gan Hashelosha National Park** ❻ (Sachne). Visit the Church of the Annunciation in **Nazareth** ❿ and the fine mosaics of **Zippori National Park** ⓫ nearby. A Christian itinerary might also include **Mt. Tabor** ⓮ and Yardenit, near **Kinneret** ㉔, on the Jordan River. For a more general approach, visit the ancient synagogue mosaics of **Bet Alfa** ❼ or **Hammat Tiberias** ㉕, the Crusader fortress of **Belvoir** ❾, and the cemetery of Kibbutz Kinneret.

If you want to concentrate on Christian sights, spend the second day around the Sea of Galilee. Join a boat ride, admire the ancient boat at **Ginosar** ⓰, contemplate the multiplication of the loaves and fishes at **Tabgha** ⓳, eat St. Peter's fish near the water, explore the ruins of **Capernaum** ⓴, and end the day in the panoramic tranquillity of the **Mount of Beatitudes** ⓲. For a more general experience, ascend the Golan Heights via **Hammat Gader** ㉒ for a spectacular view, before heading on to the Upper Galilee and Tzfat.

**If you have**
**3 days**

Spend the first day in the Jezreel Valley, including **Megiddo** ❷, visiting the scenic attractions of **Mt. Gilboa** ❸–❼, **Bet She'an** ❽, and time permitting, either the catacombs of **Bet She'arim** ❶, in the west; the Crusader castle of **Belvoir** ❾, in the east; or the church and fine views atop **Mt. Tabor** ⓮. Stay overnight in 🏨 **Tiberias** ⓯.

The Christian explorer should spend the second day as described in the first itinerary. On the morning of the third day, drive up to Banias and Caesarea Philippi, in the Upper Galilee, and then head south via the Church of the Annunciation in **Nazareth** ❿ and the ancient mosaics of **Zippori National Park** ⓫. A more general approach might include a more leisurely outdoor exploration of the Golan Heights, Upper Galilee, Nazareth, and Zippori.

## Exploring the Lower Galilee

About 50 km (31 mi) square, the Lower Galilee embraces three distinct subregions: the Jezreel and Jordan valleys, traversing the southern part of the region from west to east; Nazareth and the rugged hill country just to the north; and the Sea of Galilee. The fertile Jezreel Valley, known in Hebrew simply as Ha'emek—the Valley—is sentimentally, if not scientifically, perceived by many Israelis as distinct from the rest of the Lower Galilee. The valley towns of Afula, Migdal Ha'emek, and Bet She'an (despite its wonderful antiquities) have little to recommend them. The larger hill town of Nazareth, the region's administrative and automotive-service center—a noisy clash of pistons and politics—has more character. To the north, the steep hillsides above the Sea of Galilee (the Kinneret in Hebrew) merge into the Upper Galilee, while Route 85 west follows the Bet Hakerem Valley, the natural division between the two regions. Toward the Mediterranean Sea, the hills flatten out as you reach the coastal plain; Route 70 follows the region's western edge.

Most travelers come up Route 65 (the Wadi Ara Pass) from the Mediterranean coast, or up the Jordan Valley from Jerusalem, stopping perhaps at the national parks of Megiddo or Bet She'an, but essentially zipping through the Jezreel Valley on their way to the recreation grounds farther north. Slow down: it's worth a few hours of your time. There are no fewer than 11 national parks in this region, making the Nature and National Parks Protection Authority's pass (⇨ *See* Nature Parks and Reserves *in* Smart Travel Tips) a worthwhile investment.

## About the Restaurants

Tiberias and the Sea of Galilee are a much livelier culinary proposition than other parts of Lower Galilee. Because most travelers to this region actually stay overnight here, there are a few very good restaurants in Tiberias proper, and a few of the daytime watering holes elsewhere around the lake stay open into the evening. Tiberias no longer has the monopoly on good restaurants, however. There are some places out in the countryside worth going out of your way for, a few really good cafeterias, and many satisfying if unmemorable local eateries. Restaurant attire, even at dinner, is strictly casual.

The local specialty is the native St. Peter's fish (tilapia), though most restaurants serve the (still excellent) pond-bred variety. Meat dishes tend to be more Middle Eastern: shashlik and kebabs (ground meat grilled on skewers) accompanied by hummus, pickles, and the ubiquitous french fries. Most economical are the ever-popular *shawarma* (slices of spit-grilled turkey meat served in pita bread with salads and condiments) and the classic falafel (deep-fried chickpea balls instead of the meat).

| WHAT IT COSTS In Israeli shekels | | | | |
|---|---|---|---|---|
| $$$$ | $$$ | $$ | $ | ¢ |
| RESTAURANTS over NIS 100 | NIS 76–NIS 100 | NIS 50–NIS 75 | NIS 32–NIS 49 | under NIS 32 |

Prices are per person for a main course at dinner.

## About the Hotels

Tiberias, the region's tourist center, has a large number of hotels for every budget, from deluxe (though not top-drawer) to budget. Within a 20- to 30-minute drive are excellent motel-type guest houses, some run by kibbutzim and some on the Sea of Galilee. A few of these also rent out cheaper huts or small mobile homes called caravans, with access to the same facilities as the better accommodations.

## Ancient History

Historical, especially biblical, echoes are what make the Lower Galilee so special. In the Jezreel Valley, filled with Old Testament lore, you come face-to-face with Deborah, King Saul and Jonathan, King Solomon, and the prophet Elijah. With the Assyrian devastation of the country in the 8th century BC, the region declined, but in the Roman and Byzantine periods (1st century BC–6th century AD), vibrancy and wealth returned, as seen at the magnificent city of Bet She'an, the opulent spa of Hammat Gader, and the exquisite mosaics of Hammat Tiberias and Zippori. Christian pilgrims find the hill country and the Sea of Galilee the most compelling, for it is here that Jesus lived, healed, taught, and forged his ministry.

**5**

## Festivals

Ein Gev, on the eastern shore of the Sea of Galilee, has an Israeli-music festival in the spring. The Misgav area, at the region's western edge, is more eclectic: events take place during the week of Passover in a widespread series of venues, the better to encourage the public to mix music and sightseeing. Bet She'an revives its ancient Roman theater for a short series of events in October, and in May, Jacob's Ladder—the annual "Anglo" folk festival—fills the air above Nof Ginosar, on the Sea of Galilee, with the traditional folk and country music of the British Isles and North America.

## Swimming & Water Sports

The Sea of Galilee—really a freshwater lake—is a refreshing but rocky place for a swim. You can recline on pleasant commercial beaches with shaded lawns, facilities, cafeterias, and the occasional water park, or on free beaches with minimal facilities, particularly south of Tiberias. September's Kinneret Swim, a tradition since 1953, has both amateur (3½ km [2 mi] and 1½ km [1 mi]) and competitive (1½ km [1 mi]) categories. At several locations around the Sea of Galilee you can hire pedal boats, rowboats, and motorboats and arrange to water-ski. Serious kayakers convene for an annual international competition in March.

## Walking, Running & Bicycling

Two annual *Tza'adot* (Big Walks) take place in March or April, one along the shore of the Sea of Galilee (2½ km [1½ mi] and 9 km [5½ mi]), the other along the trails of Mt. Gilboa (routes range from 6 km [4 mi] to 40 km [25 mi] over two days). These mass scenic rambles attract folks from all over the country and abroad. A promenade suitable for jogging follows the lakeshore for about 5 km (3 mi) from Tiberias south. Dedicated runners might want to participate in the Sea of Galilee Marathon, which takes place in December or January. A noncompetitive bicycle ride around the Sea of Galilee is held at the end of October or beginning of November.

Nazareth has a few deluxe hotels and several older inexpensive ones (not all recommended), which cater primarily to organized Christian pilgrim groups but which also attract individual travelers and Israeli vacationers. Also in Nazareth, and to a lesser extent around Tiberias, are a number of hospices run by Christian denominations or orders.

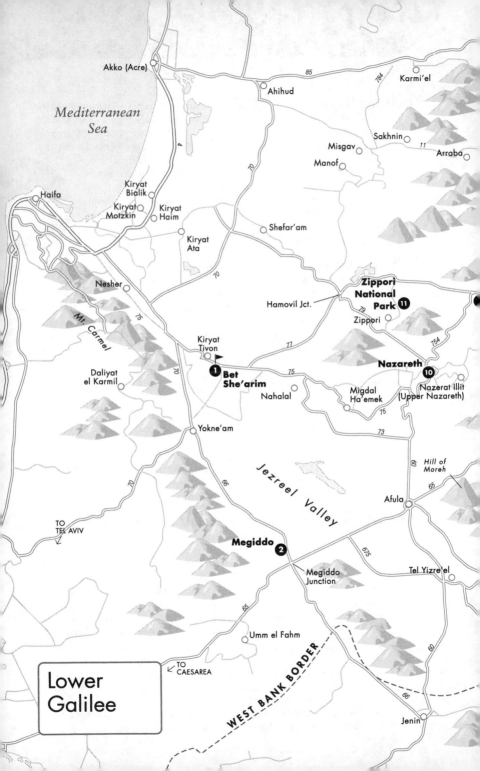

Bed-and-breakfasts have sprung up in such profusion that it's hard to keep track of them. Many are in or adjacent to private homes in rural farming communities; others are within kibbutzim, where the collective has renovated older buildings, creating units with a kitchenette and a bath. These are usually a good value, especially for families.

Youth hostels aren't what they used to be. Gone are the days of 10 people to a room with iron beds and communal showers. The Youth Hostel Association has seriously upgraded its facilities (including five in this region alone), with many hostels offering suite-type arrangements suitable for families. These are generally the cheapest deals around.

| WHAT IT COSTS In U.S. Dollars | | | | |
|---|---|---|---|---|
| $$$$ | $$$ | $$ | $ | ¢ |
| HOTELS    over $250 | $175–$250 | $111–$174 | $65–$110 | under $65 |

Prices are for two people in a standard double room in high season. Non-Israeli citizens paying in foreign currency are exempt from the 16.5% VAT tax on hotel rooms.

## Timing

By far the best time to tour the Galilee is the spring—March, April, and early May—when the weather is usually excellent and the countryside is blanketed with wildflowers. Avoid the Sea of Galilee the week of Passover (March–April), however, as well as during the High Holidays and Sukkoth (September–October). Although the weather is normally great during these periods, half the country vacations here, and rates soar. (Because they're based on the Hebrew lunar calendar, the dates of these holidays shift from year to year; be sure to verify the dates before you decide when *not* to stay in the area.) At 700 feet below sea level, the Sea of Galilee region is very hot in summer. Nevertheless, some hotels charge high-season rates for part of the summer and during the week of Christmas. Weekends in general (Thursday night through Saturday night) are more crowded as well, and some hotels raise weekend rates substantially.

# JEZREEL & JORDAN VALLEYS

"Highways of the world cross Galilee in all directions," wrote the eminent Victorian scholar George Adam Smith in 1898. The great international highway of antiquity, the Via Maris (Way of the Sea), swept up the Mediterranean coast from Egypt and broke inland along three separate passes through the hills to emerge in the Jezreel Valley before continuing northeast to Damascus and Mesopotamia. Then, as now, roads connected the valley with the hill country of the Galilee to the north and Samaria to the south. Its destiny as a kind of universal thoroughfare and its flat terrain made the Jezreel Valley a convenient and frequent battleground. In fact, the Jezreel Valley heard the clash of arms so often that the very name of its most commanding site—Har Megiddo (Mt. Megiddo), or Armageddon—became a New Testament synonym for the final cataclysmic battle of all time.

On a topographical map, the Jezreel Valley appears as an equilateral triangle with sides about 40 km (25 mi) long that are edged by low mountains and with a narrow extension east to Bet She'an, in the Jordan Rift. From there, the Jordan Valley stretches like a ribbon north to the Sea of Galilee. Your first impression will be one of lush farmland as far as the eye can see, but as recently as 50 years ago, malarial swamps still blighted the area; some early pioneering settlements had cemeteries before their first buildings were completed.

With a few good exceptions, restaurants in this rustic area are confined to roadside cafeterias, lunchtime diners at or near some parks, and small restaurants and snack bars in the towns of Afula and Bet She'an.

## Bet She'arim

▶ ❶ *20 km (12½ mi) southeast of Haifa, 25 km (15½ mi) west of Nazareth.*

Chalk slopes are honeycombed with catacombs around the attractively landscaped site of ancient Bet She'arim—today **Bet She'arim National Park.** A Jewish town flourished here after (and to some extent because of) the eclipse of Jerusalem by Titus's legions in AD 70 and its reconstruction as a pagan town by Hadrian in AD 135. For generations Jews were denied access to their holy city and the venerated burial ground of the Mount of Olives. The center of Jewish life and religious authority retreated first to Yavne, in the southern coastal plain, and then shifted to the Lower Galilee for several centuries.

By around AD 200 Bet She'arim had become the unofficial Jewish capital, owing its brief preeminence to the enormous stature of a native son. Rabbi Yehuda "Hanassi" (the Patriarch: a title conferred on the nominal leader of the Jewish community) was responsible both for the city's inner workings and for its relations with its Roman masters. Alone among his contemporaries, Yehuda Hanassi combined worldly diplomatic skills with unchallenged scholarly authority and spiritual leadership.

The rabbi eventually moved east to Zippori because of its more salubrious climate, and there he gathered the great Jewish sages of his day and compiled the Mishnah, which remains the definitive interpretation of biblical precepts for religious Jews. Nonetheless, it was in his hometown of Bet She'arim that Yehuda Hanassi was finally laid to rest. If Bet She'arim was a magnet for scholars and petitioners in his lifetime, it became a virtual shrine after his death. With Jerusalem still off-limits, the town became the most prestigious burial site in the Jewish world for almost 150 years.

Two major expeditions in the 1930s and '50s uncovered a huge series of 20 **catacombs.** The largest of these is open to the public, with 24 chambers containing more than 200 sarcophagi. A wide range of carved Jewish and Roman symbols and more than 250 funerary inscriptions in Greek, Hebrew, Aramaic, and Palmyrene throughout the site testify to the great distances some people traveled—from Yemen and Mesopotamia, for instance—to be buried here. Without exception, the sarcophagi were plundered over the centuries by grave robbers seeking the possessions with which the dead were often interred. ⊠ *Follow the* *signs in Kiryat Tivon, off Rte. 75 or 722* ☎ *04/984–1643* ⊕ *www.parks. org.il/ParksENG* ⌨ *NIS 18* ☉ *Apr.–Sept., Sat.–Thurs. 8–5, Fri. and Jewish holiday eves 8–4; Oct.–Mar., Sat.–Thurs. 8–4, Fri. and Jewish holiday eves 8–3.*

## Megiddo

★ ❷  *20 km (12½ mi) southeast of Bet She'arim, 2 km (1¼ mi) north of the Megiddo Junction, 12 km (7½ mi) west of Afula.*

This ancient city owed its great importance to its strategic position at the mouth of a pass, the main branch of the international highway between Egypt and Mesopotamia. In 1918, General Allenby swept up this ancient pass by way of Megiddo to outflank the Ottoman Turks and seal a British victory. When he was subsequently elevated to the peerage, he took the title of Viscount Allenby of Megiddo. What Megiddo is most known for, however, are the archaeological expeditions that, since the early 20th century, have exposed no fewer than 25 strata of civilization in the historical urban layer cake known as a tell (mound). Today you can see evidence of these various eras at **Tel Megiddo National Park.**

The path up to the flattop mound brings you through the partially restored remains of a Late Bronze Age gate, perhaps the very one stormed by Egyptian troops circa 1468 BC, as described in the victory stela of Pharaoh Thutmose III. A larger gate farther up was long identified with King Solomon (10th century BC)—Megiddo was one of his regional military centers—but has been redated by some scholars to the time of Ahab, king of Israel a half-century later. There is consensus, however, on the ruined stables at the summit of the tell: they were certainly built by Ahab, whose large chariot army is recorded in an Assyrian inscription.

Evidence indicates prehistoric habitation here as well, but among the earliest remains of the *city* of Megiddo are a round altar dating from the Early Bronze Age and the outlines of several Early Bronze Age temples, almost 5,000 years old, visible in the trench between the two fine lookout points.

Nothing at Megiddo is as impressive as the water system. In a masterful stroke, Ahab's engineers dug a deep shaft and a horizontal tunnel through solid rock to reach the vital subterranean spring outside the city walls. With access secure, the spring's original opening was permanently blocked. There is nothing more than a trickle today, the flow perhaps choked by subsequent earthquakes. As you descend 180 steps through the shaft, traverse the 65-yard-long tunnel under the ancient city wall, and climb up 83 steps at the other end, look for the ancient chisel marks and hewn steps. It's a 10-minute walk back to your car. If steps don't make you happy, walk back to the entrance the way you came.

A tiny museum at the site's entrance offers some good visual aids, including maps, a video, and a model of the tell itself. There is a cafeteria. ⊠ *National Park, Rte. 66* ☎ *04/659–0316* ⊕ *www.parks.org.il/ ParksENG* ⌨ *NIS 23* ☉ *Apr.–Sept., Sat.–Thurs. 8–5, Fri. and Jewish holiday eves 8–4; Oct.–Mar., Sat.–Thurs. 8–4, Fri. and Jewish holiday eves 8–3; water tunnel closes 30 mins before rest of site.*

## Shopping

**Megiddo Jewelry** (☎ 050/527–6317), a small gift shop alongside the museum, sells handsome silver and gold jewelry, some incorporating pieces of ancient Roman glass. On Saturday, call ahead to verify if it's open.

> **en route**
>
> From the Afula road (Route 65), Route 675 heads southeast through a small farming region called the Ta'anach. Just 500 yards past the intersection with Route 60, location of the Kibbutz Yizre'el, turn left (also into Yizre'el) and then immediately right to the low-rise **Tel Yizre'el.** This is the site of the Old Testament city of Jezreel, King Ahab's winter capital. Here he coveted Naboth's vineyard, and his Phoenician wife, Jezebel, met the gruesome death predicted by the prophet Elijah. The excavated ruins are indecipherable, but the site provides a magnificent view of the valley and a great place to sit and ponder those biblical passages.

## Mt. Gilboa

❸ *24 km (15 mi) southeast of Megiddo via Rtes. 675 and 667.*

FodorśChoice
★

Mt. Gilboa—actually a small, steep mountain range rather than a single peak—is geographically a spur of the far greater Samaria Range (the biblical Mt. Ephraim, today the West Bank) to the southwest. Half the mountain has been reforested with evergreens, while the other half has been left in pristine rockiness. Environmentalists prefer the latter, as it protects the profuse wildflowers that splatter the slopes with color every March and April. From the gravel parking area off Route 667 on the summit of the ridge, easy and well-marked trails wind through the natural habitat of the rare black (actually purple) iris, which draws hordes of Israelis every spring. Years of tireless efforts by environmental groups, especially the Society for the Protection of Nature in Israel (SPNI), have paid off, and well-indoctrinated preschoolers will tell you imperiously that you are not allowed to pick the wildflowers. The views of the valley below and the hills of Galilee beyond are great year-round, but on a clear winter or spring day they're amazing, reaching as far as the snowcapped Mt. Hermon, far to the north. Afternoon is the best time to come.

Three thousand years ago, the Israelites were routed by the Philistines on Mt. Gilboa. Saul, the nation's first king, was mortally wounded and took his own life on the battlefield. The next day, the Bible relates, when the Philistines came to plunder their fallen foes, they discovered the bodies of Saul and his sons. Seeking trophies, "they cut off his head, and stripped off his armor, and they fastened his body to the wall of Beth-shan [Bet She'an]" (I Samuel 31). The battle was presumably fought on the mountain's lower slopes, as the upper reaches are too craggy and steep, but from a vantage point on the crest, you can easily conjure up the din of a battle beneath you. In his lyrical eulogy for Saul and his son Jonathan, king-to-be David curses the battlefield where "thy glory, O Israel" was slain: "Let there be no dew or rain upon you" (II Samuel 1).

🐚 **④** **Ma'ayan Harod** (the Spring of Harod), at the foot of Mt. Gilboa, is a small national park with an attractive spread of lawns, huge eucalyptus trees, and a big swimming pool (open in summer) fed by a spring. Today it's a bucolic picnic spot, but almost 3,200 years ago, Gideon, the reluctant hero of the biblical Book of Judges, organized his troops to fight a Midianite army that had invaded from the desert. At God's command—in order to emphasize the miraculous nature of the coming victory—Gideon dismissed more than two-thirds of the warriors and then, to reduce the force still more, selected only those who lapped water from the spring. Equipped with swords, ram's horns, and flaming torches concealed in clay jars, this tiny army of 300 divided into three companies and surrounded the Midianite camp across the valley in the middle of the night. At a prearranged signal, the attackers shouted, blew their horns, and smashed the jars, revealing the flaming torches, whereupon the Midianites panicked and fled, securing an Israelite victory.

The spring has seen other armies in other ages. It was here in 1260 that the Egypt-based Mamluks stopped the invasion of the hitherto invincible Mongols. And in the 1930s, the woods above the spring hid clandestine Jewish self-defense squads training in defiance of British military law. There is an excellent, modern guest house of the Youth Hostel Association adjacent to the site. ✉ *National Park off Rte. 71, next to Gidona* ☎ *04/653–2211* ⊕ *www.parks.org.il/ParksENG* 💲 *NIS 33* ⏱ *Apr.–Sept., Sat.–Thurs. 8–5, Fri. and Jewish holiday eves 8–4; Oct.–Mar., Sat.–Thurs. 8–4, Fri. and Jewish holiday eves 8–2.*

> **need a break?**
>
> At Michal and Avi Barkin's **goat farm** (✉ 1 km [½ mi] east of Navot Junction [Rtes. 71 and 675], Kfar Yehezkel ☎ 054/649–2799), you can chat with them and sample their excellent cheeses over a glass of wine or coffee in the wooden reception room or enjoy a light meal of salads, toasted sandwiches, or hot stuffed pastries. The farm is open Thursday from 7 PM, Friday 10 AM–2 PM and again at 7 PM, and Saturday from 10 AM. It doesn't close until well into the evening.

**⑤** Across Route 71 from Mt. Gilboa, **Kibbutz Ein Harod (Me'uchad),** not to be confused with its neighbor to the west, Kibbutz Ein Harod (Ichud), has two interesting reasons to visit. Its **art museum,** housed in an early example of modernist architecture, has a permanent collection of Judaica (Jewish ceremonial art) and changing exhibits of both Jewish Israeli and international artists, spanning cultures and genres. The building, which uses diffused natural lighting, attracts buffs in its own right. An English-speaking guide can sometimes be arranged for a fee; call ahead. ✉ *Rte. 71, opposite gas station* ☎ *04/653–1670* ⊕ *www.museumeinharod.org.il* 💲 *NIS 16* ⏱ *Sun.–Thurs. 9–4:30, Fri. and Jewish holiday eves 9–1:30, Sat. and Jewish holidays 10–4:30.*

Also on the kibbutz, **Bet Sturman** is a museum of the region's natural history and human settlement. There is a video in English. ✉ *Rte. 71* ☎ *04/653–3284* 💲 *NIS 15* ⏱ *Sun.–Thurs. 8–3, Fri. 8–1 (call to confirm), Sat. and Jewish holidays 11–3; last entry 1 hr before closing.*

☕ ❻ The **Gan Hashelosha National Park,** commonly known as Sachne, was developed around a warm spring (28°C, or 82°F, most of the year) and a wide, still stream deep enough to dive into at spots, with artificial cascades in others. Lifeguards are on duty. Facilities include changing rooms for bathers, two snack bars, and a restaurant. The park is especially crowded on Fridays and Saturdays in good weather. Don't leave your possessions unattended on the lawns. ⊠ *Off Rte. 669* ☎ *04/658-1017* ⊕ *www.parks.org.il/ParksENG* ☒ *NIS 33* ⊙ *Apr.–Sept., Sat.–Thurs. 8–5, Fri. and Jewish holiday eves 8–4; Oct.–Mar., Sat.–Thurs. 8–4, Fri. and Jewish holiday eves 8–3.*

☕ **Gan-Garoo,** a four-acre zoo of exclusively Australian wildlife, has different kinds of kangaroo and wallabies, koala bears, and kookaburras, emus, and other exotic birds that delight children and please their parents. Call at least a day ahead for an English-speaking guide. A fun maze enhanced by distorting mirrors ends in a clearing with playground equipment and a series of mind-challenging maze games. ⊠ *Rte. 669, at entrance to Gan Hashelosha* ☎ *04/648–8060* ☒ *NIS 35* ⊙ *Sun.–Thurs. 9–4, Fri. 9–1, Sat. 9–5; usually July–Aug., Sat.–Thurs. to 8, Fri. to 4, but call to verify.*

❼ Now within a national park, the ancient synagogue of **Bet Alfa** was discovered in 1928 by members of Kibbutz Hefziba who were digging an irrigation trench. Their tools hit a hard surface, and careful excavation uncovered a multicolored mosaic floor, almost entirely preserved. The art is somewhat childlike, but that, too, is part of its charm. An Aramaic inscription dates the building to the reign of Byzantine emperor Justinian, in the second quarter of the 6th century AD; a Greek inscription credits the workmanship to one Marianos and his son, Aninas. In keeping with Jewish tradition, the synagogue faces Jerusalem, with an apse at the far end to hold the ark. The building faithfully copies the architecture of the Byzantine basilicas of the day, with a nave and two side aisles, and the doors lead to a small narthex and a onetime outdoor atrium. Stairs indicate there was once an upper story.

The classic Jewish symbols in the top mosaic panel leave no doubt that the building was a synagogue: a holy ark flanked by lions, a menorah, a shofar (ram's horn), an incense shovel once used in the temple of Jerusalem, and the *lulav* and *etrog* (palm frond and citron) used in the celebration of Sukkoth, the Feast of Tabernacles. The middle panel, however, is the most intriguing: it is filled with human figures depicting the seasons, the zodiac, and—even more incredible for a Jewish house of worship—the Greek sun god, Helios. These images indicate more liberal times theologically, when the prohibition against making graven images was perhaps not applied to two-dimensional art. The mosaic may have merely been a convenient artistic convention to symbolize the orderly cycles of the universe, since the Creator himself could not be depicted graphically. The last panel tells the story of Abraham's near-sacrifice of his son Isaac, again captioned in Hebrew. Take the time to watch the lighthearted but informative film. ⊠ *National Park on Kibbutz Hefziba, Rte. 669* ☎ *04/653–2004* ⊕ *www.parks.org.il/ParksENG* ☒ *NIS 18* ⊙ *Apr.–Sept., Sat.–Thurs. 8–5, Fri. and Jewish holiday eves 8–4;*

*Oct.–Mar., Sat.–Thurs. 8–4, Fri. and Jewish holiday eves 8–3; last entry 30 mins before closing.*

## Where to Eat

**$–$$$** ✕ **Herb Farm on Mt. Gilboa.** The sweeping panorama from the wooden
**Fodor'sChoice** deck and picture windows is attraction enough, but this family-run
★ restaurant glories in fresh herbs (25 at a time) and good produce. The menu is partly seasonal, partly weekly inspiration. Homemade bread and a "salad basket" of antipasti are fine standard starters, but try a more imaginative salad or delicacy of the day. Tempting entrées might include a tart of shallots, forest mushrooms, and goat cheese or a colorful pie of beef, lamb, goose breast, tomatoes, pine nuts, Roquefort, and basil. Less adventurous palates might prefer grilled meat or a fish or pasta dish. Desserts make for an agonizing decision, so share. ⊠ *Rte. 667, 3 km (2 mi) off Rte. 675* ☎ *04/653–1093* ⚖ *Reservations essential* ⊟ *AE, DC, MC, V* ☉ *Closed Sun.*

★ **$–$$$** ✕ **Mizra Grill.** A short drive from the Gilboa region, Mizra is best known as a superior cafeteria, but at 4:30 it becomes a good sit-down dinner restaurant. The self-service daytime menu includes several excellent cooked dishes, including grilled meats and pasta; sandwiches and a 24-item salad bar are good cheaper alternatives, and desserts are sinful. Dinner offers some of these items but adds a rich menu of starters as well as baked and grilled main courses not available for lunch. Kibbutz Mizra produces high-quality pork products, making its restaurant a magnet for those indifferent to kosher prohibitions. There is an adjacent high-end deli-supermarket. ⊠ *Rte. 60, entrance to Mizra, between Afula and Nazareth (next to gas station)* ☎ *04/642–9214* ⚖ *Reservations essential at dinner* ⊟ *AE, DC, MC, V.*

## Sports & the Outdoors

On the international calendar, the annual **Gilboa Big Walk** (Tza'adat Hagilboa) takes place over a Friday and Saturday in March, when the famous wild black irises are in bloom. The views from Mt. Gilboa are wonderful, and the weather, though sometimes unstable in this season, can be superb. For the intrepid, there are two one-day hikes of 20 km (12½ mi) each; for the more casual walker—or families—there are 6-km (4-mi) walks on both Friday and Saturday and an additional 11-km (7-mi) route on Saturday. All routes end at Ma'ayan Harod; leave your car there and take the transportation provided to the starting point. For details, contact **Hagilboa Community Centers** (⊠ M. P. Gilboa 18120 ☎ 04/653–3361).

# Bet She'an

 *23 km (14 mi) southeast of Afula, 39 km (24 mi) south of Tiberias.*

At the intersection of the Jordan and Jezreel valleys and surrounded by farms and fishponds, this town has one spectacular site, **Bet She'an National Park,** and no other attractions. Follow signs to the national park or the Roman theater. The theater was exposed in the 1960s, but the rest of Scythopolis, as this great Late Roman and Byzantine (2nd–6th centuries AD) city was known, came to light only in more recent excavations. The enormous haul of marble statuary and friezes says much about the opulence of Scythopolis in its heyday.

Scythopolis's **downtown area,** now exposed, has masterfully engineered colonnaded main streets converging on a central plaza that once boasted a pagan temple, a decorative fountain, and a monument. An elaborate Byzantine bathhouse extended over 1¼ acres. On the main thoroughfare, Sha'ul Hamelech (King Saul) Street (a few hundred yards east of Bank Leumi), are the remains of Scythopolis's amphitheater, where blood sports and gladiatorial combats were once the order of the day.

The high tell dominating the site to the north was the location of Old Testament **Canaanite/Israelite Bet She'an** 2,500–3,500 years ago. Don't climb to the top for the meager archaeological remains, but the fine panoramic view of the surrounding valleys and the superb bird's-eye view of the main excavations are worth every gasp.

The semicircular **Roman theater** was built of contrasting black basalt and white limestone blocks around AD 200, when Scythopolis was at its height. Although the upper *cavea*, or tier, has not survived, the theater is the largest and best preserved in Israel, with an estimated original capacity of 7,000–10,000 people. The large stage and part of the *scaena frons* (backdrop) behind it have been restored, and Bet She'an hosts autumn performances as in days of yore. ⊠ *National Park off Sha'ul Hamelech St., at Bank Leumi* ☎ *04/658–7189* ⊕ *www.parks. org.il/ParksENG* ▨ *NIS 23* ☽ *Apr.–Sept., Sat.–Thurs. 8–5, Fri. and Jewish holiday eves 8–4; Oct.–Mar., Sat.–Thurs. 8–4, Fri. and Jewish holiday eves 8–3.*

**need a break?**   **Bis Le'chol Kis** (⊠ Merkaz Rasco 24 ☎ 04/658–7278) translates loosely as "a bite for every budget." Falafel and shawarma are their thing, and they do it well. Instead of pita bread, you can opt to have your turkey-meat shawarma in a fresh, home-baked baguette. Air-conditioning in summer is a welcome relief. Look for this place in a small commercial center right next to the "Egged" Central Bus Station. Bon appetit!

## Where to Stay

¢   🏨 **Bet She'an Guest House.** An example of the upgraded character of the Youth Hostel Association, this limestone facility is wrapped around a courtyard with young palms and benches. Many rooms, including suites with private balconies, have great views east over the Jordan Valley. The lobby café has comfortable cane chairs in which to enjoy pizza, toasted sandwiches, and drinks. Rooms have a good layout and are simply but agreeably furnished with matching light green drapes and bedcovers. Breakfast is included; other meals are available on request. ⊠ *126 Menachem Blvd. [Rte. 90], 10900* ☎ *04/606–0760* 🖷 *04/606–0766* ⊕ *www.youth-hostels.org.il/english.html* ➾ *60 rooms, 2 suites* ⚐ *Café, dining room, minibars, cable TV, pool, basketball, Internet room, meeting rooms, free parking; no room phones* ▭ *AE, DC, MC, V* ⑩ *BP.*

**Nightlife & the Arts**
The marvelous **Roman theater** (☎ 04/658–7189) hosts concerts, mostly by Israeli artists, during the Sukkoth festival every October.

## Belvoir

❾ *Rte. 717; turnoff 12 km (7½ mi) north of Bet She'an; continue 5 km (3 mi) to site. The road from Ein Harod via Moledet is passable in dry weather but in very bad condition in places.*

The Crusaders chose their site well: Belvoir, they called it—"beautiful view"—and it was the most invincible fortress in the land. The Hebrew name "Kochav Hayarden" (the Star of the Jordan) and the Arabic "Kaukab el Hauwa" (the Star of the Wind) merely underscore its splendid isolation. Today it's part of **Kochav Hayarden National Park**. The breathtaking view of the Jordan River valley and southern Sea of Galilee, some 1,800 feet below, is best in the afternoon.

The mighty castle was completed by the Hospitallers (the Knights of St. John) in 1173. In the summer of 1187 the Crusader armies were crushed by the Arabs under Saladin at the Horns of Hattin, west of Tiberias, bringing to an end the Latin Kingdom of Jerusalem. Their remnants struggled on to Tyre (in modern Lebanon), but Belvoir alone refused to yield; 18 months of siege brought the Muslims no further than undermining the outer eastern rampart. The Crusaders, for their part, even sallied out from time to time to battle the enemy, but their lone resistance had become pointless. They struck a deal with Saladin and surrendered the stronghold in exchange for free passage, flags flying, to Tyre.

Don't follow the arrows from the parking lot; instead, take the wide gravel path to the right of the fortress. This brings you right to the panoramic view and the best spot from which to appreciate the strength of the stronghold, with its deep, dry moat; massive rock and cut-stone ramparts; and gates. Once inside the main courtyard, you're unexpectedly faced with a fortress within a fortress, a scaled-down replica of the outer defenses. It's little wonder the Muslims couldn't force its submission. Not much remains of the upper stories; in 1220, the Muslims systematically dismantled Belvoir, fearing another Crusade and the renewal of the fortress as a Frankish base. Once you've explored the modest buildings, exit over the western bridge (once a drawbridge) and spy on the postern gates (the protected and sometimes secret back doors of medieval castles). ⊠ *National Park, Rte. 717, 5 km (3 mi) west of Rte. 90* ☎ *04/ 658–1766* ⊕ *www.parks.org.il/ParksENG* 🖾 *NIS 18* ☉ *Apr.–Sept., Sat.–Thurs. 8–5, Fri. and Jewish holiday eves 8–4; Oct.–Mar., Sat.–Thurs. 8–4, Fri. and Jewish holiday eves 8–3.*

# NAZARETH & THE GALILEE HILLS

Remove the modern roads and power lines, and the landscape of this region becomes a biblical illustration. Unplanned villages are splashed seemingly haphazardly on the hillsides. Small farm-holdings crowd the valleys. Olive groves, the region's ancient resource, are everywhere. Visually arresting moments are provided by hilltop views and modern pine forests, white-and-red houses, and decorative trees that dab the countryside. There are several New Testament settings here—Nazareth, where Jesus grew up; the Cana wedding feast; and Mt. Tabor, identified with the Transfiguration—but Jewish history resonates strongly, too. Tabor and Yodefat were fortifications in the Great Revolt against the Romans; Shefar'am, Bet She'arim (in a nearby valley), and Zippori were in turn the national centers of Jewish life (2nd–4th centuries AD); and latter-day Jewish pioneers, attracted to the region's untamed scenery, put down roots where their ancestors had farmed.

## Nazareth

**❿**

**Fodor'sChoice**

**★**

*25 km (15½ mi) east of Bet She'arim, 56 km (35 mi) east of Haifa, 15 km (9½ mi) north of Afula.*

The Nazareth where Jesus grew up was an insignificant village nestled in a hollow in the Galilean hills. Today's city of 70,000 has burst out of the hollow with almost frenetic energy. It's bemusing and dissonant experience for the Christian pilgrim who seeks the spiritual Nazareth among the horn-blowing cars, vendors, and occasional donkeys (at least *they* add some scriptural authenticity!) plying Paulus VI Street. The scene is hardly quieter on Friday, the holy day for Muslims, who make up two-thirds of Nazareth's population. It calms down somewhat on Wednesday afternoon, however, when many businesses close for a midweek sabbatical, and on Sunday, the day of rest for the Christians who make up the other third of the town, it's positively placid. If you're out for local color (and traffic jams), come on Saturday, when Arab country folk come to town to sell produce and buy goods and Jewish families from the surrounding area come looking for bargains in the souk.

If you're coming from Bet She'arim or Haifa on Route 75, Route 77 breaks off to the north—to Zippori, the Golani Junction, and Tiberias. Route 75 continues to skirt the north side of the picturesque Jezreel Valley as it climbs into the hills toward Nazareth; at the crest of the hill, it's joined by Route 60 from Afula. A turn to the left takes you down to Paulus VI, Nazareth's main drag. If you pick up Route 77 from the opposite side, from Tiberias and points north, a left turn onto Route 764 takes you through a number of villages and directly into Nazareth's Paulus VI Street. For unobstructed panoramas of the town, drive to Upper Nazareth, on the eastern ridge, a Jewish town of about 45,000 that was founded as a separate municipal entity in the 1950s. Alternately, drive to the St. Gabriel Hotel, on the western ridge (accessible from the police station at the town's northern exit, where the road heads for Tiberias).

**Nazareth Village,** which opened in 2000, tries to reconstruct Jewish rural community life of 2,000 years ago. Guided tours of its indoor visual aids and its outdoor replicas of buildings, crafts, and artifacts are offered. ⊠ *Entrance at YMCA* ☎ *04/645–6042* ⊕ *www.nazarethvillage. com* ⊠ *NIS 50* ⊙ *Mon.–Sat. 9–5.*

**★** Casa Nova Street climbs steeply to the entrance of the Roman Catholic **Church of the Annunciation,** the largest church in the Middle East, consecrated in 1969. It enshrines a small ancient cave dwelling or grotto, identified by many Catholics as the home of Mary. Here, they believe, the angel Gabriel appeared to her and announced (hence "Annunciation") that she would conceive "and bear a son" and "call his name Jesus" (Luke 1). Pilgrim devotions suffuse the site throughout the day. Crusader-era walls and some restored Byzantine mosaics near the grotto bear witness to the antiquity of the tradition. The grotto is in the so-called "lower church." Look up through the "well" or opening over the grotto that connects with the "upper church" to the grand cupola, soaring 195 feet above you.

A spiral staircase leads to the vast upper church (some 70 yards long and 30 yards wide), the parish church of Nazareth's Roman Catholic community. Beautiful Italian ceramic reliefs on the huge concrete pillars represent the Stations of the Cross, captioned in the Arabic vernacular. You now have a closer view of the cupola, its ribs representing the petals of an upside-down lily—a symbol of Mary's purity—rooted in heaven. It is repeatedly inscribed with the letter *M* for her name. The huge mosaic behind the altar shows Jesus and Peter at the center and an enthroned Mary behind them, flanked by figures of the hierarchical church (to your right) and the charismatic church (to your left).

The artwork of the site, donated by Catholic communities around the world, is eclectic in the extreme but the more interesting for it. The portico around the courtyard just inside the main gate is decorated with striking contemporary mosaics, many depicting the Madonna and Child in styles and with facial features reflecting the donor nation. The massive main doors leading to the lower church relate in bronze relief the central events of Jesus's life. The dim lighting of the lower church is brilliantly counterpointed by abstract stained-glass windows. The large panels on the walls of the upper church, again on the theme of mother and child, include a vivid offering from the United States, a fine Canadian terra-cotta, and mosaics from England and Australia. Particularly interesting are the gifts from Japan (with gold leaf and real pearls), Venezuela (a carved-wood statue), and Cameroon (a stylized painting in black, white, and brick red).

In the exit courtyard, a glass-enclosed baptistery is built over what is thought to have been an ancient mikvah, a Jewish ritual immersion bath. The adjacent small Church of St. Joseph, just past Terra Sancta College, is built over a complex of rock-hewn chambers traditionally identified as the workshop of Joseph the Carpenter. Be warned that parking is hard to find; try Paulus VI Street or the side streets below it. ⊠ *Casa Nova St.* ☎ *04/657–2501* ✉ *Free* ☉ *Apr.–Sept., Mon.–Sat. 8–noon and 2–6, Sun. 2–6; Oct.–Mar., Mon.–Sat. 8–noon and 2–6, Sun. 2–5.*

**need a break?** Try the unbeatable Arab pastries at the **Mahroum** (⊠ Casa Nova and Paulus VI sts. ☎ 04/656–0214) confectionery. It's clean, has bathrooms, and serves wonderful *bourma* (cylindrical pastry filled with whole pistachio nuts), cashew baklava, and the best halvah you're likely to find anywhere. Don't confuse this place with another one nearby: look for the Arab pastries, not the gooey Western cakes.

The Greek Orthodox **Church of St. Gabriel,** about 1 km (¾ mi) north of the junction of Paulus VI and Casa Nova streets, is built over Nazareth's only natural water source, a spring dubbed Mary's Well. The Greek Orthodox, citing the noncanonical Gospel of St. James, believe it to be the place where the angel Gabriel appeared to Mary to announce the coming birth of Jesus. (On Paulus VI Street, at the bottom of the short approach to the church, is a round, white, stone structure marked MARY'S WELL, but this is merely a modern outlet.)

The ornate church was built in 1750 and contains a carved-wood pulpit and iconostasis (chancel screen), with painted New Testament scenes and silver-haloed saints. The walls are adorned with frescoes of figures from the Bible and the Greek Orthodox hagiography. A tiny "well" stands over the running water, and a modern aluminum cup gives a satisfying plop as it drops in. (The water is clean; the cup is more suspect.) ⊠ *Off Paulus VI St.* ☎ *04/657–6437* ✉ *Small donation expected* ⊙ *Mon.–Sat. 8–5, Sun. after services–5.*

Christianity speaks with many voices in Nazareth. The **Baptist Church** (⊠ Paulus VI St. ☎ 04/657–6946 or 04/657–4370), a few hundred yards north of the Church of St. Gabriel, is affiliated with the Southern Baptist Convention of the United States. Call to arrange a visit.

### Where to Stay & Eat

Travelers tend to hit the sights in Nazareth and move on, and the result is a dearth of good restaurants. There is, however, a clutch of fairly decent little Arab restaurants along Paulus VI Street, frequented mostly by locals. Dinner here means hummus, shish kebab, baklava, Turkish coffee, and the like. Decor is incidental, atmosphere a function of the clientele of the moment, and dinnertime early. Needless to say, reservations are not necessary, and dress is casual.

Nazareth tourism has been transformed by several new hotels. Roman Catholic hospices cater primarily to pilgrim groups, though some welcome individual travelers. Contact the **Government Tourist Office** (⊠ Casa Nova St. ☎ 04/657–3003) for listings.

$$ 🏨 **Plaza.** White and soft pink stone gives the first hint that Nazareth has at last acquired an upscale hotel. The deluxe guest rooms' dark wood fittings and good bathrooms confirm it. Many rooms enjoy a view of Old Nazareth; a huge gym and beauty treatments are popular draws. In a town where outside eating options are limited, the dining room is a good choice. The hotel offers guests a free tour of Old Nazareth on Saturdays; verify on check-in. ⊠ *2 Hermon St., Upper Nazareth 17000* ☎ *04/602–8200* ⊟ *04/602–8222* ➫ *185 rooms, 7 suites* ♿ *Coffee shop, dining room, snack bar, room service, in-room safes, minibars, cable TV, in-room data ports, pool, health club, bar, piano, babysitting, children's programs, dry cleaning, laundry service, Internet room, convention center, free parking, no-smoking floors* ⊟ *AE, DC, MC, V* ⊙ *BP.*

$$ 🏨 **Rimonim Nazareth.** As you walk through the doors, your first impression is likely to be of a staid establishment: quietish, with the usual marble. That's because the action is underground, where the adjoining

bar, lounge, and dining room combine to energize guests. Rooms are comfortable and well appointed; ask for one on the fourth floor with a balcony. The location—on Nazareth's main street, about 300 yards from Mary's Well in the direction of Tiberias—is a limited blessing; this is not a town that comes alive at night. Locals still know the place by its previous identity, Howard Johnson. ☒ *Paulus VI St., Nazareth 16000* ☏ *04/650–0000* ☒ *04/650–0055* ⊕ *www.rimonim.com* ☛ *226 rooms* ♿ *Coffee shop, dining room, room service, in-room safes, minibars, cable TV, in-room data ports, bar, dry cleaning, laundry service, Internet room, business services, meeting rooms, free parking* ☰ *AE, DC, MC, V* ⦿ *BP.*

**$**  ☒ **St. Gabriel.** Sitting high on the ridge that overlooks Nazareth from the west, this hotel began life as a Catholic convent, as one is reminded by the charming neo-Gothic church still in use today. Renovations extended the nuns' old cells, and half the rooms enjoy one of the city's greatest views. All rooms have private showers. The reception area is furnished with inlaid tables, chairs, and mirrors in the old Damascene style, and the dining room prides itself on its local dishes. The garden and the view make for a perfect sundowner option. ☒ *2 Salesian St., Box 2318, Nazareth 16000* ☏ *04/657–2133 or 04/656–7349* ☒ *04/655–4071* ☛ *60 rooms* ♿ *Restaurant, café, dining room, fans, cable TV, Wi-Fi, dry cleaning, laundry service, Internet room, free parking; no a/c* ☰ *AE, DC, MC, V* ⦿ *BP.*

# Zippori

*Village 5 km (3 mi) northwest of Nazareth off Rte. 79, site 3 km (2 mi) from village via bypass, 47 km (29 mi) east of Haifa.*

The ruins of ancient Zippori spread along a high ridge, surrounded by pine and cypress woods, cacti, and fruit trees, with commanding views in all directions. Archaeological excavations of the large, prosperous city of the Roman period have transformed it from a beauty spot into the much-visited **Zippori National Park.**

⑪
Fodor'sChoice
★

The Jewish town that stood here from at least the 1st century BC was also known by its Greek name, Sepphoris, and is identified in some Christian traditions as the birthplace of the Virgin Mary. Zippori's refusal to join the Great Revolt of the Jews against the Romans (AD 66–73) left a serious gap in the rebel defenses in the Galilee, angering its compatriots but sparing the town the usual Roman vengeance when the uprising failed. The real significance of Zippori for Jewish tradition, however, is that in the late 2nd or early 3rd century AD, the legendary sage Rabbi Yehuda Hanassi, head of the country's Jewish community at the time, moved here from Bet She'arim, whereupon the Sanhedrin (the Jewish high court) soon followed. For generations, rabbis here gave learned responses to real-life questions of civil and religious law, basing their judgments on the do's, don'ts, and between-the-lines principles of the Torah (the biblical Five Books of Moses). These rabbinic opinions were transmitted orally from generation to generation and, like court decisions, became legal precedents and the heart of Jewish jurisprudence. Rabbi Yehuda summoned the greatest rabbis in the land to Zippori to pool their experience and codify the so-called Oral Law. The result was the encyclopedic work known as the Mishnah. Further commentary was added in later centuries to produce the Talmud, the primary guide to Orthodox Jewish practice to this day.

Nevertheless, Zippori was a town with a cosmopolitan soul. By the 3rd century AD, it had acquired a mixed population of Jews, pagans, and Christians. The most celebrated find on the site was the mosaic floor of a Roman villa, perhaps the governor's residence, depicting a series of Dionysian drinking scenes. Its most stunning detail is the exquisite face of a woman, by far the finest mosaic ever discovered in Israel, which the popular press at once dubbed "the Mona Lisa of the Galilee." The restored mosaics are housed in an air-conditioned structure with helpful explanations. In other parts of the park, the so-called Nile Mosaic (in the ancient downtown) displays Egyptian motifs, and a mosaic synagogue floor (below the parking lot) is decorated with the signs of the zodiac, just like those found in Bet Alfa and Hammat Tiberias.

If the mosaic floors bespeak the opulence of Roman Sepphoris, the relatively small Roman theater is mute evidence of the cultural life the wealth could support. Take a few minutes to climb the watchtower for the panoramic view and the tiny museum of archaeological artifacts. One kilometer (½ mile) east of the main site—close to the entrance of the park—is a huge section of ancient Zippori's water system, once fed by springs just north of Nazareth. The ancient aqueduct-reservoir is in fact a deep, man-made, plastered canyon, and the effect is extraordinary. ⊠ *Off Rte. 79, beyond village of Zippori* ☎ *04/656–8272* ⊕ *www.parks.org.il/ParksENG* ⎙ *NIS 23* ⊙ *Apr.–Sept., Sat.–Thurs. 8–5, Fri. and Jewish holiday eves 8–4; Oct.–Mar., Sat.–Thurs. 8–4, Fri. and Jewish holiday eves 8–3; last entry 45 mins before closing.*

## Cana

**⑫** *8 km (5 mi) north of Nazareth on Rte. 754, 1 km (½ mi) south of junction of Rtes. 77 and 754; 50 km (31 mi) east of Haifa.*

Many scholars identify the large, modern Arab village of Kafr Kanna as the site of the ancient Jewish village of Cana, mentioned in the New Testament. Here Jesus performed his first miracle, turning water into wine at a wedding feast, thereby emerging from his "hidden years" to begin a three-year ministry in the Galilee. From Nazareth the road winds down through typical Galilean countryside. The profusion of olive groves, pomegranates, grapevines, fig trees, and even the occasional date palm (unusual at this altitude) is a reminder of how much local scenery is described in the Bible. Even the clutter of modern buildings, power lines, and industrial debris cannot entirely ruin the impression.

Within the village, red signs on the right (left as you come from Tiberias) lead to two rival churches—one Roman Catholic (Franciscan), the other Greek Orthodox—that enshrine the scriptural tradition. (The alleyway to these churches is just barely passable for cars, and you can sometimes park in the courtyard of the souvenir store opposite the Catholic one. If the street is blocked, park on the main road, and walk.) The present

Catholic **Cana Wedding Church** was built in the 1880s on what the Franciscans believe to be the very spot where the wedding took place. It's worth a short visit. ⊠ *Churches St.* ☎ *04/651–7011* 🖃 *Free* ☉ *Apr.–Sept., Mon.–Sat. 8–noon and 2–6, Sun. 8–noon; Oct.–Mar., Mon.–Sat. 8–noon and 2–5, Sun. 8–noon.*

## Golani Junction

**⑬** *6 km (4 mi) east of Cana at junction of Rtes. 77 and 65, 55 km (34½ mi) east of Haifa.*

One of the most strategic crossroads in the Lower Galilee, the Golani Junction is named for the Israeli brigade that captured it in the War of Independence in 1948. A monument, a museum, and a McDonald's share the northeast corner of the intersection.

Around the immediate area are new groves of evergreens planted by visitors as part of the Plant a Tree with Your Own Hands project of the Keren Kayemet (the Jewish National Fund, or JNF, in English). Since the early 1900s more than 230 million trees have been restored to barren hillsides across the country. If you want to leave something living behind, look for the **Planting Center,** a few hundred yards from the junction. For NIS 50 you can pick out a sapling, dedicate it to someone if you wish, and plant it yourself. ⊠ *Take Rte. 7707 off Rte. 77 east of Golani Junction at Lavi, then immediate left on secondary Rd.* ☎ *02/ 670–7433* ☉ *Sun.–Thurs. 8–3, Fri. 8–noon.*

### Where to Stay

**$$** 🏨 **Lavi Kibbutz Hotel.** Though under one roof, this hotel-style guest house has a fine new wing (2001), a face-lifted central wing, and an older wing slated for renovation. Rooms are spacious, and many have good views. The religious Jewish community here allows no check-ins or checkouts nor vehicle use in the village (though there's nearby parking) from sunset Friday until nightfall Saturday. That said, the atmosphere is welcoming for all, and waking to rural surroundings has much to recommend it. Professional help in planning your touring is available free; the hotel is 15 minutes from Tiberias. ⊠ *Rte. 77, 11 km (7 mi) west of Tiberias, Lower Galilee 15267* ☎ *04/679–9450* 🖶 *04/679–9399* ⊕ *www. kibbutzlavi.co.il/hotel* ➥ *172 rooms, 4 suites* ⚅ *Coffee shop, dining room, cable TV, tennis court, indoor pool, health club, hair salon, basketball, hiking, Ping-Pong, bar, shop, babysitting, children's programs, playground, dry cleaning, laundry service, Internet room, business services, convention center, free parking, no-smoking rooms* 🖃 *AE, DC, MC, V* 🍽 *BP.*

**en route**  As you head from the Golani Junction to Tiberias on Route 77, you'll see a small double hill called the **Horns of Hattin,** east of Lavi and to your left. Here, in the summer of 1187, the Arab leader Saladin crushed a Crusader army, bringing to an end the Latin Kingdom of Jerusalem. Richard the Lionhearted's Third Crusade, a few years later, restored some parts of the country to Christian control, but the power and glory of the Latin Kingdom were gone forever.

## Mt. Tabor

★  *16 km (10 mi) south of the Golani Junction off Rte. 7266, 17 km (10½ mi) northeast of Afula.*

The dome-like Mt. Tabor, at 1,929 feet the region's highest mountain, looms over one of the prettiest stretches of the Lower Galilee hill country. Quilts of farmland kaleidoscope through the seasons as different crops grow, ripen, and are harvested. Modern woods of evergreens cover the hillsides. Apart from the natural beauty, Mt. Tabor and its immediate surroundings have considerable biblical history. For example, 32 centuries ago, somewhere near the foot of the mountain, Israelite warriors of the prophetess-judge Deborah and her general, Barak, routed a Canaanite chariot army. The modern kibbutz of Ein Dor, across the highway south of the mountain, is the site of ancient Endor, where (c. 1006 BC) King Saul unsuccessfully beseeched the spirit of the prophet Samuel for help before his fateful (and fatal) battle against the Philistines.

To climb the mountain take Route 7266 through Shibli, a village of Bedouin who abandoned their nomadic life a few generations ago and became farmers. A narrow switchback road starts in a clearing between Shibli and the next village, Dabouriya. Nazareth-based taxis often wait at the bottom of the mountain to provide shuttle service to the top. Watch out for them if you're driving your own car up; they come down in overdrive like the lords of the mountain they almost are.

As far back as the Byzantine period, Christian tradition identified Mt. Tabor as the "high mountain apart" that Jesus ascended with his disciples Peter, James, and John. There, report the Gospels, "he was transfigured before them" (Matthew 17) as a radiant white figure, flanked by Moses and Elijah. The altar of the present imposing **Church of the Transfiguration,** which was consecrated in 1924, represents the tabernacle of Jesus that Peter suggested they build; those of Moses and Elijah appear as small chapels at the back of the church. Step up to the terrace to the right of the church doors for a great view of the Jezreel Valley to the west and south, and from a platform on the Byzantine and Crusader ruins to the left of the modern church (watch your step), there is a panorama east and north over the Galilean hills. Fifty yards before the church, a Franciscan pilgrim rest house has refreshments, toilets, and sometimes a meal. ☎ 04/673–2283 ✉ Free ☉ Daily 8–noon and 2–5.

The veteran farming village of **Kfar Tavor** was founded by Jewish pioneers in 1901 in the shadow of the domed mountain from which it took its name. Not everyone farms today, and the village side streets, with single-family homes and well-tended gardens, feel like a nice piece of suburbia anywhere.

An excellent time-out from regular touring, the **Tabor Winery** is a boutique outfit, founded in 1997. The quality of its wines has risen steeply in the last few years. They aren't the cheapest, but after tasting a few varietals, you might not be able to resist taking a couple of bottles home. A 12-minute film and tasting are free. From late July through September, visitors can pay to stomp grapes the traditional way—a

great family activity. ✉ *Visitors Center, Kfar Tavor* ☎ *04/676–0444*
🖥 *Free* ☉ *Sun.–Thurs. 10–5, Fri. 10–3.*

In the same compound as the winery, the charming **Marzipan Museum**
contains explanations and delectable products made from locally grown
almonds. If you have kids in tow, don't think twice about signing up
for the fun, marzipan-making workshop. (There's also a chocolate
workshop.) Best of all, you get to take your creations home. ✉ *Visitors
Center, Kfar Tavor* ☎ *04/677–2111 or 050/570–1677* 🖥 *NIS 15*
☉ *Sun.–Fri. 9–6, Sat. 10–6.*

### Where to Eat

$–$$$  ✕ **Sahara.** The menu of this Middle Eastern restaurant is a bit more so-
phisticated than its regional roadside rivals. Inside the stone building
with a landmark round tower is a spacious interior with stone floors
and arches, wooden tables, and a centerpiece water cascade. Follow the
excellent fresh meze (local salads) with traditional skewers of grilled meat,
baked lamb, or one of the fish or chicken dishes. The Jordanian *mansaf*
(a mix of rice, pine nuts, and pieces of lamb) is an interesting discov-
ery. ✉ *Rte. 65 (next to gas station)* ☎ *04/642–5959* 🍴 *Reservations
essential* 🖃 *AE, DC, MC, V.*

$–$$  ✕ **Bordeaux.** The name hints at the restaurant's location, adjacent to
the Tabor Winery. The style is "country," with warm wood decor in-
side and a great scenic deck for outside dining. With special effort made
to use excellent local farm produce, the wide-ranging menu stretches from
modestly priced pastas, salads, and sandwiches to more sophisticated
(yet still reasonable) steaks, fish, and chicken dishes. A children's menu
and good desserts contribute to the family-friendliness. That few tourists
have discovered this pretty area—just 30 minutes from Tiberias—adds
to its attraction. ✉ *Visitors Center, Kfar Tavor* ☎ *04/676–7673* 🍴 *Reservations essential Fri. and Sat.* 🖃 *AE, DC, MC, V.*

en route    If you're heading to the Sea of Galilee, take Route 767, which breaks
off Route 65 at Kfar Tavor. It's a beautiful drive of about 25 minutes.
The first village, **Kafr Kamma,** is one of two in Israel of the
Circassian (*Cherkessi*) community, Muslims from the Russian steppes
who settled here in the 19th century. The unusually decorative
minaret of the mosque is just one element of the tradition the
community vigorously continues to preserve. On the descent to the
lake, there is a parking area precisely at sea level. The Sea of Galilee
is still more than 700 feet below, and the view is superb, especially in
the afternoon. You meet Route 90 at the bottom of the road.

# TIBERIAS & THE SEA OF GALILEE

The great American writer and humorist Mark Twain was unimpressed
by the Sea of Galilee region. He passed through on horseback in 1867,
in the company of a group of pilgrims and Arab dragomans (interpreters),
and found "an unobtrusive basin of water, some mountainous desolation, and one tree." He would scarcely recognize it now. Modern agriculture and forestation projects have made the plains and hills green;

the handful of "squalid" and "reeking" villages of his day have been modernized or supplanted by thriving and well-landscaped kibbutzim; and the "unobtrusive basin of water" has become a lively resort.

The Sea of Galilee is, in fact, a freshwater lake, 21 km (13 mi) long from north to south and 11 km (7 mi) wide from east to west. The Jordan River feeds it from the north and then leaves it in the south to begin its meandering trickle to the Dead Sea. Almost completely ringed by cliffs and steep hills, the lake lies in a hollow about 700 feet below sea level, which accounts for its warm climate and subtropical vegetation. Its shores are dotted with sites hallowed by Christian tradition (note that several of these sites demand modest dress) as well as some important ancient synagogues. Tiberias itself is one of Judaism's four holy cities (along with Jerusalem, Hebron, and Tzfat). For those whose interests lie elsewhere, there are plenty of ways to relax in, on, and around the water.

The city of Tiberias is the logical starting point for exploration. Sights are described more or less in sequence as you circumvent the Sea of Galilee clockwise from Tiberias (via Routes 90, 87, 92, and 98) to Hammat Tiberias, on the city's southern edge.

## Tiberias

★ **15**  *38 km (23½ mi) north of Bet She'an, 36 km (23 mi) east of Nazareth, 70 km (43 mi) east of Haifa.*

As the only town on the Sea of Galilee, Tiberias, with a population of about 40,000, has become the natural center of the region. The city spreads all the way up a steep hillside, from 700 feet below sea level at the lake, to about 800 feet above sea level in its highest neighborhoods—a differential big enough to create significant variety in human comfort during midsummer.

The splendid panorama deserved a better sort of development. Tiberias has little beauty and less class, and although almost 2,000 years old, it still has the atmosphere of a community yet to come of age. It is at once brash and sleepy, a provincial town where hotel-lobby crooners and a couple of pubs with loud recorded music constitute the entertainment menu most nights. Its reputation as a resort town is based more on its great location and some decent hotels than on the town's own attractions. Having said that, travelers tend to see little of the town proper and confine themselves to the lakeshore strip, where most of the hotels, restaurants, and the occasional pub are clustered. Tourism, as much Israeli as foreign, is a mainstay of the town's economy. You can eat and drink well here and take in the incomparable lake view from myriad locations.

Foremost among Tiberias's many venerated resting places is the **tomb of Moses Maimonides** (1135–1204), the great sage. Born in Córdoba, Spain, Maimonides—widely known by his Hebrew acronym, the "Rambam" (for Rabbi Moshe Ben Maimon)—won international renown as a philosopher, as physician to the royal court of Saladin in Egypt, and in the Jewish world, as the greatest religious scholar and spiritual authority of the Middle Ages. To his profound knowledge of the Talmud, Maimonides brought an incisive intellect honed by his study of Aristotelian

# CloseUp
## TIBERIAS THROUGH TIME

**TIBERIAS WAS FOUNDED** in AD 18 by Herod Antipas, son of Herod the Great, and dedicated to Tiberius, then emperor of Rome. Many shunned the new town, which was built on a cemetery and considered unclean. A century later it was ceremonially purified, opening the way for settlement.

The Tiberians had little stomach for the Jewish war against Rome that broke out in AD 66. They soon surrendered, preventing the vengeful destruction visited on other Galilean towns. With Jerusalem laid waste in AD 70, the center of Jewish life gravitated to the Galilee. By the 4th century, the Sanhedrin had settled in Tiberias. Here Jewish Oral Law was compiled into what became known as the Jerusalem Talmud, and Tiberias's status as one of Judaism's holy cities was assured.

Tiberias knew hard times under the Byzantines, stabilized under the Muslim dynasties of the early Middle Ages, and declined again under the hostile Crusaders. The Arab Saladin besieged the city in 1187 and routed the Crusader army. Tiberias was in decline until 1562, when the Ottoman sultan Suleiman the Magnificent gave it to the Jewish nobleman Don Joseph Nasi. Starting in the 1700s, newcomers from Turkey and Eastern Europe swelled the Jewish population, but an 1837 earthquake left Tiberias in ruins.

Relations between Jews and Arabs were generally cordial until the Arab riots of 1936, when some 30 Jews were massacred. During the 1948 War of Independence, an attack by local Arabs brought a counterattack from Haganah (Jewish) forces, and the Arabs abandoned the town. Today its citizenry is entirely Jewish.

philosophy and the physical sciences. The result was a rationalism unusual in Jewish scholarship and a lucidity of analysis and style admired by Jewish and non-Jewish scholars alike.

Maimonides never lived in Tiberias, but after his death, in Egypt, his remains were brought to this holy Jewish city for interment. His white-washed tomb has become a shrine, dripping with candle wax and tears. To get here, walk two blocks up Hayarden Street, and turn right onto Ben Zakkai Street. The tomb is on your right, topped by a soaring spire of red steel girders. ⊠ *Ben Zakkai St.* ☎ *No phone* ⊕ *www. maimonidesheritage.org/Tomb.asp* ✆ *Free* ⊙ *Sun.–Thurs. dawn–dusk, Fri. and Jewish holiday eves until 2* PM.

### Where to Stay & Eat
At a right angle to the water-side promenade, the *midrachov* (pedestrian mall), between the Sheraton Moriah and Caesar hotels, has a wide range of affordable eating options: hamburger joints, pizzerias, ice cream parlors, a lone pub (Big Ben), and restaurants serving light meals, including a member of the nationwide Kapulsky chain, known for its sinfully rich cakes. If you're not looking for a gourmet experience, you can eat quite well for NIS 50 or less. There are also a cou-

ple of budget places on Habanim Street, on or near the top corner of the mall, and you can rub shoulders with the locals on Hagalil Street. In fact, if you're into local color, look for the tiny, modest restaurants (where English really *is* a foreign language) on Hagalil Street and in the little streets that connect it to Habanim Street, like the small, pedestrian-only Kishon Street, opposite the Jordan River Hotel. Beyond the predictable but reasonably priced fish and Middle Eastern fare, real ethnic discoveries are not unknown.

**$$–$$$$** ✕ **Decks.** Built right on a pier, Decks is at its best in fine weather. Begin with a (shared) focaccia and the unusual fried onion loaf. The kitchen specializes in good meat—steak, goose liver, or long skewers of veal and vegetables—grilled slowly over hickory wood. Fish and large salads make excellent noncarnivorous alternatives. An apple tart pan-baked at your table is the house dessert. ⊠ *Lido complex, Rte. 90, at the exit from Tiberias north* ☎ *04/672–1538* ▭ *AE, DC, MC, V* ☉ *No dinner Fri. No lunch Sat.*

★ **$$** ✕ **Pagoda and the House.** Pagoda is built as a faux-Chinese temple, with an outdoor patio overlooking the lake. The House, across the road, has a maze of more intimate rooms entered through a delightful garden. The two Chinese-Thai restaurants are essentially one, with identical menus (no pork or shrimp), but Pagoda is closed on the Sabbath and religious holidays, while the House is open only when Pagoda is not. Apart from Chinese standards, try the Thai soups (coconut based or hot-and-sour), the goose(!) spareribs, or strips of beef sautéed in satay (peanut) sauce. In truly pan-Asian spirit, there is a sushi bar as well. ⊠ *Gedud Barak St. (Rte. 90)* ☎ *04/672–5513 or 04/672–5514* ☖ *Reservations essential* ▭ *AE, DC, MC, V* ☉ *Pagoda: no dinner Fri. No lunch Sat. The House: no dinner Sat.–Thurs. No lunch Sun.–Fri.*

**$–$$** ✕ **Guy.** Stuffed vegetables are the calling card of this family-run restaurant, whose name means "valley" in Hebrew. The cook-matriarch Geula comes from a veteran Tiberias family, but her Moroccan ancestry shows through in delicious dishes like eggplant stuffed with well-seasoned ground beef. There are good, if more conventional, Middle Eastern meat and salad options, but go for the excellent soups, some *kibbeh* (a Kurdish-Iraqi specialty of seasoned ground meat and bulgur), and a platter of mixed stuffed veggies. If there are enough of you to share, experiment. The restaurant faces the lake slightly set back from the sidewalk and opposite a small traffic circle. ⊠ *63 Hagalil St.* ☎ *04/672–3036* ▭ *No credit cards* ☉ *Closed Sat. No dinner Fri.*

★ **$$$$** ▥ **Rimonim Galei Kinnereth.** The grande dame of Tiberias's up-market hotels has emerged from its most recent renovation like a butterfly from a chrysalis, ready to resume its leadership position. Its location right on the lake is unbeatable. The spa is an artistic, low-lit complex of soothing soft blues and candles; a large whirlpool gurgles away in its own glassed-in gazebo. Guest rooms have a well-matched decor of dark blue with gold patterns, but they are neither extraordinary enough nor large enough to justify the rack rate. Breakfast and either lunch or dinner are included. ⊠ *1 Eliezer Kaplan St., 14100* ☎ *04/672–8888* ▤ *04/679–0260* ⊕ *www.rimonim.com* ⟿ *113 rooms, 7 suites* ⟐ *Coffee shop, din-*

*ing room, snack bar, in-room safes, minibars, cable TV, Wi-Fi, pool, gym, spa, beach, windsurfing, boating, waterskiing, Ping-Pong, bar, lobby lounge, piano, shop, babysitting, children's programs, dry cleaning, laundry service, Internet room, meeting rooms, free parking, no-smoking floors ☰ AE, DC, MC, V ❘❍❘ MAP.*

**$$$$** ⊞ **Sheraton Moriah.** The lobby and bar are bright, comfortable places to relax, the service generally professional and accommodating. There is a new spa (2004), and a makeover of all the guest rooms is expected to raise the property to the level of its local competition. The hotel overlooks the lake but does not have lake frontage. ⊠ *Off Habanim St., 14103* ☎ *04/671–3333* 🖶 *04/679–2320* ⊕ *www.sheraton.com* ⇗ *238 rooms, 21 suites* ♨ *Coffee shop, dining room, room service, in-room safes, minibars, cable TV, pool, gym, hair salon, spa, Ping-Pong, bar, piano, shops, babysitting, children's programs, dry cleaning, laundry service, Internet room, meeting rooms, some free parking* ☰ *AE, DC, MC, V* ❘❍❘ *BP.*

**$$$** ⊞ **Caesar.** Part of a small national chain, the Caesar faces the lake and offers views from all rooms. Public areas—with much marble, brass, and leather—are arranged well, providing islands of intimacy and a superb lake view from the terrace. The spacious guest rooms have tasteful, if unexceptional, furnishings, and every suite has a whirlpool bath. The outside pool area is entirely concrete, while the warm indoor pool uses natural thermal spring water from Hammat Gader. A large gym and wide range of treatments make the spa a definite attraction. ⊠ *The Promenade, 14102* ☎ *04/672–7272* 🖶 *04/679–1013* ⊕ *www.caesarhotels.co. il/english* ⇗ *220 rooms, 7 suites* ♨ *Coffee shop, dining room, snack bar, minibars, cable TV, Wi-Fi, 2 pools (1 indoor), gym, hair salon, spa, Ping-Pong, bar, piano, recreation room, shop, babysitting, children's programs, dry cleaning, laundry service, Internet room, convention center, some free parking* ☰ *AE, DC, MC, V* ❘❍❘ *BP.*

**★ $$$** ⊞ **Club Hotel.** Cascading down the hill, far above downtown Tiberias, this all-suites hotel offers an unimpeded, breathtaking view of most of the lake. Units sleep at least four, and the rate is the same up to that number. This classic vacation property has cheerful decor and an upbeat style, an all-season team to engage the kids, and a good health club to relax their parents. Downtown is less than 10 minutes away by car or cab. ⊠ *Ahad Ha'am St., Box 680, 14222* ☎ *04/672–8000* 🖶 *04/ 672–2898* ⇗ *307 suites* ♨ *Coffee shop, dining room, in-room safes, kitchenettes, minibars, microwaves, cable TV, tennis court, pool, health club, lobby lounge, piano, video game room, shop, babysitting, children's programs, dry cleaning, laundry service, meeting rooms, free parking* ☰ *AE, DC, MC, V* ❘❍❘ *BP.*

**★ $$$** ⊞ **Gai Beach.** The rare lakeshore location is a big plus, and for some, so is its distance (still walkable) from the noisy downtown promenade. The marble lobby lounge is large and airy, yet clusters of comfortable armchairs create some intimacy. Guest rooms are well designed and tastefully furnished, if smallish; half face the lake. On two floors the rooms have private balconies. The hotel owns the adjacent water park (free to guests), which has a beach, seven water slides, a wave pool, and a children's pool, making it arguably the most family-friendly hotel in town. The guests-only policy of the fine new spa (its decor predictably Roman) gives it a more private feel. ✉ *Rte. 90, Box 274, 14102* 🖷 *04/670–0700* 🖷 *04/679–2776* ⊕ *www.gaibeachhotel.com* ⤳ *196 rooms, 2 suites* ◭ *Restaurant, coffee shop, dining room, 2 snack bars, room service, in-room safes, minibars, cable TV with movies, Wi-Fi, 4 pools (1 indoors), gym, spa, beach, bar, lobby lounge, piano, shop, babysitting, children's programs, dry cleaning, laundry service, convention center, free parking* ▭ *AE, DC, MC, V* ⏏❘ *BP.*

**$$$**  🏨 **Scots Hotel.** Formerly a Church of Scotland hospital and a pilgrim
**Fodor'sChoice**  hostelry, this place has been reinvented as Tiberias's most interesting up-
★  scale hotel. Two renovated old buildings and one entirely new one produce a pleasingly asymetrical complex (a map is provided) with surprise areas, such as an inviting lobby with deep armchairs, marble tiles, and an arch-framed lake view, and a roof terrace where you can have a drink or light meal. The aesthetics are wonderful: gold and burgundy trim in the junior suites, beige and blue carpets in the halls, and well-appointed bathrooms. The lakeside pool is open May–October. Ask for a room with a view. ✉ *Gedud Barak and Hayarden sts., Box 104, 14100* 🖷 *04/ 671–0710* 🖷 *04/671–0711* ⊕ *www.scotshotels.co.il* ⤳ *69 rooms* ◭ *Coffee shop, dining room, room service, in-room safes, minibars, cable TV, Wi-Fi, pool, massage, Turkish bath, beach, bar, shop, dry cleaning, laundry service, Internet room, meeting rooms, some free parking; no smoking* ▭ *AE, DC, MC, V* ⏏❘ *BP.*

**$$**  🏨 **Arbel Guest House.** Containing whirlpools, tile floors, and wooden balconies, the comfortable and appealing units are surrounded by a riot of greenery, including a lawn and an inviting *bustan* (a local-style garden redolent with fragrant herbs). Four apartments have a living room and a bedroom (one is wheelchair-accessible); the fifth has two bedrooms. The rustic environment, 10 minutes from Tiberias and the Sea of Galilee, is pleasing, and the dining room transforms into a good-value à la carte restaurant in the evening. ✉ *Rte. 7717, off Rte. 77, Arbel Village 15282* 🖷 *04/679–4919* 🖷 *04/673–3695* ⊕ *www.inisrael.com/shavit* ⤳ *1 room, 5 apartments* ◭ *Restaurant, dining room, BBQs, kitchenettes, microwaves, refrigerators, cable TV, basketball, playground, laundry service; no room phones* ▭ *AE, DC, MC, V* ⏏❘ *BP.*

★ **$$**  🏨 **Ron Beach.** The last hotel on Route 90 north in Tiberias, the family-run Ron Beach has rare private lake frontage, though no beach. Amenities are good for the price. Most guest rooms, in well-chosen, soft yet bright shades of gold and light blue, are in a two-story building facing the lake. The upper floor is made up of mini-suites; the lower floor opens out to lawns and the pool area. In addition, there are several very large family rooms. All in all, it's a great value. ✉ *Gedud Barak St. (Rte. 90 N), 14101* 🖷 *04/679–1350* 🖷 *04/679–1351* ⊕ *www.ronbeachhotel.com* ⤳ *70 rooms, 4 suites* ◭ *Coffee shop, dining room, room service, some minibars, cable TV, pool, waterskiing, basketball, bar, piano, shop, playground, dry cleaning, laundry service, Internet room, meeting rooms, free parking* ▭ *AE, DC, MC, V* ⏏❘ *BP.*

**$**  🏨 **Astoria.** One of Tiberias's better moderately priced hotels, the Astoria is set away from the lake, halfway uptown, with few views from guest rooms. What it lacks in aesthetics, however, it makes up for in quality. It's comfortable, clean, and family-run, with furnishings in attractive pastels. Large family rooms are available. ✉ *13 Ohel Ya'akov St., 14223*

☎ 04/672–2351  🖷 04/672–5108  ⊕ *www.astoria.co.il*  ⇔ *88 rooms* ♨ *Coffee shop, dining room, cable TV, pool, hot tub, spa, bar, dry cleaning, laundry services, Internet room, free parking, no-smoking rooms* ▭ *AE, MC, V* ⍐⌾⎮ *BP.*

★ $  🖾 **YMCA Peniel-by-Galilee.** In the 1930s, Archibald Harte, founder of the Jerusalem YMCA, built a retreat on the low cliff between the highway and the lake. The vista is grand, the pebbly beach clean, and the common room (with Damascene wood panels dating to the early 19th century) warm and inviting. Guest rooms (some family-size, most with lake views) are spacious, furnishings simple but comfortable, bathrooms have showers only, and two units have equipped kitchenettes. Most rooms are accessible only by steps. Lunch and dinner are available by prior arrangement. The quiet isolation of the place attracts a loyal Israeli clientele, making advance reservations essential. The small pool is fed by a warm natural spring. ⊹ *Off Rte. 90, 3 km (2 mi) north of Tiberias* ⊠ *Box 192, Tiberias 14101* ☎ *04/672–0685* 🖷 *02/623–5192* ⊕ *www. ymca-galilee.co.il* ⇔ *12 rooms, 1 suite* ♨ *Restaurant, dining room, some kitchenettes, refrigerators, cable TV, pool, beach, library, playground* ▭ *AE, DC, MC, V* ⍐⌾⎮ *BP.*

★ ¢  🖾 **Bet Berger.** This family-run, uptown hotel has spacious, decently furnished rooms; most have a balcony. A car is a boon, but there is frequent public transportation downtown (except on the Sabbath). The hotel is self-catering (unless there's a group in the house, when meals might be available), for which the supermarket across the street is convenient. Renovations and such frills as satellite TV have lifted the hotel's quality way above its price category. More than half of the rooms have bathtubs; the rest have showers. Management is quick to upgrade you if a larger room is available. ⊠ *27 Neiberg St., Box 535, 14105* ☎ *04/671– 5151* 🖷 *04/679–1514* ⇔ *45 rooms, 2 apartments* ♨ *Kitchenettes, refrigerators, cable TV, lounge, laundry service, Internet room, free parking* ▭ *AE, DC, MC, V.*

¢  🖾 **Meyouhas Youth Hostel.** This large basalt building fronted by a lawn and trees is in the heart of downtown Tiberias, a minute's walk from the lake, the promenade, and the mall. The term "youth" is inaccurate— the place is open to all—and though the atmosphere is hostel-like, there are en-suite facilities for half the rooms. Meals are cheap and frills are few, but it's a decent option for the budget conscious. ⊠ *Gedud Barak and Hayarden sts., Box 81, 14100* ☎ *04/672–1775 or 04/679–0350* 🖷 *04/672–0372* ⊕ *www.youth-hostels.org.il* ⇔ *56 rooms, 24 with bath* ♨ *Dining room; no room phones, no room TVs* ▭ *AE, DC, MC, V* ⍐⌾⎮ *BP.*

## Nightlife & the Arts

Much of the entertainment, especially in the larger hotels in Tiberias, is of the live-lounge-music variety: piano bars, one-man dance bands, and crooners. Thursday and Friday are "nightclub" nights at some hotels, with dance music for the weekend crowds. The clientele tends to be a bit older. Generally speaking, the younger set wouldn't be caught dead here, preferring to hang out at one of the few outside pubs, where the recorded rock music is good and loud and the beer is on tap.

## Sports & the Outdoors

BEACHES   There's good swimming at a number of beaches near Tiberias. **Blue Beach** (⊠ Rte. 90, at northern exit from Tiberias ☎ 04/672–0105) is one of the veteran establishments in the region.

**Sironit** (⊠ Rte. 90, at southern exit from Tiberias ☎ 04/672–1449) has water slides in addition to its lake access. **Gai Beach** (⊠ Rte. 90, at southern exit from Tiberias ☎ 04/670–0713), next to Sironit, has a multi-slide water park in addition to swimming.

WALKING &   A promenade follows the lakeshore for about 5 km (3 mi) to the south
JOGGING   of Tiberias.

WATER SPORTS   Waterskiing and boat rentals are available on the lake. Contact the **Tourist Information Office** (⊠ Habanim St. ☎ 04/672–5666), opposite the Sheraton Moriah Hotel, for information.

## Shopping

Tiberias relies heavily on tourism, but despite its developing infrastructure, it has little in the way of shopping. The exceptions are jewelry and souvenirs. There are a few jewelry stores near the intersection of Habanim and Yarden streets and in some of the better hotels. **Caprice** (⊠ Tabor St. ☎ 04/670–0600), a large diamond factory, introduces you to the industry with a video and a short tour of its workshops and small museum, before releasing you into its showroom.

# Ginosar

 *10 km (6 mi) north of Tiberias.*

The veteran kibbutz of Ginosar was founded here in 1937. Many Israelis know it as the home of the late Yigal Allon (1918–80), commander of the crack Palmach battalions in the War of Independence and deputy prime minister of Israel in the 1970s under Golda Meir and Yitzhak Rabin. The settlement's favorite son is immortalized in **Bet Allon** (Allon House), a good museum of the region's natural and human history.

For the traveler, the site's brilliant attraction is a wooden boat from the 1st century AD, found on the shore by local fishermen in January 1986. Three years of poor rainfall had lowered the level of the lake, and bits of the ancient wood were suddenly exposed in the mud. Excavated in a frenetic 11 days, the 28-foot-long boat became an instant media sensation. Given its age and the frequency of New Testament references to Jesus and his disciples boating on the Sea of Galilee—including coming ashore at Gennesaret, perhaps today's Ginosar—the popular press immediately dubbed it "the Jesus Boat." On the other hand, the startlingly vivid relic might have been a victim of the Roman naval victory over the rebellious Jewish townspeople of nearby Magdala in AD 67, as described by the historian Josephus Flavius. Whatever its secret history, it is the most complete boat this old ever found in an inland waterway anywhere in the world.

The ancient craft was amazingly intact but extremely fragile, its timbers sodden like wet cardboard. To move it, experts sprayed the vessel inside and out with a polyurethane mixture, giving it a buoyant "strait-

# CloseUp

## KIBBUTZ LIFE

**THE FOUNDING FATHERS AND MOTHERS** would probably be bewildered by life on a 21st-century kibbutz (collective settlement). Many if Israel's founders came from Russia in the early 20th century, inspired by Zionist ideals of returning to their ancestral homeland and a work ethic that regarded manual labor as an almost spiritual value. They were products of their time: socialists who embraced the motto "from each according to his ability, to each according to his need."

The first kibbutz was founded in 1909 on the shores of the Sea of Galilee, where a handful of pioneers began to work the land. The utopian ideology, in which individual desires were subordinated to the needs of the community, was wedded to the practical need for a close-knit communal structure, in order to cope with forbidding terrain and a hostile neighborhood. Later came the national goal of rooting Jewish settlements in Palestinian soil. Life was tough—the work arduous, and malaria rampant—but they endured and their numbers grew.

Kibbutzim played a considerable role in molding the fledgling state, absorbing immigrants, developing agriculture, and serving as border outposts. By 1950, two years after Israel's independence, there were already more than 200 kibbutzim around the country. The egalitarianism of the kibbutz meant that chores and responsibility—but also ownership of the means of production—was shared by all. So successful was the concept that the kibbutz movement became the largest communitarian movement in the world.

With time, many kibbutzim introduced light industry or tourism enterprises, and some became successful businesses. (The Kibbutz Contemporary Dance Company and the Kibbutz Orchestra are two cultural offshoots of the movement.) The standard of living improved, and kibbutzim took advantage of easy bank loans to finance development. When Israel's hyperinflation was reined in during the 1980s and interest payments became real money, many communities found themselves on the brink of economic ruin. Change became inevitable.

The movement peaked around 1990, when the almost 270 kibbutzim around Israel reached 130,000 members. (An individual kibbutz can range from fewer than 100 to more than 1,000 members.) Times change, however, and the shining ideals have dulled with the years. In a less ideological age, many young "kibbutzniks," after compulsory military service or university studies, have found the kibbutz ethos stifling and have opted for the individualism and material attractions of city life. Despite the changes, city folk, volunteers, and tourists are still drawn to this rural environment, which still offers a slower pace and a tranquil ambience.

Only some 15% of kibbutz members still work in agriculture, though they account for a significant proportion of the national production. Industry, services, and tourism are the real sources of income. Differential wage systems have been introduced, unemployment is growing, and foreign laborers often provide menial labor in fields and factories. The kibbutz has undergone a metamorphosis, down to the widespread use of personal credit cards (even to pay for meals in the communal dining room). Many members of the older generation have become deeply distressed by what they see as the contamination of the sacred principles on which they built their dream. But reality bites hard, and ironically, only those kibbutzim that succeed economically can afford to be socialist.

jacket." It was then towed a few hundred yards by rowboat and lifted by crane to a small building between the lake and the museum. The polyurethane material was removed, and for almost a decade, the boat lay immersed in a wax-based preservative solution to displace the water molecules in the wood. Today it is exhibited dry in all its modest but remarkably evocative glory in a specially built pavilion. A short video tells the story. ⊠ *Nof Ginosar, off Rte. 90* ☎ *04/672–7700* ⊕ *www. jesusboat.com* ✉ *Museum and boat NIS 20* ⊙ *Sat.–Thurs. 8–5, Fri. and Jewish holiday eves 8–1, boat only 8–4; last entry 1 hr before closing.*

## Where to Stay

**$$** 🏨 **Nof Ginosar.** Its grand location—with a private beach right on the Sea of Galilee—makes this large, veteran kibbutz guest house especially popular. The decor of the motel-like accommodations is unmemorable, and the airy, if not overly spacious, guest rooms are ready for an up-grade. However, there are sometimes evening lectures on kibbutz life and a morning tour, and the 2,000-year-old fishing boat and museum at adjacent Bet Allon are free to guests. The dinner buffet alternates between decent meat-based meals and meatless ones, the latter offering (apart from good salads, fish, and pasta) outstanding blintzes with sweetened cheese. ⊠ *Rte. 90, 14980* ☎ *04/670–0300* 🖷 *04/679–2170* ⊕ *www. ginosar.co.il* ➭ *170 rooms* ⚲ *Café, dining room, minibars, cable TV, in-room data ports, tennis court, pool, beach, boating, basketball, Ping-Pong, bar, shop, babysitting, playground, laundry service, Internet room, meeting rooms, free parking, no-smoking rooms* ▭ *AE, DC, MC, V* ⍾◎⏦ *BP.*

**en route** On Route 90, on your right a few miles north of Ginosar, is an electric substation that powers huge water pumps buried in the hill behind it. The Sea of Galilee is Israel's primary freshwater reservoir and the beginning of the National Water Carrier, a network of canals and pipelines that integrates the country's water sources and distribution lines. On the hill above is the small tell or mound of the Old Testament city of **Kinneret,** which dominated a branch of the Via Maris, the main highway of the ancient Near East. Scholars assume that the Hebrew name for the lake—Kinneret—comes from that of the most important city on its shores in antiquity. Romantics contend that the name derives from the lake's shape, which resembles the biblical *kinnor* (lyre).

## Korazim

**⑰** *Rte. 8277, at Rte. 90, 6 km (4 mi) north of Capernaum Junction.*

Built on a basalt bluff high above the Sea of Galilee, the ancient Jewish town of Korazim was renowned for its high-quality wheat. It also provided services and hospitality for travelers on the nearby high road to Damascus and the east. Korazim (or Chorasin) is mentioned in the New Testament as one of the towns rebuked by Jesus, but almost nothing survives from that era. The extensive ruins exposed in modern excavations date to the 4th or 5th century AD. The dominant building is the monumental, still-impressive synagogue, once adorned with the stone carvings of plants and animals still scattered around the site, now part of **Korazim National Park.** One remarkable artifact, a decorated and inscribed stone "armchair" dubbed the "Throne of Moses," is thought to have been used by the worthies of the community during the reading of the Torah (the Law). ⊠ *Rte. 8277* ☎ *04/693–4982* ⊕ *www.parks.org. il/ParksENG* ⊠ *NIS 18* ☉ *Apr.–Sept., Sat.–Thurs. 8–5, Fri. and Jewish holiday eves 8–4; Oct.–Mar. Sat.–Thurs. 8–4, Fri. and Jewish holiday eves 8–3.*

### Where to Stay & Eat

**$–$$**  ✕⊞ **Vered Hagalil.** The location is unbeatable, with lots of greenery and stunning views of the Sea of Galilee below. The units, from cozy cabins to suite-like cottages, successfully combine wood and dark local basalt rock, but the decor is sometimes jarring and the sofas are too firm. Especially inviting studio rooms have wood paneling and floors, and wood-burning stoves. Room TVs are available on request (for a fee). The restaurant ($–$$$) has a fine regional reputation for its hearty soups, salads, signature steaks, burgers, and chicken, but the menu is also kid-friendly. Save room for dessert, whatever your age. For many, the riding stables are still Vered Hagalil's calling card. ⊠ *Rtes. 8277 and 90, 12340* ☎ *04/693–5785* ☏ *04/693–4964* ⊕ *www.veredhagalil. co.il* ↬ *11 rooms, 8 suites* ⚷ *Restaurant, dining room, some kitchenettes, refrigerators, pool, hot tub, massage, billiards, horseback riding, Ping-Pong, bar, recreation room, babysitting, playground, dry cleaning, laundry service, Internet room, meeting rooms* ⊟ *AE, DC, MC, V.*

**$**  ⊞ **The Frenkels Bed and Breakfast.** The formerly American Frenkels retired to this rustic Galilee village on the border between the Lower and Upper Galilee (ideal for exploring either) and have made gracious hospitality a second career. Amid lovingly tended gardens and tantalizing views of the Sea of Galilee, each spacious unit has its own distinct character, courtesy of combinations of wood and stone, cane furniture, tiles, and throw rugs. The atmosphere is one of warmth and intimacy. ⊠ *Rte. 8277, 12391* ☎ *04/680–1686* ☏ *04/693–4467* ⊕ *www.thefrenkels. com* ↬ *1 room, 2 suites* ⚷ *Dining room, refrigerators, Internet room; no smoking* ⊟ *No credit cards* ❙⊙❙ *BP.*

## Mount of Beatitudes

★ ⑱  *8 km (5 mi) north of Ginosar, 3 km (2 mi) north of Capernaum Junction.*

Tradition identifies this tranquil hillside as the site of Jesus's most comprehensive teaching recorded in the New Testament as the Sermon on the Mount: "And seeing the multitudes, he went up into a mountain; and when he was set, his disciples came unto him. And he opened his mouth, and taught them, saying: 'Blessed are the poor in spirit, for theirs is the kingdom of Heaven . . .' " (Matthew 5). In 2000, Pope John Paul II celebrated mass with some 100,000 faithful a bit higher up the hill.

The domed **Roman Catholic church,** run by the Franciscan Sisters (Italian), was designed by the famous architect Barluzzi and completed in 1937. Windows are inscribed with the opening words (in Latin) of the Beatitudes, the initial "Blessed are . . ." verses from the Sermon on the

Mount. The terrace surrounding the church offers a superb view of the Sea of Galilee, best enjoyed in the afternoon, when the diffused western sun softens the light and heightens colors. Catholics and Protestants seem to feel equally at home at this site, where the sisters also run a pilgrim hospice. ⊠ *Rte. 8177, off Rte 90* ☏ *04/679–0978* ⊠ *NIS 5 per vehicle* ☉ *Apr.–Sept., daily 8–noon and 2:30–5; Oct.–Mar., daily 8–noon and 2:30–4.*

## Tabgha

**⑲**  *14 km (8 mi) north of Tiberias, at Capernaum Junction (Rtes. 90 and 87).*

The large, orange-roofed **Church of the Multiplication** was dedicated by the German Benedictines (Roman Catholic) in 1981 on the scanty remains of earlier shrines. The site has long been venerated as the "deserted place" of the Gospels, where Jesus miraculously multiplied two fish and five loaves of bread to feed the crowds that followed him. The present airy limestone building with the wooden truss ceiling was built in the style of a Byzantine basilica to give a fitting context to the beautifully wrought 5th-century mosaic floor. The nave is covered with geometric designs, but the front of the aisles is filled with flora and birds and, curiously, a Nilometer, a graded column once used to measure the flood level of the Nile for the purpose of assessing that year's collectible taxes. In front of the altar is the small and simple mosaic of the loaves and fishes, arguably the most famous mosaic in Israel. ⊠ *Rte. 87* ☏ *04/670–0180* ⊠ *Free* ☉ *Daily 8–5:20.*

The austere, black basalt **Church of the Primacy of St. Peter,** 200 yards east of the Church of the Multiplication, is built on the water's edge, over a flat rock known as Mensa Christi (the Table of Christ). After his resurrection, the New Testament relates, Jesus appeared to his disciples by the Sea of Galilee and breakfasted with them on a miraculous catch of fish. Three times Jesus asked the disciple Peter if he loved him, and after his reply of "You know that I love you," Jesus commanded him to "Feed my sheep." Some scholars see this affirmation as Peter's atonement for having thrice denied Jesus in Jerusalem after Jesus's arrest. The episode is seen as establishing Peter's "primacy" and, in the Roman Catholic tradition, that of the popes, his spiritual successors. Part of the Franciscan "Custody of the Holy Land," the site was included in the itineraries of both Pope Paul VI in 1964 and Pope John Paul II in 2000. ⊠ *Rte. 87* ☏ *04/672–4767* ⊠ *Free* ☉ *Daily 8–noon and 2–5.*

## Capernaum

**⑳**  *3 km (2 mi) east of Tabgha and the Capernaum Junction, 17 km (10½ mi) northeast of Tiberias.*

Capernaum (Kfar Nahum in Hebrew) was once a thriving town of merchants, farmers, and fishermen; today it is an archaeological site and two monasteries. The easterly monastery, distinguished by its reddomed, whitewashed church, is Greek Orthodox and is seldom visited. The westerly, Franciscan (Roman Catholic) one, at the first turnoff after Tabgha, is what you come to see.

The prosperity of this ancient Jewish community is immediately apparent from the remains of its **synagogue**, which dominates the complex. (It was excavated by the Franciscan friars in the early 20th century and partly restored.) The ancient Jewish community went to the expense of transporting white limestone blocks from afar to set the building off from the town's crudely built black-basalt houses. Stone benches line the inside walls, recalling the synagogue's original primary function as a place where the Torah was read and explained on Sabbaths and holidays. (The fixed synagogue liturgy used today was a later development.) Once thought to date to the 2nd or 3rd century AD, the synagogue is now regarded by many scholars as properly belonging to the later Byzantine period (4th–5th centuries AD). It is certainly not the actual one in which Jesus taught, but since consecrated ground was often reused, the small earlier structure in the excavation pit in the present building's southeastern corner may have been.

Jesus established his base in Capernaum for the three years of his ministry in the Galilee, where, the New Testament relates, he recruited some of his disciples ("Follow me, and I will make you fishers of men" [Matthew 4]), healed the afflicted, taught in the synagogue, and ultimately cursed the city for not heeding his message. Suspended from outer support pillars over the scanty remains of Capernaum's central Christian shrine, the **House of St. Peter** (where Jesus is believed to have lodged), a modern church follows the octagonal outline of the Byzantine basilica that once stood here.

Limestone reliefs that once graced the synagogue exterior represent a typical range of Jewish artistic motifs: the native fruits of the land, the biblical Ark of the Covenant, a seven-branched menorah, a shofar, and an incense shovel (to preserve the memory of the Jerusalem temple in which they were once used). Donors to the synagogue building fund were not forgotten: one Herod (recorded in Greek on a main column inside) and Alpheus (in Aramaic on a smaller one outside). A small 1st-century mosaic from Magdala shows a contemporary boat, complete with oars and sails—a dramatic illustration of the many New Testament and Jewish references to traffic and fishing on the lake. ✉ *Rte. 87* ☎ *04/672–1059* 🖃 *NIS 3* ⊗ *Daily 8–4:50.*

## Sports and the Outdoors

The so-called kayaks of **Abukayak** (✉ Jordan River Park, Rte. 888, north of Sea of Galilee ☎ 04/692–2245 or 04/692–1078) are really inflated rubber canoes. Abukayak offers a serene one-hour ride down the lower Jordan River, from March through November. Life jackets are provided, and the trip is appropriate for young children.

> **en route** | Route 87 continues east past Capernaum and crosses the **Jordan River**—somewhat muddy at this point—at the Arik Bridge. Those raised on spirituals extolling the Jordan's width and depth are often surprised to find how small a stream it really is: seldom more than 30 feet wide and shallow enough to wade in places. The Jordan enters the Sea of Galilee just a few hundred yards downstream. In this wetland area (now the Jordan Park, 1 km [½ mi] up Rte 888),

archaeologists have finally identified, excavated, and opened for tourism the elusive site of the ancient Jewish town of Bethsaida, Peter's birthplace according to the New Testament.

## Kursi & the Eastern Shore

*Kursi: 17 km (10½ mi) southeast of Capernaum on Rte. 92, 5 km (3 mi) north of Ein Gev.*

**㉑** Huddling under the imposing cliffs of the Golan Heights, where Route 789 climbs away from 92, **Kursi** is linked with the New Testament story of a man from Gadara (other gospels mention Gerasa) who was possessed by demons. Jesus exorcised the evil spirits, causing them to enter a herd of swine grazing nearby, which then "ran violently down a steep place into the lake, and were choked" (Matthew 8). Fifth-century Byzantine Christians identified the event with this spot (now a national park) and built a monastery here. It was an era in which the holy places, true and new, were inundated with earnest pilgrims, and the monastery prospered from their gifts. The partly restored ruins of a fine Byzantine church are a classic example of the basilica style common at the time; the ruined monastery is perched higher up the hillside. ⊠ *Rte. 92* 🏛 *04/673–1983* ⊕ *www.parks.org.il/ParksENG* 💲 *NIS 12* 🕙 *Apr.–Sep., Sat.–Thurs. 8–5, Fri. and Jewish holiday eves 8–4; Oct.–Mar., Sat.–Thurs. 8–4, Fri. and Jewish holiday eves 8–3.*

### Where to Stay & Eat

**¢–$$** ✕ **Ein Gev Fish Restaurant.** This popular establishment on the eastern shore bustles at lunchtime but is a fine dinner option as well. Famous for its St. Peter's fish (whole or filleted), it has added sea bream, trout, and gray mullet to its menu. Diners who want to avoid the baleful glare of a whole fish can opt instead for light entrées such as quiche, pizza, pasta, salads, and omelets. In fine weather, sit on the large outdoor terrace, and take in the long view across the lake to Tiberias. ⊠ *Kibbutz Ein Gev* 🏛 *04/665–8136* ⊟ *AE, DC, MC, V.*

**$$$** 🏨 **Ramot Resort Hotel.** Though high up in the foothills of the Golan Heights, this hotel is only a few minutes' drive from good beaches and a water park. Its main building has comfortable, well-appointed guest rooms, each with a very private balcony and a fabulous lake view. The deluxe wood chalets are in a different class, however, and have their own whirlpool tubs, saunas, entertainment systems, and other little perks. For a family on a more limited budget, the "nature cabins" may provide an excellent solution. Free guided tours of the area are available in summer. ⊠ *East of Rte. 92, 12490* 🏛 *04/673–2636* 🖨 *04/679–3590* ⊕ *www.ramot-nofesh.co.il* 🛏 *80 rooms, 12 chalets, 17 nature cabins* ⟡ *Coffee shop, dining room, cable TV, Wi-Fi, pool, exercise equipment, massage, Ping-Pong, bar, piano, shop, babysitting, dry cleaning, laundry service, meeting rooms, free parking* ⊟ *AE, DC, MC, V* 🍴 *BP.*

**$$** 🏨 **Ein Gev Holiday Village.** Located on the palm-shaded eastern shore, with lawns, a pebbly beach, and a view across the lake to Tiberias, the complex offers several options: spacious motel-style "hotel" rooms, some with a view; waterfront "deluxe" units, with a sunset-watching patio and barbecue; similar but larger "apartments," designed for families; and older family cottages (called "kafriot"), some close to the water, others not. All rooms have showers only; equipped kitchenettes and an on-site minimarket open up self-catering options. About a mile away, Kibbutz Ein Gev, which runs the village, has a famous fish restaurant, small harbor, and wagon-train ride. ⊠ *Rte. 92, 12 km (7½ mi) north of Tzemach Junction, Ein Gev 14940* ☎ *04/665–9800* 🖷 *04/665–9818* ⊕ *www.eingev.com* ⇥ *184 rooms* ♿ *Restaurant, kitchenettes, miniature golf, boating* ▤ *AE, DC, MC, V* ⦿ *BP.*

★ $$   🏨 **Ma'agan.** This kibbutz is located at the southern tip of the Sea of Galilee, with arguably the most enchanting view of all the properties around the lake. Furnishings are comfortable but not sumptuous. Choose between a regular guest room and a spacious suite that includes a living room (with a lake-view picture window and sofas that become beds), a small bedroom, a kitchenette, and a patio. The food is unmemorable, but the facilities—sandy beach, swimming pool near the shore, extensive lawns—make it the best deal in the area. There is a smaller pool and a play area for kids. ⊠ *Rte. 92, 1 km (½ mi) east of Tzemach Junction, M. P. Jordan Valley 15160* ☎ *04/665–4411* 🖷 *04/665–4455* ⊕ *www.maagan. com* ⇥ *36 rooms, 112 suites* ♿ *Dining room, BBQs, some kitchenettes, pool, wading pool, beach, windsurfing, boating, Ping-Pong, bar, shop, babysitting, laundry facilities, Internet room, meeting rooms, free parking* ▤ *AE, DC, MC, V* ⦿ *BP.*

¢   🏕 **Kibbutz Ha'on.** On the southeastern shore of the lake, this is a fine location for camping. There are full cooking and washing facilities, beach access, and a store, but there is no tent rental; you need to provide your own. There's also free admission to an ostrich farm with activities for kids. ⊠ *M. P. Jordan Valley 15170* ☎ *04/665–6555* 🖷 *04/665–6557* ⊕ *www.haon.co.il* ♿ *Beach, laundry service* ▤ *AE, DC, MC, V* ☉ *Closed Nov.–Mar.*

## Nightlife & the Arts

The cultural center **Bet Gabriel** (⊠ 650 feet east of Tzemach Junction, west of Ma'agan ☎ 04/675–1175 🖷 04/675–1187) is located on the southern shores of the Sea of Galilee, only a 10-minute drive from Tiberias. Its fine architecture, beautiful garden setting, and concert facilities have established its popularity in the area. Tiberias's Tourist Information Office and major hotels carry information on the month's performances and art exhibits.

The **Ein Gev Spring Festival** (⊕ bg@betgabriel.co.il), which has been going since the 1940s, once hosted the likes of Bernstein and Rampal, Dietrich and Sinatra, but its focus today is Israeli vocal music, from traditional to contemporary. It is held on Kibbutz Ein Gev during the Passover holiday but is organized by Bet Gabriel. E-mail ahead for dates and details, being sure to mention the festival in the subject line.

## Sports & the Outdoors

**Golan Beach** (⊠ Rte. 92, 7 km [4½ mi] north of Ein Gev ☎ 04/673–1750) is the veteran beach on the northeastern shore of the lake. Its wide range of attractions include powerboat, rowboat, kayak, and pedal-boat rentals; waterskiing; and the inflatable, power-towed "banana." There is no lifeguard, however.

**Dugit Beach** (⊠ Rte. 92, 8 km [5 mi] north of Ein Gev ☎ 04/673–1750) is a stone's throw north of Golan Beach. The neighbors are now under one management and provide similar recreational facilities, but Dugit has lifeguards.

**Lunagal,** a popular water park within Golan Beach, has pools, water slides, and other diversions for kids. ⊠ *Rte. 92, 7 km (4½ mi) north of Ein Gev* ☎ *04/673–1750* ☒ *NIS 60 Apr.–June and Sept.–Oct., NIS 80 July–Aug.* ☉ *Call for hours.*

**Ein Gev** (⊠ Rte. 92 ☎ 04/665–9800) has a beach near its holiday village, halfway down the lake's eastern shore.

At the southern tip of the lake, **Ma'agan** (⊠ Rte. 98 ☎ 04/665–4411) has a shaded lawn, a fine pool, and a beach.

## Hammat Gader

☾ ❷ *10 km (6 mi) east of Tzemach Junction on Rte. 98, 22 km (14 mi) southeast of Tiberias, 36 km (22½ mi) northeast of Bet She'an.*

Named for its patron city, Gadara, high up the southern bank of the Yarmuk River (today in Jordan), Hammat Gader was, in its heyday, the second-largest spa in the Roman Empire (after Baiae, near Naples). Built around three hot springs, Hammat Gader's impressive complex of baths and pools attests to the opulence that once attracted voluptuaries and invalids alike. In its time, the entrance corridor was kept dimly lit to dramatize the effect of the fine ornamental pool beyond. The large number of ancient clay oil lamps found in one small pool is proof of nighttime bathing and a hint that this area might have been set aside for lepers, to keep them out of sight of the regular patrons. Today, Hammat Gader is immensely popular among the locals, who come for the freshwater pool, giant water slide, alligator farm, performing parrots, petting zoo, and restaurants. Note: At press time, the Israel Ministry of Health had issued a warning that there were dangerous levels of bacteria in the public pools. The antiquities were currently closed, pending resolution of a dispute over jurisdiction and some safety-related renovations. The partial view from the embankment overlooking the site still gives a pretty good idea of the whole. ⊠ *Rte. 98* ☎ *04/665–9999* ⊕ *www.hamat-gader.com* ☒ *Sun.–Thurs. NIS 69; Fri., Sat., Jewish holiday eves and holidays NIS 79; after 5 PM Wed., Thurs., and Sat. NIS 50; after 8 PM Wed. and Thurs. NIS 39* ☉ *Mon.–Fri. 7 AM–11 PM, Sat. 7 AM–10 PM, Sun. 7–5; children's attractions, alligator farm, and antiquities until 5; last entry to park 1 hr before closing.*

### Where to Stay

★ **$$$$** ⊞ **Spa Village.** Though only a few yards away from the recreation park, the spa-hotel complex is a world apart. Superbly outfitted wooden cabin-suites all include Jacuzzis using thermal mineral water from the nearby springs; a few have their own saunas as well. Treatment rooms and exercise equipment are for hotel guests only. The warm mineral pool area, a serene oasis of comfort and good taste in a canyonesque landscape by day, feels almost mystical when you take the torchlit waters at night. The rest of the park is free for hotel guests. On weekends (Thursday and Friday nights), there is a minimum two-night stay. ⊠ *Hammat Gader 15171* ☎ *04/665–5555* ⊕ *www.hamat-gader.com* ⚲ *29 suites* ⚱ *Restaurant, coffee shop, snack bar, in-room safes, minibars, cable TV with movies, Wi-Fi, pool, exercise equipment, spa, dry cleaning, laundry service, Internet room, free parking* ⊟ *AE, DC, MC, V* ⍨⊙ *BP.*

## Degania & Kinneret

*Degania Alef: 10 km (6 mi) south of Tiberias, Kinneret: 2 km (1 mi) northwest of Degania Alef.*

**㉓** The first kibbutz, the collective village of **Degania Alef** was founded in 1909 by Jewish pioneers from Eastern Europe and established here at its permanent site on the banks of the Jordan River the following year. (Alef is the "A" of the Hebrew alphabet; don't confuse the kibbutz with its younger neighbor, Degania Bet ["B"].) Near the entrance is a small Syrian tank of French World War II vintage. On May 15, 1948, the day after Israel declared its independence, it was invaded from all sides by Arab armies. Syrian forces came down the Yarmuk Valley from the east, overran two other kibbutzim en route, and were only stopped here, at the gates of Degania. The lead tank was set alight by a teenager with a Molotov cocktail.

Within restored stone buildings of the early kibbutz is the museum of **Bet Gordon** (A. D. Gordon House), named for the spiritual mentor of the early pioneers. It houses two collections: one devoted to the region's natural history, the other examining the history and archaeology of human settlement in the surrounding valleys. Among the prehistoric sites represented is Ubeidiya, just south of the kibbutz and Israel's oldest human settlement, which scholars now date back to 1¼ million years ago. ⊠ *Near Rte. 90* ☎ *04/675–0040* ⚱ *NIS 13* ⊙ *Sun.–Thurs. 9–3, Fri. and Jewish holiday eves 10–1.*

**㉔** Just across the Jordan from Degania, **Kinneret** was founded in 1911 as the country's second kibbutz, taking its name from the Hebrew word for the Sea of Galilee. Two places in the immediate vicinity are of interest to travelers.

On a picturesque stretch of the Jordan, where huge eucalyptus trees droop into the quiet water, is **Yardenit,** developed in recent years as a baptism site for Christian pilgrims. The baptism of Jesus by John the Baptist is traditionally identified with the southern reaches of the Jordan River, near Jericho. However, that area was controlled by Jordan from 1949 to 1967 and then became a hostile frontier between Israel and Jordan following the Six-Day War. Pilgrims began to seek out accessible spots beyond the conflict zone. Here you will often see groups of white-robed pilgrims being immersed in the river amid prayers and hymns and expressions of joy. There are showers and changing facilities, towels and robes for rent in the souvenir shop, and a decent restaurant. ⊠ *Off Rte.*

*90 ☎ 04/675–9111 ⊕ www.yardenit.com ☉ Sat.–Thurs. 8–5, Fri. 8–4, Jewish holiday eves 8–3.*

The serene **cemetery of Kibbutz Kinneret** (✉ Off Rte. 90, 600 yards south of junction with Rte. 767 ☎ No phone) includes the grave of Rachel *Hameshoreret* (Rachel the Poetess), a virtual shrine for many Israelis. The cemetery offers a superb view of the lake, the Golan Heights, and rarely, majestic Mt. Hermon, to the north. Among the other distinguished denizens of this ground are pioneer leaders of the early Zionist movement. A few steps down from the clearing brings you to Rachel's grave, identified by the low stone seat attached to it.

The pebbles left on her grave by visitors (a token of respect in the Jewish tradition) is a tribute to Rachel's renown and to the romantic hold she has on the national imagination. Born in Russia, she immigrated in 1909 to "Eretz Yisrael", where she lived and worked on the first kibbutzim. She was in France studying agriculture when World War I broke out. Unable to get back into Ottoman Turkish Palestine because of her Russian citizenship, she spent the war years working with refugee children in Russia, where she contracted the tuberculosis that eventually took her life. She returned after the war, but died, impoverished, in 1931.

Rachel became a poet of national stature in Hebrew, an acquired language. The modern flavor and immediacy of her poems made them natural lyrics for a new genre of modern Israeli folk songs. Rachel wrote with great sensitivity of the beauty of this region and with passion— knowing that her end was near—of her frustrated dream of raising a family. Her tombstone is eloquently devoid of biographical information; it carries the only name by which she is known, Rachel, and four lines from one of her poems: "Spread out your hands, look yonder: /nothing comes. /Each man has his Nebo /in the great expanse." (It was from Mt. Nebo that Moses looked into the promised land that he knew he would never enter.) In a recess in the stone seat by the grave site is a canister containing a complete volume (in Hebrew) of Rachel's poems.

The site is not signposted, but look for it at a bend in Route 90 barely 1 km (½ mi) north of the Jordan River bridge. There is a low stone wall on the right as you travel toward Tiberias. Coming from the other direction, you cannot cross the road: continue a few hundred yards and turn around in the lot of the small gas station and general store.

## Sports & the Outdoors

In late October or early November, you can join a **bike ride around the Sea of Galilee,** which ends at the Tzemach Junction. Road distances are 12 km (7½ mi), 25 km (15½ mi), and a complete 65-km (40-mi) ring around the lake, while dirt-track options consist of 16 km (10 mi) and a very challenging 25-km (15½-mi) route.

# Hammat Tiberias

★ ㉕ *7 km (4 mi) north of Kinneret, 2 km (1 mi) south of Tiberias.*

Here in **Hammat Tiberias National Park** you'll find Israel's hottest spring, gushing out of the earth at 60°C (140°F). The healing properties of its mineral-rich waters were already recognized in antiquity, as evidenced by the ruins of ancient towns—including an exquisite 4th-century AD mosaic floor of a synagogue. Legend says that Solomon, the great king of Israel, wanted a hot bath and used his awesome authority to force some young devils below ground to heat the water. The fame of the salubrious springs spread far and wide, bringing the afflicted to seek relief. Seeing such gladness among his subjects, Solomon worried about what would happen when he died and the devils stopped their labors. In a flash of the wisdom for which he was renowned, Solomon made the hapless devils deaf. To this day, they have not heard of the king's demise and so continue to heat the water for fear of his wrath.

The scientific explanation is almost tame by comparison. This and other hot mineral springs in Israel were created by upheavals along the Great Syrian-African Rift, the world's longest fault line. Cracks in the earth's crust allow mineral-rich water to boil to the surface.

By the end of the Second Temple period (the 1st century AD), when settlement in the Sea of Galilee region was at its height, a Jewish town called Hammat (Hot Springs) stood here. With time, Hammat was overshadowed by its newer neighbor, Tiberias, and became known as Hammat Teverya (Tiberias Hot Springs). The benefits of the mineral hot springs were already legendary: a coin minted in Tiberias during the rule of Emperor Trajan, around AD 100, shows Hygeia, the goddess of health, sitting on a rock with a spring gushing out beneath it.

Parts of ancient Hammat have been uncovered on the mountain side of the road, bringing to light a number of ruined synagogues built one upon the other. The most dramatic dates from the 4th century AD, with an elaborate mosaic floor that uses motifs almost identical to those at Bet Alfa: classical Jewish symbols, human figures representing the four seasons and the signs of the zodiac, and the Greek god Helios at the center. The mosaics of Hammat Tiberias are among the finest ever found in Israel. Later cultures exploited the hot springs, too, as the small adjacent Turkish bath attests. Behind Hammat Tiberias, a turquoise dome marks the **tomb of Rabbi Meir Ba'al Ha-Ness,** the "Miracle Worker," who supposedly took a vow that he would not lie down until the Messiah came—and was therefore buried in an upright position. His name has become an emblem for charitable organizations, and many a miracle has been attributed to the power of prayer at his tomb. ⊠ *Rte. 90* ☎*04/672–5287* ⊕*www.parks.org.il/ParksENG* ⊡*NIS 12* ⊙*Apr.–Sept., Sat.–Thurs. 8–5, Fri. and Jewish holiday eves 8–4; Oct.–Mar., Sat.–Thurs. 8–4, Fri. and Jewish holiday eves 8–3.*

**Tiberias Hot Springs,** on the lake side of the road, is one of two modern spa facilities fed by the mineral spring (the other, on the mountain side of the road, is exclusively for medical use). In addition to sophisticated therapeutic services and facilities, it has a large, warm indoor mineral pool (35°C or 95°F) and a small outdoor one right near the lake's edge. A restaurant serves lunch. ⊠ *Rte. 90* ☎ *04/672–8500* ⊡ *Pools NIS 60, NIS 35 Sun.–Thurs. after 4 and Fri. after 2* ⊙ *Sun., Mon. and Wed., 8–8; Tues. and Thurs. 8 AM–11 PM; Fri. 8–4, Sat. 8:30–6.*

# LOWER GALILEE ESSENTIALS

## Transportation

### BY BOAT

At press time, scheduled sailings on the Sea of Galilee between Tiberias and Ein Gev had been discontinued. It is sometimes possible to join a chartered cruise (offered by three operators) if the primary customer is amenable. Boats, with a capacity of 60–170 passengers, can sail to any of the following anchorages: Tiberias, Ein Gev, Ginosar, and Capernaum. Most crossings take 45 minutes to an hour and are comfortable in almost all weather. The cost is about NIS 45.

🚩 **Holyland Sailing** ⊠ Tiberias Marina, Tiberias ☎ 04/672–3006 or 672–3007. **Kinneret Sailing** ⊠ Rte. 92, Kibbutz Ein Gev ☎ 04/675–8008 or 04/675–8009. **Lido Kinneret** ⊠ Gedud Barak St., Tiberias ☎ 04/672–1538.

### BY BUS

The most important sights in the region are accessible by bus, but the sometimes infrequent local service and transfers can make bus travel time-consuming. Bet She'an, Nazareth, Tiberias, and Tabgha are on the main routes; other places, such as Megiddo and the Mount of Beatitudes are a bit of a walk from a nearby junction—or even a good hike, as in the case of Bet She'arim, Capernaum, and Mt. Tabor. Belvoir and parts of Mt. Gilboa are inaccessible without a car.

The Egged bus cooperative provides regular service from Jerusalem, Tel Aviv, and Haifa to Bet She'an, Afula, Nazareth, and Tiberias. There is no direct service from Ben Gurion International Airport; change in Tel Aviv or Haifa. There are several buses an hour from Tel Aviv to Afula (1½ hours). Bus 842 (Direct, or "Yashir") is quickest; Buses 829, 830, and 835 are Express, stopping at main stations en route. Bus 823 from Afula to Nazareth (20 minutes) is infrequent—no more than six a day. The 830 and 835 continue from Afula to Tiberias (about an hour). The 829 and 843 link Afula to Bet She'an (20 minutes) three times a day. To get from Haifa to Tiberias, take the slow Bus 430 (about an hour), which leaves hourly from Merkazit Hamifratz. From the same Haifa station, the slow Bus 301 leaves two or three times an hour for Afula. Buses from Jerusalem to Bet She'an and Tiberias (Buses 961, 963, 966, and the slower 948) depart roughly hourly; change in Bet She'an for Afula, where you change again for Nazareth. Buses 961 and 963 continue to Tiberias. The ride to Bet She'an is about two hours, to Tiberias another 25 minutes. Bus 431 connects Nazareth and Tiberias once every two hours.

🚩 **Egged** ☎ 03/694–8888 or *2800 ⊕ www.egged.co.il/Eng.

### BY CAR

From Tel Aviv, the Lower Galilee can be reached by taking Route 2 north (the Tel Aviv–Haifa Highway) and then heading northeast along one of two regional roads: Route 65 (near Caesarea), emerging into the Jezreel Valley at Megiddo (80 km [50 mi], 1¼ hours), or Route 70 (near Zichron Ya'akov), emerging at Yokne'am (90 km [57 mi], 1½ hours). In good weather, traffic is heavy north out of Tel Aviv from morning to midday

Friday and returning south to Tel Aviv Saturday afternoon and early evening. Access from Haifa is on Route 75 east to Bet She'arim and Nazareth (35 km [22 mi], 45 minutes to Nazareth) or from Route 75 to Routes 70 and 66 south to Megiddo (34 km [22 mi], 40 minutes). The best routes from Jerusalem are Route 1 east to Route 90 north to Bet She'an (124 km [78 mi], 2 hours) and Route 1 west to Route 6 north to Route 65 northeast to Megiddo.

Driving is the best way to explore this region. The main roads are good—some newer four-lane highways are excellent—but some smaller roads are narrow and sometimes in need of repair. Signposting is generally clear (and in English), with route numbers clearly marked. Ask directions by destination, because most Israelis have basically ignored the innovation of route numbers. Most sights and accommodations are indicated by brown signs. You'll find gas stations and refreshment stands all over.

### BY TAXI

While fine for a local trip, a taxi is generally an uninspiring and expensive way to travel the countryside. Theoretically, cab drivers are supposed to operate their meters outside cities as well, but it is quite acceptable to negotiate a fare beforehand. It's best to get the hotel staff to set it up with the dispatcher.

🚖 **Abu el-Assal** ✉ Nazareth ☎ 04/655-4745. **Diana** ✉ Nazareth ☎ 04/655-5554. **Ha'emek** ✉ Tiberias ☎ 04/672-0131. **Hagalil** ✉ Tiberias ☎ 04/672-0353. **Yizre'el** ✉ Afula ☎ 04/652-3111.

## Contacts & Resources

### BANKS & EXCHANGING SERVICES

Standing in line at a bank to change money should be a last resort. The hours are inconvenient and rates of exchange discouraging. Most visitors prefer ATMs or, where available, private exchange bureaus. Hotels offer poor rates but great convenience: a good option if the amount is not large.

In Nazareth there is an ATM at the bottom of Casa Nova Street, below the Church of the Annunciation; two exchange bureaus are nearby on Paulus VI Street. The ATM at Bank Leumi, at the corner of the access road to the Bet She'an National Park, is a useful option. Tiberias is a far more tourist-oriented town. There are two or three ATMs and a couple of exchange bureaus on and around the intersection of Hayarden and Habanim Streets.

### EMERGENCIES

The emergency numbers for police, ambulance/first aid, and the fire department are standard throughout Israel.

Hotels generally have doctors on call. Of the Nazareth hospitals, the English Hospital may make communication easiest. Call 101 to find out what pharmacy is on late-night duty. The closest hospital to Tiberias is Poriah, but first try the 24-hour Emergency Medical Service, which has a doctor on duty, inside the Magen David Adom ambulance station, opposite the Jordan River Hotel. The local branch of the Superpharm drugstore chain is open Sunday–Thursday 8 AM–10 PM, Friday 7:30–4:30, and Saturday 10 AM–11 PM.

**⚡ Ambulance service/first aid** ☎ 101. **Emergency Medical Service** ✉ Habanim St., at Kishon St., Tiberias ☎ 04/671-7611. **English Hospital** ✉ next to YMCA, Nazareth ☎ 04/602-8888. **Fire department** ☎ 102. **Pharmacies** ☎ 101. **Police** ☎ 100. **Poriah Hospital** ✉ Poriah, Tiberias ☎ 04/665-2211. **Superpharm** ✉ 1 Hayarden St., Tiberias ☎ 04/671-6663.

### INTERNET, MAIL & SHIPPING

Nazareth and, to a much greater extent, Tiberias are the only two towns in the region that have serious tourism infrastructure. Apart from its hotels, however, Nazareth offers little technological sophistication. In Tiberias, Solan, on the midrachov (near the Caesar, Jordan River, and Sheraton Moriah hotels), offers Internet access, long-distance telephone calls, and various office services. It is open Sunday–Friday 8:30 AM–11 PM and Saturday from nightfall to 11 PM.

Apart from providing the usual mail services, some post offices change foreign currency at a decent rate (Tiberias) and offer EMS international courier service (Tiberias and Nazareth). The Nazareth branch is open Monday, Wednesday, Thursday, and Friday 8–12:30 and 4–6; Tuesday 8–1:30; and Saturday 8–1. The hours of the Tiberias downtown branch are Sunday 8–12:30 and 3:30–6:30; Monday, Tuesday, and Thursday 8–12:30 and 3:30–6; Wednesday 8–1; and Friday 8–noon. (Note that there are other branches in both towns that don't provide these services.)

**⚡ Post Office** ✉ Paulus VI St., Nazareth ☎ 04/655-4659 ✉ Ha'atzmaut (Rabin) Sq., Tiberias ☎ 04/679-0066. **Solan** ✉ Midrachov, Tiberias ☎ 04/672-6470.

### TOUR OPTIONS

The variety and frequency of guaranteed-departure, one- or two-day tours in Israel were drastically reduced because of the downturn in tourism in the early 2000s. Much of the tourism is back, but the day trips have not quite revived. At present, Galilee itineraries start from Jerusalem and Tel Aviv only; it can be tricky to link up with them if you're already in the north. Both Egged Tours and United Tours run one-day tours three times a week that take in Nazareth, Capernaum, Tabgha, the Sea of Galilee, Tiberias, and the Jordan River. Current prices are US$60 from Tel Aviv, $64 from Jerusalem. (The two companies often cooperate and combine their bookings in one bus.) United Tours also has a two-day itinerary three times a week that includes Capernaum, Tabgha, the Sea of Galilee, Tiberias, the Jordan River, Tzfat, and Banias (Upper Galilee), the Golan Heights, and Bet She'an. The cost is $198, including dinner, lodging, and breakfast.

Matan Tours, based in Tiberias, operates a guide-driven limo-van for a day tour of some Sea of Galilee sites and the Golan Heights. The cost is $45 per person, and a minimum of five passengers—an organized party or unrelated individuals—is required. A comfortable and efficient alternative is a custom tour in a guide-driven car or van. Though not cheap for a couple, custom tours become cost-effective for a larger party.

Most people traveling this way reach the region in the company of their Jerusalem- or Tel Aviv–based licensed guide.

Vered Hagalil, at Korazim Junction, specializes in short and long horseback tours above and around the Sea of Galilee. The outfit offers very comfortable accommodations and a good restaurant as well.
🚩 **Egged Tours** ⊠ 4 Bareket St., Petach Tikva ☎ 03/694-8888 or *2800 ⊕ www.egged. co.il/Eng. **Matan Tours** ⊠ Aviv Hotel, 66 Hagalil St., Tiberias 14200 ☎ 04/672-3510 or 054/461-6148. **United Tours** ⊠ 68 Mivtza Kadesh St., Bnei Brak 51200 ☎ 03/616-2656 or 03/693-3412 ⊕ www.inisrael.com/united. **Vered Hagalil** ⊠ Rte. 90, Korazim Junction 12340 ☎ 04/693-5785 🖷 04/693-4964 ⊕ www.veredhagalil.co.il.

SPECIAL-
INTEREST TOURS
The Hebrew University of Jerusalem and Tiberias Excavations run week-long programs in the summer for volunteers who want to join Tiberias's dig excavation. Tel Aviv University and The Megiddo Expedition have three- and four-week-long programs, also in the summer, to join the excavations at Megiddo, the traditional site of Armageddon.
🚩 **The Megiddo Expedition** ⊕ www.megiddo.tau.ac.il.

**Tiberias Excavation** 🖷 02/582-5548 ⊕ www.tiberiasexcavation.com.

### VISITOR INFORMATION

The Nazareth Tourist Information Office, down the street from the Church of the Annunciation (near the intersection of Paulus VI and Casa Nova streets), is open Monday–Friday 8:30–5 and Saturday 9–1. The Tiberias Tourist Information Office, which provides information for the whole Sea of Galilee region, is located in a restored Crusader building opposite the Sheraton Moriah Hotel. Its hours are Sunday–Thursday 9–4:30 and Friday 9–1. The Jordan Valley Regional Council provides information about annual Sea of Galilee area sporting events, including the fall bike ride, Kinneret Swim, and Big Walk.
🚩 **Jordan Valley Regional Council** ⊠ Tzemach Junction 15132 ☎ 04/675-7630 or 04/675-7631 🖷 04/675-7641. **Tourist Information Office** ⊠ Casa Nova St., Nazareth ☎ 04/657-3003 or 04/657-0555 ⊠ Habanim St., between Jordan River and Sheraton Moriah hotels, Tiberias ☎ 04/672-5666.

# Upper Galilee & the Golan

INCLUDING TZFAT (SAFED)

## WORD OF MOUTH

"Don't miss a visit to Tzfat (there are various spellings). It is a beautiful village with an artist's colony and lovely views. Very Orthodox, so don't go there on a Saturday—everything will be closed."

—Lisa

"For places to stay, Tzfat is okay as a base, but not quite as handy as places near the lake or in the Hula Valley, since you have to drive up and down the hills to get anywhere."

—Howard

"Look at some of the bed and breakfast places in Rosh Pina . . . it's a more convenient base, and a very beautiful one."

—Gardyloo

By Lisa Perlman

Updated by
Miriam
Feinberg
Vamosh

**THE UPPER GALILEE OFFERS A CORNUCOPIA** of attractions that have right-fully earned Israel its reputation as a destination of amazing variety. The mountain air is redolent with the fragrance of spice plants; visitors can hike, horseback ride, or cycle along trails that range from challenging to family-oriented; and opportunities for kayaking, bird-watching, and wine-tasting abound. These are the best vacation treats, all in a fascinating historical setting. The region's rustic restaurants, B&Bs, and ethnic diversity also contribute to its special personality. Travelers are attracted to major cities—Tzfat in the rugged Galilee mountains and Katzrin in the Golan Heights—which are a study in contrasts. The former is immersed in Jewish mysticism, and the latter is the result of a hardheaded determination to secure Israel's border with Syria by establishing a modern town in what was once a battlefield.

The area's diversity also extends to its topography: the undulating hills of Western Galilee push upward into sharp limestone and basalt formations, bordered on the north by Lebanon and on the east by the volcanic, mountainous Golan Heights, beyond which lies Syria. The dominant feature of the Upper Galilee and the Golan is Mt. Hermon—Israel's highest mountain (towering 9,230 feet), and the home of Israel's sole ski resort.

Mount Hermon is Israel's "sponge" as well as its ski slope: huge volumes of water from winter snow and rainfalls soak into its limestone, emerging at the base of the mountain in an abundance of springs that feed the Jordan River and its tributaries and provide half of Israel's water supply. The water also sustains lush foliage that thrives year round and is home to wildcats, hyraxes, gazelles, and hundreds of species of birds.

This water, and the strategic vantage points of the Galilee mountaintops and the Golan Heights, have made the region a source of political contention since time immemorial. Over the centuries, Egyptians, Canaanites, Israelites, Romans, Byzantines, Muslims, Crusaders, and Ottomans locked horns here; in just the previous century the borders have been changed by Russia, Britain, France, and of course, Israel and Syria.

Borders are not the only things that have shifted here. A geological fault line, the Syrian-African Rift, cuts straight through the 30-km-long (19-mi-long) Hula Valley; in 1837 Tzfat and Tiberias were razed by an earthquake, though no significant rumbles have been heard since. Extinct volcanic cones give the Golan its unusual topographic profile.

With all this water and fertile soil, the region has long been an agricultural center and is today studded with apple orchards, kiwi plantations, fish ponds, sunflowers, and vineyards. The pastoral beauty and variety of outdoor activities attract people from elsewhere in Israel and the world, providing the region's other main industry: tourism.

Proximity to Lebanon and Syria does not ordinarily deter people from visiting the Upper Galilee and the Golan. On the contrary, the combination of an exciting past with a gorgeous natural setting draws visitors from all over. In times of particular unrest, however, *see* Safety *in* Smart Travel Tips for travel advisory contact information.

**6**

A day trip to the Golan Heights from Tiberias is doable but there's something about the soft gurgling of the brooks, the lush foliage of the forests, and the crisp mountain air of the Golan Heights that slows the pace. Three or four days is ideal for a leisurely exploration of the region including wine-tasting, hiking a piece of wilderness, country meals, kayaking, or just kicking back in a room with a stunning view. The ideal way to see this area is by car, although local buses will get you almost anywhere you want to go if you have plenty of time. Note: touring in the Upper Galilee and the Golan is usually safe. If, however, security demands unusual caution, certain areas may be temporarily inaccessible to visitors.

*Numbers in the text correspond to numbers in the margin and on the Upper Galilee & the Golan map and the Tzfat (Safed) map.*

**If you have**

**1 day**

Visitors based in Tiberias or elsewhere in the Lower Galilee or Western Galilee should head straight for the northernmost part of the region, starting with a walk through the **Tel Dan** 🔟 or **Hermon River (Banias)** 🔟 nature reserve and lunching on Dan River trout. Then they can either tackle **Nimrod's Fortress** 🔟, or take a chairlift to the top of **Mt. Hermon** 🔟. Another afternoon option is to try wine-tasting in **Katzrin** 🔟–🔟. Moving in a different, direction, with variety but fewer stops, spend a morning spent strolling through the Old City in **Tzfat** 🔟–🔟 and an afternoon kayaking on the Jordan River in summer and fall.

**If you have**

**2–3 days**

The more the days, the more the options. Tiberias is a good starting point; either spend a morning by the Sea of Galilee or head for **Tzfat** 🔟–🔟 and take a walk through the Old City. Stop in **Rosh Pina** 🔟 for a look at the handicrafts boutiques; then check out the wetlands at the **Hula Nature Reserve** 🔟. Spend the night in a kibbutz guest house; the next day, head for the Golan Heights via Route 98, overlooking the Disengagement Zone between Israel and Syria. The third day is well spent outdoors—horseback riding, kayaking or rafting on the Jordan River, or Jeep touring.

Since their arrival at the turn of the 20th century, the Jews have confronted a host of hardships and hurdles. Yet the tenacious Galileans will say there's no better place to live. Only four hours' drive from hectic Tel Aviv and visceral Jerusalem, visitors find this truly is another world.

### Top 5 Reasons to Go

- **The Old City of Tzfat:** It's a study in contrasts. The tiny historic synagogues are a rare taste of Jewish houses of worship from bygone days, while the galleries, especially in the underadvertised lanes off the main tourist drag, are a palette of contemporary colors and shapes.

- **Kayaking on the Jordan River:** A cool ride downriver can be a strenuous hard-hatted adventure or a tame family float, and adds an unusual accent to northern Galilee days, not least because the very option is a surprise.

- **The Hula Nature Reserve:** A bird-watcher's paradise, the Hula Reserve provides shelter for hundreds of species of birds, some 500 million of which fly over the Hula Valley twice a year on their migrations between Europe and Africa. The sight and sound of the thousands of whooping gray cranes that winter here is a particular treat.

- **Hermon River Nature Reserve:** A hike to the Banias waterfall and the Crusader ruins is memorable, and magnificently fragrant in the spring. A freshly baked pita from the Druze mill along the way will definitely hit the spot.

- **Gamla:** The scene of the heroic last stand of its residents following a siege by the Romans in AD 67, and true in appearance to its description in ancient sources, offers a challenging hike or an easy amble, all with glimpses of wildlife, especially soaring birds of prey.

## Exploring Upper Galilee & the Golan

The northern Jordan Valley serves as the border between these two regions, with the hilly Upper Galilee lying to the west and the Golan, a basalt plateau, to the east. Together, however, they are still small enough to be combined in a weekend trip.

### About the Restaurants

The inherent attractions of the Upper Galilee and the Golan—its verdant hills, old stone dwellings, and crisp, appetite-whetting air—are an exquisite backdrop for some excellent restaurants. Tuck into hearty steaks in the middle of the forest, fresh grilled Dan River trout in shady groves on the river's banks, Middle Eastern fare prepared by Druze villagers, or home-style Jewish cooking in the heart of the holy city of Tzfat. Excellent local wines enhance any meal: try the Mt. Hermon red, Gamla cabernet sauvignon, and Yarden cabernet blanc and merlot. Most restaurants are open every day except Yom Kippur; in a few places, however (Tzfat, for example), it's hard to find one on Shabbat (Friday afternoon until Saturday sundown). Attire is always informal, but it's best to dress modestly in Tzfat.

| WHAT IT COSTS In Israeli shekels | | | | |
|---|---|---|---|---|
| **$$$$** | **$$$** | **$$** | **$** | **¢** |
| RESTAURANTS over NIS 100 | NIS 76–NIS 100 | NIS 50–NIS 75 | NIS 32–NIS 49 | under NIS 32 |

Prices are for a main course at dinner.

### About the Hotels

There are few grand hotels here, but the ample selection of guest houses and inns ranges from ranch-style to home-style. As the local tourist industry has developed, many communities, especially kibbutzim and moshavim, have added hotels (or guest wings attached to homes). Some have an extensive range of amenities including activities for children.

**6**

**Hiking** Superb nature reserves and national parks make this region a prime destination for hikers. Most trails are well marked; stick to the tracks to avoid any trouble. Always carry water and wear a hat, especially in summer; wear comfortable shoes as well. You may want to take an extra pair of shoes in case you get wet—there's an abundance of water in these parts.

**Horseback Riding** Horseback riding has really taken off in the Upper Galilee. It's an excellent way to see and appreciate Israel's beautiful northern landscape.

**Jeep Tours** Jeep tours are very popular here. Needless to say, Jeeps can cover more distance in less time than your legs or a horse's, and they add a dash of excitement.

**Kayaking & Rafting** One of the more adventurous local sports, and one that's enormously enjoyable for all ages, is skimming the Jordan River in a kayak, raft, or inner tube. Many companies rent the necessary equipment. Novices needn't worry—this is not white-water territory.

**Cycling** Cycling has become more popular among the locals, and special cycling lanes are now starting to appear, especially in the north.

---

Some kibbutz guest houses may offer lectures and tours of the community. Many also arrange kayaking and rafting, horseback riding, Jeep tours, and other sports and services both for guests and the general public. The choice can be difficult, as all are in pretty settings and have well-maintained grounds.

| WHAT IT COSTS In U.S. Dollars | | | | |
|---|---|---|---|---|
| **$$$$** | **$$$** | **$$** | **$** | **¢** |
| HOTELS | over $250 | $175–$250 | $111–$174 | $65–$110 | under $65 |

Prices are for two people in a standard double room in high season. Non-Israeli citizens paying in foreign currency are exempt from the 16.5% VAT tax on hotel rooms.

**Timing**
The best time to visit the Upper Galilee and the Golan is during winter and spring, when the range of floral colors is wondrous—although in winter, gray or rainy days are not rare. Summer days can be hot, but the region doesn't suffer the humidity of other parts of Israel. Tzfat comes alive from July through September, when more galleries are open.

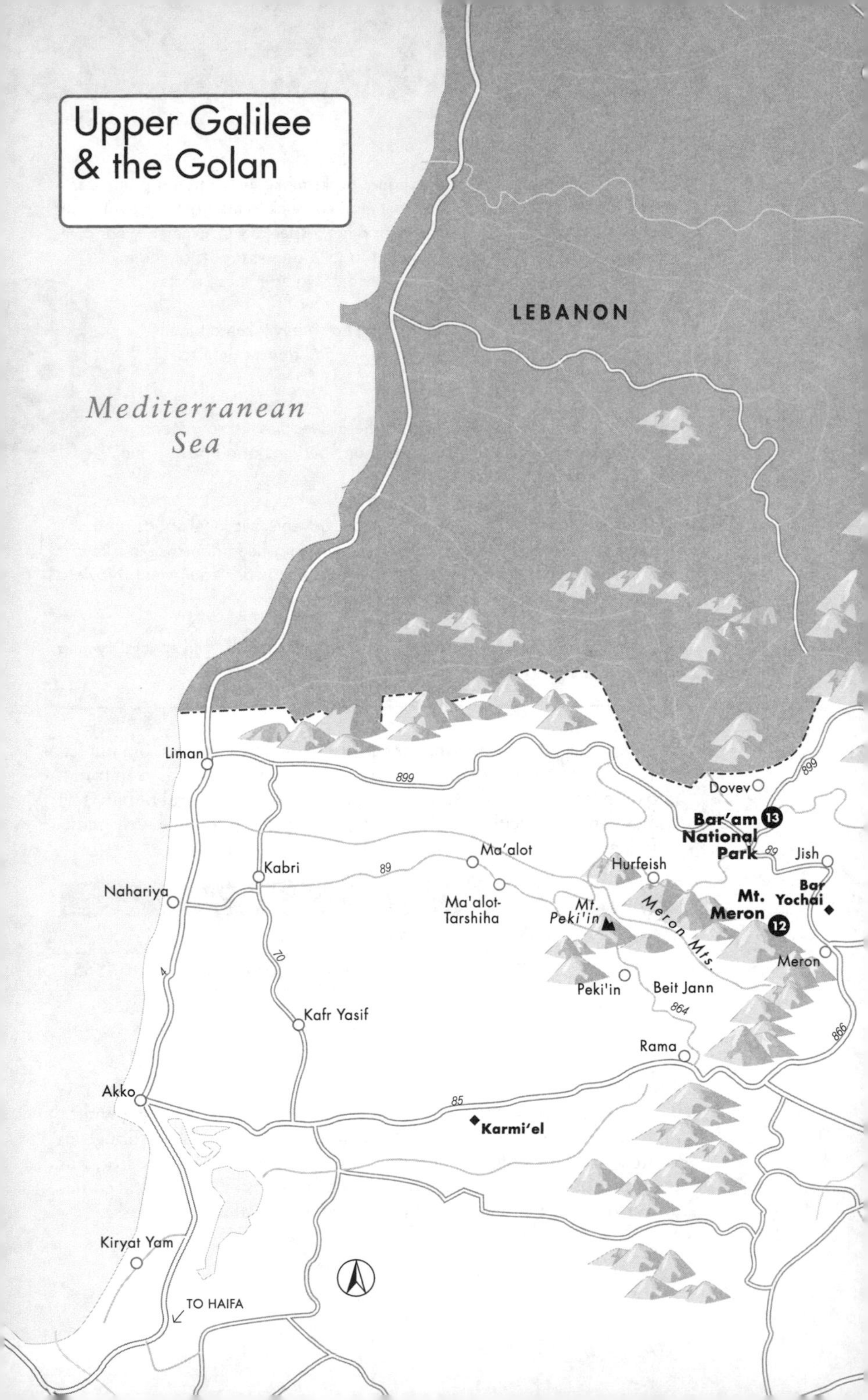

# Upper Galilee & the Golan

**LEBANON**

*Mediterranean Sea*

Liman

899

Dovev

Bar'am National Park **13**

89

Jish

Kabri

89

Ma'alot

Hurfeish

**Mt. Meron**

**Bar Yochai** ◆

Nahariya

70

Ma'alot-Tarshiha

Mt. Peki'in ▲

*Meron Mts.*

**12**

Kafr Yasif

Peki'in

Beit Jann

864

Meron

866

Akko

85

Rama

◆ **Karmi'el**

Kiryat Yam

TO HAIFA

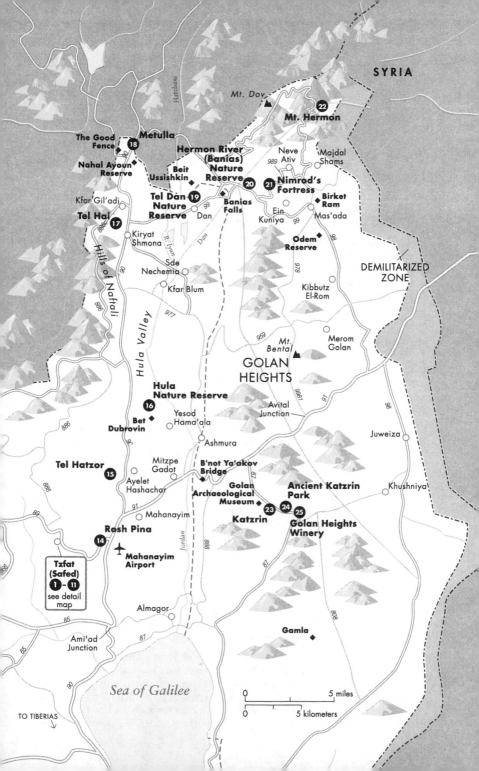

# TZFAT (SAFED) & ENVIRONS

In the southern part of the Upper Galilee, attractions range from the narrow streets and historic synagogues of Tzfat's Old City to the wilderness of the Hula Nature Reserve. Other reserves, like Mt. Meron, have both scenic appeal and spiritual importance. At Rosh Pina visitors can can shop and dine where the Galilee's first Zionist pioneers once labored. Or one can just relax at an inn or a kibbutz guest house and enjoy the wooded scenery.

## Tzfat

*33 km (20 mi) north of Tiberias, 72 km (45 mi) northeast of Haifa.*

At 3,000 feet above sea level, Tzfat is Israel's highest city. Perhaps this proximity to the heavens accounts for its reputation as the center of Jewish mysticism—Kabbalah—for although it is one of several holy cities in Israel—along with Jerusalem, Tiberias, and Hebron—Tzfat has a spiritual dimension found nowhere else.

The Crusaders built a fortress here, and a thriving Jewish settlement grew up in the shadow of the castle walls. Although it declined with the eclipse of the Crusader presence in the Galilee, the town survived rule by the Ottomans, who retained Tzfat as their capital through the 16th century. Soon after their expulsion in 1492, Jews from Spain started streaming in, among them respected rabbis and other spiritual leaders, intellectuals, and poets who gravitated to Tzfat as a center of revived Kabbalah study.

The Kabbalah—which dates to ancient times but gained popularity starting in the 12th century, possibly as a reaction against formal rabbinical Judaism—is about reading between, behind, and all around the lines. Each letter and accent of every word in the holy books has a numerical value with specific significance, offering added meaning to the literal word. During the Middle Ages, the great mystic rabbis were the soul of this city; under their tutelage, religious and mystical schools and meeting places mushroomed here. Some of these leaders would leave their mark on the age, on the generations to follow, and of course, on Tzfat itself.

Tzfat hibernates from October through June, when the city's artists move to their galleries in warmer parts of the country. This does not mean you should leave Tzfat off your itinerary during those months; there is enough to occupy the curious wanderer for at least a few hours, and much of it is free. In the summer, especially during July and August, Tzfat is abuzz with activity: galleries and shops stay open late, klezmer music (Eastern European Jewish "soul music") dances around corners, and the city extends a warm welcome to everyone.

It doesn't take long to walk all around Tzfat's Old City. Visitors can poke around the little cobbled passages that seem to lead nowhere, or linger over some minute architectural detail on a structure from another time. And it's almost impossible to get lost; Yerushalayim (Jerusalem) Street is a good orientation point—it runs through the heart of the Old City, encircles the Citadel, and from there, steps lead down to the two

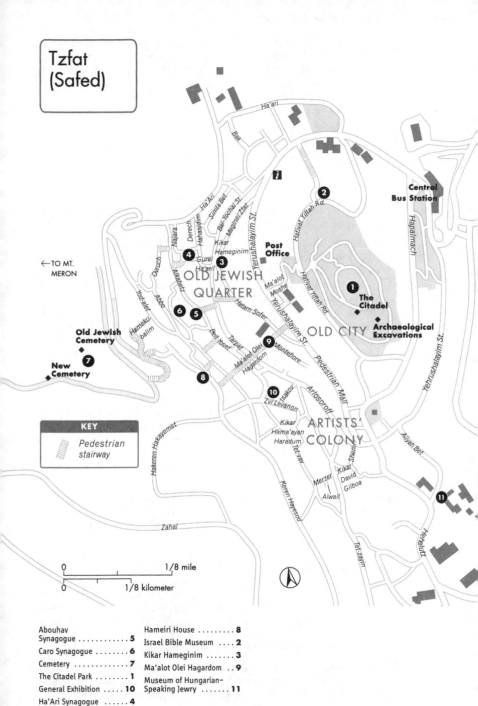

# Tzfat (Safed)

← TO MT. MERON

**Central Bus Station**

**Old Jewish Cemetery**

**New Cemetery**

OLD JEWISH QUARTER

OLD CITY

**Post Office**

**The Citadel**

**Archaeological Excavations**

ARTISTS' COLONY

### KEY

▨ Pedestrian stairway

0      1/8 mile
0      1/8 kilometer

*Street labels:* Ha'ari, Bak, Najara, Derech Hahasidim, Simta Bet, Bar-Yochai Tzfat, Meginei Tzfat, Ha'ari, Gurei, Ha'arit, Kikar Hameginim, Alkabetz, Abbo, Ortuch, Yad-Tztel, Hamekubalim, Hatam Safer, Ma'alot Moshe, Yerushalayim St., Hativat Yiftah Rd., Hapalmach, Yehrushalayim St., Bet-Yosef, Tarpat, Ma'alot Olei Hagardom, Montefiore, Pedestrian Mall, Artosoroff, Zvi Levanon, Kikar Hama'ayan Haradum, Hakeren-Hakayemet, Zahal, Keren Hayesod, Tet-vav, Merzer, Alwaji, Kikar David Gilboa, Tet-Zayin, Aiyah Bet, Herautz

| | |
|---|---|
| Abouhav Synagogue ............ **5** | Hameiri House ......... **8** |
| Caro Synagogue ........ **6** | Israel Bible Museum .... **2** |
| Cemetery ............. **7** | Kikar Hameginim ....... **3** |
| The Citadel Park ........ **1** | Ma'alot Olei Hagardom .. **9** |
| General Exhibition ..... **10** | Museum of Hungarian-Speaking Jewry ....... **11** |
| Ha'Ari Synagogue ...... **4** | |

main areas of interest, the Old Jewish Quarter and the adjacent Artists' Colony. There is no way to avoid the hilly topography, though, so do wear comfortable walking shoes. As the town is largely Orthodox, modest dress is recommended when visiting synagogues. For women, this means a longish skirt or long pants and at least a half-sleeve and, for men, long pants.

## Main Attractions

**⑤ Abouhav Synagogue.** This large Sephardic synagogue is named in honor of a 14th-century Spanish scribe, one of whose Torah scrolls found its way here with the Spanish Jewish exiles 200 years later. A look around reveals a number of differences between this synagogue and its Ashkenazi counterparts, such as the Ha'Ari; for example, the walls are painted the lively blue typical of Sephardic tradition, and the benches run along the walls instead of in rows (so that no man turns his back on his neighbor).

Every detail is loaded with significance: there are three arks—for the three forefathers, Abraham, Isaac, and Jacob (the one on the right is said to be the Abouhav original)—and 10 windows in the dome, referring to the Commandments. The charmingly naive illustrations on the squinches include a depiction of the Dome of the Rock (referring to the destruction of the Second Temple) and pomegranate trees, whose 613 seeds are equal in number to the Torah's commandments. The original building was destroyed in the 1837 earthquake, but locals swear that the southern wall—in which the Abouhav Torah scroll is set—was spared. ⊠ *Abouhav St.* ⊙ *No set visiting hrs.*

**Artists' Colony.** The colony, set in Tzfat's old Arab Quarter, was established in 1951 by six Israeli artists who saw the promise beyond Tzfat's war-torn and dilapidated condition; for them, the old buildings, the fertile landscape, and the cool mountain air fused to form a magic that would help them create. Others soon followed until, at its peak, the colony was home to more than 50 artists, some of whom are exhibited internationally. Most galleries are open only in the spring and summer, from about 10 AM to 6 PM. ⊠ *Old City of Tzfat* 🎫 *Free.*

**⑩ General Exhibition.** An important stop in the Artists' Colony, the works inside this large space are a representative sample of the work of Tzfat's artists, ranging from oils and watercolors to silk screens and sculptures, in traditional and avant-garde styles. The permission of the Muslim authorities was required to organize the Exhibition, as it is housed in the old mosque, easily identified from afar by its minaret. The Artists' Colony has recognized the growing presence of artists from the former Soviet Union, and the adjacent building holds the **Immigrant Artists' Exhibition.** In either facility, if any works catch your fancy, just ask directions to the artist's gallery for a more in-depth look at his or her work. ⊠ *Isakov and Zvi Levanon sts.* 🕾 *04/692–0087* 🎫 *Free* ⊙ *Sun.–Thurs. 9–5, Fri. 9–2, Sat. and Jewish holidays 10–2.*

**⑥ Caro Synagogue.** This is arguably the most charming synagogue in the Old City. It was named after Rabbi Yosef Caro, who arrived in Tzfat in 1535 and led its Jewish community for many years. He is the author of the Shulchan Aruch, the code of law that remains a foundation of Jewish religious interpretation to the present day, and this synagogue is said to have been Caro's study hall. It was destroyed in the great earthquake of 1837 and rebuilt in the mid-19th century. If you ask, the attendant might open the ark containing the Torah scrolls, one of which is at least 400 years old. A glass-faced cabinet at the back of the synagogue is the *geniza*, where damaged scrolls or prayer books are stored (because they carry the name of God, they cannot be destroyed). The turquoise paint here—considered the "color of heaven"—is believed to help keep away the evil eye. ☒ *Alkabetz St.* ☉ *No set visiting hrs.*

➌ **Ha'Ari Synagogue.** This Ashkenazi synagogue has associations going back to the 16th century. It is named for a rabbi who left an indelible mark on Tzfat and on Judaism; his real name was Isaac Luria, but he was known to all as the Ari, Hebrew for "lion" and an acronym for Adoneinu Rabbeinu Itzhak ("our master and teacher Isaac"). In his mere three years in Tzfat, he evolved his own system of the Kabbalah, which drew a huge following that would influence Jewish teaching and interpretation the world over, right up to the present day. Even more astounding is the fact that he died in his mid-thirties; it is generally said that one should not even consider study of the Kabbalah before the age of 40, when one reaches the requisite level of intellectual and emotional maturity.

The pale colors of this tiny Ashkenazi synagogue contrast sharply with its olive-wood Holy Ark, a dazzlingly carved tour de force with two tiers of spiral columns and vibrant plant reliefs. The synagogue was built after Luria's death, on the spot where he is said to have come with his disciples on Friday evenings to welcome the Sabbath. It was leveled by the 1837 earthquake and rebuilt in 1857. (The Sephardic Ari Synagogue, where the rabbi prayed, is farther down the quarter, by the cemetery. The oldest of Tzfat's synagogues, this 16th-century structure has especially fine carved wooden doors.) ☒ *Ha'Ari St.* ☉ *No set visiting hrs.*

➑ **Hameiri House.** This centuries-old stone building houses a museum documenting the life of the Jewish community of Tzfat over the past 200 years. ☒ *Keren Hayesod St.* ☎ *04/697–1307, 04/692–1939* 🖷 *04/692–1902* 🎫 *NIS 14* ☉ *Sun.–Thurs. 9—2:30, Fri. 9—1:30, Sat. by appointment.*

## Also Worth Seeing

➊ **The Citadel Park.** In Talmudic times, 1,600 years ago, hilltop bonfires here served as a beacon to surrounding communities heralding the beginning of the lunar month, the basis for the Jewish calendar. In the 12th century, the Crusaders grasped the strategic value of this setting and built the Citadel. It was conquered by the Muslim sultan Baybars in 1266, leaving only scattered pieces visitors see today.

The Jewish settlement outside the citadel's walls grew and prospered during and after the Crusader era, with the city becoming a center of Kabbalah studies. When the departing British Mandate forces left the town's key strategic positions to the Arab forces, the remains of the Citadel once again became a battle ground between Jews and Arabs. ☒ *Old City.*

⓫ **Museum of Hungarian-Speaking Jewry.** The founders and driving force of this museum are Tzfat residents and Holocaust survivors Hava and Yosef Lustig. The varied exhibits in the museum's few small rooms, including letters, children's books, drawings, items of clothing and more, tell of the everyday life of communities and individuals in the Hungarian-speaking Jewish pre-Holocaust world. Visitors see a 20-minute video, and can search the computer data base, which has information about 1,700 communities of Jews from Hungary, Transylvania, Slovakia, and other countries, including photographs of some 10,000 headstones ⊠ *The old Ottoman government center (the Saraya) Kikar Haatzmaut* ☎ *04/692–5881or 04/692–3880* ⊕ *www.isragen.org.il* ⊠ *Free* ☉ *Sun.–Fri. 9–1.*

❷ **Israel Bible Museum.** This stone mansion was once the home of the Ottoman governor. Today it houses the somewhat dramatic paintings and sculptures of artist Phillip Ratner, all inspired by the Bible. ⊠ *Hativat Yiftah St.,adjacent to Citadel Park* ☎ *04/699–9972* ⊕ *www.israelbiblemuseum.com* ⊠ *Free* ☉ *May–Sept. 10–4, Fri. 10–1; Oct.–Dec. Sun.–Thurs. 10–2, Fri. 10–1.*

❼ **Cemetery.** An old and a new cemetery are set into the hillside below the Old Jewish Quarter. The old plots resonate with the names and fame of the Kabbalists of yore, and their graves are identifiable by sky blue markers. It is said that if the legs of the devout suddenly get tired here, it is because they are walking over hidden graves. The new cemetery holds the graves of members of the pre-State underground Stern Gang and Irgun forces, who were executed by the British in Akko's prison ( ⇨ Chapter 4). In a separate plot, bordered by cypresses, lie the 21 Tzfat teenagers killed by terrorists in 1974—they were taken hostage while they were on a field trip and sleeping overnight in a school in the northern Galilee town of Ma'alot. ⊠ *Below Keren Hayesod St.* ⊠ *Free* ☉ *No set hours.*

❸ **Kikar Hameginim.** "Defenders' Square" is the main square of the Old Jewish Quarter and was once its social and economic heart. A sign points to a two-story house that served as the command post of the neighborhood's defense in 1948—hence the plaza's name.

❾ **Ma'alot Olei Hagardom.** Part of Tzfat's charm is its setting, on the slope of a hill. This *ma'alot*, or stairway, which extends all the way down from Yerushalayim Street, forms the boundary between the Old Jewish Quarter and the Artists' Colony. It is named for the Tzfat freedom fighters who were executed by the British during the Mandate. ⊠ *Free.*

## Where to Stay & Eat

$$$ ✕ **Bat Ya'ar.** This timbered nonkosher restaurant serves tasty steaks and salads, enhanced by the wooded mountaintop setting. A meaty bowl of bean stew, eaten by the fireplace, is a pleasure on any day. A kosher kitchen is available for reserved groups. Outside the restaurant is a playground for children. Hour-long family nature activity packages are offered, as well as horseback-riding excursions. Bat Ya'ar is 5 km (3 mi) north of Tzfat. It's best to call for directions. ⊠ *Birya Forest* ☎ *04/692–1788* ⌂ *Reservations essential on weekends* 🗎 *AE, MC, V.*

★ $$ ✕ **Ein Camonim.** The Galilee Hills make perfect pastureland for livestock—in this case, goats—and in here you can taste the fresh output of Ein

Camonim's dairy. The fixed all-you-can-eat menu contains a platter of goat cheeses, a selection of home-baked bread, a wicker basket of raw garden vegetables, local wine, coffee, and dessert. There's a half-price menu for children 12 and under. The specialty shop next door sells the cheeses and other homemade products, including the dairy's own olives, vacuum-packed rather than in glass jars, which is a boon for travelers. ⊠ *Rte. 85, 20 km (12½ mi) southwest of Tzfat, 5 km (3 mi) west of Kadarim Junction (north of highway)* ☎ *04/698–9894* ⊕ *www.ein-camonim.co.il* ▤ *AE, DC, MC, V.*

**$$** ✕ **Gan Eden.** The setting, an old stone house, lends great atmosphere to this family-run kosher eatery. Taking in the view of Mt. Meron (the restaurant's name means "paradise"), the restaurant is best known for its fish, especially its fillet of sea bream. The "Calzines a Galil" (dumplings stuffed with salty Tzfat cheese)are served with a salad of greens, tomatoes, raisins, and walnuts. Gan Eden serves no meat or chicken. ⊠ *Mt. Canaan Promenade* ☎ *04/697–2434* ▤ *AE, DC, MC, V* ☉ *Closed Sat.*

**$$** ✕ **Hamifgash.** One of the institutions on pedestrian-only Yerushalayim Street, Hamifgash (which means "meeting place") has a wide selection of options from soups and salads to substantial meat dishes. ⊠ *75 Yerushalayim St.* ☎ *04/692–0510* ▤ *AE, DC, MC, V* ☉ *Closed Fri., Sat.*

**$$–$$$** ✕🏠 **Habayit Bik'tse Hanof.** The "House at the View's Edge" is perched high in the Birya Forest with a stunning vista of the surrounding hills. In addition to a café ($–$$$) serving a selection of meat and dairy dishes, there are two spacious but utilitarian rooms with a backpacker's guest-house feel about them, accented by colorful throw rugs and pillows. A separate cottage has a whirlpool bath and some charm—it's faced with stone and looks a little like Hansel and Gretel might live there off-season. ⊠ *Birya Forest, 7 km (4 mi) from Tzfat* ☎ *04/692–3737* ⤵ *3 rooms* ⚴ *Café; no room phones, no room TVs* ▤ *AE, DC, MC, V.*

**$$$$** 🏠 **Canaan Spa.** This elegant hotel on Mt. Canaan on the outskirts of Tzfat caters to patrons seeking a luxury in-house spa experience. In addition to conventional Swedish massage, guests can enjoy reflexology or aromatic massages or hot stone treatments. Paintings and sculptures adorn public areas that are coordinated in tranquil colors, giving a feeling of refined luxury. Facilities include tennis and basketball courts and a 1.5-acre private forest. There is a minimum two-night stay. Nonguests can also enjoy the sumptuous ($$$$) buffets at lunch and dinner. ⊠*Mt. Canaan Promenade Tzfat 13214* ☎ *04/699–3000* 🖷 *04/699–3001* ⊕ *www.canaanspa.com* ⤵ *122 rooms, including six junior suites* ⚴ *Restaurant, two indoor pools; no kids under 14* ▤ *AE, DC, MC, V* ⦿ *MAP.*

★ **$$$$** 🏠 **Sea View (Mitzpe Hayamim).** This serene hotel located halfway between Tzfat and Rosh Pina has a splendid view of the Sea of Galilee and specializes in spa packages. All rooms are nonsmoking; some suites and junior suites have whirlpools. The lobby has an herbal tea corner open around the clock. A gallery exhibits and sells Israeli artwork, and a gift shop offers homemade breads, cheeses, and other local products. ⊠ *Box 27, Rosh Pina 12000* ☎ *04/699–4555* 🖷 *04/699–9555* ⊕ *www.mizpehayamim.com* ⤵ *89 rooms* ⚴ *Restaurant, pool, gym, hot tub, massage, sauna; no-smoking rooms* ▤ *AE, DC, MC, V* ⦿ *MAP.*

★ **$$$** 🏨 **Ruth Rimonim.** Two hundred years ago, this gracious old building was the local post office. Over the years, rooms were added and it became a *khan*, or inn. Since opening as a hotel in 1961, it has enjoyed a reputation for charm and excellence. The stone-walled rooms have a comfortable, rustic feel; the former stables serve as a dining room. Half the rooms have mountain views. Children's programs are offered in the summer. ✉ *Artists' Quarter, Box 1011, Tzfat 13110* 🕾 *04/699–4666* 🖷 *04/692–0456* ⊕ *www.rimonim.co.il* ↻ *76 rooms* ♨ *2 restaurants, pool, gym, sauna, bar, children's programs (ages 3–6)* ⊟ *AE, DC, MC, V.*

**$$** 🏨 **Ron.** The rooms in this unassuming and somewhat old-fashioned hotel are spacious and light-filled; half have mountain views. The Ron is centrally located, making it a good choice for Orthodox travelers on the Sabbath. The pool is only open in the summer. ✉ *Near the Citadel Park, Hativat Yiftah, Box 22, Tzfat 13214* 🕾 *04/697–2590* 🖷 *04/697–2363* ↻ *50 rooms* ♨ *Restaurant, pool* ⊟ *AE, DC, MC, V.*

**$** 🏨 **Joseph's Well.** All the rooms at Joseph's Well, which is on Kibbutz Amiad, 10 km (6 mi) south of Tzfat, are on the ground floor, in clusters of three with a shared patio—and each room is like a cozy studio apartment, with pine furniture, coordinated tablecloths and sheets, and chintz curtains. They all have a coffee corner with an electric kettle, and tea and coffee. Meals are served in the kibbutz dining room. Unlike the bigger kibbutz hotels, Joseph's Well offers few activities, but is a good location for a base to explore both the Upper Galilee and the Panhandle. ✉ *M.P. Upper Galilee 12335* 🕾 *04/690–9829* 🖷 *04/690–9307* ⊕ *www.amiad-inn.com* ↻ *27 rooms* ♨ *Dining room, pool; no room phones* ⊟ *AE, DC, MC, V.*

## Nightlife & the Arts

Tzfat hosts a **klezmer festival** every summer, usually in July, and there could be no better setting for three days of "Jewish soul music" than this mystical, cobbled-lane city. Some of klezmer's roots are Hasidic, making it plaintive and almost prayer-like in tone, especially with its emphasis on wind and string instruments. Many events are street performances and therefore free. Keep in mind, though, that Tzfat practically bursts at the seams at this time, with revelers both religious and secular.

## Sports & the Outdoors

★ ☾ **Bat Ya'ar** (🕾 04/692–1788), in the Birya Forest 5 km (3 mi) from Tzfat, is a steak house with a playground, which also offers an hour package of outdoor fun for the whole family including pony rides, a "rope park" with rope bridges between trees, and outdoor bowling with wooden lanes and balls. The cost is NIS 67.50 per person for groups up to 10 or NIS 45 per person for groups of more than 10. Horseback riding and ATV trips of two hours to two days can be arranged; children must be at least 10.

## Shopping

☾ **Tzfat Candles** (✉ Najara Street near the Ari Synagogue 🕾 04-682—2068 ◷ weekdays 9-7; Fri. 9-12:30). From the original one-room store and workshop a decade ago, Tzfat Candles has grown to include a museum of intricate wax sculptures as well as the shop, which is permeated with the pleasant aroma of the beeswax candles and bright with a rainbow range of Sabbath, Havdalah, and Hanukkah candles. Groups can get a demonstration of the process.

## Mt. Meron

**12** *21 km (13 mi) west of Tzfat on Rte. 89.*

The spiritual importance of Tzfat extends beyond the city limits to Mt. Meron, which is a pilgrimage site both for ultra-Orthodox Jews and nature lovers.

The village of Meron has for centuries drawn thousands upon thousands of Orthodox Jews to pay homage to several of the great rabbis of the Roman era who are buried at the eastern foot of the mount. The most important site—and one of the holiest places in Israel—is the **Tomb of Rabbi Shimon Bar Yochai,** survivor of the Bar Kochba Revolt of almost 2,000 years ago. Bar Yochai is said to have fled from the Romans with his son Elazar after the fall of Jerusalem to a cave at Peki'in, not far from here, where he remained for 13 years. The faithful, beginning with the 16th-century mystics who settled in Tzfat, believe that from his cave-hideout Bar Yochai penned the Zohar (the Book of Splendor), his commentary on the first five books of the Hebrew Bible. Others claim that the Zohar dates from 13th-century Spain. Nevertheless, the constant flow of visitors is evidence of the pilgrims' devotion to the great rabbi and rebel.

The pilgrimage is still celebrated en masse on Lag Ba'Omer, the festive 33rd day of the seven solemn weeks that begin with Passover and end with Shavuot (Pentecost). At this time Mt. Meron comes alive as a grand procession arrives on foot from Tzfat, carrying Torah scrolls and singing fervently. Bonfires are lighted, with celebrations lasting days. Many ultra-Orthodox Jews still uphold the tradition of bringing their three-year-old sons here on Lag Ba'Omer for their first haircuts.

### Where to Stay & Eat

★ **$$$-$$$$** 🏨 **Amirim Holiday Village.** Moshav Amirim offers something quite different from the typical lodging—almost all of its 135 families are vegetarian and several of them offer lodgings; there are a number of homey restaurants and cafés with a range of vegetarian fare, and a specialty bakery; and the location, on top of a hill with a magnificent view of the Sea of Galilee, is incomparable. This is a real get-away-from-it-all kind of place and guests have a choice of health and beauty treatments, including those at "Spa in the Forest," where the treatment room with whirlpool bath was built around the branch of an old oak tree. Lodgings at Amirim are owned and run by different families, who clearly put their heart into the details. They run from single to several rooms, and from plain to lap-of-luxury. There are two wheelchair-accessible units. Former Englishman and village resident Phillip Campbell serves as a clearing house for reservations and advice. ✉ *Moshav Amirim, near Mt. Meron (about 4 km/2½ mi north of the junction of Rte. 89 and Rte. 886), M. P. Carmiel 20115* ☎ *04/698-9571* 🖷 *04/698-7824* ⊕ *alitamirim@hotmail.com* ♿ *Some kitchenettes, some room TVs, some A/C, some room phones.* ▤ *AE, DC, MC, V* ⦿ *BP.*

$ 🔲 **Al Jermak.** This family-owned bed-and-breakfast is in the Druze village of Beit Jann, about 25 km west of Tzfat on the southern slope of Mt. Meron. The rooms are basic but cozy rooms—some have balconies—with lovely views of the wooded slopes of Mt. Meron and fine mountain air. There is a good measure of the famous Druze hospitality, which really makes the stay here unique. ⊠ *Beit Jann 13214* 🕾 *04/ 980–2962* 📑 *8 rooms* ⚭ *Restaurant* 🚍 *AE, DC, MC, V.*

$$$ ✗ **Dalia's.** The cheerful owner of this restaurant, the oldest dining establishment in Moshav Amirim, is a former nutritionist who is also the chef. The set menu includes, among other items, almond and peanut patties in onion sauce and tomatoes stuffed with wheat and barley, as well as a beautiful array of salads, and soup. Dessert, consisting of yogurt with fresh fruit, is served with a big helping of fresh air and scenery, on the balcony. Call for directions. ⊠ *On the main road in Amirim right-hand side when driving in* 🕾 *04/698–9349* ⚭ *Reservations essential* 🚍 *AE, DC, MC, V.*

★ $$$$ ✗ **Hase'uda Ha'aharona.** This restaurant's peculiar choice of name (it means "The Last Supper") shouldn't stop you from enjoying its magnificent combination of tasty fare and pleasing, country-style decor. The excellent vegetarian cuisine—enriched by any number of the 45 herbs that owner-chef Bella grows in her garden—has made this one of the region's best-known eateries. Try the ginger soup or scrumptious and beautifully presented phyllo basket, filled either with a soy mix or with egglant. The menu is fixed, but changes weekly. It's useful to call ahead for directions. ⊠ *Near the entrance to Moshav Amirim, 4th house on the right when driving in* 🕾 *04/698–9788* ⊕ *www.haseudah-haacharonah.com* ⚭ *Reservations essential* 🚍 *AE, DC, MC, V* ⊗ *closed Mon.–Wed.*

$ ✗ **Stupp's.** Esther and Mordechai are not only the biblical characters who gave us Purim; they are also the Stupps, originally from Canada, who own and run this small kosher dairy establishment. The menu has something for everyone, or at least for every vegetarian, including a selection of pastas and sauces, a couple of tofu dishes, and the large salads typical of Israeli dairy restaurants. ⊠ *On the main road into Amirim near the entrance, on the left when driving in* 🕾 *04/698–0946* 🚍 *AE, DC, MC, V* ⊗ *Sat. and Jewish holidays.*

## Sports & the Outdoors

Mt. Meron, over a thousand acres of which is a nature reserve, is crisscrossed with hiking trails. One relatively easy loop-trail, which takes about an hour and a half to complete leisurely, wends gradually upward and around the area near the 900-meter-high peak, revealing beautiful views in every direction from several lookouts created by the Israel Nature and Parks Authority (INPA). Depending on the time of year, wild flowers, including bright yellow Sternbergia and meadow saffron, may grace the trail, and bright red anemones and delicate pink cyclamens might peep out from among several species of hardy oak. A left turn about a mile and a half southwest of the Sasa junction, marked with an INPA directional sign, leads to a parking lot, from which the trail starts.

**Eretz Hagalil Jeeps.** Yoram Zarchi, whose extended family also owns several B&Bs in Amirim, picks up off-road aficionados at their accommodations throughout the Galilee, and plans excursions of two hours to a day in the Galilee and the Golan, taking in sites of natural beauty and historical significance hidden from ordinary travelers. A two-hour tour in a seven-seater Jeep is NIS 550 per person. ✉ *Moshav Amirim* ☎ *04/698–0434, 050/531–6140* ⊕ *www.eretzhagalil.co.il.*

**Malkiya Stables** (✉ Kibbutz Malkiya ☎ 052–281–6293), off road 899, 29 km (18 mi) north of the Hiram junction on the new northern road, has spectacular mountain views all along the road. They offer trail rides of one to four hours by appointment, for ages 7 and up.

| off the beaten path |
| :---: |

**PEKI'IN** – Peki'in—a day trip from Amirim (or Tiberias or Akko) is high above the Bet Kerem valley and its main town of Karmiel, almost exactly halfway between the Mediterranean and the Jordan River. Its location, high in the mountains north of the main Akko-Tzfat highway, means that it is still a truly off-the-beaten-track destination. It's an ancient village whose 12,000 inhabitants—Druze, Christians, Muslims, and Jews—are doing their best to forge a community. Pomegranates and carob trees still dot the yards of some of the old stone houses. Some houses, like the *mukhtar's* (headman's), in the center of the village near the spring, have been abandoned for so many years that grape vines as thick as tree trunks wend their way in and out of windows and doorways. Visitors get the rare feeling in Peki'in of a glimpse of unspoiled local color. The town's synagogue, last restored in 1890 and open intermittently, has carvings the locals say were brought from the Jerusalem Temple after the Roman destruction, and a piece of ancient Torah scroll preserved in glass above the Holy Ark. The tiny candlelit cave where Rabbi Shimon Bar Yochai hid from the Romans is an attraction for Jewish pilgrims. On the main street is the factory and shop where the Druze "Savta [Grandma] Jamila" makes the "secret recipe" olive oil soap that has become famous in Israel, and even has a following abroad.

## Bar'am National Park

**⑬** *15 km (9 mi) northwest of Meron, 40 km (25 mi) northwest of Tzfat.*

In an otherwise deserted spot lie the ruins of **Bar'am**, one of the best-preserved ancient synagogues anywhere, dating from the 3rd century AD. Although Bar'am is less grand than the synagogue at Capernaum, on the Sea of Galilee (⇨ Chapter 5), the community that built it must have devoted considerable funds and energy to their most important building. Like most other synagogues uncovered in this area, it faces south, toward Jerusalem; unlike any other, however, this one has lavish architectural elements, such as an entrance with a segmental pediment, and freestanding giant columns in front.

The interior, which resembles that of other Galilean synagogues of the talmudic period (3rd–8th centuries AD), is in a worse state of repair than the facade. Rows of pillars in the prayer hall apparently served as supports for the ceiling, and the building may have had a second story. A section of the facade's lintel, now in the Louvre in Paris, contains the Hebrew inscription "May there be peace in this place, and in all the places of Israel. This lintel was made by Jose the Levite. Blessings upon his works. Shalom." ⊠ *Rte. 899* ☎ *04/698–9301* 🖻 *NIS 12* ⊙ *Apr.–Sept. 8–5; Oct.–Mar. 8–4, Fri. 8–3.*

## Where to Eat

¢–$$  ✕ **Jascala.** Departing from the usual Middle Eastern plate of hummus and pita with chips, Jascala, in the village of Jish, offers flavors of Lebanon cooked with the assistance of the owner's mother. Specialties include salads based on greens like chard and mallow that grow wild in the hills (in spring), and melt-in-the-mouth pastry stuffed with mushrooms cooked in tangy yogurt sauce. The vine leaves come with or without meat; the fried *koubeh*, a small bulgur wheat pocket, is filled with either meat or hummus. ⊠ *Jish* ☎ *04/698–7762* 🖃 *AE, DC, MC, V.*

# Rosh Pina

**⑭**  *10 km (6 mi) east of Tzfat, 25 km (15½ mi) north of Tiberias.*

Fodor'sChoice
★  The restored village of Rosh Pina is a gift shop and gallery browser's delight, and the dilapidated wooden doors and stone work of some still-abandoned premises are part of the charm.

Rosh Pina—literally "cornerstone"—gets its name from Psalm 118:22: "The stone that the builders rejected has become the chief cornerstone." This verse inspired the Galilee's first Zionist pioneers, who came from Romania in 1882, determined to build a village. They bought this land, 1,500 feet above sea level at the foot of the mountain ridge east of Tzfat, and arrived with all they needed for their new home, right down to the timber for construction.

The Romanians derived their main livelihood at Rosh Pina from the production of silk by silkworms; the philanthropist Baron Edmond de Rothschild donated the necessary mulberry trees. However, the desired results were elusive: residents walked around in silk scarves and socks but had nothing to eat. Eventually, the immigrants moved away to other settlements, leaving only squatters for decades to follow.

The two-story **Schwartz Hotel,** on Ha'elyon Street, built in 1890, was the first rest house in the Galilee. Today it is a mere skeleton of the original, but try to imagine what it was like to check in here after a long, tiring journey on foot and enjoy the tranquil view of the Sea of Galilee below and white-capped Mt. Hermon to the north.

The **synagogue** (⊠ Ha'elyon St.) is usually locked. However, someone in the office of Old Rosh Pina (☎ 04/693–6603), a development company next door to the restaurant at the bottom of Ha'elyon Street, may be able to open it. The interior of the synagogue remains as it was when it was built in the mid-1880s; the dark pews and Ark made of the timber brought from Romania have aged gracefully. The ceiling has painted depictions of palm trees and biblical motifs.

The **Old Rosh Pina office,** which oversees the restoration and maintenance of Old Rosh Pina, occupies the house that belonged to Professor Gideon Mer, a leading expert on malaria in the 1930s. Legend has it that Mer used to inject his wife and children with experimental remedies in his efforts to combat malaria in this region. (All survived.) The British were so impressed with Mer's work that they sent him to Burma to fight malaria epidemics there. Implements and household items from the early days of Rosh Pina are on display. Admission is free. Next door, a colorful audiovisual presentation showcases the founding of this pioneering community. ☎ 04/693–6603 *for English viewings* ☎ *NIS 15* ☉ *Sun.–Thurs. 8:30–5; Fri.–Sat. 8:30–1 or by appointment.*

## Where to Stay & Eat

Rosh Pina is a budding center of tourism for this region, and many residents are now opening their homes as bed-and-breakfasts. There is no central reservation center, but the various tourist information centers can help you find simple, pleasant accommodations.

**$$$–$$$$** ✕ **Black Steer.** This red-roof steak house is part of a South African chain specializing in spareribs. Outdoor dining is especially pleasant here, as the garden is leafy and surprisingly private. The location—right off the road—is handy for those on the move. Business lunches on weekdays from noon until 5 PM are an added savings. ✉ *Opposite police station on west side of Rte. 90, at bottom of Rosh Pina* ☎ *04/693–6250* 🖃 *AE, DC, MC, V.*

**$–$$$$** ✕ **Babayit Shel Rafa** ("Rafa's"). Owner and chef Rafa infuses the menu with gastronomic memories of his native Argentina. The best starters are the pickled tongue and the two kinds (meat or corn) of empanadas. Entrées include steaks, chicken, and a choice of fish, but the house specialty is casseroles—hefty meals-in-a-pot. Try the lamb casserole with celery, rosemary, lemon, potatoes, and sweet potatoes; or the piquant beef and chorizo *asado* (roasted). Vegetarians will enjoy the rich vegetable, mozzarella, prune, and almond combination, served with polenta. ✉ *Old Rosh Pina restoration site next to the Rosh Pina office* ☎ *04/693–6192* 🗇 *Reservations essential Fri. dinner and Sat. lunch* 🖃 *AE, DC, MC, V.*

**$–$$$** ✕ **Ja'uni.** The houses and street where this restaurant are located were built when Baron Rothschild founded the town: Ja'uni is in a century-old structure used by the British as a post office and, later, as an arms hideout. The menu is seasonal and eclectic; one specialty is their Spanish-style *tapas* (small bites), which change daily and may include roast peppers; zucchini or fried cabbage in tahini; and eggplant in ginger, honey, and soy sauce. Outdoor seating is pleasant, especially in the evening and early morning. Brain-teaser puzzles for the nimble-fingered of all ages keep hungry diners busy until the food arrives. Good service and a separate room for nonsmokers earn extra points. There is live music on summer evenings. ✉ *30 David Shub St.* ☎ *04/693–1881* 🖃 *AE, DC, MC, V.*

**$** ✕ **Choclolata.** One difference between this dairy restaurant and others of its genre is its historic premises–the original arched stone basement of the old synagogue. The other is given away by its name: in addition to the usual Israeli salads, pasta, and sandwiches, they serva a host of chocolate delights, including 37 different kinds of pralines made by the house chocolatier. ✉ *Old Rosh Pina, east lower entrance to the synagogue.* ☎ *04/686–0219* 🖃 *AE, DC, MC, V.*

★ **$$** ✕▦ **Auberge Shulamit.** This charming inn takes its name from the original Hotel Shulamit, where the 1948 Armistice Treaty was signed. Among the menu's delectables—along with the home-smoked meats—are chestnut soup (in season), shrimp with wild rice, and an elegant array of desserts. The Auberge has three French country–style guest rooms and a suite with an outdoor whirlpool. ⊠ *David Shub St., Box 259, Rosh Pina 12105* ☎ *04/693–1485 or 04/693–1494* 🖷 *04/693–1495* ⊕ *www. shulamit.co.il* ⚱ *Reservations essential* ☌ *4 rooms* ⚘ *Restaurant, minibars* ▤ *AE, DC, MC, V.*

**$** ▦ **Village Inn.** These accommodations at Kibbutz Kfar Hanassi give you a *real* taste of kibbutz life. The one- and two-room units look out onto a garden, each has a barbecue, and a few share a kitchenette. Boldly colored sheets and dhurrie rugs add a country touch. Meals are in the kibbutz's communal dining room. Several artists live and work at Kfar Hanassi, and you're welcome to visit their studios. Guided hikes to the mountainous Jordan River area northeast of the kibbutz can be arranged. ⊠ *Kibbutz Kfar Hanassi, near Mahanayim Airport (10 km, or 6 mi, from Rosh Pina), M.P. Upper Galilee 12305* ☎ *04/691–4870* 🖷 *04/691–4077* ⊕ *www.villageinn.co.il* ☌ *32 units* ⚘ *Dining room, kitchenettes, 2 tennis courts, pool, massage, basketball,* ▤ *AE, DC, MC, V.*

## Shopping

**The Shop Around the Corner.** Sigal and her husband Inbar pick their merchandise from among all that is authentic in the Galilee—including handicrafts, packaged food, and drinks. Unique items like sage incense bundles and unusual Judaica can be found alongside herbal remedies and homemade limoncello. ⊠ *Old Rosh Pina, around the corner from the synagogue* ☎ *04/693–0340* ☉ *Tues.–Sat. 10:30–6; Sun.–Mon. 10:30–3.*

## Nightlife & the Arts

**The Well.** What better name for the local watering hole? Especially since it really does have its own well, complete with goldfish, in addition to a small orchard. The warm atmosphere comes from more than the fireplace. Light meals are served, along with the house drink, homemade limoncello ⊠ *Adjacent to the Old Rosh Pina vistors' parking lot* ☎ *04/693–0340.*

**Blues Brothers Pub.** The atmosphere in this small stone basement premises may best be described as "happy Gothic." Light meals are served to the mainly youthful clientele. ⊠ *32 David Shub St., Villa Tehila* ☎ *04/693–5336, 04/693–7788.*

# Tel Hatzor

🔟⑮ *8 km (5 mi) north of Rosh Pina.*

Tel Hatzor is a good stop for archaeology buffs as the remnants of 21 cities create its large mound. The excavation and restoration of some antiquities have produced fascinating results.

Situated on the Via Maris—the major trade route linking Egypt and Mesopotamia—Hatzor is referred to several times in documents from ancient archives in both lands, and scholars believe a huge archive may someday be found here as well.

The Book of Joshua (Joshua 11:13) notes that Joshua destroyed Canaanite Hatzor in the 13th century BC, and Israelites resettled it. Its next heyday came three centuries later, when King Solomon decided it would serve him well as a regional military and administrative center, like Megiddo and Gezer. In 732 BC, Hatzor met its end when invading Assyrian king Tiglath Pileser III conquered the Galilee and forced its Israelite inhabitants off the land in chains and into exile.

The huge site is divided into two areas: the *tell,* or **Upper City,** which comprised the oldest settlements, and the **Lower City,** first settled in the 18th century BC. Only the tell, covering less than a fifth of the total excavation site, is open to the public. The **Hatzor Museum** (on the grounds of Kibbutz Ayelet Hashachar, across the highway) houses figurines, weapons, stone pots, and other artifacts unearthed in the two areas; others are at the Israel Museum in Jerusalem. ⊠ *Tel Hatzor National Park, off Rte. 90* ☎ *04/693–7290* ⊠ *NIS 18 ($4.00)* ☉ *Park and museum Apr.–Sept. Sat.–Thurs. 8–5, Fri. 8–4; Oct.–Mar. Sat.–Thurs. 8–4, Fri. 8–3.*

## Where to Stay

**$$** ⊡ **Pausa–Gourmet Galilee Inn** This boutique hotel has eight suites, each beautifully designed in a minimalist style. The carefully landscaped and tranquil setting includes a bocce court, herb and vegetable gardens, and orchards that produce the ingredients used in preparing the dishes for the inn's slow-food cuisine. Meals are served family style; dinner begins with a cocktail where guests get acquainted. ⊠ *Moshav She'ar Yashuv, rt. 99, northeast of Kiryat Shemona 12240* ☎ *04/690–4434* ⊟ *04/690–4435* ⊕ *www.pausa-inn.co.il* ⊃ *8 rooms* ⌂ *Restaurant, Wi-Fi; no room phones, no children under 14* ⊟ *AE, DC, MC, V* ¡◎¡ *MAP.*

# Hula Nature Reserve

★ ⑯ *8 km (5 mi) north of Tel Hatzor.*

The Hula Nature Reserve contains the last vestige of wetlands preserved after the rest were drained in the 1950s to create arable land. Over the years it was realized that in addition to affecting water quality in the Sea of Galilee, the project had destroyed the habitat for millions of birds that migrate across the Hula Valley between Europe and Africa.

Pelicans, wild geese, storks, cranes, plovers, and raptors once again have their sanctuary, but they would not be here if not for the swampy waters that abound with carp, catfish, and perch, and a reed habitat boasting rare thickets of papyrus through which you might see a water buffalo or two. The visitor center has complete information about the 800-acre reserve, an observation tower, and a snack bar. Hunting and fishing are strictly forbidden. The main path is wheelchair accessible. A new visitor center has recently opened. ⊠ *East of Rte. 90* ☎ *04/693–7069* ⊠ *NIS 18 for park, additional 15 NIS for visitor center* ☉ *Park open daily 8–4; visitor center open daily 9–4.*

**need a break?** For a rest stop with a bit of history, try **Bet Dubrovin** (✉ Yesod Hama'ala ☎ 04/693–7371), near the entrance to the Hula Nature Reserve. This reconstructed farmhouse-cum-museum was once owned by the Dubrovins, Russian immigrants who converted from Christianity to Judaism. Old man Dubrovin brought his family to the swamps of the Hula in 1904, and despite the hardships, these pioneers set up a farm. The property was eventually donated to the Jewish National Fund and was opened to the public in 1986. An exhibit in the former family home highlights the old days and includes an audiovisual presentation. There is also a ceramics store selling locally made pieces, and a kosher restaurant specializing in smoked meat dishes. The museum entrance fee (NIS 7) is free for restaurant patrons, who are charged a small fee for the audiovisual presentation only, and who also receive a 20% discount at the Hula Nature Reserve.

# UPPER HULA VALLEY

The sights that hug the border with Lebanon show contrasting sides of Israel. The bustling town of Kiryat Shmona and sleepy Metulla bear eloquent witness to the varying fortunes of Israel's relationships with its Arab neighbors. Tel Dan Nature Reserve, on the other hand, draws visitors with its antiquities, surging river, and lush, wild beauty.

## Kiryat Shmona

*45 km (28 mi) north of Tiberias, 30 km (19 mi) north of Tzfat.*

The major urban center in the Upper Hula Valley, Kiryat Shmona offers fast food, a pharmacy, and other shopping in the mall on Route 90; the Manara Cable Car is its major tourist attraction. For years, the instablility in neighboring Lebanon profoundly affected life in the town, and by 1982 the spate of terrorist attacks had reached such proportions that Israel responded by invading Lebanon, the first stage of what would become the war with Lebanon. Kiryat Shmona was again in the news in 1996 when Hezbollah terrorists launched a focused and continued attack on the town and its environs using katyusha rockets. The Israel Defense Forces responded by targeting Hezbollah's bases in southern Lebanon in a campaign that became known as the Grapes of Wrath.

The Kiryat Shmona–Kibbutz Manara **Manara Cable Car** (☎ 04/690–4680) runs regularly from 9:30 AM to 5 PM daily and costs NIS 49. There is one station midway on the 1,890-yard trip, where the adventurous can step out and do some rappelling and dry-sliding (a roller-coaster-like activity), or try the climbing wall. One option is to take the cable car up and mountain bike down. There's also the thrill of a 600-foot zip line— a harnessed, partially free-fall jump down a cable to the ground. If you opt to remain in the cable car, the trip takes eight minutes each way, overlooking cliffs and green hills from a height of some 850 yards. There is wheelchair access to the cable car and upper station.

**17** Perched on the northern edge of Kiryat Shmona is **Tel Hai,** meaning "hill of life" in Hebrew. In a sense, the hill did become a monument to life after a memorable battle in 1920. In the aftermath of World War I, while Britain and France bickered over who should have final control of the upper Hula Valley, bands of Arabs often harassed the tiny Jewish farming settlements. They overran Tel Hai, and caused a temporary abandonment of the old village of Metulla; only Kibbutz Kfar Giladi was successful in defending itself, and it has since gone on to become one of the largest and most prosperous kibbutzim.

Following the Tel Hai incident, in which two defenders were killed, Tel Hai resident Josef Trumpeldor and seven comrades were called on to protect the place. Trumpeldor already had a reputation as a leader in the czar's army in his native Russia, where he lost an arm fighting. Fired by Zionist ideals, he moved to Palestine in 1912 at the age of 32 with a group of followers in tow. During the final battle in 1920 Trumpeldor and his comrades were killed and it is for them that Kiryat Shmona—City of the Eight—is named. It is said that Trumpeldor's last words were: "It is good to die for our country." He is buried just up the road from the museum, beneath the stone statue of a lion.

The heroic last stand at Tel Hai's came to have two important consequences for the area: one is that it was the first modern instance of Jewish armed self-defense, and the second is that the survival of at least two of the Jewish settlements determined that when the final borders were drawn by the League of Nations in 1922, these settlements were included in the British-mandated territory of Palestine and thus, after 1948, in the State of Israel.

The **Tel Hai Courtyard Museum** displays agricultural tools used in Trumpeldor's time. A moving audiovisual show highlights the history of the place. The museum is currently being remodeled, but you can still go in. The admission price may change in late 2006. ⊠ *Off Rte. 886* ☎ *04/695–1333* ⊠ *NIS 14* ☉ *Sun.–Thurs. 8–4, Fri. and Jewish holiday eves 10–3, interim days of Passover, Succot, and July and Aug., 8–5; Sat. visits for groups only by prior reservation.*

### Where to Stay & Eat
In addition to the guest houses here, there is a large (200-bed) **youth hostel** (⊠ Mobile Post, Tel Hai Upper Galilee 12210 ☎ 04/694–0043 🖷 04/694–1743). For camping or bungalows, head for the **Hurshat Tal National Park** (⊠ East of Hagoshrim on Rte. 99, 8 km [5 mi] east of Kiryat Shmona ☎ 04/694–2360 🖷 04/695–9360), opposite Kibbutz Dafna, but remember that it gets pretty cold here at night once summer is over.

For food options, the **Alonim Mall** (⊠ Off Rte. 99 near Kiryat Shmona, opposite Kibbutz Ma'ayan Baruch), a strip mall also known as Gan Hatzafon ("the northern garden"), has a number of eateries, including falafel and shwarma places.

**$$$** ✕ **Dag al Hadan.** Fresh trout and a cool glass of wine, in a shady woodlet by the gurgling Dan River—it's as good as it sounds, except on crowded weekends. This was the first restaurant in the region to specialize in the fish the Dan yields in abundance; you can see the trout ponds in a small installation on the grounds. The same management also runs a café next door where light vegetarian meals are served. The restaurant is tucked away behind the main road, but it's large and well signposted. ⊠ *Off Rte. 99 near Kiryat Shmona, opposite Kibbutz Hagoshrim* ☎ *04/695– 0225* ⚄ *Reservations essential on weekends* ⊟ *AE, DC, MC, V.*

**$$$**  ✕ **Jordan Pagoda.** Unlikely, but somehow, it works: a Chinese-Thai restaurant and sushi bar in a pagoda made of timber on the banks of the Jordan River. The restaurant, which caters to families, is part of the Jordan Sources complex, which has 10 very reasonably priced wooden cabins. The complex is on the grounds of Kibbutz Sde Nechemia. ⊠ *Kibbutz Sde Nechemia (8 km, or 5 mi, from Kiryat Shmona), Rte. 918* ☎ *04/ 694–7447* ⊟ *AE, DC, MC, V.*

**$–$$**  ✕ **The Foccacia Bar.** This family restaurant in the Alonim Mall serves a good selection of pastas and pizzas, as well as meat dishes with a Middle Eastern touch. ⊠ *Off Rte. 99 near Kiryat Shmona, opposite Kibbutz Ma'ayan Baruch* ☎ *04/690–04474* ⊟ *AE, DC, MC, V.*

★ **$$$–$$$$**  ⌂ **Kfar Blum Guest House.** Tucked in the northern Hula Valley, Kfar Blum's home-style hospitality is enhanced by its garden setting. The spacious rooms in their new wing are far above the usual kibbutz hotel standard. One of the kibbutz's major attractions is its kayaks—what better way to experience the Jordan River? (Guests receive a 20% discount.) Kfar Blum hosts an annual chamber music festival in summer. ⊠ *North of Rte. 977, near Kiryat Shmona, Upper Galilee 12150* ☎ *04/683–6611* ⊞ *04/683–6600* ⊕ *www.net-travel.org/kibbutz/kibbutzhotels/kfarblum. htm* ⇨ *130 rooms* ⚄ *Restaurant, tennis courts, pool, kayaking, bar* ⊟ *AE, DC, MC, V.*

**$$**  ⌂ **Hagoshrim Kibbutz Hotel.** The waters of the Hermon River flow right through Hagoshrim—under a glass-topped channel in the ceramic tile of the lobby and then through the property, creating a uniquely natural setting. While the rooms are simply decorated, the lobby is especially pleasant, with blond wood furniture and colorful cushions and throw rugs. Gosh ($–$$$), the hotel restaurant, specializes in fish and homemade cheeses. Kayaking and guided walking tours are available. ⊠ *Rte. 99, east of Kiryat Shmona, Upper Galilee 12225* ☎ *04/681–6000* ⊞ *04/ 681–6002* ⊕ *www.hagoshrim-hotel.co.il* ⇨ *180 rooms* ⚄ *Restaurant, cafeteria, squash court, pool, pub* ⊟ *AE, DC, MC, V.*

**$$**  ⌂ **Kibbutz Hotel Kfar Giladi.** Atop a hill behind Tel Hai is one of the oldest and largest kibbutz hotels in Israel. It's run very efficiently, but it still retains a homey atmosphere. Typical to kibbutz hotels, the rooms are on the plain side, but some have lovely views of the Hula Valley and Mt. Hermon. The gift shop has some unusual handcrafted items, many made by senior members of the kibbutz. The Bet Hashomer Museum, which explores the pre-State history of the kibbutz and the vicinity, is on the grounds. ⊠ *Rte. 886, Upper Galilee 12210* ☎ *04/690–0000* ⊞ *04/690– 0069* ⊕ *www.kibbutz.co.il/kibbutzhotels/kfargiladi.htm* ⇨ *180 rooms* ⚄ *Snack bar, pool, health club, sauna, minibars* ⊟ *AE, DC, MC, V.*

### The Arts
For the classically minded, **Kibbutz Kfar Blum** (⊠ Upper Galilee 12150 ☎ 04/683–6611) hosts **Chamber Music Days** each year in late July and early August, a nationally renowned festival of chamber music in a pastoral setting.

### Sports & the Outdoors

A plethora of outfits organize water sport trips in this region, and almost all hotels can make reservations for you. The minimum age for kayaks and other water "vehicles" is usually six.

KAYAKING **Hagoshrim Kayaks** (☎ 04/681–6034) has a 5-km (3-mi) "family" course that lasts 1½ hours and a 6-km (4-mi) "stormy" course that expands on the family course and lasts almost two hours. The family course costs NIS 68 per person, the stormy course NIS 90 per person.

**Kibbutz Kfar Blum** (☎ 04/690–2616) rents two-person rubber kayaks for 1½-hour or 2-hour runs. The cost is NIS 98 per person for the short course and NIS 105 per person for the long course. Kayaks are available from March through October; call ahead to inquire at other times of the year. At the same site, they also have a climbing wall, a rope park, a zip line across the water, and archery, at NIS 68 per person for the package.

**Jordan Sources** (✉ On the grounds of Kibbutz Sde Nechemia ☎ 04/694–7447) runs a 3½-hour kayaking trip (this one can be rough) costing NIS 75 per person and a 1½-hour trip for NIS 50 per person.

TUBING **Sde Nechemia** (✉ Kibbutz Huliot ☎ 04/694–6010), near Kiryat Shmona along Route 99, rents inner tubes for NIS 50 for an hour or so.

OFF-ROAD **Easy Track,** a company based in Moshav She'ar Yashuv in the northern VEHICLES Hula Valley, offers wind-in-your-hair ways to explore the countryside, including self-drive dune buggies (driver's license required) or a 1½-hour guided mini-Jeep trips, as well as bicycle rentals. ✉ *Moshav She'ar Yashuv* ☎ *04/690–4440* ⊕ *www.mbez.co.il.*

## Metulla

 *7 km (4 mi) north of Kiryat Shmona.*

Israel's northernmost town, Metulla, is so picturesque that it's hard to believe this tranquil spot is just a stone's throw from its foes in Lebanon.

The tensions of the Middle East dissipate here in the charm of the European-style limestone buildings that line Metulla's main street, and the city itself seems to have changed little since its founding as a farming settlement in 1896. The Continental atmosphere is enhanced by the numerous signs offering ZIMMER (German for "room") for rent. Even the weather is decidedly un-Mediterranean, with refreshingly cool mountain breezes carrying whiffs of cypress and spice plants in summer, and snow in winter.

In June 2000 a new chapter (but certainly not the last) of the old story was written, when the Good Fence border-crossing at Metulla, through which hundreds of Lebanese civilians used to come to Israel to work, was closed in the wake of the pullback of Israeli troops from southern Lebanon.

**need a break?** Take a picnic to the **Nahal Ayoun Nature Reserve,** just south of Metulla next to Route 90. Just a 10-minute walk from the picnic area is a spring. (✉ East of Rte. 90, south of entrance to Metulla ☎ 04/

695–1519 🖪 NIS 18 ⊙ Apr.–Sept., Sat.–Thurs. 8–5, Fri. 8–4; Oct.–Mar., Sat.–Thurs. 8–4, Fri. 8–3)

### Sports & the Outdoors

The multistory, multipurpose **Canada Centre** (⊠ 1 Harishonim St. ☎ 04/695–0370), at the top of the hill, has just about everything a sports complex can offer. For the price of admission (NIS 69) you can spend the whole day here, playing basketball, ice-skating, working out, bowling, swimming, zooming down the water slide, or taking aim on the shooting range. If it gets to be too much, the spa offers a sauna, hot tub, and massages. The complex is open daily 10–8 and contains a restaurant in case you're afraid you burned too many calories.

The ice-skating rink is one of only two in the Middle East; the other is in Saudi Arabia, but what the Saudis cannot boast are world-class former Soviet skaters, several of whom now live in Metulla and teach the sport at the center. If you're lucky, you might catch a demonstration of their dazzling skills.

## Tel Dan Nature Reserve

**19**
Fodor'sChoice
★
*25 km (15½ mi) southeast of Metulla, 15 km (9 mi) northeast of Kiryat Shmona.*

Tel Dan is hard to beat for sheer natural beauty. A river surges through it, and luxuriant trees provide shade. A host of small mammals live here— many partial to water, such as the otter and the mongoose—as well as the biblical coney, also known as the hyrax. This is also the home of Israel's largest rodent, the nocturnal Indian crested porcupine, and its smallest predator, the marbled polecat. The reserve has several hiking trails; a short segment, on a raised wooden walkway, is wheelchair accessible.

Dan was a majestic city in biblical times. According to Genesis, Abraham came here to rescue his nephew Lot and, five centuries later, Joshua led the Israelites through the area to victory. Fine ruins from several epochs lie here. Among them are the 9th-century BC city gate and the cultic site where King Jeroboam set up a golden calf to rival the Jerusalem Temple. Just inside the city gate was discovered the platform for a throne, where the king of the city pronounced judgment. One of the site's most extraordinary finds was an arched gateway dating from the 18th century BC Canaanite period, more than a millennium before the time scholars previously believed the arch was invented. ⊠ *North of Rte. 99* ☎ *04/695–1579* 🖪 *NIS 23* ⊙ *Apr.–Sept., Sat.–Thurs. 8–5, Fri. 8–4; Oct.–Mar., Sat.–Thurs. 8–4, Fri. 8—3. Last entrance one hour before closing.*

## Bet Ussishkin

*1 km (½ mi) from Tel Dan Nature Reserve.*

☺ Adjacent to the Tel Dan Nature Reserve, the **Bet Ussishkin Museum** can really enhance a visit to the Dan Nature Reserve. Children will appreciate the displays here, which document the flora, fauna, and geology found around the Hula Valley, the Golan Heights, and the Jordan River.

The audiovisual presentations are concise and informative. ⊠ *Off Rte. 99* ☎ *04/694–1704* ⊕ *www.zimmer.co.il/ussishkin/indexe.html* 💳 *NIS 18* ⊙ *Sun.–Thurs. 8–4, Fri. and Jewish holiday eves 8–3, Sat. 9:30–4:30.*

# GOLAN HEIGHTS

Geologically distinct from the limestone massif of Mt. Hermon, to its north, the basalt slopes of the Golan Heights extend about 60 km (37 mi) from north to south and between 15 km and 25 km (between 9 mi and 15½ mi) across. The whole region was once volcanic, and many symmetrical volcanic cones and pronounced reliefs still dominate the landscape, particularly in the upper Golan. Where the dark basalt rock has weathered or been cleared, the mineral-rich soil supports a wide variety of crops. The Golan's gentle terrain and climate have historically attracted far more settlement than the less hospitable northern Upper Galilee. In spring the region, already greened by winter rains, comes alive with wildflowers, but when the summer heat has frizzled everything to a uniform yellow-brown, it seems a land of desolation. Sights here range from nature reserves in the north, to a winery and archaeological sites near Katzrin, in the south. The Golan was part of Syria and was taken by Israel in the 1967 War.

## Hermon River (Banias) Nature Reserve

★ ⑳ *20 km (12½ mi) east of Kiryat Shmona.*

One of the most stunning parts of Israel, this reserve contains gushing waterfalls, dense foliage along riverbanks, and the remains of a temple dedicated to the god Pan. There are two entrances, each with a parking lot: the first is indicated on a sign as BANIAS WATERFALL; the other is 1 km (½ mi) farther along the same road and marked BANIAS.

The **Banias Spring** emanates at the foot of mostly limestone Mt. Hermon, just where it meets the basalt layers of the Golan Heights. The most popular short route in the reserve is up to the **Banias Cave,** via the path that crosses the spring. Excavations reveal the five niches hewed out of the rock to the right of the cave; these are what remain of Hellenistic and Roman temples, depicted in interesting artist's renderings. Three of the niches bear inscriptions in Greek mentioning Pan, the lover of tunes; Echo, the mountain nymph; and Galerius, one of Pan's priests. All early references to the cave identify it as the source of the spring, but earthquakes over the years have changed the landscapes formations, and the water now emerges at the foot of the cave rather than from within it.

Altogether the Banias Reserve offers three interconnected hiking trails—ask for the English trail map and advice at the cashier's booth. One, which passes a Crusader gate, walls, and moat, takes about 45 minutes. The second, also about 45 minutes, explores the magnificent 1,613-square-foot palace complex dating to the reign of Herod's grandson Agrippa II, on top of which are the ruins of what is thought to have been the marketplace of the day: a string of single chambers along a well-preserved section of wall might well have been shops. The third is a 90-minute trail leading past the **Officers' Pool,** built by the Syrians, and a

# CloseUp

## THE CITY OF PAN

**THE NAME BANIAS** is an Arabic corruption of the Greek Panias (Arabic has no p), the original name given to the area that, in the early 4th century BC, was dedicated to the colorful Greek god Pan, the half-goat–half-human deity of herdsmen, music, and wild nature—and of homosexuals and nymphs. The Banias Reserve encompasses the ruins of this ancient city.

Herod the Great ruled the city in the 1st century AD; his son Philip inherited it and changed the city's name to to Caesarea Philippi, to distinguish it from the Caesarea his father had founded on the Mediterranean coast. Roman rule in this part of the kingdom did not last another generation past Philip, but Panias continued to flourish until after the Muslim conquest in the 7th century AD, when it declined into no more than a village. In the 10th century AD Muslim immigration brought renewed settlement and Jews also came to Banias (as it became known

sometime during the 7th century), and the town also became an important center for the Karaite sect (an offshoot of Judaism).

In the early 12th century, Banias was held by Crusaders, who saw it as a natural border between their kingdom and the neighboring Muslim realm, whose center was Damascus. The Muslims recaptured Banias in 1132, but the city declined in importance and was taken over by Bedouin chieftains. It became a small village, which it remained until the area was conquered by the IDF in the 1967 Six-Day War and was abandoned by its inhabitants.

water-operated flour mill, to the thundering 33-meter high **Banias Waterfall.** The trails are spiced with the pungent aroma of mint and figs, and studded with blackberry bushes. If time is short, you may prefer to take a brief walk to the falls, return to your car, then drive on to the second entrance to see the caves and the spring where the Hermon River originates. The cost of admission covers entry to both sites.

For those ready for a real hiking challenge, who have the possibility of a car waiting at the other end, a long, very steep trail leads from the parking lot at the Banias Nature Reserve through the oak and thorny broom forest up to Nimrod's Fortress, a 40- to 60-minute climb.

✉ Off Rte. 99 ☎ 04/695–0272 💲 NIS 23 ⊙ Apr.–Sept., Sat.–Thurs. 8–5, Fri. 8–4; Oct.–Mar., Sat.–Thurs. 8–4, Fri. 8–3.

**need a break?** A few minutes' walk along the trail leading to the Crusader ruins and the waterfall is the ancient flour mill and a **stall** where Druze villagers make their traditional pita (bigger and flatter than the commercial version), which is not only baked on the premises but also milled here. Until a few decades ago, this was where local Druze villagers milled their own flour. Now the mill and "bakery" service hungry hikers.

Pull up a rock, and for a few shekels you'll be served a large rolled-up pita with *labane* (white goat's cheese) and Turkish coffee.

> **off the beaten path**
>
> **THE GOLANI LOOKOUT –** The large number of monuments to fallen soldiers in the Golan is a reminder of the region's strategic importance—and the price paid to attain it. Among the easily accessible sites, where pre-1967 Syrian bunkers give a gunner's-eye view of the valley below, is the Golani Lookout, known in Arabic as Tel Faher, in the northern Golan. Here visitors can explore the trenches and bunkers that now stand silent. Caution: beyond the fences and clearly marked paths are old Syrian minefields that have not been completely detonated. ⊠ *Off Rte. 99; turn right just above Banias.*

## Nimrod's Fortress

★ ☾ ㉑ *5 km (3 mi) east of Hermon River (Banias) Nature Reserve.*

The dramatic views of this towering, burly fortress perched above Banias, appearing and disappearing behind each curve of the narrow road that leads to it, are part of the treat of a visit to Nimrod's Fortress (Kal'at Namrud). And once you're there, the fortress commands superb vistas, especially through the frames of its arched windows and the narrow archers' slits in its walls.

This fortress was built in 1218 by the Mameluke warlord al-Malik al-Aziz Othman to guard the vital route from Damascus via the Golan and Banias, to Lebanon and to the Mediterranean coast against a Crusader *reconquista* after their 1187 defeat. It changed hands between Muslims and Christians in the centuries to follow as both vied for control of the region. During one of its more interesting periods, from 1126 to 1129, Nimrod's Fortress was occupied by a fanatic sect of Muslims famous as murderers. Before heading out to track down their enemies, the cutthroats are said to have indulged in hashish, thus earning the nickname *hashashin* (hashish users), from which the word *assassin* is derived.

Nimrod's fortress is a highlight for kids, with a ladder-climb down to a vaulted cistern, a shadowy spiral staircase, and unexpected nooks and crannies. A path leads up to the fortress's central tower, or keep, where the feudal lord would have lived. ⊠ *Nimrod's Fortress National Park, Rte. 989 (off Rte. 99)* ☎ *04/694–9277* 🎟 *NIS 18* ☾ *Apr.–Sept., Sat.–Thurs. 8–5, Fri. 8–4; Oct.–Mar., Sat.–Thurs. 8–4, Fri. 8–3; Last entrance one hour before closing.*

## Mt. Hermon

㉒ *12 km (7½ mi) northeast of Nimrod's Fortress, 25 km (15½ mi) northeast of Kiryat Shmona.*

The summit of Mt. Hermon—famous as Israel's highest mountain, at 9,230 feet above sea level—is actually in Syrian territory. Its lower slopes attract Israelis to the country's only ski resort. Summer is arguably the most interesting time on the Hermon, though: after the winter snows melt, hikers can discover chasms and hidden valleys here, the long-term result of extremes in temperature. Moreover, a powerful array of colors and scents emerges from the earth as cockscomb, chamomile, and scores of other flowers and wild herbs are drawn out by the summer sun. Approaching from Nimrod's Fortress, you'll pass **Moshav Neve Ativ,** designed to look like a little piece of the Alps in the Middle East, replete with A-frame chalet-style houses, a handful of which have guest rooms. A detour through the old Druze village of **Majdal Shams** offers a number of good eateries.

## Skiing

The slopes of **Mt. Hermon** (☎ 04/698–1337) can't compare with those in Europe or the Americas, but there is a certain thrill to having a ski resort in a hot Mediterranean country—and for Israelis it's a bargain compared with flying to the Alps (figure about NIS 315 per day for admission to the site, lift tickets, and equipment rental). Frankly, though, Mt. Hermon has little to offer the serious, or even the novice, skier. There is a chair-lift ride to the top, year-round—NIS 50 for entrance and the lift—the better to enjoy the place in summer, when it's bursting with wildflowers. A track sled that spirals down a 950-yard course is another attraction. To get to Mt. Hermon, take Route 99 east to Route 989 north to Neve Ativ.

en route    **Ein Kiniya,** which appears across a valley on your left as you head east into the Golan on Route 99, is the most picturesque of the several Druze villages around here. The houses are built of the black basalt so prevalent in the Golan.

## Merom Golan

*20 km (12½ mi) south of Mt. Hermon.*

Kibbutz Merom Golan was the first settlement built in the Golan after the Six-Day War. Its fields and orchards are typical of local kibbutzim. Apples are especially good in these parts, but man cannot live by apples alone, so Merom Golan runs Cowboys' Restaurant, with good steaks.

### Where to Eat

$$  ✕ **Cowboys' Restaurant.** This is the best corral this side of the Israel-Syria Disengagement Zone. Saddle-shape stools at the bar and cattle hides on the walls contribute to the frontier atmosphere. But it's the grub—specifically the hearty steaks and the house specialty—chicken breast stuffed with smoked meat—that packs 'em in. ⊠ *Kibbutz Merom Golan, off Rte. 959* ☎ *04/696–0206* ▭ *AE, DC, MC, V.*

## Mt. Bental Observatory

*20 km (12½ mi) south of Mt. Hermon.*

From the top of this volcanic cone, once a military outpost, Mt. Hermon rises majestically to the north and the Syrian side of the Golan stretches eastward like it's on the palm of your hand. Opposite is the ruined town of Kuneitra, captured by Israel in 1967, lost and regained in the 1973 Yom Kippur War, and returned to Syria in the subsequent Disengagement

Agreement—it is now a demilitarized zone. Modern Kuneitra is in the distance. The cluster of white buildings south of old Kuneitra houses the United Nations Disengagement Observer Force. The pine-cabin shop that serves delicious herb teas and snacks is the perfect place to get out of the wind that often sweeps this peak. ☒ *Off Rte. 9981 near Kibbutz Merom Golan, north of the Avital junction with Rte. 91.*

## Katzrin

**㉓** *20 km (12½ mi) south of Merom Golan, 38 km (23½ mi) northeast of Tiberias, 35 km (22 mi) northeast of Tzfat.*

The commercial center of Katzrin, the "capital" of the Golan Heights, has a number of falafel stands, a couple of restaurants, a pharmacy, a pizzeria, a minimart, and several museums, all of which make it a perfect midday stop for travelers.

Katzrin, founded in 1977 near the site of a 3rd-century town of the same name, has a suburban feel, despite its strategic location and attendant sensitivity. The water here, which comes straight from the basalt bedrock, is delicious and makes your skin feel like silk. To get here from the northern Golan, take Route 91 west, and then go south on Route 87.

The **Golan Archaeological Museum** has a fascinating collection of animal bones, stones, and artifacts that put the region into historical and geographical perspective. Among the exhibits is a Bronze Age dwelling reconstructed from materials excavated nearby. Don't miss the moving film on the history and last stand of Gamla, the "Masada of the North," during the Great Revolt against the Romans (AD 66) and its rediscovery by archaeologists 1,900 years later. The museum is run in conjunction with the Ancient Katzrin Park. ☒ *Katzrin commercial center* ☎ *04/696–1350* ⊕ *www.golan.org.il/museum* ☒ *NIS 24, includes Ancient Katzrin Park* ☉ *Sept–May, Sun.–Thurs. 9–4, Fri. and Jewish holiday eves 9–2; June–Aug. and the interim days of Passover and Sukkoth, Sun–Thurs. 9–6, Fri and Jewish holiday eves 9–4. Sat. groups only by prior reservation.*

**㉔** **Ancient Katzrin Park,** 2 km (1 mi) east of Katzrin's business center, is a partially restored 3rd-century Jewish village, whose economy was based on the production of olive oil. The Katzrin synagogue has decorative architectural details, such as a wreath of pomegranates and amphorae in relief on the lintel above the entrance. The complexity of its ornamentation reflects the importance of the city. Built of basalt, the synagogue was used for 400 years until it was partly destroyed, possibly by an earthquake, in 749.

The park's two reconstructed buildings, the so-called House of Uzi and House of Rabbi Abun (presumably a Talmudic sage), are attractively decorated with rope baskets, weavings, baking vessels, and pottery (based on remnants of the originals), and lighted with little clay oil lamps.

☾ An audiovisual presentation, in a reconstructed building, helps makes connections between Talmudic times and the present. ☒ *Rte. 87* ☎ *04/ 696–2412* ⊕ *www.golan.org.il/park* ☒ *NIS 24, includes Golan Ar-*

*chaeological Museum* ⊙ *Sept.–May, Sun.–Thurs. 9–4, Fri. and Jewish holiday eves 9–2; June–Aug. and the interim days of Passover and Sukkoth, Sun–Thurs. 9–6, Fri. and Jewish holiday eves 9–4. Sat, groups only by prior reservation.*

**㉕** The **Golan Heights Winery,** in Katzrin's industrial zone, is one of Israel's top businesses; it launched the country into the international wine-making arena with its Yarden, Gamla, and Golan labels. The area's volcanic soil, cold winters, and cool summers, together with state-of-the-art wine-making, have proven a recipe for success. Wine-tasting tours are generally available if reserved in advance. The shop sells the full line of wines, including the Katzrin Chardonnay, the Yarden Gewürtztraminer, and the Yarden Cabernet Sauvignion, as well as sophisticated accessories for the oenophile. ✉ *Rte. 87 (east of town center)* ☎ *04/696–8420 for tours* ⊕ *www.golanwines.co.il* ✆ *Tour and tasting NIS 20* ⊙ *Sun.–Thurs. 8–5, Fri. 8–1:30; July and Aug., Sun–Thurs. until 6:30, Fri. until 2:30.*

## Where to Eat

$ ✕⌨ **The Yemenite-Eastern.** The name may be plain, but the food in this tiny eatery in the Katzrin commercial center is rich with Yemenite flavors and aromas. Shalom, the owner, chief cook, and bottle washer, makes a hearty meat soup, served alongside airy Yemenite pitas to dip in tangy fenugreek salsa. Middle Eastern salads, hamburgers, and other local favorites are also on offer. ✉ *Katzrin commercial center* ☎ *04/696–2412.*

## Nightlife

Within Katzrin Park, there's a **pub** (☎ 050/687–7617) in a century-old Syrian dwelling, with a selection of 10 different beers on tap and a dairy menu. The sheer experience of having a drink among the ancient ruins is worth a detour if you're lodging in this area. The pub is open from Saturday to Thursday, from 9 PM until the last patrons leave.

> **off the beaten path**
>
> **MITZPE GADOT –** If you continue northwest on Route 87 from Katzrin and then west on Route 91, you'll pass this tall, triangular concrete monument to fallen Israeli soldiers of the Golani Brigade. Caution: The site is safe, but don't explore beyond any marked paths, because there may be undetonated Syrian minefields.

# Gamla Nature Reserve

★ *20 km (12 mi) southeast of Katzrin; take Rte. 87 to Rte. 808 and watch for Gamla signpost*

Aside from the inspiring history of "the Masada of the north," the beauty of Gamla's rugged terrain, softened in spring by greenery and wildflowers, is truly breathtaking. Griffon vultures soar above and gazelles can often be seen bounding through the grasses. The main story of the camel-shaped Gamla (the name *Gamla* comes from *gamal,* the Hebrew word for "camel") goes back to the year AD 67, when at the beginning of the Great Revolt, Vespasian launched a bloody attack here that ended seven months later, when the 9,000 surviving Jews flung themselves to their deaths in the abyss below the town. The vivid descriptions of the battle, as written by Flavius Josephus in *The Jewish War,* are engraved in stones along the trail site. " . . . Built against the almost vertical flank, the town seemed to be hung in the air . . ."—exactly the impression visitors still have as they approach the site.

Because Gamla was never rebuilt, the relics of the battlefield still eerily match the ancient sources; among them the fortifications, 2,000 "missile stones," and a large number of arrowheads. From a much earlier period (probably the 2nd millennium BC) there are about 200 **dolmens** scattered in the area—strange basalt structures shaped like the Greek letter "pi," probably used for burial. There is an excellent film on the story of Gamla at the Golan Archaeological Museum in Katzrin. ⊠ *Off Rte. 808* ☎ *04/682–2282* ✉ *NIS 23* ☉ *Apr.–Sept., Sat.–Thurs. 8–4, Fri. 8–3; Oct.–Mar., Sat.–Thurs. 8–3, Fri. 8—2. Last entrance one hour before closing.*

# UPPER GALILEE & THE GOLAN ESSENTIALS

## Transportation

### BY AIR

Arkia Airlines operates three flights daily from Sde Dov Airport in Tel Aviv to the small Galilee airport of **Mahanayim**, near Rosh Pina. The flight takes ½ an hour. From the airport it is 10 km (6 mi) to Tzfat and 30 km (19 mi) to Kiryat Shmona.
🎦 Arkia Israeli Airlines ☎ 800/444-888.

### BY BUS

Local Egged buses stop at all major sights in this region (there is always a kibbutz, a town, or some other small residential settlement nearby), but you should avoid buses if you're on a tight schedule, as they tend to be infrequent. Call Egged for schedules. If you have trouble getting through to Egged, you can try the local bus stations.

From Tel Aviv, Egged runs 15 buses daily (22 on Sunday) to Kiryat Shmona (Bus 842) and 1 bus daily to Tzfat (Bus 846); from Jerusalem 4 buses daily to Kiryat Shmona (Bus 963) and 8 buses daily to Tzfat (Bus 982); from Haifa 16 buses daily (20 on Sunday) to Kiryat Shmona (Bus 500 or 501) and 33 buses daily (35 on Sunday) to Tzfat (Bus 361 or 362); and from Tiberias 11 buses daily (14 on Sunday) to Kiryat Shmona (Buses 841 and 963) and 12 buses daily to Tzfat (Bus 459).
🎦 Egged ☎ *2800 ⊕ www.egged.co.il Local depots ☎ Kiryat Shmona 04/681-8222, Tzfat 04/682-2044.

### BY CAR

It's much easier to rent a car in Tiberias ( ⇨ Lower Galilee Essentials *in* Chapter 5), Tel Aviv, Jerusalem, or Haifa than to search for a dependable rental agency in the tiny towns of the Upper Galilee. For those flying to the Galilee, Arkia Israeli Airlines can arrange for a rental car to be waiting at Mahanayim Airport, outside Rosh Pina.

The state of Israel's roads is generally fair-to-good, but in the Upper Galilee in particular, some roads are still two-lane. Drive cautiously! Try to avoid driving during peak hours (usually late Saturday afternoons), when city folk crowd the roads back to Jerusalem and Tel Aviv after a day out in the country.

Gas stations are numerous along Route 90 and in the towns, such as Katzrin (Route 87) and Tzfat (Route 89). Most are open daily but close by 9 PM, so it's best to fill up during the day.

The Upper Galilee and the Golan are a three-hour, 180-km (112-mi) drive from Tel Aviv; a 1½-hour, 60-km (37-mi) drive from both Akko and Nahariya; and four hours from Jerusalem, which is 200 km (124 mi) to the south. There are numerous routes to approach the area. From Tiberias and the Sea of Galilee, Route 90 runs north between the Hula Valley, on the east, and the hills of Naftali, on the west. The more rugged Route 98 runs from the eastern side of the Sea of Galilee up through the Golan Heights to Mt. Hermon. Near the top of Route 98 you can pick up Route 91, which heads west into the Upper Galilee.

From the Mediterranean coast there are several options, but the main one is Route 85 from Akko. Route 89 runs parallel to Route 85 a little farther north, from Nahariya, and has some gorgeous scenery. From Haifa take Route 75 to Route 77, turning onto Route 90 at Tiberias, or Route 70 north onto Route 85 east. If you're starting from Tel Aviv, drive north on Route 4 or 2 to Hadera; from there you'll head northwest on Route 65, exiting onto Route 85 east.

The main north–south roads in the region are Route 90, which goes all the way up to Metulla at the Lebanese border; the Tiberias–Metulla Road; and the less-traveled Route 98, which runs from the eastern side of the Sea of Galilee through the Golan Heights (along the Disengagement Zone) to Mt. Hermon. The main west–east highways are Route 85, which runs from Akko to Ami'ad, and Route 89, which connects Nahariya and Tzfat.

**BY TAXI**

The Hamavreek taxi company in Tzfat and the Hatzafon taxi company in Kiryat Shemona will pick up incoming travelers at the Mahanayim Airport who are bound for various destinations in the region. Otherwise, you can hail a taxi in the street.

🚖 **Hamavreek** 📞 04/697-4222

## Contacts & Resources

### BANKS & EXCHANGING SERVICES

As elsewhere in Israel, foreign bank cards can be used to withdraw Israeli currency from most automatic tellers. Currency exchange services are available at the reception desks of hotels and kibbutz guest houses and banks.

🏦 **Bank Hapoalim** ✉ Pedestrian Mall, Tzfat; Rosh Pina Mall 📞 *2497 contacts all Hapoalim banks ⊙ Sun., Tues., Wed., 8:30–1:15; Mon., Thurs. 8:30–1, 4–6:30 **Bank Leumi** ✉ Commercial center, Katzrin 📞 04/685-9333 ⊙ Mon.–Thurs. 8:30–1:30, Tues.–Wed. 4:30–7, Fri. 8:30–12:30. **First International** ✉ Pedestrian Mall, Tzfat 📞 04/690-9200 **Otzar Hahayal** ✉ Rosh Pina Mall 📞 04/693-5349 ⊙ Tues., Wed. 9–1:30; Mon., Thurs. 9–1:30, 3–5:30; Fri., 9–1

## EMERGENCIES

Emergency calls from public phones do not require tokens or telecards. The main police station in the Upper Galilee is in Kiryat Shmona. Magen David Adom, near the central bus station, handles medical and dental emergencies 24 hours a day. The largest hospital in the north outside Haifa is the Rivka Sieff General Hospital. Buses 6 and 7 from the Tzfat bus station stop here.

There are no 24-hour pharmacies in the north of Israel but there are several with extended hours.

**⚑ Ambulance** ☏ 101. **Fire** ☏ 102. **Magen David Adom** ⊠ 3 Tchernichovsky St., in Kiryat Shmona ☏ 04/694–4334 or 04/694–4335. **Police** ☏ 100. **Police station** ⊠ 1 Salinger St. Kiryat Shmona ☏ 04/694–3445. **Rivka Sieff General Hospital** ⊠ Harambam Rd., Tzfat ☏ 04/682–8811.

**New-Pharm Pharmacy** ⊠ Rosh Pina Mall, junction of road 90 and the Rosh Pina turnoff Rosh Pina ☏ 04/686–0645, 04/686–0058 ☾ Sun.–Thurs. 9–10, Fri. 9–6; Sat. 10–11 **Super-Pharm Pharmacy** ⊠ Nehemia Mall, junction of road 90 and road 99 Kiryat Shmona ☏ 04/690–5111 ☾ Sun.–Thurs. 8:30–10, Fri. 8–5, one hour earlier in winter

## INTERNET, MAIL & SHIPPING

Internet access is available in the lobbies of most of the region's kibbutz guest houses, and stamps are available for sale at the reception counters. Wi-Fi is not widely available in the region. Visitors can obtain dial-up access through the sales department at the local Internet server Netvision.

Post office hours are somewhat complicated, but the same at all branches: Sun.–Tues., Thurs. 8–12:30, Mon.–Tues., Thurs. 3:30–6, Sun. 3:30–6:30, Wed. 8–1, Fri. 8–12. The big names of package shipping—FedEx, DHL and UPS—are all well established in Israel.

**DHL** (☏ 700–707–345) **FedEx** (☏ 700–700–378) **Katzrin Post Office** (⊠ Commercial Center ☏ 04/696–1202) **Kiryat Shmona Post Office** (⊠ Tzahal Square 110, Commercial Center ☏ 04/694—0220) **Netvision** (☏ 800/017–017 ⊕ www.netvision.co.il) **Rosh Pina Post Office** (⊠ Gai-Oni St. next to the local council office ☏ 04/693—5710) **Tzfat Internet Café and Gallery** (⊠ Old City, near the Judith Gallery ☏ 04/682—0981 ☾ Sun.–Thurs. 9:30–1 AM, Fri. 9:30–4 PM; Sat. night from 1 hour after sunset–1 AM)

## TOUR OPTIONS

Both of Israel's major bus companies, Egged and United, used to offer one- and two-day guided tours of the region, departing from Tel Aviv and Jerusalem, but both have cut this service in recent years. There is some speculation that United may renew this service in 2006. Visitors can, however ask their hotel or B&B host about private guides. You can also contact the Fodor's writers ( ⇨ *See* Sightseeing Guides *in* Smart Travel Tips).

**⚑ Egged Tlalim** ⊠ 59 Ben Yehuda St., Tel Aviv ☏ 03/527–1212 ⊠ 8 Shlomzion Hamalka St., Jerusalem ☏ 02/622–1999. **United Tours** ⊠ 113 Hayarkon St., Tel Aviv ☏ 03/522–2008 or 03/693–3412 ⊠ King David Hotel Annex, Jerusalem ☏ 02/625–2187.

### VISITOR INFORMATION

All hotels and kibbutz guest houses can provide tourist information, and many will arrange tours as well.

Bet Ussishkin Museum has information about area nature reserves, natural history, and bird-watching. The Golan Tourist Association has a wealth of information about the Golan. The Israel Nature and Parks Authority staff at any of their sites are good resources for planning itineraries that include their sites in other parts of the region and the country. The visitor information service at Moshav Beit Hillel is especially helpful, with a wide selection of bed and breakfast accommodations in the moshave, which is in the heart of the Hula Valley tourist region. The Rosh Pina Information Center provides tips on touring Tzfat and Rosh Pina. The Tiberias Tourist Information Office can furnish information on the entire region. The Tourist Information Center–Upper Galilee can also provide information; it's open weekends and holidays only.

🚹 **Bet Ussishkin Museum** ✉ Kibbutz Dan, M.P. Upper Galilee 12245 ☎ 04/694-1704. **Golan Tourist Association** ✉ Box 171, Katzrin 12315 ☎ 04/696-2885 ⊕ www.tour.golan. org.il. **Israel Nature and Parks Authority Northern District** ✉ Megiddo National Park ☎ 04/659-0316 ⊕ www.parks.org.il. **Moshav Beit Hillel** ✉ Upper Galilee ☎ 04/690-4001, 04/694-2728. **Rosh Pina Information Center** ✉ Rte. 90, at the Rosh Pina Junction ☎ 04/684-1465. **Tiberias Tourist Information Office** (TIO) ✉ Habanim St., at the Mahanayim Junction, next to the gas station. Tiberias ☎ 04/672-5666. **Tourist Information Center–Upper Galilee** ✉ Mahanayim Junction ☎ 04/693-6945.

### WHERE TO STAY

Rooms in kibbutz guest houses can be reserved directly or through Kibbutz Hotels Chain, a central reservation service based in Tel Aviv, although not all the kibbutzim are represented. Moshav Beit Hillel also makes kibbutz and bed-and-breakfast reservations.

🚹 **Kibbutz Hotels Chain** ✉ 90 Ben Yehuda St. ☎ 03/560-8118 🖶 03/527-8088 ⊕ www.kibbutz.co.il **Moshav Beit Hillel** ✉ M.P. Upper Galilee 12255 ☎ 04/690-4001, 04/694-2728.

# Eilat & the Negev

WITH A SIDE TRIP TO PETRA

By Judy Stacey Goldman

**THE NEGEV IS ISRAEL'S** southernmost region, an upside-down triangle that constitutes about half the country's land mass, but is home to only about 6% of the population. The Negev's northern border, the base of this triangle, lies about 27 km (17 mi) north of Beersheva, which is the capital of the Negev and the only large city within its borders. The Jordanian and Egyptian borders mark its eastern and western limits, respectively, and Eilat, a resort town on the Gulf of Eilat at the gateway to the Red Sea, is at its southernmost tip.

The word "negev" means dry; it is a semiarid and arid desert. If this sounds rather dull, it isn't—a flamboyant, intriguing world awaits visitors. The Negev contains Israel's most dramatic natural scenery as well as pampering luxuries, from the gigantic *makhtesh* (erosion crater) in the rugged highlands to sparkling ultramodern hotels and classy restaurants in Eilat; from multicolored, layered mountains of the vast Timna Valley park to opulent spa hotels at the Dead Sea, the lowest point on earth. You can visit the kibbutz home and grave of Israel's first prime minister—David Ben-Gurion, the man who first dreamed of settling the desert—and on the same day you can tour the millennia-old ruins at Tel Beer Sheva, visited by the biblical patriarch Abraham. At the Red Sea city of Eilat you can snorkel past multicolored tropical fish and coral formations, and in both Eilat and Ein Bokek you can indulge in spa treatments. You can learn to scuba dive, eat foie gras followed by grilled fish, take a camel trip at sunset, bike, hike, lie in the year-round sun, take a Dead Sea–mud bath, drink coffee made over a fire in the mountains, meditate on a cliff, buy an Israeli-designer swimsuit or Roman glass earrings, and gaze at migrating storks.

If all this isn't enough, another option is a day trip or overnight visit to Petra in Jordan. The rose-red remains of this ancient city of the wealthy Nabateans, who controlled a spice route that stretched from Arabia to the Mediterranean, are carved into towering sandstone cliffs. Petra's gigantic monuments and royal tombs, 2,000 years old, are treasures even in a region filled with antiquities.

The Negev has a long and varied human history. The ancient Israelites had fortifications here, as did the Nabateans and the Romans after them. The region's first kibbutzim were established in the early 1940s, with new immigrants sent south after the War of Independence, in 1948. Two years later, people started trickling into Eilat, which was nothing but a few rickety huts. Arad put down its roots in 1961. The desert itself was pushed back, and the semiarid areas between Tel Aviv and Beersheva became fertile farmland. Today, agricultural settlements throughout the Negev make use of brackish water to raise tomatoes, melons, olives, and dates that are sent to winter markets in Europe. Fishponds and vineyards can now be seen in the dry landscape. Throughout these periods, the area has been home to the Bedouin, whose distinctive way of desert life can still be seen today.

The army has been deployed over a large part of the Negev since the Sinai was handed back to Egypt in 1982. You'll feel a military presence at roadside diners, where soldiers stop to eat; at bus stations, where they're in transit; and at tent-filled compounds here and there. Signs declaring

The following itineraries cover the major (and some off-the-beaten-path) Negev sights for travelers who are driving and have a limited amount of time. All assume that you're coming from Tel Aviv or Jerusalem. You can reach a few places by bus, but this is definitely not the most comfortable way to get around. You might combine one of these itineraries with a short guided tour.

*Numbers in the text correspond to numbers in the margin and on the Eilat & the Negev map.*

**7**

**If you have 1 or 2 days**

You can cram a lot of Negev sights into a day or two; just get an early start from Jerusalem or Tel Aviv. You can stop at the **Museum of Bedouin Culture ❶** or drive straight to Beersheva on your way to see the reconstruction of a 1943 military desert outpost at **Mitzpe Revivim ❷**. Next, visit renowned prime minister **David Ben-Gurion's desert home ❸** and **grave ❹**, overlooking the Wilderness of Zin. Head down the twisting road near the grave site to get to **Ein Avdat ❺**, a welcome respite of splashing waterfalls in the blazing summer and a green and picturesque sight in winter. It's a short drive from Ein Avdat to the 2,000-year-old Nabatean hilltop stronghold of **Avdat ❻**, which you can explore on foot. If you have only one day, skip Ein Avdat and Avdat and drive straight to the visitor center at **Mitzpe Ramon ❼** to see the **Makhtesh Ramon ❼**. If you have two days, spend the night in Mitzpe Ramon and explore the immense crater the next morning. (If you've brought children, they'll appreciate a visit to the Alpaca Farm, just outside town.) Your return trip brings you back to **Beersheva ❽**, where you can choose between visiting **Tel Beer Sheva ❿** and the possible site of Abraham's Well and stopping at the **Israel Air Force Museum ❾**, in Hatzerim, to see a field full of planes.

**If you have 5 days**

Start at the **Museum of Bedouin Culture ❶** for a look at the lifestyle of Israel's nomads. The sandy landscape along Route 31 takes you through ancient **Tel Arad ⓫** and modern **Arad ⓬**. From Arad drive the dramatic 24-km (15-mi) descent on sharply curving Route 31 to the Dead Sea, the lowest point on Earth. Stay overnight in 🏨 **Ein Bokek ⓭** and devote the next morning to floating in the Dead Sea and enjoying your hotel's spa facilities. By afternoon you'll be well relaxed and ready to drive south to 🏨 **Eilat ⓮**, where you can spend two more days relaxing on the beach in an entirely different setting. (Feeling energetic? Take a trip to the ancient city of Petra, in Jordan, on one of those days to see its dramatic monuments.) Back on the road on the fourth day, going north, drive through the **Makhtesh Ramon ❼** to reach 🏨 **Mitzpe Ramon ❼**, on the crater's edge; spend the night there. You might have time to go to the visitor center or at least enjoy the cliffside promenade before dark. On your last day head back to Tel Aviv or Jerusalem, stopping at either **Arad ⓬**, **Ben-Gurion's desert home ❸**, **Ben-Gurion's grave ❹**, **Mitzpe Revivim ❷**, or the **Israel Air Force Museum ❾** (you won't have time to see them all).

**If you have 9 days**

Follow the first three days of the itinerary above, spending the third and fourth nights in **Eilat ⓮**. On the fourth and fifth days, kick back, learn to dive, swim with dolphins, bird-watch, hike, or take a guided tour of the Eilat area. Another option is to make a side trip to Jordan to see the rose-red remains of ancient Petra. On Day 6 drive north to the **Makhtesh Ramon ⑦**. Stay overnight in ▨ **Mitzpe Ramon ⑦**. On Day 7 you might take a Jeep tour, and perhaps visit the Alpaca Farm. Heading north on Route 40 on Day 8, visit ancient **Avdat ⑥**, **Ben-Gurion's home ③**, **Ben-Gurion's grave ④**, or **Ein Avdat ⑤** on your way to ▨ **Beersheva ⑧** for the night. If your last day (spent in Beersheva) is a Thursday, you can get an early start at the Bedouin market or visit **Tel Beer Sheva ⑩**—or the **Israel Air Force Museum ⑨** or **Mitzpe Revivim ②**—on your way to Tel Aviv or Jerusalem.

---

FIRING ZONES indicate areas that the public may not enter, and checkpoints—where a smile and a wave-through are the order of the day—are scattered throughout.

## Top 5 Reasons to Go

- **Makhtesh Ramon:** Explore Israel's most spectacular natural site—by foot, mountain bike, or Jeep. The giant crater is a geological phenomenon with hundreds of rock formations and different-color layers of rocky cliffs formed over thousands of years.

- **Coral Reserve, Eilat:** Put on your snorkel, swim around, and marvel at the brilliant-color fish and entrancing corals at one of the finest protected areas of its kind in the world.

- **Spas and more spas:** Luxuriate in hedonistic bliss at one of the lush resort spas by the Dead Sea, which has the lowest elevation on Earth.

- **A camel ride at sunset:** Travel up into the mountains around Eilat on your own "ship of the desert" to see the sunset turn the Gulf of Eilat red, and wave at Jordan, Egypt, and Saudi Arabia in the distance.

- **Scuba diving:** Dive centers in Eilat take PADI divers on safaris to explore off-shore Aqaba and Jordan, and to get personal with dolphins, coral reefs, tropical plant life, and Day-Glo fish.

# Exploring Eilat & the Negev

Our peregrinations cover three basic areas in the inverted triangle of the Negev. The first is the Negev's heart, with sites such as David Ben-Gurion's home and grave, the ancient Nabatean-Roman-Byzantine ruins at Tel Avdat, and the amazing Ramon Crater (the makhtesh). The second, in the north, includes the capital city of Beersheva, the spa-resort town of Ein Bokek at the Dead Sea, the ancient city of Tel Arad, and the modern city of Arad. The third, and southern, tip of the triangle encompasses carefree Eilat, the Underwater Observatory at Coral Beach, and Timna Park. Eilat is also the jumping-off point for a trip to Jordan and the ruins of the ancient city of Petra.

As you travel through the Negev, you'll pass stretches of flat, uninhabited countryside under hot, blue skies, punctuated by the odd acacia tree, twisting wadi, or craggy mountain. In winter you'll see delicate desert flowers along the road. If you want to skip the desert-driving experience, you might limit your trip here to Eilat or Ein Bokek. In Eilat you can stay at a luxurious hotel, relax on the sunny shore, and dive or snorkel. In Ein Bokek you can settle into one of the numerous health and beauty spas that make use of the Dead Sea waters and medicinal mud.

## About the Restaurants

If the word "dining" conjures up starched and draped tablecloths, gliding waiters, and gleaming silver, head for the upscale restaurants and luxury hotels of Eilat and Ein Bokek. Although Eilat is at the southern tip of a desert, it has all the essentials—including Ben & Jerry's. Tastes range from Italian, Indian, and French to Argentinian, Yemenite, and Thai. Specialty fish restaurants abound—excellent sea fish, including delicacies such as *denise* (sea bream) and the Israeli specialty *forel* (salmontrout bred in the Dan River up north), make wonderful meals.

In the rest of the Negev, with the notable exception of the Mitzpe Ramon Inn, plan to dine in humble surroundings—typically a roadside diner—on meals that are apt to reflect the cook's ethnic background. You might find Tunisian carrot salad, Moroccan *cigarim* (flaky pastry with a meat or potato filling), or standard Middle Eastern fare: hummus, pita, grilled meat, french fries (known here as chips), chopped or shredded vegetable salads (*salatim*), strong coffee in small cups, and fruit or chocolate mousse for dessert. Keep in mind that outside Eilat, restaurants close early on Friday, and since the main meal of the day is served at noon in the desert, lunch may be history if you arrive after 1:30.

If people are dressed up anywhere, it will be at the better restaurants (and nightclubs and discos) in Eilat and Ein Bokek, though ties are never required. Everywhere else, the finest attire you'll see is a clean T-shirt. It's always a good idea to make reservations at Eilat and Ein Bokek restaurants, especially on Friday and Saturday night.

| WHAT IT COSTS in Israeli shekels | | | | |
|---|---|---|---|---|
| $$$$ | $$$ | $$ | $ | ¢ |
| AT DINNER  over NIS 100 | NIS 76–NIS 100 | NIS 50–NIS 75 | NIS 32–NIS 49 | Under NIS 32 |

Prices are for a main course at dinner.

## About the Hotels

Hotels in sunny Eilat and Ein Bokek (Dead Sea) run from family-style to huge, lush, and luxurious. Pleasure comes first: business facilities on a modest scale are available in larger hotels, whereas a beautiful and luxurious spa with a wide range of facilities is an important feature of each large hotel. Even many of the smaller hotels have installed spas. In Eilat, a few hotels operate on an all-inclusive basis.

Keep in mind that prices rise during high season and holidays. High season is Hanukkah/Christmas, Passover/Easter, and July and August, when Israelis take a break (and hotels are crowded with families). At Ein Bokek, high season is mid-March to mid-June and mid-September to the end of November. Eilat's hotels are crowded with Europeans from October until April. Reserve well in advance at any time of year.

| WHAT IT COSTS | | | | |
|---|---|---|---|---|
| $$$$ | $$$ | $$ | $ | ¢ |
| EILAT AND EIN BOKEK HOTELS | | | | |
| over $400 | $300–$400 | $231–$299 | $160–$230 | under $160 |
| OTHER AREA HOTELS | | | | |
| over $250 | $175–$250 | $111–$174 | $65–$110 | under $65 |

Prices are for two people in a standard double room in high season. Non-Israeli citizens paying in foreign currency are exempt from the 16.5% VAT tax on hotel rooms.

## Timing

October through May is the best time to explore the Negev. In the winter months of January and February it's dry and cold. Scorching-hot conditions prevail in the summer, from June through late September (though it's very dry), so your best bet then is to stay by the water, in Eilat. Ein Bokek, with its unique hotels and spas by the Dead Sea, attracts visitors even in the wildly hot summer. In early March, you'll be treated to the sight of scarlet, bright yellow, white, and hot pink desert flowers bursting out against the brown desert earth; March is also when Eilat's International Bird-watchers' Festival takes place.

Most Negev sites open at 8:30 AM and close by 4 PM in winter and 5 PM in summer. Restaurants (except those in Ein Bokek and Eilat) serve their main meal of the day (hot food) at noon and often close by early evening. Most places close early on Friday; roadside diners close at around 1:30 PM. If you plan to add Petra to your itinerary, allow a full day or an overnight.

Get an early start; plan to be inside or resting at midday in summer; and make every effort to reach your destination by nightfall. Always lock your car, take your valuables when you leave it, and stash your bags where they're not visible from the outside. Women should not hitchhike.

## Desert Precautions

To remain comfortable, happy, and *safe,* you must observe certain rules of the desert. You should drink two quarts of water a day in the winter, and if you're active, one quart per hour in the summer; dehydration sets in quickly in the desert. Keep a jerrican (which holds five gallons) of water in your car, plus extra bottles. You'll find water fountains along the way, but they don't always function. Wear sunblock, sunglasses, protective lip balm, and a hat—a must year-round. Light hiking shoes and a small knapsack are indispensable for walks and hikes, as are bug spray and a flashlight.

Although it may seem incongruous in the desert, road flooding is a very real danger from September through March, especially the day after a rainfall farther north. In the spring, low-pressure systems from the Red Sea can bring torrential rains. If it's raining or has recently rained, call the **police** (☎ 100) for advice on road conditions. You can also call the 24-hour operations center of the **Society for the Protection of Nature in**

**7**

Adventure Tours A thrilling way to see the Negev is by Jeep or camel, in the company of an expert guide who is not only familiar with every facet of desert life but also knows how to prepare open-air meals and brew tea from desert plants (your guide might be a resident of a desert settlement). If you have time, take a several-day trek through the desert, an unforgettable experience; tour outfits provide the camping equipment. Certain desert expeditions combine hiking, camel riding, and rappelling. It's wise to reserve in advance; you can often do so through a travel agency or your hotel. Note that some tours don't operate in the summer, when it's very hot.

Hiking the Desert Exploring the splendid scenery, rugged heights, and steep cliff faces of the Negev requires knowledge and skill. In summer the heat is extreme, and in winter the danger of floods is ever present. Hiking on your own is not recommended unless you're well versed in the art of reading topographical maps. The best way to hike the Negev is to join one of several excellent organizations. If you do venture out without a guide, give the details to someone who is staying behind—where you're headed, the route you plan to follow, and when you expect to be back. Always follow the desert guidelines for water consumption.

Natural Wonders The star of the Negev is the Makhtesh Ramon (Ramon Crater), one of a group of geological formations found only in Israel. But knockout views abound throughout the area: the changing colors of the Wilderness of Zin as the day progresses; the sunsets that stain Eilat's waters a deep red; the snow-white blocks of salt clumped on the surface of the Dead Sea; and the fantastic, eroded rock formations surrounded by brooding mountains in Timna Park.

Scuba Diving Eilat is at the gateway to the Red Sea, one of the best dive sites in the world. Its dive centers run regular dive safaris over the border to Egypt. Amazing coral formations, underwater tropical plants, and a dazzling array of fish live in waters that stay warm year-round (22°C, or 72°F, in winter). The reefs are a mere 10 yards offshore, with an immediate deep drop, so a dive is just a walk away. Divers should bring their license, insurance certification, and appropriate footwear—the sea floor is rough, and so are the sea urchins. Top-level diving courses are widely available.

**Israel** (sometimes in Hebrew only; ☎ 03/638-8666) to ask if the road you intend to take is in passable condition. If you're already in the Negev, contact the local tourist office for an update. If, while traveling, you see even a small amount of water flowing across the road in front of you, stop and wait, even if it takes a while for the water to subside. Water on the road is a warning of possible imminent flooding. When hiking, do not enter canyons or dry riverbeds on rainy days, or days when it has just rained farther north.

Mediterranean Sea

GAZA STRIP

Gaza

TO TEL AVIV

EDOM MOUNTAINS

Dead Sea

Ein Gedi

Masada

Hebron

TO JERUSALEM

WEST BANK BORDER

Beit Qama Jct.

Lahav

Rahat

Negev Brigade Memorial

1 Museum of Bedouin Culture

Omer

Shoket Jct.

10 Tel Beer Sheva

8 Beersheva

9 Israel Air Force Museum

2 Mitzpe Revivim

Mashabim Jct.

Mashabei Sade

Haggay Observation Point

Nizzana

11 Tel Arad

12 Arad

13 Ein Bokek

Dead Sea Works

Zohar-Arad Jct.

2499

Arava Jct.

Neot HaKikar

Dimona

Mamshit

Makhtesh HaGadol

Sde Boker College

Sde Boker

Haluqim Jct.

En Avdat Observation Point

3 Ben-Gurion's Desert Home

4 Ben-Gurion's Burial Place

5 Ein Avdat

6 Avdat

Zin R.

Wilderness of Zin

Ein Hazeva

Arava Rd.

Ein Yahav

ARAVA

NEGEV DESERT

7 Mitzpe Ramon Visitors Center

Makhtesh Ramon

Kadesh Barnea

Zin R.

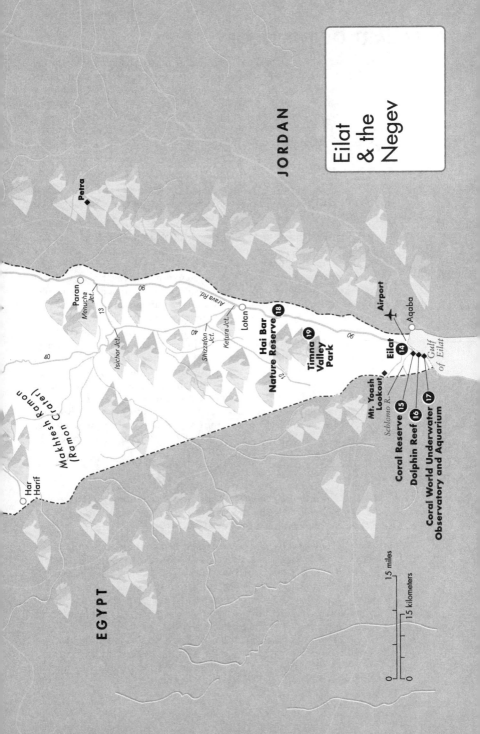

Eilat
& the
Negev

JORDAN

EGYPT

Petra

Menucha Jct.
Paran
13
90
Arava Rd.
Isichor Jct.
40
40
Har Harif
Makhtesh Ramon
(Ramon Crater)
Shizzafon Jct.
Ketura Jct.
Lotan
Hai Bar Nature Reserve
18
Timna Valley Park
19
90
Airport
Aqaba
Eilat
14
Gulf of Eilat
Mt. Yoash Lookout
Shlomo R.
Coral Reserve
15
Dolphin Reef
16
Coral World Underwater Observatory and Aquarium
17

15 miles
15 kilometers
0
0

# THE HEART OF THE NEGEV

The area extending from the Negev Highlands to Eilat has a whole range of sights: the Museum of Bedouin Culture, Mitzpe Revivim, a reconstructed desert outpost; David Ben-Gurion's kibbutz home and grave site; an icy desert pool at Ein Avdat; the 2,000-year-old Nabatean hilltop stronghold of Avdat; and the immense Makhtesh Ramon (Ramon Crater). The first stop on this tour will give you an introduction to the Negev's indigenous people, the Bedouin.

## Museum of Bedouin Culture

★ ☾ ❶ *95 km (57 mi) south of Tel Aviv, 24 km (14 mi) north of Beersheva. At the Lahavim Junction, turn east onto Rte. 31, and turn in at the sign for the Joe Alon Center.*

Once off the main road, you'll drive through a pine forest to reach the Joe Alon Center, whose centerpiece is this one-of-a-kind museum that focuses on the Bedouin people, who have long populated the Negev. The study center (marked with an orange sign) is named for the late Colonel Joe Alon, a pilot who took a great interest in this area and its people. Housed in a circular, tentlike building, the museum takes an authentic look at the Bedouin's rapidly changing lifestyle through tableaux containing life-size mannequins. The tableaux are grouped by subject: wool spinning and carpet weaving, bread baking, the Bedouin coffee ceremony, wedding finery (including a camel elaborately decorated for the event), donkeys and camels at work, and toys made from found objects such as pieces of wire and wood. The tools and artifacts—most handmade, and many already out of use in modern Bedouin life—form an outstanding collection. Admission includes a cup of thick coffee in a real Bedouin tent, where the sheikh performs the coffee ceremony over an open fire. ⊠ *Rte. 325 off Rte. 31* ☏ *08/991–8597 or 08/991–3322* 🎟 *NIS 20* ⊙ *Sun.–Thurs. 9–4, Fri. 9–2, Sat. 9–4.*

## Mitzpe Revivim

❷ *36 km (22 mi) southeast of Beersheva. On Rte. 40 turn right onto Rte. 222 after Kibbutz Mashabei Sade, then drive 9 km (6 mi) to turnoff to Retamim, following signs to the Mitzpe.*

Mitzpe Revivim is the site of an early desert outpost, and an interesting example of early Jewish settlement history. In 1943, in a desolate and empty Negev, three such outposts were set up to gauge the feasibility of Jewish settlement in the southernmost part of the country; one of these was Mitzpe Revivim (*mitzpe* means "lookout," and *revivim* means "rain showers"). Revivim's very presence, along with a handful of other Negev settlements, influenced the U.N.'s decision to include the Negev as part of the State of Israel in the 1947 partition plan. During the War of Independence, isolated Mitzpe Revivim was besieged by Egyptian soldiers, and a hard battle was won by a small band of pioneers and Palmach soldiers. The defenders' fort and living quarters have been preserved: the radio room (the radio crackles original messages), ammunition

# BEDOUIN CULTURE

For Israelis and visitors alike, the Bedouin are a fascinating people. Dressed in flowing black embroidered dresses, their heads covered in white scarves, Bedouin women tending flocks of goats are the brightest touch of color in the treeless, waterless, and harsh Negev desert. Since Israel became an independent state in 1948, the Negev Bedouin men, most of whom are Israeli citizens, have served in the Israeli army, and some have lost their lives doing so. Ironically, however, they are at odds with government authorities, who would like the Bedouin to settle in specially built towns near Beersheva, the capital of the Negev. Their simple, nomadic way of life becomes more difficult to maintain each year as they resist these policies.

**The Bedouin today.** Currently, about 60,000 Bedouin have settled down in towns, while another 60,000 or so remain in the desert. There were 11,000 Bedouin in the area when Israel was established in 1948.

The present-day Bedouin of the Negev (and the Sinai) trace their origins to nomads of the Arabian peninsula who wandered west 400 to 600 years ago. The exceptions are members of the Jebeliya tribe, descendants of East European slaves sent by Emperor Justinian to serve Greek monks at St. Catherine's Monastery at Mt. Sinai. The slaves slowly adopted the Bedouin way of life, and they still serve the monks from their desert nearby.

**Earning a living.** The Bedouin's main livelihood is the raising of livestock, camels and black goats in particular. The animals supply milk, meat, hair for weaving, and dung for burning as fuel. The wanderings of the Bedouin are driven by the unending search for grazing land and water for their flocks. Marriages are arranged, taking family interests into

account. It is not uncommon today for a man to have two wives, the first wife and a younger one to help her.

The family is structured as a business. Men make decisions about buying and selling livestock as well as finding new pastures. Women and children do the cooking, weaving, searching for firewood, and often caring for the flocks.

**Hospitality and heritage.** Bedouin are known for their warm hospitality. It is not only a pleasure to extend hospitality but the Bedouin see it as a duty. A Bedouin host would never fail to invite a stranger into his tent. And refusing a Bedouin's invitation would be unthinkable because it would deny the host an opportunity to display his kindness. Having the honor of being invited by a Bedouin host to drink sweet tea or coffee, made over an open fire in his tent, is an unforgettable experience.

A rich heritage of poetry has been passed down through the generations by word of mouth. Only in the past few years have these words been recorded, written in their original Arabic, and preserved by scholars who recognize that the Bedouin way of life is rapidly slipping away.

room, and kitchen contain original equipment. Outside are a cave where a medical clinic was set up, and two airplanes used to bring supplies and evacuate the wounded. The one-page "self guide" brings the rooms to life. Snacks, drinks, and Revivim's fine "Halutza" olive oil are available at the visitor center. ⊠ *Rte. 222* ☎ *08/656–2570* ✆ *NIS 14* ⊙ *Sun.–Thurs. 8–4, Fri. and Jewish holiday eves 8–noon.*

**off the beaten path**

**NEVEH MIDBAR –** This health spa (for daytime visits) centers on a pool of natural thermo-mineral waters pumped up from deep underground, at a temperature of 39°C (around 102 °F). The spa also has two freshwater pools (one with a slide for those with disabilities) and a shallow pool for babies. A hot tub, sauna, various massages, and aromatherapy treatments make for an unusual desert experience. A gift shop, restaurant, and coffee shop share the premises. ⊠ *Rte. 40, 20 minutes' drive from Beersheva* ☎ *08/657–9666* ⊙ *Sun., Mon., Wed., and Sat. 9–6; Tues. and Thurs. 9 AM–10 PM; Fri. 9–4.*

**en route**

Proceed south along Route 40 and you'll come to the gas station at **Mashabim Junction,** which also serves as a roadside café (good for stocking up on bottled water). Continue on Route 40 for 2 km (1 mi) past the station and make a left at the sign for Mitzpe Ramon, at Telalim Junction. Heading southwest along this stretch of road, you'll pass through areas where signs announce FIRING ZONE. The signs indicate closed military areas, which you may not enter without proper authorization. It's perfectly safe to travel on the main roads; just don't wander off them.

Continuing along Route 40, you'll see a sign on the right for the **Haggay Observation Point.** The parking lot is on the opposite side of the highway at a curve in the road. After parking the car, carefully cross the road to the observation point for a glorious first view of the **Wilderness of Zin**—stark, flat, beige terrain—and **Kibbutz Sde Boker.** Except for the greenery of the kibbutz, the area looks just as it did to the wandering Children of Israel making their way from Egypt to the Land of Canaan more than 3,000 years ago, no doubt complaining all the while about the lack of figs, vines, and water.

## Ben-Gurion's Desert Home

**❸** *24 km (15 mi) south of Mitzpe Revivim. Sign for Ben-Gurion's Home is just after Kibbutz Sde Boker.*

Thousands of people make their way to this pilgrimage site every year. Ben-Gurion himself hoped that tens of thousands would actually settle in the Negev, though his dream has not come true. A film showing the footage of kibbutz members actually voting on his acceptance to their community is shown in the **visitor center;** the shop here sells gifts, jewelry, and books about the "Old Man," as he was known locally.

Amid the waving eucalyptus trees is Paula and David Ben-Gurion's simple dwelling. Ben-Gurion (1886–1973), Israel's first prime minister, was one of the 20th century's great statesmen, yet his small Negev home is commonly known as "the hut," owing to its humble appearance. It's a one-story wooden home with a small kitchen, an eating corner with a table and two chairs, and simple furniture throughout. Visitors such as United Nations Secretary-General Dag Hammarskjöld drank tea with Ben-Gurion in the modest living room. Ben-Gurion's library shelves contain 5,000 books (there are 20,000 more in his Tel Aviv home). His bedroom, with its single picture of Mahatma Gandhi, holds the iron cot on which he slept (only three hours a night) and his slippers on the floor beside it. The house is exactly as he left it.

Next door, in another painted-wood building, is an exhibition whose themes are the biography of Ben-Gurion's extraordinary life, original documents that show the leader's strong ties to the Negev, and the Negev today in light of Ben-Gurion's dream.

When Ben-Gurion resigned from government in 1953 (later to return), he and his wife moved to the isolated, brand-new **Kibbutz Sde Boker** to provide an example for others. "Neither money nor propaganda builds a country," he announced. "Only the man who lives and creates in the country can build it." And so, the George Washington of Israel—whose interests were history, philosophy, and politics, took up his new role in the kibbutz sheepfold. In February 1955 he became prime minister once more, but he returned here to live when he retired in 1963. (He moved back to his Tel Aviv residence some months before his death, at the age of 87, in 1973.) ☎ 08/655–8444 ⊕ http://bgarchives.bgu.ac.il/moreshet ▨ 10 NIS ⊗ Sun.–Thurs. 8:30–4, Fri. and Jewish holiday eves 8:30–2, Sat. and Jewish holidays 9–2:30. Arrive ½ hr before closing time.

> **need a break?**
> Looking for zinfandel (or cabernet sauvignon or merlot) in the desert? Call San Francisco–born kibbutznik **Zvi Remak** (☎ 050/757–9212), and he'll lead you on his bicycle to his garage winery behind Ben-Gurion's home. Tasting is done on a barrel by the front door of what was once a kibbutz shower room.

By the gas station just to the south of the entrance to Ben-Gurion's Desert Home is a small café called **Menta** (☎ 08/657–9938), with heaven-sent cappuccinos, espressos, muffins, and sandwiches.

## Ben-Gurion's Burial Place

**❹** *3 km (2 mi) southwest of Ben-Gurion's home, to the right of the main gate for Sde Boker College.*

Ben-Gurion's grave is not far from his former home. Walk through the beautiful garden until you reach the quiet, windswept plaza; in the center are the simple raised stone slabs marking the graves of David and Paula Ben-Gurion (she died five years before her husband). The couple's final resting place—selected by Ben-Gurion himself—overlooks Zin Valley's geological finery: a vast, undulating drape of velvety-looking stone in shades of cream, ivory, coffee, and soft brown that slowly changes hue as the day goes on. The cluster of greenery and palm trees to the right on the valley floor indicates Ein Avdat (Avdat Spring).

# CloseUp

## KIDS IN THE NEGEV

**THE NEGEV IS A HUGE SANDBOX** *for kids. People are friendly here and genuinely like children. There's lots to do and enjoy: alpaca rides, camel trips, Jeep rides, swimming with dolphins, learning to dive, snorkeling, floating in the Dead Sea, smearing on mud. And children like the kind of food prevalent in the Negev, such as french fries and shnitzel (fried breaded chicken cutlets). Even fancy restaurants have these on their menus, to please the young ones. It is amazing how the hotels*

*in Eilat and Ein Bokek (Dead Sea) cater to kids: the lush hotels outdo one another with their children's sections, often called Kiddyland. These are separate facilities on the hotel grounds, filled with every imaginable distraction, from toys and crafts to Playstations, and there are trained attendants on hand. Many hotels employ staff trained to keep kids entertained. And even in upscale restaurants at night you're apt to see baby strollers parked beside the candlelit tables.*

## Sde Boker College

*Enter through the gate with the traffic arm, next to the* BEN-GURION'S MEMORIAL *sign.*

Ben-Gurion envisioned a place of learning in the desert. This campus became part of Ben-Gurion University of the Negev, whose main campus is in Beersheva. Although there isn't much to see here, the **National Solar Energy Center** (☎ 08/659–6736), where a research program investigates new ideas for the harnessing of solar energy, is interesting. For the traveler, the college is primarily a place to eat and possibly spend the night. The commercial center, in the middle of the campus, has a restaurant, a supermarket open until 8 PM, a post office, and the field school of the **Society for the Protection of Nature in Israel.** ☎ 08/653–2016 ⊕ *www.boker.org.il.*

### Where to Stay & Eat

$ ✕ **Zin Inn.** Stop for a bite here if you're very hungry; otherwise, it's best to push on. This modest spot is where everyone hangs out—desert researchers from overseas, soldiers from the nearby base, visiting schoolchildren, and field-school guides. The menu is the usual desert-restaurant fare (plus croissants at breakfast): soup, schnitzel, chicken, falafel, salad, ice cream, and coffee. It's open until 11 PM from Sunday to Wednesday, closes at 7 PM on Thursday, and 2 PM on Friday. ⊠ *Sde Boker campus* ☎ 08/653–2811 ⊟ *AE, MC, V* ⊙ *Closed Sat.*

¢–$ 🏠 **Sde Boker Field School Hostel and Hamburg Guest House.** Known locally as "midreshet Sde Boker" and just a short walk from the commercial center, these two facilities have the same ownership and both make especially good options for budget-minded families. At the hostel, the octagonal units each contain a large room with a skylight, two bunk beds, two twin beds, and a private bathroom. At Hamburg House, the rooms are in a single building and, although modest, are comfortable—each has a TV and a refrigerator. Lunch and dinner are available in the pleasant dining room. ⊠ *Sde Boker campus, 84990* ☎ *08/653–2016* 🖷 *08/653–2721* ⊕ *www.boker.org.il* 🛏 *330 beds* ♨ *Dining room, some cable TV* ▭ *No credit cards* ⍾◎⍾ *BP.*

## Ein Avdat

★ ⍾ **5**   *3 km (2 mi) south of Ben-Gurion's grave and Sde Boker College.*

Ein Avdat (Avdat Spring) lies at the foot of the canyon, dividing the plateau between the ancient Nabatean city of Avdat and Kibbutz Sde Boker, in **Ein Avdat National Park.** To get to the spring from Ben-Gurion's grave, head down the curving road to a clump of palm trees. Ask for the explanatory leaflet when you pay. Lock the car, taking valuables with you. Walk toward the thickets of rushes, and look for ibex tracks, made with pointed hoofs that enable these agile creatures to climb sheer rock faces. It's not easy to spot an ibex—their coats have striped markings that resemble the rock's many strata. Rock pigeons, Egyptian vultures (black-and-white feathers, bright yellow beak, and long, pinkish legs), and sooty falcons nest in the natural holes in the soft rock and in cliff ledges.

The big surprise at Ein Avdat is the pool of ice-cold, spring-fed water, complete with splashing waterfall. To reach this cool oasis, shaded by the surrounding cliffs, walk carefully along the spring and across the dam toward the waterfall. Swimming and drinking the water are not allowed (you'll not be *sorely* tempted, though—the water is swarming with tadpoles), but enjoying the sight and sound of water in the arid Negev certainly is. The trail continues up the cliffside (using ladders and stone steps), but you can't follow it unless your party has two cars and leaves one at the destination, the Observation Point; the descent is considered too dangerous and is prohibited. ⊠ *Ein Avdat National Park* ☎ *08/655–5684* ⊕ *www.us-israel.org/jsource/Archaeology/Avdat.html* 🅿 *Parking NIS 12* ☉ *Apr.–Sept., Sun.–Thurs. 8–5, Fri. and Jewish holiday eves 8–4; Oct.–Mar., Sun.–Thurs. 8–4, Fri. and Jewish holiday eves 8–3.*

**en route**   For an eagle's-eye view of the waterfall and spring below, turn off Route 40 at the orange sign for Ein Avdat to get to the **Ein Avdat Observation Point.** Below you is the white canyon carved out by the Zin River, with its waterfall (most of the year) tumbling into a pool, surrounded by greenery. From the lookout, a path leads around the top of the cliff (be very careful), enabling you to see the rope marks in the rock; these have been created over the years by Bedouin pulling up water buckets. For information on the hike from here to ancient Avdat, consult the SPNI Field School at Sde Boker College.

## Avdat

**❻**

**Fodor'sChoice**
**★**

*About 20 km (12 mi) south of Ben-Gurion's desert home and grave.*

The Nabatean city of Avdat, a 12-acre acropolis, looms on a hilltop. Here you can see the ancient stronghold and urban ruins of three peoples who have left their mark all over the Negev: the Nabateans, the Romans, and the Byzantines.

The Nabateans were seminomadic pagans who came here from northern Arabia in the 3rd century BC. Establishing prosperous caravan routes connecting the desert hinterland with the port city of Gaza, on the Mediterranean coast, they soon rose to glory with a vast kingdom whose capital was Petra (in present-day Jordan). Strongholds to protect the caravans—which carried gold, precious stones, and spices—were established along these routes, usually a day's journey apart.

The name "Avdat" is the Hebrew version of Oboda (30 BC–9 BC), a deified king who may have been buried here. Another king of Avdat, Aretas, is mentioned in the New Testament. The prominent local dynasty intermarried with the family of Herod the Great, and the Nabatean kingdom was finally abolished by the Romans in AD 106. Most of the remains on the acropolis date from the 3rd, 4th, and 5th centuries—the Christian Byzantine period. The city was sacked by the Persians in AD 620 and was rediscovered only in the 20th century.

Start at the **visitor center** (the Avdat Data Shop), where you can learn about the Nabateans in a 10-minute video, see examples of what these ancient traders actually transported across the desert, and examine archaeological artifacts found in the excavations. Be sure to pick up the Nature and National Parks Authority's excellent explanatory brochure and map of the site. Drive up the road (save your energy for walking around the site itself), stopping first at the sign for the **Roman burial cave**. Park and walk the 300 feet for a quick peek. The 20 burial niches cut into the rock date from the 3rd century BC.

Back in your car, drive up to the lookout point at the restored Roman building. The cultivated fields below were re-created in 1959 in order to see if the ancient Nabatean and Byzantine methods of conserving the meager rainfall (measured in millimeters) for desert farming would still work. The proof is in the cultivated crops and orchards before you.

Using Nature and National Parks Authority's map, you can trace the lifestyle of these former locals at sites that include a reconstructed three-story Roman tower; a rare Nabatean pottery workshop; a winepress; cisterns; two Byzantine churches; and a large baptismal font (to accommodate the converted). Near the baptismal font you can walk down the steps to see 6th-century AD Byzantine dwellings, each consisting of a cave (possibly used as a wine cellar) with a stone house in front of it. At the bottom of the hill, north of the gas station, is a Byzantine bathhouse. There is an eatery that serves light meals at the visitor center. ☒ *Rte. 40* ☏ *08/658–6391* ⊕ *www.parks.org.il* ☺ *NIS 18* ☽ *Apr.–Sept., Sat.–Thurs. 8–5, Fri. and Jewish holiday eves 8–4; Oct.–Mar., Sat.–Thurs. 8–4, Fri. and Jewish holiday eves 8–3.*

## Makhtesh Ramon & Mitzpe Ramon

**❼**
**Fodor'sChoice**
**★**

*21 km (13 mi) south of Avdat, 80 km (50 mi) south of Beersheva.*

**Makhtesh Ramon** (the Ramon Crater) is Israel's most spectacular natural sight, an immense depression 40 km (25 mi) long, 10 km (6 mi) wide, and at its deepest, measuring 2,400 feet. Because it's a phenomenon known only in this country (there are three others in the Negev), the Hebrew term *makhtesh*—meaning mortar, as in mortar and pestle—is now accepted usage. By definition, a makhtesh is an erosion valley walled with steep cliffs on all sides and drained by a single watercourse.

**Mitzpe Ramon** is a tiny town on the edge of the crater. The populace numbers 5,500 people, including recently arrived Russian immigrants. Its raison d'être is the magnificent giant crater, and visitors love the area because of its serenity, pure refreshing air, and natural beauty. The local main road runs through the crater (eventually arriving in Eilat), a promenade winds along its edge, and a huge sculpture park sits on its rim. Outdoor enthusiasts will enjoy exploring the geology, nature (note the metal fences around the trees to keep the ibex from eating the leaves), and stunning scenery by foot, mountain bike, or Jeep. The weather here in November, December, and January is cool and pleasant.

If you're continuing south to Eilat, you can still see the crater, as Route 40 goes right through it; just try to plan your day so that you won't be driving to Eilat after dark. There are no gas stations between Mitzpe Roman and Yotvata, a distance of more than 100 km (62 mi).

The impressive **visitor center**, at the very edge of the makhtesh, is built in the shape of an ammonite fossil (a spiral-shape sea creature that lived here when everything was under water, millions of years ago). The helpful staff are rangers with the Israel Nature and National Parks Protection Authority; they can suggest hiking routes in the makhtesh.

For a clear understanding of the makhtesh phenomenon, the center offers a full-color, sound-and-screen presentation with a walk-around model of the makhtesh—this definitely outshines the 12-minute film shown in the auditorium. On the way to the top-floor lookout there are informative, wall-size panels describing the makhtesh's geological makeup, ecology, vegetation, and settlement.

As you stand behind the glass, you peer out at a world formed millions of years ago. The crater's walls are made from layer upon layer of different-color rock beds containing fossils of shells, plants, and trees. The makhtesh floor is covered with heaps of black basalt, the peaks of ancient volcanoes, jagged chunks of quartzite, huge blocks of overturned rock, and beds of multicolor clays.

Just outside the center's front door, and included in its admission, is **Bio Ramon,** a garden of usually hidden small desert animals, such as snakes, sand rats, beetles, turtles, and hedgehogs, who dwell in conditions that imitate their natural surroundings. ✉ *On main road in Mitzpe Ramon* ☎ *08/658–8755* 🎫 *NIS 12* ☉ *Sun.–Thurs. 8–5, Fri. 8–4, Sat. 8–5.*

★ You can take a walk (about 1 km, or ½ mi) along the **Albert Promenade,** which winds east to west along the edge of the crater from the visitor center to the cantilevered observation platform. This is not the time to forget a camera—the view is overwhelming. The promenade is fashioned from local stone, as is the huge sculpture by Israel Hadani, the back of which faces town and represents the crater's geological layers.

With the crater as a magnificent backdrop, the **Desert Sculpture Park** exhibits a far-flung collection of huge stone sculptures. The park took shape in 1962 with the work of a group of Israeli and foreign sculptors under the direction of Negev artist Ezra Orion. Their idea was to add to the natural stone "sculptures" with geometrical rock formations of similar design. The sculptors brought their chosen rocks and formed their desert works of art with minimal hand shaping. ⊠ *Turn off near gas station on main road at sign marked* MA'ALE NOAH.

For a look at one of the crater's geological subphenomena, drive into the makhtesh to see the **Carpentry.** A path goes up to a wooden walkway, built to protect nature's artwork from travelers' feet. Long ago, the sandstone was probably hardened and slightly warmed by volcanic steam, and the rocks split into prisms, owing either to cooling joints or to another unknown process. The formations look like wooden chips piled up in a carpentry shop. ⊠ *Along Rte. 40, going south.*

Another of nature's works is the **Ammonite Wall,** which is on the right as you drive through the crater. A sign indicates a distance of 5 km (3 mi), which applies to the marked hike in the crater (for fit walkers only—take water). The rock face contains hundreds of ammonite fossils, which look like rams' horns and are indeed named for the Egyptian god Ammon, who had the head of a ram.

ᗣ Just outside town is the **Alpaca Farm,** with its large herd of 600 sweet-faced alpacas and llamas. Young and old get a kick out of feeding the animals, even if they receive the occasional spit in the face from these long-eyelashed creatures. Children weighing less than about 50 pounds can take a llama ride; horseback rides and tours are available to all. Everyone loves to watch the shearing at Passover. ⊠ *Turn off main road opposite gas station* ☎ *08/658–8047 or 08/658–6067* ⊕ *www.alpaca.co. il* ✑ *NIS 25* ⊙ *Daily 8:30–6:30 (9–4:30 in winter).*

en route   It's a **scenic drive** through the Ramon Crater on Route 40. The Negev wadis increase in size from their source, in the Sinai, and cut through the Negev on their way to the Arava Valley, to the east. The sight of the Edom Mountains on the eastern horizon is beautiful, especially in the light of late afternoon. After the Tsichor Junction with Route 13 (which connects with the nearby north–south highway Route 90), you'll see limestone strata that have "folded" over the millennia. After the Ketura Junction (where Route 40 ends), there are breathtaking views of the Arava Valley (on your left), which marks the Israel-Jordan border and is part of the Great Syrian-African Rift, a fault line formed millions of years ago. From here, Route 90 leads straight to Eilat (52 km, or 33 mi). It's not advisable to take Route 12 to Eilat if you're finishing this tour after a long day's drive or toward dark; Route 90 is the better and safer road.

## Where to Stay & Eat

**$**  ✕ **Havit.** If you're lucky enough to get a window table at Havit ("beer barrel"), you'll be sitting right on the edge of the crater, and the scenery may just overshadow whatever's on your plate. At this pub-restaurant, you can choose from fairly predictable fare including onion soup, pasta, meatballs, chicken, schnitzel, pasta, hummus, and stuffed mushrooms. You can raise a toast to the spectacular view with beer or wine. On Tuesday night, Havit morphs into a disco, and soldiers come to dance the night away. ✉ *Beside Mitzpe Ramon Visitors Center* ☎ *08/658–8226* ⚠ *Reservations not accepted* ▭ *DC, MC, V.*

**$**  ✕ **Misedet Hanna.** A roadside-diner atmosphere—Formica tables and chairs and fluorescent lighting—prevails in this wayfarer's restaurant at the gas station opposite the Mitzpe Ramon visitor center. David, the owner, knows everyone and talks warmly to multiple guests at the same time. Hanna and her daughters prepare the food, and patrons serve themselves, cafeteria-style. Offerings include soups, salads, schnitzel, chicken, fish, spaghetti, rice, and on Tuesday and Friday, a tasty couscous with meatballs. Hanna's never stays open past 6 PM, so only early dinners are available. ✉ *Paz gas station* ☎ *08/658–8158* ⚠ *Reservations not accepted* ▭ *No credit cards* ☉ *No dinner Fri. Closed Sat.*

★ **¢**  ✕ **Cafeneto.** Ah, the taste of a flaky croissant and the enticing scent of cappuccino—in the desert! You can get a full Israeli breakfast here (including local cheese, omelets, and vegetables) as well as sandwiches such as the "Baghdadi" (hard-boiled egg, roasted eggplant, tomato, cucumbers, scallions, parsley, and tahini). Or you might try a salad of finely chopped vegetables with mint, coriander, lemon, and olive oil. Sip an iced chai, fresh juice, espresso, or a latte with shredded chocolate on the terrace. ✉ *Nahal Tsiah* ☎ *08/658–7777* ⚠ *Reservations not accepted* ▭ *AE, DC, MC, V.*

★ **$$$**  ✕▦ **Ramon Inn.** There's nothing rugged about a stay at this charming desert hotel. The four-story building has no elevator, but the accommodations are entirely comfortable, and the staff is well known for its helpfulness. Stay in a pastel-and-white studio apartment (for one or two) or a two- or three-room suite (for four to six people); suites have well-equipped kitchenettes. The lobby has an open fireplace for chilly winter nights. The 20-yard-long heated swimming pool would not be out of place at any luxury hotel. Even if you're not staying here, the restaurant is worth a visit; hearty buffet meals are enlivened by condiments made by local cooks. ✉ *Box 318, Mitzpe Ramon, 80600* ☎ *08/658–8822* ⊟ *08/658–8151* ⊕ *www.isrotel.co.il* ⬍ *64 suites* ⚛ *Restaurant, room service, in-room safes, kitchenettes, refrigerators, pool, gym, massage, sauna, mountain bikes, Ping-Pong, lobby lounge, laundry facilities, no-smoking rooms* ▭ *AE, DC, MC, V* ⏐◉⏐ *CP.*

★ **$$**  ▦ **Desert Home.** Here's a little piece of heaven: a building with five lovely guest rooms, each with a covered terrace facing creamy-brown desert hills. In this two-story, sand-colored, adult-oriented inn that's fenced with tree branches, each room has a bleached-wood floor and pale lime, mauve, or blue walls, a double bed with bright-white pillows and taupe spread, a white fan overhead (in addition to individual air-conditioning), and a blue sofa with Moroccan cushions. The wood kitchenette sparkles with shiny utensils, and there's a microwave. Your breakfast of local delicacies is delivered to your room each morning. ⊠ *70 En Shaviv, 80600* ☎ *052/322–9496* 🖹 *08/658–6327* ☞ *5 rooms* ⌂ *Cable TV; no room phones, no kids under 16* ⊟ *No credit cards* ⦿ *BP.*

★ $$    🔲 **Succah in the Desert.** In the middle of nowhere (but accessible by road) is this out-of-the-ordinary encampment of huts (like the portable dwellings used by the Children of Israel when they wandered in this desert). On a rocky hillside are eight isolated dwellings, each made of stone and wood, with a palm-frond roof. It's an appealing combination: the starkness and purity of the desert and some modern amenities. Each succah has a carpet on its earthen floor and a mattress with cozy blankets; household essentials include a tea corner, a clay water jar, and copper bowls for ablutions. There's an ecological-toilet cabin. Guests eat homemade vegetarian breakfasts and dinners (included in the price) in the communal succah. ⊠ *On road to Alpaca Farm, 7 km (4½ mi) west of Mitzpe Ramon, Box 272, 80600* ☎ *08/658–6280* ⊕ *www.succah.co.il* ☞ *8 units that sleep 2, 1 unit that sleeps 10, all with shared bath* ⊟ *AE, DC, MC, V* ⦿ *MAP.*

$    🔲 **Youth Hostel.** Known in Israel for its high standards, at least as hostels go, this property must be booked well in advance (June and September are the busiest months). Fine for families, the place is done in bright colors and has a cheerfully decorated dining room. Several room sizes are available, from those with three bunk beds and one cot, to rooms with just one bunk bed (none have double beds); each room has its own bathroom. Food is inexpensive and plentiful, and you can order box lunches; nonguests must reserve for dinner. ⊠ *Opposite Mitzpe Ramon Visitors Center, 80600* ☎ *08/658–8443* 🖹 *08/658–8074* ☞ *276 beds* ⌂ *Dining room, snack bar, dance club* ⊟ *DC, MC, V* ⦿ *CP.*

## Sports & the Outdoors

DESERT ARCHERY    **Desert Archery** (☎ 050/534–4598) offers trips where you hike through a desert course while shooting arrows at targets.

JEEP AND HIKING    A hike or a ride in a Jeep is an unforgettable way to immerse yourself
TOURS    in the landscape. The staff at the **visitor center** (☎ 08/658–8691) in Mitzpe Ramon can help you plan local hikes, though the explanatory maps are in Hebrew.

Camel-supported Jeep trips and hikes are run by **Adam Sela Tours** (☎ 050/ 530–8272 ⊕ www.adamsela.com), which offers ecological tours and
★    Bedouin visits as well. Desert hikes and Jeep tours are ably led by **Desert Eco Lodge** (☎ 054/627–7413 or 08/658–6229 ⊕ www.desert-shade. com). Contact **Hadar Desert Tour** (☎ 052/270–3451) for Jeep and hiking tours of 2½ hours to 5 hours into Ramon Crater. Nature Guide **Peter Bugel** (☎ 08/658–8958) offers intensive tailor-made desert trips.

**Society for the Protection of Nature in Israel** (SPNI; ☎ 03/638–8666) often includes the Negev heartland in its trips.

MOUNTAIN    Treat yourself to a thrilling bike ride: **Negevland (Siurei Midbar)** (☎ 08/
BIKING    659–5555 or 050/865–4777 ⊕ www.negevland.co.il) rents bikes for
★    the day.

RAPPELLING **Negevland** (☎ 08/659–5555 or 050/865–4777 ⊕ www.negevland.co.il) takes groups to the crater cliffs; call ahead for details. Note that rappelling is known as "snappelling" in Israel.

SWIMMING You'll find a large indoor pool at **Mitzpe Ramon Inn** (☎ 08/658–8151).

The **Municipal Pool** (☎ 08/659–6222) is at the entrance to town, opposite the gas station. Call for times and admission fees.

### Shopping
At the visitor center, the **Amonit Gallery** (☎ 08/658–6166) has a rather unusual selection: jewelry and batiks made by the owner, Bedouin drums, Armenian pottery, T-shirts with pictures of local animals, and desert stones and fossils.

**Alpaca Farm** (☎ 08/658–8047) sells skeins of alpaca wool—light as a feather, soft as down, and warm as toast. There are cozy hats, too.

★ For all-natural, family-made, deliciously scented body-care products, visit **Naturescent** (☎ 08/653–9333 ⊕ www.naturescent.co.il) in the Industrial Area.

# BEERSHEVA TO EIN BOKEK

This area in the north of the region stretches east from Beersheva, known as the capital of the Negev, to the resort town of Ein Bokek, on the Dead Sea. In between are ancient Tel Arad and modern Arad. Between Beersheva and Arad you'll encounter scenes that look strikingly biblical—black tents, Bedouin shepherds with robes flying, and sheep and goats bumbling around. And after several twists of the road from Arad, you'll arrive at the spa-resort area of Ein Bokek, at the southernmost part of the Dead Sea, the lowest point on earth.

## Beersheva

**8** *24 km (14 mi) south of Museum of Bedouin Culture, 113 km (70 mi) southeast of Tel Aviv.*

Beersheva's emblem consists of a tamarisk tree, representing the biblical past, and a pipe through which water flows, symbolizing the city's modern revival. It was here that the patriarch Abraham constructed his well (*be'er* in Hebrew) and swore an oath (*shevua* in Hebrew) over seven (*sheva* in Hebrew) ewes with the king of Gerar, who vowed to prevent his men from seizing the well. And it was here that Abraham planted a grove of tamarisk trees. The Book of Genesis describes other patriarchal figures who lived in this area as well. It's easy to envision these scenes today thanks to the cloaked figures of Bedouin shepherds with their sheep and goats in the hillside surrounding the city.

Tel Beer Sheva, just outside the city, is the site of biblical Beersheva and could easily be the site of Abraham's well. An expression from the Book of Judges, "from Dan to Beersheva," once marked the northern and southern boundaries of the Land of Israel. It was declared a World Heritage site by UNESCO in July 2005.

Romans and Byzantines built garrisons in Beersheva, but the city was later abandoned. In 1900 the Ottoman Turks, who had ruled Palestine since 1517, rebuilt Beersheva as their Negev district center (the present Old City). They set aside an area for a Bedouin market, which still takes place every Thursday. During World War I, the British took Beersheva from the Turks; in 1948 it was conquered by Israel.

Beersheva is now the the fourth-largest city in Israel, with its own university, named after David Ben-Gurion, and a regional hospital serving Bedouin shepherds, kibbutzniks, and other desert dwellers. Largely blue-collar, the city is struggling to provide housing for thousands of recent immigrants, many from Ethiopia and the former Soviet Union.

The famed Bedouin Market, once a source of some of Israel's best ethnic handicrafts, has been hit by modern times (items from the Far East offer competition), and isn't what it used to be. But it now has a permanent location, and it's interesting to visit with the hope that you'll find something authentic. Most intriguing are the Bedouin themselves, sitting cross-legged with their goods spread out on the ground.

Considering the short distances from Tel Aviv and Jerusalem, the city is more of a jumping-off point for Negev travel—main roads branch out from here; buses serving the Negev depart from here; trains from the north end up in Beersheva. If your schedule permits, stay overnight in Beersheva for a glimpse of a growing desert city with an interesting citizenry.

## Where to Stay & Eat

**$$$$** ✕ **Ahuzat Halperin.** On a tree-lined street with old-fashioned street lights, you'll find this perfect venue for a rarified dining experience. The old stone building has high ceilings, leafy potted plants, floors enhanced with arabesque tiles, and an inner courtyard. Candle boxes hang from the walls, and dark-wood padded chairs and beautifully set tables give serene elegance to the lovely setting. The creatively prepared dishes don't disappoint: start with furnace-baked camembert or smoked duck in aspic and move on to such main courses as saffron salmon, roasted eggplant ravioli, lamb osso buco, and fillet of beef. ⊠ 23 Smilansky, Old City ☎ 050/751–5154 or 599/506–507 ⚠ Reservations essential ☰ AE, DC, MC, V ⊗ No lunch weekdays.

**$** ✕ **Bulgarit.** The family-run Bulgarit ("Bulgarian"), on the pedestrian mall in the Old City, has been in business for more than five decades; the third generation is now at the helm. The owner sits with his cronies at a corner table and reels off the selections from his international, Bulgarian-influenced menu: roast lamb and grilled meats, oven-baked fish, moussaka, vegetables stuffed with meat and rice, *gvetch* (an assortment of vegetables cooked together), and coconut parfait or pears in wine for dessert. If you speak Bulgarian, your meal comes with stories of pioneer days; if not, you still get friendly, efficient service. ⊠ K.K. le Israel St. ☎ 08/ 623–8504 ⚠ Reservations not accepted ☰ DC, MC, V ⊗ Closed Fri.

**$** ✕ **Pitput.** The name means "chattering" in Hebrew, and the young crowd definitely lives up to this moniker. The washed beige walls are hung with shadow boxes filled with wine corks and coins. The staff here is congenial and the food attractively presented. Sitting outside on the busy sidewalk or inside listening to recorded jazz or blues, desert diners have a range of selections: salads, omelets, blintzes from cheese to salmon, pasta, grilled fish with grilled vegetables, and pizza. Cheese sandwiches are made on sesame-seed rolls called *begeles.* Half bottles of Yarden wine may be ordered. You can't go wrong by finishing with hot homemade pecan pie or cheesecake with fresh fruit. ⊠ *122 Herzl St.* ☎ *08/ 623-7708* ⌂ *Reservations not accepted* ▭ *AE, DC, MC, V.*

$$$  📺 **Paradise Negev.** It's the only hotel in town, and it provides up-to-date lodgings. The building's beige-and-brown stone reflects its desert surroundings, and arched windows soften the city's square look. Guest rooms are comfortably outfitted with wicker chairs, and the curtains and bedspreads form a snappy color scheme of red, green, and butterscotch. Good reading lights are a welcome touch. Rooms on the business floor are equipped with safes and minibars. The breezy outdoor patio, with bubbling fountains, is a cool place to relax in the hot desert climate. ⊠ *Henrietta Szold St., near City Hall, 84100* ☎ *08/640–5444* 🖷 *08/640– 5445* ⊕ *www.fattal.co.il* ⤴ *210 rooms, 48 suites* ⌂ *Restaurant, room service, cable TV, some kitchenettes, pool, wading pool, gym, spa, lobby lounge, shop, laundry service, Internet* ▭ *AE, DC, MC, V* ⎮◯⎮ *BP.*

## Nightlife & the Arts

**Beer Sheva Sinfionetta** (☎ 08/623–1616) is a well-regarded symphonic group. Once a year, in March or April, **Light Opera Group of the Negev** presents two performances of Gilbert and Sullivan in English; contact the tourist office in Beersheva for details.

Join Ben Gurion University students for a beer and delicious pub food at **Coca Bar and Restaurant** (☎ 08/623-3303), behind the student dorms.

★ Savor a long evening of wine and tapas at **Hatzer Hayain Wine Bar** (☎ 08/ 623–8135), a popular spot in the Artists' Quarter. Proprietor, wine expert, and congenial host Michael will guide you through the intricacies of Israeli and other wines from 7:30 PM till very late. It closes weekends.

## Shopping

The Negev is still the home of the Bedouin, but today's Bedouin women are less interested than yesterday's in staying home all day to weave and embroider. That's why you need an eagle's eye and a saint's patience to search through the bundles and stacks of rather ordinary stuff at the **Bedouin market,** where you should try to find goods made by elder generations. The market starts at daybreak each Thursday and lasts until early afternoon; it's on the eastern side of the huge outdoor market site near the bridge, at Derech Eilat and Derech Hebron streets. (A goat and sheep sale takes place once in a while.) The best time to be there is 6 AM, an hour or so later in winter. Walk to the back, passing coffee and tea sellers. For sale, if you can find them, are embroidered dresses, yokes, and side panels from dresses; woven camel bags; rugs; earrings, bracelets, amulets, and nose rings; coin headbands (used as dowry gifts); tassels; copperware; and *finjans* (Bedouin coffee utensils).

The popular **Dalia Schen's Gift Shop** (☎ 08/628–2785 or 050/751–3496) is right in the Paradise Hotel. An expert in Israeli handicrafts, Dalia seeks out the unusual and offers a small but careful selection of weavings, artifacts, Ethiopian crafts, old and new Yemenite and Bedouin jewelry, locally made rugs, and other pieces by local artists. Ask to see her unusual T-shirts and blouses decorated with old Bedouin embroidery.

An elegant desert wine shop? You may be surprised by the state-of-the-art design, stock of imported and local wines, and well-informed staff at **Wine Aficionado** (⊠ 117 Trumpeldor St. ☎ 08/628–9444).

en route    On Route 40 northeast from Beersheva to Arad is the large and impressive **Negev Brigade Memorial,** designed by Israeli artist Danny Karavan. The monument's 15 symbolic parts and Hebrew text tell the story of the battle of the Palmach's Negev Brigade against the Egyptians after the birth of the State of Israel. The tower offers a great view of Beersheva and the surrounding desert.

**Kafriat Shoket,** a kibbutz-run way station, has a large cafeteria with two sections, one for grilled meat dishes, the other serving dairy food: sandwiches, salads, and cakes. Eat inside or outside under the tamarisk trees. ⊠ *Intersection of Rte. 31 and Rte. 60* ☎ *08/646–9421* ☉ *Sun. and Thurs. 6 AM–9 PM; Fri. 6–6; Mon., Tues., and Wed. 7 AM–8 PM; Sat. 7 AM–9 PM.*

## Israel Air Force Museum

★ ☾ **9** *7 km (4½ mi) west of Beersheva.*

For plane lovers, this is a field of dreams. The open-air Israel Air Force Museum (also known as Hatzerim) is a gigantic concrete field with 90 airplanes parked in rows. The fighter, transport, and training (plus a few enemy) aircraft tell the story of Israel's aeronautic history, from the Messerschmitt—obtained in 1948 from Czechoslovakia, and one of four such planes to help halt the Egyptian advance in the War of Independence— to the *Kfir,* Israel's first fighter plane. The young air force personnel who staff the museum lead tours that take about 1½ hours and include a movie shown in an air-conditioned Boeing 707 used in the 1977 rescue of Israeli passengers held hostage in a hijacked Air France plane in Entebbe, Uganda. Another attention-getting display is a shiny, black Supermarine Spitfire with a red lightning bolt on its side, flown by Ezer Weizmann, the IAF's first pilot. As of this writing, a memorial exhibit is planned for Col. Ilan Ramon, Israel's first astronaut, who died in the *Columbia* space shuttle disaster in 2003. ⊠ *Rte. 233* ☎ *08/990–6855 or 08/990–6888* ⊕ *www.fai.org/education/museums/isr_iaf* ⊠*NIS 26* ☉ *Sun.–Thurs. 8–5, Fri. 8–noon.*

## Tel Beer Sheva

★ **10** *2 km (1¼ mi) east of Beersheva.*

Tel Beer Sheva, biblical Beersheva—traditionally associated with the patriarch Abraham—is an artificial tell created by nine successive settlements between 3500 BC and 600 BC. The tell is a recent addition to the Nature and National Parks Authority's roster; ask for the excellent explanatory leaflet.

At the top of the tell is the only planned Israelite city uncovered in its entirety. Most of the visible remains date from the 10th to 7th centuries BC. A fine example of a circular layout typical of the Iron Age, the city is believed to have been destroyed around 706 BC by Sennacherib of Assyria. In the northeast, outside the 3,000-year-old city gate, is a huge well more than 6 feet in diameter, which apparently once reached groundwater 90 feet below (it has not been completely excavated). This ancient well served the city from its earliest times, and scholars speculate that it could be the well that is documented in the Bible as Abraham's Well (Genesis 21:22–32). The observation tower is rather ugly, but it does afford beautiful views. ⊠ *Rte. 60* ☎ *08/646–7286* ⊕ *www. parks.org.il* ⌦ *NIS 12* ⊙ *Apr.–Sept., Sun.–Thurs. 8–5, Fri. and Jewish holiday eves 8–3; Oct.–Mar., Sun.–Thurs. 8–4, Fri. and Jewish holiday eves 8–2, Sat. 8–4.*

**en route** On the way to 3,000-year old Tel Arad, you might stop to check out the modern **Yatir Winery** (☎ 08/995–9090 ⊕ www.yatir.net), a boutique-style vineyard established in 2000. The first wines were launched in 2004. There are two labels: Yatir Forest (cabernet sauvignon), and Yatir (cabernet sauvignon, sauvignon blanc, merlot, and shiraz), which are made from several varieties of grapes. Call ahead for a visit and tasting.

## Tel Arad

**⑪** *38 km (23 mi) east of Beersheva, 8 km (5 mi) west of Arad.*

Approaching Tel Arad, the 25-acre site of the biblical city of Arad, from the west takes you through flat fields of the low shrub called *rotem* (white broom). At the entrance, pick up the National Parks Authority's pamphlet, which explains the ongoing excavations, and purchase (for NIS 8) the plan of the early Canaanite city of Arad, with a map, recommended walking tour, and diagrams of the typical Arad house.

Arad was first settled during the Chalcolithic period (4000–3000 BC) by seminomadic pastoralists who lived and traveled together, herding and farming. It was they who first developed bronze. Arad was continually occupied until the end of the Early Bronze Age (3500–3200 BC), but the city you see most clearly is from the Early Bronze Age II (2950–2650 BC). Here you can walk around a walled urban community and enter the carefully reconstructed one-room "Arad houses."

After the Early Bronze Age II, Arad was abandoned and hidden beneath the light loess soil for nearly 2,000 years, until the10th century BC, when a fortress—one of many in the Negev (the first may have been built by Solomon)—was built on the site's highest point. It's worth the trek up the somewhat steep path. Take a moment to appreciate the view as you take your leave of the Early Bronze Age; at the top, you step into the Iron Age (10th–6th centuries BC). The small, square fortress served the area intermittently until Roman times; most of the visible remains date from the end of the First Temple period (935–586 BC). Note the small Israelite temple sanctuary, with its two standing stones (these are replicas—the originals are in the Israel Museum, in Jerusalem) and sacrificial altar of unhewn stone. In the 7th century BC, the southern part of the Israelite kingdom of Judah reached as far as today's Eilat. ⊠ *Off Rte. 31* ☎ *08/995–7690* ⊕ *www.parks.org.il* ☎ *NIS 12* ⊙ *Apr.–Sept., Sun.–Thurs. 8–5, Fri. and Jewish holiday eves 8–4; Oct.–Mar., Sun.–Thurs. 8–4, Fri. and Jewish holidays eves 8–3.*

# Arad

❷ *46 km (28½ mi) east of Beersheva, 8 km (5 mi) east of Tel Arad.*

The modern town of Arad was established as a planned community in 1961. Arad's population of nearly 25,000 now includes immigrants from Russia and Ethiopia, as well as the acclaimed Israeli writer Amos Oz. Breathe deeply: the town sits 2,000 feet above sea level and is famous for its dry, pollution-free air and mild climate. Arad has made a name for itself as a healthy home for asthma sufferers. Arad could be a base for excursions to sites in the Dead Sea area, notably to Masada, and is the only approach (via Route 31) to Masada's sound-and-light show.

The **Arad Tourist Information Center** (☎ 08/995–1622) is open Thursday–Saturday 9–4. It's behind the Paz gas station opposite the entrance to Arad; you'll see a yellow sign with the "i" for Information on it. A small supply of maps, brochures, and hiking information is available; a simple 24/7 café called Yellow is next to the gas pumps.

Gideon Fridman, one of the founders of Arad, uses recycled glass in his personally developed fusing methods to create "talking glass" sculptures in ovens he built himself. These intriguing pieces are three-dimensional, and each is one-of-a-kind. Find this exciting work at the **Glass Museum Gallery** (☎ 08/995–3388 or 050/766–7080 ⊕ www.warmglassil.com) on the road to the tourist information center. Pass the gas station on your left, turn right at the roundabout, take the second right, go to the end of the street, and it's on the left. A trip here is worth the effort.

## Where to Stay & Eat

★ $ ✗ **Muza.** With chunky wood furniture, a ceiling crammed with bar mats, soccer scarves draped along one wall, and a bar lined with beer bottles, this is a classic pub. It's on Route 31, at the entrance to Arad, next to the gas station. The place is warm and cozy, staffed by wide-smiling servers and filled with locals and travelers enjoying meat on skewers, hummus, hearty salads, and *malawach* (a flaky Yemenite pastry eaten with tomato sauce). Here you can also indulge your yen for an American-style tuna melt: request "toast," the Israeli term for a grilled cheese sandwich, with tuna salad, satisfyingly accompanied by Muza's signature home-cut, crunchy "chips" (french fries). A covered terrace with a billiard table at one end serves alfresco diners. ⊠ *Rte. 31* ☎ *08/997–5555* ♿ *Reservations not accepted* ☰ *AE, DC, MC, V.*

$$ ▥ **Inbar.** At the entrace to Arad is the only lodging option in town, the five-story Inbar hotel, built of white stone with orange trim. The welcoming and warm staff makes up in friendliness what this property lacks in luxury. The upstairs lobby feels inviting with its blue and yellow ceiling lamps; there's a metal-sculpted divider with birds on it at the entrance

to the dining room, which overlooks the street. Rooms are petite, done in a palette of beige and olive. Minibars are available on request. ⊠ *38 Yehuda St., 89109* ☎ *08/997–3303* 🖷 *08/997–3322* ⊕ *www.hotel-inbar.com* ⬠ *96 rooms, 7 suites* ⚒ *Restaurant, in-room safes, pool, wading pool, exercise equipment, sauna, hot tub* ☰*AE, DC, MC, V* ⍥*CP.*

## The Road to the Dead Sea

*The steep, 24-km (15-mi) descent to the Dead Sea on Rte. 31 has one sharp curve after another. Watch for the sign on the right indicating that you've reached sea level.*

The drama of this drive is enhanced by the stunning canyons and clefts that unfold on every side. Two observation points soon appear on the left. You can't cross to the first—Metsad Zohar—from your side of the road. The second—Nahal Zohar—looks down on an ancient, dry riverbed, the last vestige of an eons-old body of water that once covered this area. The Dead Sea lies directly east, with the Edom Mountains of Jordan on the other side. To the right (south) is Mt. Sodom.

You'll soon see, from above, the southern end of the Dead Sea, sectioned off into the huge evaporation pools of the Dead Sea Works, where potash and salts such as bromine and magnesium are extracted. On land are row after row of plastic "tunnels," which act as hothouses for fruit (often tomatoes and melons) that is sold to Europe in winter.

Two roads lead from Route 90 to the Ein Bokek hotel area; once there, you are at *the bottom of the world*: 1,292 feet below sea level.

## Ein Bokek

**⑬**  *8 km (5 mi) north of Zohar–Arad Junction on Rte. 90.*

**Fodor'sChoice**
★

The sudden and startling sight, in this bare landscape, of multilevel, hot-white, ultramodern hotels surrounded by waving palm trees signals your arrival at the spa-resort area of Ein Bokek, at the southern tip of the Dead Sea. According to the Bible, it was along these shores that the Lord rained fire and brimstone on the people of Sodom and Gomorrah (Genesis 19:24) and later turned Lot's wife into a pillar of salt (Genesis 26). Here, at the lowest point on earth, the hot, sulfur-pungent air hangs heavy, the odd cry of the indigenous grackle bird is heard, and there is often a haze over the Dead Sea itself. You can float, but you cannot sink, in the soup-warm, oily water.

The legendary Dead Sea, whose rare physical properties attracted glitterati such as King Herod and Cleopatra in their day, retains its unusual attractions 2,000 years later. Its salt content (six times denser than that of the Mediterranean), high content of special minerals (bromine, for example, which calms the nervous system), and thick, black mud, enriched with organic elements, are sought out for their curative and beautifying properties. They are found nowhere else in the world.

Ein Bokek also has sulfur-rich hot springs with a temperature of 31°C (88°F). Many hotels have tapped into these for their spas; the water is used along with Dead Sea water and mud to treat rheumatic and arthritic problems—even tennis elbow or a sore back. The combination of sunshine (it's sunny 320 days a year), Dead Sea water, and mineral-rich mud seems to work wonders on psoriasis and other skin problems.

Once upon a time, Ein Bokek comprised a handful of hotels, each with a "spa" of perhaps three or four treatment rooms, with a pebbly beach out front. Today, it's a collection of large and luxurious hotels with curvy pools and grassy, sprawling outdoor areas; each has a state-of-the-art spa equipped to provide beauty and health treatments and a rooftop solarium, and some have private beaches. Each hotel has a pretty good restaurant. There are no full-service restaurants outside the hotels, although a few casual eating places are set along the beach and in the two shopping centers. The cluster of hotels in the main area is linked by a promenade to two hotels at the very southern end of the area.

Ein Bokek is a 30-minute drive from Masada and a 45-minute drive from Ein Gedi. You can enjoy Jeep trips through the lunarlike landscape east of the hotel area and explore interesting local sights, such as the nearby white-marl **Flour Cave** (from which you emerge dusted with white powder) with a driver-guide arranged through your hotel concierge or through a tour company.

## Where to Stay & Eat

$$ ✕ **Tapuah Sodom.** The name means "apple of Sodom," and the sign outside is only in Hebrew, but this place can't be missed as it's beside a shopping center and is usually quite crowded. Glass-enclosed, with a view of the public beach outside, it's a favorite wayfarer's stop. You can change into a bathing suit downstairs, and stoke up on braised chicken, steak, pasta, fish, fresh salads, and sandwiches, plus beer and wine. It's open daily 8 AM to 11 PM. ✉ *Next to shopping center* ☎ *08/658–4382* ♙ *Reservations not accepted* ▭ *AE, DC, MC.*

$$ ✕▥ **Crowne Plaza.** Built in 1997, this 12-floor hotel is not as lavish as many of its neighbors, though its spa facilities are top-notch. And it's right on the beach. The Sato Bistrot ($$$$), a restaurant serving Asian fusion cuisine, is a treat in an area with a dearth of good eateries. About 90 rooms afford direct panoramic views of the Dead Sea, while the others have balconies from which you can view the sea (balcony furniture is available on request). Carpets, curtains, and bedspreads please the eye with their taupe and navy color schemes. The pool has a central island reached by a bridge, and one section is marked off for swimming laps. ✉ *M. P. Dead Sea, 86930* ☎ *08/659–1919* ⊕ *www.crowneplaza.com* ↹ *290 rooms, 14 suites* ⋄ *2 restaurants, room service, minibars, cable TV, Wi-Fi, 2 pools, wading pool, fitness classes, gym, hot tub, spa, beach, billiards, ping-pong, lobby lounge, nightclub, shop, babysitting, children's programs (ages 3–10), playground, laundry service, Internet, business services, no-smoking rooms* ▭ *AE, DC, MC, V* ⑩ *CP.*

$$$$ ▥ **Royal.** A crown topped with the letter R sits perched atop this 18-story tower, the largest and newest of the Dead Sea hotels. Built in 2001, the hotel has a spare, minimalist entrance, whereas the stunning indoor pool area has more color: striped lounge chairs face windows that soar two floors high and overlook the sand-colored mountains. The actual pool, with hot tub, is immense. At the lavish spa with 52 treatment rooms,

you can enjoy the fitness room and soak in the personal sulfur and therapeutic baths. Peach walls in the guest rooms are set off by rust-colored curtains and bedcovers. Twenty-five rooms are wheelchair equipped. The beach is across the street. ⊠ *M. P. Dead Sea, 86930* ☎ *08/668–8555* 🖷 *08/668–8500* 🖥 *394 rooms, 26 suites* ♿ *2 restaurants, coffee shop, room service, in-room safes, refrigerators, cable TV, pool, wading pool, hair salon, spa, billiards, lobby lounge, pub, video game room, shops, children's program (ages 3–10), laundry service, Internet, no-smoking rooms* ☰ *AE, DC, MC, V* ⧉ *CP.*

**$$$** 🏨 **Caesar Premier.** Bright white both inside and out, the terraced, nine-story Caesar Premier is across the road from the beach. Two 6-foot-high silver urns furnish the lofty lobby, and glass elevators add to the airy feel. Each room has a balcony; suites have balconies with whirlpool baths. The wooden wall at the entrance to the dining room is carved in a distinctive bas-relief with date palms, fish, flowers, and fruit. The gracious, ultra-equipped spa (small fee for guests) features a bath for two with an underwater aromatic-oil massage, and two sulfur pools. The Dead Sea–water pool starts inside the hotel and ends outside. A motorized trolley transports guests to the private beach. ⊠ *M. P. Dead Sea, 86980* ☎ *08/668–9666* 🖷 *08/652–0301* ⊕ *www.caesarhotels.co.il/english* 🖥 *298 rooms* ♿ *Restaurant, room service, in-room safes, refrigerators, cable TV, some in-room data ports, some Wi-Fi, 2 pools, wading pool, hair salon, spa, billiards, Ping-Pong, lobby lounge, shop, children's programs (ages 3–10), playground, Internet room, no-smoking rooms* ☰ *AE, DC, MC, V* ⧉ *CP.*

**$$$** 🏨 **Golden Tulip Privilege.** Many architectural elements are present in the Golden Tulip: two terraced wings, arched windows here and there, a tower, and an undulating front wall that swirls around a huge flower-shape pool. The public rooms are on the plain side, but the guest accommodations are well appointed, most with a sofa that opens into an additional bed. There's a bowling alley, and the dining room serves several styles of cuisine each evening. There's a shuttle to the beach. ⊠ *M. P. Dead Sea, 86930* ☎ *08/668–9999* 🖷 *08/668–9900* ⊕ *www.fattal. co.il* 🖥 *292 rooms, 10 suites* ♿ *Restaurant, room service, in-room safes, minibars, cable TV, some Wi-Fi, tennis, pool, wading pool, gym, hair salon, hot tub, spa, basketball, billiards, Ping-Pong, volleyball, lobby lounge, pub, dance club, children programs (ages 3-10), Internet room, no-smoking rooms* ☰ *AE, D, MC, V* ⧉ *CP.*

**$$** 🏨 **Magic Nirvana Club.** You might consider bringing the whole family to this all-inclusive property, where guests enjoy four meals daily (the last one being a midnight supper), plus popsicles are available to kids 24/7. The hotel is at the southern end of the promenade, and its nicest "deluxe" section was added in 1999. Huge windows in the reception lobby look out at the dolphin-shaped pool and the Lagoon with umbrellas in the water. Colors of soft green, sunny yellow, and tobacco decorate the rooms—request one with a balcony. Suites have hot tubs on the balcony. ⊠ *M. P. Dead Sea, 84960* ☎ *08/668–9444* 🖷 *08/668–9400* ⊕ *www.fattal.co.il* 🖥 *345 rooms, 43 suites* ♿ *Restaurant, in-room safes, refrigerators, in-room data ports, cable TV, miniature golf, pool, wading pool, exercise equipment, spa, beach, billiards, lobby lounge,* *video game room, shop, children's programs (ages 3–10), no-smoking rooms* ☰ *AE, DC, MC, V* ❙❂❙ *FAP.*

★ $ ▥ **Hod Hamidbar.** Comprising thirteen floors of homey comfort, the Hod was completely renovated from top to toe in 2000 and still looks great today. A distinctive feature here is the private beach, reached via a walkway lined with 10-foot-high Roman-style pillars. Guest rooms are not especially large, but they are handsomely furnished in blond wood with taupe and gray carpets and curtains; be sure to request a sea view if that's important to you. The contemporary lobby, in shades of sand with red stone, gives way to a pillared terrace. The dining room has a view of the Dead Sea. ✉ *M. P. Dead Sea, 86930* ☎ *08/668–8222* 🖷 *08/ 658–4606* ⊕ *www.hodhotel.co.il* ⇦ *203 rooms* ♨ *Restaurant, room service, in-room safes, refrigerators, cable TV, 2 pools, wading pool, exercise equipment, hair salon, spa, Turkish bath, beach, Ping-Pong, lobby lounge, piano bar, dance club, babysitting, playground, laundry service, internet room, no-smoking rooms* ☰ *AE, DC, MC, V* ❙❂❙ *CP.*

★ $ ▥ **Le Meridien.** Formerly a Hyatt resort and now managed by a local hotel chain, Fattal, Le Meridien stands out for its stunning parquet-floor lobby and other inviting public spaces filled with paintings and sculptures by Israeli artists. The hotel is set against a backdrop of small palm trees and gurgling waterfalls. Treatments in the sparkling-white spa include the use of therapeutic mud; the medical center offers services such as sports medicine, postsurgery recovery, and alternative medical treatments. The comfortable rooms, all of which face the water, are decorated in shades of calm brown. Puffy white bedcovers are a pleasant touch. A shuttle zips guests to the hotel's private beach. ✉ *M. P. Dead Sea, 86980* ☎ *08/659–1234* 🖷 *08/659–1235* ⊕ *www.fattal.co.il* ⇦ *509 rooms, 68 suites* ♨ *Restaurant, room service, in-room data ports, cable TV, some Wi-Fi, tennis court, pool, wading pool, fitness classes, health club, hair salon, spa, billiards, Ping-Pong, squash, lobby lounge, pub, nightclub, piano bar, shops, babysitting, children's programs (ages 3- 10), playground, laundry service, concierge, Internet room, business services, no smoking* ☰ *AE, DC, MC, V* ❙❂❙ *CP.*

$ ▥ **Lot.** The exterior of this property does not impress, but inside the welcome is warm. Europeans are drawn to the cheerful and friendly atmosphere of this seven-story hotel where all the rooms—in sprightly combinations of marine blue, bright yellow, and dark red—look about the same and each has a balcony with views either of the mountains or the sea. Unwinding is easy at the private beach, in the rooftop solarium, or on the terrace overlooking a colorful garden. The fancy hotels up the road are for glitz—the Lot is for a rewarding stay that won't break the bank. ✉ *M. P. Dead Sea,, 86930* ☎ *08/668–9200* 🖷 *08/658–4623* ⊕ *www.lothotel.co.il* ⇦ *199 rooms* ♨ *Restaurant, room service, in-room safes, refrigerators, cable TV, in-room data ports, pool, wading pool, gym, hair salon, hot tub, spa, beach, billiards, Ping-Pong, lobby lounge, pub, nightclub, shop, laundry facilities* ☰ *AE, DC, MC, V* ❙❂❙ *CP.*

## Outdoor Activities & Spas

In Ein Bokek, **Yoel Tours** (✉ Gardens Hotel ☎ 052/256–2563) operates a half-day minibus tour to the Bedouin market in Beersheva followed by a cup of coffee with a Bedouin family. The trip costs NIS 210 and runs every Thursday. Yoel also offers a one-day trip (on Tuesday, and priced at NIS 290) to Eilat, which includes the Underwater Observatory and a swim in the Red Sea; a yacht trip and snorkeling are optional. If you'd like to see the famed Mountain of Sodom, where Lot's wife looked back, Yoel's trip goes for half a day and includes a stop at the Flour Cave, for NIS 140. Desert agriculture tours are also available.

BEACHES    The Tamar Local Council has beautified the beaches of Ein Bokek. They're free to the public and are usually fairly crowded. Regrettably, there are no facilities for changing; the only option is having a bite at Tapuah Sodom restaurant and using their restrooms. A lifeguard is on duty year-round. There is ample parking alongside the promenade. Keep in mind that the only water sport in the Dead Sea is floating!

SPAS    Luxurious **spas** are an understood feature of Ein Bokek's hotels, but
★    note that you must reserve treatments in advance and there's an extra charge. Make arrangements with your hotel upon arrival. You can certainly sample the sybaritic delights if you're in Ein Bokek only for a day; again, reserve treatments in advance. Many spas are operated under medical supervision; each has an indoor Dead Sea–water pool, a sauna, and a hot tub, and offers a range of beauty and health treatments using curative substances from the Dead Sea. Sample prices for individual treatments are as follows: NIS 150 for a half-hour massage; NIS 50 for a sulfur bath; and NIS 200 for a 50-minute mud treatment. Hotel guests pay lower fees. Other facilities and services include fitness rooms, private solariums, and cosmetic treatments. Some hotels offer spa packages.

## Shopping

★    Several companies manufacture excellent **Dead Sea bath and beauty products** made from mud, salts, and minerals; the actual mud is sold in squishy, leak-proof packages. Ahava, DSD, and Jericho are three popular brands whose products are sold at Tapuah Sodom restaurant, next door at the shopping center, and at the shops in most hotels.

Diamonds and jewelery are sold at the **Dead Sea Diamond Center** (☎ 08/ 995-8777 or 057/755-4004). Call for a shuttle to pick you up. The center is closed Thursday and Sunday.

**Miri** (✉ Le Meridien ☎ 08/995–6543) creates unusual, handmade, soft-body dolls, about 2 feet high, as well as droll-face puppets.

**Petra Kanion** (✉ near Le Meridien) shopping center contains a minimarket that sells wine and liquor, a currency exchange kiosk, and two swimwear and resort wear boutiques.

en route    **Arava Road** (Route 90) traverses the Arava Valley south from Ein Bokek to Eilat and parallels the Jordanian border, almost touching it at some points. To the east you'll see the spiky, red-brown mountains of Moab, in Jordan. The road follows an ancient route mentioned in biblical descriptions of the journeys of the Children of Israel. The Arava (meaning "valley") is part of the Syrian-African Rift, that great crack in the earth stretching from Turkey to East Africa, the result of an ancient shift of land masses. Just south of Ein Bokek, you'll pass signs for the settlements Neot HaKikar and Ein Tamar, whose date palms draw water from underground springs rather than irrigation. With the Edom Mountains rising in the east, the road continues along the southern Dead Sea Valley. You'll cross one of the largest dry riverbeds in the Negev, Nahal Zin.

About halfway between Ein Bokek and Eilat is **Kushi Rimon,** named for the eccentric Shimon Rimon (nicknamed Kushi) and the legendary army unit in which he served. This huge, offbeat road stop is landscaped with palm trees and metal-and-wire sculptures. Peacocks and ducks wander about, cages house a monkey and a tiger. Inside is a cafeteria with hot food, a bar, and a minimart. ⊠ *Km 101 on Arava Rd.* ☎ *08/634–5101* ⊙ *Daily 24 hrs, except Yom Kippur.*

# EILAT & ENVIRONS

The Arava Plain comes to an abrupt end where it meets the Bay of Eilat, site of the country's southernmost town: the sun-drenched resort of Eilat. The Gulf of Eilat gives way to the Red Sea, which lies between the Sinai Mountains, to the west, and Jordan's Edom Mountains, to the east. The Jordanian port of Aqaba is directly across the bay—Eilat residents will eagerly point out the Jordanian royals' yacht and vacation villa—and to the southeast is Saudi Arabia. The Sinai Desert is just over the Egyptian border.

Most travelers fly into or whiz down to Eilat to flop down on its beaches and snorkel or scuba dive among its tropical reefs. But if you have time, see the vast desert landscape to the north of Eilat. You'll find cliffs, canyons, and unique formations at Timna Park and indigenous animals at Hai Bar Nature Reserve. Both make good side trips from Eilat; just leave time for a sunset stop at Mt. Yoash. Another option is to explore ancient Petra, over the border in Jordan.

## Eilat

**⑭** *307 km (190 mi) south of Jerusalem, 356 km (221 mi) south of Tel Aviv.*

A legend says that after the Creation, the angels painted the earth. When they got tired, they spilled their paints: the blue became the waters of Eilat, and the other colors became its fish and the corals. Whether or not this is true, add to this rainbow of color Eilat's year-round warm weather, its superb natural surroundings of sculptural red-orange mountains, and its situation on the sparkling Red Sea—whose coral reefs attract divers from all over the world—and you've got a first-rate resort.

Eilat is now Israel's prototypical "sun-and-fun" destination, but its strategic location as a crossroads between Asia and Africa has given it a long place in history. The Children of Israel stopped here as they fled from Egypt into the Promised Land, and it was long thought that King Solomon kept his fleet in the area between Aqaba and Eilat. Later, because of its position on a main trade and travel route, Eilat was conquered by every major power: the Romans, Byzantines, Arabs, Crusaders, Mamluks, Ottoman Turks, and, most recently, the British, whose isolated police station (headquarters of their camel corps) was taken by the Israelis in March 1949. Called Umm Rash Rash, this was the first building in modern-day Eilat, a town founded in 1951 and developed as a port in 1956 after the Egyptian blockade of the Tiran Straits was lifted.

Most travelers decide that Eilat's natural assets more than make up for undistinguished architecture and overdevelopment. For wherever you are in Eilat, a glance eastward presents you with the dramatic sight of the granite mountain range of Edom, whose predominant shades of red intensify and fade with the light of day, culminating in a red-gold sunset blaze over the Red Sea. This incongruous name for a body of water that's brilliantly turquoise along the shore is the result of a 17th-century typographical error by an English printer: in setting the type for an English translation of a Latin version of the Bible, the printer left out an "e" and thus "Reed Sea" became "Red Sea." The name was easily accepted because of the sea's red appearance at sunset.

With an average annual rainfall of about 7½ inches and an average winter temperature of 21°C (70°F), Eilat is a haven from the cold winter of Israel's north. Eilat's high season is mid-October to April, but the city is also crowded during Jewish and Christian holidays. It's hottest here in July and August (39°C or 102°F)—many travel agencies close their doors, and Jeep trips and hikes are curtailed. The burning summer brings a dry heat, though, without any mugginess. The wind picks up in late afternoon, and beaches, hotel terraces, and outdoor cafés fill up with loungers sitting, sipping, and watching the Edom Mountains turn red and the Saudi Arabian hills go purple. Summer walking in Eilat is pleasant in the early morning and the late afternoon; save indoor attractions, shopping, and siestas for midday.

Arava Road (Route 90) runs north–south through the town, bordered by the airport on the east. The main intersection just south of the airport is Durban Road, site of the tourist office (behind the Burger Ranch). The section of Eilat called the North Beach includes the promenade south to the main marina and past the Lagoon and contains many of the town's luxury hotels, restaurants, and boutiques. Eilat's residential area and the Central Bus Station are in the foothills of the Eilat Mountains, which rise west of Route 90.

South of Eilat, Route 90 (now called Eilat–Taba Road) continues past the port and navy base to Coral Beach; then passes Coral Reserve, Dolphin Reef, and the Coral World Underwater Observatory and Aquarium; and finally reaches the Taba border crossing to the Sinai, in Egypt. To reach sights south of Eilat, take Bus 15 (from the hotel area; the Central Bus Station, on HaTmarim Boulevard; or Arava Road) or grab a taxi. Although the sights are close enough together that you can walk, inexpensive taxis are a good alternative in the afternoon heat.

Start exploring Eilat with a walk along the **promenade**, beginning at Herod's Hotel, near the Jordanian border. The 3-km (2-mi) promenade is also known as the Peace Walk, since it is hoped that one day it will continue to Aqaba, Jordan. Purple and pink bougainvillea pour down from the Royal Beach Hotel's terrace above; add to your enjoyment by stopping for an ice cream (say, mango) from one of the stands. If you're here at sunset, sit and savor the show-stopping view of the Red Sea turning red, with the dark, reddish-gray shapes of the Edom Mountains to the east and the rugged Eilat Mountains to the west. On a clear day, you can see as far as Saudi Arabia and Egypt.

A stroll past swanky hotels and loads of shops, coffee bars, and restaurants, with palmy beaches on the other side, brings you to the Dutch Bridge, which opens for tall-masted vessels. On one side is the Lagoon, or inner marina, where yachts are anchored and various small craft are for hire; on the other is the marina, where cruise boats of all types wait to sally forth. The promenade winds along beside more beaches, covered with folks reddening in the sun. The scene includes sophisticated strollers, the backpack crowd, artists doing quick portraits, vendors selling earrings, tattoo artists, all accompanied by strolling street musicians. At the intersection of Durban and Arava streets (at the roundabout), you can continue along the waterfront, with the Sea Gate Mall on your right, until you reach a small palm-filled plaza with a tiny, cement block-shape building with a statue of four fighters boosting a comrade aloft while a flag "flies" above. This is Umm Rash Rash, where the Israelis first took control of the Gulf of Eilat in March 1949, as determined by the U.N.'s Partition Plan. The small building—the only one that existed then—is a far cry from today's luxury resorts.

**need a break?** At the western end of the promenade, at the Mul Yam (Mall Yam) Shopping Mall (identified by the seahorse over its entrance), is the outdoor **Mul HaYam** café, which feeds the crowd with ice cream, sweet drinks, and good coffee. Locals turn out in force here to sip, chat, and watch the tourists go by.

ℭ **Kings City.** This gigantic fairy-tale castle looms behind the hotels on the northern beach. Kings City, a biblical theme park complex on three levels, offers three distinct sections of sophisticated entertainment, and there's a high-flying water ride to boot. The **Cave of Illusions** has, among other diversions, hands-on games that test your mental acuity, a jail to test your ability to escape, a huge maze, and a large, endless kaleidescope. Next, you reach the **Bible Cave** in an elevator that descends almost 200 feet underground to a gigantic cave where humanlike robots reenact Bible stories about King Solomon and other tales. In the **Journey to the Past** you see 3-D films of pharaohs in ancient Egypt, and then there's the thrilling 10-minute waterfall ride that ends in a pool (you're in a boat). There is a restaurant (with kid stuff like pizza and burgers), a café, a bar, and a gift shop, too. You'll need three to four hours to do this park justice. Note that children under 1 meter tall (about 3 feet) are not admitted, and the park is handicapped-accessible. ⊠ *East Lagoon* ☎ *08/ 630–4444* ⊕ *www.kingscity.co.il* ☞ *NIS 118* ☉ *Daily 10–10.*

★ ⑮ Less than 1 km (½ mi) south of Eilat, the **Coral Reserve** is one of the finest such protected areas in the world. Close to the shoreline, its coral reef is 1¼ km (¾ mi) long and is zealously guarded by the Nature and National Parks Protection Authority. It's the most northern reef in the world. You don't need experience to scuba dive here; the 15-minute movie explains everything and the crew provides continual assistance. In the Lagoon, divers and snorklers take two bridges, or a trail marked by buoys, to get to the reef wall. Stunning multicolored fish and soft and hard corals are your rich reward. There are hot showers and a snack bar on the premises. Kids should be over 5 to snorkel—younger ones can fool around on the beach. ⊠ *Rte. 90 (Eilat–Taba Rd.)* ☎ *08/637–6829* ⊕ *www.parks.org.il* 🖃 *NIS 23* ⊙ *Mid-Apr.–mid-Oct., Sat.–Thurs. 9–5, Fri. 9–4; mid-Oct.–mid-Apr., Sat.–Thurs. 9–4, Fri 9–3.*

★ ⓒ ⑯ **Dolphin Reef,** 1 km (½ mi) south of Eilat, was developed for the study of marine mammals, specifically dolphins, in their natural habitat. Dolphin Reef allows you the novel experience of meeting bottle-nosed dolphins face-to-face: you can actually swim, snorkel, or scuba dive with them. The guide who introduces you to these friendly creatures is there to protect them from people, not the other way around. It's fun to watch the dolphins being fed, daily at 10, noon, 2, and 4. Facilities include a dive center, a snorkel rental, and a photo shop with on-the-spot film and video developing. Don't miss the Relaxation Pools, freshwater, highly concentrated saltwater, and sea water, surrounded by a botanical garden. There's a beach here and at one end is the Reef Bar, a thatched roof pub and restaurant. Note: you must reserve a specific time to swim or dive with the dolphins; call in advance. ⊠ *Rte. 90 (Eilat–Taba Rd.)* ☎ *08/637–1846* ⊕ *www.dolphinreef.co.il* 🖃 *NIS 42* ⊙ *Daily 9–5.*

★ ⓒ ⑰ The **Coral World Underwater Observatory and Aquarium,** one of Eilat's star attractions, is recognizable by the tall space-needle structure that floats offshore. Plan to spend many hours here (there's a casual restaurant for lunch on the premises). The **Aquarium's** 12 windows provide views of rare fish so magnificent and so Day-Glo colorful that it's hard to believe they're real; there's an unlighted room where phosphorescent fish and other sea creatures glow in the dark. Don't miss feeding time (11 AM) in the **Shark Pool.** The anaconda snakes, poisonous frogs, and piranha are fed the **Amazonas** at 3 PM. Capt. Jaws takes you on a sea journey during an audiovisual show presented in a simulated-motion theater with moving seats at the **Oceanarium.**

The **Underwater Observatory** is reached by a 330-foot wooden bridge. Head down the spiral staircase and into the sea—you are now 15 feet underwater, in a round, glass-windowed room, looking at a huge coral reef. Swimming outside are thousands of exotic tropical fish. The **Observatory Tower**—reached by elevator or stairs—gives coastal views of Israel's neighboring countries. There's a café up here. ⊠ *Rte. 90 (Eilat–Taba Rd.)* ☎ *08/636–4200* ⊕ *www.coralworld.com* 🖃 *NIS 80 with Oceanarium, NIS 70 without* ⊙ *Sat.–Thurs. 8:30–4, Fri. and Jewish holiday eves 8:30–3.*

## Where to Eat

Eilat has so many restaurants that you can easily dine on a different cuisine each night over a long holiday. Savor the finest local seafood and fresh fish; charcoal-grilled meats of every kind; or Chinese, Indian, Thai, and Italian cuisine and other ethnic meals, reflecting Israel's many waves of immigration. Many restaurants have outdoor seating, often near the water or amid pots of pink bougainvillea. Outdoor cafés serve café *hafuch* (strong coffee with a frothy, hot-milk topping) and light food, such as cheese toast (grilled-cheese sandwiches) and salads, as well as rich cakes, ice cream, iced drinks, and various other coffees.

**$$$** ✗ **Cucina.** Right here on the North Beach Promenade you'll find a little slice of Tuscany at this restaurant with arched wooden windows, paintings of Italian cities, a fireplace, and bougainvillea spilling over the outdoor terrace. If you love thin-crust pizza, try Cucina's, which is crunchy as a cracker and especially delicious when topped with seafood. Other good bets are fried spinach ravioli with ricotta cheese, and peppered fillet of beef medallions in a waistline-inflating cream and Gorgonzola sauce. Passion fruit and forest berry sherbet flavored with lemongrass makes a cool ending. ⊠ *North Beach Promenade near the Royal Beach* ☎ *08/ 636–8932* ♣ *Reservations essential* ☰ *AE, D, MC, V.*

**$$$** ✗ **Eddie's Hideaway.** As the name suggests, Eddie's is slightly hard to find. But the highly affable Eddie prepares delicious food, which makes it easy to understand why his hideaway is so worth seeking out and earns such stellar reviews, especially for delicious steaks. Devotees also appreciate the shrimp and fish dishes. Try Filet Dijon (filet mignon graced with mustard and brown sugar) or Shanghai fish with hot soybean paste. If you can pack it in, try the pecan pie. Inquire if Eddie has prepared a "daily"— a dish he particularly likes to cook. Eddie does lunch only on Saturday. ⊠ *68 Almogim St. (enter from Elot St.)* ☎ *08/637–1137* ♣ *Reservations essential* ☰ *AE, DC, MC, V* ☻ *Closed Sun. No lunch.*

★ **$$$** ✗ **La Coquille.** Chef Robert and his wife, Zari, run this French haute-cuisine establishment. Petite and intimate, the restaurant is set up with red velvet chairs and tables with starched linen tablecloths. French watercolors line the walls, lending a charming air. La Coquille's fine reputation is well earned with such memorable fare as shrimp sautéed in champagne, stuffed crab, grilled lobster, delicate trout sautéed with almonds, and filet mignon. On weekdays, a three-course business lunch quells noontime hunger pangs. ⊠ *Derech Hayam, 2nd floor* ☎ *08/ 637–3461* ♣ *Reservations essential* ☰ *AE, DC, MC, V.*

**$$$** ✗ **Last Refuge.** Eilatis hold this fine restaurant in high regard and take
**FodorsChoice** their guests from "up north" here as a real treat. The dining room, with
★ dark wooden paneling and predictable nautical motifs, extends outside to a spacious balcony, where diners eat beside the water, looking at Jordan across the way. Presented with a flourish are fish or crab soups, just-caught charcoal-grilled Red Sea fish, lobster (order in advance), jumbo shrimp, and creamed seafood served in a seashell. A Refuge specialty is stir-fried, small, spicy sea crabs, prepared in olive oil and garlic. Friday night is extra busy, so it's smart to reserve even four days ahead (ask for balcony seating). ⊠ *Rte. 90 near overhead bridge, Coral Beach* ☎ *08/637–3627* ♣ *Reservations essential* ☰ *AE, DC, MC, V.*

**$$** ✗ **Lalo.** Here's a top-drawer example of ethnic cooking, by a mother-and-son team. Upon your arrival, five different salads (including eggplant and hot peppers) are set quickly upon the table. The menu may confront you with foods you've never eaten before, but this food rewards any adventuresome choices you make. Consider such delicacies as beef cooked with hummus (a house specialty), calves' brains served straight-up with Moroccan spices, couscous with vegetables and chicken, and spicy-hot fish. No fancy pitas are served here—just plain bread. Dessert is specially prepared fruit, such as oranges cooked till thick and soft, accompanied by tea with mint. ⊠ *259 Horev St., Shkunat Alef* ☎ *08/ 633–0578* ☐ *AE, D, MC, V* ⊘ *Closed Fri.–Sat. No dinner.*

**$$** ✕ **Red Sea Star.** You can do lunch or dinner in this inside-out aquarium 20 feet under the sea, while Technicolor fish glide by, an eel gives you the eye, and spiny sea urchins float amid the corals outside the window. The window frames are wavy, the red tables project inward like continuations of the coral outside, and a watery light filters through from the water's surface above—all adding to the underwater feel. To reach the Star, diners walk about 85 yards along a wooden walkway over the water. Start with a salad of lettuce and vegetables with shrimp, calamari, and tiny squid; then move on to main courses like sea bream in paprika cream; mussels in garlic, chili, and mustard; veal steak; or spareribs in melon and chili sauce. ⊠ *Arava Rd., near Reef hotel* ☎ *08/634–7777* ⏦ *Reservations essential* ☐ *AE, DC, MC, V.*

**$$** ✕ **Tandoori.** First-rate Indian cuisine is graciously presented amid embroidered wall hangings, authentic Indian wood carvings, and brass table appointments. The food is prepared to order; while you wait, sip a *lassi* (a refreshing Indian drink of yogurt, fruit, and saffron) or one of the many cocktails on the menu. House specialties are various succulent meats cooked in a tandoor (a charcoal-fired clay oven), curries, and a selection of vegetarian dishes. Lamb curry with green masala sauce is a treat. The business lunch (from noon to 3:30) is moderately priced. ⊠ *King's Wharf at the Lagoon (below Lagoona Hotel)* ☎ *08/633–3879* ⏦ *Reservations essential* ☐ *AE, DC, MC, V.*

**★ $** ✕ **Ginger Asian Kitchen and Bar.** A duo of Thai chefs presents Thai, Japanese, and Indonesian food at Ginger's, a spiffy New York look-alike. It's small, and the menu's huge. Recessed lighting contributes to the hip vibe, as do the pale gray walls and black leather chairs. Start with plump *kioza* dumplings stuffed with chicken, goose, and vegetables or shrimp tempura on avocado with miso sauce, then try the Jakarta (chicken or beef with eggplant and zucchini with an Indonesian sweet sauce) or Exotica (seafood dressed with coconut milk and chili paste and scattered with basil leaves). Finish off with an almond and butter pastry, topped with carmelized bananas and ginger parfait. A lighter bar menu is served from midnight till 3 AM Thursday–Sunday night. ⊠ *Yotam St. near Imax* ☎ *08/637–2517* ⏦ *Reservations essential* ☐ *AE, MC, DC, V.*

**★ $** ✕ **Shauli and Guy.** Two brothers and their dad run this place, inviting guests to feast on special Algerian-Tripolitan–style grilled meats such as veal chops, lamb chops, and skewers of lamb (there's fish, too). These guys know what they're about: three generations of butchers work in the family-run butcher shop next door. You can get right down to it, Israeli-style, by sampling the fresh salads and succulent skewers of meat as well as luxurious goose liver (fois gras). As a warm-up, try homemade hummus and grilled eggplant, then tuck in to skewers of grilled chicken, lamb, beef or turkey, goose liver or ground-meat kebabs, steak, or the daily catch of local fish, accompanied by beer, wine, or Turkish coffee. The plain and simple dining room is both spotless and homey. It's in the middle of the Industrial Zone, so you shouldn't walk here; but taxi drivers know this place well. ⊠ *"Azore Hatassia" (Industrial Zone)* 🕾 *08/633–1930* ⬧ *Reservations not accepted* ▤ *AE, DC, MC, V* ☺ *No lunch Sat. No dinner Fri.*

$  ✕ **Spring Onion.** Vegetarians, front and center! Here's the place to get garden-fresh salads with interesting toppings, as well as delicately cooked vegetable quiches, fresh fish, blintzes, and wonderfully authentic pizzas. Noodles tossed with vegetables in ginger and soy sauce make an appetizing dish. There's also a selection of "cheese toast" (grilled-cheese sandwiches)—try the one with Bulgarian cheese, olive oil, and black olives. Portions are large (it's acceptable to split a dish); if you have room, try a wedge of cream cake. Beer and wine are available. Both floors are always crowded (the top floor is no-smoking), but there's plenty of outdoor seating. ⊠ *Bridge House, near the bridge* 🕾 *08/ 637–7434* ▤ *MC, V.*

## Where to Stay

★ $$$$ 🏨 **Dan Eilat.** The 14-floor, U-shape Dan is on the North Beach Promenade near the Jordanian border. The decor, by internationally acclaimed Israeli architect Adam Tihani, effectively combines snazzy high-style with comfort. The two connecting two-story lobbies feature a winding glass stairway (as scary as it sounds), craggy rock walls with a water cascade, floating ceiling sculptures, a huge aviary, and a rock pool with iguanas. The spacious blue and terra-cotta rooms have blond-wood furnishings, and the dresser mirror can be adjusted to reflect the sea. A 20-meter pool for serious swimmers anchors the large, lush outdoor area. ⊠ *Promenade, North Beach, 88000* 🕾 *08/636–2222* 🖷 *08/636–2333* ⊕ *www. danhotels.co.il* ⏎ *325 rooms, 48 suites* ⬧ *2 restaurants, in-room safes, minibars, cable TV, 2 pools, wading pool, gym, hair salon, hot tub, spa, Turkish bath, squash, lobby lounge, bar, piano, video game room, shop, babysitting, children's programs (ages 3–10), playground, dry cleaning, laundry service, concierge, Internet room, no-smoking rooms* ▤ *AE, DC, MC, V* ⥙ *CP.*

★ $$$$ 🏨 **Herod's Palace.** Herod's—designed with the legendary king in mind— is all about over-the-top opulence and palatial pizzazz. It's part of a hotel complex opposite the beach, with Jordan's mountains as a backdrop. Luxury is found throughout, from the minaret towers that greet you outside to the dramatic 12-story lobby, decorated with Italian wrought-iron chandeliers, carved marble planters, and mosaics. Romanesque domes, arches, bridges, and niches are everywhere. Rooms are spacious, with warm, dark-wood furniture and lush curtains. A Roman-style pool sits at the end of an avenue of palm trees—it looks as though it flows straight into the sea. The Vitalis Spa Hotel is next door. ⊠ *North Beach, Box 4201, 88000* 🕾 *08/638–0000* ⊕ *www.herods.co.il* ⏎ *265 rooms, 31 suites* ⬧ *3 restaurants, room service, in-room safes, minibars, cable TV, some in-room DVDs, some in-room VCRs, some Wi-Fi, 2 pools, 2 wading pools, spa, beach, bicycles, bar, lobby lounge, piano bar, video game room, shop, babysitting, children's programs (ages 2–12), laun-*

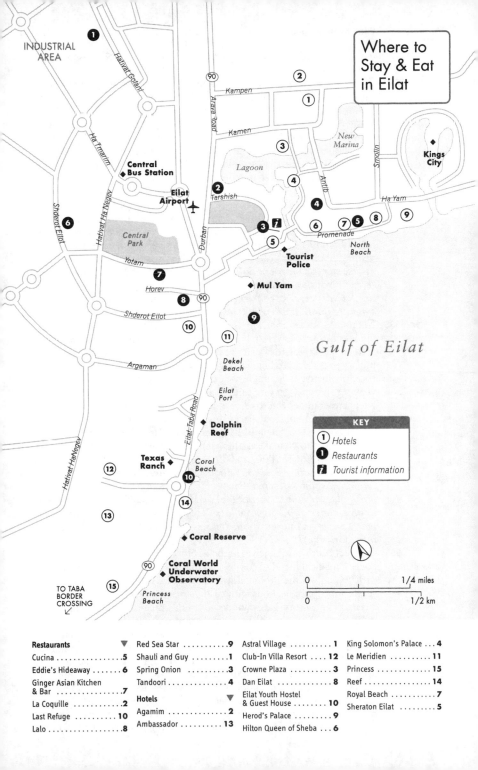

# Where to Stay & Eat in Eilat

INDUSTRIAL AREA

Kampen

Kamen

New Marina

Kings City

Central Bus Station

Eilat Airport

Tarshish

Lagoon

Central Park

Tourist Police

North Beach

Promenade

Mul Yam

Horev

Yotam

Shderot Eilot

Argaman

Dekel Beach

Eilat Port

Gulf of Eilat

Dolphin Reef

Texas Ranch

Coral Beach

Coral Reserve

Coral World Underwater Observatory

Princess Beach

TO TABA BORDER CROSSING

**KEY**
① Hotels
❶ Restaurants
𝒊 Tourist information

0       1/4 miles
0       1/2 km

*dry service, concierge, concierge floor, Internet room, business services, no-smoking floors* $\equiv$ *AE, DC, MC, V* ⊠ *CP.*

**$$$$** ⊞ **Hilton Queen of Sheba.** The imaginary palace King Solomon built for the queen is what Hilton International set out to construct with this imposing example of grandeur: a palatial entrance capped with a pillared dome rises between two turrets, with a wing of more than 200 rooms on either side. Khaki-color curtains cover the windows of the 40-foot-high lobby, and Italian mosaics of biblical animals cover the floor. The queen must have loved cats—images of them are everywhere. The bedrooms have gold-framed mirrors, taupe and orange carpeting, Egyptian-motif black and taupe bedspreads and curtains, and marble bathrooms with hand-painted murals. Rooms on even-numbered floors have balconies facing the sea or the marina. ⊠ *North Beach, Box 2228, 88121* ☎ *08/630–6666* ⊟ *08/630–6677* ⊕ *www.hiltonworldresorts.com* ⊃ *488 rooms* ⚹ *4 restaurants, in-room safes, minibars, cable TV, 3 pools, wading pool, fitness classes, health club, hair salon, hot tub, massage, sauna, spa, steam room, lobby lounge, dance club, video game room, shop, babysitting, children's programs (ages 3–10), playground, dry cleaning, laundry service, concierge, Internet room, no-smoking rooms, no-smoking floors* $\equiv$ *AE, DC, MC, V* ⊠ *CP.*

**★ $$$$** ⊞ **Princess.** Geographically the final hotel you'll reach in Israel (it's five minutes from the Egyptian border), the Princess has a light-filled reception area facing a two-story sheer rock cliff through a soaring glass wall; the public spaces are dazzlingly white with gold trim. The pool area is a country club in itself. Squiggle-shape pools connected by bridges afford views of charcoal-gray mountains and cliffs. Down at the beach, reached by a tunnel under the road, two jetties lead to the water, and sun-tanning beds beckon. The spa in this self-contained world-class resort is ultramodern. The splendid Kings nightclub and disco is another plus. A shuttle into town makes sightseeing convenient. ⊠ *Rte. 90 (Eilat–Taba Rd.), Box 2323, 88000* ☎ *08/636–5555* ⊟ *08/637–6333* ⊕ *www.inisrael.com/princess* ⊃ *355 rooms, 65 suites* ⚹ *2 restaurants, room service, in-room safes, minibars, cable TV, 2 tennis courts, 2 pools, wading pool, gym, hair salon, hot tub, spa, beach, billiards, Ping-Pong, lobby lounge, dance club, shops, children's programs (ages 3–10), laundry service, concierge, Internet room, business services, free parking, no-smoking floors* $\equiv$ *AE, DC, MC, V* ⊠ *CP.*

**$$$$** ⊞ **Royal Beach.** At the jewel in the Isrotel company's crown, guests discover a magical blend of comfort, glamour, and sophistication. Opened in 1994, across the Promenade from the beach, the Royal Beach has a serene lobby that beckons with cushy, smoky-green leather couches and chairs. Three-story glass windows bring graceful bamboo and palm trees inside. The oversized terrace—crammed with multicolored flowers, white overhead fans, and kilim rugs—faces the Gulf of Eilat, providing a stunning view at sundown. Rooms are decorated in warm blue and pale rose; all have comfortable sofas and chairs, and a balcony. Two are hearing impairment–equipped, and five are handicapped-equipped. Suites come with whirlpool tubs. ⊠ *North Beach* ☎ *08/636–8888* ⊟ *08/636–8811* ⊕ *www.isrotel.co.il* ⊃ *363 rooms; 19 suites* ⚹ *4 restaurants, room service, in-room safes, minibars, cable TV, some in-room hot tubs, Wi-Fi, 3 pools, hot tub, wading pool, spa, beach, lobby*

**FodorśChoice** **★**

*lounge, piano bar, babysitting, children's programs (ages 3–10), laundry service, concierge, no-smoking floors* ▤ *AE, DC, MC, V* ▢◎ *CP.*

★ **$$$** ▥ **King Solomon's Palace.** Solomon's entire court could easily have been accommodated at this venerable member of Isrotel's chain. It's a huge and comfortably utilitarian place with an expansive lobby furnished in beige wicker with gray upholstery. The staff attends to guests' every need, and everything runs like clockwork. The commodious dining room is open market–style and serves Chinese and other foods. Breakfast selections are vast, and eating on the leafy, shaded terrace is a pleasure. Palm-fringed pools (one with a 50-meter slide), overlook the Lagoon. The children's "house" offers all-day entertainment. Garden-terrace suites have their own hot tubs. ⊠ *Promenade, North Beach, 88000* ☎ *08/636–3444* ▭ *08/ 633–4189* ⊕ *www.isrotel.co.il* ⋚ *398 rooms, 22 suites* ⚭ *Restaurant, room service, in-room safes, some in-room hot tubs, refrigerators, cable TV, some Wi-Fi, in-room data ports, 2 pools, wading pool, gym, spa, billiards, Ping-Pong, lobby lounge, pub, dance club, video game room, shop, children's programs (ages 2–10), playground, laundry service, concierge, no-smoking floors* ▤ *AE, DC, MC, V* ▢◎ *CP.*

★ **$$** ▥ **Agamim.** With a name that means "lakes," this water-garden hotel has been designed with pure relaxation in mind. Built in 2002, the compound of four-floor buildings is set amid palm trees, emerald grass, and tropical plants, around a lagoon-shaped pool with hammocks and swing chairs. Pale green wicker chairs invite leisure time on the nearby terrace. Many rooms (all the same size) sit right at the curving waterways that flow from the pool, and all have balconies. Recessed lighting in the guest rooms gives a soft cast to striped sofas, bedspreads, and curtains of tobacco, blue, dark green, and dark rose, along with dark turquoise rugs. It's a 10-minute walk to the beach. ⊠ *Kampan, 88000* ☎ *08/630–0300* ▭ *08/630–0302* ⊕ *www.isrotel.co.il* ⚭ *2 restaurants, in-room safes, refrigerators, cable TV, 4 pools, wading pool, gym, spa, billiards, lobby lounge, video game room, shop, children's programs (ages 3–12), laundry service, Internet room, no-smoking rooms* ▤ *AE, DC, MC, V* ▢◎ *CP.*

★ **$$** ▥ **Ambassador.** Near the Coral Beach, this swank hotel is made up of an L-shape, three-floor wing called the Ambassador, where the rooms (all with balconies) face the sea; the Garden Wing, comprising two three-floor buildings with rooms and suites that have private gardens; and the Diver's Wing, which faces the Manta Dive Center and has nine rooms that can each accommodate four guests. The hotel's entrance, facing the Eilat Mountains, is up a palm-lined drive; inside, the decor is ultramodern and lively. The color scheme of the guest rooms is particularly attractive, with marine blue, khaki, and sunny yellow tones. Just across the road is the beach and a seafood restaurant. ⊠ *Rte. 90 (Eilat–Taba Rd.), 88000* ☎ *08/638–2222* ▭ *08/638–2200* ⊕ *www. isrotel.co.il* ⋚ *237 rooms, 14 suites* ⚭ *Restaurant, in-room safes, cable TV, refrigerators, pool, 2 wading pools, gym, hair salon, spa, dive shop, billiards, Ping-Pong, video game room, shops, lobby lounge, sports bar, children's programs (ages 3–10), laundry service, Internet room, no-smoking rooms* ▤ *AE, DC, MC, V* ▢◎ *CP.*

**$$** ⊞ **Club-In Villa Resort.** This midprice resort comprises a bilevel complex of connected, self-contained villas set into the mountainside opposite the Coral Beach Reserve. Each unit has two bedrooms (comfortably accommodating up to six guests), a kitchenette with a microwave (there's a minimart on the premises), a balcony, and a living room with a TV. Picking up on the desert colors outside, rooms are beige with sky blue ceilings and cacti painted on some walls. Front units face the pool; those in the rear have mountain views. ⊠ *Rte. 90 (Eilat–Taba Rd.), Box 1505, Coral Beach 88000* ☎ *08/638–5555* 🖷 *08/638–5533* ⊕ *www. clubhotels.co.il* �'➚ *168 units* ⚬ *Restaurant, grocery, cable TV, tennis court, pool, gym, bar, lobby lounge, dance club, children's programs (ages 3–10)* ⊟ *AE, DC, MC, V* ⦿⊙⦿ *CP.*

★ **$$** ⊞ **Le Meridien.** Enter this dandy hotel, and the first thing you'll see through its glass walls is a breathtaking view of the shimmering sea and Jordanian mountains beyond. This all-suite lodging (rooms house four to six guests) has a refined air. The spacious lobby lounge has a bar and a dance floor (there's a quiet lobby as well), and waiters sing in the pub at night. Parents can keep an eye on their children in the Kids' Club via a closed-circuit system transmitted to their in-room TV. The spa offers the last word in beauty and health treatments, and there's a beach exclusively for hotel guests. ⊠ *Arava Rd., Box 2120, 88119* ☎ *08/638–3333* 🖷 *08/638–3300* ⊕ *www.fattal.co.il* ➚ *245 suites* ⚬ *2 restaurants, room service, in-room safes, refrigerators, cable TV, some Wi-Fi, pool, wading pool, gym, hair salon, hot tub, spa, beach, lobby lounge, pub, children's programs (ages 3–10), laundry service, Internet room, no-smoking floors* ⊟ *AE, DC, MC, V* ⦿⊙⦿ *CP.*

**$$** ⊞ **Sheraton Eilat.** The location couldn't be better here at the Sheraton—the hotel faces the beach from the promenade near the marina, and everything is within walking distance. A decorator's touch is needed in the pedestrian lobby and reception area. That being said, the pleasant dining room was renovated in 2004, and the western wing received a makeover in 2005. The rooms, along outside corridors, have blue, light blue, and white-patterned carpets; bedspreads of dark blue; and curtains of gold and blue. Most rooms face the sea or pool, and 14 have in-room hot tubs. American tour groups and French visitors are partial to this property. The fourth-floor business lounge has fax and Internet facilities. ⊠ *Promenade, Box 135, Eilat 88000* ☎ *08/636–1111* 🖷 *08/633–4158* ⊕ *www.sheraton.com* ➚ *299 rooms, 7 suites* ⚬ *2 restaurants, room service, in-room safes, refrigerators, cable TV, some in-room hot tubs, Wi-Fi, 2 pools, wading pool, exercise equipment, hair salon, outdoor hot tub, spa, beach, billiards, Ping-Pong, lobby lounge, shop, video game room, children's programs (ages 4–10), laundry service, Internet room, no-smoking rooms, business services* ⊟ *AE, DC, MC, V* ⦿⊙⦿ *CP.*

**$** ⊞ **Astral Village.** Otherwordly, no. Fun for a family, yes. This relatively affordable compound opened in 2005 consists of small, trim cottages constructed of beige stucco, with wood shutters and red-tile roofs. White-frame windows with red-and-white flowers planted out front sit in adjoining pairs all around the huge pool, where holiday activity is centered. Music plays, palm trees sway. The cheerful turquoise-trimmed dining room is off the lobby, with its pale gray–and–beige floor and comfortable beige and rust-hued chairs. The staff is eager to please. It's just a 10-minute walk to the beach. ✉ *Kempen St. near King Solomon's Palace hotel* ☎ *08/636–6888* 🖷 *08/638–8889* ⊕ *www.eilatinhotels.co.il* ⟿ *170 rooms, 12 suites* ⚲ *Restaurant, in-room safes, refrigerators, pool, wading pool, gym, spa, lobby bar, children's programs (3–10)* ▤ *AE, MC, DC, V* ⍩ *CP.*

$ ⊡ **Crowne Plaza.** Once you've admired this hotel's blue, yellow, and green painted-glass entrance, and the glass-domed ceiling in the reception area, you'll encounter the lobby's fat fake trees with huge snakes (also fake), bananas, and lotus flowers. You can count on competent service at this nine-floor hotel, which faces the Lagoon. Renovations were carried out in the public areas in 2005—as of this writing, similar overhauls were planned for the guest rooms. In the meantime, the rooms are still quite presentable, done up in bronze, tobacco, and blue; most have balconies. There's a waterfall to sit in at the pool. The fifth floor and public areas are non-smoking. ✉ *Lagoon, North Beach, 88101* ☎ *08/ 636–7777* 🖷 *08/633–0821* ⊕ *www.crowneplaza.com* ⟿ *247 rooms; 18 suites* ⚲ *Restaurant, room service, minibars, cable TV, Wi-Fi, pool, health club, hair salon, spa, billiards, Ping-Pong, lobby lounge, video game room, shop, children's programs (ages 3–10), laundry service, Internet room, no-smoking rooms* ▤ *AE, DC, MC, V* ⍩ *CP.*

★ ¢ ⊡ **Eilat Youth Hostel & Guest House.** The word *hostel* takes on new meaning here: each room is air-conditioned and has its own bathroom. The pleasant rooms are simply furnished and sleep two to six (in bunks); certain rooms have coffee corners and/or refrigerators. Bed linens and towels are provided. Two rooms are wheelchair-equipped. A mere 10-minute walk from the central bus station and right across the highway from the beach, this hostel is wildly popular with the backpack crowd, so make reservations well ahead of time. The dining room serves lunch and dinner if ordered ahead. A competent and friendly staff are a plus. ✉ *Arava Rd., Box 152, 88101* ☎ *08/637–0088* 🖷 *08/637–5835* ⊕ *www.iyha.org.il/english.html* ⟿ *106 rooms* ⚲ *Lobby lounge, laundry service, Internet room; no room phones* ▤ *AE, DC, MC, V* ⍩ *BP.*

¢ ⊡ **Reef.** Modest and unassuming, this two-story stucco beachfront hotel occupies a quiet spot, away from the clutch of hotels farther north. A notable plus is your direct access to the beach from the Reef's wooden sundeck and pool area. Water-sports outfits, including a dive center, are but a splash away. The small lobby has a corner bar; the modern rooms are in light green and mauve; all have balconies. There are rooms around the pool on the ground level. Built in 1992, the Reef doesn't pretend to be luxurious; with its friendly staff, however, it's a good value. ✉ *Rte. 90 (Eilat–Taba Rd.), Box 3367, 88100* ☎ *08/636–4444* 🖷 *08/636–4488* ⊕ *www.reefhotel.co.il* ⟿ *71 rooms, 8 suites* ⚲ *Pool, wading pool, hot tub, spa, bar, billiards* ▤ *AE, DC, MC, V* ⍩ *CP.*

## Nightlife & the Arts

For an overview of local events, pick up a copy of the detailed leaflet "Events and Places of Interest," available at the tourist information office. For the coming week's arts and entertainment information, check out Friday's *Jerusalem Post* magazine, or the *Herald Tribune*'s *Ha Aretz Guide,* both of which carry listings for Eilat.

**BARS & CLUBS**  Most hotels in Eilat have a piano bar (some with space for cutting loose), and many have dance clubs; all are open to the public. Pubs also abound; top bands perform at several, and at many you can even get a decent meal. Other dancing options are beach parties, where bronzed bodies groove to recorded music all night; keep an eye out in town for English-language posters listing times and places. Admission is free. On Friday night, join Eilatis who gather at the Aqua Sport beach at sunset.

**Dolphin Reef** (⊠ Eilat–Taba Rd. ☎ 08/637–1846) is a good example of a bar-pub-restaurant on the beach. At the Princess Hotel, **King's** (⊠ Eilat–Taba Rd. ☎ 08/636–5555) tops the disco bill, with mirrored walls, fluted columns, and a checkered dance floor. **Platinum** (⊠ Promenade ☎ 08/636–3444) at King Solomon's Palace hotel has laser light ★ shows. Good bands are the claim to fame at the very popular **Three Monkeys** (⊠ Royal Beach Promenade ☎ 08/636–8888) club.

**CONCERTS**  Two of the country's most important music events have taken place in Eilat for many years. Both festivals feature internationally acclaimed musicians. Check with the tourist office for details. **Music by the Red Sea,** a ★ series of chamber music concerts, takes place in late December. The **Red Sea Jazz Festival** (⊕ redseajazzeilat.com) is held in Eilat's cargo port during the last four days of August.

★ ☾ **WOW** (⊠ Royal Gardens Hotel ☎ 08/638–6701 ⊕ www.isrotel.co.il ☒ NIS 95). This 1½-hour show (performances are daily 11 AM–9 PM) has vaudeville sketches, magicians, and acrobats flying over the audience—all in a 3-D video-art setting.

**ISRAELI FOLK**  At **Neamat Hall** (⊠ Eilot St. ☎ 052/352–9588), a dance hall, you can
**DANCING**  show off your stuff, or learn how to folk dance, on Sunday and Thursday (call ahead to verify).

**LOCAL**  Have a cup of tea with **Mrs. Morris** (☎ 08/637–2344), the entertaining
**HOSPITALITY**  former U.S. consul in Eilat, and meet her crocodile.

Every Tuesday at 8 PM **Nurit** (☎ (08/635–8726 or 052/392–0884) takes groups (minimum of 10) around Kibbutz Elot, which is 3 km (2 mi) from Eilat, to meet a longtime member, listen to some gossip, and enjoy coffee and homemade jam and cake.

**WINE TASTINGS**  For an early evening sampling of "Private Collection" Carmel wines (produced north of Tel Aviv in the Shomron area), drop by Eilat's oldest wine shop, **Ha Martef** (⊠ 3 Haniyot Shva ☎ 08/637–2787). Owner Itzik Ben Adiva will happily bring you up to date on Israel's burgeoning viniculture scene in his modest, jam-packed shop. It's in the Industrial Area close to Eddie's Hideaway—look for wall-size murals of women treading grapes. Ha Martef is open Sunday through Thursday, 9 to 1 and 5 to 8, and Friday 9 to 3.

## Sports & the Outdoors
Many of the activities outlined below can be arranged through your hotel or a travel agency. Several tour operators maintain desks in hotel lobbies and will take reservations there.

BEACHES
★
Eilat's **beachfront**—the North Beach and the South Beach—is operated by beach managers who ensure the cleanliness of their section and provide open-air showers and (for a fee) deck chairs. Look for beaches with the large white sign that says A PUBLIC, AUTHORIZED SWIMMING ZONE, along with the wood lifeguard huts (on stilts); lifeguards are usually on duty until 4 or 5 in the afternoon. Most of the beaches are free, and some have a clublike atmosphere, with thatched-roof restaurants and pubs, contemporary music, and dancing day and night. Beach No. 2, at the Sheraton Moriah, and Beach No. 3, on the northern promenade near the Dan Hotel, are particularly pleasant.

Families favor North Beach, which runs northeast from the intersection of Durban and Arava streets up to the marina and the bridge. Here you can go paragliding or rent paddle boats or a "banana" (a plastic boat towed by a motorboat). Farther along, after the Bridge and opposite the Queen of Sheba, Royal Beach, Dan, and Herod's hotels, lies a beautifully landscaped series of beaches. Young people tend to hang out at the southernmost beaches, where the dive centers are (south of the port, along the Eilat–Taba Road). The southern beaches share the coast with the Underwater Observatory, Dolphin Reef, and the Coral Reserve.

BIRD-WATCHING
★
**International Birding and Reserach** (⊠ Entrance to Eilat, at Dor gas station ☎ 08/633–5339) holds Thursday lectures at 6 PM at Le Meridien Hotel and also organizes Jeep bird-watching tours.

BOATING
There are boat-rental and water-sports facilities at both Eilat's marina (near the Bridge) and Coral Beach, the area south of the port on the Eilat–Taba Road (Route 90).

The **Red Sea Sports Club** (⊠ Bridge House ☎ 08/633–3666 ⊠ Coral Beach ☎ 08/637–6569) rents paddleboats, canoes, and minispeedboats. You can also charter a 150-horsepower speedboat piloted by a water-ski instructor for about NIS 550 per hour.

HORSEBACK RIDING
In Coral Beach, **Texas Ranch** (⊠ Rte. 90 ☎ 08/637–6663 or 08/637–9685) takes riders on trails through Wadi Shlomo (Solomon's Valley) and into the desert. The sunset rides are particularly popular. The cost is NIS 165; call ahead to reserve a horse. Children over 12 who know how to ride are welcome on the trails, and younger children may ride in the ring for NIS 80 for 30 minutes.

PARASAILING
**Red Sea Sports Club** (⊠ Bridge House ☎ 08/633–3666 ⊠ Coral Beach ☎ 08/637–6569) offers guests a bird's-eye view of all those beach loafers for NIS 165 per 10 minutes.

RAPPELLING
**Jeep See** (⊠ Bridge House, near the marina, Box 4188 ☎ 08/633–0133) runs rappelling (known as snappelling in Israel) trips for both novices and more experienced rappellers. Call ahead to reserve. The cost is NIS 160 per person, with a minimum of 10 participants.

SCUBA DIVING & SNORKELING
★
You'll find everything from courses and cruises to safaris at PADI 5-star centers; **snorkeling and scuba diving** are extremely popular activities in Eilat.

**Aqua Sport International Red Sea Diving Center** (⊠ Coral Beach ☎ 08/633–4404 ⊕ www.aqua-sport.com) operates daily boat and shore diving trips to Sinai.

Families (it's open to ages 8 and over) have fun "snuba"-diving at **Caves Reef** (☎ 08/637–2722), south of the Underwater Observatory. In this snorkeling-diving hybrid, you breathe through tubes connected to tanks carried in a rubber boat. The price, NIS 180 per person, includes instruction, a practice session, and a guided underwater tour that goes no deeper than 20 feet. Reserve in advance.

**Coral Reserve** (⊠ Eilat–Taba Rd., Coral Beach ☎ 08/637–6829) is a great place for qualified divers to observe the region's fabulous fish and corals. Facilities include hot showers, lockers, and a small restaurant.

At **Dolphin Reef** (⊠ Eilat–Taba Rd., Coral Beach ☎ 08/637–1846) you can "dive with dolphins" using snorkel equipment (NIS 150, for half an hour), and preserve the experience on video for posterity (for an extra charge). Call ahead for a reservation. Dolphin Reef also runs a professional dive center.

**Lucky Divers** (⊠ 5 Simtat Zukim, near the Mul Yam Shopping Center ☎ 08/633–5990 ⊕ www.luckydivers.com) is a reliable full-service dive center.

At the Ambassador hotel, **Manta Diving Club** (⊠ Eilat–Taba Rd., Coral Beach ☎ 08/637–6569 ⊕ www.redseasports.co.il) is an excellent diving center.

**TENNIS &** The two squash courts at the **Dan Hotel** (☎ 08/636–2222) are available
**SQUASH** to guests and nonguests for NIS 45 for 40 minutes.

Courts at the **Sport Hotel Country Club** (⊠ North Beach ☎ 08/630–3333) are open to guests of the several Isrotel properties at the hourly rate of NIS 40; you can rent racket and balls.

**WATER SPORTS** You've got to get out in the water if you're in Eilat, so choose your sport.
★ **Aqua Sport International Red Sea Diving Center** (⊠ Coral Beach ☎ 08/633–4404 ⊕ www.aqua-sport.com) rents windsurfing equipment and provides lessons (NIS 75 per hour), and also rents Jet Skis (NIS 30 per 10 minutes), skippered speed boats (NIS 60 per half-hour), laser dinghies (NIS 40 per hour), and catamarans (NIS 50 per hour).

**Red Sea Sports Club** (⊠ Bridge House ☎ 08/633–3666 ✉ Coral Beach ☎ 08/637–6569) rents water-skiing equipment and boats (NIS 75 per half-hour).

## Shopping

Eilat is a tax-free zone, meaning that all items are exempt from VAT (Value-Added Tax) and/or purchase tax. Articles such as bathing suits and jewelry sold in chain stores are less expensive in Eilat branches. Items that are price-controlled, such as gas, beer, cigarettes, and alcohol, are also cheaper.

**MALLS** One of Eilat's two shopping malls, **Mul Yam** (⊠ Arava Rd. and Yotam St.) is at the very entrance to town and is noted for made-in-Israel products. Here you can stroll along with the chattering crowd, stop for a drink of freshly squeezed orange or carrot juice, and perhaps pick up a lottery ticket at the stand outside the Israel Jewelry Exchange shop. Then check out such stores as **Intima** for women's soft and sexy lingerie; **Gottex** for famous swimwear; **Honigman** for women's sweaters, shirts, and skirts; and **Fox** for cheeky casual clothing for adults and children. There's also a postal agency, bookstore, drugstore, and several coffee shops. Outside the mall, on the Promenade going west, are one-after-the-other tacky but fun stalls selling hats, T-shirts, and earrings. Also, a branch of **Rockport** sells Teva sandals and other shoes.

The two sections of **Kanion Adom and Shalom Plaza** (⊠ HaTmarim Blvd.) are connected by a café-filled passage. You'll find a variety of shops, but this is on a smaller scale than Mul Yam. There is notable absence of tacky souvenir and gift shops.

HOTEL BOUTIQUES On the western side of the Marina Bridge, Eilat's largest hotels sit tall and splendid. On the ground level of each hotel, along the beachside promenade, is one luxury shop after another. You'll find at least 40 stores along with numerous restaurants, pubs, and coffeehouses—Cafe Aroma, which is open 24/7, is a good bet for a chocolate croissant, Greek salad, or orange cake. If you'd rather sun and play during the day, you'll still have plenty of time to shop at night—these places are open until 9 PM or later (except Friday night). Here's a sampling of some of the best.

At Herod's Palace hotel, **Cardo** (☎ 08/638–0000) is an intriguing marketplace carrying unusual paintings, sculptures, Judaica, old-style objets d'art, Moroccan furnishings such as painted and inlaid mirrors, boxes and frames, gifts, and wall hangings. Stop at **Emporium** (☎ 08/633–9495) on the Promenade near Herod's Palace to browse familiar designer names, such as DKNY, Polo, and Calvin Klein. **H. Stern** (⊠ Queen of Sheba hotel ☎ 08/633–1525) has an excellent reputation for high-quality gold and diamond pieces, pearls, and also a small selection of silver sculptures by the well-known artist Frank Meisler. **Laline** (⊠ Promenade near Queen of Sheba hotel ☎ 08/633–5713) features Israeli-made soap, body-care products, and candles. Look for Breitling timepieces at **Padani** (⊠ Royal Beach hotel ☎ 08/636–8872). Shop at **Red Sea Sportswear** (☎ 08/633–0825) for the latest in swim and surf wear. You'll find everything from resort wear and cosmetics to T-shirts, jewelry, and toys at **Royal Beach Rotunda** (⊠ Royal Beach Hotel ☎ 08/636–8811).

## Hai Bar Nature Reserve

**⑱** *35 km (21½ mi) north of Eilat on Rte. 90. Look for the sign for Hai Bar and Predator Center, opposite entrance to Kibbutz Samar. Drive 1½ km (1 mi) to entrance.*

The Hai Bar Nature Reserve makes a good day trip from Eilat and can be combined with a visit to the Timna Park. Try to be here in the morning, when the animals are most active. You need a car and a CD player if you want a "guided tour"; you rent the CD for a few shekels and off you go. It takes about 45 minutes. Call ahead for winter hours.

The Hai Bar Nature Reserve consists of a 12-square-km (4½-square-mi) natural habitat for biblical-era animals and birds and the Predator Center. The reserve was created not only as a refuge for animals that were almost extinct in the region but also as a breeding place; the animals are then set free in the Negev. Opened to the public in 1977, the area re-creates the ancient savanna landscape, with lots of acacia trees; roaming around are the striped-legged wild ass, onagers (another species of wild ass), addaxes, gazelles and ibex, and white oryx. Ostriches come prancing over, ready to stick their heads into the car windows.

The 20-square-km (7¾-square-mi) **Predator Center** is where local birds and beasts of prey are raised and displayed. As you watch the hyena, notice that his front legs are stronger than his rear legs, enabling him to carry his heavy prey a long distance. The birds of prey hang out in gigantic cages, where you'll see, among other species, the only lappet-face vultures left in Israel, with average wingspans of about 10 feet. In the pitch-black **Nightlife Room,** watch nocturnal animals who are active when we sleep: owls, hedgehogs, scorpions, and bats. ⊠ *Rte. 90, 35 km (21 mi) north of Eilat* ☎ *08/637–3057 or 08/637–6018* ⊕ *www. redseadesert.com* ✉ *NIS 40 (Predator Center only, NIS 20)* ☉ *Sun.–Thurs. 8:30–5, Fri.–Sat. 8:30–3:30.*

**need a break?**

If you're looking for fantastic ice cream—made on a kibbutz—stop by **Yotvata Rest Inn** (☎ (08/635–7229), at a gas station on Rte. 90 between Hai Bar and Timna Park (40 km [25 mi]) north of Eilat. The kibbutz of the same name is across the way, and from their dairy come products much loved by Israelis: cheeses, chocolate milk, yogurt, puddings, and ice cream (try the pitaya, or dragonfruit, flavor). Hot dishes (chicken or beef) and sandwiches are available as well. There's also a tourist information center at the entrance.

## Timna Park

**19**

**Fodor's**Choice

★

*From Hai Bar Nature Reserve, return to Rte. 90 south toward Eilat. Turn right after 15 km (9 mi) at sign for Timna Park and Timna Lake. A 3-km (2-mi) access road (which passes Kibbutz Elifaz) leads to entrance booth.*

This desert park is a lunarlike landscape of wide spaces interspersed with amazing geological shapes and ancient archaeological sites, surrounded by beautifully colored cliffs in a range of shades from sandy beige to rich red and dusky black. The Timna Mountains (whose highest peak is 2,550 feet) encompass the park's spectacular collection of rock formations and canyons. Millions of years of erosion have sculpted shapes of amazing beauty, such as the red-hued Solomon's Pillars (created by nature, *not* by the biblical king) and the 20-foot-high freestanding Mushroom. The late-afternoon hours provide unusual light for both spectators and photographers.

When you arrive, ask for the explanatory pamphlet, which shows the driving route in red. Because of the park's size (60 square km [23 square mi]), we suggest driving from sight to sight, each of which can then be explored on foot (some of the sights are several kilometers apart). A small building just inside the entrance screens a video detailing humanity's 6,000-year-old relationship with the Timna area. Wall panels explain the valley's fascinating geological makeup.

Experienced hikers can pick up a map that details various serious hikes, which take from 7 to 10 hours to complete. They're best done in winter (the summer heat is scorching). Watch out for old mine shafts, take lots of water, and *be sure* to let the person at the gate know you are going, and when you plan to return.

People have also left their mark here. Near the Pillars are the remains of a small **temple** built by Egyptians who worked the mines 3,400 years ago, during the Egyptian New Kingdom (the time of Moses); the temple was dedicated to the cow-eared goddess Hathor. Archaeologists discovered in the temple a snake made of copper (*nehushtan* in Hebrew)—according to Numbers 21:4–9, Moses made a serpent in the wilderness to heal people suffering from snake bites, and the snake remains a symbol of healing to this day. Near the temple, a path and stairway lead up to the observation platform overlooking the valley. Above the platform is a rock-cut inscription whose hieroglyph you can see clearly with the aid of a sighting tube—it shows Ramses III offering a sacrifice to Hathor. ⊠ *Rte. 90* ☎ *08/635–6215* ⊕ *www.redseadesert.com* ✉ *NIS 38* ⊗ *Sat.–Thurs. 8–4, Fri. 8–2.*

**need a break?** Here's a surprise in the desert landscape, right in Timna Park: a lake (man-made). Nearby sits an authentic **Bedouin tent** with goodies for the worn-out traveler. Big, flat, crispy pita is baked on a traditional *saj* (a concave metal disc over a fire). You then wrap it around falafel, creamy hummus, and salad and wash it down with sweet tea or coffee. ⊠ *Timna Park* ☎ *08/635–6215.*

**off the beaten path** **MT. YOASH –** This fine lookout along the border road with Egypt is an easy trip from Eilat. Notice the huge tanks as you drive along Route 12; they belong to the Eilat–Ashkelon oil pipeline. After you pass the tanks, you enter the Eilat Mountains Nature Reserve, with Nahal Shlomo, a dry riverbed, on your left. Drive in 12 km (7½ mi) and turn left at the orange sign for Mt. Yoash; then drive another 1 km (½ mi), bearing right up a rough, steep, and winding stone road. Park and take in knockout views of the alternating light and dark ridges of the Eilat Mountains; Eilat and Aqaba; the mountains of Edom, behind Aqaba; the start of the Saudi Arabian coastline and the Nahal Geshron gorge, emptying into the Red Sea at Taba; and the plain of Moon Valley and the mountains of Sinai, in Egypt. To get to Mt. Yoash, leave Eilat from the junction of Route 90 (Arava Rd.) and Yotam Boulevard, traveling west on Yotam (which becomes Route 12), with New Tourist Center on the left.

# SIDE TRIP TO PETRA

By Miriam
Feinberg
Vamosh

Poet Dean Burgon described Petra as the "rose-red city, half as old as time." Petra is about three hours north of Eilat, in Jordan, and its boulevards, temples, and splendid tombs secreted among the high cliffs have an incomparable mystery and grandeur. Once inaccessible to all but an intrepid few, it is now easier to reach and has become an increasingly popular destination since the Israel-Jordan border was opened in 1994.

Petra lies in the biblical region of Edom. According to Genesis, the Edomites were descendants of Esau, Jacob's brother and rival. Edom's fertile land was a magnet that desert dwellers couldn't ignore, but the Edomites were careful to keep it exclusive. When Moses led the Israelites to the Promise Land and asked to pass through Edom, he was denied. By the 4th century BC, a new group had arrived from Arabia: the Nabateans. It is their spectacular tombs and urban monuments that draw travelers to Petra today. Early writings describe the Nabateans as shepherds, but they later became traders in frankincense and myrrh, the most valuable of biblical spices, and were the wealthy masters of the region's trade routes.

Most of Petra's famous tombs were carved during the first century AD. Although the combination of a necropolis and a capital city may seem strange today, this custom was common among ancient peoples, who established cemeteries at the entrances to many of their capitals. The presence of tombs of the rich and powerful near the city's major monuments was perhaps part of a cult of the dead. When travelers came to the city, they would leave offerings at the tombs to ensure the success of their journeys.

Gradually, Christianity replaced the old religion, and churches were built in Petra. By this time, the rise of sea trade precipitated Petra's decline, as ancient traders learned that they could use prevailing winds to hasten ships across the sea. Some Arabian goods began to come to Egypt and its Mediterranean ports via the Red Sea. It didn't help that a series of earthquakes left a ruinous mark on the city.

After Petra's takeover by the Muslims in 633, alliances and crossroads changed and the world lost interest in the area. The Crusaders built fortifications among the ruins in the 11th century, but after their 1189 surrender to the Muslim warrior Saladin, the city sank into oblivion. It was not until 1812 that Swiss explorer Johann Ludwig Burckhardt rediscovered Petra, providing the Western world with its first contemporary description of the marvels of the ancient city.

**Practical notes:** The closest border crossing to Petra is at Eilat. Most visitors take a taxi to the Jordan border from Eilat, walk across, and catch a taxi to Petra on the other side. A parking area on the Israeli side of the border makes it possible to drive a rental car there, but only cars registered to their drivers can be taken into Jordan. For those taking longer trips, rental cars are available in Aqaba and Petra.

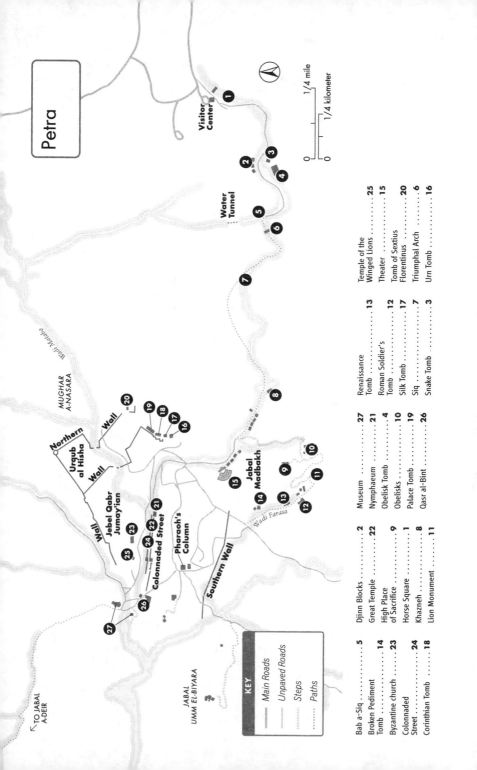

Petra

Visitor Center

Water Tunnel

MUGHAR A-NASARA

Wadi Mataha

Northern Wall

Urqub al Hisha

Wall

Jebel Qabr Jumay'ian

Wall

Colonnaded Street

Pharaoh's Column

Southern Wall

Jabal Madbakh

Wadi Farasa

JABAL UMM EL-BIYARA

TO JABAL A-DEIR

1/4 mile

1/4 kilometer

0

0

**KEY**

—— Main Roads

——— Unpaved Roads

|||||| Steps

······· Paths

Bab a-Siq ............ **5**
Broken Pediment
Tomb ............ **14**
Byzantine church ...... **23**
Colonnaded
Street ............ **24**
Corinthian Tomb ...... **18**

Djinn Blocks .......... **2**
Great Temple ........ **22**
High Place
of Sacrifice ......... **9**
Horse Square ......... **1**
Khazneh ............ **8**
Lion Monument ...... **11**

Museum ............ **27**
Nymphaeum ........ **21**
Obelisk Tomb ........ **4**
Obelisks ............ **10**
Palace Tomb ......... **19**
Qasr al-Bint ........ **26**

Renaissance
Tomb ............ **13**
Roman Soldier's
Tomb ............ **12**
Silk Tomb ........... **17**
Siq ............... **7**
Snake Tomb ......... **3**

Temple of the
Winged Lions ...... **25**
Theater ............ **15**
Tomb of Sextius
Florentinus ........ **20**
Triumphal Arch ...... **6**
Urn Tomb ........... **16**

Americans need a visa to enter the country, which can be bought on the spot for about NIS 88 everywhere except at the Allenby Bridge crossing. It's advisable to cross the border early in the morning to avoid crowds. Petra is open daily from 6 AM to 7 PM; the city is gated and has an entrance fee of 21 JD for a one-day visit with a discount for multiple entries.

Before traveling to Jordan, make sure to check your government's travel advisory and always exercise caution.

## Exploring Petra

An overnight (two-day) trip to Petra will allow visitors to see many of the area's highlights. Begin early in the afternoon at the Horse Square, and walk through the narrow and mysterious Siq to the Khazneh (the treasury), Petra's most magnificent tomb. Be sure to take a peek through a slit in the rock at the end of the Siq for an awe-inspiring view. From there, continue along a route that was once the city's main street, lined with monuments from Petra's glory days. End with a walk along the Colonnaded Street to The Basin for a good lunch. Although the route back is the same, the sun striking the rocks at different angles in the late afternoon reveals new beauty. In the evening, take a moment to enjoy the sunset from a hotel balcony or rooftop terrace. On the second day, visitors can return to the Khazneh and explore other sites. Afterward, spend a little time souvenir shopping in Wadi Musa before heading back to Eilat.

### Main Attractions

**㉔ Colonnaded Street.** The Romans built the main street of Petra in the early 1st century BC. In typical Roman style, it became the city's major thoroughfare, suitable for both commerce and grand ceremonial processions. After the Roman annexation of the Nabatean kingdom, the street was restored, as noted in an inscription dated AD 114 and dedicated to Emperor Trajan. The remains of statues of deities still stand, including Hermes and Tyche. In 363 an earthquake devastated Petra and the entire surrounding region, and the street never returned to its former glory.

**㉒ The Great Temple.** No one can say for sure who was worshipped at this temple, or if it was the seat of the city's government. The dozens of columns that adorned its courtyards attest to its ancient grandeur; it even had its own theater, which some scholars believe may have been a meeting hall for Petra's rulers.

★ **❽ Khazneh.** Petra's most famous monument, this 130-foot-high structure has a splendid frontage graced by a number of mythological figures adopted by the Nabateans from Greek and Roman worship. Castor and Pollux (who after their death became the two brightest stars in the constellation Gemini), Amazons, Gorgons, eagles, and other creatures march across the Khazneh's rosy facade. Between the columns of the *tholos* (the rounded section above the tympanum) are the remains of a female deity holding a cornucopia; she is believed to be al-

Uzza, the patroness of Petra and the Nabatean version of Aphrodite, goddess of love.

The Arabic name for this monument means "treasury"—its full name is Khaznet Fara'un, the Pharaoh's Treasury. It was assumed by archaeologists to be a tomb, but legends of treasures allegedly secreted within have led grave robbers here for centuries. The urn carved at the top of the tholos was thought to be the hiding place for the hoard. The Bedouin have been taking potshots at it for generations in the hopes of dislodging its contents, a practice whose results are still visible.

**❼ Siq.** The Siq (meaning "cleft"), a rocky passage between towering walls of stone, leads visitors to the main ruins. The colors of the rock are astounding, varying in hues of red and purple. Nabatean paving is still visible in two locations along the way. Niches, some of which contain inscriptions dating from the 2nd and 3rd centuries AD, show that this road was as much a ceremonial path as a passageway. One niche is carved into a small outcropping of rock near one of the paved patches; it's unusual in that it faces away from the approach and may have been designed to bestow a blessing on those leaving the city. Film buffs may recall Harrison Ford riding through this area in some of the concluding scenes of *Indiana Jones and the Last Crusade.*

## Also Worth Seeing

**❺ Bab a-Siq.** The Gate of the Cleft is near the Siq, the canyon-lined passageway leading to the main sights. From here you can spot the remains of a Nabatean water tunnel, built to divert flood waters from coursing through the narrow cleft and flooding the necropolis. A dam, constructed for the same purpose in the second half of the 1st century AD, was restored by the Jordanians after particularly serious flooding some years ago.

**⑭ Broken Pediment Tomb.** This tomb is characterized by the broken-off gable of its roof, supported by four pilasters topped with capitals in the unique Nabatean style.

**㉓ Byzantine church.** Richly decorated with mosaics in the style of the period, this church appears to have been destroyed by fire soon after its construction, perhaps in a severe earthquake that took place in AD 551. The remains have undergone only partial conservation.

**⑱ Corinthian Tomb.** Set among some of Petra's finest tombs is one named for the large number of Corinthian capitals, now badly deteriorated, that once decorated its facade.

**❷ Djinn Blocks.** The function of these large structures is unclear; they may have been connected to Nabatean worship, perhaps symbolizing one of their deities. In Arabic, *djinn* means "spirits," a common theme in Arab folklore.

**★ ❾ High Place of Sacrifice.** An ancient flight of stairs—restored in recent years by the Jordanian Department of Antiquities—leads to the top of Jabal Madhbah, the Mount of the Altar. At its peak is a rectangular court surrounded on three sides by benches in the triclinium style of the Roman dining room; in the center of the court is a raised block of stone, on which the priest may have stood. To the west are two altars accessed by steps, in front of which is a channel into which the blood of the sacrificial animal may have pooled.

**❶ Horse Square.** Horses used to be the conveyance of choice for the approximately 1-[km] (1/2-mi) trip to Petra's main antiquities. The growning number of visitors has made this impractical, but you can still hire horses for the first 800 yards before the path narrows to become the Siq.

**⓫ Lion Monument.** Surface runoff fed this fountain via a channel leading to the lion's mouth, from which water once streamed.

**㉗ Museum.** Petra's museum, and also its restrooms, is in the same building as the Basin restaurant. Displays include a small number of Nabatean artifacts, such as jewelry and pottery.

**㉑ Nymphaeum.** Dedicated to the water nymphs, this fountain was used for both refreshment and worship. The fountains of the two-story structure were fed by a water channel that continued along Petra's main street.

**❹ Obelisk Tomb.** This upper story of a two-story tomb is named for the four freestanding obelisks that decorate its facade. The lower story, the Triclinium Tomb, was so named because three walls of the empty room are lined with triclinia, a Latin word for this kind of bench. In other settings, diners would recline on these.

**❿ Obelisks.** These two 20-foot-tall obelisks are examples of a common method of representing deities in the ancient Near East. Some scholars believe them to be representations of Dushara and al-Uzza; others believe they are simply the remains of quarrying activity.

**⓳ Palace Tomb.** This unfinished tomb is one of the few in Petra not carved entirely out of the rock. Many of the tomb's constructed segments have fallen away, so it's hard to ascertain its original dimensions. At the base of the Palace Tomb are the remains of the northern city wall, built after the 1st century BC.

**㉖ Qasr al-Bint.** This structure's full name, which translates as the "Palace of the Daughter of Pharaoh," stems from a legend that the pharaoh's daughter promised she would marry the man who could channel water to the city where she lived. When she had to choose between two winners, she asked each how he had managed his appointed task. The one whose answer she preferred won her hand. In fact, the structure is a temple, built in the early 1st century AD. As in the Temple of the Winged Lions, the identity of the deity worshiped here isn't known, but a statue depicting him or her—perhaps Dushara, the greatest deity of the Nabatean pantheon—certainly stood in the temple's inner sanctum.

**⓭ Renaissance Tomb.** This tomb bears a resemblance to the Tomb of Sextius Florentinus, in the main part of the city. It may have been created around the same time, the first third of the 1st century AD.

⑫ **Roman Soldier's Tomb.** The figure in the niche of this tomb's facade is dressed in typical Roman military garb, while the friezes and capitals appear more typical of Nabatean architecture before the Roman annexation. Directly opposite the Roman Soldier's Tomb is a triclinium; the rubble in between was probably once a courtyard connecting the two edifices.

⑰ **Silk Tomb.** The striations of natural color in the Silk Tomb's rock make it one of Petra's finest and certainly aid in identification. They flow across the facade like a multicolor silk scarf blowing gently in the wind.

❸ **Snake Tomb.** No outward decoration marks this tomb, but 12 burial niches are carved into the floor inside. The name comes from a wall relief that shows two snakes attacking what may be a dog.

㉕ **Temple of the Winged Lions.** This impressive building takes its name from the sculptures that serve as capitals for its columns. The identity of the deity worshiped within is unknown, but figurines suggest that it may have been Isis, Egyptian goddess of the heavens and patroness of fertility. An inscription dates the construction of the temple to around AD 27.

⑮ **Theater.** This semicircular hallmark of Roman culture is a clear sign of the extent to which the Nabateans, like most other peoples of this region, had adopted the Roman way of life. The Nabateans apparently had no qualms about building a theater in a cemetery; their stone masons even cut into some of the existing tombs (the remains of which you can see at the back of the rock-cut theater) to do so. The capacity of the theater has been estimated at 10,000.

⑳ **Tomb of Sextius Florentinus.** The name of this Roman governor of Arabia appears in the tomb's inscription. Historical records indicate that he died in office in AD 128.

❻ **Triumphal arch.** Today, all that's left of this arch near the Siq are niches with the remains of statues that decorated the point where the arch's springs were built. The arch collapsed in 1895.

⑯ **Urn Tomb.** Named for the vase-like decoration at the top of its pediment, this tomb is supported by a series of vaults at its lower level, dubbed *al makhamah* (the law court) by the locals for some long-forgotten reason; the upper level was called *a-sijn* (the prison). According to an inscription within, Petra's Byzantine Christians turned the Urn Tomb into a church in AD 446.

## Where to Stay & Eat

Dining in the town closest to the antiquities of Petra—Wadi Musa—represents both ends of the scale, from very simple, inexpensive fare to the very elegant and pricey. There is little in between. Both dining experiences have one thing in common: courteous service and a warmly welcoming spirit. Don't be put off by the plainness of center-village eateries mentioned here. The locals enjoying their meal at the next table will remind you that the best fare is often to be had at such restaurants.

Petra offers numerous accommodation options. You can choose from luxurious to money-saving accommodations; both types can be found adjacent or near the site. The hotels closest to the site obviously provide the most convenient access to Petra and save you taxi money. A short car drive away in Wadi Musa are several good hotels, with some on the ridge above Wadi Musa. Taybet Zeman, in the village of Taybeh 9 km (5½ mi) from Petra, is the farthest from the site, but its uniquely authentic flavor is well worth the ride. All rooms have a private bath unless otherwise indicated.

| WHAT IT COSTS | | | |
|---|---|---|---|
| | **$$** | **$** | **¢** |
| RESTAURANTS | over 7JD | 5JD–7JD | under 5JD |
| HOTELS | over $110 | $65–$110 | under $65 |

Restaurant prices are in Jordanian Dinar, for one main course at dinner. Hotel prices are in U.S. dollars, for two people in a standard double room in high season.

**$$** ✕ **The Basin.** This buffet restaurant, owned by the Petra Crowne Plaza Hotel, is in the antiquities site of Petra at the end of the Colonnaded Street. It serves mainly salads and meat-and-potato dishes, so it may not be the most imaginative meal you'll ever have but it caters to groups and the shady outdoor section is pleasant. It's definitely the best place to stop for a substantial lunch around the midpoint of your Petra tour day. ✉ *Petra* ☎ *03/215–6266* ⊟ *AE, MC, V.*

**$** ✕ **Arabi.** This is a good place for lunch on a budget, where diners can get a substantial meal, including mixed grill (their specialty), barbecued meats, and hummus. ✉ *Main St., Wadi Musa* ☎ *03/215–7661* ⊟ *AE, MC, V.*

**$** ✕ **Petra Zeman.** The specialty here is *maklouba*, a chicken-and-rice dish which the locals call "upside down," because servers seem to enjoy diners' reaction as they turn the pot upside down with a flourish on the serving tray at the table. This is also a great place to try the Jordanian national dish *mansaf*—lamb meat in a tangy yoghurt sauce served over rice. Dessert, here and everywhere in town, means a tiny cup of strong coffee spiced with *hel* (cardamom) and a dish of baklava, or one of the many kindred versions of this Middle Eastern honey-and-pistachio sweet. ✉ *Main St., Wadi Musa* ☎ *777/993–913* ⊟ *AE, MC, V.*

★ **$$$** ✕⌕ **Taybet Zeman.** Nine kilometers (5½ miles) from Petra, on the outskirts of the town of Taybeh, this unique lodging was once a Bedouin village. Abandoned for years, it was eventually revamped into a hotel that has every modern amenity but has been designed to steep its guests in aspects of Jordanian-Bedouin culture that have all but disappeared. Located high above Petra, Taybet Zeman has an incomparable view of the mountains of Edom, especially from the Diwan, its garden terrace. Rooms are very spacious and decorated in authentic Bedouin style with throw rugs and wall hangings—a colorful counterpoint to the natural stone walls. At the hotel's souk (market), you can watch unusual handcrafted items being made. The central courtyard has a spice garden, and its yields are served in the hotel's excellent restaurant, whose menu mixes Eastern and Western favorites. The buffet is worth a trip in itself. The hotel has one wheelchair-accessible room. ⊠ *Queen Ranya St., Wadi Musa* ☎ *03/215–0111* ☒ *03/215–0101* ⊕ ↝ *105 rooms* ৬ *Restaurant, sauna* ☐ *AE, MC, V.*

**$$$** ⊡ **Crowne Plaza Petra.** The Crowne Plaza is conveniently located adjacent to Petra's entrance. Next door is the Petra Cave, the hotel's bar-discothèque, with nightly live Arabic and Western music, and "hubbly-bubblies"—water-pipes—for those who want to try smoking tobacco the traditional Middle Eastern way. ⊠ *Tourism St., Wadi Musa* ☎ *03/215–6246* ☒ *03/215–6977* ⊕ *www.petra.crowneplaza.com* ↝ *147 rooms* ৬ *2 restaurants, bar, fitness room, sauna, whirlpool, tennis court, 24-hour Internet in the business center* ☐ *MC, V.*

**$$** ⊡ **Hidab Hotel.** This is a very good option for those on a budget, and has a central location with a view of Wadi Musa and the Petra mountains, with a terrace for catching the beautiful sunset. In the summer, check out a live nightly performance on the terrace under a Bedouin tent. ⊠ *Box 142, Wadi Musa* ☎ *03/215–6763* ☒ *03/215–7496* ⊕ *www.hidabhotel.com* ↝ *40 rooms* ৬ *Turkish bath, massage, whirlpool, Internet service in the lobby* ☐ *AE, MC, V.*

## Nightlife & the Arts

A **candle-lit tour** of Petra is one of the city's attractions. A stroll through the Siq as shadows play on the canyon walls is a dramatic way to discover aspects hidden by day. Music is played and stories told in front of the Khazneh at the end of the walk. Check for availability at the Petra visitor center.

## Shopping

Petra's handicraft specialty is the work of its "sand artists"—artisans who fill bottles with sand in a variety of hues and complex designs. They can customize the purchase by writing a name or other text in the sand. The artists work and sell their unique wares in shops in Wadi Musa, as well as in the Siq.

# PETRA ESSENTIALS

## Transportation

### BY AIR
El Al and Royal Jordanian Airlines fly to Amman, Jordan's capital, from Tel Aviv's Ben Gurion Airport. This option has limited appeal, as you must be at the airport two hours before flight time for the 15-minute flight, then drive three hours from Amman to Petra.

🚪 **Ben Gurion International Airport** ☎ 03/971–0000 for information ⊕ www.iaa.gov. il. **El Al Airlines** ☎ 03/971–6111 for information ⊕ www.elal.co.il. **Royal Jordanian Airlines** ☎ 03/516–5566 for information ⊕ www.rja.com.jo.

**BY BUS**

There is no bus service from the Arava side of the border to Petra. There are two buses a day from Aqaba to Petra at a cost of 1.75 JD but there is no specific timetable.

🚩Alpha Daily Tours Reservaton Department ☎ 06/585-5196.

**BY CAR**

The closest border crossing to Petra is at Eilat. Cross the border early in the morning to be in Petra before noon.

The Arava border crossing, just north of Eilat in Israel, is open Sunday–Thursday 6:30 AM–10 PM, Friday–Saturday 8–8. The crossing is closed on the religious holidays Yom Kippur and Id el Fitr. There is a border tax of about NIS 71 on the Israeli side.

Two other border crossings might be convenient under certain circumstances. The Allenby Bridge crossing (four hours' drive from Petra) is about 45 minutes from Jerusalem. If you plan to enter Jordan here, you'll need to obtain your visa ahead of time at the Jordanian Embassy in Tel Aviv or in your country of origin. Bring a passport photo. The Beit She'an border crossing (five hours' drive from Petra) is approximately 40 minutes from Tiberias.

Hidab Hotel can book rental cars from local agencies. There is an Avis agency in the Movenpick Hotel in Petra and in Aqaba. The Hertz office in Petra is located next to the Palace Hotel on the main street of Wadi Musa.

Driving the narrow, winding Aqaba–Petra Highway is an experience. Remember to stay well to the right, but bear in mind that the driver coming from the opposite direction may not be so inclined.

🚩**Avis** ✉ Housing Bank Building, Beach Road, Aqaba ☎ 03/610-5982. **Hertz** ☎ 03/215-6981 or 777/762-842. **Hidab Hotel** ✉ Box 142, Wadi Musa ☎ 03/215-6763 🖷 03/215-7496 ⊕ www.hidabhotel.com.

**BY TAXI**

Shared taxis are available on the Jordanian side of the Arava border to take you into Aqaba, where you can rent a car or take the bus to Petra if the scheduling is right. A shared taxi to Aqaba costs about about 5 JD, which is divided among all passengers; a private taxi from the border to Petra or from Aqaba to Petra is about 40–45 JD, but this price is negotiable.

If your time in Petra is limited, consider taking the direct although costlier route by taxi from the Arava border rather than sharing a taxi to Aqaba and taking the bus.

## Contacts & Resources

**BANKS & EXCHANGING SERVICES**

The Jordanian unit of currency is the dinar, abbreviated JD. The exchange rate at press time was approximately .66 JD to the U.S. dollar.

**EMERGENCIES**

There is a private clinic in Wadi Musa next to the Arab Bank. The closest hospital is the Queen Rania Hospital, 7 km south of Wadi Musa. It has a 24-hour emergency service and English is spoken.

The few pharmacies carry basic items. There are no 24-hour pharmacies in Petra.

**⑦ Modern Pharmacy** ⊠ Tourism St. ☎ 03/215-6444. **The Petra Medical Clinic** ⊠ Tourism St., next to the Arab Bank ☎ 03/215-6694. **Petra Pharmacy** ⊠ Tourism St. ☎ 03/215-6999. **Queen Rania Hospital** ⊠ Queen Rania Rd. ☎ 03/215-0634/5.

**INTERNET, MAIL & SHIPPING**

There is a post office located on Tourism Street next to the Housing Bank, but no private express shipping services.

**MEDIA**

The English-language daily, *The Jordan Times,* is for sale at the reception desks of major hotels. CNN and CNBC are available in hotels with cable service.

**TELEPHONES**

The international country code for Jordan is 962. When dialing from Israel, dial 00962 and the area code 3 before land line numbers in Petra; for Amman, use 00962 and the area code 6. When dialing within Jordan, add a 0 before the area code.

**TOUR OPTIONS**

A number of operators run tours to Petra that you can reserve in advance. These are a good option if you want to see the highlights without having to worry about logistics. Note that summer days can be very hot; on any tour of Petra, even the most basic one, drinking water and a hat are a must.

**⑦ Geographical Tours** ⊠ 1 Odem St., Petah Tikva ☎ 03/927-9000 ⊕ www.geotours.co.il.

**VISITOR INFORMATION**

Petra's visitor center, located right next to the entrance of the site, has brochures and a computerized information service about Jordan as well as a well-stocked souvenir shop. The friendly staff will answer all your questions. You can also arrange a local guide for a basic two-hour Petra tour here for a flat fee of 15 JD.

**⑦** ☎ 03/215-6029.

# EILAT & THE NEGEV ESSENTIALS

## Transportation

**BY AIR**

Flights to Eilat take off from Ben Gurion Airport (about halfway between Jerusalem and Tel Aviv), Sde Dov Airport in north Tel Aviv, and Haifa Airport. In Eilat, the airport is actually in the middle of the city, and thus a five-minute cab ride from hotels and a five-minute walk to the center of town. Charter flights from Europe arrive at Ovda Airport (also known as Eilat West), 60 km (37 mi) north of Eilat; transportation to Eilat is arranged by the travel agents who book the flights.

Arkia Israeli Airlines serves Eilat from all three airports mentioned above. There are between four and eight round-trip flights daily from Ben Gurion and Sde Dov airports. There are two to three flights, Sunday–Thursday, between Haifa and Eilat, as well as one flight on Friday and one on Saturday night. Israir Airlines takes to the air from Tel Aviv's Ben Gurion Airport to Eilat—and back—three times a day. Israir flights run between Sde Dov Airport and Eilat eight times daily.

🛫 **Arkia Israeli Airlines** ☎ 1/700-700-255 or *5758 general reservations and information, 08/638-4888 in Eilat ⊕ www.arkia.co.il. **Eilat Airport** ☎ 08/636-3838 or 1-700/705-022. **Israir Airlines** ☎ 03/795-5777 ⊕ www.israir.co.il. **Ovda Airport** ☎ 08/637-5880.

## BY BUS

Bus service in Israel, and particularly in the Negev, is excellent. Keep in mind, however, that buses do not run on Saturday (except for a few routes that resume after sunset). Sunday morning, Israel's first work day, sees very heavy traffic on all bus routes. It's a good idea to get the first bus, or travel after 9:30 or so, when the rush is over. The national bus company, Egged, has a very good Web site and is updated frequently, Egged provides frequent bus service to Beersheva from Tel Aviv's Central Bus Station (Levinsky St.) and Arlozoroff Station (Arlozoroff St. and Haifa Rd.), and from Jerusalem's Central Bus Station (Jaffa Rd.); the trip takes 1½ hours. From the Beersheva Central Bus Station, buses depart four times a day for Arad, Avdat, Ein Bokek, Mitzpe Ramon, and Sde Boker. For Ein Bokek, there's also a daily 8:30 AM bus from Tel Aviv's Central Bus Station and several buses from Jerusalem. Buses can be very crowded, especially on Friday and Sunday. You cannot buy tickets *or* reserve seats by phone for the above routes; you must go to the bus station, and you should arrive early.

Egged buses run from Tel Aviv to Eilat at least four times a day and twice at night. A round-trip ticket costs NIS 110, and the ride takes 4½ to 5 hours each way. There's also daily service from Jerusalem to Eilat; the trip takes about 5½ hours and costs NIS 110. You can reserve Eilat bus tickets by phone, using a credit card, up to two weeks in advance (definitely book ahead, especially for weekend travel). If you'd rather pay by cash, you can do so at the bus station, but again, book well ahead, and be sure to reserve your seat for the return trip when you arrive at Eilat's Central Bus Station.

In theory, you can explore the Negev independently by bus, but in practice, you'll waste a lot of time waiting for connections, and the heat can make standing at a bus stop uncomfortable. Moreover, buses don't go everywhere. However, Egged connects Beersheva (the transfer point for buses from Tel Aviv and Jerusalem) with all major Negev towns.

Within Eilat, the No. 15 bus starts at the Central Bus Station (entrance to town) and runs through the hotel area to pick up passengers and take them south to the Coral Reserve, Dolphin Reef, and the Underwater Observatory. There is no bus service in Mitzpe Ramon, where taxis are your best bet. And in Ein Bokek, shuttle buses link hotels with each other and the center of town.

**ℹ Beersheva Central Bus Station** ✉ Ben Zvi St. **Egged** ☎ 03/694-8888 or *2800 ⊕ www.egged.co.il. **Eilat Central Bus Station** ✉ Rte. 90, at northern entrance to town.

### BY CAR

The only way to see the Negev Desert comfortably and efficiently is to drive (air-conditioning in summer is a must). All roads have two lanes. The conditions of secondary roads vary; only those in good condition are mentioned here. Roads marked in Hebrew only are not for public travel. To avoid dangerous wintertime floods, proceed with caution when there is any indication of rain. Driving at night in the Negev is not recommended; plan to reach your destination by 5 PM in winter and by 8 PM in summer.

Beersheva is 113 km (70 mi) southeast of Tel Aviv and 83 km (52 mi) south of Jerusalem. The drive from either Tel Aviv or Jerusalem takes about 1½ hours. To Beersheva from Tel Aviv, take Route 2 (the Ayalon Highway) south until the turnoff marked BEERSHEVA–ASHDOD. After this you'll be on Route 41, which runs into Route 40 after 6 km (4 mi). Continue on Route 40 to Beersheva; there are clear signs all the way.

To reach Beersheva from Jerusalem, take Route 1 west to the Bet Shemesh turnoff (onto Route 38); traveling south, follow Route 38, then Route 32, which turns into Route 35, to Kiryat Gat. Here you'll pick up Route 40 south to Beersheva.

To drive to Ein Bokek from Tel Aviv, leave Tel Aviv via the Ayalon Highway (Route 2) south and join Route 1, following signs to AIRPORT–JERUSALEM. As you approach Jerusalem, stay left, on Route 1, which is marked JERICHO–DEAD SEA. Continue 30 km (18 mi) to the unmarked Almog Junction (where Route 1 meets Route 90; there is a turnoff on the left, heading north, marked JERICHO). Stay on the same road, now Route 90, for 10 km (6 mi) to the Dead Sea. Bear right (due south) and follow Route 90 along the coast, passing Qumran, Ein Gedi, and Masada, until you reach Ein Bokek. To get to Eilat, continue south along Route 90 (Arava Road) for another 177 km (111 mi). The trip to Ein Bokek takes about an hour and a half.

The most direct way from Tel Aviv to Eilat is Route 40 south to Beersheva. Leave Beersheva via Route 25 (marked DIMONA–EILAT), driving 69 km (43 mi) to the Arava Junction. Turn right (south) onto Route 90 (Arava Road), and travel straight to Eilat. The trip takes about five hours.

Apart from those in towns and cities, there are gas stations at Tel Avdat (near Sde Boker), Ketziyot (near Nizzana), Mashabei Sade Junction (40 km, or 25 mi, south of Beersheva), Zohar–Arad Junction (near Ein Bokek), Ramat Hovev, and Shoket Junction (on the way to Arad). You'll find gas stations on Route 90 (Arava Road) at Ein Hazeva, Ein

Yahav, Ketura (tires fixed here), and Yotvata. There's a tire-repair shop in the industrial area just before the entrance to Mitzpe Ramon. Most gas stations share space with a roadside café, and a majority are open 24 hours a day.

The following are the main roads in the Negev: Route 40 goes through the Negev highlands to Eilat via Sde Boker, Mitzpe Ramon, and Makhtesh Ramon; Route 90 (called Arava Road in the Negev), which starts in Metulla near the Lebanese border, runs through Ein Bokek and along the Jordanian border and ends in Eilat; and Route 31 runs from Beersheva to the Shoket Junction, Arad, and Ein Bokek. Most of your driving will be along straight roads; the exceptions are the winding (and in some parts rough) road through Makhtesh Ramon, and the steep road between Arad and Ein Bokek (one hairpin turn after another). Beersheva is 45 km (28 mi) from Arad, 80 km (50 mi) from Mitzpe Ramon, and 241 km (151 mi) from Eilat. Mitzpe Ramon is 148 km (93 mi) from Eilat. Ein Bokek is 177 km (111 mi) from Eilat.

### BY TAXI

In Eilat, the preferred (and air-conditioned) way of hopping from one place to another is by taxi. Rides don't usually cost much more than NIS 35; you can hail a taxi on the street or order one from Taba, and restaurants can call one for you. In Beersheva, Netz Taxis operates seven days a week. Taxis are not necessary in Ein Bokek or Mitzpe Ramon.

🚩 **Taba** ☎ 08/633-3339. **Netz Taxis** ☎ 08/627-0808.

### BY TRAIN

Israel Railways provides service only between Tel Aviv and Beersheva, the hub city in the northern Negev, from which buses continue to all destinations in the Negev. There is frequent service (except on Saturday, when just two trains run, and both late in the evening) from the north to Beersheva all day; the trip takes 1½ hours and round-trip fare is NIS 46. On Friday, the last train departs just before noon, and on Saturday, service resumes at 10 PM. Trains run from Tel Aviv's Central Station (also called Arlozoroff Station, and known in Hebrew as "Ha Merkaz").

🚩 **Israel Railways** ☎ 03/577-4000 or *5770 ⊕ www.israrail.org.il.

## Contacts & Resources

### BANKS & EXCHANGING SERVICES

Generally, bank hours in this region are Sunday and Tuesday–Thursday 8:30–12:30 and 4–5:30, and Monday, Friday, and Jewish holiday eves 8:30–noon. Banks in the Negev towns and Eilat have their own hours and closing days, which vary. Foreign currency exchange can be carried out, for a fee, as well as other banking services. Called "caspomats" in Israel, ATM machines are generally not enclosed but rather installed in a wall, usually next to a bank. In Eilat, there's an ATM machine beside the Tourist Office at Bridge House, and there are several at the Mul Yam shopping mall. In Ein Bokek, there's an ATM at the shopping center near Tapuah Sodom restaurant.

🖪 **Bank Hapoalim** ✉ 3 Hativat Hanegev, Eilat ☎ 08/636-1222 ✉ 1 Sderot Ben Gurion, Mitzpe Ramon ☎ 08/659-6107. **Bank Leumi** ✉ Sderot Hatamarim Shopping Center, Beersheva ☎ 08/636-4111.

## EMERGENCIES

Magen David Adom is Israel's health, medical, blood, and disaster service; both they and the police force are always on call, and English is spoken. Magen David may be contacted for assistance with emergency prescriptions (bring yours to Israel with you). Two hospitals serve the Negev, Soroka in Beersheva, and Yoseftal in Eilat; both have English-speakers on staff. Each has a 24-hour emergency room (bring your insurance documents). Both may be approached for emergency dental problems. If you're anywhere else, call Magen David Adom.

In Eilat, the Michlin Pharmacy will deliver to your hotel and is open Sunday–Thursday 8–2 and 4–8:30, Friday 8–3. Superpharm is open daily 9:30 AM–1 AM. There are also pharmacies in Arad, Beersheva, and Mitzpe Ramon.

🖪 **Ambulance** ☎ 101, 911 for English-speaking operator. **Fire** ☎ 102. **Magen David Adom Medical Service** ☎ 101 ⊕ www.magendavidadom.org. **Michlin Pharmacy** ✉ Opposite Central Bus Station, Eilat ☎ 08/637-2434. **Police** ☎ 100. **Soroka Hospital (Beersheva)** ✉ Hanessi'im St. ☎ 08/640-0111 ⊕ www.soroka.org. **Superpharm** ✉ Kanion Mul Yam, Eilat ☎ 08/634-0880. **Yoseftal Hospital (Eilat)** ✉ Yotam St. ☎ 08/635-8011.

## INTERNET, MAIL & SHIPPING

At the Eilat Central Bus Station, ESurf sells drinks and snacks and offers Internet access. The Israel Postal Authority offers Express Mail Service, a guaranteed worldwide courier service, at area post offices.

🖪 **ESurf** ☎ 08/634-4331 ⊕ www.esurfeilat.com. **Israel Postal Authority** ☎ 1/700-5001 ⊕ www.postil.com.

## MEDIA

The daily (except Saturday) *Jerusalem Post* and *Ha Aretz* newspaper (published with the *Herald Tribune*) each have weekend magazines—*Billboard* in the *Post* and *The Guide* in *Ha Aretz*—that include information about events in the Negev (along with the rest of the country).

Steimatzky's, a chain that sells English-language books, magazines and newspapers, is located inside Eilat's Central Bus Station.

🖪 **Steimatzky's** ✉ Central Bus Station ☎ 08/637-5084 ⊕ www.ibooks.co.il.

## TOUR OPTIONS

AIRPLANE TOURS From Sde Dov Airport in Tel Aviv, Ayt Aviation & Tourism Ltd. provides two-hour flights over the Negev's *makhteshim* (canyonlike craters), the spring and waterfall of Ein Avdat, and the Dead Sea; the cost is about NIS 1,200 per person.

BEDOUIN EXPERIENCE In his Bedouin tent at Coral Beach, Yusuf presents with a flourish a desert dinner of *labane* (thick, tangy yogurt), hummus, fresh-baked pita, meat on skewers, and coffee or mint tea—sometimes there's even belly dancing. You can smoke a *nargilla* (water pipe) with him, too.

BIRD-WATCHING TOURS    Every spring and fall, millions of birds fly over Eilat on their journey between winter grounds in Africa and summer breeding grounds in Eurasia. Migration takes place between mid-February and the end of May, and between the beginning of September to the end of November (spring is the larger of the two migrations). The International Birding and Research Center, just north of Eilat, is aflutter year-round (except August, when it closes); it's open Sunday–Thursday 8:30–5. The center conducts half- and full-day trips with names like "Morning Birder," "Desert Birding Trip," and "The Grouser." The center provides binoculars for better views of birds of prey, waterfowl, and songbirds, among others. Prices range from NIS 15 to NIS 230 per person per trip.

BOAT TOURS    Take in the spectacular underwater phenomena near Eilat—coral and colorful fish—from one of the glass-bottom boats at Eilat's marina. The *Jules Verne Explorer*, a mobile underwater observatory with two upper decks and a glass-sided underwater section, takes a two-hour trip past the Coral Reserve twice a day. The cost is NIS 50, and reservations are suggested. *Israel Yam* casts off three times a day and charges NIS 60.

Enjoy a day at sea in the Gulf of Eilat (Aqaba) with Zorba Cruises; you sail to Coral Island, actually in Egypt, 17 km (10 mi) south of Eilat, with time to explore a Crusader fortress, have a barbecue lunch, and most important, engage in the highly recommended scuba diving at the Coral Reef—all for about NIS 240. (You'll need to present your passport a day before, for visa processing.) Zorba also offers a cruise to Taba, leaving at 11 and returning at 3; this includes barbecue lunch, swimming, and snorkeling and costs NIS 135. You can also tour the Gulf of Eilat on the Red Sea Sports Club's *Orionia*, a classic Spanish-built sailing yacht whose skipper explains what's to see at sea; it's wise to reserve ahead. The cost is NIS 180 for a four-hour sail. In addition, Red Sea Sports Club offers a four-hour cruise on a wooden, Cutty Sark–style schooner that anchors at the Lighthouse, near Taba; the cost is NIS 180. While out at sea, you'll have the chance (for an additional fee) to go parasailing or waterskiing, or to take an introductory scuba dive.

If you're itching for more active sailing, contact Ziki Sailing School, which offers day trips on a 35-foot sloop, on which guests enjoy a chance to take the helm and hoist the sails. Snorkels and masks are provided, and for an extra fee you can try waterskiing, parasailing, and scuba diving. The trip costs NIS 150 and includes a barbecue lunch, with wine.

CAMEL TOURS    A desert experience wouldn't be the same without a camel ride. The Camel Ranch (enter just after the Texas Ranch opposite Coral Beach) offers tours for every taste: a daily tour at 4:30 ventures into the desert mountains and canyons (affording fabulous sunset views). Or try the two-hour tour on which you ride for an hour, then savor a desert meal including vegetables and goat cheese. Finally, you might try the family ride, which lasts 1½ hours. The Ranch is closed Sunday.

DIGS    If you fancy working all day in the dust under a blazing sun with the hope of finding Abraham's tent peg (and perhaps contributing to Holy Land archaeology and meeting interesting people), check out this Web site for the latest information on digs that need volunteers: www.israel-mfa.gov.il/archdigs. (It's so popular that they'll no longer give out their phone number.)

ECOLOGICAL TOURS    Every Saturday at 9:30 and at 3, you can tour Kibbutz Lotan, which is 55 km (33 mi) from Eilat, to see how a community tries to live according to an environmentally sensitive lifestyle. Visitors learn how the kibbutz deals ecologically with waste disposal, grows organic agriculture, reuses solid waste for alternative building, composts, and recycles creatively.

HIKING TOURS    A safe—and highly interesting—alternative to venturing out on your own is an off-the-beaten-track hike led by guides from the SPNI (Society for the Protection of Nature in Israel). Although some one-day hikes are conducted in English, don't dismiss hikes conducted in Hebrew; English-speakers in the group are often glad to translate, and the outings are a good way to get to know nature-loving Israelis. SPNI day trips are planned only a short time in advance, so call to see what's happening.

The expert guides at Hadar Desert Tours take hikers down and around the phenomenal Ramon Crater.

The Eilat Field School staff are helpful and friendly—it's a branch of the SPNI. They'll supply full details of local hikes as well as maps in English. The office is opposite Coral Beach, and it's open Sunday through Thursday 8–8, Friday and Jewish holidays until noon, and Saturday until 11 AM. Though few of the myriad hikes are led in English, and most are designed for groups, you can call to see what's on the roster.

JEEP TOURS    From Eilat, the well-established Red Sea Sports Club leads Jeep safaris through the Granite Mountains around Eilat to lookout points above Moon Valley, with a descent into the Red Canyon where you walk for an hour in natural beauty. The cost is NIS 140 per person. Another experienced company, Jeep See, offers a 1½-hour "Desert Glimpse," with a view of the hot-pink flamingos near Eilat; the cost is NIS 65. Jeep See also provides a four-hour trip to the Red Canyon (including hiking) for NIS 140 per person.

**Ayt Aviation & Tourism Ltd.** ☎ 03/699-0185 or 054/478-0096. **Camel Ranch** ☎ 08/637-0022. **Eilat Field School** ☎ 08/637-2021. **Hadar Desert Tours** ☎ 052/270-3451. **International Birding and Research Center** ✉ Main highway, near Dor gas station, outside Eilat ☎ 08/633-5339. *Israel Yam* ☎ 08/637-5528 ⊕ www.israel-yam.co.il. **Jeep See** ✉ Bridge House, near the marina, Eilat ☎ 08/633-0133 ⊕ www.jeepsee.com. *Jules Verne Explorer* ☎ 08/631-6348 or 631/6377 ⊕ www.hofhananya.co.il. **Kibbutz Lotan** ☎ 08/635-6935. **Negevland Tours** ☎ 08/655-5788. **Red Sea Sports Club** ✉ Bridge House, Eilat ☎ 08/633-3666 ✉ Coral Beach ☎ 08/637-6569 ⊕ www.redseasports.co.il. **SPNI** ✉ 13 Hashfela St., Tel Aviv 66183 ☎ 03/638-8677 ✉ 13 Helene Hamalka St., Jerusalem 96101 ☎ 02/625-2357. **Yusef** ☎ 050/550-3826 **Ziki Sailing School** ☎ 050/528-6334 ⊕ www.sailingschool.co.il. *Zorba Cruises* ☎ 052/441-5656.

**VISITOR INFORMATION**

Hours vary greatly among the region's tourist information offices and visitor centers—it's best to phone ahead. In Eilat, be sure to pick up the useful "Events in Eilat" brochure from the tourist information office. Eilat Friendly Tours provides advice about hotels, tours, and activities; does booking; and offers guide service in and around Eilat.

🚩 Arad Tourist Information Center ✉ Industrial Center ☎ 09/995-1622. **Eilat Friendly Tours** ⊕ http://friendlytours-online.com. **Beersheva Tourist Information Office** ✉ 1 Derech Hebron, near the Central Bus Station, Beersheva 84104 ☎ 08/623-4613. **Eilat Tourist Information Office** ✉ Bridge House, North Beach Promenade, Box 14, Eilat 88100 ☎ 08/630-9111. **Ein Bokek Tourist Information Office** ✉ the shopping center ☎ 08/997-5010 ⊕ www.deadsea.co.il. **Mitzpe Ramon Visitor Center** ✉ Top of the main street, Box 340, Mitzpe Ramon ☎ 08/658-8691 or 08/658-8620. **Yotvata Tourist Information Office** ✉ Rte. 90, north of Eilat ☎ 08/635-7229.

# UNDERSTANDING ISRAEL

# ISRAEL AT A GLANCE

## Fast Facts

**Nickname:** The Holy Land, The Land of Milk and Honey, Palestine
**Type of government:** Parliamentary democracy with legislative, executive, and judicial branches.
**Population:** 6.94 million
**Population Density:** 300 persons per square kilometer.
**Median age:** 28.3

**Life expectancy:** Men: 77 years. Women: 81 years.
**Language:** Hebrew, Arabic
**Ethnic groups:** Jews 81%, Arabs 19%
**Religion:** Jewish 76.5%, Muslim 15.9%, Christian 2.1%, Druze 1.6%
**National Anthem:** *Hatikva,* "The Hope." Written in 1886 by poet Naftali Herz Imber.

## Geography & Environment

Israel is located in the Middle East, at the crossroads of three continents—Asia, Africa, and Europe—and is bounded by the Mediterranean Sea to the west, the Great Syrian-African Rift to the east, and the Red Sea to the south. Israel shares borders with Jordan, Egypt, Lebanon, and Syria. Mt. Hermon on the Golan Heights is the highest point in the country at 9,230 feet above sea level. At the other end of the spectrum is the Dead Sea, the lowest point on earth, with its surface at 1,369 feet below sea level. Despite its small size (covering an area of 7,849 sqare miles, it's slightly smaller than New Jersey), Israel has a variegated landscape that includes deserts, mountain ranges, fertile valleys, and a coastal plain with a rich variety of flora and fauna. A central environmental challenge in this small area is population growth; since the creation of the state in 1948, Israel's population has jumped from 800,000 to 6.9 million. Today, 92 percent of the population is concentrated in the Central Plain area, north of Beersheva. Water conservation and maintaining air quality are the two leading environmental issues facing Israel in the next twenty years.

**Latitude:** 31⅓° N
**Longitude:** 34½° E
**Elevation:** From 9,230 feet at Mt. Hermon in the north to −1,369 feet at the Dead Sea
**Land area:** 7,849 sq. miles; slightly smaller than New Jersey
**Parkland:** There are 54 national parks in Israel
**Terrain:** Desert in the south; low coastal plain on the eastern shore of the Mediterranean; hills that cover most of the country west of the Jordan River; the Jordan Rift Valley forms the eastern border of the country; two internal bodies of water—the Sea of Galilee and the Dead Sea—are also found in the center of the country
**Natural hazards:** Sandstorms; desert flash floods in winter; earthquakes (infrequent)

## Economy

**Per capita income:** $19,620
**Unemployment:** 9.0%
**Work force:** 2.084 million in 2004; manufacturing 17.2%; motor vehicle trade and repair 12.5%; health, welfare, and social assistance 11.3%; banking, finance, and insurance 3.5%; educational services 14%;

accommodation and food services
4.4%; business activities 12.6%;
construction 5.1%; information and
cultural industries 3.9%; other services
(except public administration) 4%;

public administration 5.4%; real estate
and rental and leasing 2%; utilities
0.9%
**Major industries:** Aircraft, high-tech,
tourism, food, diamond-cutting

## Did You Know?

• The world's largest manufacturer of
generic pharmaceuticals, Teva Pharmaceuticals, is based in Israel. One out of
every 16 prescriptions filled in the
United States is for a Teva product.

• The small southern Israeli town of
Beersheva has eight chess grand masters, a higher percentage per capita than
any other city worldwide. The majority
of them are immigrants from the former
Soviet Union; the city of 183,000 has
one grand master per 22,875 residents.
In October 2005, Beersheva hosted the
Chess World team Championships.

• Israel has ten sites recognized by UN-
ESCO as World Heritage Sites. They in-
clude the biblical archeological sites of
Tel Megiddo, Hazor, and Beer Sheva.
The Negev desert cities of Haluza,
Mamshit, Avdat, and Shivta are part of

the ancient Nabatean spice route that
operated between the 3rd century BC
and the 3rd century AD. Spices, incense,
silver, and gold flowed from Yemen to
the Mediterranean Sea through the
Negev. The other three Israeli UNESCO
World Heritage Sites are Masada, the
Old City of Akko, and Tel Aviv (for it's
"White City," Bauhaus architecture).

• Israel is the only country in the world
to end the 20th century with more trees
than it had at the beginning. More than
240 million trees were planted in Israel
during the 20th century.

• Every spring and fall more than half a
billion birds from three continents fly
across Israel. During migration seasons,
Israel has the highest concentration of
birds per square yard of any country in
the world.

# SMALL COUNTRY, BIG HISTORY

**ISRAEL IS A LAND OF PASTEL** landscapes and primary-color people; a land where the beauty of nature is subtle but the natives often are not. The sometimes rambunctious Israeli affability may envelop you as soon as you board your flight to Tel Aviv, especially if you're flying El Al, Israel's national carrier. Cries of recognition and the chatter of passengers exchanging stories about their trips and their duty-free bargains recall first days back at school after summer vacations. Some passengers greet El Al touchdowns on Holy Land soil with spontaneous applause, but these are the sentimental tourists; the red-blooded Israelis are already on their feet collecting their bags, despite pleas from the cabin staff.

The feistiness of many Israelis can come across as assertive, intrusive, even aggressive; their fighter-pilot style of driving may be the best example of this. At the same time, many claim that this attitude is what helped Israel survive in a hostile political and natural environment. The related lack of inhibition leads to fast and genuinely warm human contacts that are a refreshing surprise to many visitors from more reserved cultures.

Hospitality has been a deeply ingrained tradition in this part of the world since the days of Abraham's tent. If an Israeli even casually invites you home for coffee or a meal, he or she probably expects that you'll accept the invitation. Do. There is no better way to dive into the culture, and you'll probably pick up instant expertise on local politics, ethnic differences, food, the cost of buying a house, and what your host earns. Be prepared for similar questions about *your* life; there are fewer conversational taboos in Israel than in most English-speaking countries. An oft-quoted anecdote is that of the Israeli company rep sent abroad, who was advised to avoid discussing politics, religion, and sex

in social situations. "What *else* is there to talk about?" asked the astonished Israeli.

An important key to understanding Israel is this: the founding generation saw it as a modern reincarnation of the ancient Jewish nation-state. Israel was the "Promised Land" of Abraham and Moses, the Israelite kingdom of David and Solomon, and the home of Jesus of Nazareth and the Jewish Talmudic sages. Although the Jewish presence in the country has been unbroken for more than 3,000 years, several massive exiles—first by the Babylonians in 586 BC and then by the Romans in AD 70—created a diaspora, a dispersion of the Jewish people throughout the world. The sense of historical roots still resonates for many, probably most, Jewish Israelis; and bringing their brethren home has been a national priority from the beginning.

The attachment to the ancient homeland, and a yearning for the restoration of "Zion and Jerusalem," weaves through the entire fabric of Jewish history and religious tradition. Over the centuries, many Jews trickled back to Eretz Yisrael (the Land of Israel) while others looked forward to fulfilling their dream of return in some future—many felt imminent—messianic age. Not all were prepared to wait for divine intervention, however, and in the late 19th century, a variety of Jewish nationalist organizations emerged, bent on creating a home for their people in Israel (then Palestine). Zionism was founded as a political movement to give structure and impetus to that idea.

Some early Zionist leaders, like founding father Theodor Herzl, believed that the urgent priority was simply a Jewish haven safe from persecution, wherever that haven might be. Argentina was suggested, and Great Britain offered Uganda. In light of Jewish historical and emotional links to the land of Israel, most Zionists rejected these "territorialist" proposals. British statesman Arthur James Balfour (later Lord Balfour) was perplexed by this attitude and asked Zionist leader Chaim Weizmann—later Israel's first president—to explain it. "Mr. Balfour," Dr. Weizmann responded, "if I were to offer you Paris instead of London, would you accept it?" "Of course not," Balfour replied, "London is our capital." "Precisely," said Weizmann, "and Jerusalem was *our* capital when London was still a marsh!"

The establishment of the state of Israel did not, of course, meet with universal rejoicing. To the Arab world, it was anathema, an alien implant in a Muslim Middle East. Palestinian Arabs today mark Israel's independence as the *Nakba,* the Catastrophe, when their own national aspirations were thwarted. To many ultra-Orthodox Jews, the founding of Israel was an arrogant preempting of God's divine plan; and to make matters worse, the new state was blatantly secular, despite its concessions to religious interests. This internal battle over the character of the Jewish state, and the implacable hostility of Israel's neighbors—which has resulted in more than half a century of almost constant conflict—have been the two main issues engaging the country since its birth.

### The People

Of Israel's 7 million citizens, about 76% (5.3 million) are Jewish. Some proudly trace their family roots back many generations on local soil; others are first- to fourth-generation *olim* (immigrants) from dozens of different countries. The first modern pioneers arrived from Russia in 1882, purchased land, and set about developing it with romantic zeal. A decade or two later, inspired by the socialist ideas then current in Eastern Europe, a much larger wave founded the first *kibbutzim*—collective villages or communes. In time, these fiercely idealistic farmers became something of a moral elite, having little financial power but providing a greatly dis-

proportionate percentage of the country's political leadership, military officer cadre, and intelligentsia. "We are workers," they liked to say, "but not working-class!" Individual kibbutz members may still wield some influence in one area or another, and the movement as a whole is still a factor in the Israeli economy, but the ideology has pretty much run out of steam. A more personally ambitious younger generation has increasingly eschewed the communal lifestyle in favor of the lures of the big city; and in almost all the 270 kibbutzim across the country, modern economic realities have undermined the old socialist structure, and some degree of privatization is the order of the day.

The State of Israel was founded just three years after the end of World War II, in which the Nazis annihilated fully two-thirds of European Jewry. In light of the urgency of providing a haven for remnants of those shattered communities, the Law of Return was passed in 1949 granting any Jew the automatic right to Israeli citizenship. Most who immigrated before Israel's independence in 1948 were Ashkenazi Jews (those of Central or Eastern European descent), but the biggest waves of immigration in the first decade of statehood were of Sephardic Jews, who came from the Arab lands of North Africa and the Middle East. Israel's Jewish population—600,000 at the time of its independence—doubled within 3½ years and tripled within 10.

The national system that was developed to facilitate immigration and immigrant absorption has generally been very successful, but its resources and creativity were sorely taxed in the 1980s and early '90s, when some one million newcomers inundated the country, most from the former Soviet Union, and a lesser number from Ethiopia. In relative terms, it was equivalent to the United States absorbing the entire population of France in the space of a decade.

For a long time, the visible differences between the haves and have-nots in Israel broke down along the lines of the more established and better-educated Ashkenazim and the poorer, unskilled Sephardim. The old prejudices and resentment this created have not quite disappeared, but the lines have become fuzzier, as many of the recent immigrants join the ranks of the country's poor. Israel's increasingly free-market economy is more robust than ever, but the wealth is not spread around. The disturbingly high percentage of Israelis living in poverty—and what to do about it—has become the single hottest issue in the land (after national security concerns, of course).

The vast majority of Israel's 1.4 million Arabic-speaking citizens are Muslims (among them about 100,000 Bedouin), followed by about 100,000 Christian Arabs, and a similar number of Druze (a separate religious group). All are equal under the law, and vote for and may serve in the Knesset, the Israeli parliament. (Not included are the 2.5–3 million Palestinian Arabs of the partly autonomous West Bank and the completely autonomous Gaza Strip, who are not Israeli citizens.) A new demographic factor is the 300,000 Russian-speakers who appear on the census as "other": these are immigrants who were eligible for Israeli citizenship because of their Jewish ancestry, but are not Jewish by practice or religious definition.

Social and economic gaps between the Arab and Jewish sectors continue to rankle. Arab complaints of government neglect and unequal allocation of resources have sometimes spilled into angry street demonstrations and other anti-establishment activity. Although the Muslims in Israel, mainstream Sunnis, are regarded as both politically and religiously moderate by the standards of the region, there has been considerable radicalization in recent years of the community's youth, who identify politically with the Palestinian liberation movement and/or religiously with the Islamic revival that has swept the Middle East.

Of the Christian Arabs, most belong to the Greek Catholic, Greek Orthodox, or Roman Catholic church; a handful of Eastern denominations and a few tiny Protestant groups account for the rest. The Western Christian community is minuscule, consisting mainly of clergy, and temporary sojourners such as diplomats and foreign professionals on assignment.

The Druze, though Arabic-speaking, follow a separate and secret religion that broke from Islam about 1,000 years ago. Larger kindred communities exist in long-hostile Syria and Lebanon, but Israeli Druze have solidly identified with Israel, and the community's young men are routinely drafted into the Israeli army. The Arab community itself is not liable for military service, in order to avoid the risk of battlefield confrontations with kinsmen from neighboring countries.

### Religion and State

There is no firm separation of religion and state in Israel. Matters of personal status—marriage, divorce, adoption, and burial—are the preserve of the religious authorities of the community concerned. For this reason there is no civil marriage; if one partner does not convert to the faith of the other, the couple must marry abroad. Within the Jewish community, such functions fall under the supervision of the Orthodox chief rabbinate, much to the dismay of members of the tiny but growing Conservative and Reform movements (many of whom are American expatriates) and of the large number of nonobservant Jews.

The confrontation between secular Israelis and the hard-line ultra-Orthodox has escalated over the years, as the religious community tries to impose on what it considers an apostate citizenry its vision of how a Jewish state should behave. One volatile issue is the Orthodox contention that only someone who meets the Orthodox definition of a Jew (either born of a Jewish mother or converted by strict Orthodox procedures) should be eligible for Israeli citizenship under the Law of Return. Disagreements about public observance of the Sabbath and of dietary laws are old sources of tension as well. For many nonreligious Israelis, already irked by what they consider religious coercion, the fact that most ultra-Orthodox Jewish men avoid military service on the grounds of continuing religious studies just rubs salt in the wound.

Israel prides itself on being the only true democracy in the Middle East, and it sometimes seems bent on politically tearing itself apart in the democratic process. This is how the system works (or doesn't): once every four years, prior to national elections, every party publishes a list of its candidates for the 120-member Knesset. There are no constituencies or voting districts; each party that breaks the minimum threshold of 2% of the *national* vote gets in, winning the same percentage of Knesset seats as its *proportion* of nationwide votes (hence the term "proportional representation").

The good news is that the system is intensely democratic. A relatively small grouping of like-minded voters *countrywide* (currently about 60,000) can elect an M.K. (Member of the Knesset) to represent its views. The largest party able to gain a parliamentary majority through a coalition with other parties forms the government, and its leader becomes the prime minister. The bad news is that the system spawns a plethora of small parties, whose collective support the government needs in order to rule. Since no party has ever won enough seats to rule alone, Israeli governments have always been based on compromise, with small parties exerting a degree of political influence often quite out of proportion to their actual size. Attempts to change the system have been doomed to failure, because the small parties, which stand to lose if the system is changed, are precisely those on whose support the *current* government depends.

## The Land

Israel is a small country—just 470 km (under 300 mi) long, from Metulla, on the northern border with Lebanon, to Eilat, on the Red Sea; 110 km (69 mi) wide at its widest, across the Negev Desert; and as little as 50 km (31 mi) wide across the Galilee. In area Israel is exactly the size of Wales, or just larger than the land area of Massachusetts or New Jersey. The American writer Mark Twain was astonished by the smallness of the Holy Land when he visited in 1867. He had envisioned, he wrote, "a country as large as the United States . . . I suppose it was because I could not conceive of a small country having so large a history."

Mark Twain's astonishment is instructive: in Israel the past is more present than almost anywhere else on earth. There is something about the place that seeps into one's soul. For the Jewish visitor, it's a feeling of coming home, of returning to one's roots. For the Christian, it's the awe of retracing Jesus's footsteps in the Scripture's actual landscape, of seeing the Bible take on entirely new meaning. For a Muslim, it's the opportunity to pray at the third holiest shrine in Islam.

Indeed, the country's biblical past has made names like Jerusalem, the Galilee, and the Jordan River household words for almost half the human race. Many a pilgrim has reached Israel expecting a Jerusalem preserved as a pristine shrine, a Galilee of donkey traffic and tiny fishing boats, and a Jordan River "deep and wide." The reality hits as you find the ancient names shouted from store billboards and highway signs. You discover that Jerusalem is a modern metropolis of 700,000 people and Galilee is the name of a professional basketball team. To top it all off, the Jordan River is for the most part a very modest stream.

The past is far from forgotten, however. Archaeology is almost a national sport here (though less for today's video-game generation than for its parents), and any unusual find in one of the ongoing excavations is sure to make the prime-time news. There are prehistoric settlement sites more than a million years old; the world's oldest walled town, at Jericho (now in the West Bank); echoes of the biblical patriarchs; and evidence of the kings of Israel. You can stand on the Temple Mount steps that Jesus almost certainly climbed, or marvel at a 1st-century wooden boat by the Sea of Galilee. The word "ancient" has a particular currency here.

Despite its small size, Israel offers an astonishing diversity of climate and terrain. Drive east from Tel Aviv via Jerusalem to the Dead Sea, and in 1½ hours you pass from classic Mediterranean white beaches and orange groves through olive-draped hills and up rugged pine-wooded mountains, only to plunge almost 4,000 feet down the other side, through wild, barren desert, to the subtropical oasis of Jericho and the Dead Sea, the lowest point on the planet.

Half of Israel is desert, but don't picture endless sand dunes. Awesome canyons slice through the Judean Desert to the Dead Sea, a few with sweet waterfalls and brilliant shocks of greenery. The Negev highlands, south of Beersheva, are punctuated by three huge craters caused by eons of water erosion, the only such formations in the world. The resort city of Eilat sits on the coral-reef Red Sea against a backdrop of jagged granite peaks and desert moonscapes. And in the spring, after the meager winter rains, the deserts burst into startling bloom, the hard landscapes softened by a fuzz of grass and multicolored wildflowers. A desert excursion here—by foot, Jeep, or camel—is not quickly forgotten.

The northern and western parts of the country are a complete antidote to the desert. True, it's also hot in the summer and somewhat parched in the rainless season from May through October, but it's a land of good winter rains, some springs and streams, miles of Mediterranean beaches, extensive irrigated fields and orchards, mountainsides of evergreen forests, lush nature reserves, and the freshwater "Sea" of Galilee.

### Israel Today

Despite its heritage and location—think of it as Eastern Mediterranean rather than Middle Eastern—Israel is as European as it is Levantine. Scientifically, the country is at the forefront of computer technology and software, lasers, medicine, biotechnology, aeronautics, electronics, and agriculture. Seven universities, some world-renowned, set exceptional standards, and there have been four Israeli Nobel laureates in Economics and the sciences just since 2002. Israel's health system is groaning under the weight of financial deficits, and hospital conditions sometimes reflect this, but the country's high medical standards do not seem to have been compromised. Doctors on call for your hotel will speak English and likely be on par with physicians back home.

Violent crime is relatively low in Israel, though there has been a worrying increase in incidents involving teenagers in the last few years. The wave of politically motivated Palestinian violence (the *intifada*) that began in late 2000 seems to have subsided. Radical organizations that reject any accommodation with Israel still attempt to disrupt life in the country, but the resurgence of tourism and the relaxed atmosphere of daily activity in Israel's cities are an indication of how seldom they succeed. You *will* occasionally see automatic weapons on the street, obviously in the hands of uniformed security personnel, but also sometimes over the shoulder of a young off-duty soldier in civvies. The Israeli Defense Force is a people's army: almost all Jews serve, and a national serviceman or servicewoman, once issued a weapon, is *wedded* to it for the duration. The criminal misuse of army-issue firearms is very, very rare.

There are many small cities in Israel, but only three major ones. Jerusalem, the capital and spiritual center, lies 60 km (38 mi) inland, at an elevation of 762 meters (2,500 feet), and is a limestone blend of the ancient and the modern. Tel Aviv, on the Mediterranean coast, is not beautiful but very lively—the country's commercial and entertainment center, the city that never sleeps. Two out of every five Israelis live within its metropolitan area. Haifa, 100 km (63 mi) north of Tel Aviv, sprawls up the slopes of Mt. Carmel, offering sweeping views and serving as one of the country's two main ports and industrial areas.

Urban life, at least in the metropolis, has changed dramatically over the years. Greater affluence and a sharp sense of international fashion and style have produced a consumerism not unlike that of North America or Western Europe. You can see it in the delis and supermarkets, the boutiques and home-furnishing stores. The growing popularity of dining out as an evening activity has created a clientele with sophisticated expectations, which are reflected in the large number of great restaurants and local fine wines. A good climate and fine beaches have spawned a burgeoning leisure industry as well. Add all of this to Israel's physical attractions, historical fascination, and profound religious impact, and you have one of the most intriguing destinations around.

— Mike Rogoff

# BOOKS & MOVIES

## Books

**History & Biography.** If you haven't opened the Bible in a while, this is a good time to review biblical narratives; better yet, bring it along on your trip. Bruce Feiler's *Walking the Bible* is a thought-provoking account of the author's 10,000-mile, 2-year-long journey through biblical lands, reading the stories of the bible in their "natural surroundings." (It was also made into a PBS mini-series.) For a modern take on the Bible, take a look at *Genesis and the Big Bang*, by Gerald Schroeder. *A History of Israel: From the Rise of Zionism to Our Times*, by Howard M. Sachar, is the classic comprehensive history of how Israel came into being. Karen Armstrong's *Jerusalem: One City, Three Faiths* traces the city's physical history and spiritual meaning from its beginning to the present day. Last, but far from least, is Flavius Josephus's *The Jewish War*. The Jewish commander who defected to the Romans during the Great Revolt wrote a still-fascinating account of the Roman campaigns.

To better understand some of the leading players in Israel's modern history, try one of the following. *Warrior: The Autobiography of Ariel Sharon*, by Ariel Sharon, and *Soldier of Peace: The Life of Yitzhak Rabin*, by Dan Kurzman, detail the lives of two key political figures. *O Jerusalem*, by Larry Collins and Dominique Lapierre, is a dramatic account of the establishment of the Israeli state.

*The Book of Our Heritage*, by Eliayahv Kitov, is a superb guide to Jewish holidays and traditions.

**Fiction & Poetry.** *Exodus*, a novel by Leon Uris, deals with the founding of the State of Israel. *The Source*, by James Michener, is the novelist's epic look at Israel's early history. Naomi Ragen writes about how one Israeli family is affected by the violence of the second intifada in *The Covenant*.

*Closing the Sea*, by Yehudit Katzir, is a book of short stories set in Israel. *The Same Sea*, by Amos Oz, blends prose and poetry in a tale of family love and longing. The poetry of C. N. Bialik (1873-1934), has been hugely influential, both to artists and politicians, and among the works of the late poet Yehuda Amichai is *Poems of Jerusalem*. Other contemporary Israeli writers worth looking out for are A. B. Yehoshua, Meir Shalev, David Grossman, Irit Linor, Orly Castel-Bloom, Etgar Keret, Edna Mazya, Michal Govrin, S. Yizhar, Shulamit Hareven, Ruth Almog, Batya Gur, and S.Y. Agnin—Israel's only winner of the Nobel Prize for Literature.

**Modern Israel.** *The Israelis*, by Donna Rosenthal, is an in-depth look at the diverse people who make up the Jewish state and *In the Land of Israel*, by Amos Oz, is a series of articles depicting various settlements and towns and conversations with local people. *Cain's Field*, by Matt Rees, delves into the internal workings of Palestinian and Israeli society. In *Jerusalem Diaries: In Tense Times*, journalist Judy Lash Balint, who also updated parts of *Fodor's Israel*, describes life in the holy city during the early days of the second intifada. In *My Enemy, Myself*, Yoram Binur, an Israeli journalist, imagines himself a Palestinian. Former Israeli prime minister Benjamin Netanyahu lays out his view of Israel in *A Durable Peace: Israel's Place Among the Nations*. For a closer look at two important Israeli cities, past and present, read *Jerusalem in the Twentieth Century*, by Martin Gilbert, and *Safed, the Mystical City*, by David Rossoff.

## Movies

The Israeli film industry has burgeoned over the past few years, producing several dramas and comedies that have won awards from prestigious film festivals around the world. Documentary films made between 2002 and 2006 tend to be heavily political and portray the country almost exclusively in terms of the Arab-Israeli conflict.

**Documentaries.** *Tkuma* (1998), meaning "Rebirth," is a comprehensive and unflinching account of the birth of the modern Jewish state. A look at one of the food staples of the Middle East, *Hummous for Two* (1997) portrays the search for the perfect chickpea spread in Jerusalem's Jewish and Arab neighborhoods. In *Israel–A Nation Is Born* (1994), the late Abba Eban, Israeli Ambassador to the United Nations, narrates an engrossing and dramatic six-part chronicle of the birth and development of the Jewish state.

**Drama.** *Turn Left at the End of the World* (2004) depicts life for new immigrants in an Israeli development town, while *James' Journey to Jerusalem* (2003) is a look at the life of a young African Christian who wants to become a pastor, and the Israel he encounters. *Nina's Tragedies* (2003) is a bittersweet drama of family life influenced by the tension of living with the ever-present threat of terror in Israel, viewed through the eyes of a forlorn teenager. In *Campfire* (2004), director Joseph Cedar tells the story of a 42-year-old widow and her two daughters who are looking to start their lives over in a settlement. *Ushpizin* (2004) is an engaging comedy-drama set in an ultra-Orthodox neighborhood in Jerusalem.

# CHRONOLOGY

As the only land bridge between Africa and Asia, Israel has always been a thoroughfare, a distinction that made it desirable to foreign powers and often turned it into a battleground. Moreover, the country's geography—isolated mountain areas and well-traveled valleys, and its position between the desert and the Mediterranean Sea—has determined its climate, its economy, and by extension, the character of those who conquered and settled the land.

Israel was once called Canaan, then the Land of Israel (Eretz Yisrael, in Hebrew), then Israel. Later, the name "Israel" came to represent only the northern Israelite kingdom, including Samaria and Galilee, while the southern kingdom was called Judah. Judah became the Greek "Judea," first applied only to a small part of the country centered on Jerusalem but later to a much larger territory. After the Bar Kochba Revolt (2nd century AD), the Roman emperor Hadrian changed the name of the province to Palaestina (after the long-gone Philistines) in order to dissociate the country from its Jewish identity. Palestine later became the name of this tiny district in the huge Muslim empires of the Middle Ages. To Christians it was always the Holy Land; to Jews, Eretz Yisrael. The use of the name "Israel" in the following chronology does not always imply any specific set of borders, past or present, but the country as a whole, the ancient Land of Israel.

## Prehistoric Israel

**ca. 1.2 million years ago**  Earliest known human habitation in Israel (Lower Paleolithic period), period), at Ubeidiya, in Jordan Valley.

**ca. 7800 BC**  The establishment of Jericho (Neolithic pre-pottery period), the oldest walled town ever found.

## Canaanite Period (Bronze Age) ca. 3200 BC–1250 BC

**ca. 3200–2150**  Writing is developed in Mesopotamia; beginning of recorded history. Early Bronze Age in Israel. Major cities are built: Megiddo, Hatzor, and (apparently) Jerusalem.

**ca. 2150–1550**  Age of the Patriarchs: Abraham, Isaac, and Jacob. Middle Bronze Age.

**ca. 1550–1250**  Time of Hebrews' enslavement in Egypt. Decline of Egyptian power. Moses believed to have led Hebrews in exodus from Egypt. Late Bronze Age: Israel divided into Canaanite city-kingdoms.

**ca. 1290**  The Hebrews—the "Children of Israel"—receive the Torah (the Law) at Mt. Sinai. The nation of Israel is formed, the basis of its religion established, and its relationship with the one God defined. Forty years of desert wandering separate the nation from its Promised Land.

## Old Testament/First Temple Period (Iron Age) ca. 1250 BC–586 BC

ca. 1250   Moses dies within sight of the Promised Land. Joshua leads the nation across the Jordan River and embarks on the conquest of Canaan, beginning with Jericho.

ca. 1200–1025   Period of the Judges (e.g., Deborah, Gideon, Samson), charismatic regional leaders.

ca. 1150   The Philistines invade from the west and establish a league of five city-states in the coastal plain. Israelites appeal to the prophet Samuel for a king.

1025   Saul, of humble origin, is the first King of Israel.

1006   Saul and three sons, including Jonathan, are killed fighting the Philistines. David rules Judah.

1000   David conquers Jerusalem, a Jebusite enclave, and makes it the capital of a unified Israel. He brings the sacred Ark of the Covenant to Jerusalem and establishes the city as the new religious center.

968   Solomon becomes king, consolidates David's kingdom, and ca. 950 builds the First Temple of the Lord, in Jerusalem.

928   Solomon dies and the kindom splits. The northern tribes, under Jeroboam, secede and form the Kingdom of Israel. The southern tribes, now known as the Kingdom of Judah, are ruled from Jerusalem by Solomon's weak son, Rehoboam.

ca. 865   Ahab rules as King of Israel (871–851) and Jehosophat as King of Judah (867–843). Peace exists between the two kingdoms. Ahab's wife, Jezebel, reintroduces pagan idol-worship, incurring the wrath of the prophet Elijah.

721   The Kingdom of Israel is destroyed by the Assyrians (now the region's superpower) and its population (the "Ten Lost Tribes") exiled. Judah comes under the Assyrian yoke.

701   Hezekiah, King of Judah, revolts against Assyria. The Assyrians lay siege to Jerusalem, but with new fortifications and a clever water system, the city survives.

609   Josiah, the last great king of Judah (640–609) and a religious reformer, is killed at Megiddo trying to block an Egyptian advance. Jeremiah prophesies national catastrophe.

586   The Assyrians are defeated by a new power, the Babylonians, whose king, Nebuchadnezzar, conquers Judah and destroys Jerusalem and the Temple. Of those who survive, large numbers are exiled to the "rivers of Babylon."

## Second Temple Period, 538 BC–AD 70

During this period the Babylonians succumb to the rising Persian empire, which allows the Jews to rebuild the Temple in Jerusalem. The sacrificial rites are restored; but the Land of Israel must now share its preeminence with important Jewish centers in Babylon, Egypt, and elsewhere. Starting in the 3rd century bc, deep divisions appear within the Jewish nation over theological issues and the response to the seductive Hellenistic culture, introduced to the region by Alexander the Great. The Sadducees, who draw their strength from the upper classes, take a literal, Bible-based view and are willing to accommodate elements of Hellenism. The Pharisees, a Jewish group of the common people, add the Oral Law (the unwritten rabbinic interpretation of the Torah) to the authority of the Scriptures; they reject pagan culture and spin-off moralistic splinter-groups like the ascetic Essenes, the militant Zealots, and the followers of Jesus.

**538**  Cyrus, King of Persia, conquers Babylon and allows the Jewish exiles to return home and rebuild the Temple (completed circa 516). In Babylon, the synagogue develops as a communal place of assembly, with an emphasis on the reading of the Torah and (eventually) on prayer.

**445**  Nehemiah, a Jewish nobleman, is sent to Jerusalem by the Persian king, with the authority to rebuild the city's walls and rule the district.

**333**  The Persian Empire is defeated by Alexander the Great, and the entire Near East comes under Hellenistic sway.

**323**  Alexander's death precipitates a struggle for succession. His empire is split up: Ptolemy rules in Egypt; Seleucus in Syria and Mesopotamia.

**301**  Ptolemy establishes control over the whole land of Israel. Egypt's now Greek-speaking Jewish population expands. The Bible is translated into Greek and called the Septuagint.

**198**  The Syrian Seleucids defeat the Egyptian Ptolemies at Banias, the headwaters of the Jordan, annex the country, and establish good relations with the Jewish community.

**167**  The Seleucid king Antiochus IV outlaws all Jewish religious practices, sparking the Maccabean Revolt.

**165**  After four decisive victories over Hellenistic armies, Judah the Maccabee (Judas Maccabeus) enters the desecrated Temple in Jerusalem, purifying and rededicating it (commemorated by the Jewish festival of Channukah).

**142**  Simon, brother of Judah the Maccabee, achieves independence for Judea and establishes the Hasmonean dynasty.

**63**  Pompey, the Roman general, enters the country to settle a civil war between the last Hasmonean princes and annexes it as a Roman province.

**48**  The influential royal counselor Antipater, a convert to Judaism, appoints his sons, among them Herod, to key administrative positions.

**40**  Mark Antony appoints Herod as king of the Jews.

**37**  After fighting his way through the country, Herod claims his throne in Jerusalem. Hated by the Jews, he seeks to legitimize his reign by marrying a Hasmonean princess (whom he later murders).

31 Antony is defeated by Octavian, now the emperor Caesar Augustus. Herod pays homage to Augustus in Rome and is confirmed in his titles and territories. He rebuilds the Second Temple in Jerusalem on a grand scale, winning great esteem.

ca. 5 BC Birth of Jesus in Bethlehem.

4 BC Death of Herod, called by history "the Great." His kingdom is divided among three sons: Archelaus rules in Jerusalem for 10 years (and is replaced by a Roman procurator); Herod Antipas rules the Galilee and Perea (east of the Jordan River); and Philip controls Golan, Bashan, and the sources of the Jordan River.

ca. AD 26 Beginning of Jesus's Galilean ministry. He calls his disciples, heals and performs miracles, teaches, and preaches, mostly around the Sea of Galilee.

ca. 29 Jesus and his disciples celebrate Passover in Jerusalem. Arrest, trial, and crucifixion of Jesus by the Romans on orders of the governor, Pontius Pilate. For the Romans, the claim of Jesus as the Messiah (Hebrew for "the anointed one"), with its implication of kingship, is tantamount to high treason. The New Testament relates that Jesus's death and resurrection were divinely determined, an expiation for the sins of humanity. Identification with this event as the way to personal salvation becomes the basis for the community of faith that is Christianity.

66 Start of Great Revolt against Roman oppression. Jews briefly reassert their political independence.

67 Galilee falls to the Romans. The Jewish commander defects to the enemy. Romanizing his name to Josephus Flavius, he follows the Roman campaigns, eventually recording them in *The Jewish War*.

69 Before the fall of Jerusalem, the sage Yochanan Ben Zakkai leaves the city, settling with his disciples in the town of Yavneh in the coastal plain, by grant of Roman general and Caesar-elect Vespasian.

70 Jerusalem, torn by internal faction fighting, falls to the Roman general Titus after a long siege. The Second Temple is destroyed. Slaughter and enslavement of Jews follow. The revolt is officially at an end.

73 The last Jewish stronghold, at Masada, falls. Its defenders take their own lives rather than surrender. Yavneh becomes the seat of the Sanhedrin, the Jewish High Court. Its sages find religious responses to the new reality of Judaism without the Temple, and the spiritual and legal authority of Yavneh is established.

## Late Roman & Byzantine Period, AD 73–640

132 When the Roman emperor Hadrian threatens to rebuild Jerusalem as a pagan city, another Jewish revolt breaks out, led by Bar Kochba and supported by Rabbi Akiva. Secret preparations and a strong unified command bring spectacular initial successes.

**135** Death of Bar Kochba. The revolt is brutally suppressed, but only after severe Roman losses. Hadrian plows over Jerusalem and builds in its place Aelia Capitolina, a pagan city off-limits to Jews. The name of the country is changed to Palaestina, and Jewish religious practice is outlawed. The Sanhedrin relocates to the Lower Galilee.

**ca. 200** At Zippori or Sepphoris, in the Galilee, Judah the Nasi (patriarch), spiritual and political head of the Jewish community, compiles the Mishnah, the summary of the Oral Law, which is the basis of Jewish jurisprudence. A period of peace and prosperity ensues under the tolerant Severan emperors.

**325** Emperor Constantine the Great makes Christianity the imperial religion. His mother, Helena, comes to the Holy Land in 326 and initiates the building of major churches—the Holy Sepulcher in Jerusalem and the Nativity in Bethlehem.

**330** Constantine transfers his capital from Rome to Byzantium, now renamed Constantinople. Beginning of the Byzantine Period. Judaism is on the defensive.

**351** A Jewish revolt, primarily in the Galilee, against the Roman ruler Gallus is brutally suppressed.

**361** Emperor Julian the Apostate (circa 361–363) tries to reintroduce pagan cults.

**ca. 400** Final codification of the so-called Jerusalem Talmud, the result of years of rabbinic elaboration of the Mishnah. (The Babylonian Talmud, codified a century later, is regarded as more authoritative.)

**527–565** The reign of Emperor Justinian. Many important churches were built or rebuilt, among them the present Church of the Nativity in Bethlehem. Vibrant Jewish community despite persecution.

**614** Persian invasion, with destruction of churches and monasteries.

**622** Muhammad's *hejira* (flight) from Mecca to Medina in Arabia; beginnings of Islam. This is Year One on the Muslim calendar.

**628** Persians defeated and Byzantine rule restored in Israel.

**632** Death of Muhammad. His followers, ruled by a series of caliphs, burst out of Arabia and create a Muslim empire that within a century would extend from India to Spain.

**636–640** Arab invasion of Israel. Byzantine Jerusalem falls to the caliph Omar ibn-Katib in 638.

## Medieval Period, 640–1516

**691** Caliph Abd al-Malik builds the Dome of the Rock in Jerusalem.

**1099** Sworn to wrest Christian holy places from Muslim control, the European armies of the First Crusade reach the Holy Land. Jerusalem is taken, and most of its population, Muslim and Jew alike, is massacred.

1100   Establishment of the Latin Kingdom of Jerusalem, with Baldwin I at its head. Chronic shortage of manpower puts the burden of defense on the monastic orders (the Hospitallers and Templars, for example) who build castles—among them Belvoir, in the Lower Galilee, and the underground quarter in Akko (also called Acre).

1110   Most coastal cities in Crusader hands.

1187   The Crusader army is routed by the Arab ruler Saladin at the Horns of Hattin, near Tiberias. The Crusaders are expelled from the country.

1191   The Third Crusade arrives, led by Richard the Lionheart of England and Philip II (Augustus) of France. The Latin Kingdom of Jerusalem never regains its former size and glory. The Crusaders content themselves with the coast from Tyre to Jaffa and the Galilee. Akko becomes the royal capital.

1228   The Crusaders gain Jerusalem by treaty but lose the city again in 1244.

1250   The militant Mamluk class seizes power in Egypt. The Crusade of King Louis IX (St. Louis) against Egypt fails. He is captured but comes to the Holy Land after his release.

1260   The Mamluks check the Mongol invasion at Ayn Jalout (Ein Harod), in the Jezreel Valley.

1265   Muslim reconquest of the land begins under the Mamluk sultan Baybars.

1291   Akko falls and the Crusader kingdom comes to an end. Commerce and trade decline with the destruction of coastal cities. Beginning of a period of outstanding architecture, especially in Jerusalem's Temple Mount (Haram esh-Sharif) and Muslim Quarter, and in the Cave of Machpelah in Hebron.

1492   Expulsion of the Jewish community from Spain. Many of these Sephardic Jews later immigrate to Israel.

## The Modern Period, 1516–Present

1516   Mamluk armies defeated in Syria by the Ottoman Turks, who extend control over the land of Israel (Palestine) as well. Sephardic Jews (Spanish exiles) settle throughout the country. Tzfat (also called Safed) becomes the center of Kabbalah (Jewish mysticism).

1520–1566   Suleiman the Magnificent reigns. Among his many projects is the rebuilding of Jerusalem's walls.

1700   A large contingent of Ashkenazi (Eastern European) Jews settles in Jerusalem.

1799   Napoléon Bonaparte's military campaign founders at Akko.

1832   Egyptian nationalists under Muhammad Ali and Ibrahim Pasha take control of Israel but are expelled in 1840 with the help of European nations.

1853   The Crimean War breaks out in Europe. A contributing factor is the continuing confrontation between Roman Catholic France and Orthodox Russia over the custody of holy places and the patronage of religious communities in the Holy Land and elsewhere in the Ottoman Empire.

1882   First Aliyah (wave of Jewish immigration) of mostly idealistic Eastern European Jews. Baron Edmond de Rothschild establishes new villages and wineries in the coastal plain and the Galilee.

1897   First World Zionist Conference, organized by Theodor Herzl in Basel, Switzerland, gives great impetus to the idea of a "Jewish national home."

1906   The Second Aliyah, or wave of immigration, of young Jewish pioneers from Russia and Poland, including David Ben Gurion, who would eventually become Israel's first prime minister.

1909   Tel Aviv is founded. Degania, the first kibbutz, is established on the southern shore of the Sea of Galilee.

1914   Outbreak of the Great War (World War I). The Ottoman Turks plunder the country to support their war needs.

1917   The British government issues the Balfour Declaration expressing support for a "Jewish national home" in Palestine. General Edmund Allenby captures Jerusalem.

1918   Ottoman Turkey, which had sided with Germany during the War, abandons Palestine.

1920–1939   As Arab nationalism rises in the post-Ottoman Middle East, tensions increase between Jews and Arabs in Palestine, peaking in the massacres of Jews in 1920, 1929, and 1936. Jewish militias form to counter the violence. Substantial immigration of European Jews, who come with growing urgency, as Nazis take power in Germany.

1921   Transjordan is separated from Palestine.

1922   The newly formed League of Nations confirms the Mandate entrusting the rule of Palestine to Great Britain, incorporating the text of the Balfour Declaration in its Terms of Reference.

1939   The British Government issues a White Paper restricting Jewish immigration to Palestine and Jewish purchase of land there, in an attempt to secure Arab goodwill in the coming war. In World War II, Jews enlist on the Allied side. "We shall fight the war as if there were no White Paper," said Palestinian Jewish leader David Ben Gurion, "but we shall fight the White Paper as if there were no war."

1945   End of World War II, in which two-thirds of the Jewish population of Europe was annihilated by the Nazis. When British policy does not change, underground movements challenge British authority. Illegal immigrants, most of them Holocaust survivors, are brought in on ships; many don't get through the British blockade. Clashes with Arabs increase.

1947  United Nations Special Commission on Palestine recommends a plan to partition the country into a Jewish state and an Arab state (three disconnected territorial segments in each) and to internationalize Jerusalem and Bethlehem, with the result of Jewish euphoria and Arab rejection. Beginning of Israel's War of Independence. Discovery of the first Dead Sea Scrolls at Qumran.

1948  May 14: Last British forces depart, ending the British Mandate. David Ben Gurion declares Israel an independent state. The new state survives invasion by the armies of seven Arab countries.

1949  End of fighting in January. U.N.-supervised cease-fire agreements signed. Transjordan annexes the West Bank (of the Jordan River) and East Jerusalem, which it captured in the war, and changes the country's name to the Hashemite Kingdom of Jordan. Egypt annexes the Gaza Strip along the southern Mediterranean coast. Palestinian Arabs who fled or were expelled during the conflict are housed in refugee camps in neighboring countries; those who remain behind become citizens of Israel. First elections to the Knesset, Israel's parliament. David Ben Gurion is elected prime minister; Dr. Chaim Weizmann, first president.

1949–1952  Israel absorbs great numbers of Jewish refugees, tripling its Jewish population by the end of the decade.

1950  The Knesset enacts the Law of Return, giving any Jew the right to Israeli citizenship.

1956  Sinai Campaign, in which British, French, and Israeli forces oppose Egyptian nationalization of the Suez Canal. Fedayeen terrorist attacks from Egyptian-controlled Gaza Strip become less frequent, but sporadic Syrian shelling of Israeli villages below the Golan Heights is a major security issue into the 1960s.

1964  Formation of the Palestine Liberation Organization (PLO), which seeks an independent state for Palestinians and refuses to recognize the legitimacy of the State of Israel.

1967  June: Outbreak of Six-Day War. Egypt, Jordan, and Syria are routed; Israel occupies the Sinai Peninsula, Gaza Strip, West Bank, East Jerusalem, and the Golan Heights, and finds itself in control of almost one million Palestinian Arabs. Some Jewish settlements are established in the West Bank and Golan Heights.

1973  Egypt and Syria attack Israel on the holiest Jewish holiday, the Day of Atonement (hence the name "Yom Kippur War"). Israel beats off the invasion but the euphoria and self-confidence of '67 are shattered.

1974–1975  Signing of Disengagement Agreement on the Golan with Syria and the Interim Agreement with Egypt.

1976  Dramatic Israeli commando raid frees Air France passengers taken hostage in Entebbe, Uganda, by Palestinian hijackers.

1977   Menachem Begin's Likud Party comes to power in May, ending almost four decades of Labor domination of Israeli politics. Egyptian president Anwar Sadat visits Israel.

1978   Camp David Accords give direction to Egypt-Israel peace talks and produce guidelines for a solution to the Palestinian problem.

1979   Israel-Egypt peace agreement signed.

1980   Israeli prime minister Menachem Begin and Egyptian president Anwar Sadat share the Nobel Peace Prize.

1982   Israeli forces cross into southern Lebanon in pursuit of Palestinians shelling civilian settlements in Israel. This escalates into the Lebanon War (1982–85), which is met with unprecedented opposition within Israel.

1987   A road accident in the Gaza Strip triggers the beginning of the *intifada* (uprising), sustained Palestinian Arab street violence, demonstrations, strikes, and sporadic terrorist activity.

1989–1992   Israel absorbs more than 500,000 Soviet Jewish immigrants.

1991   Persian Gulf War; Israel under constant attack but restrained from retaliating. June: 14,500 Ethiopian Jews airlifted to Israel. December: Peace talks in Madrid between Israel and Jordan, Syria, Lebanon, and the Palestinians.

1992   In June the Labor Party under Yitzhak Rabin, vowing to step up the peace process and halt Israeli "political" settlements in West Bank, wins the general elections and forms the government.

1993–1994   The Oslo Accords provide for mutual recognition of Israel and the PLO, as well as Palestinian autonomy in the Gaza Strip and Jericho. Nobel Peace Prize shared by Yitzhak Rabin, Shimon Peres, and Yasser Arafat.

1995   Six more Palestinian Arab West Bank cities are given autonomy. Prime minister Yitzhak Rabin is assassinated in November by an Israeli, a tragic climax to a year of rancorous national debate on the "territory for peace" concept.

1996   New law for direct election of the prime minister brings Likud's Binyamin Netanyahu to power by a margin of less than 1%. Contrary to expectations, the major parties lose much strength, with the religious parties—now powerful partners in a new, far more conservative government—the big winners.

1997   Israel and the Palestinians sign the Hebron Agreement.

1998   Israel celebrates its 50th anniversary.

1999   Ehud Barak, of One Israel (a Labor-led coalition), is elected prime minister by a landslide. Among his campaign promises is that Israel withdraw from Lebanon by July 2000. One of the biggest election surprises is the huge increase in Knesset seats won by the ultra-Orthodox Shas Party.

2000 March: Pope John Paul II visits Jerusalem and the Galilee, only the second papal visit ever to the Holy Land. May: Israel withdraws from Lebanon almost overnight—two months before Barak's pledge. July: Prime minister Barak and Palestinian Authority chairman Yasser Arafat meet with President Clinton at Camp David, but fail to make headway on the peace talks. August: Likud's Moshe Katsav is sworn in as eighth President of Israel. September: Palestinian violence breaks out in the West Bank and Gaza.

2001 Ariel Sharon and his Likud party win new elections and form a broad-based ruling coalition. The second *intifada*, or Palestinian uprising, gathers momentum, with use of firearms and explosives, amid suspicions that it was orchestrated, not spontaneous.

2002 Israel launches a large-scale military response to the wave of suicide bombings on civilian targets. Ultimately, over four years of intifada, more than three thousand Israelis and Palestinians will lose their lives.

2003 January: Early elections confirm Ariel Sharon as prime minister; he forms a conservative government. February: Israel's first astronaut, Ilan Ramon, dies in the Columbia disaster. The construction of Israel's antiterror fence around many parts of the West Bank gets under way, amid controversy abroad and at home.

2004 The small Israeli town of Sderot starts becoming a target for Qassam rockets fired from the Gaza Strip. Maccabi Tel Aviv, Israel's perennial basketball champs, take the European crown for the fourth time. Yasser Arafat dies; Mahmoud Abbas (Abu Mazen) assumes leadership of the Palestinian Authority.

2005 The intifada subsides, sparking hope for a resolution of the conflict in the post-Arafat era. Maccabi Tel Aviv win again in Europe. Amid fierce domestic opposition, Ariel Sharon makes good on his promise to evacuate all Jewish settlements in the Gaza Strip. At year's end, the political fall-out of that event leads Sharon to leave the Likud and form a new party; new elections are called for March 2006; and the Israeli parliamentary scene is even more intriguing than usual.

2006 The year gets off to a disquieting start as Ariel Sharon is incapacitated by a stroke in early January and Hamas, unexpectedly, has a landslide win in Palestinean elections. In March elections, Israelis vote Kadima, the new Centrist party founded by Sharon when he broke with Likud, into power. Kadima's leader, Ehud Olmert, becomes prime minister.

# NATIONAL & RELIGIOUS HOLIDAYS

Time is figured in different ways in Israel. The Western Gregorian calendar—the solar year from January to December—is the basis of day-to-day life and commerce, but the school year, for example, which runs from September through June, follows the *Hebrew* lunar calendar (dated to when Creation is believed to have occurred). Thus fall 2006–fall 2007 is the Hebrew year 5767, reckoned from Rosh Hashanah, the Jewish New Year, which usually falls in September. Since the lunar year is 11 days shorter than the solar year, Jewish holidays are out of sync with the Gregorian calendar and fall on different dates (though within the same season) from one year to the next. Jewish religious festivals are observed as national public holidays, when businesses and some museums are closed (on Yom Kippur, the Day of Atonement, *all* sites are closed).

The Muslim calendar is also lunar, but without the compensatory leap-year mechanism of its Hebrew counterpart. Muslim holidays thus drift through the seasons and can fall at any time of the year.

Even the Christian calendar is not uniform: Christmas in Bethlehem is celebrated on different days by the Roman Catholic ("Latin") community, the Greek Orthodox Church, and the Armenian Orthodox Church.

In addition to the information below, for up-to-date holiday information, contact the Israel Government Tourist Office (IGTO) in your country or region, or in Jerusalem the **Christian Information Center** (☎ 02/628-7647).

## Jewish Holidays

Here is a calendar of holidays as they're observed in Israel. Remember that Jewish holidays begin at sundown the previous evening and end at nightfall; the dates listed for Jewish holidays in 2006 and 2007 are for the day itself, not for the beginning of the holiday on the previous evening. The phrase "Not religious" in the text indicates that the holiday might be part of the religious tradition, but few or no public restrictions apply. On holy days, when the text indicates "Religious," most of the Sabbath restrictions apply.

**Shabbat (Sabbath)** The Day of Rest in Israel is Saturday, the Jewish Sabbath, which begins at sundown Friday and ends at nightfall Saturday. By Friday afternoon, you can feel the country winding down, as most Jewish-owned businesses close until Saturday night or Sunday morning. Religious neighborhoods grow frantic as families do last-minute cooking and cleaning before the Sabbath begins. Torah-observant Jews do not cook, travel, answer the telephone, or use money or writing materials during the Shabbat, hence the Sabbath ban on photography at Jewish holy sites like the Western Wall. In Jerusalem, where religious influence is strong, the downtown area clears out on Friday afternoon, and some religious neighborhoods are even closed to traffic.

Kosher restaurants close on the Sabbath, except for the main hotel restaurants, where some menu restrictions apply. In the Holy City itself, your dining choices are considerably reduced. Outside Jerusalem, however, you'll scarcely be affected; in fact, many restaurants do their best business of the week on the Sabbath because nonreligious Israelis take to the roads.

In Arab areas, such as East Jerusalem and Nazareth, Muslims take time off for the week's most important devotions at midday Friday, but the traveler will notice this much less than on Sunday, when most Christian shopkeepers in those towns close their doors. Saturday is market day, and these towns buzz with activity.

There is no public intercity transportation on the Sabbath, although the private *sherut* taxis drive between the main cities. Urban buses operate only in Nazareth and, on a reduced schedule, in Haifa. Shabbat is also the busiest day for nature reserves and national parks—indeed, anywhere the city folk can get away for a day. Keep this in mind if you fancy a long drive; the highways toward the main cities can be choked with returning weekend traffic on Saturday afternoon.

Sunday, then, is the first day of the regular work week (in Israel, says the old quip, the Monday-morning blues begin on Sunday). The country has adopted a five-day work week, but unlike in Western countries, the weekend includes Friday—already a half day and holy to the country's Muslim minority—and Saturday, the Jewish Sabbath. The public sector and most corporations work Sunday through Thursday only.

**Rosh Hashanah (Jewish New Year)** Sept. 24–25, 2006, and Sept. 13–14, 2007. Yom Kippur and this two-day holiday are collectively known as the High Holy Days. Rosh Hashanah traditionally begins a 10-day period of introspection and repentance. Observant Jews attend relatively long synagogue services and eat festive meals, including apples and honey to symbolize the hoped-for sweetness of the new year. Nonobservant Jews often use this holiday to picnic and go to the beach.

**Yom Kippur (Day of Atonement)** Oct. 2, 2006, and Sept. 22, 2007. Yom Kippur is the most solemn day of the Jewish year. Observant Jews fast, wear white clothing, and avoid leather footwear. There are no radio and television broadcasts. All sites, entertainment venues, and most restaurants are closed. Much of the country comes to a halt, and in Jerusalem and other cities towns like Jerusalem the roads are almost completely empty aside from emergency vehicles. It is considered a privilege to be invited to someone's house to "break fast" as the holiday ends, at nightfall.

**Sukkoth (Feast of Tabernacles)** Oct. 8–14, 2006, and Sept. 27–Oct. 4, 2007. First and last days religious. Jews build open-roof "huts" or shelters called *sukkot* (singular *sukkah*) on porches and in backyards to remember the makeshift lodgings of the biblical Israelites as they wandered in the desert. The more observant will eat as many of their meals as possible in their sukkah, and even sleep there for the duration of the holiday.

Right before Sukkoth, colorful street markets sell special decorations and the four kinds of "species" used in the Sukkoth ceremonies—the *etrog* (citron, like a yellow lime) and the elements that make up the *lulav* (a palm frond and sprigs of willow and myrtle). The first day is observed like the Sabbath, except that food can be cooked. The intervening days are half holidays, and shopkeepers often take vacations. Many Israelis, and some tourists, join in the hugely colorful annual hike to Jerusalem through the surrounding hills. Many Evangelical Christians come to Israel to celebrate this festival as well, obeying the passage in the prophecy of Zechariah 14.

**Simhat Torah** The last day of Sukkoth (⇨ *above*), this holiday marks the end—and the immediate recommencement—of the annual cycle of the reading of the Torah, the Five Books of Moses. The evening and morning synagogue services are characterized by joyful singing and dancing (often in the street) as people carry the Torah scrolls.

**Hanukkah** Dec. 17–23, 2006, and Dec. 5–12, 2007. Not religious. A Jewish rebellion in the 2nd century BC renewed Jewish control of Jerusalem. In the re-cleansed and rededicated Temple, the tradition tells, a vessel was found with enough oil to burn for a day. It miraculously burned for eight days, hence the eight-day holiday marked by the lighting of an increasing number of candles (on a candelabrum called a *hanukkiah*) from night to night. Customary foods are potato pancakes (latkes or *levivot*) and a local version of the jelly doughnut called *sufganiah*.

Schools take a winter break. Shops, businesses, and services all remain open.

**Tu B'Shevat** Feb. 3, 2007, and Jan. 22, 2008. Not religious. Israelis eat fruit and plant trees on the New Year of Trees, when the white- and pink-blossomed almond trees are in bloom.

**Purim** Mar. 4, 2007, and Mar. 21, 2008 (one day later in Jerusalem). Not religious. Children dress up in costumes on the days leading up to Purim. In synagogues and on public television, devout Jews read the Scroll of Esther, the story of the valiant Jewish queen who prevented the massacre of her people in ancient Persia. On Purim day, it's customary to exchange gifts of prepared foods with neighbors and friends. Many towns hold street festivals.

**Pesach (Passover)** Apr. 13–20, 2006, and Apr. 3–9, 2007. First and last days religious; dietary restrictions in force throughout. Passover is preceded by vigorous spring cleaning to remove all traces of leavened bread and related products from the household. During the seven-day holiday itself, no bread is sold in Jewish stores, and the crackerlike matzo replaces bread in most hotels and restaurants. On the first evening of the holiday, Jewish families gather to retell the ancient story of their people's exodus from Egyptian bondage and to eat a festive and highly symbolic meal called the seder (Hebrew for "order"). Hotels have communal seders, and the Ministry of Tourism can sometimes arrange for tourists to join Israeli families for Passover in their homes.

**Yom Hasho'ah (Holocaust Memorial Day)** Apr. 25, 2006, and Apr. 15, 2007. Not religious. Special services take place at Jerusalem's Yad Vashem Holocaust Memorial and elsewhere in the country. Entertainment venues are closed, and at 11 AM all stand silent as a siren sounds in memory of the 6 million Jews who were annihilated by the Nazis in World War II.

**Yom Hazikaron (Memorial Day)** May 2, 2006, and Apr. 22, 2007. Not religious.

This is a day of mourning for Israel's war dead. Commemorative ceremonies are held around the country, entertainment sites are closed, and at 11 AM a siren sounds in memory of the fallen.

**Yom Ha'atzma'ut (Independence Day)** May 3, 2006, and Apr. 23, 2007. Not religious. Israel achieved independence in May 1948; the exact date of Yom Ha'atzma'ut follows the Hebrew calendar. Although there are gala events, fireworks displays, and military parades all over the country, most Israelis go picnicking or swimming. Stores and a few tourist sites are closed, but public transportation runs.

**Lag Ba'omer** May 16, 2006, and May 6, 2007. Not religious. The 33rd day between Passover and Shavuot marks both the end of the anniversaries of a string of historic tragedies, and the commemoration of the death of the great 2nd-century AD Rabbi Shimon Bar Yochai. Kids build bonfires, and the devout visit the rabbi's grave in Meron, near Tzfat (also called Safed).

**Shavuot (Feast of Weeks)** June 2, 2006, and May 23, 2007. This holiday, seven weeks after Passover, marks the harvest of the first fruits and, according to tradition, the day on which Moses received the Torah ("the law") on Mt. Sinai. Many observant Jews stay up all night studying the Torah. It is customary to eat meatless meals with an emphasis on dairy products.

**Tisha B'Av (The Ninth of Av)** Aug. 3, 2006, and July 24, 2007. Not religious. Among the calamities believed to have occurred on this day was the destruction of both the First and Second Temples. Observant Jews fast and recite the biblical Book of Lamentations. Entertainment venues and many restaurants are closed.

## Christian Holidays

**Easter** April 16, 2006, and April 8, 2007. This major festival celebrates the resurrection of Jesus. The nature and timing of its ceremonies and services are colorfully different in each Christian tradition represented in the Holy Land—Roman

Catholic, Protestant, Greek Orthodox, Armenian Orthodox, Ethiopian, and so on. The dates above are for the Western Easters, which are the basis for public holidays, and are the dates observed by the Western churches—Roman Catholic and Protestant. Check the dates for different groups such as the Orthodox Armenian, Greek, and Russian churches, who base their holidays on the Julian calendar, converted to the Gregorian calendar now commonly in use.

**Christmas** Except in towns with a large indigenous Christian population, such as Nazareth and Bethlehem, Christmas is not a high-visibility holiday in Israel. The Christmas of the Catholic and Protestant traditions is, of course, celebrated on December 25, but the Greek Orthodox calendar observes it on January 7, and the Armenian Orthodox wait until January 19. Shuttle buses from Jerusalem run to Bethlehem's Manger Square on Christmas Eve (December 24) for the annual international choir assembly and the Roman Catholic midnight mass. For more information on Christmas celebrations, contact the **Bethlehem Peace Center** ☎ 02/276–6677 ⊕ www.peacecenter.org in Bethlehem. In Jerusalem contact the Christian Information Center ( ⇨ *above*).

## Muslim Holidays

Muslims observe Friday as their holy day, but it's accompanied by none of the restrictions and far less of the solemnity than those of the Jewish Shabbat and the Christian Sabbath (in their strictest forms). The noontime prayer on Friday is the most important of the week and is typically preceded by a sermon, often broadcast from the loudspeakers of the mosques.

The dates of Muslim holidays vary widely each year because of the lunar calendar.

**Ramadan** Beginning Sept. 24, 2006, and Sept. 13, 2007. This monthlong fast commemorates the month in which the Koran was first revealed to Muhammad. Devout Muslims must abstain from food, drink, tobacco, and sex during daylight hours; the conclusion of the period is then marked by the three-day festival of Id el-Fitr. The dates are affected by the sighting of the new moon and can change slightly at the very last moment. The Muslim holy sites on Jerusalem's Temple Mount (Haram esh-Sharif) offer only short morning visiting hours during this time and are closed to tourists during Id el-Fitr.

**Eid al-Adha** Dec. 31, 2006, and Dec. 20, 2007. This festival commemorating Abraham's willingness to sacrifice his son marks the end of the annual Haj, or pilgrimage to Mecca. Muslim families throughout Israel celebrate Eid al-Adha by slaughtering a sheep or goat.

# HEBREW VOCABULARY

Many people in Israel speak at least one other language, in addition to Hebrew, and most can get by in English. So the chances of getting too lost for words are slim. At the same time, your traveling experience can be enriched by having at least a few words to share in conversation or to use while touring and shopping, even at the local grocery store. Here are some basic words and expressions that may be of use during your stay. Please note that the letters "kh" in this glossary are pronounced like the "ch" in *chanuka* or the Scottish *loch*.

| English | Hebrew Transliteration | Pronunciation |
|---|---|---|
| **Greetings and Basics** | | |
| Hello/good-bye/peace | Shalom | shah-**lohm** |
| Nice to meet you | Na'im me'od | nah-**eem** meh-**ohd** |
| Good morning | Boker tov | boh-ker **tohv** |
| Good evening | Erev tov | eh-rev **tohv** |
| Good night | Layla tov | lahy-lah tohv |
| How are you? (to a woman) | Ma shlomekh? | mah shloh-**maykh** |
| How are you? (to a man) | Ma shlomkha? | mah shlohm-**khah** |
| How are you? | Ma nishma? | mah-nee-**shmah** |
| Fine | Beseder | beh-**say-dehr** |
| Everything is fine | Hakol beseder | hah-kohl beh-**say-dehr** |
| Is everything okay? | Hakol beseder? | hah-kohl beh-**say-dehr** |
| Very well | Tov me'od | tohv-meh-**ohd** |
| Excellent/terrific | Metzuyan | meh-tzoo-**yahn** |
| Send regards! | Timsor dash! | teem-sohr **dahsh** |
| Thank you | Toda | toh-**dah** |
| Thank you very much | Toda raba | toh-dah rah-**bah** |
| See you again | Lehitra'ot | leh-heet-rah-**oht** |
| Yes | Ken | kehn |
| No | Lo | lo |
| Maybe | Oolai | **oo**-ligh |
| Excuse me/Sorry | Slicha | slee-**khah** |
| Again/Could you repeat that? | Od pa'am | ohd pah-**ahm** |

## Days

| Today | Hayom | hah-**yohm** |
|---|---|---|
| Tomorrow | Machar | mah-**khahr** |
| Yesterday | Etmol | eht-**mohl** |
| Sunday | Yom Rishon | yohm ree-**shohn** |
| Monday | Yom Sheni | yohm sheh-**nee** |
| Tuesday | Yom Shlishi | yohm sh-lee**shee** |
| Wednesday | Yom Revi'i | yohm reh-**vee** |
| Thursday | Yom Chamishi | yohm kha-mee-**shee** |
| Friday | Yom Shishi | yohm shee-**shee** |
| Saturday, Sabbath | Shabbat | yohm shah-**bat** |

## Numbers

| 1 | Echad | eh-**khad** |
|---|---|---|
| 2 | Shtayim | shtah-**yeem** |
| 3 | Shalosh | shah-**lohsh** |
| 4 | Arba | ah-**rbah** |
| 5 | Chamesh | chah-**maysh** |
| 6 | Shesh | shehsh |
| 7 | Sheva | **sheh**-vah |
| 8 | Shmoneh | **shmoh**-neh |
| 9 | Teisha | **tay**-shah |
| 10 | Esser | **eh**-sehr |
| 11 | Achad esreh | ah-**chahd** eh-**sreh** |
| 12 | Shteim esreh | sh**taym** eh-**sreh** |
| 20 | Esrim | eh-**sreem** |
| 50 | Chamishim | khah-mee-**sheem** |
| 100 | Me'a | may-**ah** |
| 200 | Ma'tayim | mah-**tah-yeem** |

## Useful Phrases

| Do you speak English? | Ata medaber anglit? | ah-ta meh-dah-ber ahng-**leet** |
|---|---|---|
| I don't understand (man) | Ani lo mevin | a-**nee** loh meh-**veen** |
| I don't understand (woman) | Ani lo m'vina | a-**nee** m'veena |
| I don't know (man) | Ani lo yodea | a-nee loh yoh-**day**-ah |
| I don't know (woman) | Ani lo yodaat | a-nee loh yoh-**dah**-aht |

| I am lost (man) | Ani avud | a-nee ah-**vood** |
| I am lost (woman) | Ani avuda | a-nee ahvoo-**dah** |
| I am American | Ani Amerika'i | ah-nee ah-mer-ee-**kah**-ee |
| I am British | Ani Briti | ah-**nee bree**-tee |
| I am Canadian | Ani Canadi | ah-**nee** kah-**nah**-dee |
| What is the time? | Ma hasha'a? | mah hah-shah-**ah** |
| Just a minute | Rak rega | rahk **reh**-gah |
| Minute, moment | Rega | **reh**-gah |
| Now | Achshav | ahkh-**shahv** |
| Not yet | Od lo | ohd loh |
| Later | Achar kach | ah-**khahr** kahkh |
| I would like | Hayiti mevakesh | hah-**yee**-tee m-vah-**kehsh** |
| Where is..? | Eifo..? | **ay**foh |
| The central bus station | Hatachana hamerkazit | hah-tah-khah-**nah** hah-mehr-kah-**zeet** |
| The bus stop | Tachanat ha'autobus | tah-khah-**naht** hah-oh-toh-**boos** |
| The train station | Tachanat harakevet | tah-khah-**naht** hah-rah-**keh-veht** |
| The city center | Merkaz ha'ir | mehr kahz hah-**eer** |
| The post office | Hado'ar | hah-**doh**-ahr |
| A pharmacy | Beit mirkachat | bayt meer-**kah**-khaht |
| A public telephone | Telefon tziburi | teh-leh-**fohn** tzee-boo-ree |
| A good restaurant | Mis'ada tova | mee-sah-**dah toh-vah** |
| The rest rooms | Hasherutim | hah-shay-roo-**teem** |
| Right | Yemina | yeh-**mee**-nah |
| Left | Smola | s-**moh**-lah |
| Straight ahead | Yashar | yah-**shar** |
| Here | Kan | kahn |
| There | Sham | shahm |
| Do you have a (vacant) room? | Yesh lachem cheder (panui)? | yehsh lah-**chehm khed**-ehr (pah-**nooy**) |
| Is it possible to order a taxi? | Efshar lehazmin monit? | ehf-**shahr** leh-hahz-**meen** moh-**neet** |
| Taxi | Monit | moh-**neet** |
| A little | k'tzat | keh-**tzaht** |
| A lot | harbe | hahr-**beh** |
| Enough | maspik | mah-**speek** |

| | | |
|---|---|---|
| I have a problem | Yesh li ba'aya | yehsh lee bah-**yah** |
| I don't feel well (man) | Ani lo margish tov | ah-**nee** loh mahr-**geesh** tohv |
| I don't feel well (woman) | Ani lo margisha tov | ah-**nee** loh mahr-**geeshah** tohv |
| I need a doctor (man) | Ani tzarich rofe | ah-**nee** tzah-**reech** roh-**feh** |
| I need a doctor (woman) | Ani tzricha rofe | ah-**nee** tzree-**khah** roh-**feh** |
| Help | Ezra | eh-**zrah** |
| Fire | Dleika | duh-leh-**kah** |

## Dining

| | | |
|---|---|---|
| I would like | Hayiti mevakesh | hah-**yee**-tee m-vah-**kehsh** |
| Some water, please | Mayim, bevakasha | mah-**yeem** beh-vah-kah-**shah** |
| Bread | Lechem | **leh**-khehm |
| Soup | Marak | mah-**rahk** |
| Meat | Bassar | bah-**ssahr** |
| Chicken | Off | ohf |
| Vegetables | Yerakot | yeh-rah-**koht** |
| Dessert | Kinuach | kee-**noo**-ahkh |
| Cake | Ooga | **oo**-gah |
| Fruit | Perot | peh-**roht** |
| Coffee | Cafe | kah-**feh** |
| Tea | Te | teh |
| fork | Mazleg | mahz-**lehg** |
| spoon | Kapit | kah-**peet** |
| knife | Sakin | sah-**keen** |
| plate | Tzalachat | tzah-**lah**-chaht |
| Napkin | Mapit | mah-**peet** |
| Food | Ochel | **oh**-khehl |
| Meal | Arucha | ah-roo-**khah** |
| Breakfast | Aruchat boker | ah-roo-**khaht boh**-ker |
| Lunch | Aruchat tzaharayim | ah-roo-khaht tzah-hah-**rah**-yeem |
| Dinner | Aruchat erev | ahroo-**khaht eh**-rehv |
| Do you have a menu in English? | Yesh tafrit be'anglit? | yehsh tahf-**reet** beh-ahng-**leet** |
| A pita filled with felafel | Manat felafel | mah-naht feh-**lah**-fehl |
| Without hot sauce | Bli charif | blee khah-**reef** |
| It's tasty, delicious | Zeh ta'im | zeh tah-**eem** |

| I don't like the taste | Zeh lo ta'im li | zeh loh tah-**eem** lee |
| The check, please | Cheshbon, bevakasha | khehsh-bohn beh-vah-kah-**shah** |

## Shopping

| Do you have..? | Yesh lecha..? | yesh leh-khah |
| Milk | Chalav | khah-**lahv** |
| (Orange) Juice | Mitz (tapuzim) | meetz (tah-poo-**zeem**) |
| Butter | Chem'a | khem-**ah** |
| Cream cheese | Gevina levana | geh-vee-**nah** leh-vah-**nah** |
| Hard cheese | Gevina tzehuba | gevee-**nah** tzeh-**hoo**-bah |
| Sausage | Naknik | nahk-**neek** |
| Jelly | Riba | **ree**-bah |
| Sugar | Sukar | **soo**-kahr |
| Ice cream | Glida | **glee**-da |
| Map | Mapa | **mah**-pa |
| Cigarettes | Sigariyot | see-gahr-ee-**yoht** |
| Telephone card (for public phones) | Telecart | teh-leh-**kahrt** |
| That one, please | Et zeh, bevakasha | eht zeh, beh-vah-kah-**shah** |
| May I see it? | Efshar lir'ot? | ehf-**shahr** leer-**oht** |
| How much does it cost? | Kama zeh oleh? | **kah**-ma zeh **ohleh** |
| That's expensive! | Yakar! | yah-**kahr** |
| No, it's too expensive | Lo, zeh yakar midai | loh, zeh yah-**kahr** meed-**igh** |
| Too big | Gadol midai | gah-dohl meed-**igh** |
| Too small | Katan midai | kah-tan meed-**igh** |
| Perhaps there is a discount ? | Yesh hanacha oolai? | yehsh hah-na-**khah** oo-**ligh** |
| I'll take it | Ani ekach et zeh | ah-nee eh-**kakh** eht zeh |

# PALESTINIAN ARABIC VOCABULARY

Arabic is spoken by all Arab citizens of Israel, (about 20% of the Israeli population) and in the West Bank and Gaza. The areas where you're most likely to hear Arabic are East Jerusalem, Jaffa, and Nazareth, and in the popular sites of the West Bank, Bethlehem and Jericho (when these are open to travelers). Many people in these areas speak some English, but a little Arabic will come in handy with some vendors and taxi drivers or when you are in more rural areas and villages. It helps to have a written address for a taxi ride as well. You may run into small differences in dialect and accent between villages and cities, but for the most part Palestinians dialects are similar.

Some letters in Arabic do not have English equivalents. This glossary tries to approximate Arabic sounds. The letter 'r' is always rolled. When you see 'gh' at the start of a word, pronounce it like a French 'r', lightly gargled at the back of the throat. Any double letters should be extended: 'aa' is pronounced as an extended 'ah'; 'hh' is an extended 'h' sound; 'ss' is an extended hiss.

| English | Arabic Transliteration | Pronunciation |
|---------|------------------------|---------------|
| **Greetings and Basics** | | |
| Hello/ peace be upon you | salamou alaikom | sah-**lah**-moo **aah-lay**-kom |
| (reply) Hello/ and peace be upon you | wa aalaikom essalaam | wah aah-**lay**-kom **ehss**-sah-**ahm** |
| Good-bye | maa issalameh | **maah** is-**ah-lah**-meh |
| Mr./ Sir | sayyed | **sigh**-yed |
| Mrs./ Madam | sayyida | **sigh**-yee-dah |
| Miss | anisseh | **ah**-niss-say |
| How are you? (man speaking) | keif hhalak | kayf **hah**-luck |
| How are you? (woman speaking) | keif hhalik | kayf **hah**-lik |
| Fine, thank you | bi kheir elhhamdilla | bee **khayr** el-**ham**-dihl-lah |
| Pleased to meet you | tsharrafna | tshahr-**ruhf**-nah |
| Please (man) | min fadlak | min **fahd**-lahk |
| Please (woman) | min fadlik | min **fahd**-lik |
| Thank you | shokran | shohk-rahn |
| God willing | Inshallah | ihn-**shahl-lah** |
| Yes | aah or naam | aah or naahm |
| No | la | lah |

| | | |
|---|---|---|
| I'm Sorry (man) | mit assif | miht **ass**-sef |
| I'm Sorry (woman) | mit assfeh | miht **ass**-feh |

## Days

| | | |
|---|---|---|
| Today | eliom | el-**yohm** |
| Tomorrow | bokra | bok-rah |
| Yesterday | embarehh | ehm-**bah**-rehh |
| Sunday | il ahhad | **il ah**-had |
| Monday | ittinein | it-tee-**nayn** |
| Tuesday | ittalata | it-tah-**lah**-tah |
| Wednesday | il 'arbaa | il **ahr**-bah-**aah** |
| Thursday | il khamees | il khah-**mees** |
| Friday | iljumaa | il zhum-**aah** |
| Saturday | issabet | **iss-sah**-bet |

## Numbers

| | | |
|---|---|---|
| 1 | wahed | **wah**-hed |
| 2 | tinein | tee-**nayn** |
| 3 | talati | tah-**lah**-tee |
| 4 | arbaa | **ahr**-bah-aah |
| 5 | khamseh | **khahm**-seh |
| 6 | sitteh | **sit**-teh |
| 7 | sabaa | sub-**aah** |
| 8 | tamanyeh | tah-**mah**-nee-**yeh** |
| 9 | tisaa | **tiss**-aah |
| 10 | aashara | **aah**-shah-rah |
| 11 | ihhdaaesh | ihh-**dah**-ehsh |
| 12 | itnaaesh | it-**nah**-ehsh |
| 20 | ishreen | iish-**reen** |
| 50 | khamseen | khahm-**seen** |
| 100 | meyyeh | **may**-yeh |
| 200 | mitein | **mee**-tain |

## Useful Phrases

| | | |
|---|---|---|
| Do you speak English? | btihki inglizi? | btih-**kee** in-**glee**-zee? |
| I don't understand (man) | mish fahem | mish **fah**-him |
| I don't understand (woman) | mish fahmi | mish **fah**-meh |

| I don't know (man) | mish aarif | mish **aah**-ref |
|---|---|---|
| I don't know (woman) | mish aarfi | mish **aahr**-fee |
| I'm lost (man) | ana dayih | ah-nah **dah**-yeh |
| I'm lost (woman) | ana dayaa | ah-nah **dah**-ye-aah |
| I am American (man) | ana amriki | ah-nah ahm-**ree**-**kee** |
| I am American (woman) | ana amrikiyya | ah-nah ahm-**ree**-**key**-yah |
| I am British (man) | ana baritani | ah-nah bah-**ree**-**tah**-**nee** |
| I am British (woman) | ana baritaniya | ah-nah bah-**ree**-**tah**-**nay**-yah |
| What is this? | eish hada? | aysh **hah**-dah? |
| What time is it? | Addeish el wa'ed? | Ahd-**daysh**-el **wah**-ed |
| Where is? | wein? | wayn? |
| The train station | mahattit iltrain | mah-**huht**-**tit il-train** |
| The bus station | mahattit el buss | mah-**huht**-tit el **buhss** |
| The intracity bus station | mahattit el bus eddakheli | mah-**huht**-**tit el** buhss **ed**-dah-**khe**-**lee** |
| The taxi station | mujammaa el takasi | moo-**jam**-maah el tah-**kah**-see |
| The airport | el matar | el mah-**tahr** |
| The hotel | el oteil | el **ooh**-tayl |
| The cafe | el ahwi | el ah-**weh** |
| The restaurant | el mataam | el **matt**-**aahm** |
| The telephone | el tiliphon | el tih-lih-**fohn** |
| The hospital | el mostashfa | el moos-**tash**-fah |
| The post office | el bareed | el bah-**reed** |
| The rest room | el hammam | el huhm-**mahm** |
| The pharmacy | el saydaleyyeh | el sigh-dah-**lay**-**yeh** |
| The bank | el bank | el bahnk |
| The embassy | el safara | el sah-fah-**rah** |
| Right | yameen | yah-meen |
| Left | shmal | shmahl |
| Straight ahead | doughri | doo-ghree |
| I would like a room | beddi ghorfi | bed-dee **ghor-fih** |
| A little | shway or aleel | shway or ah-leel |
| A lot | kteer | kteer |
| Enough | bikaffi | bee-kaf-fee |
| I have a problem | aandi moshkili | aahn-dee **moosh**-keh-lee |
| I am ill | ana mareed | ah-nah mah-reed |
| I need a doctor | beddi daktor | bed-**dee** dac-**tor** |

| Help | saadoonee | **saah-doo**-nee |
|---|---|---|
| Fire | naar or harika | naahr or hah-**ree**-kah |
| Caution/ look out | entebeh or owaa | in-teh-beh or ohw-**aah** |

## Dining

| I would like | beddi | behd-dee |
|---|---|---|
| Water | mayy | muhyy |
| Bread | khobez | kho-bihz |
| Vegetables | khodra | khod-rah |
| Meat | lahhmi | **lahh**-meh |
| Fruits | fawakeh | fah-**wah**-keh |
| Cakes/ Sweets | helou/ halaweyyat | **heh**-loo/ hah-lah-**way**-yaht |
| Tea | shay | shahy |
| Coffee | ahwi | ah-weh |
| A fork | shokeh | show-keh |
| A spoon | maala a | **maah**-lah ah |
| A knife | sikkeen | sick-**keen** |
| A plate | sahin | sah-hin |

## Shopping

| I would like to buy | beddi ashtri | bed-**dee** ahsh-tree |
|---|---|---|
| cigarettes | sagayer or dokhkhan | sah-**gah**-yer or dokh-**khahn** |
| a city map | khareeta lal madeeni | khah-**ree**-tah lahl mah-**dee**-nee |
| a road map | khareeta lal tareek | khah-**ree**-tah lahl tah-**reek** |
| How much is it? | addaish ha o | **ad**-daysh **ha** oh |
| It's expensive | ghali | **ghah**-lee |

# INDEX

## PHOTO CREDITS

# NOTES

# NOTES

# NOTES

# NOTES

# NOTES

# NOTES

# NOTES

# NOTES

# ABOUT OUR WRITERS

Our success in helping to make your trip the best of all possible vacations is a credit to the hard work of our extraordinary writers and editors.

**Judy Lash Balint** is an award-winning Jerusalem-based writer and the author of *Jerusalem Diaries: In Tense Times*. Born in England, Judy fell in love with Jerusalem on her first trip as a teenager, and shares her passion for the holy city with visitors from all over the world.

**Judy Stacey Goldman** was born in Montreal and has lived in Israel for the past 30 years, where she has worked enthusiastically as a professional tour guide for over a decade. Her many–faceted Jerusalem Walk has become a highlight experience. She has co-authored three books with culinary and off-the-beaten-track themes about Jerusalem and Tel Aviv. Her Fodor's territories include the Northern Coast & Western Galilee, Eilat, and the Negev.

**Mike Hollander** was born in Canada and has lived in Israel since 1988. He has worked for over twenty years as a Jewish educator, and has been a professional tour guide in Israel for the last 12 years. His passion is taking visitors of all ages and all faiths on an inter-disciplinary historical, theological, sociological, political, and environmental "Israel Experience." This is his first time writing for Fodor's, and he updated the Around Jerusalem chapter.

**Mike Rogoff**, a professional tour guide and writer, has been exploring the byways of Israel and exciting visitors of all persuasions since the early 1970s. South African-born and Jerusalem-based, Mike is a recipient of the Israel government's Guide of the Year award, and has contributed to *Fodor's Israel* since 1985. This year he updated the Jerusalem and Lower Galilee chapters, and the essay "Small Country, Big History."

**Miriam Feinberg Vamosh**, who hails from New Jersey, is a long-time tour educator specializing in Christian pilgrimage and tours for Jewish families. She is the author of numerous articles, brochures, and four books about biblical Israel's history and lore: *Food in the Bible: from Adam's Apple to the Last Supper, Daily Life at the Time of Jesus, Israel, Land of the Bible*, and *Pathways through the Land of the Hart*. In addition to updating the chapters on her favorite areas of Israel—the Upper Galilee & the Golan, and Tel Aviv—Miriam is the writer and updater of our section on Petra.